WILDLIFE BIOLOGY

WILDLIFE BIOLOGY
An Indian Perspective

GOUTAM KUMAR SAHA
Professor and Former Head
Department of Zoology
University of Calcutta

SUBHENDU MAZUMDAR
Assistant Professor and Head
Department of Zoology
Shibpur Dinobundhoo Institution (College)
Howrah, West Bengal

PHI Learning Private Limited
Delhi-110092
2025

In fond memory of ***Shri Asoke K. Ghosh*** *(October 1942 – February 2024), Founder Chairman and Managing Director of PHI Learning, whose vision endlessly inspires.*

The Legacy Continues....

Published by Pushpita Ghosh, PHI Learning Private Limited, Rimjhim House, 111, Patparganj Industrial Estate, Delhi-110092 and Printed by Syndicate Binders, A-20, Hosiery Complex, Noida, Phase-II Extension, Noida-201305 (N.C.R. Delhi).

₹995.00

WILDLIFE BIOLOGY—AN INDIAN PERSPECTIVE
Goutam Kumar Saha and Subhendu Mazumdar

ISBN-978-81-203-5313-8 (Print Book)
ISBN-978-93-90669-96-7 (e-Book)

The export rights of the book are vested solely with the publisher.

CONTENTS

PREFACE

Wildlife biology is an upcoming subject in the present day curriculum. It is either offered as an independent course at undergraduate and postgraduate level or is taught in the course curriculum of zoology and environmental biology. The term 'wildlife' means different things to different people. From a purely objective standpoint, wildlife should include all animals and their associated habitats. The subject is unique in encompassing vast arena like wildlife ecology, details of wildlife habitats, biology and ecology of wild animals, threats of wildlife, *in-situ* and *ex-situ* conservation processes, wildlife laws and ethical issues, etc. Although numbers of books are available on this subject, yet most of them are written by foreign authors, published by foreign publishers and mainly based on studies and examples of exotic animals and situations, which are not common in the Indian perspective. So far we gather, there is no such title available in the market which discusses the subject based on Indian situation and examples in a comprehensive manner. Therefore, the present effort is to bring together the concepts of wildlife biology in a single volume encompassing the requirement of undergraduate and postgraduate courses offered by most of the Indian Universities, as well as, to make the book reasonably priced and affordable for our students. The book will help students to understand wildlife biology in a comprehensive way and will also serve as an important resource for wildlife researchers, academicians, policy makers, naturalists and wildlife enthusiasts to get an insight into the wildlife wealth, its problems and relevant conservation initiatives in our country.

Our goal is to impart knowledge of various facets of Indian wildlife, inculcate basic understanding of tools and techniques associated with faunal research and thus to stimulate a passion for wildlife amongst the readers of this book.

Goutam Kumar Saha
Subhendu Mazumdar

ACKNOWLEDGEMENTS

We are inundated to Prof. Asutosh Ghosh, Vice Chancellor, University of Calcutta for his encouragement and kind patronage towards this endevour. We also express our deep sense of gratitude to Prof. Subrata Roy, Prof. Sajal Roy, Dr. Parthiba Basu, Dr. Rakesh Tamang and Principal, Shibpur Dinabundhoo Institution (College), Howrah for their inspiration and providing valuable inputs. Special thanks are also due to Dr. Dipankar Ghose, Dr. Sunita Pradhan. Dr. Sarala Khaling, Dr. Gautam Aditya, Dr. S. Sathyakumar, Dr. Soumyajit Banerjee, Dr. Tapajit Bhattacharya, Mrs. Soujita Pramanik, Mrs. Gargi Nandi, Mrs. Bidisa Mazumdar, Ms. Sampa Banerjee, Sk. Habibur Rahaman, Mr. Anupam Chakraborty and Master Susmit Saha for their help and suggestions during the preparation of manuscript. We are grateful to Ms. Swarnali Mukherjee for critically going through this manuscript and performing the most tedious job of proofreading and also for providing technical help. We extend our sincere thanks to Dr. Dipankar Ghose (WWF-India), Dr. Abesh Kr. Sanyal (WII), Mr. Rudra Prasad Das (WBBB) and Mr. Supriyo Dalui (CU) for their kind permission to use some of their line drawings and photographs in this book. We are also thankful to PHI Learning, Delhi for timely publication of this volume. A good number of books, technical monographs, reports as well as websites of both Government and Non-Government Organizations have been consulted and some tables, figures and ideas have been incorporated in the present textbook with proper citation which is gratefully acknowledged.

Goutam Kumar Saha
Subhendu Mazumdar

1

INDIAN WILDLIFE — THEIR IMPORTANCE AND CONSERVATION STATUS

1.1 BASIC CONCEPT OF WILDLIFE

The term 'Wildlife' is commonly referred to as all wild and undomesticated animals in their natural habitats. According to the other school of thought, all wild vertebrates and larger invertebrates important from aesthetic, sporting, utilitarian and nuisance point should come under the purview of wildlife. Philosophically, it should include all the biotic elements that evolved and flourished as a consequence of evolution. From ecological point of view, it includes all flora and fauna in their natural habitats. In other words, wildlife may simply be defined as all non-cultivated and undomesticated life forms. According to Wildlife (Protection) Act of India, 1972, wildlife includes any animal, bees, butterflies and moths, crustaceans, fish and aquatic and land vegetation which forms part of a habitat. On one hand, the term is often associated with the management, control and conservation of animal population and, whereas on the other hand, wildlife is defined as all living creatures of nature that are not under direct control, manipulation or management of human beings. Hence, the term 'wildlife' has a broad expression, which varies according to the perspective, often not implying any uniform meaning. Hence, it is quite challenging to define wildlife. The most accepted definition was provided by the Indian scientist E.P. Gee in the year 1964, which states that wildlife embraces all living creatures and implies their conservation.

1.2 IMPORTANCE OF WILDLIFE

1.2.1 Ecological Value

Wildlife, being an integral part of any ecosystem, plays a vital role in maintaining ecological balance. In any ecosystem, anything is related to everything else and each biotic component, by virtue of its position in the food chain, biogeochemical cycles and through positive and negative population regulation, maintains the delicate balance of an ecosystem. Therefore, decline or extinction of a component species results in a chain of events which adversely affect a number of other species as well (ripple effect). If a species is lost, it may upset the balance of nature and make the entire system vulnerable which, often results in unfavourable and undesirable outcome that ultimately affects mankind. For example, loss of one mature tropical plant leads to the loss of 10–30 species of insects that have highly specialized foraging habits. Destruction of carnivores will lead to the increase of herbivores, which in turn will affect the forest vegetation. Once the forest vegetation is reduced, herbivores will start invading cultivated lands leading to conflict with farmers. The reduction in the extent of the forest will affect rains and thereby affect the economy of our land. On the other hand, tigers turn man eaters and hyenas become child lifters often because humans interfere with their natural food. Wild animals also provide various 'ecological services' to mankind. Birds serve as pollinating agents, assist in fruit and seed dispersion, eat a large number of harmful insects and other pests, as well as, play the vital role of scavengers in many ecosystems. One of the most important roles of snakes is to check the rodent population in agricultural fields. Thus, illegal killing of snakes (for illegal skin trade or from fear or taboo) leads to the increase of the rodent population, which ultimately results in huge economic loss in terms of loss of certain quantity of crop, as well as, increased cost towards pest management by using rodenticides.

1.2.2 Economic Value

Wildlife is an important natural wealth and, if carefully conserved and sustainably exploited, may significantly contribute towards national economy. Communities dwelling in the fringe and wilderness areas rely heavily on forests and wildlife. Various products obtained from wildlife include timber, fire wood, natural rubber, gums, resins, tannins, essential oils, honey etc. Wild medicinal plants are source of a number of medicines. In various countries abroad, revenue is generated through fees against grant of hunting permits and through duties imposed for import of arms and ammunitions. Animal products like hides, horns, ivory, fur etc. are good sources of income for many countries. However, hunting of wildlife and trade in wildlife parts is prohibited under law in India. In this country, wild animals are used as non-consumptive source of income like tourism, wildlife photography etc. Wildlife sanctuaries and national parks of this country are most popular tourist destinations, which also attract several foreign tourists, and thus, good amount of foreign exchange is earned. The zoological gardens and botanical gardens of this country also earn good amount of revenue as entry fees. Collection of live and dead specimens, respectively, for zoos and museums also generates a lot of revenue.

1.2.3 Sports and Enjoyment

Wild animals are also good source of game, fun and recreation to people from all walks of life. In some countries, people spend a large amount of money on hunting, fishing, bull fight, cock fight, etc. A visit to the protected areas and viewing wild animals in their natural surroundings is often a thrilling experience. 'Bird watching' and 'Wildlife photography' are two very popular and growing hobbies for many people. Many educational institutions regularly conduct study tours to various protected areas to generate awareness and compassion for wildlife among the educated youth of this country.

1.2.4 Scientific Value

Many wild species are of immense value for the scientific community and for the mankind perse. Several life-saving drugs have been discovered from different species of flora and fauna. Efficacy of new medicine or any new surgical method is often tested first on animals. Sea urchins helped to understand human embryology, rhesus macaques to understand human blood group, antlers of deer are used to study radioactive contamination and feathers of birds help to assess the heavy metal pollution in environment. Animals like monkeys, guinea pigs, rats are commonly used as experimental models in medical research. Similarly, several species of fauna also serve as experimental models for various scientific studies and experiments on animal behaviour, physiology, anatomy, genetics, etc. to generate wealth of new information for mankind. Likewise, several naturalists carry out research on diversity and ecology of wild flora and fauna in their natural habitats.

1.2.5 Genetic Resource

Wildlife often comprises of pure breeds that act as important genetic resources. Genes from wild flora and fauna are used to devise better and more productive crop varieties and breeds through genetic engineering. Thus, wildlife serves as resource for traits like higher productivity, better disease and pest resistance, greater climatic adaptability etc. For improvement and progress in agriculture, animal husbandry and aquaculture, genes from various wild species are preserved in 'gene banks' and are utilized in different breeding programmes. In addition, several wild species may also serve as potential source of future life-saving drugs.

1.2.6 Aesthetic Value

Wild creatures are nature's gifts which help adorn the natural beauty by their unique ways of existence. Thus, wildlife is also of important aesthetic value adding pleasure and happiness to mankind. Forests often become melodious with the calls of diverse song birds. Ornamental wild plants, wild flowers (like rhododendrons, orchids, etc.), colourful insects, birds and mammals all have magnificent aesthetic value. Pleasure and enjoyment gained through the taste of wild berries, softness of moss or grass beds, fragrance and colours of wild flowers, melodious calls of birds rejuvenate human beings, which is often essential to overcome stress and lead a healthy life. This world would indeed be bleak and bare without dense forests, graceful beasts, vibrant and colourful flowers, butterflies and birds.

1.2.7 Cultural and Religious Value

Wildlife is intertwined with various traditional beliefs, culture and religion of this country. Wildlife is protected by different cultures like the *Bishnois* of Rajasthan protecting and worshipping blackbuck, some indigenous tribes in Arunachal Pradesh protecting sacred groves, etc. Animal symbols were found on the seals of early *Indus* civilization. Almost all epics, mythologies and ancient literatures bear descriptions of wild flora and fauna. Epics such as *Ramayana* and *Mahabharata*, depicted that deers, birds and several animals and plants were protected and roamed freely in the vicinity of the *ashramas* of the saints. Tales of *Panchatantra* revolves around various animal characters. We, like most of the Indian children, grew up listening to these tales that helped us to develop an inherent compassion for wild flora and fauna. Animals are considered sacred in Hindu religion and thus they receive very important place. *Matsya*, *Narasimha* and *Hanuman* are worshipped as animal gods. All Hindu gods and goddesses are also associated with some wild fauna as their rider, like Lord *Vishnu* sleeps on snakes and rides on *lammergeiers* (*garura*). Lord *Mahadev* rides on bull, goddess *Durga* rides on lion, *Laxmi* on barn owl, *Saraswati* on swan, *Kartikeya* on peacock and *Ganapati* on a mouse. About 30 different mammals are mentioned in the *Vedas*. Furthermore, in *vedic* literatures, Earth is personified as goddess *bhumi* or *prithvi*, an abundant mother who always showers mercy to all living creatures who are considered to be her children. *Vedas* also contain hymns praising several wild animals.

1.2.8 Ethical Value

Every single species on this planet are an outcome of evolution and hence, has equal right to survive. Most of the religions usually agree that human beings should have the responsibility as to how they use the creation. Human responsibility towards creation is a common theme in Buddhism. Particularly the Chinese Buddhists emphasized intimate connections between all things of nature. Such theme of stewardship of the natural world is also found in recent literatures of Christianity, Islam and other religions.

1.3 WILDLIFE WEALTH OF INDIA

India is the seventh largest country in the world and the second largest nation in Asia covering a geographical area of 3,287,263 sq km with a land frontier of around 15,200 km with neighbouring five countries and a coastline of 7,516 km. India is unique in its richness and diversity of wildlife and hosts some of the most biodiversity rich regions of the world. This country is also bestowed with diverse ecological habitats like cold and hot deserts, snow-capped mountains, moist evergreen forests, tropical rainforests, deciduous forests, high alpine and central Indian grasslands, inland and coastal wetlands, mangroves and oceanic islands. Such rich habitat diversity of this country, in turn, favours immense diversity of flora and fauna. Apart from natural wilderness areas, several wild species are also found in human dominated areas, such as in rural areas, and even in most developed urban centres.

Species of various flora and fauna of this country historically have descended from various parent taxa originating in Gondwana. Volcanic eruptions and subsequent massive change of the climate (around 20 million years ago) had led to the extinction of many endemic Indian forms. Later many species immigrated to this country from other parts of Asia through two passes on either side of the emerging Himalayas. Presently this country harbours around 8 percent of the global biodiversity comprising of more than 46000 floral species and over 81000 faunal species and is designated as one of the 17 megadiversity countries of the world for its rich biological heritage.

Endemism is also very high in this country. Endemic species are those with distribution restricted to a particular geographical area (country), found nowhere else in the world. Due to such very limited geographical range, threat of extinction looms large on the endemic species and once lost they (like any other species) can no way be recovered. Around 33 percent Indian plants belonging to 140 genera (Botanical Survey of India 1983) are endemic. Again out of around 5150 endemic plant species, 4950 are angiosperms and 200 are pteridophytes. High endemism has also been recorded for various faunal taxa, like insects, marine worms, centipedes, mayflies and freshwater sponges found in this country. About 400 species of higher vertebrates found in this country are also endemic. Some endemic species of this country have been enlisted in Table 1.1.

Table 1.1 List of Endemic Species Belonging to Different Taxa Found in India

Taxa	*Examples*
Mammals	Lion-tailed macaque *Macaca silenus* Nilgiri thar *Hemitragus hylocrius* Indian giant squirrel *Ratufa indica* Namdapha flying squirrel *Biswamoyopterus biswasi*
Birds	Narcondam hornbill *Aceros narcondami* Nicobar megapode *Megapodius nicobariensis* Andaman crake *Rallina canningi* Nilgiri flycatcher *Eumyias albicaudata* Grey junglefowl *Gallus sonneratii* Great Indian bustard *Ardeotis nigriceps* Forest owlet *Heteroglaux blewitti* Jerdon's courser *Rhinoptilus bitorquatus*
Reptiles	Assam keelback *Amphiesma pealii* Darjeeling kukri snake *Oligodon juglandifer* Andaman cobra *Naja sagittifera* Nilgiri forest lizard *Calotes nemoricola*
Amphibia	Malabar toad *Duttaphrynus hololius* Nagaland toad *Duttaphrynus nagalandensis*
Freshwater Fish (Osteichthyes)	Malabar ricefish *Horaichthys setnai* Mahanadi rita *Rita chrysea* Western ghat loach *Bhavania australis* Hillstream spineless eel *Pillaia indica* Deccan barb *Puntius deccanensis* Dwarf mahseer *Tor kulkarnii* Gangetic bola *Johnius gangeticus*

(*Contd...*)

Table 1.1 List of Endemic Species Belonging to Different Taxa Found in India (*Contd.*)

Taxa	*Examples*
Marine Fish (Chondrichthyes)	Godavari thryssa *Thryssa kammalensoides* Bengal Spaghetti-eel *Moringua arundinacea* Quilon electric ray *Heteronarce prabhui*
Butterflies	Nilgiri tiger *Parantica nilgiriensis* Malabar banded swallowtail *Papilio liomedon* Malabar banded peacock *Papilio buddha* Andaman mormon *Papilio mayo*

Western Ghats, Northeast India, Eastern Himalayas and Andaman and Nicobar Islands are the regions with high endemism. Amongst all endemic plant species of this country, 3500 species are found in the Himalayas, 1600 species in Western Ghats and 220 species in Andaman and Nicobar Islands.

Biodiversity Hotspot: A region which on one hand is a significant reservoir of biodiversity and, on the other hand, is threatened with destruction is designated as 'biodiversity hotspot'. Myers et al., (2000) defined global biodiversity 'hotspots' as areas of high biological diversity with high endemism which are also under severe anthropogenic threats. Apart from high endemic species richness and considerable threat, other features for demarcation of an area as 'biodiversity hotspot' include following three criteria:

- The area should include diverse range of habitats.
- The area should support adequate number of 'specialist species' adapted to specific edaphic conditions.
- The area should contain important gene pools of valuable and potentially useful plants.

Thirty four global biodiversity hotspots (Figure 1.1) cover just about 0.5 percent of the total land area of Earth, but harbour about 49,955 species of endemic plants. The geographical boundary of this country encompasses three such 'biodiversity hotspots' *viz.* Western Ghats (parts of Western Ghats and Sri Lanka Hotspot), Eastern Himalayas (parts of Indo-Burma Hotspot) and Andaman and Nicobar Islands (parts of Sundaland Hotspot).

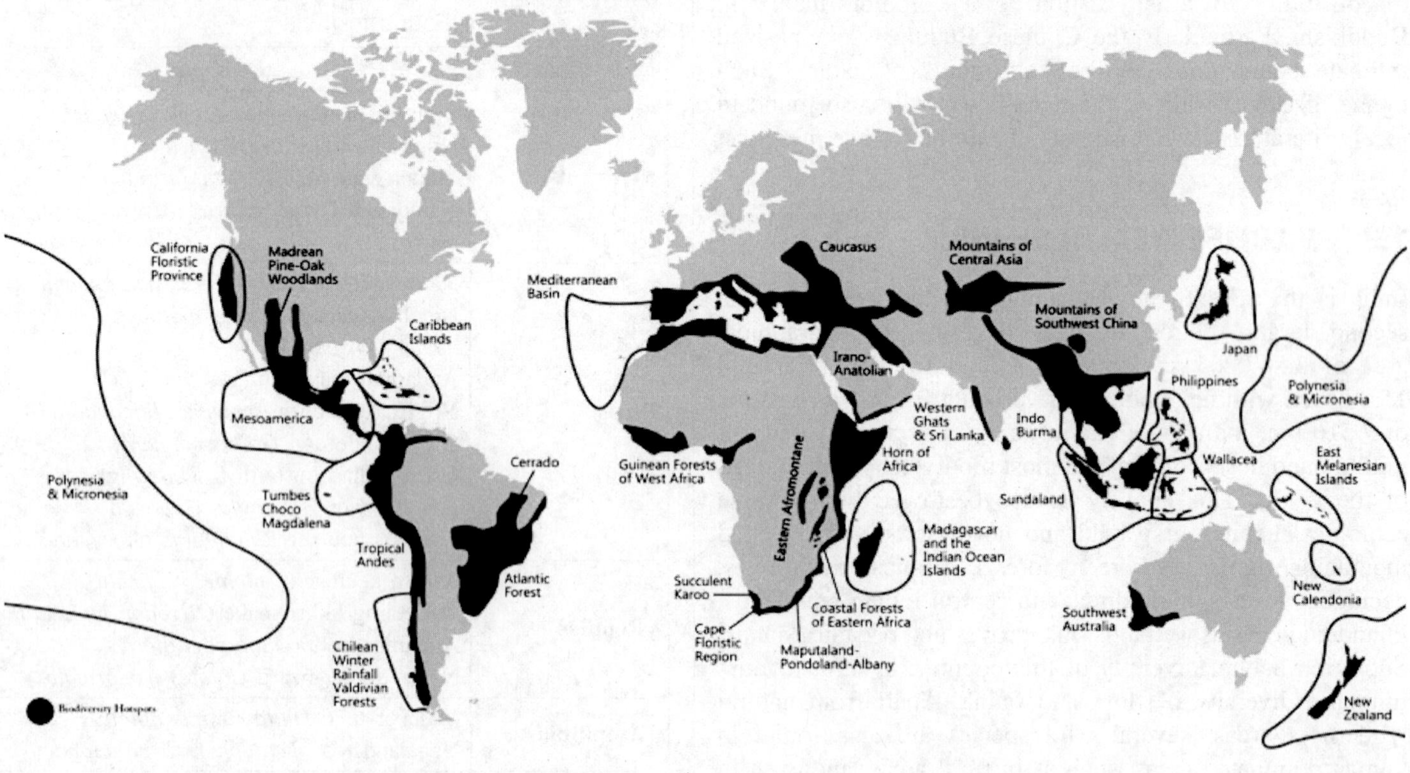

FIGURE 1.1 Biodiversity hotspots of the world. (Source: Conservation International)

1.4 THREATS TO INDIAN WILDLIFE

Wildlife across the globe is facing various types of threats and India is no exception. Most ecosystems are facing multiple threats (sometimes termed as 'stressors'), which operate alone or are interlinked, and more often one threat triggers several others. With a constantly changing environment, all organisms need to adapt to new temperature, climate and other atmospheric conditions, as well as should develop capacity to overcome the natural catastrophic events like earthquakes, landslides, volcanic eruptions, meteor strikes, severe storms and other natural calamities. In addition to these abiotic stresses, species are further challenged to adapt to several biotic stresses like intra and inter-specific competition, predation, parasitism, disease etc. Wildlife is also threatened by different anthropogenic activities like degradation, fragmentation and destruction of habitat, poaching, spreading of invasive species and diseases. Each new threat, in combination with others, puts additional stress on already weakened ecosystem and threatens the existence of several wild flora and fauna thriving therein. For example, rapid population expansion has led to the conversion of various natural landscapes into human habitations and agricultural lands, thereby degrading and reducing habitat of many wild fauna. If a species is unable to successfully cope with these stressors (abiotic, biotic and anthropogenic) through successful adaptation, then the individuals often fail to reproduce successfully and/or die. As a consequence, the entire species might face extinction. In the recent evolutionary history, many species have already become extinct and numerous others are on the verge of extinction. Many scientists believe that we are now experiencing the 'sixth mass extinction' in the history of life on Earth.

To have an overview, the threats to wildlife have been classified into the following categories:

1.4.1 Habitat Loss

Habitat loss is the major threat to the survival of wildlife throughout the globe. Once a particular area is altered by human activities, it may no longer be able to provide food, water, cover (shelter) and places to raise young for the resident species, thus posing a threat to their survival. Tropical forests though cover a very large area along the tropics, yet are also being destroyed rapidly at a perilous rate. If the current rate of deforestation continues, all the existing rain forests of the world will vanish within 100 years (Urquhart et al., 2001). Massive deforestation has already been reported from Thailand. In contrast to 53 percent forested land in 1961, forest cover in Thailand has decreased to only 23 percent in 1995 (FAO 1999) and 17 percent by 1999 (Prayurasiddhi et al., 1999).

Habitat loss is a grave concern as it threatens the survival of wildlife in the following manner:

- **Absence of cover or shelter:** Destruction of trees, herbs and shrubs from a particular area reduces the cover for the wildlife dwelling in that habitat patch. Once cover is absent, the animal species would not survive, even if the food and water is plenty.
- **Reduction in the area of free movement:** Deforestation and fragmentation of forests has been scientifically proven to be one of the biggest threats to wildlife. It reduces the area of movement especially to habitat specialist and large vertebrates which require vast stretches of undisturbed forests for food, water and home ranges as the key determinants for their survival. Reduction in the area for free movement often retards the reproductive capacity of certain wild vertebrates like rhinoceros, tiger, bison etc.
- **Lack of food, water and other resources for survival:** Destruction or degradation of habitat, especially a forest patch, often reduces the availability of water, food and shelter for several species. As many species are often associated with a single tree, hence, destruction of single tree often affects the survival of many wild species.

Habitat loss can be classified into following four broad categories:

Habitat Destruction

Habitat destruction is the process in which natural habitat is rendered functionally unable to support the species present. This occurs when an area is dramatically changed by human activities in such a way that it is no longer able to provide food, water or cover for the resident species. In this process, the organisms which previously used the site are either displaced or destroyed, affecting biodiversity of the region. Habitat destruction is caused by several human activities like mining, logging, trawling, harvesting natural resources for industry, clearing of natural habitats for agriculture and urban sprawl. Destruction of habitat also occurs from pressures like, flood, drought, as well as, due to drainage, logging etc.

Habitat destruction is currently ranked as the primary cause of species extinction worldwide. A proportion of habitat available to a particular species may simply be destroyed for urban and industrial development or for the production of certain natural resources (such as, timber). Forest clearance has been and is still the most pervasive force for habitat destruction. In the developed countries much of the temperate forests have already been destroyed and at present more than 1 percent of the rain forests are being destroyed annually in the tropics.

Habitat Fragmentation

Splitting up of a continuous habitat to several smaller discontinuous patches due to several unplanned and unsustainable developmental activities is termed as habitat fragmentation. Due to habitat fragmentation habitats are increasingly subdivided into smaller units, resulting in their increased insularity, as well as, loss of total habitat area. Continuous terrestrial wildlife habitats are often been fragmented by roads, railway tracks, dams and other infrastructural developments. Similarly aquatic habitats have also been fragmented by construction of dams. Often these fragmented habitats are neither large nor connected enough to support species requiring large territory or home range. Therefore, fragmented habitats frequently confine wildlife populations to small, isolated patches of their original habitat.

There are many examples of habitat loss due to unplanned development and other anthropogenic activities. Kabini reservoir has cut movement corridors for wildlife between Nagarahole and Bandipur Tiger Reserves along with submergence of over 30,000 acres of prime wildlife habitat. Similarly, mine located in the heart of Kudremukh National Park caused irreparable damage through destruction of large areas of forests and threatening the habitat of the lion-tailed macaque.

Habitat Degradation

Pollution, introduction of invasive species, climate change and subsequent disruption of ecosystem processes may degrade a particular habitat in such a way that it no longer supports native wildlife. Pollution, indiscriminate use of pesticides, acid rain, land use changes and improper disposal of wastes, apart from degrading the terrestrial habitats, also degrade the aquatic habitats in the form of run-offs. Besides, water impoundment and abstraction may also profoundly affect the quality and flow pattern of water. In a degraded habitat, several specialized species are often replaced by more generalist species.

Habitat Disturbance

Though not as disastrous as destruction, fragmentation or degradation of habitats, yet certain species are particularly vulnerable to various kinds of disturbances. Some wilderness areas face habitat disturbances particularly due to increased sound and vehicular movements caused by increased number of tourist visits. Vehicular noise on the roads cutting across through some of the pristine forests of this country also disturbs wildlife dwelling there.

1.4.2 Grazing of Livestock

Livestock grazing has severely threatened our wildlife and their habitats in various ways. The decline of wild herbivore population is the most noticeable effect as they have to compete with livestock for food. If more cattle graze in a particular habitat, then they often eliminate palatable native plant species leaving only the unpalatable natural vegetation for wild herbivores. As a result, the plant species composition of the area is altered. In addition to that, the recruitment rate and regeneration of trees and other plant species are also affected as livestock voraciously graze on young saplings. Thus, heavy grazing increases soil erosion in forest areas. Besides, livestock grazing aids in the spread of communicable diseases from domestic to wild animals often causing death of wild ungulates. Moreover, livestock grazing in forests serve as easy prey for wild carnivores, which subsequently might lead to human-wildlife conflict.

1.4.3 Mining Activities

Iron ore mining and quarrying for granite leads to large scale habitat loss and takes severe toll in many wildlife habitats. Species like tigers, Asiatic elephants, wild dogs, lion-tailed macaques, great pied hornbill etc. require large home ranges and/or are sensitive to disturbances. Therefore, they are seriously affected by the mining activities. Mining also changes hydrological profile of an area and affects both quantity and quality of water by degrading the catchments. It increases run-offs during monsoons and also pollutes rivers and streams that flow through mining areas. Mining on fragile hillsides exposes the area to erosion, taking the mud directly into nearby streams and rivers adding further to the siltation load of these lotic ecosystems. Reservoirs are often clogged with mine silt which decrease their water holding capacity. Moreover, dust generated by quarrying accumulates on leaves affecting photosynthesis of plants. Small-scale mining (such as sand mining and granite mining) also occur in forest areas. Most such activities are illegal, and destroy important ecological habitats in the forests. For example, many parts of the Western Ghats have been blighted by mining and quarrying which ultimately resulted in irreversible degradation of wildlife habitats.

1.4.4 Forest Fires

Forest fires are one of the major threats to wildlife. In contrary to the popular belief that forest fires are natural, they are entirely anthropogenic in India. There are various reasons of forest fire. Repeated forest fires are mainly caused by grazers, minor forest produce collectors, hunters and sometimes by careless tourists. Cattle grazers set fire in the dry pastures in the hope of new flush of grass for their livestock. Honey collectors accidentally set fire in their urgency to smoke out bees from the hives. Devastating fires have also been sparked by careless tourists or villagers discarding *bidi* and cigarette butts and sometimes due to negligence by forest staff while burning of fire lines. The sources of forest fires indicate that they are set either intentionally or negligently.

Ground fires burn the undergrowths leading to a shortage of food for herbivores like elephant, gaur, sambar, chital, wild boar etc. Fires destroy seedlings, affecting regeneration of native plant species and replace edible plant species with inedible exotic species like *Chromolaena*, *Parthenium* and

Lantana. Due to the shortage of food, herbivores raid crops which elevate human-wildlife conflict. Furthermore, forest fires are known to kill numerous small, slow-moving and ground-nesting species of mammals, birds, reptiles, insects, micro organisms and even the dependent young ones of large vertebrates.

1.4.5 Constructions of Roads and Railway Tracts

Roads and railway tracts spanning linearly often break the contiguity of forest, resulting in their fragmentation and act as physical barriers restricting free movement of animals. Tree dwelling wildlife such as lion-tailed macaque, giant squirrel and flying squirrel would be unable to move to different patches of forests as roads and railway lines break tree canopy continuity affecting their range for foraging food. Besides, they also impose significant impact on wildlife behaviour and survival. Roads and railway lines running through forests lead to the accidents and often death of several wild animals, which are being hit by fast-moving vehicles and trains. Nocturnal animals (such as mouse deer, civet, black-naped hare, leopard and sambar) are more commonly killed on roads and raillines due to poor visibility in night hours. However, there have also been several instances of tiger, elephant calves, chital, dhole, sloth bear, wolf, blackbuck and other large mammals killed due to road and train accidents. Vehicular traffic in protected areas kills numerous reptiles, birds and amphibians which often goes unnoticed. In addition to road kills, highways and bridges can harm wildlife and destroy habitat in less obvious ways. For instance, construction of such passageways subsequently leads to residential and commercial growth in its vicinity, which leads to further destruction, fragmentation and disturbance of wildernes areas.

1.4.6 Invasive Species

Invasive species are briefly defined as plants, animals, and microbes that are out of place and out of control. In recent times, invasive species are considered as one of the most serious threats to wildlife. Invasive species cause harm to wildlife in many ways. Direct threats to wildlife by the invasive species includes preying on native species, out-competing native species for food or other resources, spreading disease, preventing native species from reproducing and/or killing their young.

Once a new and aggressive species is introduced into an ecosystem, it might not have any natural predators (or controls) and, therefore, can quickly breed and spread threatening the survival of native flora and fauna. Besides, native wildlife may not have evolved necessary defenses against the invader or they cannot compete with a species that has no predators. Invasive species often degrade the quality of a healthy habitat, thereby forcing both predators and prey to search for other more suitable habitat. Some invasive species are capable of changing soil chemistry, can increase the intensity of wildfires and alter natural fire regimes. Invasive species, thus, provide inferior habitat with lesser nutritional values for native species and ultimately deplete biodiversity of a region.

An ideal example of invasive species is water hyacinth (*Eichhornea crassipes*) which was introduced to India from South America as an ornamental plant. These floating macrophytes form dense mats, reduce sunlight for submerged plants and other aquatic organisms, threaten the existence of many native wild aquatic plants and also clog waterways.

1.4.7 Overexploitation

Overexploitation is defined as the irrational and over use of several species of wild flora and fauna by people for their self-interested need. People have depended on wildlife and plants for food, clothing, medicine, shelter and many other needs since time immemorial. But in recent times due to excessive need and greed, people have started exploiting certain natural resources beyond the capacity that the natural world could supply. Consequently, the demand has overshot the sustainable yield. This has become a serious threat for many wild species. Overexploitation not only threatens the survival of the species that is collected from nature, but it also leads to the depletion of many other species that are dependent on that very species for survival.

Forests provide a large number of non-timber forest products (NTFPs) like fruit, seed, resin, medicine, honey, cane and bark which have been collected from the forests for commercial use. Constant and large-scale collections of such products cause destruction of the habitat and deprive wildlife of their food sources. Goose berries harvested during summer often deplete the food source of several species dependent on it like chital, sambar, wild boar, langur, elephant, different species of herbivores and many birds. Besides, NTFPs harvesting methods are often unscientific and have severe impact on forests. Often entire branches are cut to harvest fruits or nuts, sometimes even killing the very source of these products. At present, 34 percent of mammals and 37 percent of birds are threatened due to overexploitation.

With the advancement of boats and fishing gears, harvesting of fish and shellfish has become much efficient. As a result of expansion of the fishing industry and the increasing demands for seafood, many fishes have been exploited beyond sustainable level. As a consequence, fishes like swordfish, cod and tuna, have undergone dramatic declines. Horseshoe crabs, whose eggs provide food for migratory birds, fish and other organisms, are being harvested largely to be used as bait for eel and whelk fishing. Octopuses are suffering decline world-wide due to heavy fishing pressure. Sharks provide an interesting example in this context. Annually 200 million sharks are estimated to be killed for sport and commercial fishing and many others are killed to prepare 'shark fin soup'. Evidences are mounting that due to their late maturity, slow reproductive rate and low fecundity, many species of sharks are declining. Sharks are one of the top predators in the marine environments, and their forced rarity may lead to further adverse consequences in the ocean community.

1.4.8 Poaching and Illegal Wildlife Trade

Poaching of wild animals to cater the illegal trade of wildlife articles is one of the greatest threats to wildlife. Illegal trade is considered to be the second largest threat after arms and ammunitions. Poaching directly reduces the number of animals of a population. Moreover, hunting of herbivores has a direct effect on carnivores, as they are directly dependent on them for food. Animals are mostly killed for the local and/or international demand of their different parts as food, medicine (mainly in traditional medicinal practices like *Ayurveda*, Tibetan and Unani), clothes and decorative items. In most cases poachers target the tropical and biodiversity rich countries to cater the demand of the economically rich end users in the countries like United States, Australia, China, Japan and other Far East countries.

Tigers, leopards and other big cats are mostly killed for their skin, bones, nails and other body parts, elephants are killed for tusks, rhinoceros for horns, different species of wild ungulates for their antlers, Himalayan black bears and sloth bears for bile and gallbladder, Tibetan antelope (*Chiru*) for their fur (under wool) and mongooses for their hair. Besides, peafowl, jungle fowl and many other species of birds are trapped and killed for their colourful feathers. Amphibians are collected and shipped all over the world for medicine, education, scientific research, as well as, for pet trade and food. Skins of crocodile, python and monitor lizards are traded as these are highly prized leathers in grey markets. In addition, spotted deer, sambar, barking deer, mouse deer, wild boar, gaur and other smaller mammals like giant squirrel, hare, porcupine, pangolin, civet and birds like pigeons, quails and hornbills are regular targets of local poachers for their meat and other body parts.

Country-made shotguns are most commonly used, while noose and snares, electrocution through live wires and traps (pitfall traps, leg traps, jaw traps, etc.) set in the trail of wild animals, poison baiting etc. are some other techniques used by the poachers. In addition to poaching, many species of wild animals, as well as, orchids and other medicinal plants are also collected from the wild and traded as live animals and plants. A number of tree species that are prized for their wood and are often illegally cut and smuggled from the forests.

1.4.9 Diseases

Wildlife populations are often affected by a series of emerging diseases, some of which lead to serious declines and pose significant threat to their conservation. For example, squirrel poxvirus is contributing to the decline of the red squirrel population and crayfish plague is considered responsible for declines in native white clawed crayfish numbers. Diseases caused by or carried by invasive species are particularly threatening, as native wildlife may have no natural immunity to them. Though diseases are a normal phenomenon in nature, but human interventions can directly lead to disease outbreaks in wildlife. The diseased animals, in turn, may act as reservoirs of pathogens which not only threaten allied wild animals, but can be transmitted to domestic animals and also affect human health.

1.4.10 Pollution, Global Warming and Climate Change

Pollution often kill or impair the health of several species of wild animals. For example, the bald eagle, peregrine falcon and brown pelican nearly became extinct before scientists discovered that the synthetic chemical DDT was the cause of 'egg-shell thinning' and devastating reproductive failure in these species. The destruction of the ozone layer by chlorofluorocarbons may lead to excessive ultraviolet radiation which exerts detrimental effect on wildlife and their food sources. Synthetic chemicals, oil, toxic metals and acid rains are also included in the category of 'toxic pollutants'. Oil spills immediately affect the population of seabirds. Oil spread over the oceanic waters kills many other marine fauna of the region as well. Other forms of pollution affect wildlife in a more indirect manner by altering or destroying wildlife habitat. For instance, dumping of solid wastes often destroys several wetlands, marshes, and grasslands.

The impact of rising temperature and the subsequent climate change is multifarious and is threatening the very existence of many species throughout the globe. Some of the prominent impacts of climate change on wildlife are as follows:

- Many species show 'shifting of range' northwards to higher altitudes or in colder regions in search of favourable climate and are termed as 'climate refugees'. The areas with favourable climate then show evidences of higher competition for resources between the natives and refugees.
- Arctic ice is melting at a faster pace threatening many Arctic mammals, such as polar bears, walrus and seals those who depend on sea ice for hunting and survival.
- Glaciers are melting at a faster rate and many glaciers in different part of the globe have already

disappeared. This might lead to the decrease in the water flow of various rivers originating from those glaciers, which in turn might have an adverse impact on the wildlife depending on the glacier itself or the river for their survival.

- Sea-level is rising and the frequency and intensity of the extreme weather events are also escalating, which will inundate beaches, marshes and other low-lying areas, diminishing habitat for birds, invertebrates, fishes and other coastal wildlife.
- With the rise of the sea-surface temperature the events of coral bleaching is also increasing, threatening numerous other flora and fauna surviving on those coral reefs.
- Warming and drought stress might lead to the death of trees or else making them more vulnerable to various insect infestations. Infestations will be more severe as pests will take advantage of drought-inflicted and weakened plants, ultimately leading to widespread forest loss.
- Changing climate might also create favourable conditions for the spread of several invasive species.
- Pathogens will also spread to new areas with higher temperatures along with their hosts.
- Besides, many species take their cues about the time of migration, flowering, nesting or breeding from seasonal changes in temperature, precipitation and daylight (phenology). The changes in the climate parameters compel wildlife to alter life cycle and the timing of other natural and seasonal events like migration, nesting and breeding, flowering etc. often leading to a 'phenological mismatch', which means, some animals are laying eggs, migrating or emerging from hibernation much earlier than they used to, only to find that the plants or the insects they need for food have not yet emerged.

In a nutshell, the survival of numerous species as well as our own existence may well be in jeopardy due to global warming and climate change. Hence it is considered to be the largest threat to wildlife and mankind as well.

1.4.11 Human–Animal Conflict

With the ever increasing demand for land and other resources, forests and other wildlife habitats are often encroached by the proliferating human population in India for agriculture, large-scale developmental activities, livestock grazing, collection of various non-timber forest products etc. Besides, habitat loss and degradation of habitats force wild animals to stray into human habitation that surround forest areas leading to loss of crop, livestock and injury to both humans and animals. Human–animal conflict is intense in different parts of India. This often result in retaliatory killing of wild animals, such as electrocution of elephants, killing of leopards, bears and other species.

1.4.12 Excessive Tourism

Tourism in the protected areas is very essential to understand and build public support for the issues related to wildlife conservation. But, unplanned tourism may pose a threat to wildlife. Roads and developmental activities to aid tourism, fragment wildlife habitats, often leading to disturbances and behavioural changes in wildlife and might also indirectly aid spread of exotic plant species (like *Parthenium*, *Lantana*, *Eupatorium,* etc.). High density of tourists in the protected areas, unruly behaviour of some tourists, uncontrolled traffic into protected areas, littering of forests, passive harassment of wildlife and driving at high speeds inside protected areas resulting in road-kills are some of the other activities that not only create nuisance in those eco-sensitive areas, but also disturb wildlife and their habitat. Therefore, strict guidelines should be implemented for tourists inside protected areas and any deviation from those guidelines must be strictly dealt with.

1.4.13 Population Explosion, Poverty, Lack of Awareness and Activism

Human population explosion and subsequent encroachment in natural landscapes are some of the greatest threats to Indian wildlife. Exponential growth in population resulting in increasing need for food, housing, services, transportation and other infrastructure pose ever increasing demands on land, water and other natural resources. In India, people below poverty line and without education are often so much engaged with their struggle for survival that they hardly bother to even think about wildlife. Poor people inhabiting villages in the forest fringe areas are often exploited by the wildlife traders to collect the wildlife articles. Being mostly unaware of the legal provisions, they often commit crime. Besides, awareness for wildlife conservation is also deficient among the general masses. Despite of being included in the curriculum, even the students fail to realize the importances of wildlife and their threats. As a consequence, activism for conservation of wildlife and their habitat is still poor in this country.

1.4.14 Legal Lapse

India though possesses stringent laws for the conservation of wildlife, yet proper implementation of laws is often lacking. The importance of wildlife conservation is often not properly realized by the enforcement officials and some legal personnel in the judiciary. There are instances that a person despite of committing some of the heinous wildlife crime, was granted bail. The person being free in bail was found involved in repeat offence. Also, the process of litigation is often very slow.

1.4.15 Other Threats

Some threats are not as obvious as the others mentioned above. In the past, due to lack of knowledge and understanding of wildlife management, several decisions have been carried out which were not in tune with the needs of wildlife. Instead of understanding the underlying ecological principles, certain solutions were proposed and implemented based on the wishful thinking or to show political obedience of the authority.

For instance, exotic tree species are planted in natural grasslands of the Western Ghats. It has been documented that different types of waste such as plastic, food and even carcass of livestock, rotten fruits and vegetables, as well as medical wastes are being dumped inside wildlife habitats, which apart from polluting habitats also cause communicable diseases to wildlife. Dead livestock carrying dangerous diseases such as Foot and Mouth (F&M) and Anthrax once thrown inside forests might lead to the spread of these deadly diseases to wild ungulates resulting in their death.

Underlying Causes — At A Glance

- Population pressure vis-à-vis poverty
- Administrative legacy and policy failure
- Environmental laws — weak enforcement
- Unsustainable developmental projects
- International trade factors
- Resource documentation poor
- Habitat loss and fragmentation
- Overexploitation of resources
- People's participation —
    - Lack of awareness
    - Indifferent attitude

1.5 THREATENED WILDLIFE

Threatened animals are those whose numbers are fewer than normal and whose habitats are constricted with several disturbances, or fragmented or destroyed altogether due to anthropogenic or natural causes. To highlight the status of threatened species for the purpose of conservation, the International Union for Conservation of Nature and Natural Resources (IUCN) has established eight main conservation categories on the basis of two basic criteria a) the existing population size b) degree of threats to their survival. Animals are categorized into *data deficient*, *least concern*, *near threatened*, *vulnerable*, *endangered*, *critically endangered*, *extinct in the wild* and *extinct*. Of all vertebrate species worldwide, 6.69 percent are considered threatened and, of all invertebrate species, only 0.16 percent are considered threatened.

1.5.1 Extinct (EX)

A taxon is declared 'Extinct' when exhaustive surveys in known and/or expected habitat, at appropriate times (diurnal, seasonal, annual), throughout the historic range of the species over a time frame appropriate to the taxon's life cycle and life form reveals that there is no reasonable doubt that the last individual has died and no longer exist in captivity, as well as, in the wild.

Example: Desert bandicoot (*Perameles eremiana*), dodo (*Raphus cucullatus*), passenger pigeon (*Ectopistes migratorius*), etc.

1.5.2 Extinct in the Wild (EW)

A taxon is considered 'Extinct in the Wild' when exhaustive surveys in its known and/or expected habitat, throughout the historic range of the species for over a considerable time have failed to record single individual and is known only to survive in cultivation (for plants) or in captivity (for animals) as a naturalized population (or populations) well outside the past range.

Example: Black soft-shell turtle (*Nilssonia nigricans*).

1.5.3 Critically Endangered (CR)

A taxon is 'Critically Endangered' when the best available evidence indicates that it is facing an extremely high risk of extinction in the wild in immediate future.

Example: Namdapha flying squirrel (*Biswamoyopterus biswasi*), white-rumped vulture (*Gyps bengalensis*), great Indian bustard (*Ardeotis nigriceps*), gharial (*Gavialis gangeticus*).

1.5.4 Endangered (EN)

A taxon is 'Endangered' when the best available evidence indicates that it is facing a very high risk of extinction in the wild and may become critically endangered in the near future because populations of the species are decreasing in size throughout its range.

Example: Hog deer (*Axis porcinus*), hispid hare (*Caprolagus hispidus*), dhole (*Cuon alpinus*), Asian elephant (*Elephas maximus*), Himalayan musk deer (*Moschus leucogaster*), tiger (*Panthera tigris*), Ganges river dolphin (*Platanista gangetica*), fishing cat (*Prionailurus viverrinus*), etc.

1.5.5 Vulnerable (VU)

A taxon is 'Vulnerable' when the best available evidence indicates that it is facing high risk of extinction in the wild and may become endangered in near future because populations of the species are decreasing in size throughout its range.

Example: Gaur (*Bos gaurus*), leopard (*Panthera pardus*), clouded leopard (*Neofelis nebulosa*), greater one-horned rhinoceros (*Rhinoceros unicornis*), binturong (*Arctictis binturong*), sarus crane (*Antigone antigone*), lesser adjutant (*Leptoptilos javanicus*), king cobra (*Ophiophagus hannah*), etc.

1.5.6 Near Threatened (NT)

A taxon is 'Near Threatened' when it has been evaluated against the Red Data Book criteria but does not qualify for Critically Endangered, Endangered or Vulnerable at present, but is close to qualifying for or is likely to qualify for a threatened category in near future.

Example: Asiatic golden cat (*Catopuma temminckii*), striped hyaena (*Hyaena hyaena*), blackbuck (*Antilope cervicapra*), Assam macaque (*Macaca assamensis*), Asiatic wild ass (*Equus hemionus*), oriental darter (*Anhinga melanogaster*), painted stork (*Mycteria leucocephala*), Alexandrine parakeet (*Psittacula eupatria*), etc.

1.5.7 Least Concern (LC)

A taxon is 'Least Concern' when it has been evaluated according to the Red Data Book criteria and does not qualify for Critically Endangered, Endangered, Vulnerable or Near Threatened at present as well as estimated to have a good chance to perpetuate in future. Widespread and abundant taxa are included in this category.

Example: Black kite (*Milvus migrans*), chital (*Axis axis*), golden jackal (*Canis aureus*).

1.5.8 Data Deficient (DD)

A taxon is 'Data Deficient' when there is inadequate information to make a direct, or indirect, assessment of its risk of extinction based on its distribution and/or population status. A taxon in this category may be well studied, and its biology is well known, but appropriate data on abundance and/or distribution are lacking. Data Deficient is therefore not a category of threat. Listing of taxa in this category indicates that more information is required and acknowledges the possibility that future research will show that threatened classification is appropriate.

Example: Long-snout Seahorse (*Hippocampus reidi*), Somali pigeon (*Columba oliviae*), *Duttaphrynus crocus*,

1.5.9 Not Evaluated (NE)

A taxon is 'Not Evaluated' when it is has not yet been evaluated against the criteria.

Example: Reticulated python (*Python reticulatus*)

1.6 RED DATA BOOK AND IUCN RED LIST OF THREATENED ANIMALS

The IUCN maintains record of animals that are known to be in danger in the "Red Data Book". Based on the above-mentioned IUCN categories, the World Conservation Monitoring Centre (WCMC) has evaluated and described threats of about 60000 plant and 2000 animal species in its series of Red Data Books. Although, great majority of the species on these lists are plants, there are also species of fish, amphibians, reptiles, invertebrates, birds and mammals. The IUCN system has been applied to specific geographical areas as a way to highlight conservation priorities. IUCN has also begun to issue lists of the world's most threatened plants and animals to help focus attention on the threatened species which need immediate conservation efforts. These lists, therefore, include species of unique conservation value. On a global basis, the IUCN has estimated that about 10 percent of the world's vascular plant species (totaling about 20,000–25,000 species) are under varying degrees of threat. IUCN published the "IUCN Red List of Threatened Animals" for the first time in 1988, which is a compilation of endangered wildlife species. On the other hand, the Red Data Book provides data on population status of the species included in the Red List. Both the Red List and Red Data Book show the risk of extinction based on the biological data. They have no legal definition but serve as the scientific basis for the promotion of conservation of endangered wildlife. The first Red Data Book of animals was compiled in 1991 by the Environment Agency. But, it was realized that Red Data Books need periodical revisions as the distribution and habitat of wildlife changes constantly. For that reason, the Environment Agency had set up a group of specialists in mammals, birds, amphibians, reptiles and so on. Subsequently, a revised set of Red List Categories was adopted by IUCN in December 1994 with the help of the IUCN Species Survival Commission (SSC). Since 1995, the Red List and Red Data Book is being regularly updated.

1.7 AIMS AND OBJECTIVES OF WILDLIFE CONSERVATION

Wildlife management emerged as a branch of science in the 1930s. But, during the initial years, till 1960s, it primarily revolved around management of game animals. During 1970s, this trend shifted as many people increasingly took interest and initiative to manage and protect several non-game species, especially the song-birds. Human perception, ethics, culture and legal concepts often intermingle with wildlife management practices.

The term 'conservation' was coined by Dr. Gifford Pinchot in 1908 from two Latin words – *con* (=together) and *servare* (=guard). Conservation is one of the major applications of ecology to ensure scientific and sustainable utilization of resources. Conservation may be defined as the scientific management of natural resources, both living and its associated non-living attributes, in order to yield sustainable benefits to the present generations, as well as, safeguarding the potentiality of the resources to meet the needs and aspirations of the future generations in the days to come.

Wildlife conservation is commonly known as the practice of protecting endangered flora and fauna and their habitat to ensure the existence of wildlife and wilderness areas and their values for future generations. Wildlife conservation has become increasingly important due to adverse impacts of various anthropogenic activities on nature in the recent time.

Objectives of Conservation

Conservation is chiefly concerned with the protection, preservation, propagation and judicious control of population for rare species of plants and animals in their natural habitats and can be achieved through intelligent exploitation of nature keeping all its biological and physical components in its original form as far as practicable. Actually conservation of wildlife is equated with the proper management of nature. Following are the different objectives of conservation—

1. To study the interrelationship of plants and animals in their natural habitat.
2. To protect and preserve the rare species of plants and animals from extinction.
3. To preserve the breeding stock of wildlife.
4. To prevent deforestation.
5. To maintain the balance of nature.

1.8 WILDLIFE CONSERVATION IN INDIA — THROUGH AGES

Indian culture is based on an ardent faith of conservation and shows a tradition of love, respect and reverence for all life forms. Several monks, saints and religious leaders asked common people to be more compassionate for all living creatures around them. Through religion or ancient folklores, the message of conservation was spread among the common people. As a consequence, admiration for wildlife became a part of their lifestyle and culture. During the 3rd century B.C., Emperor Ashoka defined a king's duty as "not only to protect the citizens and maintain law and order, but also to preserve animal life and forests as well". Embracing Buddhism, he brought about significant changes in his style of governance in the later part of his reign. He protected many birds and animals by imposing ban on the royal hunt and also introduced a fine of 100 *panas* or coins for poaching deer inside the forests. This is one of the earliest conservation laws and is considered to be the pioneering effort for the conservation of Indian wildlife (Rangarajan, 2005). *Ahimsa* (non-violence) indeed became the central concept of the religious belief of Buddhism and Jainism in the 7th and 6th centuries B.C. Jain's religious beliefs even speak to avoid harming the worms and insects. These ideas later formed a part of the Hindu religion and were passed through centuries that followed. Hindu religion has many deities with animal attributes that reflect the relation between man and nature. Several wild species being thus associated with the deities have been safeguarded from perishing in the hands of the humans through ages.

Certain flora, fauna and habitats have been considered to be 'sacred' in different traditional and religious beliefs, which, in turn, contributed towards their conservation by the communities through ages. Several tribal rituals in our country also reflect the age old respect for wild flora and fauna. The *Warli* tribe in the north of Mumbai worships *Vaghadeva*, the tiger god. Tigers are worshipped in several other parts of the country as well. The *Baghel Rajputs* in central India never take part in the pursuit of the tigers as they claim to be the descendents of these big cats. In Sunderbans, the forest dwellers, as well as, the people entering inside the forest worship *Banabibi*, who is believed to be the goddess of the mangrove forests and will protect them from all evil forces inside the forests.

The *Bishnois*, an ethnic group of Rajasthan, strictly follow the 29 principles laid down by their religious prophet Jameshwarji Maharaj. Many of those principles are based on certain ecological attributes. They worship the Khejri trees (*Prosopis cineraria*) and believe that the spirits of their ancestors reside in blackbuck. In 1730, soldiers of the then Maharaja came to cut Khejri trees in a *Bishnoi* village. Amrita devi, a *bishnoi* woman, protested and many other villagers embraced Khejri trees to save them from the soldiers. In the ensuing slaughter, 362 villagers along with Amrita devi and her children died. This incidence of sacrifice was considered to be the inspiration for *Chipko* movement.

In the past, peacocks were supposed to save crop field from snakes and insect pests and was, therefore, guarded from hunters. Even the creatures that were potentially dangerous were not always killed. Co-existence was a part of human lifestyle. Many ethnic communities traditionally protect certain forest patches from certain religious beliefs and social taboos. These sanctified areas of forests are termed as 'sacred groves' and felling of trees, collection of forest produces and killing of animals are forbidden in these areas. As a result, these areas are found to be teeming in biodiversity and often serve as last refuge for several flora and fauna. There are evidences that several forest tribes worship certain parts of the forests. In addition to that, there are several old trees in every village, which are worshipped as 'sacred trees'.

The ecological map of the entire south Asia was indeed strikingly different from the one we know today. It was mostly covered by the forests with fewer cultivated lands in between. The Chinese traveller, Hiuen Tsang, in his travel across the India during 17th century A.D. repeatedly refers to the dense forests tracts that made his journey difficult. Perhaps due to low density of human population and large areas of forest and fallow, human-animal conflicts were also limited in the past.

Before colonialism, the *Mughal* states honoured the local customs and were very much conscious about harming local sentiments. However, during this period hunting was an essential practice related to warfare. During winter, the ruler used to hunt with thousands of his soldiers in a patch of jungle. All animals caught were considered as ruler's prey — a part of which was often sold and few were also distributed among the poor. Rulers used to declare few areas of the forests as 'reserved' where intrusion of common people was restricted. These areas supplied many valuable animals, like cheetahs for hunting, elephants for warfare, etc.

With the establishment of British colonialism, the traditional scenario of wildlife conservation in India changed radically. *Shikar* not only replaced *ahimsa*, but also became a part of the culture and festive occasions of the elites. Sport hunting rapidly depleted the population of several wild species. Several species disappeared and many other were on the edge of extinction with a dwindling population. Worried by this sharp decline in animal population, officials realized the need for animal conservation. Thus, a new regime for conservation of wildlife arose. However, conservation of wildlife initiated not just to save animals, but primarily to continue with hunting as an imperial sport. Forest legislation in India dates back to 1865 when first Indian Forest Act was passed, which was later revised in 1878. First regular policy statement relating to forestry in India was issued in 1894. The present form of Indian Forest Act came into force in 1927. The Indian Forests Act of 1865 extended the British Colonial claims over forests in India and empowered the British government to declare any land covered with trees as a government forest and make rules to manage it. The Forest Act of 1878 truncated the centuries-old use of forests by traditional communities and secured the colonial governments control over the forestry. Thus, most of the then forest laws were introduced to protect forests from grazing, trapping, gleaning and to establish their control over commercially valuable timber and other forest produces. So the colonial forest laws and game laws were introduced actually to exclude the locals from being a part of the conservation processes.

Serious conservation efforts were taken in the post independent era. Pandit Jawaharlal Nehru, the first Prime Minister of India, initiated immediate measures to protect Indian wildlife and formed the Indian Board of Wildlife (IBWL) in 1952. In this very year, a new National Forest Policy was enunciated. However, *shikar* still continued in different parts of independent India and the princes further depleted several wild species as a consequence of 'trophy hunting'. A major breakthrough occurred in 1969, as the then Prime Minister, Mrs. Indira Gandhi, addressed a major international conference to put this gloomy situation to an end. As a result, 1970s saw a new beginning and more resolute initiative towards wildlife conservation. Serious concern had been expressed about several threatened species and shrinking wilderness of India in 1969, a national ban on tiger hunting was imposed in 1970 and in 1972, Wildlife (Protection) Act with stronger punitive powers and a long list of protected species, came into force. Further, Forest (Conservation) Act was passed in 1980 to protect the forest covers in India and prevent indiscriminate conversion of forest lands for non-forestry purposes. National Wildlife Action Plan has been adopted in 1983 for the protection of dwindling wildlife. Environment (Protection) Act was enacted in the year 1986 to protect the environment parse. The Biological Diversity Act was implemented in 2002, which is one of the most recent legislations associated with the conservation, documentation and sustainable use of biodiversity and the traditional knowledge associated therewith. The Scheduled Tribes and Other Traditional Forest Dwellers (Recognition of Forest Rights) Act, 2006 is a major legal provision implemented in the recent times to ensure the rights of tribal people over the forests where they had inhabited for centuries and thus include them in the process of wildlife conservation in this country.

Project Tiger was launched in 1973 and many other species conservation programmes followed. Another major Central Government sponsored species conservation programme was 'Project Elephant', which was initiated in 1992 to conserve these mega herbivores in their natural habitat. Later, as another conservation initiative, several wild flora and fauna were provided with a 'status quo' and were declared as state/national flora and fauna. States were entrusted with the responsibility to take necessary steps to increase their population especially in the relevant conservation areas within the state.

At present, the policy framework for wildlife conservation in the country is provided by the National Board of Wildlife (NBWL) which is chaired by the Prime Minister of India. In 2002, the National Wildlife Action Plan (2002–2016) was adopted which —

- Is based on the philosophy of identifying and protecting representative wild habitats across all ecosystems.
- Emphasized people's support and active participation in wildlife conservation.

1.9 DIFFERENT APPROACHES OF WILDLIFE CONSERVATION

- Conservation through laws
- Establishment of protected areas
- Species preservation scheme
- Prevent deforestation
- Habitat improvement
- Preservation of breeding stock
- Periodic census
- People's participation
- Inclusion of conservation biology in school/ college curricula.

1.10 MODES OF CONSERVATION

There are two distinct modes of conservation *viz., in-situ* conservation and *ex-situ* conservation.

1.10.1 *In-situ* Conservation

Conservation of a species (or genetic resources) within their original habitat is termed as *in-situ* conservation. For *in-situ* conservation, the area with most potential resource base needs to be identified and the area is to be demarcated as protected area. As the species is conserved in their natural habitat, hence, this type of conservation is also commonly called as 'on-site conservation'.

India is carrying out *in-situ* conservation since long back through establishing a network of protected areas (PAs) throughout the country safeguarding the natural habitats of several threatened species. Such PAs are of various categories *viz.* species oriented wildlife reserves, national parks, wildlife sanctuaries, biosphere reserves, community reserves, conservation reserves, cultural landscapes, etc.

It is to be noted that *in-situ* conservation is very difficult to adopt in the following situations where:

- the target species remain very few in number, which is well below the 'minimum viable population' (MVP).
- the reproductive success of the species is very low.
- the habitat of the species could not be designated as a 'protected area' due to the conflict with certain socio-economic issues.

Therefore, in spite of such long history of wildlife conservation in this country, only 4.58 percent of the geographical area is presently conserved under PA network.

1.10.2 *Ex-situ* Conservation

Conservation of a particular species, or a part of it, outside its original habitat is known as *ex-situ* conservation. In this mode of conservation, the sample population is usually kept in a simulated environment and is perpetuated in genetic resource centres, zoological parks, botanical gardens, etc. Besides, gene pools and gametes are stored in germplasm banks for seeds, pollens, semen, ova, cells, tissues etc. Therefore, *ex-situ* conservation is commonly referred to as 'outside habitat conservation'. In addition to protection of a species in captivity, the objective of *ex-situ* conservation is also to reintroduce the individuals of wild species back to the nature.

India has a chain of 45 zoological parks and 61 botanical gardens and in some of them *ex-situ* conservation is practiced mainly through captive breeding of animals and culture of representative plants. Plants are relatively easier to conserve through *ex-situ* conservation where botanical gardens, seed banks, pollen storage stations, tissue culture and genetic engineering laboratories play vital roles. Besides, certain faunal species are protected through 'conservation breeding programmes' carried out in various zoos throughout the globe, as well as, in India.

Different modes of wildlife conservation have been schematically represented in Figure 1.2.

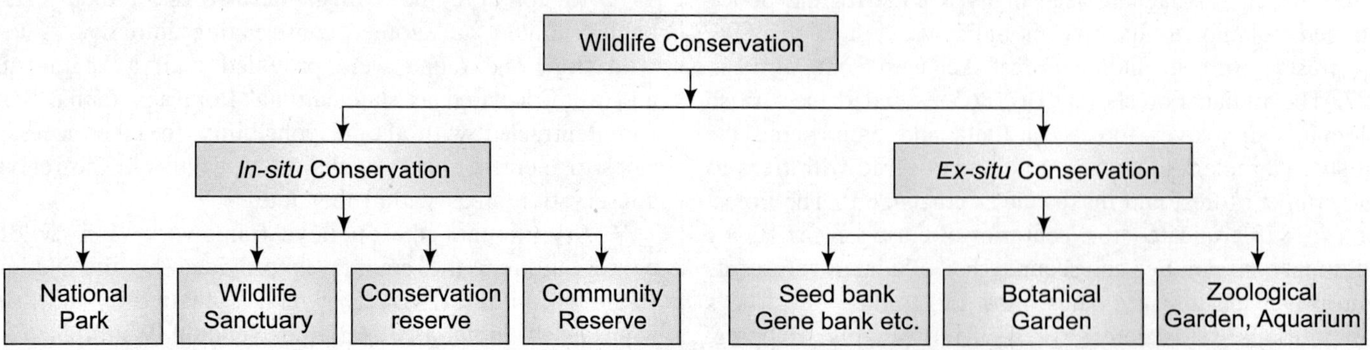

FIGURE 1.2 Schematic diagram of different modes of wildlife conservation.

1.11 NECESSITY FOR WILDLIFE CONSERVATION

Wildlife conservation has been advocated over the years by many government and non-government organizations throughout the globe and there is more than one reason for which conservation of wild flora and fauna is considered of utmost importance in the present time.

First of all, we must understand that evolution and wildlife is intricately linked. Diverse flora and fauna of today has undergone adaptations, adaptive radiations, speciation and extinctions and is ultimately a product of 3.5 billion years of evolution. On the other hand, it has become increasingly clear through various evolutionary studies that a family or genus with greater diversity of species has better chance to adapt environmental changes and survive. Variety of species and their habitats play an important role in ecosystem functioning and provide vital ecological services like nutrient and water cycling, soil formation and retention, resistance against invasive species, plant pollination, climate regulation, as well as, pest and pollution control. From time immemorial, the efficiency of new medicines or any new surgical method is often tested on several species of animals. Around 50,000–70,000 plant species are used in traditional and modern medicine worldwide and more than a third of pharmaceuticals originated from wild plants. There are 121 clinically useful prescription drugs worldwide, that are derived from plants (Payne, et al., 1991) of which, about 70 percent have attracted the attention of pharmaceutical industry due to their wide application in traditional medicine (Abelson 1990). In India, about 18000 species of angiosperms are used in indigenous systems of medicine like *Ayurveda* and Unani, of which about 3000 species are considered as important sources of medicinal and aromatic chemical compounds (Gupta et al., 2013).

FAO (2009), estimated that 119.2 million tones of wild aquatic organisms (including fishes, molluscs and crustaceans) are harvested annually from the oceans, which significantly contribute towards food security of a major human population of the globe. Besides, in many countries people inflicted with sheer poverty and food insecurity often rely heavily on meat from wild animals. The value of goods and services provided by ecosystems is estimated to be about 33 trillion dollars annually, which is nearly twice the global production resulting from human activities (Costanza et al., 1997).

Despite knowing such importance of wildlife for a long time, human activity has been causing massive extinctions. The Millennium Ecosystem Assessment (2005) highlighted a substantial and largely irreversible loss in the diversity of life on earth due to human actions, with some 10–30 percent of the mammal, bird and amphibian species threatened with extinction. After the five 'mass extinction events' in geological history (i.e., Cretaceous–Paleogcene extinction event, Triassic–Jurassic extinction event, Permian–Triassic extinction event, Late Devonian extinction, Ordovician–Silurian extinction event), the present scenario of species extinction is caused by various anthropogenic activities and is often referred to as "the sixth extinction crisis". The rapid loss of species as estimated by experts to be between 1,000 and 10,000 times higher than the *natural extinction rate* (means the rate of species extinctions that would occur if we humans were not around). Such escalating biodiversity loss has widespread implications for both human and environmental security. Experts calculate that with the present extinction rate between 0.01 and 0.1 percent of all species will become extinct each year. Over the centuries scientists have discovered and catalogued between 1.4 and 1.8 million species, which means between 200 and 2,000 species, will potentially be extinct every year. Furthermore, Mora et al., (2011) predicts that our planet is home to 8.7 (± 1.3) million species, which means that only around 20 percent of species present in this planet have so far been cataloged. In addition to this fact, only 2.5 percent of the described species have so far been assessed by IUCN. Taking all these issues into consideration and with increased current extinction rates, it may so happen that many unknown organisms will disappear even before they are discovered.

Conservation of wildlife is essential as it ensures not only a proper ecological balance, but also ensures the survival of mankind. It is pertinent to mention here that the absence of wildlife due to lack of conservation initiatives is attributed to be one of the causes for the culmination of the *Mohenjodaro* civilization by some historians. Most of the people of this area were good hunters who relentlessly killed the carnivores. As a consequence, number of herbivores increased, who voraciously fed on the vegetation, subsequently destroyed the forests and grasslands. Consequently, the adjoining deserts advanced and finally led to the end of an enviable civilization. This gives us a useful snapshot and highlights the pressing need for wildlife conservation.

Wildlife and biodiversity are undoubtedly the fundamental components of life on earth. They create complex ecosystems that could never be made by humans. The value of biodiversity, both intrinsically and to humans, is immense and therefore must be protected at all costs. We should not forget that our descendants and future generations will inherit the situation that we create today through our own attitude and action towards the environment.

Aldo Leopold, a Professor at the University of Wisconsin and an American author mentioned that "wildlife had once fed us and shaped our culture. It still yields up pleasure in leisure hours, but we try to reap that pleasure by modern machinery and thus destroy part of its value. Reaping it by modern mentality would yield not only pleasure, but wisdom as well. .... It has now become essential that we support the active conservation of wildlife for reasons which reflect the different facets of our relationship with the natural world".

REVIEW QUESTIONS

1. Define Wildlife. State the importance of Wildlife. Give an impression on the Wildlife wealth of India.
2. What do you mean by endemism? Cite examples.
3. Define Biodiversity hotspot. Name the Biodiversity hotspots of India. What do you mean by Megadiversity Country? India is considered to be a megadiversity country — why?
4. Enumerate the underlying reasons for depletion of Indian Wildlife.
5. Elaborate the impact of invasive species on native Wildlife.
6. What do mean by threatened fauna? Distinguish between Endangered and Vulnerable species with example.
7. What is meant by extinct fauna? Cite example.
8. What do you mean by 'Sixth mass extiction'?
9. What is 'Phenological mismatch'?
10. What is Red Data Book? Give the full form of 1. WWF, 2. BNHS, 3. WII, 4. CITES, 5. WCMC 6. SSC
11. What are the aims and objectives of conservation of Wildlife? Why conservation of wildlife is an urgent agenda?
12. Elaborate the different approaches of wildlife conservation.
13. Distinguish between *in-situ* and *ex-situ* modes of conservation.
14. Give an account on the conservation of Indian Wildlife through ages.
15. Justify the role of sacred groves in wildlife conservation.
16. Explain the role of climate change on wildlife. What do you mean by 'Climate refugees'?
17. Define 'eco-sensitive area'. Explain how excessive tourism leads to disturbance to animal community inside the protected areas.

REFERENCES

Abelson P.H., Medicine from plants, *Science,* **247**, 513, 1990.

Botanical Survey of India, *Flora and Vegetation of India - An Outline*. Botanical Survey of India, Howrah, 1983.

Costanza R., dArge R., de Groot R., Farber S., Grasso M., Hannon B., Limburg K., Naeem S., Oneill R.V., Paruelo, J., Raskin, R.G., Sutton, P. and van den Belt, M., The value of the world's ecosystem services and natural capital, *Nature*, **387**, 253–260, 1997.

FAO, *The State of World's Forest*, Food and Agriculture Organization of the United Nations. Rome, Italy, 1999.

FAO, *The State of World Fisheries and Aquaculture 2008*, Food and Agriculture Organization of the United Nations. Rome, Italy, 2009. Retrieved from: www.fao.org/docrep/011/i0250e/i0250e00.htm

Gee, E.P., *The Wildlife of India*, Collins, London, 1964.

Gupta, M., Thakur, S., Sharma, A. and Gupta, S., Qualitative and Quantitative Analysis of Phytochemicals and Pharmacological Value of Some Dye Yielding Medicinal Plants, *Oriental Journal of Chemistry*, **29,** 2, 475–481, 2013.

Millennium Ecosystem Assessment (MEA), *Ecosystems and Human Well-Being: Synthesis*, Island Press, Washington, DC, 2005.

Mora, C., Tittensor, D.P., Adl, S., Simpson, A.G.B. and Worm, B., How Many Species Are There on Earth and in the Ocean? *PLoS Biol*, **9**, 8, e1001127, 2011.

Myers, N., Mittermeier, R.A., Mittermeier, C.G., de Fonseca, G.A.B. and Kent, J., Biodiversity hotspots for conservation priorities, *Nature*, **403**, 853–858, 2000.

Payne, G.F., Bringi, V., Prince, C. and Shuler, M.L., *Plant cell and tissue culture in liquid systems*, Hanser Publications, Munich, 1991.

Pinchot, G., *The conservation of natural resources*, U.S. Deptt. of Agriculture, Washington, 1908.

Prayurasiddhi, T., Chaiwatana, S. and Naporn, S., *Forest Complexes in Thailand*, Prueksirin Printing, Royal Forest Department, Bangkok, 1999.

Rangarajan, M., *India's Wildlife History: An Introduction*, Permanent Black, Delhi, 2005.

Urquhart, G., Chomentowski, W., Skole, D. and Barber, C., *Tropical deforestation*, NASA, Earth Observatory, 2001. Retrieved from: http://earthobservatory.nasa.gov/Features/Deforestation/tropical_deforestation_2001.pdf

2

WILDLIFE HABITAT ECOLOGY

2.1 CONCEPT OF BIOME

Earth contains diverse life forms, which vary from simple unicellular organisms to complex flora and fauna. All these living beings are interdependent on other biotic components and abiotic factors of their surroundings, as well as, on their environment. Hence, any change in one part of the environment leads to a 'ripple effect' on other parts and influences the entire floral and faunal community of that particular environment. Moreover, the environment of different parts of the globe varies significantly from each other. As a consequence, the floral and faunal compositions of several regions are often distinct from each other. However, despite being situated in geographically different regions, many places spread over large area on Earth share similar climatic conditions and create a typical ecosystem. Such major ecosystems spread over large geographical areas with unique physical and climatic parameters and distinct ecological communities are termed as *biomes*. The plants and animals are well adapted to the physical environment of the biomes.

There is no unanimity among the scientists as far as the definition and classification of biome is concerned. The vegetation of a biome is also called *plant formation*. Similar biomes in different parts of the globe without any operational or transitional connection are termed as *biome types*. For example, tropical rainforests are present in the African, Oriental and Australasian, Central and South American and Madagascar regions without any continuity between them. So, tropical rainforests in each of these continents would be termed as *tropical rainforest biome type*. This is true for many other biomes like grasslands, deserts, etc. Furthermore, a large landmass contains various *biotic provinces*, which are continuous geographic areas with typical flora and fauna distinguishable (at species or subspecies level) from adjacent such areas.

2.1.1 Definition

Biomes may be defined as a biotic community formation in a large geographical area characterized by distinctive plant and animal groups, which are adapted to that particular environment and are often represented by the dominant growth forms of the region.

Kendeigh (1975) defined a biome as "a biotic community characterized by distinctiveness in life forms of the important climax species". According to Campbell (1996), biomes are "the world's major communities, classified according to the predominant vegetation and characterized by adaptations of organisms to that particular environment".

Rodgers et al., (2000) opined that a biome is an ecological unit, not a biogeographic unit. While according to Bird Life International, biome is defined as "a major regional ecological community, characterized by distinctive life forms and principal plant species".

2.1.2 Characteristic Features of Biome

Present day distribution and species composition of the biomes of the globe is governed by three set of factors *viz.*:

(i) Environmental Factors

These include biotic factors (food, cover, reproduction, competition, etc.) and abiotic factors (substratum, climate, rainfall, etc.).

(ii) Zoogeographic Factors

These include the place of origin, dispersal path, barrier, adaptability and evolution of the characteristic flora and fauna.

(iii) Anthropogenic Factors

These include the rapid destruction or alteration of habitat for developmental, agro-industrial, urban economy oriented anthropogenic activities.

Each biome is, thus, characterized by a major vegetation type or life form of animals or some other identifying feature of landscape. The distribution of terrestrial biomes is correlated with the regional climate, especially temperature and precipitation. Because, temperature and precipitation collectively determine the kind of vegetation that can develop at a particular site. There are various factors which affect the size, location, and character of a biome. Important factors are as follows:

(i) Length of day light and darkness.
(ii) Length of growing season.
(iii) Mean temperature, as well as, diurnal and annual difference in temperature.
(iv) Precipitation including total amount, intensity and variations over time.
(v) Speed, direction, duration and frequency of wind flow.
(vi) Soil type, slope and drainage.
(vii) Other plant and animal species.

2.2 BIOMES OF THE WORLD—AN OVERVIEW

Biomes of the world can be grouped into two broad categories—**terrestrial biomes** and **aquatic biomes**. Although terrestrial biomes are differentiated and often recognized based on predominant life form of climax vegetation, yet the species vary topographically in different parts of same biome and also on biomes of different continents. Along with the climax vegetation, persistent sub-climax communities and associated successional communities are also present.

The major terrestrial biomes are: *Tundra*, *Temperate boreal forests* (Taiga), *Temperate broadleaf deciduous forests*, *Chaparral*, *Desert, Grasslands* and *Tropical forests* (de Blij and Miller, 1996). The boundaries between the biomes may appear to be sharp on the map (Figure 2.1). However, there are often transitional areas are often present between biomes on the ground.

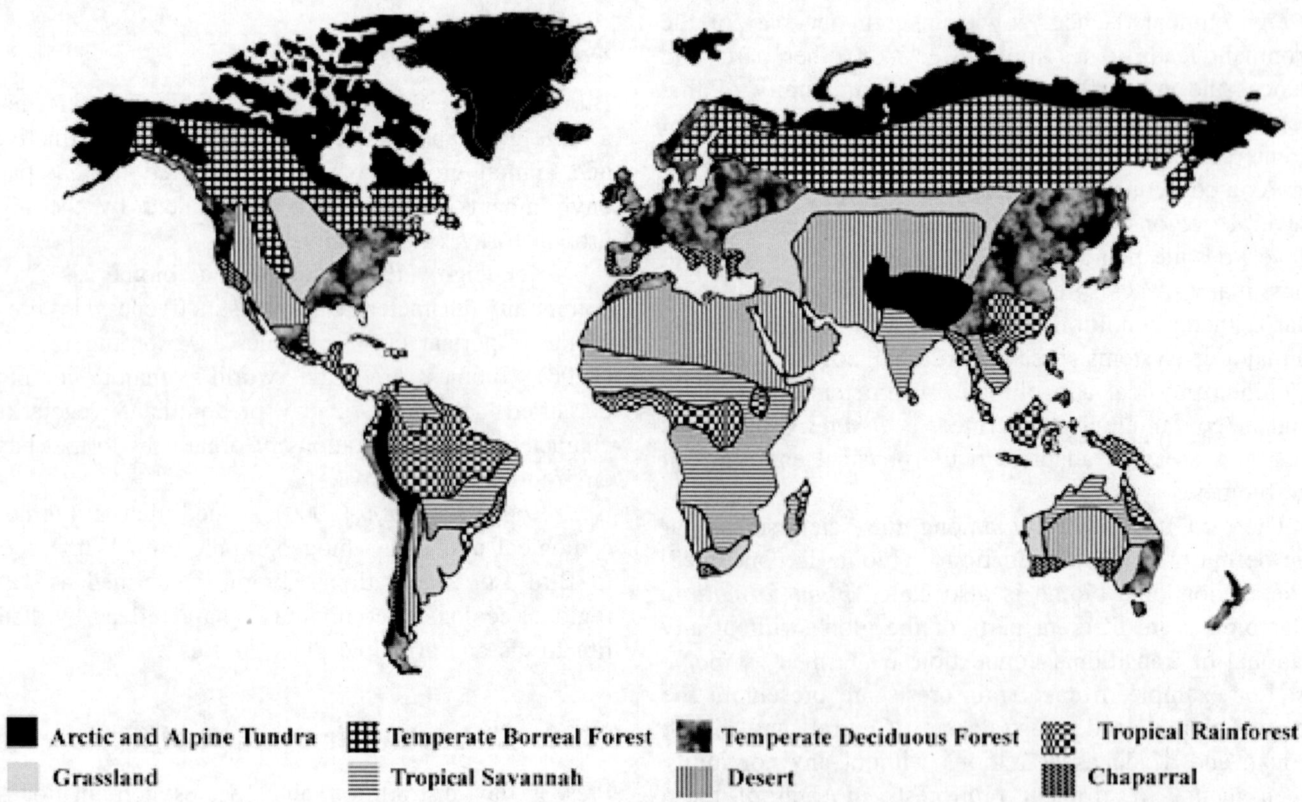

FIGURE 2.1 Distribution of the Earth's major terrestrial biomes. (Adapted from: de Blij and Miller 1996).

2.3 BIOME TYPES OF INDIA

Five major terrestrial biome types are found in India *viz.* Alpine Tundra, Montane Temperate, Tropical Forests, Grasslands and Deserts. Biome types in India are often equated to the broad forest vegetation types classified by Champion and Seth (1968), with the addition of non-forest categories such as grassland, wetland, etc. (Rodgers et al., 2000). All these biome types are described below in detail:

2.3.1 Alpine Tundra

Alpine tundra biomes are found above *tree line* usually at an altitude of around 3,000 m or more and lie just below the snow lines of the great mountain ranges around the world including the Andes, Alps, Rocky and Himalayan mountains.

Tibetan plateau and Himalayan mountains constitute the largest alpine area of the world. The Himalayan alpine range makes a curve of more than 2,400 km through southern Asia and is located in the countries of Nepal, Tibet, China, India, Pakistan and Bhutan. In India, the alpine tundra biome-type is found high up along the Himalayan ranges between 3600–4500 m beyond the tree line and below the snow line. Soil is thin, unstable and well drained and the steep topography results in rapid run off of water. This Himalayan biome is becoming more polluted due to increased amount of trekking, mountain climbing and tourism in these pristine ecosystems.

Climate: The climate of alpine tundra biomes of this country is very cold, snowy and windy with rapid radiation at night. Due to such harsh climate, it is hard to survive in most parts. There are two distinct seasons — long and very cold winter (October to May) and short and cool summer (June to September). The mean annual temperature of this region is usually below 7°C. In summer, the temperature range from 10 to 15°C, while in winter the temperature sharply drops and is often below freezing point (0°C). Winter of this region is severe with heavy snowfall. Wind coupled with high solar radiation can promote extremely high rates of evaporation and transpiration. Since, it is situated at a high altitude where the air is very thin and dry, the rainfall is fairly low and precipitation mostly occurs in the form of snowfall. However, the temperatures in the alpine biome can change from mildly warm to freezing in one day depending on wind flow, precipitation and other climate parameters. Besides, the air density is low with low oxygen, carbon-dioxide and water vapour contents. This zone is also characterized by cold, snow cover, greater penetration of light, increased rate of desiccation and high wind velocity. Since there is less atmosphere to filter UV rays from the sun, the animals and plants face very high UV-exposure.

Vegetation: Alpine vegetation varies greatly from place to place. At such high altitudes there is very little CO_2, which is necessary for photosynthesis by the plants. The soil is also less nutrient rich as the dead plants animals and other organic matters do not quickly decompose due to cold. Hence, the vegetation of alpine tundra is very sparse and mostly consists of grasses, lichens, mosses, perennial forbs, sedges and shrubs. Because of the cold and wind, most plants grow and reproduce slowly. They are often small and perennial plants which protect themselves from cold and wind by hugging the ground. Most alpine plants can grow in sandy and rocky soil and have also adapted to the dry conditions of alpine biome. There are only around 200 species of alpine plants found in this country. Trees are even sparse in this region.

Faunal Richness: Due to harsh climate and challenging landscape, animal communities are sparse in the alpine tundra zone of Himalaya which includes a few warm blooded animals, birds and some insects. Very few mammals (like yellow-bellied marmots, moles, voles, etc.) dwell in alpine tundra throughout the year. Other mammalian species are seasonally present in the alpine zone of Himalayas which include Himalayan musk deer (*Moschus moschiferus*), bharal (*Ovis nahura*), great pamir sheep (*Ovis poli*), Himalayan tahr (*Hemitragus jemlahicus*), Tibetan wild yak (*Bos grunniens*), Tibetan argali (*Ovis ammon hodgsoni*), marco polo sheep (*Ovis ammon polii*), ibex (*Capra sibirica*), markhor (*Capra falconeri*), wild goat (*Capra aegagrus*), Himalayan mouse hare (*Lagomys roylei*), *Chinchilla* spp., snow leopard (*Panthera uncia*), lynx (*Felis lynx*), martens, etc. Avifaunas of this region are common raven (*Corvus corax*), snow partridge (*Lerwa nivicola*), pipits, rosy finches, horned larks etc. Among other vertebrates, reptiles are very few and amphibians and fishes are almost absent. However, pelobatid frog (*Aleurophryne mammata*) has been reported from an altitude of 4,500m in Himalayas. Large number of insects and arachnids are best adapted invertebrates of this zone. Some of the common terrestrial insects are black bog ant (*Formica picea*), bumble bees (*Lapidariobombus separandus*), butterflies (*Colias* spp., *Argynnis* spp., *Parnassius* spp.), grasshoppers (*Bryodema* spp., *Gomphomastax* spp.). Aquatic forms are represented by mayfly (*Ephemeroptera* spp.), stonefly (*Rhabdiopteryx lunata*), caddis flies (*Trichoptera* spp.), beetles (*Amphizoa* spp.), hemipteran bugs etc.

Animal Adaptations: The animals living in alpine tundra show formidable adaptations and adjustments to survive in these great heights. In order to reduce heat loss, birds and mammals of this region are usually with large, compact bodies (Bergmann's rule) and the legs, tails, ears and other extremities of the body are shorter (Allen's rule). Alpine animals also have larger lungs and more hemoglobin-rich blood cells for efficient respiration through better oxygen uptake. This is vital for survival in these high altitude habitats with less oxygen. Some animals develop a thick insulating cover of fur or feather. The coat colours usually changes seasonally - usually white in winter and brown in summer. They also accumulate thick deposits of fat during the short growing season and this fat acts as insulation layer and energy reservour during the long winter season. During winter, some animals (like marmots and ground squirrels) undergo hibernation. Yellow-bellied marmots have been reported to hibernate for, as many as, eight months in a year. Pikas do not hibernate, but they hide under rocks in boulder fields, store food in hay piles and munch them until real food is available. Several others (mountain ungulates like sheep and goats and many species of avifauna) migrate to warmer regions at lower altitude to avoid extreme cold in harsh winters. Insects and birds usually stay close to the ground and fly as little as possible to cope up with strong winds blowing throughout the year. During the breeding season, alpine birds build compact nests to protect the eggs from cold. They also place their nests behind some trees, rocks or other similar features, which serve as an obstacle and protect the nest from direct wind. Some others crawl into holes and crevices.

2.3.2 Grassland Biome

Grasslands are biomes where vegetation is dominated by grasses (Poaceae) and other herbaceous (non-woody) plants (forbs) along with floral species of Cyperaceae and Juncaceae families. According to IUCN (2009), the vegetation-based, ecological definition of **natural grassland** is "lands covered with herbaceous plants which have less than 10 percent tree and shrub cover," and **wooded grassland** (or savanna) is "lands covered with grassland which have 10-40 percent tree or shrub cover".

The stratification of grasslands is simple. Grasslands usually consist of three strata — root layer, ground or mulch layer and herbaceous layer. Grasses may be tall (1.5–3.0 m), mid (0.5–1.5 m) or short (less than 0.5 m). Some grass species develop as distinct clumps (bunches), whereas sod forming grasses form a solid mat of grass over the ground.

Grasslands are not climax communities and often tend to be gradually replaced by shrubs or woodlands during succession. But, various climatic, edaphic and biotic factors keep grasslands in a delicate equilibrium. Grasslands are generally found in areas where the soil depth and quality is poor and the rainfall is usually low. These two geoclimatic features primarily prevent the growth of large number of trees and support the growth of grass cover during monsoon. Fires during dry season are an integral phenomenon of *savanna*. Frequent fires and grazing also prevents the succession of grasslands into forests. In grasslands, many of the grasses and other small herbs become dry during the summer months and their part above the ground dies. But, in the next monsoon the grass cover grows back from the root stock and the seeds of the previous year present in the soil. For this reason, grasslands are highly seasonal in appearance.

Types of Grasslands in India

(i) **Himalayan grasslands:** The Himalayan grasslands extends up to snowline. At lower altitudes, grasslands are present in patches along with coniferous or broadleaved forests. These grasslands are of great importance in forming the habitat of Himalayan wildlife, which require both the forest and the grassland ecosystem to survive.

(ii) **Terai–Duars grasslands:** About 25 km wide stretches of Terai-Duars grasslands are located in the low-lying waterlogged areas (marshes) at the base of the Himalayas. Vegetation of these mesophilous grasslands are a mosaic of tall riverside grasslands, savannas, evergreen and deciduous forests. Some of the tallest grasslands of the world consisting of elephant grass (which grows to a height of about five meters) are found in this region. These grasslands extend as a belt in the south of the Himalayan foothills. These grasslands are colloquially called '*Terai*' in the Ganges basin east to Nepal, then '*Duars*' in West Bengal, Bangladesh, Bhutan and Assam east to the Brahmaputra river. In India, wet grasslands, swamps and densely vegetated river valleys are largely found in Manas National Park, Namdapha National Park and Indravati National Park.

(iii) **Semi-arid grasslands:** Semi-arid (or xerophilous) grasslands are usually found in the semi desert conditions. The semi-arid plains of western India, central India and the Deccan are covered by grassland tracts with patches of thorn forests.

(iv) **Shola grasslands:** The *Shola* grasslands are the patches of undulating grasslands on hill-slopes between the *Shola* forests on the Western Ghats, Nilgiri and Annamalai ranges above 2,000 m from sea level. This forms a patchwork of grassland on the slopes and forest habitats along the streams and low-lying areas. The mosaic of *shola* and grassland together form the shola-grassland complex.

Climate: Tropical grasslands are usually found in areas with tropical wet and dry climate, which is characterized by high average temperature, a prolonged dry season followed by a season of heavy rain. The climate for grasslands is basically dry. The mean temperature ranges from 15° to 35°C and annual precipitation (rainfall) usually lies within 25–250 cm. In India, natural grasslands appear in areas with 25–90 cm annual rainfall (usually never more than 100 cm per year). However, grasslands may exist naturally in areas with higher rainfall when other edaphic, biotic or anthropogenic factors prevent forest growth. On the contrary, man-made (anthropogenic) grasslands may be present in much higher rainfall zones (as high as 200 cm).

In grasslands, dry season (with low sun period and almost no rain) is usually followed by a long and hot summer (often leading to drought conditions). The dry season may last as long as eight months. During this period, the entire grasslands becomes completely dry and fires often burn dry grasses. Then the *savannas* receive heavy rainfall when new shoots of grasses sprout. The climate is warm and humid during rainy season.

Vegetation: Grassland vegetation can vary in height from very short to quite tall. Woody plants, shrubs or trees, may occur on some grasslands — forming savannas, scrubby grassland or semi-wooded grassland. The Himalayan pasture belts have a large variety of grasses and herbs along with thousands of colourful flowering plants and medicinal plants. *Saccharum–Vetiveria* association is common in the Terai-Duars mesophilous grasslands and *kans* grass (*Saccharum spontaneum*) is often found to be the dominant grass species here. In these grasslands Sal (*Shorea robusta*) is the dominant tree in the hilly region and the riverside tropical deciduous forests comprise of trees like monkey-face tree (*Mallotus philippensis*), jamun tree (*Syzygium cumini*), cotton tree (*Bombax ceiba*), false white teak tree (*Trewia nudiflora*) and garuga tree (*Garuga pinnata*). Wet *savannas* or hygrophilous grasslands found in marshy areas are made up of *Erianthus-Phragmites* association. The scrublands of the Deccan plateau are covered with various seasonal grasses and herbs. The dominant families of flora in the *shola* grasslands belong to Graminae (mainly *Chrysopogon* spp., *Arundinella* spp., *Themeda* spp., *Ischaemum* spp., *Heteropogon* spp., etc.), and Compositae (mainly *Anaphalis* spp.) families. Marshes and streams often occur in the grasslands where floral species belonging to families Cyperaceae, Erioculaceae, Juncaceae, etc. are abundant.

Faunal Richness: Faunal diversity in Indian tropical grasslands ranges from tiny insects to large mammals. Herbivores are undoubtedly the dominant faunal groups of these grasslands. Himlayan tahr (*Hemitragus jemlahicus*), bharal or blue sheep (*Pseudois nayaur*) and other mountain ungulates migrate up into the Himalayan grasslands in summer and move down to the forests in winter. Snow leopard (*Panthera uncia*) is one of the prime carnivores of these high altitude grasslands. Terai–Duars grasslands habitats are very rich in mammalian and avian diversity. Some of the very important herbivores of these grasslands include five species of deer, *viz.* barasingha or swamp deer (*Rucervus duvaucelii*), sambar (*Rusa unicolor*), chital or spotted deer (*Axis axis*), hog deer (*Axis porcinus*) and barking deer (*Muntiacus muntjak*), along with other large grazing animals like Asiatic elephant (*Elephas maximus*), greater one-horned rhinoceros (*Rhinoceros unicornis*), gaur (*Bos gaurus*), wild water buffalo (*Bubalus arnee*) and nilgai (*Boselaphus tragocamelus*). Near-endemic hispid hare (*Caprolagus hispidus*) are also found in the Terai-Duars grasslands. Being attracted by the assemblage of such large number of herbivores, many predatory carnivores like Bengal tiger (*Panthera tigris tigris*), clouded leopard (*Neofelis nebulosa*), common leopard (*Panthera pardus*), jungle cat (*Felis chaus*) etc. strive in these mesophilous and hygrophilous grasslands. These grasslands are also home to a number of reptiles including the gharial (*Gavialis gangeticus*), mugger or marsh crocodile (*Crocodylus palustris*) and soft-shelled turtles. There are three near-endemic bird species including the vulnerable Manipur bush quail (*Perdicula manipurensis*). The 44 threatened and declining bird species are present in those grasslands. Some of them are Bengal florican (*Houbaropsis bengalensis*), lesser florican (*Sypheotides indicus*), sarus crane (*Grus antigone*) and rufous-rumped grassbird (*Graminicola bengalensis*).

The semi-arid grasslands are often found to be teaming with insect life. Many insectivorous birds are, therefore, also dependent on these grasslands to feed on these insects. Mammals such as Indian *wolf* (*Canis lupus pallipes*), blackbuck (*Antilope cervicapra*) and chinkara (*Gazella bennettii*), and birds such as the Great-Indian bustard (*Ardeotis nigriceps*), lesser florican (*Sypheotides indicus*), Malabar lark (*Galerida malabarica*), green avadavat (*Amandava formosa*), rock bush quail (*Perdicula argoondah*) and brown rock chat (*Cercomela fusca*) are adapted to these arid conditions.

The shola–grassland ecosystem–mosaic provides habitat for many threatened species including Bengal tiger (*Panthera tigris tigris*), dhole (*Cuon alpinus*), gaur (*Bos gaurus*) etc. Endemic mammals like Nilgiri tahr (*Nilgiritragus hylocrius*), Nilgiri langur (*Trachypithecus johnii*) and Nilgiri marten (*Martes gwatkinsii*) and several endemic avifauna like Nilgiri laughing thrush (*Garrulax cachinnans*), black-and-orange flycatcher (*Ficedula nigrorufa*), Nilgiri pipit (*Anthus nilghiriensis*) are found in the *shola* grasslands of the Western Ghats.

Floral Adaptations: Grassland flora, specially adapted to survive and grow in the dry seasons with long periods of droughts, usually possess extensive root systems with long tap roots to reach water table. Coarse savanna grasses possess vertical leaves exposing less surface area to sun in order to conserve water. Some tree trunks are specially modified to store water. Leaves usually drop during the dry season to reduce transpiration. During fire, above-ground portions of grasses perish, but the root portions survive to sprout again from near their base. Some other plants possess thick bark to resist annual fires. Certain grasses are bitter to taste, possess poisonous chemicals, or are with sharp edges that protect them from the grazing herbivores. Many plants of *savanna* possess storage organs (like bulbs, corns) to store food for the dry season. Extensive root systems prevent grazing animals from pulling roots out of the ground.

Animal Adaptations: Most animals of *savannas* show cursorial adaptation as speed is the only strategy to capture prey or escape from the predators in these open terrains. Hence, most of the mammalian species in *savanna* possess long legs for swift running and birds have strong wings to migrate long distances. Most of the grassland mammals have strong forelegs, long and strong hind ones and have developed hopping locomotion which enables them to get above the grass level for locomotion and also allow better visibility. The inhabitants also possess keen vision. Many herbivores forage in groups with some of the members always keeping a vigil. These *sentinels* give alarm signals or alarm calls once a prowling predator is observed or any other danger is perceived. At such slightest notion of danger, the whole group of such gregarious herbivores quickly moves to safety. Some carnivores, like lions and hyenas, also hunt in groups to drive the weaker animals away from the protection of the herd and predate. Small mammals, birds and insects of the grasslands often rely on their protective colouration and mimicry to evade from the predators. Some animals migrate out of the semi-arid xerophilous grasslands, particularly during dry and hot summer. Some other species (like many species of insects, reptiles, rodents and lagomorphs) are fossorial and dwell in the burrows beneath ground to escape from heat. Many burrowing animals go into a state of dormancy during the period of drought. Some are capable of drinking morning dew and deriving water from their food. Savanna mammals tend to give birth during the rainy season when food is plentiful. This eventually ensures sufficient nutrition for the mother to nurse her offspring and the young are more likely to survive. Scavengers like vultures and hyenas forage on the remains of other predator's kill. Fires in the tropical grasslands kill numerous insects, which again provide a feast to many birds and other animals. *Savanna* is a perfect place for birds of prey like kites, eagles, hawks and buzzards. The wide, open plains provide them with a clear view of their prey, hot air updrafts keep them soaring and they suddenly swoop down at great speed to capture prey. Occasional trees present in grasslands serve as perching, roosting or nesting sites for these raptors. Many resident and migratory waterfowls are also found in grasslands adjoining river or other wetlands.

Importance of Grasslands

Grasslands play a crucial role in wildlife management as they provide excellent forage for herbivores. Grasslands are an important part of ecosystem as they cover nearly one third of the earth's land surface and supply three quarters of the energy budget of the world.

(i) **Ecosystem services of grasslands:** Grasslands have diverse species of insects that pollinate crops, thus, increasing productivity of an ecosystem. On the other hand, insectivorous animals of grasslands help to control insect pests in adjoining agricultural lands. Besides, water seeping through vast stretches of grasslands help to replenish ground water and raise the water table. Grasslands also reduce soil erosion and presence of grasslands along the rivers reduces siltation load to a large extent. The grasslands also serve as important catchment for rivers, streams, reservoirs, dams, check-dams and village ponds, as well as, act as barrier towards desertification of land. They serve as critical wildlife habitats and support an amazing variety of animals and plants including a good number of endemic fauna. Grasslands are also used by many wild fauna as corridors for dispersal (migration).

(ii) **Anthropogenic uses of grasslands:** Many rural communities of this country often graze their livestock in natural grasslands. Besides, fodder is also collected and stored to feed cattle when there is no grass left for them to graze in summer. Grass is also used to build thatch houses and farm sheds. The thorny bushes and branches of trees growing in the semi-arid grasslands are often collected and used as a major source of fuel-wood, particularly in central and western India. Himalayan meadows have always been of major tourist attraction, particularly during spring when the grassland flowers are in full bloom. Riverine grasslands present inside many protected areas of this country are important tourist destinations for wildlife viewing.

Threats to Grasslands: About 16 percent of tropical grasslands have been converted for agriculture or urban development. The grassland cover presently comprises of only 3.7 percent of land in the country. In recent time, desertification is a significant threat to the grasslands due to change in rainfall patterns as a result of continued global warming. Frequent burning of grasses and poor agricultural practices can ruin soil and turn grasslands into lifeless, barren spaces. Besides, development of urban areas is increasingly cutting into grassland habitat. Some other major threats to Indian grasslands include overgrazing of grasslands, poaching, change in soil characteristics, clearing of the land for crops, introduction of (exotic) weeds and inappropriate plantation of trees.

Conservation of Grasslands: Conservation of various natural and important grasslands of India has to be a national priority and 'management plans' need to be developed for the major important grasslands. Conservation of grasslands should take into account that these ecosystems often serve as the habitat for various specialized fauna. Therefore, the management plans should adopt appropriate measures to preserve all the unique species of plants and animals of grasslands. Rocks, leaf litter and woody debris in natural grasslands need to be kept intact which provide niches to many plants and animals. Random and unscientific plantation of trees in grasslands might reduce the natural features of this ecosystem resulting in the destruction of this unique habitat for wildlife. In hilly areas, soil and water management in each micro-catchment helps grasslands to return to a naturally highly productive ecosystem. Periodic chemical and mechanical control of weeds is also very essential to conserve grassland habitats. Fires can have positive influence, but frequent fires must be prevented. If fire breaks out in one part of a grassland, then it needs to be rapidly controlled in order to save the habitat and diversity present in its other parts. Grasslands should not be overgrazed and it is always better to collect grass for 'stall feeding' cattle. But, if large numbers of cattle needs to graze on natural grasslands, then 'rotational grazing patterns' must be established and the degraded grasslands should be closed for grazing. Moreover, the less disturbed grassland patches which have retained their plants and animals need to be urgently protected by creating national parks and wildlife sanctuaries.

In addition to all these, campaigns to create awareness among people about the value of the grasslands is very essential. The voice of a sizeable number of local people expressing concern for disappearing grasslands along with their wonderful wildlife might motivate the Government to protect them.

2.3.3 Forest Biome

A forest is a complex ecosystem or assemblage of ecosystems dominated by trees and other woody vegetation and supports a myriad of life forms. More than 250 definitions of the term "forest" exists and all definitions stress the importance of trees in the system and include places where tree cover ranges from 25 percent to as high as 100 percent. Forest is best defined as an area that is dominated by trees having usually a single stem and a mature or potentially mature stand height exceeding 2 m and with existing or potential crown cover of overstorey strata ≥ 25 percent. In spite of being dominated by trees, the flora of a forest biome also includes large number of diverse shrubs, herbs, climbers, ferns, mosses, algae and fungi. According to the U.S. National Vegetation Classification system, forests consist of trees with overlapping crowns usually forming 60 to 100 percent cover, whereas woodlands are more open, with 25 to 60 percent cover. Depending on the constituent tree species, the forests are of several distinct types and the landscapes also appear very different from each other. Forest type is, therefore, defined as 'a unit of vegetation that possesses broad characteristics in physiognomy and structure, which are sufficiently pronounced to permit its differentiation from other such units' (Champion and Seth, 1968). Each forest type serve as habitat for a distinct community of animals adapted to live therein.

Forest Types of India

According to the, 'State of Forests' report of the Forest Survey of India, 63.3 million hectare corresponding to 19.27 percent of the geographic area of India is the actual forest cover. The Indian forests are of various types ranging from evergreen tropical rain forests (in Andaman and Nicobar Islands, the Western Ghats, and the north-eastern states) to dry alpine scrubs (in the high altitudes of Himalayas). Between these two extremes, there are semi-evergreen rain forests, deciduous monsoon forests, thorn forests, subtropical pine forests in the lower montane zone and temperate montane forests. Each Indian forest is rich in floral diversity, which provides shelter for a wide range of faunal species.

Champion and Seth (1968) classified Indian forests into six major groups, 16 major types and more than 200 minor types based mainly on natural vegetation and climatic factors of the particular ecosystem (Figure 2.2).

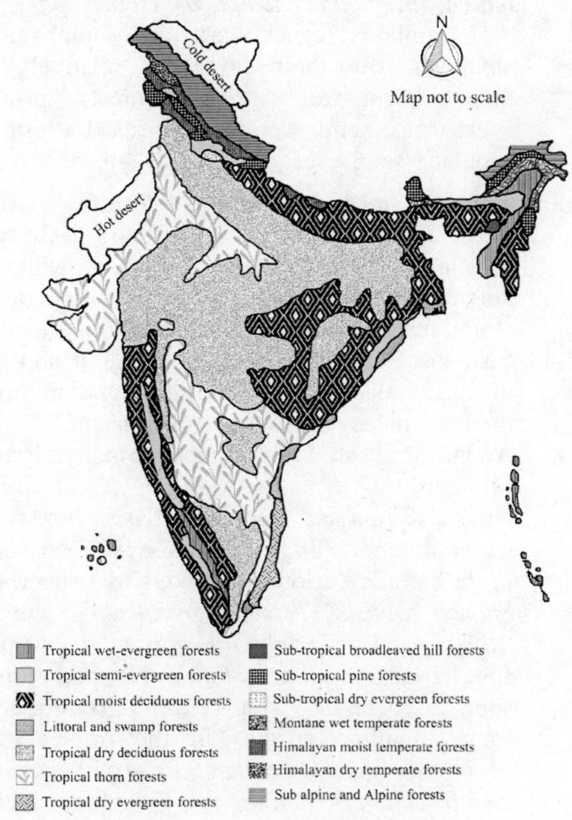

FIGURE 2.2 Distribution of Forest Types in India (based on Champion and Seth, 1968).

1. ***Tropical wet-evergreen forests:*** Tropical wet evergreen forests are present in parts of Western Ghats, upper Assam, Arunachal Pradesh, hilly areas in north-east India and in the Andaman and Nicobar Islands. These are tall, dense and multilayered forests characterized by very high rainfall (>250 cm) with thick humus layer on the forest floor. These forest types harbour rich biodiversity. The flora generally comprises of trees with greater foliage like *Dipterocarpus macrocarpus*, *Shorea assamica*, *Mesua ferrea*, *Atrocarpus* spp., *Terminalia* spp. etc. Ferns and epiphytes are fairly common throughout the forests, while bamboos and canes are present in specific locations.
2. ***Tropical semi-evergreen forests:*** Tropical semi-evergreen forests are the transitional forest types between evergreen and moist deciduous forests and are often found in areas adjoining the tropical wet evergreen forests. In India, they are found in patches in Western Ghats, Assam, Arunachal Pradesh, Orissa and in the Andaman and Nicobar Islands. These forests are characterized by a mean temperature of about 26°C and comprise of a mixture of tall (larger than 30m in height), evergreen and deciduous trees like *Dipterocarpus* spp., *Shorea assamica*, *Mesua ferrea*, *Atrocarpus* spp., *Terminalia* spp., *Bombax ceiba*, *Mangifera indica*, *Michelia champaca*, *Hopea parviflora*, etc. Bamboos, canes, ferns and epiphytes are abundant. But their growth is relatively poor than tropical wet evergreen forests. Example: West Coast semi-evergreen forests, Eastern Sub-Montane semi-evergreen forests, etc.
3. ***Tropical moist deciduous forests:*** Tropical moist deciduous forests are usually 2–3 layered and are particularly grow in areas with 100–200 cm annual rainfall. They occur as a strip along the foothills of Himalayas, in the north-east, in a large area of Chhotonagpur and along the eastern side of Western Ghats and are present in the states of Assam, Arunachal Pradesh, Andhra Pradesh, Uttar Pradesh, Madhya Pradesh, Maharashtra, Mizoram, Bihar, West Bengal, Orissa, Kerala and Karnataka. These forests have lesser diversity than the semi-evergreen forests. Flora include various deciduous tree species like *Shorea robusta*, *Tectona grandis*, *Grewia* spp., *Albizia* spp., *Terminalia* spp., *Lagerstroemia* spp., *Dalbergia* spp., *Bauhinia* spp., *Bombax* spp., *Anogeissus* spp. etc. Two commonly found bamboo species in the tropical moist deciduous forests are *Bambusa arundinacea* and *Dendrocalamus hamiltonii*. Example: Southern moist mixed deciduous forests, Eastern bhabar sal forests, etc.
4. ***Littoral and swamp forests:*** Littoral and swamp forests are found along the coastal tracts and are characterized by trees of medium height, annual mean temperature of 27.5°C and rainfall for more than 100 days per annum. These are more or less gregarious forests consisting of evergreen species of varying density and height, which are dependent upon the wetness of the region. Swamp forests occur in north-east India along the major rivers. They are also present in the deltas of some of the large rivers of this country. Mangrove forests consist of *Rhizophora* sp., *Bruguiera* sp., *Ceriops* sp., *Heritiera* sp., the tidal and swamp forests generally comprise of several evergreen and semi-evergreen tree species like *Barringtonia* spp., *Syzygium cumini*, *Dillenia* spp., *Erythrina* sp. and the freshwater swamps contain species like *Terminalia arjuna*, *Lagerstroemia speciosa*, *Trewia nudiflora*, *Myristica* spp., etc. Example: Mangrove forests, Tropical freshwater swamp forests, etc.
5. ***Tropical dry deciduous forests:*** Tropical dry deciduous forests are usually found in areas with dry arid climate with 75–125 cm rainfall and are present as discontinuous wide stretches in the states of Rajasthan, Maharashtra, Madhya Pradesh, Uttar Pradesh, Orissa, Andhra Pradesh, Karnataka and Tamil Nadu. These forests are almost entirely of deciduous species of low or moderate height. The trees are usually 20–25 m in height, less branched and form a light canopy. About 80 percent of tiger population of this country thrives in these forests. The main tree species are *Shorea robusta*, *Tectona grandis*, *Anogeissus pendula*, *Boswellia serrata*, *Hardwickia binata*, *Acacia nilotica*, *Acacia catechu*, *Madhucha indica*, *Butea monosperma*, *Bombax ceiba*, *Dalbergia sissoo*, *Lannea* sp., *Sterculia* sp., *Flacourtia* sp., *Mallotus* sp. etc. Some of the common shrubs are *Adhatoda* sp., *Gymnosporia* sp., *Indigofera* sp.
6. ***Tropical thorn forests:*** Tropical thorn forests extend from western border of the country and gradually merge with the dry deciduous mixed forests of the Aravalli hills and the south-eastern plateau. These forests are present as a large strip in southern Punjab, Haryana, northern Gujarat and in almost entire Rajasthan in the semi-arid regions where the rainfall varies from 25 to 75 cm and the summer temperature is as high as 50°C. Such forest types are also present in patches in the Gangetic plains and Deccan plateau. These low and open forests primarily consist of xerophytic thorny species like *Acacia* spp., *Prosopis* spp., *Salvadora oleoides*, *Tamarix aphylla*, *Capparis* spp., *Ziziphus* spp., *Cassia* spp., *Flacourtia* spp. etc. Shrubs of all sizes are found in these forest

types. Due to large scale grazing and other biotic factors these forests often get degraded into very open, low thorny scrubs of *Euphorbia* sp., *Ziziphus* spp., etc. Example: Southern thorn forests, Desert thorn forests, etc.

7. ***Tropical dry evergreen forests:*** Tropical dry evergreen forests are found in relatively small areas in southern India. These forests are typically low and open forests comprising of broadleaved and thorny evergreen trees like *Canthium dicoccum*, *Carissa carandas*, *Maba buxifolia*, *Memecylon edule*, etc. Example: Forests in Satpura conservation area.
8. ***Sub-tropical broadleaved hill forests:*** Subtropical broadleaved hill forests occur in the foothills and low hills in peninsular and northern India. These forests are found in the states of West Bengal, Assam, Bihar, Maharashtra, Madhya Pradesh and Tamilnadu on the lower slopes of the Himalayas and on other hill ranges like Khasi, Nilgiri, Mahabaleshwar, Panchmarhi, Amarkantak and Parshwanath. Tree species of these forest types include *Syzygium cumini*, *Alnus nepalensis*, *Ficus* spp., *Quercus* sp., *Castanopsis* sp. etc. Example: Nilgiri sub-tropical hill forests, Western sub-tropical hill forests, East Himalayan sub-tropical hill forests, Khasi sub-tropical wet hill forests etc.
9. ***Sub-tropical pine forests:*** Distributed in various Hiamalayan states, these are open pine forests found between 900 m and 1,700 m elevation in Himalayas often without a dry evergreen shrub layer and little or no underwood. Characteristic species of these forests are *chir* pine (*Pinus roxburghii*) in the western and central Himalayas and *Khasi* pine (*Pinus kesiya*) in the north eastern hills in similar altitudes. Example: Himalayan sub-tropical pine forests, Assam sub-tropical pine forests, etc.
10. ***Sub-tropical dry evergreen forests:*** Sub-tropical dry evergreen forests comprise of xerophytic thorny and small leaved evergreen trees and are restricted in the north-western part of this country. They are mainly found in areas of Himlayan foothills in Jammu and Kashmir with 50–100cm rainfall. *Olea cuspidata* and *Acacia modesta* are the typical species in the top canopy, whereas *Dodonea* shrubs are found in degraded forests. These forest types resemble the Mediterranean scrub type of vegetation in appearance.
11. ***Montane wet temperate forests:*** Montane wet temperate forests are usually found in high rainfall areas between 1,800–3,000 m elevations. These are evergreen forests with thick canopy cover. Apart from the Himalayas, such forest types are also found in Penninsular India in some of the hill tops (like Nilagiri hills). *Quercus* sp., *Castanopsis* sp., *Michelia nilagirica*, *Acer cambellii*, *Rhododendron* sp. etc. are some of the characteristic species of these forest type in Himalayas, whereas *Syzygium* spp., *Ternstroemia* spp. are some important species in the southern hills. In the Nilgiri hills, montane wet temperate forests are luxuriant with dense undergrowth and *Rhododendron arboretum nilagiricum* is an important flora of these forests. Example: Southern Montane wet temperate forests, Northern Montane wet temperate forests, etc.
12. ***Himalayan moist temperate forests:*** Himalayan moist temperate forests are found between 1,500–3,000 m altitudes and are particularly localized in the central and western Himalayas, except in areas with mean annual rainfall below 100 cm. These thick evergreen forests are broadly grouped into two distinct categories—the ***upper forms*** and the ***lower forms***. Both the zones contain many commercially important species. The upper forms consist of *Abies* sp., *Picea smithiana*, *Quercus semecarpifolia*, while the lower forms include *Quercus leucotrichophora*, *Quercus dilatata*, *Pinus wallichiana*, *Cedrus deodara,* etc. Besides, *Quercus lineata*, *Quercus lamellosa*, *Quercus pachyphylla*, *Tsuga dumosa*, *Picea spinulosa*, *Abies densa* are some of the conspicuous species found in the eastern Himalayas. Example: Upper West Himalayan temperate forests, East Himalayan mixed temperate forests etc.
13. ***Himalayan dry temperate forests:*** Himalayan dry temperate forests are found in the higher ridges of Himalaya with low rainfall. These thick evergreen forests with open scrub undergrowth consist of both coniferous and broad-leaved species. In the eastern Himalayas *Abies* and *Picea* are common and *Juniperus wallichiana* are present in the higher elevations. On the other hand, *Pinus gerardiana*, *Cedrus deodara*, *Queropoda ilex* and *Juniperus macropoda* (in higher elevations) are found in western Himalayas. Some other tree species like *Larix griffithiana*, *Populus euphytica*, *Salix* spp., *Hippophae* spp., *Myricaria* spp., *Quercus* spp., etc. are present between 2,500–4,000 m elevations. Example: Dry mixed temperate forests, High level dry Blue Pine forests, Dry Juniper forests etc.
14. ***Sub-alpine forests:*** This forest type occurs throughout the Himalayas above 3,000 m elevation upto the tree line and consist of dense growth of small and stunted trees with scattered patches of coniferous over wood. The tree species found in the sub-alpine forests include *Taxus baccata*, *Pinus wallichiana*, *Abies densa*, *Abies*

spp., *Betula* spp., etc. *Rhododendron* spp. is frequently found in the understorey. Besides, stands of blue pine (*Pinus wallichiana*) are found in exposed sites. Example: Sub-alpine Birch Pine forests, Sub-alpine Fir forests, etc.

15. ***Moist alpine scrub:*** Moist alpine scrubs are present above tree line up to 5,500 m just below the snowline in the Himalayas. These regions are practically devoid of trees and shrubs are rarely more than 1m in height. Some of the plant species of this forest type include *Rhododendron campanulatum*, *Viburnum nervosum*, *Salix* spp., *Juniperus* spp., *Betula* spp. etc. Example: Birch Rhododendron scrub forests, dwarf Rhododendron forests etc.
16. ***Dry alpine scrub:*** Dry alpine scrubs are also present below the snowline in the dry desert regions of inner Himalayas with less than 40 cm of annual rainfall. Vegetation of these regions consists of open xerophytic dwarf scrub. *Armeria* sp., *Artemisia* spp., *Salix* spp., *Juniperus* spp., *Carangana* sp., *Eurotia* sp., *Myricaria* sp. etc. are some of the common floral species of this forest type. Example: Dwarf juniper scrub forests etc.

Tropical Rain Forest—A Unique Biome

Tropical rain forests are usually found along the equator between 10° N and 10° S latitudes at elevations below 1,000 m and are the most complex biomes of the globe. Three distinct zones of tropical rain forests are situated in (1) **Neotrophical** (Amazon basin in South America to central America), (2) **African** (West and Central Africa and east coast of Madagascar) and (3) **Indo-Malaysian and New Guinea regions** (West coast of India, Assam, southeast Asia, New Guinea & Queensland, Australia). Species diversity is highest in the Neotropical regions followed by Indo-Malayan and is generally lowest in the African rainforests.

Tropical rain forests are among the most productive biomes of the world with a mean net primary productivity of 21.6 metric ton/ hectare/ year. Occupying less than 6 percent of the land surface of this planet, this biome produces 40 percent of the Earth's oxygen. They also exhibit a staggering diversity of life and serve as home to an estimated more than half to two-third of the world's terrestrial floral and faunal species. On the other hand, this is amongst the most threatened biomes of this planet. According to an estimate, around 150,000 sq km of rainforest is destroyed every year in different corner of the globe for timber, minerals, agriculture, human settlements, as well as, to cater to various other anthropogenic needs.

Characteristic Features of Tropical Rain Forests

Tropical rain forests are usually found in wet climate regimes with optimal growing conditions. The length of day and night is fairly equal. These forests are generally moist and warm round the year. The temperature typically ranges between 18–34°C throughout the year with the mean annual temperature of about 26°C. The thick vegetations of these forests absorb moisture, which then evaporates and falls back as rain. Rainfall is abundant (between 125 and 660 cm annually) and is generally evenly distributed throughout the year. Relative humidity is also high, the annual mean of which lies between 77 and 88 percent and seldom drops below 60 percent. The top soil of these forests is very shallow and is poor in nutrients. But a lot of litter fall on the ground that are quickly degraded by heat, humidity and by the action of numerous decomposers present in the forest floor. The organic matter is then absorbed by the shallow roots of the trees. Hence, tropical trees are shallow rooted, with their feeder roots concentrated in the upper 15 cm of humus and only a few penetrate the upper layer of mineral soil. Symbiotically associated with these roots are abundant mycorrhizal fungi that attach these roots to dead organic matter by hyphae and rhizomorph tissue. Minerals are transferred from dead branches or leaves to living roots through fungal hyphae. In such a direct mode of mineral cycling, minerals remain tied up in living and dead organic matter, with minimum leakage into the soil.

Tropical Rain Forests in India

Three main areas of wet-evergreen tropical rain forests are present in India—(i) in the north-east India like a strip running from north-east to south-west direction across Arunachal Pradesh, Upper Assam, Nagaland, Manipur, Mizoram and Tripura upto a height of 1,070 m; (ii) in the Western Ghats along the west coast of peninsular India between 500 and 1,370 m above sea level and (iii) in the Andaman and Nicobar Islands. However, there are substantial differences in both the flora and fauna between the three major rain forest regions of this country. In addition, small remnants of wet-evergreen tropical rain forests are also found in the state of Orissa.

Semi-evergreen tropical rain forest is more extensive than the evergreen formations in India, partly because evergreen forests tend to degrade to semi-evergreen with human interference. These forests are found on the Western coast, Assam, lower slopes of the Eastern Himalayas, Orissa and Andamans.

(i) **Tropical rain forests of the north-east India** Tropical rain forests of north-east India comprise of evergreen and semi-evergreen rain forests, moist deciduous monsoon forests, riparian forests, swamps and grasslands and occur at elevations up to 900 m. These forests are present in the states of Assam, Nagaland, Manipur, Mizoram, Tripura, Meghalaya and Arunachal Pradesh. Evergreen tropical rain forests are typically present in the foothills of the eastern Himalayas of Assam Valley, as well as in the lower parts of the Naga Hills, Meghalaya, Mizoram, Manipur, as well as, in the plains of Arunachal Pradesh, where the annual rain fall exceeds 2,300 mm.

Dipterocarpus macrocarpus and *Shorea assamica* are frequently found in the Assam Valley. Some of these trees are huge and such single giant tree might occasionally attain a girth of seven metre and a height of 50 m. *Shorea robusta* also widely occur in this region particularly, in the monsoon moist sal forests.

Thirty two species of mammals, more than 300 species of birds and several other rare and endemic wild species are found in these forests. This rainforest is also one of the important elephant zones in India. Every year more than 2,000 elephants migrate to these forests. The region also manifests high degree of endemism. Some of the characteristic vertebrate fauna of the tropical rainforests in north-east India include rhesus macaque (*Macaca mulatta*), Assamese macaque (*Macaca assamensis*), northern pig-tailed macaque (*Macaca leonina*), slow loris (*Nycticebus* sp.), capped langur (*Trachypithecus pileatus*), golden langur (*Trachypithecus geei*), hoolock gibbon (*Hoolock hoolock* and *Hoolock leuconedys*), Malayan giant squirrel (*Ratufa bicolor*), bearcat or binturong (*Arctictis binturong*) and red panda (*Ailurus fulgens*). Many species of bats and civets also dwell in these tropical rain forests.

(ii) **Tropical rain forests of the Western Ghats:** Tropical rain forests in the Western Ghats range are present both on the western and eastern margins of the Ghats. Wet evergreen forests are very rich in biodiversity and are mostly confined to the areas of Western Ghats where annual rainfall exceeds 2,000 mm.

Enormous numbers of tree species are present in these rain forests. Several commercially important tree species (like *Dalbergia latifolia*, *Pterocarpus marsupium*, *Terminalia paniculata*, *Tectona grandis*, etc.) are present in these forests. Throughout these evergreen and semi-evergreen forests of south-west India, clumps of bamboo occur along streams or in poorly drained hollows, particularly in areas once cleared for shifting agriculture.

Tropical rain forests of the Western Ghats are home to the world's largest population of Asiatic elephants (*Elephas maximus*) and ten percent of the Bengal tigers (*Panthera tigris*) remaining in the world (WWF, 2011). Around 120 mammalian species, more than 500 species of birds, 225 species of reptiles, 117 amphibian species, 288 species of fish and 330 butterfly species have been recorded from this region. However, knowledge on the invertebrate fauna of the Western Ghats is comparatively poor. Tropical rain forests of the Western Ghats also serve as home to many endemic fauna including 22 species of birds, 89 species of amphibia, 118 species of pisces, more than 100 species of tiger beetles and a family of primitive burrowing snakes (Uropeltidae). Nilgiri tahr (*Hemitragus hylocrius*), lion-tailed macaque (*Macaca silenus*), Salim Ali's fruit bat (*Latidens salimalii*), Nilgiri flycatcher (*Eumyias albicaudatus*), Nilgiri wood pigeon (*Columba elphinstonii*) and Nilgiri blue robin (*Myiomela major*), Cochin forest cane turtle (*Vijayachelys silvatica*), purple frog (*Nasikabatrachus sahyadrensis*), Denison barb fish (*Puntius denisonii*), Travencore evening brown butterfly (*Parantirrhoea marshalli*) etc. are some endemic fauna of this region. The other mammalian species found in this region are Nilgiri langur (*Trachypithecus johnii*), stripe-necked mongoose (*Herpestes vitticollis*), grey slender loris (*Loris lydekkerianus*) and Malabar large-spotted civet (*Viverra civettina*).

According to Bawa et al., (2007) only one third of the Western Ghats still clings to its natural vegetation, and the remaining forests are under tremendous pressure from a variety of human activities, facing the threat of increasing degradation and are becoming highly fragmented. Selective logging, conversion of land to agriculture and forest clearance for the construction of reservoirs, roads and railways have all played a part in this habitat loss (Conservation International, 2011). Unfortunately, not even protected areas are safe from such threats, as hunting, firewood extraction, timber felling and livestock grazing apply pressure on the fringes of these important refuges (Conservation International, 2011).

(iii) **Tropical rain forests in Andaman and Nicobar islands** Tropical evergreen rain forests, tropical semi-evergreen rain forests as well as tropical monsoon moist monsoon forests are present in the Andaman and Nicobar islands (IUCN 1986). However, stature and species richness in these tropical evergreen rain forests is slightly less than on the mainland.

Floristically, the Andamans have much more in common with north-east India. North Andamans is characterized by the wet evergreen type, with plenty of woody climbers. There are about 200 species of trees of which padauk, gurjain, silver-gray, etc. are prominent. *Dipterocarpus grandiflorus* is the dominant species in hilly areas, *Dipterocarpus kerrii* is dominant on some islands in the southern parts of the archipelago while *Pterocarpus dalbergioides* and *Terminalia* spp. are the dominant species of the monsoon forests in the Andamans. Dominant tree species (like *Dipterocarpus grandiflorus, D. turbinatus, Sideroxylon longipetiolatum, Endospermum malaccense, Hopea odorata* and *Planchonia andamanica*) reach heights of 40–60 m,

Despite their isolation from adjacent landmasses, as well as, from the tropical rain forests of Andaman Nicobar Islands are surprisingly enriched with faunal species and also exhibit high degree of endemism. There are 16 species of bats and 13 species of rats. Five mammalian species including Andaman wild pig (*Sus scrofa andamanensis*), Crab eating macaque (*Macaca fascicularis umbrosa*), Andaman masked palm civet (*Paguma larvata tytlerii*) are strictly endemic to this region. The islands have no native herbivores except for endemic wild pig. Native carnivores and larger mammals are also absent. Elephants (*Elephas maximus*) were brought over from mainland India in the 1880s, while several species of deer were introduced in the Island during 1920s. Similarly, there are eight strictly endemic birds, *viz.* Andaman serpent eagle (*Spilornis elgini*), Andaman crake (*Rallina canningi*), Andaman coucal or brown coucal (*Centropus andamanensis*), Andaman scops-owl (*Otus balli*), Narcondam hornbill (*Aceros narcondami*), Andaman woodpecker (*Dryocopus hodgei*), Andaman drongo (*Dicrurus andamanensis*) and Andaman treepie (*Dendrocitta bayleyi*). Likewise, 13 out of 45 species of terrestrial reptiles, 7 out of 12 amphibian species and 10 out of 225 species of butterflies found in the tropical rain forests of these islands are endemic. Some other unique faunal species of these tropical forests include Andaman spiny shrew (*Crocidura hispida*), Nicobar tree shrew (*Tupaia nicobarica*), Andaman horse-shoe bat (*Rhinolophus cognatus*), lesser short-nosed fruit bat (*Cynopterus brachyotis*), Andaman teal (*Anas albogularis*), Nicobar megapode (*Megapodius nicobariensis*), Nicobar pigeon (*Caloenas nicobarica*), Nicobar parakeet (*Psittacula caniceps*), green imperial pigeon (*Ducula aenea*), crested serpent eagle (*Spilornis cheela*), white-bellied sea eagle (*Haliaeetus leucogaster*), edible-nest swiftlet (*Aerodramus fuciphagus*) and emerald dove (*Chalcophaps indica*). Many species of snakes also inhabit these forests including reticulate python (*Malayopython reticulatus*) and king cobra (*Ophiophagus hannah*), etc.

Adaptations

Floral adaptations: Tropical trees usually possess certain characteristic features which are distinct from the trees present in higher latitudes. All the plant species coexisting in tropical rain forests mainly compete for sunlight and nutrients. The trees are mostly evergreen with large dark-green leaves and are tall, slender, often unbranched excepting the top. In many species, base of the tree trunk possesses certain broad, woody flanges known as 'buttresses'. In addition to providing mechanical support to the tree, these buttresses also regulate stem flow in such a way that the dissolved nutrients pass on to the roots. Many trees also have stilt roots for extra support in shallow wet soils of the rain forests. Trees, particularly the growing saplings and young trees beneath the closed canopy usually have large leaves to optimally intercept light. Some trees have leaf stalks that move with the movement of the sun. In some emergent species, small leaves are present in upper canopy and large leaves in sub-canopy layer of the same tree. "Drip tips", "drip spouts" or "grooved leaves" not only promote transpiration, but also prevent the growth of molds by draining the rain water off the leaves. Some leaves have oily coatings. Other unique adaptive features of trees in tropical rain forests include smooth and thin bark, development of flowers from trunk rather than at the tip of branches (known as cauliflory) and large fleshy fruits. Epiphytes grow in the upper canopy on larger trees to receive sunlight.

Faunal adaptations: Very rich diversity of animal life is found in the tropical rain forests. However, animal life in this biome is largely inconspicuous, either due to being hidden behind dense foliage or because of nocturnal habit of many species. Animals are usually brightly coloured with distinct patterns and loud vocalizations. Many of the faunal species are also obligatory frugivores. Some others exhibit protective colouration.

Very few animals live near the ground level in the tropical rain forests. Most of the animals live on trees and manifest arboreal adaptations. Animals in these forests prefer to live on treetop as productivity is highest there, and treetops are beyond the reach of many predators (except some large raptors). Many animals are able to hang from the trees and are almost inaccessible to the attack by predators. Arboreal animals are broadly classified as:

— **Branch runners:** Animals that walk or even run on tree branches. *Example:* squirrels, lemurs, chameleons etc.

— **Suspended forms:** These are unable to walk on branches, instead they hang down from branches and move in their upside down posture clinging on the branches with claws. *Example:* bats, sloths, etc.

— **Brachiators:** These animals move from branch to branch with great speed and accuracy by swinging their forelimbs. *Example:* apes and monkeys.

These arboreal forms often exhibit some of the following unique adaptive features to successfully thrive on tree tops:

- Body is slender, small and of light weight. Birds and mammals are smaller than their relatives in temperate forests.
- Strong chest, ribs and limb girdles.
- Thorax sub-circular with more curved ribs. In some species, numbers of ribs have increased to give support to the viscera during inverted position.
- Lumbar vertebrae are elongated and number increased.
- Pectoral girdle is strongly built as the forelimb support the body weight while hanging. The clavicle and scapula are prominent to withstand the strain caused by the contraction of powerful breast muscles.
- Ilium bone of the pelvic girdle is broad to support the viscera (in sloth).
- There is a trend of reduction in the number of digits. In koala, the 2nd and 3rd toes are syndactylous, whereas in chameleons, the digits of both fore and hind limbs are arranged into opposable bundles of 2 or 3 digits helping them to hold branches.
- Long and curved claws are common in bats, squirrels and lizards. In sloths, the claws are modified into powerful hooks. In many species of tree frogs, digits are provided with adhesive discs or suction discs.
- Long prehensile tails with spines and scales are one of the most common and striking adaptive features among the arboreal forms. This prehensile tail often act as '*the fifth limb*' and help in balancing.
- Arboreal animals usually possess a keen sense of hearing.

In this biome there is no definite period of bird migration and breeding. Flocking is more prevalent and breeding territories are less firmly established. Invertebrates are diverse and occur in great numbers in forest floor, particularly in the wet season. Besides, many protozoans, rotifers, leeches, many arthropods and small frogs inhabit the tiny pools of water present in the epiphytes or in the clump of leathery leaves.

2.3.4 Desert Biome

Deserts are usually located along the Tropic of Cancer or the Tropic of Capricorn covering about 20 percent of the Earth and are present on every continent except Europe. Some parts of deserts do not receive any rain at all in a year due to lack of moisture resulting in droughts. Desert is usually defined as an area that has very little moisture and receives insufficient precipitation in the form of either rain or snow (less than 25 cm of precipitation annually) to support normal life. The deserts located near the mountains are formed by the "rain shadow" effect. Most hot deserts have a drastic day-night difference in temperature. Days are warm with about 38°C daytime average temperature, while the night temperature is even subzero at certain places in winter. Lack of moisture and extremes of temperature lead to strong air currents. Dust storms occur almost every evening, which at times can be up to 1.5 km high and travel at a speed of over 160 km per hour. Scarcity of water, extremes of diurnal and nocturnal temperatures and dust storms often make the deserts inhospitable for many species. Hence, the number of flora and fauna is relatively less as compared to other biomes. Nevertheless, the life forms found in deserts are specially adapted for this unique biome.

Types of Desert in India

In India, deserts extend over 4,42,289 sq km covering 13.52 percent of the country's geographical area. Physiographic conditions of Indian deserts widely vary in terms of landscape, soil structure, precipitation, temperature, humidity and evaporation. Based on the meteorological observations, desert regions of India have been classified into hot and cold deserts.

Hot Deserts: Deserts that receive rain (about 25 cm or less per year) as their main form of precipitation are referred to as 'hot deserts'. The sandy desert spread over a large part of the north-western part of the country, particularly west to the Aravalli range, are known as *Thar* deserts (Figure 2.3).

This is a unique example of hot desert in India. Beyond the last major city of Jaisalmer, *Thar* desert stretches to the horizon and covers eastern Sindh province and some areas of Punjab in south-east Pakistan as well. This desert is bound by the Sutlej river to the north, the Aravalli range to the east, salt marsh to the south, and the Indus river to the west covering an area of 208,110 sq km. It is also referred to as the Great Indian Desert and is considered as the seventh largest desert in the world. These arid and semi-arid regions are found in 36 districts, mostly in the states of Rajasthan, and are also extended into some portion of Haryana, Punjab and in the Rann of Kutch in Gujarat. Stretches of sand in the desert are interspersed by hillocks, as well as, sandy and gravel plains. The region is drained by *Luni* river and its tributaries. Most of the region has closed drainage and forms shallow saline inland lakes. There are eleven protected areas in the Great *Thar* Desert ecosystem.

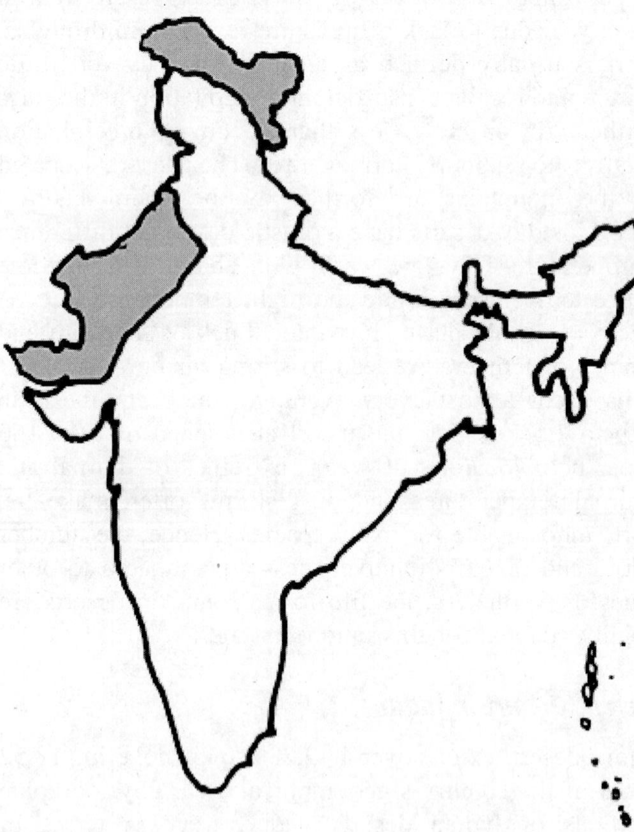

FIGURE 2.3 Distribution of Hot and Cold Deserts in India.

Climate: Warm-dry continental climate of the *Thar* desert shows extreme variation in diurnal and seasonal temperatures. Annual temperature can range from sub-zero in the winter to more than 45°C during the summer. The summer begins with progressive rise in temperature during March and the maximum temperature in May-June reaches 50°C. Low erratic rainfall and high temperature are the most conspicuous characteristics of hot desert climate. Drought is quite a common phenomenon in the desert biomes. Few mild rainfall occur during January-March and dust storms are regular during April-June. The main rainy season is during July and August when almost 80 percent of the annual rain occurs. Annual rainfall decreases from about 500 mm over east Rajasthan to about 100 mm over extreme western parts of the west Rajasthan. Such marked decrease in rainfall in the west of *Aravalli* range makes western Rajasthan the most arid part of this country. Winter season remains from December through February with marked decline in minimum temperature in December and January. The minimum temperature reaches –3°C or even less in extreme cold wave conditions. A sharp decline in diurnal temperatures is also experienced in night throughout the arid and semi-arid zone of western Rajasthan due to quick thermal radiation from sandy soil soon after the dusk.

Vegetation: Usually vegetation in the desert region is sparse. 'Northern Desert Thorn Forests' comprising of small and scattered clumps of more or less open scrub vegetation are the unique feature of this arid region. Scrub vegetation consists of low, small trees and shrubs (such as *Acacia*, *Euphorbia*, etc.) along with some of the xerophytic grasses and herbs of *Thar* desert. Density and size of these natural patches increase from west to east following the increase in rainfall.

Faunal Richness: In spite of hostile climatic conditions and barren appearance, desert fauna in India is quite diverse comprising of about 1,200 species. Camels (*Camelus dromedarius*) are the first animal that come to mind while discussing about wildlife in desert. *Thar* desert has become a safe haven for 68 species of mammals including chinkara (*Gazella bennetti*), blackbuck (*Antelope cervicapra*), nilgai (*Boselaphus tragocamelus*), long-eared hedgehog (*Hemeichinus auritus*), desert cat (*Felis silvestris*), caracal (*Felis caracal*), desert fox (*Vulpes vulpes pusilla*), Indian fox (*Vulpes bengalensis*), Asiatic jackal (*Canis aureus*) and grey wolf (*Canis lupus*). The sand dune dominated, tree-less region in the extreme western zone of Jaisalmer and Barmer districts is largely inhabited by Indian desert hare (*Lepus nigricollis*), cutch rock-rat (*Cremnomys cutchicus*), Indian crested porcupine (*Hystrix indica*) and the endemic Indian hairy-footed gerbil (*Gerbillus gleadowi*). In addition, 350 species of birds, 23 species of lizards, 25 species of snakes, 142 species of fish, five species of amphibians and countless insects are found in these unique biome types. The spiny-tailed lizard (*Uromastyx* sp.) is a vulnerable species found only in the *Thar* deserts and saw scaled viper (*Echis* sp.) and black cobra (*Naja naja oxiana*) are some of the deadliest snakes. The region is also a haven for migratory and resident birds like short-toed eagle (*Circaetus gallicus*), tawny eagle (*Aquila rapax*), greater spotted eagle (*Aquila clanga*), laggar falcon (*Falco jugger*), red spurfowl (*Galloper dixspadicea*), painted spurfowl (*Galloperdix lunulata*), great Indian bustard (*Ardeotis nigriceps*) and blue peafowl (*Pavo cristatus*). The great Indian bustard is one of the heaviest of the flying birds found in India and are mostly present in the arid habitats of *Thar* deserts. Different species of harriers, buzzards, kestrel and vultures are also fairly common. The Rann of Kutch is the only breeding ground for greater flamingo (*Phoenicopterus roseus*) and lesser flamingo (*Phoenicopterus minor*) in the South Asian region and the only known population of Asiatic wild ass (*Equus hemionus khur*). The larger caves and caverns are occupied by about 16 species of micro chiropteran bats, and sometimes also by wolves, jackals, hyaenas, etc. (Prakash 1997). Apart from these vertebrate fauna, 755 species of invertebrates also thrive in these arid conditions. More than 40 species of termites and four species of locusts (*viz.* desert locust *Schistocerca gregaria*, migratory locust *Locusta migratoria*, Bombay locust *Nomadacris succincta* and tree locust *Anacridium* sp.) are reported from *Thar*. The solitary phase of most dreadful desert locusts has been reported from time to time at some locations in the states of Rajasthan and Gujarat. The Scheduled Desert Area (SDA) is spread over an area of 2.05 sq km in the state of Rajasthan, Gujarat and Haryana.

However, desert is losing its xeric fauna due to rapid alteration in land use pattern in recent time. The Asiatic cheetah (*Acinonyx jubatus venaticus*) was once commonly found around Jaipur (Seshadri 1969). Many other species of desert fauna also sharply declined since 1950s and some of them have completely vanished from these regions.

Adaptations

Aridity and extremes of temperature (sweltering hot day and freezing cold night) are the major challenges for survival in hot deserts. Desert flora and fauna face an unfavourable environment in terms of thermal extremes, paucity of drinking water and food and lack of shelter. Hence, they have to develop specialized strategies and adaptive features to survive in those evidently difficult, adverse climatic conditions.

Floral Adaptations: Adaptations include the morphological and behavioural responses of desert flora to maximize their chances of survival in arid regions. Plants evincing adaptations to arid conditions are termed xerophytes. Desert plants survive the long rainless periods with three main adaptive strategies: succulence, drought tolerance, and drought evasion.

- ***Succulent plants*** have extensive, shallow root systems and store water in their fleshy leaves, stems, roots or within cells from where water is not easily lost. All cacti are succulents. The stems and leaves of most succulent species have waxy cuticles that make them nearly waterproof when their stomatas are closed. Most succulents have few leaves (agaves) or no leaf at all (most cacti) thereby reducing surface areas to conserve water. Stored water in an arid environment also requires protection from thirsty animals. Hence, most succulent plants are spiny, bitter or toxic, and often all three.
- ***Drought-tolerant plants*** often appear to be dead or dying during the dry seasons. To tolerate the adverse conditions plants have developed special adaptations like mechanism of storing water in the leaves or stems, reduction in the number of leaves or waxy coverings on the leaves to reduce water loss, long tap roots that can penetrate the deep water table.
- ***Drought-evading plants*** (ephemerals) are a smaller group of annual species that grow only in response to summer rains. Some of these plants even undergo dormancy for over half the year and only grow when water becomes available.

In addition to these, microphylly (the trait of having small leaves) is primarily an adaptation to avoid overheating and it also reduces water loss. Some plants open their stomata only at night when evaporation rates are lowest. Leaf or stem colour, orientation and self-shading are some other ways to adapt to intense light and heat. Desert foliage is rarely typical leaf-green and more often gray-green, blue-green, gray or even white.

Faunal Adaptations: Despite harsh and unfavourable climate of the deserts, many different species of animals live there. They have evolved remarkable adaptations over time to successfully thrive in the inhospitable desert conditions.

- Since vegetation does not grow very tall, so the desert animals are smaller. These animals can escape the harsh sun by hiding under small scrubs or hiding in burrows. Large animals including the carnivores are scarce.
- Body color is mostly pale which resembles the colour of the landscape. Many desert animals have light-colored fur, feathers or scales, which absorb less heat and also help the animals to hide in the sand.
- Possession of venom is another important aspect for self protection. Most of the desert spiders, snakes and lizards are poisonous.
- Many animals, including 80 percent of the mammals found in these deserts are nocturnal. They spend the day sleeping and come out at night when the temperatures are more tolerable. On the other hand, many of these nocturnal animals even cease their activities and take refuge in their hideouts during extreme cold hours in night, particularly in winters when the temperature fall below 5°C.

- The diurnal animals spend the extreme hot hours under shade or inside their hideouts to avoid scorching heat of sun and excessive water loss due to evaporation. They are usually found to be active during early morning and evening.
- According to Prakash (1997), 56 percent of the small mammals of *Thar* Desert are reported to be fossorial (i.e., burrow dwellers). Some insects and amphibians also seal themselves in burrows with gelatinous secretions and remain dormant for eight or nine months until plenty of water is available after heavy rains.
- Desert animals can survive for a longer duration without drinking water. Some others survive even just by only obtaining moisture. Herbivores get sufficient water by feeding on succulent plants. Some of the predatory animals (like snakes) obtain water from the body fluid of their prey. Certain desert animals even absorb dew drops. Skin of certain animals like *Moloch* is hygroscopic in nature and can absorb water like a blotting paper. Camels have developed the ability to store large amounts of water for long periods of time.
- Some species develop impermeable thick hide, often accompanied by scales and spines to avoid water loss by perspiration; sweat glands are much less in number, even totally absent.
- Excretion with less water elimination like concentrated or semisolid urine.
- As the body fat retains heat, many desert animals have an adaptation that allows them to store all their body fat in one area of their body. For example, camels stores large amount of body fat in its hump. The blubbery fat of hump is also oxidized to produce metabolic water.
- Many animals also develop long legs, which not only help them in swift running, jumping but also lift their body above ground to avoid direct contact with burning sand (leaf hoppers). Their wide soles are often padded (camel) or covered with hair (desert cat).
- For protection against sand storms the nostrils are either reduced to small pinhole or protected with valves (in camels) or turned upwards (in sand-swimming lizards); eyelids are capable of closing without hindering the vision or formation of nictitating membrane; ears are protected with fringes, scales or hairs. In some animals, ear aperture may altogether be absent.
- Most of the animals have also developed a wide range of dietary habit depending on the availability of food in the deserts.
- The breeding season of most mammalian fauna were found to coincide with the monsoons due to the prevalence of green food and favourable environmental conditions. Some insects lay eggs that remain dormant until the environmental conditions are suitable for hatching.
- Organs of sight, smell and hearing are specially developed.

Cold Deserts

Cold desert is possibly the strangest of all deserts that receive either fog or snow as their main form of precipitation. In India, this desert type covers a vast area of 109,990 sq km, including 87,780 sq km in Ladakh (Jammu and Kashmir), 22,210 sq km in Lahaul-Spiti-Kinnaur-Bharmour (Himachal Pradesh) and some areas of northern Uttaranchal and Sikkim (Figure 2.3). In the high Himalayan mountains, cold deserts were formed primarily due to 'rain shadow effect'. On the other hand, trans-Himalayan cold deserts are physiographically a part of the vast Tibetan plateau with an average elevation of 3,000 m and extends like flat tableland towards north. Zanskar and Karakoram are two major mountain ranges that dissect these cold deserts and Indus, Chenub, Saltuz, Bhagirathi-Alakananda are a few rivers that flow across these regions. Soil type varies in different parts of this area, but overall texture of the soil is heavy, alkaline and often porous.

***Climate*:** Climate of these cold deserts varies from dry temperate to arctic with very little precipitation (annual mean < 50 cm and often range within 15–26 cm) and most of the precipitation is in the form of heavy snowfall. Summer and winter are two pronounced seasons in most of the cold deserts. Summer season is brief, moist, and moderately warm extending from June to September. The maximum temperature in summer months lies between 20–25°C. However, the temperature drops quickly in winter and mostly remains below freezing point. Snowfall usually begins from mid October and lasts till end of May. Thick layer of ice and snow covers the ground during most of the winter season.

Vegetation: Cold deserts in India represent unique floral assemblages in terms of wide variety of economically and medicinally important plants along with several endemic and rare flora. The harsh climate and low temperature, limit the number and type of vegetation found in cold deserts. Greenish patches of vegetation can be seen round the riverbanks and along the snow line, certain varieties of willow groves, wild roses and herbs grow. Tree species in these cold desert regions include *Juniperus* sp., *Pinus* sp., *Taxus* sp., *Quercus* spp., etc.

Moreover, these areas are considered as a treasure trove of medicinal plants. An extensive ethno-medico-botanical survey of different parts of Indian cold desert has documented 425 plant species. The important medicinal taxa are *Artemisia* spp., *Aconitum heterophyllum*, *Cremanthodium ellisii*, *Gentiana algida*, *Oxytropis microphylla*, *Podophyllum hexandrum*, *Saussurea obvallata* etc. Besides, more than 40 mushroom species were reported from various locations of Ladakh. There are certain narrow valleys in the region which are quite fertile where certain agricultural crops are grown. Apart from this, 44 important species of flora found in the cold desert are being used for edible purpose. Some species of scrub and perennial herbs also grow in the marshes around some of the lakes present therein. Trees are very scarce on such rough terrain. Apart from some trees along riverbanks and valleys, cold deserts possess virtually no natural forests. In the lower elevation, dry forests of juniper, *Populus-Salix* forests and subalpine dry birch-fir forests are found.

Faunal Richness: The cold deserts of this country harbours very rich diversity of wild sheep and goats and are home to the endangered Tibetan wild ass or kiang (*Equus kiang*), which is a close relative of the Indian wild ass found the Rann of Kutch. Among the sheeps of this cold desert, Tibetan argali (*Ovis ammon hodgsoni*) is the largest and Ladakh urial or shapu (*Ovis orientalis vignei*) is the smallest wild sheep in the world. Similarly wild yak (*Bos grunniens*) is the largest animal and blue sheep or bharal (*Pseudois nayaur*) is the most wide spread sheep in the Ladakh region. Himalayan marmot (*Marmota himalayana*), Tibetan woolly hare (*Lepus oiostolus*), cape hare (*Lepus capensis*) and several varieties of pika or mouse hare (*Ochotona* spp.) and vole (*Alticola* spp.) are some smaller animals found in Ladakh region. Other animals of this region include long-tailed marmot (*Marmota caudata*), Himalayan ibex (*Capra ibex sibirica*), Tibetan antelope or chiru (*Pantholops hodgsonii*), Tibetan gazelle (*Procapra picticaudata*), Kabul markhor (*Capra falconeri megaceros*), Himalayan marmot (*Marmota himalayana*), wooly flying squirrel (*Eupetaurus cinereus*) etc. Carnivorous species are snow leopard (*Uncia uncia*), Himalayan lynx (*Felix lynx isabellina*), Pallas's cat (*Otocolobus manul*), Tibetan wolf (*Canis lupus chanko*), red fox (*Vulpes vulpes*), Tibetan sand fox (*Vulpes ferrilata*), Himalayan weasel (*Mustela ermenia*), Tibetan polecat (*Mustela putorius*) etc. Apart from these, brown bear (*Ursus arctos isabellinus*) is also occasionally reported from Ladakh near Dras and upper Suru Valley.

In spite of being an arid area, cold deserts of this country exhibit a great diversity of around 310 species of birds, most of which are breeding migrants. Black-necked crane (*Grus nigricollis*), one of the rarest birds in the world, is found scattered in the Tibetan plateau, and is also found nesting in summer in parts of Ladakh. Other migratory birds which breed in Ladakh are ruddy shelduck (*Tadorna ferruginea*), bar-headed goose (*Anser indicus*) and great-crested grebe (*Podiceps cristatus*). Threatened raptors like Lammergeier (*Gypaetus barbatus*) and the golden eagle (*Aquila chrysaetos*) are fairly common here. Tibetan sandgrouse (*Syrrhaptes tibetanus*), Tibetan partridge (*Perdix hodgsoniae*), Tibetan snowcock (*Tetraogallus tibetanus*) and the chukar partridge (*Alectoris chukar*) are few other threatened avian species found in the cold deserts. Apart from these, Tibetan raven (*Corvus corax tibetanus*), red-billed chough (*Pyrrhocorax pyrrhocorax*), greater sand plover (*Charadrius leschenaultia*), lesser sand plover (*Charadrius mongolus*), desert wheatear (*Oenanthe deserti*), horned lark (*Eremophila alpestris*), fire-capped tit (*Cephalopyrus flammiceps*), white-tailed rubythroat (*Luscinia pectoralis*), long-billed bush warbler (*Bradypterus major*), little forktail (*Enicurus scouleri*), wallcreeper (*Tichodroma muraria*), brown dipper (*Cinclus pallasii*) and many species of finches, robins, redstarts and the hoopoe are common in summer (Chandan et al., 2011). Many of these birds reside or breed at high-altitude wetlands such as Tso Moriri. Many insect species are also found to be endemic to these regions.

Adaptations

Cold deserts are very arid regions due to lack of rain. Here mineral deposits are often exposed and get shifted around, mixing salt into the soil.

Floral adaptations During severe cold and arid conditions xerophytes in cold deserts tend to be deciduous, either completely (shed all leaves) or partially (shed some of their leaves). They also have spiny leaves, which can help prevent evapotranspiration and also protect the plant from the herbivores. Their shallow and widely spread root systems help to absorb as much water as possible. These high-altitude xerophytes thrive on enough soil moisture but the atmosphere is dry. In addition to aridity, in some parts of cold deserts plants also need to thrive in highly saline soil conditions. **Halophytes** usually grow in saline soils. Plant heights largely vary ranging from 15 to 120 cm.

Faunal Adaptations The animal species also demonstrate an excellent ecological adaptation to flourish in such inhospitable conditions. Animals, which have adapted to the rigorous conditions usually thrive on minimal vegetation, poor shelter, rocky terrain and bitter cold. Animals that live in cold deserts must be able to conserve energy and live in the cold.

- Warm blooded mammals with highly insulated thick coats of fur are more likely to appear in cold deserts (than reptiles or amphibians), as they are better adapted to deal with freezing winters.
- Some animals have broad feet and fur on its paws to efficiently walk over the cold and often snow covered terrain (as in snow leopards). Some others possess a big, bushy tail that the animal can

put around its body for additional warmth (as in Tibetan fox).

- Large mammals of these cold deserts molt in early winter and grow an extremely white coat to camouflage with the snow in their habitat.
- Many creatures, notably the ungulates, migrate to lower regions in winter (seasonal migration) while others, like the brown bear and marmots, usually hibernate.
- Most of the animals in the cold desert, even the cold-blooded carnivores and reptiles, are fossorial. It is to be noted that in hot and dry deserts animals live inside their burrows to stay cool, whereas in cold deserts animals burrow into the ground to stay warm. In cold deserts, animals usually come out of their burrow when the temperature is warmest.

2.3.5 Aquatic Biomes

Water covers major portion of the earth's surface, providing abode to numerous species of organisms. The terrestrial biomes are usually identified and classified on the basis of dominant vegetation. In contrast, the aquatic biomes are distinguished on the basis of physical attributes such as salinity, strength of water current, availability of light, oxygen content, etc. Global aquatic biomes have been classified into two broad categories—the **marine biomes** and **freshwater biomes**.

Marine Biomes

Marine biomes are undoubtedly the largest among all the terrestrial and aquatic biomes covering about 71 percent of the earth's surface. This biome includes oceans and its associated ecosystems like coral reefs, sea shores, estuaries, as well as, tidal marshes and swamps.

All oceans are very deep, interconnected and play important role in regulating the regional atmosphere, global climate and in the functioning of major mineral cycles. Marine regions are very rich in biodiversity. Various life forms extend to all its depth, but their diversity and abundance is much higher in relatively shallow regions near the margins of continents and islands. In spite of being interconnected, the physical factors like temperature, salinity and depth are the main barriers against free movement of marine organisms.

Characteristic features: Sea water is alkaline (pH = 8.2), highly saline and is also strongly buffered. In the open ocean, salinity lies within very narrow limits but is widely variable in estuarine waters. Majority of this salinity of the marine waters is contributed by sodium chloride and the rest by calcium, magnesium and potassium salts. The major anions in sea water are chloride, sulfate, bicarbonate, carbonate and bromide. Numerous other elements are also present in oceans. Temperature, pressure and light are the other important factors in marine life of organisms. Oceans store large amount of heat from sun and thereby regulate the temperature of the world. The surface water, particularly in the shallow coasts, is coolest at dawn and warmest at dusk ranging from –3°C to 40°C. Seasonal and daily temperature changes in the open sea is not very pronounced, but remarkably vary in coastal and estuarine waters. Pressure increases proportionately with the depth in the ocean and this also has prime effect on the vertical distribution of marine life. Light influences photosynthesis, water heating, radiations and vision of the inhabitants. Light penetrates only up to 100 – 200 m in the ocean and this zone near surface is termed as the 'euphotic zone'. The vast zone below 200 m is completely dark as sunlight does not penetrate and is termed as 'aphotic zone'.

***Vegetation*:** The euphotic zone is considered as the 'producing zone' of the marine ecosystems and are rich in phytoplankton (producers), as well as, primary and secondary consumers. On the contrary, producers are absent in the aphotic zone and secondary consumers are the main heterotrophs thriving there. The volume of surface area receiving sunlight is small in all oceans as compared to the total volume of ocean water.

Faunal Richness: The near shore coastal waters of India are extremely rich fishing grounds, from where the total commercial marine catch (ranging between 1.4–1.6 million tonnes) are harvested annually. Around 30 percent of the commercial marine fishes are sardines (*Sardinella* spp.), Indian shad or hilsa (*Tenulosa ilisha*) and whitebait (*Stolephorus* sp.). Coral reefs are found only in a few sections along mainland coasts (mainly in the Gulf of Mannar, Gulf of Kutch, off the southern mainland coast). Coral reefs are also found around a number of islands in Andaman, Nicobar and Lakshadweep. Besides, sea-grass beds present on the shallow sedimentary areas of continental shelfs are important feeding areas for the dugong (*Dugong dugong*), along with several species of marine turtle. Five species of marine turtle occur in Indian marine waters *viz.* green turtle (*Chelonia mydas*), loggerhead turtle (*Caretta caretta*), olive ridley turtle (*Lepidochelys olivacea*), hawksbill turtle (*Eretmochelys imbricate*) and leatherback turtle (*Dermochelys coriacea*). Some other commercially important marine species found in Indian coasts and coral reefs include spiny lobsters (*Panulirus* spp.), tiger prawns (*Penaeus spp.),* pearl oysters (*Pinctada* spp.), sea fans (*Gorgonia* spp.), seaweeds, ornamental shells, chanks and many species of ornamental aquarium fishes.

Adaptations

Organisms in this biome must adapt in order to survive in unique marine conditions.

Floral Adaptations Plant adaptations are common in the ocean. Flora found in the ocean are seaweed, sea cabbage, kelp, algae and planktons. Some species of seaweed have air bladders to make them float. They come in colors that range from green, blue-green, red or blue. Marine plants and algae also attach firmly to rocks and other substratum, so that the ocean currents and waves do not displace them from their preferred habitat. Certain seaweeds are tough and leathery, which protects them from being torn or dried out by the sun. The plants provide food and shelter for the animals. Animals often remain behind such dense foliage to hide from their predators.

Faunal Adaptations Adaptations in most marine fishes include sleek spindle-shaped bodies to reduce friction while moving in the water. Such body shape helps them glide smoothly through the water and the fins help them swim and maneuver. Besides, they also possess gills, which allow them to intake the salt water and breath under ocean using the dissolved oxygen of marine water. Most animals, especially the cartilaginous marine fishes, have eyes on the sides of their heads so that they can see the approaching predators. Colours of their body often blend with the surroundings helping them to camouflage and hide from their enemies. Small fish in the marine biomes are often herbivores and the larger ones are carnivores. Nevertheless, there are some predatory small fishes (like piranhas), which live and predate in large groups. All predatory fishes possess razor sharp teeth, which help them to tear the flesh of their prey. Many marine organisms are well adapted to live in high salinities. Hence, different marine invertebrates and fishes have adopted different strategies for osmoregulation in marine environment. Organisms of open oceans are usually stenohaline whereas organisms of inshore brackish waters are generally euryhaline. Pressure also has pronounced effect on the distribution of life. Therefore, certain organisms are restricted to surface waters, whereas others are adapted to immense pressure at great depths. Some marine organisms, such as sperm whales and certain seals are eurybathic which can dive to great depths and return to the surface without difficulty. Sea anemones are like plants and possess specialized cells (cnidoblast cells containing nematocysts) in their tentacles that act as poison stings. To sustain in the cold waters in deep oceans most marine mammals (such as whales) have thick layer of fat beneath their skin known as 'blubber'. In addition to these basic adaptations, there are many adaptive features specific for the conditions where the animals or plants inhabit.

Freshwater Biomes

Freshwater biomes are found in relatively small portion as compared to marine and terrestrial habitats and occupy less than five percent of the earth's surface. But their importance to humans is greater as they are the most convenient and cheapest source of water for domestic and industrial use. Freshwater habitats are divided into two groups:

A. Lentic (or standing-water) Ecosystems: *Lentic* ecosystems are geographically isolated inland depressions containing standing water, which are scattered throughout the earth's surface such as lakes and ponds. They vary in size (from just a few square meters to thousands of square kilometers) and depth (from one meter to over 1,000 m deep). Aquatic organisms often move from one part of aquatic body to other. However, the distribution and abundance of biotic communities in lentic habitats is largely influenced by the availability of light, oxygen and nutrients. So, biotic communities often vary in different zones as many of them restrict themselves to a particular zone. Based on the availability of light, *lentic* ecosystems have well defined and characteristic stratification:

(a) **Littoral zone:** It is the shallow water zone near the shore of a lake or pond in which light penetrates up to the bottom. It is typically occupied by rooted and floating aquatic plants. Aquatic life is richest and most abundant in this littoral zone. In ponds and lakes, littoral zone is relatively large.

(b) **Limnetic zone:** It is the near-surface zone in the open water that extends up to the depth of effective light penetration and is usually surrounded by littoral zone. Planktons (both phytoplankton and zooplankton) and nektons (fishes) are the abundant biotic forms of the limnetic zone.

Both littoral and limnetic zones constitute the euphotic zone where light penetrates and production is greater than respiration ($P/R > 1$).

(c) **Profundal zone:** The deep water zone present beyond the depth of effective light penetration is the profundal zone. This is also termed as aphotic zone where light does not reach and respiration is greater than production ($P/R < 1$). Producers are absent and heterotrophs usually inhabit this zone. The consumers are mainly detritus feeders and carnivores. Such profundal zones are usually present in marine and deep freshwater ecosystems, but are usually small or even absent in shallow waterbodies (like ponds).

(d) **Compensation level:** Between the limnetic and profundal zone lies another strata where production equals respiration (i.e., $P/R = 1$) is known as compensation level.

(e) **Benthic zone:** Benthic zone is the bottom region of both littoral and profundal zones. In this zone the dead bodies of plants and animals, organic debris and the materials washed in by inflowing water settle and mainly decomposition takes place. The major community constituents are bacteria, fungi, chironomid larvae, bottom dwelling annelids, clams, etc.

Periphytons are closely associated with the benthic community and are found moving on or attached to leaves of submerged plants, sticks, rocks and other debris. They consist primarily of blue-green algae, diatoms, water mosses and sponges.

***B. Lotic (or running-water) Ecosystems*:** *Lotic* ecosystems are the continuously flowing bodies of water (such as springs, streams and rivers), where the water mostly flows in one direction. The direction and rate of flow is determined by the slope, topography and underlying rock condition. Fast flowing water moving downstream causes extensive erosion that cuts the channel wider, deeper and carries lot of debris that sooner or later are deposited within or along the stream where flow of water is less. Land-water interchange is relatively more extensive in this open ecosystem than any other aquatic ecosystems. Detritus carried from the surrounding land are the major source of nutrients in these ecosystems.

Unlike lentic ecosystems, lotic ecosystems are neither vertically stratified nor exhibit any horizontal zonation. However, in a given stretch of stream two zones are generally recognized:

(a) **Rapid zone:** This is the shallow water zone with very high water current. Therefore, the bottom substrate is rocky and is devoid of any silt or other loose material. Organisms specialized to firmly attach or cling to the substrate or those can swim against the current are found in this zone. Plants of streams such as algae, mosses and encrusting diatoms are found attached to stones and logs. A few animals such as freshwater sponges, coelenterates (e.g., *Hydra*) and caddis fly larvae are found fixed to stones.

(b) **Pool zone:** This is the deep water zone where the velocity of current is relatively low. Hence, the sand and silt settle and provide a soft bottom favourable for burrowing and swimming animals, rooted plants and even planktons.

Wetlands

In addition to these *lotic* and *lentic* ecosystems, there is another type of unique freshwater biome called *wetlands*. In wetlands, water is at or near the surface or the land and is usually covered by shallow water such as swamps, marshes and bogs.

Wetlands are the unique transitional conditions between terrestrial land and deep water bodies consisting primarily of hydric soil which is saturated with water, either permanently or seasonally, and supports characteristic vegetations adapted to their unique soil conditions. Wetlands are also regarded as *ecotones* providing transition between dry land and water bodies. So these unique ecosystems serve as an interface between terrestrial and aquatic ecosystems. Wetlands, including rivers, lakes, reservoirs, etc. are the most precious life-sustaining water resources and play crucial role in the hydrological cycle. Typical wetlands show a vegetation cover of over 50 percent annually and support plants adapted to the wetland habitat. Many wetlands show a seasonal appearance, where free overlying water is noticed during the rainy season and during summer they become almost marshy or dry. Such periodic fluctuations in water level influence the productivity and species composition of wetland community.

Wetlands account only for about six percent land surface of the earth, but they serve as potential source of 'carbon sequestration' and are the most productive ecosystems of the world.

Definitions Wetlands are defined as 'lands transitional between terrestrial and aquatic ecosystems where the water table is usually at or near the surface of land and the land surface is saturated or covered with shallow standing water at least part of the year during which time they support predominately hydrophytes'.

According to the **Ramsar Convention** "wetlands are areas of submerged or water saturated lands, both natural or artificial, permanent or temporary, with water that is static or flowing, fresh or brackish or salty including areas of marine water, the depth of which at low tide does not exceed six meters." This definition is widely used in the Indian context. Thus, all inland water bodies and even the rice fields are considered as wetlands. Wetlands may be defined in many other ways and different countries have their own definition of wetlands, often for legal purposes.

Characteristics of Wetlands

Wetlands are often characterized by:

- Presence and predominance of hydric soils.
- Areas inundated or saturated by surface or ground water for a considerable period.
- Prevalence of hydrophytic vegetation.

Types of wetlands

Wetlands are broadly classified as natural and artificial wetlands. Natural wetlands are found in every continent, except Antarctica. There are various types of freshwater wetlands, like marshes, swamps, peatlands, flood plains etc. Amazon river basin and the west Siberian plains harbour some of the largest wetlands in the world. The natural wetlands of this country include temporary or permanent freshwater ponds, lakes, floodplain marshes and swamps. Nevertheless, there are some wetlands which have high salt concentrations, such as inland saline marshes, coastal salt marshes and mangrove swamps. Estuaries and coastal lagoons are also considered as brackish water wetlands. Therefore, wetlands often overlap with the freshwater and marine biomes. There are also numerous artificial (man-made) wetlands constructed for water management and are found in areas influenced by human activities. Substantial waterlogged areas with wetland vegetation, which are formed by spillover from irrigation channels or reservoirs are the examples of such man-made wetlands. In India, more than 1,550 large reservoirs cover a total area of more than 14,500 sq km and 100,000 small and medium reservoirs that cover another 11,000 sq km. Innumerable fishponds and extensive paddy fields are also considered as wetlands, which are often modified from the earlier marshes (Garg, et al. 1998). Besides, numerous small reservoirs have been built in the drier regions. These artificial wetlands are usually devoid of hydric soils.

Some of the prominent types of wetlands are discussed below:

1. ***Marshes:*** Marshes are permanently low lying wet areas usually dominated by emergent vegetations (like reeds, grasses, sages, cattails, etc.) that grow with roots in soil, with stems partly in bottom sediment and partly out of water and leaves are held above water. Trees are usually absent in marshes. These wetlands are often not dependent on precipitations and develop along the margins of lakes and ponds or in shallow basins with an inflow and outflow of water. Marshes are also present on tidal flats along the lower reaches of large rivers and in coastal plains. The substratums of these wetlands are rich in mineral soil. The productivity of marshes is much higher than the surrounding uplands. Marshes serve as the breeding and wintering grounds for ducks, geese, herons, shorebirds and 'stopover points' for many migrating waterfowl and shorebirds. These wetlands also exhibit rich diversity of amphibians, reptiles, birds and function as nurseries for many fishes.
2. ***Swamps:*** Swamps generally contain saturated soils and may be described as the wetlands with wooded vegetation (trees and shrubs). They are flooded for most of the growing season. Deepwater swamps are dominated by swamp oaks and cyprus trees; shrub swamps are dominated by monospecific stands of *Typha* spp., *Phragmites* spp. etc., and mangrove swamps show presence of different mangrove species. Swamps may also be tidal or non-tidal based on its location. Forested woodlands along large river systems are occasionally flooded by river waters which form another type of swamp wetland.
3. ***Peatlands:*** Peatlands are waterlogged areas saturated by water (groundwater or rainwater) and accumulates partially decayed organic matter. Anoxic environment, poor nutrient content, hyper acidity are some features often associated with these wetlands. Nutrients are locked up in peat. Undecomposed plant matter accumulation provide energy. Primary productivity in peatlands is low due to low temperatures, acidity and nutrient immobilization. Slightly acidic peatlands which are dominated by reeds, sedges and other herbs, fed by water moving through mineral soil and receive inflow of water washed from mineral rich catchments are called *fens*. *Carex* spp., *Salix* spp., etc. are some of the characteristic herbs of *fens*. The dominant herbivores of bog community are insects, grouse, hares, bog lemmings and sheep and the predators include spiders, ground beetles, frogs, shrews, warblers, weasels and owls.
4. ***Floodplains:*** Wetlands present adjacent to river in riverine ecosystem which are inundated regularly or seasonally and rich in alluvial deposits are called *floodplains*. They may also be tidal or non-tidal, may be associated with coastal lowland and often end in estuaries or deltas. Based on their origin, floodplains are of different types *viz.* river channel myandas, natural levees, oxbow lakes, back swamps etc. Characteristic vegetations of freshwager floodplains are *Ipomoea aquatica*, *Sagittaria sagittifolia*, *Narenga porphyrocoma* etc. while dominant species of saline habitats are *Porteresia* sp., *Nypa fruticans*, *Heritiera* spp., *Avicennia* spp., *Sonneratia* spp., *Bruguiera* sp., etc.
5. ***Lakes:*** Lakes are permanent water bodies having steady standing water table. Shallow parts of a lake may be considered wetlands. Water quality of a lake may vary from fresh to saline. Shallow part of the lake is usually vegetated by grass species. Floating-leaf, floating-stem and emergent plant species are also present. Unmanaged lakes are totally covered by few floating hydrophytes. Sometimes eutrophic conditions are also noticed.
6. ***Estuaries:*** Estuaries are deep water wetlands receiving regular tidal flush, but the water here is diluted with freshwater washes from the catchments. They include intertidal mudflats and sandflats, salt marshes, mangroves etc. Estuaries are main important centres of inland capture fisheries.
7. ***Man-made Wetlands:*** Wetlands excavated or transformed for human need are called as man-made or artificial wetlands. They include paddy fields, fish ponds, reservoirs, etc. Water qualities of these wetlands are dependent on the nature of exploitation. There there are many instances where water quality of a man-made wetland has drastically changed due to overexploitation. Vegetation covers in these wetlands are generally man-managed. Sometimes perennial reservoirs are good abode for many endemic species.

Wetlands of India

India has a rich variety of wetland habitats due to varied topography and eco-climatic regimes across the country. First survey undertaken by the Department of Science and Technology in 1976, revealed a total of 1,193 wetlands in India, covering an area of 39,045 sq km, of which 572 were natural, 542 were man-made, seven included both natural and man-made habitats and the remainder were unclassified. Of these wetlands, majority were freshwater, followed by brackish water and coastal wetlands. These wetlands were used for irrigation purposes, fishing, fish culture, grazing, waste disposal and reed-gathering. At many sites, there were multiple uses, for example, used both for fishing and irrigation. Most of the wetlands were small. Over 690 had an area of less than 1 sq km, and only five wetlands were larger than 1,000 sq km. Second survey revealed the total area of wetlands (excluding rivers) in India is 5,82,860 sq km (18.4 percent of the country's area), of which 70 percent are paddy cultivation areas.

Climate: About 70 percent of the annual rainfalls for the entire Indian subcontinent occur during the south-west monsoon, which largely influences the development of wetland vegetation. The environment of wetlands is usually moist with relatively high humidity. Nevertheless, temperature, rainfall and other climatic parameters largely vary depending on the wetland location. Even same wetland may show noticeable variations in different years. Dissolved oxygen content of the wetlands usually lies between 4–10 ppm.

Vegetation: Wetlands in India support more than 1,500 aquatic and wetland species. More than 40 percent algae and over 12 percent of the pteridophytes of India are found in the freshwater wetlands. Types of wetland plants are also remarkably diverse owing to the large scale variation in topography, huge climatic gradient across the country and due to local variation in rainfall. All wetland plants have been grouped under following broad categories *viz.* free-floating hydrophytes (*Eichhornia crassipes*, *Lemna perpusilla*, *Pistia stratiotes*, etc.), suspended hydrophytes (*Hydrilla* sp., *Utricularia* sp., etc.), submerged-anchored hydrophytes (*Aponogeton appendiculatus*, *Vallisneria* sp. *Potamogitum* sp. etc.), anchored hydrophytes with floating leaves (*Aponogeton natans*, *Nelumbo nucifera*, etc.), anchored hydrophytes with floating shoots (*Ipomoea aquatica*, *Trapa maximowiczii* etc.) and emergent-anchored hydrophytes (*Bacopa monnieri*, *Eleocharis spiralis*, *Hydrocera triflora*, *Limnocharis flava*, *Limnophila aromatic*, *L. heterophylla*, *Monochoria vaginalis*, *Typha* spp. etc.)

Faunal richness: It is estimated that at least 12,280 faunal species belonging to various taxa are found in freshwater environment which account for about 16 percent of the known faunal diversity of India. Many species of indigenous fishes are largely dependent on these ecosystems. Mangroves serve as critical hatching and nursery grounds and coral reefs are good sources of food for many tropical fish species. 131 species under 67 genera, 28 families and 10 orders of cartilaginous fishes (Chondrichthyes) are found in the brackish or saltwater wetlands of Indian region (Kar et al., 2000). On the other hand, 2415 species of bony fishes (Osteichthyes) belonging to 902 genera, 226 families and 30 orders are reported from the freshwater wetlands of this country (Prasad et al., 2002). Some families of these bony fishes (viz. Parapsilorhynchidae, Psilorhynchidae, Olyridae, Horaichthyidae) are endemic to India. These endemic fish families form 2.21 percent of the total bony fish families of the Indian region. A total of 223 endemic fish species are found in wetlands, which constitute 8.75 percent of the total fish species known from the Indian region. *Parapsilorhynchus* spp., *Olytra* spp., *Horaichthys setnai* are some endemic fishes of small streams and other wetlands of hilly terrains in India (Prasad et al., 2002). Frogs are the major amphibian species in most wetlands as they require both terrestrial and aquatic habitats. The tadpoles control algal populations and the adults forage on insects and thereby serve as an indicator of wetland health. Saltwater or estuarine crocodiles (*Crocodylus porosus*) are found in the brackish waters along the coast, estuaries and mangroves (like Bhitarkanika, Sundarbans etc.). Marsh crocodiles or *muggers* (*Crocodylus palustris*) and gharials (*Gavialis gangeticus*) are found in some rivers of this country (like Chambal river, Narmada river, Vishwamitri river etc.). Various kinds of snakes, lizards and turtles are also fairly common in wetland habitats. Moreover, several species of small mammals along with some large herbivores (viz. wild water buffalo *Bubalus arnee*, swamp deer *Rucervus duvaucelii*, Manipur brow-antlered deer *Cervus eldi eldi,* etc.) live within and around wetlands. Many species of invertebrates (including various insects) are also found submerged in water or in the soils, as well as, on the surface water of the wetlands.

Adaptations

Wetlands are some of the most diverse wildlife habitats on earth. In spite of the abundance of water and nutrients, flora and fauna of wetlands need to adapt to survive in periods of both flood and drought conditions. The organisms often need to survive in conditions with reduced oxygen in both the soil and water, as well as, contend with accumulated salts or other pollutants. Finding food, shelter and successful mating is also challenging in wetland habitats and must be accomplished properly to ensure survival. Therefore, wetland plants and animals develop a variety of physical and behavioural adaptations to deal with the particular set of challenges in these unique biomes.

Floral Adaptations In order to successfully meet the demand of oxygen for respiration, many wetland plants have developed several strategies to survive in an oxygen-depleted environment, as well as, to deal with anaerobic conditions in the sediment and soil. Wetland bacteria use sulfate in lieu of oxygen for respiration, and thus have a unique way of dealing with anaerobic conditions. Many emergent wetland plants (like cattail) have developed air spaces (called *aerenchyma*) throughout the structures of their emergent parts (the part above water), which help in the entry of oxygen and its transportation to their submerged roots. Some other plants also have hollow stems for oxygen transport to the roots. Some mangrove trees have developed upwardly projected roots (called *pneumatophores*), which grow above the soil to deal with the problems of growing in a wet and salty place. Plants growing in tidal wetlands are called *halophytes* which are adapted to high level of salinity.

Faunal Adaptations Some air-breathing invertebrate species deviced novel ways to find air — some of them come to surface to breathe, while some others carry air bubbles. In fishes, hemoglobin oxygen delivery increase in low dissolved oxygen conditions. Some faunal species tolerate wide salinity fluctuations (*euryhaline*) whereas others tolerate only very limited salinity ranges (*stenohaline*). Migratory fishes (such as *Tenulosa ilisha*) can survive all levels of salinity in their migration through river, estuarine and coastal wetlands. The resident fishes (like freshwater carps) cannot tolerate wide range of salinity. Some are obligate air-breathers (lungfish, electric eel, etc.) and some others are facultative air-breathers (*Jeol* fishes like *Anabas*, *Clarias,* etc.). Freshwater animals excrete dilute urine whereas the saltwater fauna often release concentrated urine to maintain body water and ion balance. Salt excretion glands or cells are also present in some wetland birds, fishes, reptiles and mammals. Animals that live in wetlands also have specialized ways of reproducing and feeding. Otters have webbed feet, and a broad flat tail for swimming and a thick, waterproof coat. They close off nose and ears while swimming underwater. Some insects also possess specialized, paddle like legs that enable the insect to move over the surface of the water. Based on the feeding strategies the wetland fauna are grouped as bottom feeders (or scrapers), surface feeders, sit and wait predators, active predators, shredders and suspension feeders and each type has specially adapted body parts to successfully procure food (or capture prey). Life history strategies adopted by the faunal species during dry period in the wetlands include aestivation (amphibians, reptiles), switching to terrestrial life stages (amphibians, insects) and dormancy of eggs (invertebrates). On the other hand, antifreeze or controlled freezing is adopted by many invertebrates, amphibians, fishes as overwinter survival strategies, particularly in wetlands where temperature drops below freezing point. Many faunal species (like insects, birds, fishes) simply migrate out of the wetland in search of better conditions. Reproduction in many wetland fauna is also timed depending on water presence (insects, amphibians, birds), water temperature (fish, insects, amphibians), food presence/abundance (most groups) or predator absence (insects, amphibians). Besides, the timing of egg-hatching and maturation is also timed with the favourable conditions.

Wetland Values Each wetland is ecologically unique, provides many commodities, performs a number of vital ecological functions and significantly contributes towards healthy environment. Although wetlands occupy only two percent of the Earth's surface, they play important role in global cycling of sulfur, nitrogen, phosphorus and carbon. Wetlands are often described as "kidneys of landscape". Valuable functions of a wetland include recycling of nutrients, water purification, flood control, maintenance of stream flow and groundwater recharge (Prasad et al., 2002). In addition to providing drinking water, fish, fodder, fuel, wildlife habitat and recreation to the society, wetlands also control the rate of runoff in urban area and serve as buffer against shoreline erosion (Prasad et al., 2002).

Some of the important ecological services rendered by the natural wetlands are discussed below:

1. ***Storage reservoir and flood attenuation:*** Wetlands also provide an important ecological service in storing flood waters. Floodplains are formed in the downstream of major rivers and act as natural storage reservoirs. During flood, volume and speed of excess water gets reduced as they spread over wide area of these floodplains, thereby preventing sudden and damaging effects of flood.
2. ***Groundwater replenishment:*** Drinking water and irrigation of crops across the country largely depends on groundwater. In wetlands, water usually filters down through porous sediments, layers of soils and overlying rocks into aquifers. Some other wetland systems are directly linked to groundwater. Thus, wetlands play crucial role in replenishment of groundwater and thus regulate its quality and quantity.
3. ***Shoreline stabilization and protection:*** Tidal and inter tidal wetlands protect and stabilize coastal zones. Similarly, coral reefs and mangroves also act as a protective barrier in parts of the coastline of this country. Mangroves absorbs the impact of sea storms and significantly decrease the near surface wind speed. Similarly, the coral reefs, tidal and inter-tidal wetlands effectively reduce the speed and height of tidal surges and storm waters.
4. ***Water purification:*** Wetlands improve water quality by acting as natural water purification systems, removing silt and absorbing nutrients

and toxins. Purification of water is rendered by the vegetations in two ways – through nutrient retention and sediment traps. Many wetland flora absorb certain nutrients in some of their body parts and those nutrients are retained in the system until the plant dies or is harvested. Besides, reed beds and submerged vegetations present in the wetlands act as physical barriers, slow down the water flow and trap nutrients in the sediments. Some hydrophytes also have the capacity to remove toxic substances and heavy metals. Water hyacinth (*Eichhornia crassipes*), duckweeds (*Lemna* spp.) and waterferns (*Azolla* spp.) store iron and copper commonly found in wastewater. Many fast-growing emergent wetland plants such as cattail (*Typha* spp.) and reed plants (*Phragmites* spp.) also aid in the uptake of heavy metals from water. Oysters can filter more than 200 liters of water per day while grazing for food and in the process they remove nutrients, suspended sediments and chemical contaminants from water.

5. ***Reservoir of biodiversity:*** Wetlands are rich in biodiversity, harbour many endemic species, sustain specialized flora and fauna and serve as suitable habitat for fish and other aquatic fauna. Some wetlands also serve as important nursery for several commercial fish stalks. Species richness and productivity are higher in many mudflats, salt marshes, mangroves and sea grass beds. Freshwater wetlands alone support 20 percent of the known biodiversity in this country (Deepa and Ramachandra, 1999). In addition, wetlands are important feeding, breeding and nesting sites for a number of endangered species. They also serve as 'stop-over site' for many migratory birds and act as refuge for various species of waterfowls. Abundance of invertebrates in the mud of inter-tidal mudflats often serve as major foraging ground for many species of migratory avifauna, particularly waders.

6. ***Wetland products:*** Wetlands often provide livelihood for numerous people living around them. Many species of wetland flora and fauna are harvested by the local communities for personal and commercial use. Cultivation of paddy, jute and pisciculture are three most significant and conventional traditional practices associated to the wetland ecosystems. In addition, cattail (*Typha* spp.), mat stick (*Cyperus* spp.), etc. are few commercially viable products derived from wetland flora. *Euryale ferox* (locally called *makhana*) is another highly valued dry fruit crop that is extensively cultivated in the wetlands of northern Bihar. Cultivation of water chestnut (*Trapa natans* var. *bispinosa*) along with pisciculture is also quite popular in parts of Uttar Pradesh, Bihar and West Bengal. Some of the major supplementary vegetables include water spinach (*Ipomoea aquatic*), helencha (*Enhydra fluctuans*), alligator weed (*Alternanthera philoxeroides*), vegetable fern (*Diplazium esculentum*), taro (*Colocasia esculenta*), marsh barbel (*Hygrophila schulli*), Asiatic pennywort (*Hydrocotyle sibthorpioides*), narenga (*Narenga porphyrocoma*), waterlily (*Nymphaea spp.),* etc. Some medicinal plants of wetlands are brahmi (*Bacopa monnieri*), gotu kola (*Centella asiatica*), sweet flag or *vacha* (*Acorus calamus*), watercress (*Nasturtium officinale*), lady's tresses orchid (*Spiranthes* spp.). *Hydrilla* spp., *Aponogiton* spp., *Vallisneria natans* etc. are often used as aquarium plants. Some of the products derived from mangrove wetlands are fuel wood, traditional medicines prepared from mangrove bark, fibers for textiles, dyes, tannins, animal fodder and tiger prawn seed. However, over exploitation of some of these commercially important products has emerged as one of the major problem for the sustainable use of wetlands.

7. ***Climate change mitigation:*** Wetlands perform two-fold functions in mitigating the climate change. On one hand various wetlands, particularly tropical mangroves and coastal salt marshes act as carbon sinks. It has been estimated that globally all wetlands store approximately 44.6 Tg of carbon every year. On the other hand, wetlands also reduce the devastating effects of storms, tidal surge and sea-water rise through their ability to store and regulate water.

Thus, wetlands being dynamic and influenced by both natural and man-made activities, need frequent monitoring.

2.4 BIOGEOGRAPHIC ZONES OF INDIA

Biogeography is the study of the distribution of species and ecosystems in geographic space and through geological time. The biogeographic zone is a large distinctive unit of similar ecology, biome representation, community and species. The biotic province is a secondary unit within a biogeographic zone, giving weight to particular communities separated by dispersal barriers or gradual change in environmental factors. On the other hand, the biome is an ecological unit and not a biogeographic unit (Rodgers et al., 2000). Therefore, a biome can be found in several biogeographic zones or provinces.

A wide range of latitudes and longitudes together with varied climatic regimes, have resulted in an astounding range of bio-physical environments, ecosystems and habitats in

India. Moreover, India has a legacy of co-existence of humans and nature, and a longstanding tradition of conservation. As a result, India has a rich floral and faunal diversity and is considered as one of the 'megadiversity countries' of this planet. Biogeographic classification of India is, thus, one of the major recent approaches of division of the diverse ecosystems of this country based on known information on biogeographic characters (Rodgers and Panwar, 1988) in order to enable conservation planning both at the national and local levels. India has 10 different biogeographic zones and 26 biotic provinces, which was made based on various factors such as altitude, moisture, topography, rainfall, etc. (Rodgers and Panwar 1988; WII 2000).

The biogeographic zones of this country are Trans-Himalayan zone, Himalayan zone, desert zone, semi-arid zone, western ghats zone, deccan plateau zone (or deccan penninsula), Gangetic plains zone, northeast zone, coastal zone and islands (Figure 2.4):

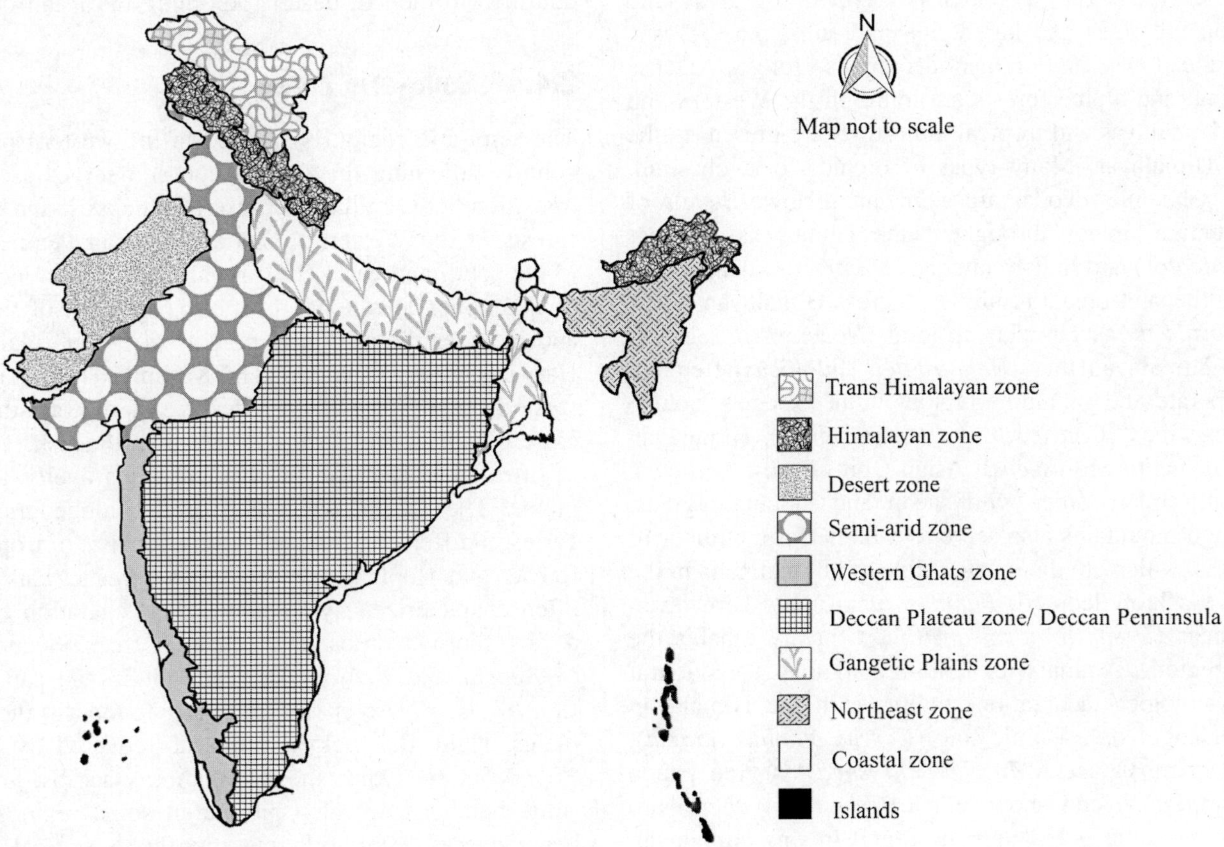

Figure 2.4 Distribution of various Biogeographic Zones in India (based on Rodgers and Panwar, 1988).

2.4.1 Trans Himalayan Zone

The Trans-Himalayan region is present in the immediate north of Great Himalayan range and constitutes 5.6 percent of the country's geographical area. This is the most elevated zone on the earth, which includes cold and arid mountain areas, as well as, the cold deserts of the Tibetan Plateau. Altitude varies from 2,800 m in the Indus to over 7,000 m in the Himalayan and Karakoram ranges. This biogeographic zone is present mainly in Ladakh and Kargil (Jammu and Kashmir); the Spiti valley, Lahaul valley and Kinnaur (Himachal Pradesh); as well as, in small rain shadow areas of Nanda Devi range (Uttaranchal) and Kangchendzonga range (Sikkim). The climate of this region is very cold and arid. Bare rock and glaciers form major portion of the habitat. This zone supports some of the biggest populations of wild sheep and goats that subsist on the sparse vegetation found only in the alpine steppe. Some other major fauna of this region are snow leopard (*Panthera uncia*), marbled cat (*Pardofelis marmorata*), Himalayan marmot (*Marmota himalayana*) and migratory black-necked crane (*Grus nigricollis*).

2.4.2 Himalayan Zone

The Himalayan zone exhibits a wide altitudinal gradient consisting of the entire Himalayan mountain range. This zone covers 6.4 percent of the total land surface of the country and is further classified into Northwest Himalayas (Kashmir to the *Sutlej* river in Himachal Pradesh), West Himalayas (*Sutlej* river in northern India to the *Gandak* river in Nepal), Central Himalayas (*Gandak* river in Nepal through West Bengal and Sikkim to central Bhutan) and East Himalayas (central Bhutan to Arunachal Pradesh). The Himalayas is the youngest mountain chain in the world and is very rich in biodiversity. Floral and faunal diversity in different parts of the Himalayan zone is mainly is determined by the altitude and climate of the area. This zone is characterized by extensive growth of grass and evergreen tall trees and has alpine and sub-alpine forests, grassy meadows and moist deciduous forests. Dense subtropical and alpine forests are found in the Western and Central Himalayas and tropical rainforests are present in the Eastern Himalayas. Many types of orchids, oak, chestnut, conifer, ash, pine, deodar are abundant in lower levels of the mountain ranges throughout the Himalayas. Sambar (*Rusa unicolor*) and Indian muntjac (*Muntiacus muntjak*) are found in the subtropical foothills, whereas Himalayan serow (*Capricornis thar*), Himalayan goral (*Naemorhedus goral*) and the Himalayan thar (*Hemitragus jemlahicus*) frequent the temperate and subalpine regions. Other species include Himalayan ibex (*Capra sibirica hemalayanus*), Himalayan shrew (*Soriculus nigrescens*), Asian tapir (*Tapirus indicus*), along with many other wild sheep and mountain goats. These high mountains also serve as a home for a number of carnivores, which are the most elusive of all mammals in the Himalayas. Snow leopard (*Panthera uncia*) and Himalayan brown bear (*Ursus arctos isabellinus*) mostly inhabit the alpine region. Animals exhibit remarkable behavioural and physiological adaptations to thrive in the Himalayan region. Hangul or Kashmir stag (*Cervus elaphus hangul*), Himalayan musk deer (*Moschus chrysogaster*), red panda (*Ailurus fulgens*) and snow leopard (*Panthera uncia*) are some of the endangered animals found in this Himalayan zone.

2.4.3 Desert Zone

This region consists of 6.6 percent of the India's geographical area and is spread in parts of Rajasthan, Delhi and Kutch region of Gujarat. The elevation of this region ranges from about 350–450 m above sea level at the Aravalli range in the east, about 100 m in the south and west and about 20 m in the Rann of Kutch. Very hot and dry summer, cold winter and very little annual rainfall are the unique climatic features of this zone. Tropical thorn forests with xerophytic plants are the typical natural vegetation of the Indian desert. Tropical dry deciduous forests of babul, kikar, wild palm grows in areas with moderate rainfall. Numerous insect species along with 43 reptile species are found here. Birds are present in almost every habitat of Indian Thar desert. Grasslands in parts of this region support an endangered avian species – the great Indian bustard (*Ardeotis nigriceps*). This is also the only breeding site in the Indian subcontinent for the greater flamingo (*Phoenicopterus roseus*). Some characteristic mammalian species of this zone include Indian camel (*Camelus dromedarius*), blackbuck (*Antilope cervicapra*), Indian gazelle or chinkara (*Gazella bennettii*), nilgai (*Boselaphus tragocamelus*), Indian desert fox (*Vulpes vulpes pusilla*), Indian desert cat (*Felis silvestris ornata*), etc. The Indian wild ass (*Equus hemionus khur*) is now confined to the salt deserts adjoining the Rann of Kutch.

2.4.4 Semi-arid Zone

The semi-arid region is situated in the western part of this country adjoining the desert zone and serves as a zone of transition between the true desert in the west and the denser forests of the Western Ghats and Deccan Peninsular India to the south and east. The Aravalli hills constitute the heart of this zone. This zone covers 16.6 percent of the country and includes the semi-arid regions of Punjab plains, Delhi, Haryana, fringes of Jammu and Kashmir, Himachal Pradesh, western edges of Uttar Pradesh, eastern Rajasthan, south eastern Gujarat and northwest Madhya Pradesh. The habitat is often characterized by dry, rocky, gravelly and sandy plains. The natural vegetation of this biogeographic zone varies in different parts and mainly consists of tropical thorn forests and tropical dry deciduous forests. This region is often characterized by discontinuous vegetation cover with a few thorny scrubs and scattered trees. Scattered trees of *Acacia* and *Prosopis* are present in the sandy plains, *Calotropis*, *Gymnosporia* etc. are found in the gravelly plains, while the rocky terrains are covered by bushes of *Euphorbia* sp. Other species of thorny scrubs, grasses and some bamboos are also present in some regions. Despite being overall semi-arid, this zone holds several lakes and marshlands. Critically endangered Asiatic lion (*Panthera leo persica*) is the endemic species in this biogeographic zone and are found only in Gir National Park in Gujarat.

2.4.5 Western Ghats Zone

Western Ghats is a mountain range extending about 1,600 km from *Tapti* river (21°N) in the north to Kanyakumari (8°N) in the south along the western coast of peninsular India. The Western Ghats is present in the states of Gujarat, Maharashtra, Goa, Karnataka, Tamil Nadu and Kerala. The mountains rise to average altitudes between 900 and 1,500 m above sea level, intercepting monsoon winds from the south-west and creating a rain shadow in the region to their east. This is one of the major tropical evergreen forested regions in India. However, the natural vegetation is diverse ranging from evergreen to dry deciduous. The varied climate and diverse topography create a wide array of habitats that support unique sets of plant and animal species. This biogeographic zone is very rich in biodiversity and is also known for their high levels of endemism among the higher and lower taxa of flora and fauna. Occupying only about 4 percent of the terrestrial land of this country, this biogeographic zone harbours nearly 27 percent of the total flora in India. Out of more than 4,000 species of flowering plants occurring in the region, about 1,500 species are endemic (Mackinnon and Mackinnon, 1986). Most of the Western Ghat endemic plants are associated with evergreen forests. But, expansion of traditional agriculture and the spread of particularly rubber, tea, coffee and forest tree plantations have wiped out large pockets of primary forests in the valleys of the Western Ghats. There are several endemic faunal species as well, such as Nilgiri langur (*Trachypithecus johnii*), lion-tailed macaque (*Macaca silenus*), Nilgiri thar (*Nilgiritragus hylocrius*), Malabar pied hornbill (*Anthracoceros coronatus*) and Malabar grey hornbill (*Ocyceros griseus*). The Western Ghats are well known for harbouring several endemic species of amphibia including 14 endemic species of caecilians (legless amphibians). Hence, Western Ghats are designated as one of the 'biodiversity hotspots' in the world. Apart from biological diversity, many indigenous people inhabit forests of this region, for which Western Ghats also boasts of high levels of cultural diversity.

2.4.6 Deccan Plateau Zone (or Deccan Penninsula)

Deccan Plateau (or Deccan Penninsula) is a semi-arid region lying in the 'rain shadow' of the Western Ghats occupying about 42 percent of the total land surface of this country. This biogeographic zone is present in the states of Maharashtra, Madhya Pradesh, Uttar Pradesh, Karnataka, Tamil Nadu, Andhra Pradesh, Orissa and Bihar encompassing the Vindhya and Satpura hill ranges, Chhota Nagpur plateau, Eastern Ghats, Tamil Nadu plains and Karnataka plateau. The elevation of the plateau ranges from 300 m in the east to 900 m in the west. This zone is relatively homogenous, known for a rich diversity of flora and are covered with different types of forests varying from semi-arid to moist deciduous or semi-evergreen type. Tropical forests are the main natural vegetation of Deccan Penninsula. The northern, central and southern part of the plateau contain tropical dry deciduous forests, whereas moist deciduous forests are present in the eastern part of the plateau in Andhra Pradesh, Madhya Pradesh and Orissa. Indian tiger (*Panthera tigris tigris*), sloth bear (*Melursus ursinus*), wild boar (*Sus scrofa*), gaur (*Bos gaurus*), sambar (*Rusa unicolor*), spotted deer or *chital* (*Axis axis*), four-horned antelope or *chousingha* (*Tetracerus quadricornis*), as well as, small populations of swamp deer or *barasingha* (*Rucervus duvaucelii*), wild water buffaloes (*Bubalus arnee*) and Asiatic elephant (*Elephas maximus*) are some of the characteristic fauna of this biogeographic zone.

2.4.7 Gangetic Plains Zone

The Gangetic plains is the largest unit of the 'great plain' of India spanning over 7,24,000 sq km area encompassing 10.8 percent of the country's geographical area. These alluvial zones are fairly uniform topographically with the Ganges and the Brahmaputra forming the main drainage axes. However, Ganges is the main river and this plain is mainly formed by the alluvial deposits of the river Ganges and its tributaries. These plains stretches from eastern Rajasthan in the west to West Bengal in the east and extends up to the Himalayan foothills in the north. This zone is one of the most fertile regions of India, hence, is mostly under agriculture. This zone is further divided into the Upper Gangetic plain, the Middle Gangetic plain and the Lower Gangetic plain. The physiogeographic features greatly vary from arid and semi-arid landscapes of the Rajasthan plains to the humid landscapes of the delta and Assam valley in the east. Based on geomorphology, the Gangetic plains include four distinct regions *viz. Bhabar* (pebble studded zone with porous beds), *Terai* (marshy tracts), *Bhangar* (older alluvium of the floodplains) and *Khadar* (newer alluvium). Along with some of the important grasslands of this country, large stretches of tropical dry deciduous forests are also present in this region. Some of the economically important trees belonging to these forests are teak, sal, shisham, mahua, khair etc. The southeastern end of the Gangetic plain merges with the littoral zones and mangroves of the Sunderbans. The reptiles of this region includes various species of snakes, freshwater turtles, monitor lizard (*Varanus bengalensis*), marsh crocodile (*Crocodylus palustris*), gharial (*Gavialis gangeticus*) etc. In addition to a large abundance and diversity of avifauna including waterfowl, many threatened and conservation dependent birds also thrive here. Bengal florican (*Houbaropsis bengalensis*) is one such unique threatened species found in this biogeographic region. Some of the important mammalian species are greater one-horned rhinoceros (*Rhinoceros unicornis*), Asiatic elephant (*Elephas maximus*), wild water buffaloes (*Bubalus arnee*), hispid hare (*Carprolagus hispidus*), Indian tiger (*Panthera tigris tigris*), sloth bear (*Melursus ursinus*), wild boar (*Sus scrofa*), gaur (*Bos gaurus*), swamp deer or *barasingha* (*Rucervus duvaucelii*), hog deer (*Axis porcinus*), sambar (*Rusa unicolor*), spotted deer or *chital* (*Axis axis*), etc.

2.4.8 Northeast Zone

Characterized by diverse habitats and long-term geological stability, the northeast zone is located at the junction of the Indian, Indo-Malayan and Indo-Chinese bio-geographical regions. The region spans over eight states, viz. Arunachal Pradesh, Assam, Manipur, Meghalaya, Mizoram, Nagaland, Sikkim and Tripura and covers 5.2 percent of India's geographical area. Due to its location, it is also considered a 'gateway' for much of India's flora and fauna. Diverse topography of this region, in turn, supports large number of flora and fauna. Hence, in addition to the Western Ghats, Northeast India is also designated as a 'biodiversity hotspot' for its biodiversity and significant levels of endemism in all floral and faunal groups. With several species of orchids, bamboos, ferns and other plants, the northeast India represents one of the richest floristic diversity in the country. The tropical vegetation of northeast India is rich in evergreen and semievergreen rain forests, moist deciduous forests, swamps and grasslands. The wild relatives of cultivated plants such as banana, mango, citrus and pepper are also found here. Mammalian fauna includes 390 species of which 63 percent are found in Assam. Highest population of Asiatic elephants (*Elephas maximus*) of this country is reported from this zone. The area is also very rich in lesser carnivores. Some other charismatic vertebrate fauna of this region include greater one-horned rhinoceros (*Rhinoceros unicornis*), wild water buffaloes (*Bubalus arnee*), red panda (*Ailurus fulgens*), capped langur (*Trachypithecus pileatus*), golden langur (*Trachypithecus geei*), Phayre's leaf monkey (*Trachypithecus phayrei*), sloth bear (*Melursus ursinus*), slow loris (*Nycticebus bengalensis*), Manipur brow-antlered deer or *sangai* (*Cervus eldi eldi*), Himalayan musk deer (*Moschus chrysogaster*), clouded leopard (*Neofelis nebulosa*), Manipur bush quail (*Perdicula manipurensis*) etc.

2.4.9 Coastal Zone

India has a coastline extending over 5,500 km stretching from Gujarat to Cape Comorin (Kanyakumari) in the west, and from Cape Comorin to the Sundarbans in the east. The Indian coasts vary in their characteristics and structures. The west coast is narrow except around the Gulf of Cambay and the Gulf of Kutch. In the extreme south, however, it is somewhat wider along the south *Sahyadri*. On the contrary, the east coast plains are broader due to depositional activities of the east-flowing rivers. Extensive deltas of the Mahanadi, Godavari, Krishna and Kaveri are the characteristic features of this coast. The coastal zone constitutes 2.5 percent geographical area of India, which covers the beaches, backwaters, mangroves, mud flats, coral reefs and marine angiosperm pastures. Coconut trees (*Cocos nucifera*) grow all along the coastlines. The natural vegetation also consists of mangroves. Mangrove vegetation is particularly characteristic of estuarine tracts present along the coast. Sundarbans is the largest contiguous patch of mangrove forest in the world and is present in the delta of river Ganges, Padma and their tributaries in India and Bangladesh adjoining the Bay of Bengal. The long stretch of coastline in the mainland has a very diverse set of biotic communities. In India, 26 species of fresh water turtles and five species of marine turtles inhabit and feed in coastal waters and lay their eggs on suitable beaches. Over 200,000 olive ridley turtles (*Lepidochelys olivacea*) come to coastal areas of Orissa to lay eggs. These areas are called 'arribadas' and are very important areas of coastal zone for turtle conservation. Besides, highest tiger population of this country is found in the mangroves of Sundarbans. Dugong (*Dugong dugon*), Ganges river dolphin (*Platanista gangetica*), irrawaddy dolphin (*Orcaella brevirostris*), marsh crocodile (*Crocodylus palustris*), water monitor lizard (*Varanus salvator*), along with many species of avifauna and sea snakes are some other characteristic vertebrate fauna of this biogeographic zone.

2.4.10 Islands

This biogeographic zone covers only 0.3 percent of the country's geographical area, but is very important from the biodiversity perspective. Islands are essentially grouped into the Lakshadweep islands and the Andaman and Nicobar islands. Origin and physical characteristics of these two groups of islands (i.e. the Arabian Sea islands and Bay of Bengal Islands) significantly differ.

The ***Andaman and Nicobar Islands*** are a group of 325 islands oriented in north-south direction in the Bay of Bengal stretching for 590 km from 6° to 13° N latitude and 92° to 93° E longitude. Five islands close together constitute the Great Andaman (300 km long), and the Little Andaman lies to the south. The Nicobar groups of islands are separated from the Andamans, as well as, internally from each other by deep channels. Rainfall is heavy and caused by both northeast and southwest monsoons. The natural vegetation of the Andaman and Nicobar Islands include tropical evergreen forests, tropical semi-evergreen forests, as well as, moist deciduous forests, littoral forests and mangroves. The Andaman and Nicobar islands also show high degree of endemism. About 2,200 species of higher plants are found here, of which 200 are endemic. Coral reefs are stretched over an area of 11,000 sq km in the Andamans and 2,700 sq km in Nicobar. The coconut crab or giant robber crab (*Birgus latro*) found in these islands are considered to be the largest land-living arthropod in the world. Andaman day gecko (*Phelsuma andamanense*), the Andaman Islands water monitor (*Varanus salvator andamanensis*), etc. are some unique reptiles of these islands. One hundred and twelve endemic species of avifauna are found in these islands including Narcondam hornbill (*Rhyticeros narcondami*), edible-nest swiftlet (*Aerodramus fuciphagus*) and Nicobar megapode (*Megapodius nicobariensis*). Endemic mammals include Andaman spiny shrew (*Crocidura hispida*),

Andaman shrew (*Crocidura andamanensis*), Jenkins' shrew (*Crocidura jenkinsi*), Andaman rat (*Rattus stoicus*) and Andaman horseshoe bat (*Rhinolophus cognatus*).

The ***Lakshadweep islands***, on the other hand, are the biodiversity-rich reef lagoon system consisting of 36 major islands, 12 atolls, three reefs and five submerged coral banks. Stretching from 8° to 12° N latitude and 71° to 74° E longitude, these islands are situated more than 300 km to the west of the Kerala in the Arabian sea and cover an area of 32 sq km. Lakshadweep islands also have some of the best-preserved evergreen forests of India. The vegetation of Lakshadweep islands is typical of Indo-Pacific coral island flora. Neither flora nor fauna of these islands has much significant endemism. Mainly 41 species of sponges, 36 species of crabs and 12 species of bivalves are present in those islands. Some of the islands are fringed with coral reefs comprising of 104 scleractinian corals belonging to 37 genera. Many invertebrates, including two endemic butterflies (*Hypolimnas bolina euphorioides* and *Junonia villida chagoensis*) and two amphbians (*Rana breviceps* and *Bufo melanostictus*) are recorded from the islands (Zuhair, 1997). The most common reptiles are house lizards (*Gecko* sp., *Hemidactylus* sp.), garden lizards (*Calotes versicolar* and *Calotes liocephalus*) and skinks (*Riopa albopunktata* and *Mabuya carinata*). Snakes are quite uncommon in these islands and very few species (like *Lycodon aulicus* and *Typhlos braminus*) have been documented. Coral snakes are occasionally seen in the reef area during low tide. These islands are important nesting sites for the endangered green turtle (*Chelonia mydas*) (Olson and Dinerstein 1998). Other sea turtles likely using the islands are the olive ridley turtle (*Lepidochelys olivacea*), leatherback turtle (*Dermochelys coriancea*), loggerhead turtle (*Caretta caretta gigas*) and hawksbill turtle (*Eretmochelys ambricata*) (Zuhair, 1997), which are plentiful in Lakshadweep waters. House crow (*Corveus splendens*) is not uniformly found in the islands. Common resident birds of these islands are *Sterna fuscata*, *Sterna bergiivelox*, *Sterna anethetus*, *Anous stolidus piletus*, etc., and some of the migratory birds are *Pluvialis dominical*, *Nuemenius phaeopus*, *Arenaria interpries*, etc. About 14 species of seabirds are known to nest on these oceanic islands. Maldivian pond heron (*Ardeola grayii phillipsi*), white tern (*Gygis alba monte*), lesser frigate (*Fregata ariel iredalei*), black-naped tern (*Sterna sumatrana*), brown-winged tern (*S. anaethetus*) and large-crested tern (*S. bergi*) are some endemic avifauna of Lakshadweep. Two fruit bats (*Pteropus giganteus ariel* and *Pteropus hypomelanus maris*) are endemic to the archipelago on the islands and both are of conservation concern. Other important marine mammals are Dugong (*Dugong dugong*), short-beaked saddleback dolphin (*Delphinus delphis*) and Cuvier's beaked whale (*Ziphius cavirostris indicus*). Besides, many ornamental fishes and dugongs are found in the waters around Lakshadweep islands.

REVIEW QUESTIONS

1. Define Biome. What do you mean by "biotic provinces"? State the characteristic features of biome. Mention the name of different Biomes of the world.
2. Give an account on the Alpine Tundra biome of India with special reference to distribution, climate, vegetation and faunal assemblage. Comment on the faunal adaptations of Alpine Tundra.
3. What different types of grass lands are found in India? State the importance of grassland biome as ecosystem service providers. Give an account on the grassland fauna of India with a note on their adaptive features.
4. Give an exhaustive account on the forest types of India. State the characteristic features of Tropical rain forest. What do you mean by vertical stratification of tropical rain forest? Describe different tropical rain forest of India.
5. Why Tropical Rain forest support large faunal assemblage? Comment on types of vegetation and unique floral adaptations of Tropical rain forest.
6. Elaborate different modes of adaptations encountered among the animal community of Tropical rain forest. "Tropical rain forest support unique types of arboreal adaptations" — Elaborate.
7. Give an account on the faunal assemblage of desert biome. How they overcome the problems associated with temperature extremes?
8. Give an impression on the adaptive features of desert flora.
9. What do you mean by cold desert? Distinguish between hot and cold desert with special reference to animal adaptation. Comment on the faunal richness of Cold mountain desert of Trans- Himalayas with special reference to their adaptive modes.
10. What do you mean by compensation level? Distinguish between Euphotic and Aphotic Zone. Mention important adaptive features of deep sea fauna.
11. Distinguish between Rapid zone and Pool zone of freshwater biotic ecosystem.

- ❒ What do you mean by Wetlands? "Wetlands are the most productive ecosystem of the earth"—Justify.
- ❒ What different types of wetlands are usually found? Elaborate the role of wetlands as ecosystem service provider.

REFERENCES

Bawa, K.S., Das, A., Krishnaswamy, J., Karanth, K.U., Kumar, N.S., and Rao, M., *Ecosystem Profile: Western Ghats and Sri Lanka Biodiversity Hotspot - Western Ghats Region*. Critical Ecosystems Partnership Fund, Virginia, 2007.

Campbell, N.A., *Biology* (4th ed.), The Benjamin/Cummings Publishing Company, Inc., Menlo Park, California, 1996.

Champion, H.G. and Seth, S.K. *A Revised Survey of the Forest Types of India*, Govt of India Press, Delh, 1968.

Chandan, P., Abbas, M. and Gautam, P., *Field Guide — Birds of Ladakh,* WWF-India, 2011. Retrieved from: http://awsassets.wwfindia.org/downloads/field_guide_birds_of_ladakh.pdf

Conservation International, *Biodiversity Hotspots*, Conservation International, Arlington, VA, 2011, Retrieved from: http://www.conservation.org/where/priority_areas/hotspots/asia-pacific/Western-Ghats-and-SriLanka/Pages/default.aspx

de Blij, H.J. and Miller, P.O., *Physical Geography of the Global Environment*, John Wiley, New York, 1996.

Deepa, R.S. and Ramachandra, T.V., *Impact of Urbanization in the Interconnectivity of Wetlands*. Paper presented at the National Symposium on Remote Sensing Applications for Natural Resources: Retrospective and Perspective (XIX–XXI 1999), Indian Society of Remote Sensing, Banglore, 1999.

Garg, J.K., Singh, T.S. and Murthy, T.V.R. *Wetlands of India (Project Report: RSAM/sac/resa/pr/01/98, June 1998),* Space Applications Centre, Ahmedabad, 1998.

International Union for Conservation of Nature (IUCN), *Review of the Protected Areas System in the Indo-Malayan Realm.* IUCN, Gland, Switzerland and Cambridge, U.K., 1986.

International Union for Conservation of Nature (IUCN), *Defining Grasslands and Highly Biodiverse Grasslands (Information Paper tabled to the European Commission for Support Activities for the Development of Practical Measures to Facilitate the Implementation of the Biofuels Sustainability Scheme. Draft, 17 September 2009)*, Ecofys, Netherlands, 2009.

Kar, D., Nagarathna, A.V., and Ramachandra, T.V., Fish diversity and conservation aspects in an aquatic ecosystem in India. In: *INTECOL, 6th International Wetland Symposium, August VI–XII,* 2000, *Quebec, Canada*, International Association of Ecology and Society of Wetland Scientists, Canada, 2000.

Kendeigh, S.C., *Ecology with Special Reference to Man and Animals*, Prentice Hall, New York, 1975.

MacKinnon, J. and MacKinnon, K., *Review of the Protected Areas System in the Indo-Malayan Realm.* International Union for the Conservation of Nature and Natural Resources, Gland, Switzerland and Cambridge, U.K., 1986.

Olson, D. and Dinerstein E, The global 200: a representation approach to conserving the earth's distinctive ecoregions. World Wildlife Fund, Washington, D.C., 1998.

Prakash, I., Ecology of desert mammals. *Current Science*, **72**, 1, 31-34, 1997.

Prasad, S.N., Ramachandra, T.V., Ahalya, N., Sengupta, T., Kumar, A., Tiwari, A.K., Vijayan, V.S. and Vijayan, L., Conservation of wetlands of India – a review. *Tropical Ecology*, **43**, 1, 173-186, 2002.

Rodgers, W.A. and Panwar, H.S., *Planning a wildlife protected area network in India,* (Project FO: IND/82/003. FAO), Wildlife Institute of India, Dehra Dun, 1988.

Rodgers, W.A., Panwar, H.S. and Mathur, V.B., *Biogeographical Classification of India in Wildlife Protected Area Network in India: A Review*. Wildlife Institute of India, Dehra Dun, 2000.

Seshadri, B. *The twilight of India's wild life.* John Baker Publishers, London, 1969.

Wildlife Institute of India (WII), (*Wildlife Protected Area Network in India: A Review*, Wildlife Institute of India, Dehra Dun, India, 2000.

WWF, Western Ghats, 2011, Retrieved from: http://wwf.panda.org/what_we_do/where_we_work/western_ghats/

Zuhair, M., *Country Report – Maldives* (Asia–Pacific Forestry Sector Outlook Study Working Paper Series, Working Paper No. APFSOS/WP/30), FAO, Rome, 1997.

3

PROTECTED AREA CONCEPT

3.1 PROTECTED AREAS — CONCEPT AND DESIGN

Protected Areas (PAs) are one of the most important *in-situ* conservation strategies to reduce deforestation and sustain the ecological integrity of forest ecosystems. Over 130,000 PAs have so far been designated worldwide covering more than 12 percent of the land surface throughout the globe. Although, 7,74,700 sq km land area (23.57 percent of the total land area) of India has been estimated to have forest cover, yet only about one-fifth of those forested land could so far been designated as 'Protected Areas'. Jim Corbett National Park was the first protected area of India declared in 1935. Since independence, and more precisely after the enactment of the Wildlife (Protection) Act in 1972, there has been a steady increase in the number of protected areas in this country. The National Protected Area Network in India initiated with the establishment of tiger reserves in 1973. Wildlife (Protection) Act, 1972 was amended in 2003 when two new categories of protected areas, namely 'conservation reserve' and 'community reserve' has been included to facilitate peoples' involvement in establishment and management of such protected areas. So far a network of 732 PAs has been established comprising of 103 'National Parks', 536 'Wildlife Sanctuaries', 67 'Conservation Reserves' and 26 'Community Reserves'. All these protected areas presently extend over an area of 1,60,901.77 sq km occupying around 4.9 percent of the total geographical area of this country (Forest Survey of India, 2015). In addition, 50 'Tiger Reserves' (Project Tiger, 2016) and 32 'Elephant Reserves' (MoEF, 2010) have also been designated for species specific management of tiger and elephant habitats, respectively. Seven protected areas have been declared as 'Natural World Heritage Sites' by UNESCO and 26 important wetlands have been declared as 'Ramsar sites' thereby giving international recognition to those sites. In addition to these, there are 131 marine protected areas (25 in peninsular India and 106 in islands) (Saravanan et al., 2011; Sivakumar 2013; Sivakumar et al., 2013). Birdlife International have identified 467 Important Bird Areas (IBAs) in India (Islam and Rahmani, 2004) and 62 sites along the west coast and 44 sites along the east coast have been identified as Important Coastal and Marine Areas (ICMBAs) by the Wildlife Institute of India (Saravanan et al., 2013).

Protected areas, comprising of one or more ecosystems, actually serve as refuge for many threatened species. Hence, designs of such areas are crucial to ensure maximum conservation benefits for the flora and fauna, which are on the brink of extinction. The essential features of any protected area, therefore, should include the following:

- Adequate information on the species and its dependence on the habitat under consideration needs to be gathered before designating any area. For instance, migratory species cannot be protected throughout the year in a single area. Rather, reserves may be created on the roosting and breeding sites along with protecting their feeding sites and corridors or stop-over sites. Resident species, on the other hand, may be conserved relatively easily in a single reserve.

- The area should be large enough to hold a viable population of the species to be conserved.
- Genetic variability of the focal species should be maintained.
- One large reserve is better than many small ones (Figure 3.1).
- The reserve should preferably be surrounded by similar habitats as buffer zones (Figure 3.1).
- The designated area should have smallest amount of edge-to-area ratio. However, this is often predetermined by natural features of the designated area (such as river banks, cliffs, mountain top, etc.).
- In ideal situation, the protected areas should preferably be large, interconnected and compact in shape (usually circular) with surrounding buffer zones as shown in Figure 3.1.

However, every case is different. Therefore, to ensure optimum conservation benefit, the site-structure and the requirement of local communities must be considered separately and with due importance before setting up a protected area.

Once a protected area is declared, proper maintenance and scientific management of the designated area is one of the most important tasks and quite a challenging job. Regulation of human interference, succession of natural vegetation, management of invasive exotic species, ensuring proper regeneration of existing native vegetation, as well as, maintaining the delicate balance and productivity of the entire ecosystem are the major challenges for any conservation manager.

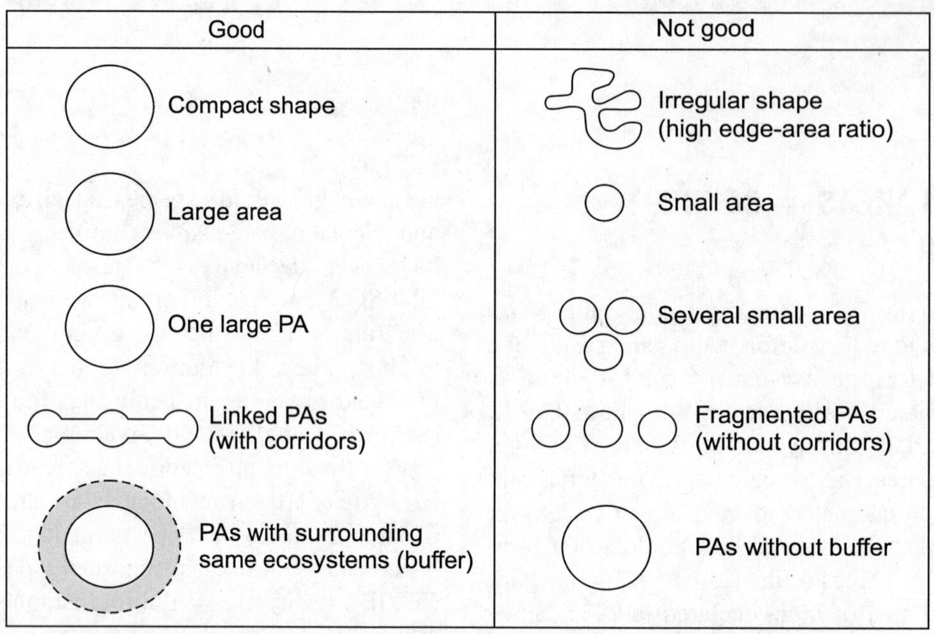

FIGURE 3.1 Basic guidelines regarding the shape and size of Protected Areas.

3.1.1 Types of Protected Areas in India

The Protected Areas have been classified into the four categories, *viz.* Wildlife Sanctuary, National Park, Conservation Reserve and Community Reserve.

A. Wildlife Sanctuary

Sanctuary is an area with adequate ecological, floral, faunal, geo-morphological or natural significance and is usually declared with a purpose of protecting, propagating or developing wildlife and its environment. Wildlife sanctuaries are, therefore, protected areas that provide protection and optimum living conditions to wild animals, where conservation focus is mainly species-oriented and may be formed by an executive order. During the settlement of claims before final notification, the Collector, in consultation with the Chief Wildlife Warden, may decide upon the continuation of certain rights of persons over any land within the limit of the proposed sanctuary. Hunting, killing or capturing of any species is prohibited. However, sometimes such activities are only allowed for management of the sanctuary with special permission from the highest authority of the concerned department. Private ownership and certain forestry activities that do not have any adverse effect on wildlife are also permitted within the sanctuaries. Vedanthangal Bird Sanctuary in Tamil Nadu is the first wildlife sanctuary in India which was designated to conserve birds.

Text Box 3.1 Declaration of a Sanctuary or National Park

According to the Wildlife (Protection) Act, 1972, if the State Government realizes that an area needs to be designated as a Wildlife Sanctuary or National Park for the purpose of protection and propagation of wildlife and environment for its ecological, floral, faunal, or geo-morphological significance then–

1. State Government shall publish a notification specifying the limits of the area and also mention the date from when the area is to be designated as Sanctuary or National Park.
2. Prior concurrence of the Central Government has to be obtained by the State Government for inclusion of any part of the territorial waters. The limits of the area of the territorial waters to be included in the Sanctuary or National Park shall be determined in consultation with the Chief Naval Hydrographer of the Central Government and after taking adequate measures to protect the occupational interests of the local fishermen.
3. After designating a protected area, no alteration of its boundaries shall be made, except on a resolution passed by the Legislation of the State.

If an area appears to be of adequate floral, faunal, ecological, geo-morphological or natural significance, the Central Government may also declare such area as a Sanctuary or National Park under Section 38 of the Wildlife (Protection) Act, 1972. In such cases, the State Government either leases or transfers the area under its control and the Central Government designates and declares the area through notification. In relation to a Sanctuary or National Park declared by the Central Government, the powers and duties of the Chief Wildlife Warden shall be exercised and discharged by the Director or any other officer authorized by the Director.

B. National Park

National Park is an area with adequate ecological, floral, faunal, geo-morphological or natural significance and is usually declared with a purpose of protecting, propagating or developing wildlife and its environment, like that of a sanctuary. However, National Parks enjoy higher status than wildlife sanctuaries and are usually set up by the approval of legislature for preserving flora, fauna, historic landscapes, cultural assets where all private rights are non-existent. Within the boundary of a National Park, activities like grazing of domestic animals, collection of non-timber forest produce and fuel wood, as well as, several other forestry operations are prohibited. Removal or exploitation of wildlife or forest produce from the National Parks requires recommendations of the National Board for Wildlife (NBWL). In broader sense, the national parks are dedicated to conserve the environment and wildlife of the area *per se*. According to the IUCN (1975), national parks are relatively large areas where

- one or several ecosystems are protected from human exploitation.
- plant and animal species, habitats of special scientific, educative, recreational interest and unique natural landscapes are protected.
- highest competent authority of the country usually takes steps to prevent and eliminate all possible occupations that exploit natural resources within the entire designated area.
- tourism is permitted in certain parts, but should be developed in such a way that it does not scare or disturb wildlife and visitors are allowed to enter for inspirational, cultural and recreational purposes with special permission.
- efforts are given to effectively restore the ecological, geomorphological or aesthetic features of the area for which it has been designated.

C. Conservation Reserve

Any government-owned vested land with adequate conservation significance can be declared by the State Government as Conservation Reserve. Such conservation reserves are usually set up in areas adjacent to the National Parks and Sanctuaries that serve as a link between the two PAs. In consultation with the local communities, Conservation Reserves are declared for the purpose of protecting landscapes, seascapes, flora, fauna and their habitat. The rights of people living inside Conservation Reserves are not affected.

D. Community Reserve

Community Reserves can be declared by the State Government in any private or community-owned lands not situated within any National Park, Sanctuary or Conservation Reserve. In such cases the land is usually donated voluntarily by an individual or by the community for the conservation of wildlife and its habitat. Along with protecting flora and fauna of the area, Community Reserves also focus to preserve traditional and cultural conservation values and practices. The rights of people dwelling inside Community Reserves are also not affected.

3.1.2 Problems and Prospects of Protected Area Concept

For management and *in-situ* conservation of wildlife and their habitat, protected area networks (in brief, PA networks) have been created in India covering the forests with relatively higher density. The abundance of certain focal species, their habitat and other associated ecological components are also taken into consideration. Management plans for a stipulated time period are supposed to be prepared on sound scientific knowledge for every protected area. However, all protected areas of this country are under tremendous stress caused by human interventions. Disproportionately large human and livestock populations have made setting aside this 4.9 percent of country's geographical area under the protected area system increasingly difficult. Almost 40 percent of these protected areas are affected by traditional livestock grazing, fodder extraction, timber extraction and non-timber forest produce collection. More than 45 percent have public thoroughfares dissecting them into smaller parts. Almost all have human habitations in or around them. A conflict of interest pervades in the interface areas between the gene-pool reserves and the exploiters of the forest resources. These pressures are increasing with the rapid rise in the population of the country. People are not aware that more than 300 rivers originate in India's national parks and sanctuaries and many others do so in the forest lands outside these protected areas. Since the role of these natural life-sustaining systems is invisible to most people, our consumerist preoccupation for exploitation of forest lands and the life forms inhabiting there for short-term gains, has created a barrier of indifference, resistance and even misdirected opposition against conservation of the nation's biodiversity. In spite of all odds, it is to be admitted that the PA network of this country has played a paramount role in wildlife conservation and over the years has protected a large number of species, which otherwise would have been extinct by now.

In addition to the designated protected areas, there are numerous 'sacred groves' and many small areas where various wild flora and fauna are conserved through traditional beliefs. In India, neither the concept of protected area, as defined in the Wildlife (Protection) Act, nor other administrative categories like Biosphere Reserves, World Heritage Sites, etc. conserve these sacred groves. But, these areas also undoubtedly play a significant role in the conservation of many flora and fauna of this country.

3.2 CONCEPT OF BIOSPHERE RESERVE

The concept of setting up of Biosphere Reserves evolved in the UNESCO conference on 'Rational Use and Conservation of the Resources of the Biosphere' in 1968, which ultimately resulted in Man and Biosphere (MAB) programme, initiated in 1971. The Biosphere Reserves are now considered separate from other protected areas as they take into account the structure and dynamics of regional landscapes, integrate the concept of ecosystems, incorporates the presence of human settlements and gives equal emphasis to the development objectives (Ishwaran et al., 2008). In brief, Biosphere Reserves are the only conservation strategy that include human beings and take the cultural diversity of the surrounding areas into consideration. The purpose is to conserve all forms of life *in situ*, along with its support system in totality, so that the designated area could serve as a referral system for monitoring and evaluating changes in natural ecosystems. The ecosystems and landscapes designated as Biosphere Reserves:

- are devoted to conserve the entire biological diversity of the area
- promote research and monitoring of flora and fauna
- provide models of sustainable development in the service of human beings
- facilitate conservation of unique features of the representative landscapes of exceptionally pristine nature along with their rich biological diversity and cultural heritage
- foster economic and human development which is culturally and ecologically sustainable
- provide support for research, monitoring, education and information exchange

Finally, declaration of a particular area as 'Biosphere Reserve' facilitates international recognition and attracts additional funding to those sites as well.

Definition: Biosphere Reserves are the internationally recognized areas of terrestrial and coastal ecosystems, which are aimed at reconciling the utilization and long-term conservation of their biodiversity.

3.2.1 Zones of a Biosphere Reserve

Biosphere reserves are traditionally organized into three interrelated zones known as: core area, buffer area and a transition zone or area of cooperation (Figure 3.2).

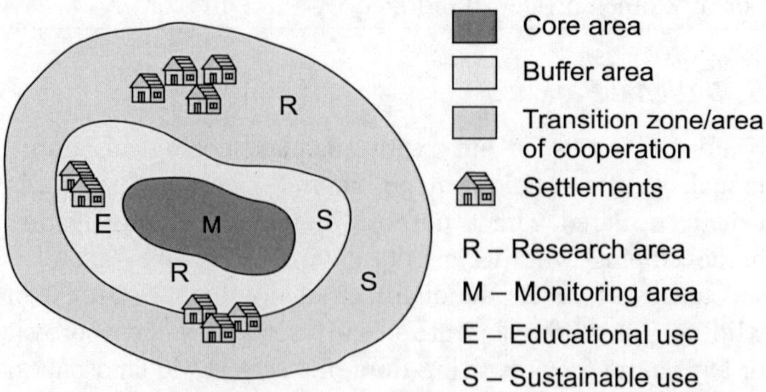

FIGURE 3.2 Illustration of zonation in a model Biosphere Reserve.

- **Core Area:** The core area justifies the creation of a Biosphere Reserve and seeks to protect its biodiversity. Core area should be set aside and be free from all kinds of external human pressures to the system. This area is secured through legal protection, but allows management and research activities that do not affect natural processes and wildlife.

- **Buffer zone:** The buffer zone surrounds the core area and has the major function of protecting the core area from high human impact. Thus surrounding buffer zone ensures low-impact activities in the form of sustainable land-use. Besides, recreational activities, tourism, fishing and grazing are permitted to a limited extent. Barzetti (1993) states that buffer zones are important for the conservation of species with high mobility. The benefits of buffer zones for wildlife are:
  - (i) Physical barrier from human encroachment.
  - (ii) Protection from storm and other extreme climatic events.
  - (iii) Enlarge the natural habitat.
  - (iv) Reduce edge effects.
  - (v) Enhance the environmental services provided by the reserve.

  On the other hand, social benefits rendered by the buffer zones include reduced damage to crops by wildlife, as well as, lesser risk from wild animals and wild fires for the population living close to the parks. In many Biosphere Reserves, human use is less intensive in the buffer zones than the transition zone.

- **Transition zone:** The buffer zone is surrounded externally by the transition area where the focus is on cooperation with the local stakeholders. Transition zone is the outermost part of a Biosphere Reserve and is usually not a delimited one. This area is also termed as an 'area of cooperation' where conservation, knowledge and management skills are applied together. Transition zone often includes settlements, croplands, managed forests and area for intensive recreation and other economic activities that are prevalent in the region (Biswal et al., 2013). This area underscores the role of cooperation as the main tool to achieve the objectives of the biosphere reserve. In this area the local communities, conservation agencies, scientists, civil associations, cultural groups, business personals and other stakeholders usually work together to manage and use the area in a sustainable way to benefit the people residing there.

  However, such concept of zones is flexible to some extent and is designated to address local needs and conditions.

Similarly, core and buffer zonation are also noticed in various protected areas and tiger reserves. Restrictions are placed upon resource use or special development measures in areas peripheral to a National Park or equivalent reserve to enhance the conservation values of the area. Partial restrictions are also imposed on areas adjacent to protected areas to give an added layer of protection to the protected area itself while providing valued benefits to neighbouring rural communities. According to Wildlife (Protection) Act 1972, the State Governments are to notify the core and buffer areas of tiger reserves within their jurisdiction. In the tiger reserves, core zones are the critical tiger habitats where the animals reside, feed and breed. As per law, the Government should prevent any disturbance (including tourism) in such areas. Buffer zones usually lie in the periphery of the core zones and constitute the fringing areas of tiger reserves up to 10 km.

3.2.2 Biosphere Reserves in India

In India, the National Biosphere Reserve Programme (NBRP) was initiated in 1986. Since then 18 biosphere reserves have been set up in this country of which 10 have been included in World Network of Biosphere Reserves by UNESCO. These important biosphere reserves are Nilgiri Biosphere Reserve, Gulf of Mannar Biosphere Reserve, Sundarbans Biosphere Reserve, Nanda Devi Biosphere Reserve, Nokrek Biosphere Reserve, Pachmarhi Biosphere Reserve, Simlipal Biosphere Reserve, Achanakmar-Amarkantak Biosphere Reserve, Great Nicobar Biosphere Reserve and Agasthyamala Biosphere Reserve. Ministry of Environment and Forests, Government of India provides the State Governments with financial assistance for conservation and management of these Biosphere Reserves.

Text Box 3.2 Sundarbans — A Unique Biosphere Reserve

Sundarbans (Latitude: 21°32″ – 22°40″ N; Longitude: 88°30″– 89°00″ E) are the largest deltaic mangrove region of the world extending through India (one third) and Bangladesh (two third) covering a total area of about 26,000 sq km. This is the largest single stretch of mangrove vegetation. Indian Sundarban covers an area of 9,630 sq km and is present in two districts (North & South 24 Parganas) of West Bengal.

Climate

- Average annual temperature 25°C.
- Summer: March - June (29°C).

- Winter: December - February (20°C).
- Rainfall: Annual rainfall 192 cm.

Riverine Network: This is a unique Riverine ecosystem. River *Hugli* and its tributaries like Matla, Ichamati, Raimongal, Bidyadhari, Kalindi, Gousaba, Thakuran, Saptamukhani, Hatania-Doania etc. and innumerable criss-cross channels form this unique riverine network.

Vegetation: Sundarbans show the greatest concentration of mangroves restricted to inner-tidal zone at the land-sea interface. The flora of this mangrove is naturally exposed to high and low tides twice in 24 hours. A total of 84 floral species have been identified of which 34 are true mangrove species (comprising of 70% of the world mangrove species). Some common plants include bakul (*Bruguiera cylindrical*), sundari (*Heritiera fomes*), bhola (*Hibiscus tilliaceous*), golpata (*Nypa fruticans*), hental (*Phoneix paludosa*), keya (*Pandanus tectorius*), garjan (*Rhizophora apiculata*), keora (*Sonneratia apetala*) and kankra (*Bruguiera gymnorhiza*).

Mangrove plants have the ability to maintain a suitable water balance in spite of high salinity of soil and water. Some mangrove plants even excrete salts from their leaves. They have excellent anchoring mechanism and modified roots, through which they can stand firmly on mud. They spread horizontally as roots just below the surface and provide necessary anchorage. Thus some mangrove species play vital role to withstand cyclone and prevent soil erosion (e.g. garjan). They have also evolved special aerial roots, tip of which protrude out of the mud upwards like spikes and are called pneumatophores (e.g. keora). These pneumatophores ensure sufficient oxygen supply to the deeper roots. Some mangrove plants show viviparous germinations.

Avian Life: Sunderbans are very rich in avian diversity. Upper canopy layer is mainly used by the birds of prey like osprey, brahminy kite and white belled sea eagle. Rose-ringed parakeets, flycatchers, warblers, small minivet, bee-eaters, golden backed wood pecker, orioles, barbets inhabit middle tier, while 7 species of kingfishers (pied, white breasted, common blue, black capped, collard, brown winged and ruddy kingfisher) are predominantly found in the lowest tier. Sand pipers, shanks, water hens, lesser adjutant storks, open billed storks, egrets, herons are common in the mud flats. Gadwalls, northern pintails, northern shovellers, common pochard, brown headed and black headed gulls are the most common trans-Himalayan migratory wetland birds of this biosphere reserve.

Reptiles: Reptiles of Sunderbans include Estuarine crocodile, Olive ridley turtle (*Lepidochelys olivacea*), river terrapin (*Batagur baska*) and green turtle (*Chelonia mydas*) and various species of snakes (like non-venomous ornamental and vine snakes, as well as, poisonous common krait, Indian cobra, Russell's viper etc.).

Mammals: Royal Bengal tiger (*Panthera tigris tigris*), fishing cat (*Felis viverrina*), Rhesus macaque (*Macaca mulatta*), chital (*Axis axis*), Indian wild boar (*Sus scrofa*), finless porpoise (*Neophocaena phocaenoides*), Gangetic dolphin (*Platanista gangetica*), smooth Indian otter (*Lutra perspicillata*) and Irawaddi dolphin (*Orcaella brevirostris*) are some of the most charismatic mammals of this unique ecosystem.

Extinct Mammals: Javan rhinoceros (*Rhinoceros sondaicus*), swamp deer (*Cervus duvauceli*), wild buffalo (*Bubalus bubalis*) and barking deer or muntjac (*Muntiacus muntjak*).

People

- Out of 108 islands present in this deltaic region, 54 are inhabited by around 5 million people.
- Mono cropping agriculture, honey collection, fishing, prawn seed collection are the major occupations.
- Despite belonging to different caste, creed and religion, people of Sunderbans are culturally very rich.

Management Practices

- ***Protection:***
  - (a) Establishment of observation camps, watch towers and deploying guards with modern arms and ammunitions
  - (b) Patrolling vessels and mobile camps
- ***Afforestation:***
  - (a) With pure mangrove species—for bank protection and to prevent soil erosion
  - (b) Distribution of seedlings to local people free of costs
- ***Habitat improvement***
- ***Reduction of man-animal conflict***
- ***Eco-development projects***
  - (a) Community Development projects: Construction of irrigation canals, sweet water ponds, village brick paths, jetties, tube wells, embankments, along with organization of regular medical camps

(b) Individual beneficiaries oriented scheme: Apiary, mushroom cultivation, piggery, vocational training for cottage industries

- Periodic census of important prey and predatory species
- Introduction of GIS – upgrade forest/vegetation and topography map to update the management plan

Importance of Mangroves

- They produce economically significant products like timber, firewood, honey, wax, tannins and other medicines.
- They produce leaf litter and debris which fulfill the nutritional requirements of the young prawns, adult shrimps, molluscs and fish of high economic value.
- They act as the breeding and feeding ground of shell and fin fishes.
- They directly protect the coastline (and indirectly the mainland) from the devastating impacts from storms, sea surges, tropical cyclones, high winds etc.
- The Sundarban are the only deltaic mangrove swamp where a significant number of Indian tiger population of the country thrive.
- It protects the human settlements and even metropolitan Kolkata from the frequent gales originating in the Bay of Bengal.

3.3 CONCEPT OF CORRIDOR

In recent times, the concept of wildlife corridors has become a widely adopted strategy for conservation of wildlife in fragmented landscapes. Habitat fragmentation is a global issue that leads to the conversion of a linear habitat into a landscape mosaic consisting of modified environments and residual stands of remnant vegetation. The process of habitat fragmentation leads to the overall loss of original habitat, reduction in patch size and increased isolation of patches. As a consequence, smaller remnant habitats get isolated both from each other and from any remaining continuous habitats. They often differ greatly in size, structure, complexity and resource availability from the original habitat type. Thus, fragmentation increases the incidences of inbreeding among the meta-populations and thereby significantly increases the potential risk of extinction due to stochastic processes.

Wildlife corridors are permanent linear stretches of habitat, differing in structure and vegetation type to that of the landscape elements of the surrounding habitat (matrix), which links at least two habitat patches that would otherwise be isolated from each other. Hence, the existence of a corridor effectively integrates the meta-populations into a single demographic unit through increased level of connectivity.

This concept of wildlife corridors has its origin in the 'Island Biogeography Theory' and was originally referred to the strips connecting nature reserves. Narrow strips of forested habitat within agricultural landscapes are the most widely studied corridor type and are most frequently adopted for conservation purposes.

Definition: Wildlife corridor may be defined as strips of habitat which serve to connect otherwise isolated habitat patches that were once connected in the historical past (Saunders and Hobbs, 1991).

It has also been suggested that the definition of a wildlife corridor should include a functional element and only those linear strips that provide the means for organisms to move along them should be termed as wildlife corridor (Lidicker, 1999).

3.3.1 Animals Using Wildlife Corridors

Wildlife corridors are essential for larger animals with wide home ranges and often serve as ecological connectors between two or more remnant patches. Nevertheless, they are also vital for smaller animals. Animals using a wildlife corridor may broadly be categorized as:

Passage Users: They use the corridors for a short period for various events like seasonal migration, dispersal of juveniles or moving between different patches of a large home range.
Example: Large herbivores, medium to large carnivores, migratory species etc.

Corridor Dwellers: If all the resources for survival are optimally available then some individuals of certain population may stay in the corridor for a relatively longer period, which, depending on the species and individual, may vary from a few days to several years. These individuals residing in the corridors are then called 'corridor dwellers'.
Example: Various species of amphibians, reptiles, birds and small mammals etc.

3.3.2 Types of Wildlife Corridors

Corridors can be established either in land or water. Water corridors are often called **riparian ribbons**, which include rivers and streams. On the other hand, land or **terrestrial corridors** are usually wooded strips connecting larger woodlands. However, as a primary condition, any of these types should serve as linkage between the isolated habitats and allow the dispersal of animals.

Width to length ratio, design and quality plays vital role in creating a perfect corridor. The use of a corridor by animals is usually directly proportional to its width. Hence, according to the width, wildlife corridors are usually categorized as:

Regional: These wildlife corridors connect major ecological gradients and are usually more than 500 m wide. *Example:* migratory pathways.

Sub-regional: These wildlife corridors generally connect large vegetated landscapes and are more than 300 m wide. *Example:* ridgelines.

Local: These wildlife corridors connect smaller landscapes and are often less than 50 m wide. *Example:* strips of vegetations connecting remnant patches, narrow stretch of water connecting two wetlands etc.

Besides, wildlife corridors are also grouped based on their continuity (Figure 3.3), such as:

Linear Corridors: These are long, uninterrupted continuous strips of vegetation between two isolated patches that are not broken up, such as hedges, strips of forest and the vegetation growing on banks of rivers and streams etc.

Stepping Stone Corridors: These type of corridors consist of a series of discontinuous small patches of suitable habitats arranged in a line between the isolated habitats which are often used to find shelter, food or to rest.

Landscape Corridors: These consist of diverse, uninterrupted landscape elements which offer sufficient cover for a safe journey from one core area to another.

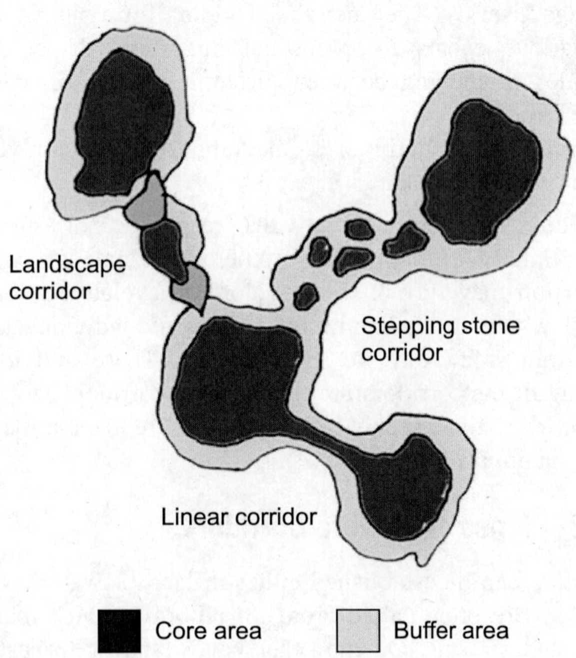

FIGURE 3.3 Schematic diagram of different types of corridors.

3.3.3 Advantages of Wildlife Corridors

In absence of connectivity, the small isolated populations residing within the remanant patches are isolated and their population size is largely reduced. Isolation of small populations might lead to the loss of alleles, decrease heterozygosity, increase homozygosity of deleterious alleles, resulting in inbreeding depression, ultimately reducing individual fitness. Such populations with reduced genetic variations have limited adaptability and are more prone to extinction, at least locally. The process of such local extinctions in patches might subsequently lead to regional extinction. The impacts of stochastic processes and catastrophic events are thus more pronounced on small and isolated meta-populations. Wildlife corridors offer a potential solution to such problems of isolation through establishment of connectivity between two patches. They usually stabilize a declining population by means of three distinct phenomena:

1. **Interbreeding between different meta-population:** Animals dwelling in remnant patches get the opportunities to interbreed with new individuals if they move through the corridors to new areas or else mate with some individuals of other meta-population appearing through the corridor.
2. **Colonization:** Animals often move through corridors and occupy new habitats in other remnant patches in search of food and other resources for their survival, which were lacking or depleting in their resident patch.
3. **Migration:** Effective and safe dispersal (seasonal or annual) of animals can only take place through corridors without any interference with the human dominated landscapes.

In brief, wildlife corridors are beneficial, as they:

- alter ecological isolation of the demographic and genetic sub-units
- potentially increase the effective population size and increase population viability
- might assist in recolonization of a remnant patch where a population has gone extinct locally
- effectively assist in transfer of individuals between habitats which supplement the number of individuals in a declining population, arrest the declining trend and increase the effective population size (**rescue effec**)
- introduce new genes into the population by incorporation of new individuals and such increased gene flow might potentially reduce inbreeding, as well as, enhance genetic diversity
- decrease susceptibility of the population to demographic changes and increase viability of the population

- provide breeding links between the population of connected habitat patches, which efficiently increase the size of breeding population through transit of new individuals from one patch to another
- corridor itself might serve as suitable breeding area
- increase area and resource availability through connectedness
- provide safe passage for large mammals to move from one patch to another without entering adjacent anthropogenic landscapes, thereby help to reduce human-wildlife conflicts

3.3.4 Problems Associated with Wildlife Corridors

In spite of several advantages, many wildlife corridors are inflicted with several problems.

1. It is very difficult to set aside land for wildlife corridors due to increasing demand of land for anthropogenic use, developmental activities and urban sprawl.
2. Wildlife corridors are often species-specific and even all individuals of same species might not use a particular corridor.
3. Species movements through landscapes are often guided by daily and seasonal movement patterns, as well as, innate and learning behaviour. Hence, the dispersing animals may not necessarily follow the corridors designated and conserved for them and may use altogether different habitat strips.
4. Wildlife corridors without proper buffer zones and with very high amount of disturbance and developmental activities in its vicinity may hardly be used by the animals for dispersal and thus protecting such a corridor might prove to be a futile effort.

3.4 UNESCO WORLD HERITAGE SITE

Government of India had received funding support from UNESCO for conservation of outstanding natural sites. Recognition of an area as 'World Heritage Site' has many fold benefits like:

- It enhances the importance of the site to the international community.
- Elevates the conservation values and status of the site.
- Generates awareness among the masses.
- Socio-economic development of the site through enhanced funding support.
- Increased fund flow through eco-tourism.

3.5 CONCEPT OF JOINT FOREST MANAGEMENT (JFM)

Joint Forest Management (JFM) is a unique initiative in forest management to protect and safe guard forest and its resources through a joint effort by the state forest department and local communities. In such agreement, usually village committee known as the Forest Protection Committee (FPC) and the Forest Department jointly perform their duties for the cause of a healthy and sustainable forest. Villagers agree to assist in the safeguarding of forest resources through protection from fire, grazing, and illegal harvesting. In exchange of this they receive non-timber forest products and a share of the revenue from the sale of timber products.

The concept of Joint Forest Management was first proposed by Mr. Ajit Kumar Banerjee, a Silviculturist and the then Divisional Forest Officer of Midnapore. JFM was initiated at the Arabari Forest Range in West Midnapore, on trial and error basis in 1971. The major hardwood of Arabari is sal, which is a commercially profitable forest crop and was constantly under threat due to grazing and illegal harvesting by the local people. To overcome this nuisance, the forest department took special drive to actively involve the local people for protecting forests. The JFM is based on the principle of 'Care and Share'. People are encouraged to protect forests in lieu of which they are awarded a share in the usufructs from the forests. The initial programme involved 612 families managing 12.7 sq km of degraded forests and, as per agreement, 25 percent of profits from the forests were shared with the villagers. The experiment was successful and was expanded to other parts of the state. West Bengal is the pioneer in the field of JFM in India. Later, in 1977, the idea of JFM was implemented in the state of Haryana to prevent soil erosion and deforestation and the programme led to reforestation of many hills in the state. After the initial success in West Bengal and Haryana, the JFM schemes received national importance in the legislation of 1988. As of 2011, 29 states and Union Territories of India had various JFM schemes. Presently about 1,20,000 JFM committees (with the involvement of 1,45,18,219 families) are protecting 2,29,388.14 sq km of forested land of this country.

3.5.1 Recognition

The Government of West Bengal played a key role in promoting JFM further in the state. In recognition to the successful 'Arabari Model', the Government of West Bengal issued the 'Usufruct Right for Arabari Socio-economic Project' in the year 1987. The policies and objectives of Joint Forest Management are detailed out in the Indian Comprehensive National Forest Policy of 1988.

It was further substantiated by the resolution yielding statutory recognition to this Joint Forest Management (JFM) regime in the year 1989. Encouraged by the success of the Arabari Model, the Ministry of Environment and Forests, Government of India, issued guidelines in June 1990, to all the states and the Union Territories for involvement of village communities and voluntary agencies in regeneration, management and protection of forest lands. Other state governments in India soon ratified this participatory forest management and implemented Joint Forest Management (JFM) regime.

3.5.2 Advantages of JFM

- A reasonably friendly relationship and faith has developed between the Forest Department and local communities.
- Certain amount of sustained income from JFM contributes positively to the livelihood of local communities.
- Different local activities (like rural development, micro credits, self help groups, ecotourism, etc.) have received some institutional support from the Forest Department.
- Improvement in biodiversity and forest quality.
- Employment opportunities have increased.

3.5.3 Limitations of JFM

- Initially, only degraded forests were considered under the ambit of JFM. But, later the Government of India allowed the closed forests to be included, as well.
- NGOs have not been encouraged to be a part of the JFM scheme.
- JFM micro plans fail to reflect local people's needs and livelihood improvement is not satisfactory as expected.
- Forest Departments fail to technically manage the forests to achieve JFM objectives. For example, no innovative or experimental work has been done to improve the productivity, which ultimately can help to improve the subsistence of the poorer sections of the community.
- No compensation was given to the deprived section on implementation of JFM scheme.
- JFM has achieved limited success in establishing traditional rights of the indigenous people over forest resources.
- Lack of transparency in FPCs and the nature and level of democracy among FPC members.
- Lacunae in the monitoring processes for JFM activities, corruption in benefit distribution, livelihood changes, gender issues. Although some women FPCs are working, overall the voice of the women in the JFM operation is minimal.
- There is no regular or systematic supervision of FPCs, either by the Forest Department, by the FPC themselves or their executive committees, nor are there any regular reporting systems.
- Lack of interest and devotion of many forest officials in the promotion of JFM. Foresters are sometimes unwilling to empower local people to manage forests. This is very unfortunate, as the Forest Department has also singularly failed to use their expertise in forest management.

Text Box 3.3 Arabari Model – A Classic Example of JFM

Arabari is a moist deciduous forest range in West Midnapore district of West Bengal, India contiguous with the *Dalma* range of East Singhbhum, Jharkhand in the Upper Gangetic Plains and predominated by sal forest. A forest conservation model was started in 1980's in this remote village which became a widely popular mode of conservation motivating about 32,000 residents to join it. Subsequently, this model received national and international acceptance. There are two distinct schools of thought regarding the origin of JFM. According to some, the genesis of JFM lies in the efforts of some progressive foresters followed by the *Arabari* experience. While others claimed that it was a spontaneous movement of the local community. However, it's a fact that some frontline staff of the forest department played an important role in promoting JFM in West Bengal. Based on the encouraging results of the Arabari experiment, the Government of West Bengal has prepared an ambitious programme to regenerate some 2,590 sq km of *sal* forest under the joint forest protection scheme. At present, there are about 1,266 FPCs in the Western Circle protecting and managing about 1,520 sq km of forest land which account for about 37 percent of the total forest area in the Western Circle of West Bengal.

Socio-ecological Impact: This project has very positive social, ecological and economic impacts, because it has also economically benefited the local people. Villagers use the majority of this income for community development purposes like construction of roads for their village, provision for drinking water or rural electrification, school buildings or the village sanitation. Apart from that, primary health centres and community halls have been constructed from the community fund. The entire exercise is thus gradually bringing development and prosperity to a hitherto socially and economically backward region mostly inhabited by families belonging to the minority communities and backward classes. Forest officials were buoyant with the success of this model. Then several plans for support activities like lending of paddy thrashers, setting up of self help groups (SHGs) for cottage industries etc. have now been set rolling. In addition, The West Bengal Forest Development Corporation Limited also encouraged the members of the FPCs and EDCs in running its eco-resorts and for arranging catering facilities for the tourists. Thus, JFM became an effective tool for making the local people a stakeholder of the forests and other natural assets in their vicinity. JFM also ensured continuous support of the local residents in protecting and, in exchange, ensure their economic and social up gradation. Local people are employed as tourist-guides and encouraged to arrange transport facilities for the tourists as well. In many areas, local people provide 'home-stays' for tourists, run their own resorts and manage picnic sites. They run small shops on the fringe of eco-resorts and sell local handicrafts to the tourists as souvenirs. In broader sense, JFM thus generates rural employment and income.

The execution of Joint Forest Management (JFM) is a paradigm shift in the history of Indian forest conservation policy. The success of JFM in West Bengal lies in the fact that it resulted in a revolutionary change of mindset of the forest bureaucracy and implementation of "people first" concept into practice. This concept has drastically metamorphosed the attitude of the forest department and restored the rights of common people at the grass root level. In wildlife-depredation-prone areas, this joint venture has played an important role at the mitigation of several conflicts between the authority and the locals and gained remarkable achievements. Not only has the model been widely adopted today as an effective strategy for forest management, but the concept has presently been promoted widely in other sectors of management related to common property natural resources like fisheries, grazing land, distribution of irrigational water sources, etc. by several international bodies, including the World Bank. With the concept of participatory governance at the grassroots level inculcating community involvement, there is a good scope for the furtherance of Government-People partnership strategy in future.

REVIEW QUESTIONS

1. Mention the importance of Protected Area Concept in wildlife conservation in India. What are its limitations? Distinguish between Sanctuary and National Park. What do you mean by conservation reserve? How does it differ from community reserve?
2. State the basic objectives of Biosphere Reserve. What are the core and buffer zones?
3. Explain the ecological importance of a Mangrove forest.
4. What is a corridor and mention its advantage. Enumerate the problems associated with wildlife corridors.
5. What do you mean by Joint Forest Management? Mention advantages of JFM. What are its limitations? Elaborate Arabari model with a note on its socio-ecological impact.

REFERENCES

Barzetti, V., *Parks and Progress: Protected Areas and Economic Development in Latin America and the Caribbean*, World Conservation Union, Washington D.C., 1993.

Biswal, A., Jeyaram, A., Mukherjee, S. and Kumar, U., Ecological significance of core, buffer and transition boundaries in biosphere reserve: A remote sensing study in Similipal, Odisha, India. *Computational Ecology and Software*, **3**,4, 126–137, 2013.

Forest Survey of India. *India State of Forest Report 2015*, Forest Survey of India (Ministry of Environment & Forests), Dehradun, India, 2015.

Ishwaran, N., Persic, A. and Tri, N.H., Concept and practice: the case of UNESCO biosphere reserves. *International Journal of Environment and Sustainable Development*, **7**, 118–131, 2008. http://dx.doi org/10.1504/IJESD.2008.018358

Islam, M.Z. and Rahmani, A.R., Important Bird Areas in India: Priority sites for conservation, Indian Bird Conservation Network, Bombay Natural History Society and Bird Life International, UK, 200, p. 2004.

IUCN, *World Directory of National Parks and Other Protected Areas*, IUCN, Morges, 1975.

Lidicker, Jr. W.Z., Responses of mammals to habitat edges: an overview. *Landscape Ecology*, **14**, 4, 333–343, 1999.

Ministry of Environment and Forests (MoEF), Gajah: Securing the Future for Elephants in India The

Report of the Elephant Task Force, Elephant Task Force, Ministry of Environment and Forests, New Delhi, 2010.

Saravanan, K.R, Sivakumar, K. and Choudhury, B.C. *Status of Marine and Coastal environments and developing a Marine Protected Area Network in India*. Wildlife Insitute of India. Dehradun, pp. 334, 2011.

Saravanan, K.R., Sivakumar, K. and Choudhury, B.C. Important Coastal and Marine Biodiversity Areas of India, pp. 134–188, In: *Coastal and Marine Protected Areas in India: Challenges and Way Forward, ENVIS Bulletin: Wildlife & Protected Areas*, Vol. 15 (Ed.: Sivakumar K.) Wildlife Institute of India, Dehradun, India, 2013.

Saunders, D.A. and Hobbs, R.J. The role of corridors in conservation: what do we know and where do we go? In: *Nature Conservation 2: The role of corridors* (Eds. Saunders DA and Hobbs RJ). Surrey Beatty and Sons, Sydney, 1991.

Sivakumar, K. Coastal and Marine Biodiversity Protected Areas in India: Challenges and Way Forward, *Ecology and Conservation of Tropical Marine Faunal Communities* (Eds. Venkataraman K. et al.) Springer–Verlag, Berlin Heidelberg, 2013.

Sivakumar, K., Mathur, V.B. and Pande A. Coastal and Marine Protected Areas in India: Challenges and Way Forward. pp. 292-298, In: *Coastal and Marine Protected Areas in India: Challenges and Way Forward, ENVIS Bulletin: Wildlife & Protected Areas.* Vol. 15 (Ed. Sivakumar K.) Wildlife Institute of India, Dehradun, India, 2013.

4

BIO-ECOLOGY OF SOME IMPORTANT INDIAN WILD ANIMALS

4.1 HIMALAYAN SALAMANDER (*see* Plate I)

Order: Caudata
Family: Salamandridae
Scientific Name: *Tylototriton verrucosus* Anderson

Present Status

Wildlife (Protection) Act, 1972	Schedule – II
IUCN	Least Concern
CITES	Not listed
Population Trend	?

Distinctive Features

- The Himalayan newt (*Tylototriton verrucosus*) is considered as one of the most primitive species amongst living salamanders (Das, 1987). This is the only one in which the larval tail is retained throughout its life (like its aquatic ancestors) and therefore, is regarded as a 'living fossil'.
- This Himalayan newt has rough-skin, with large parotid glands measuring about 160 mm to 170 mm at full adulthood. The body is 3–3.5 times as long as the head.
- The entire newt is uniformly blackish brown with slightly paler regions on the lips, snout, chin, throat and under surface of limbs. There is a series of 15 or 16 knob-like porous glands along the sides with the last three situated behind the leg.
- Tail compressed laterally, with a well-developed fin fold and the lower edge of the tail is orange-yellow.
- The tongue is small and is free on the sides and only slightly towards its base.
- The teeth on the palate are in two oblique rows that meet at the front of their mouth.
- The skull has a thick and bony fronto-squamosal arch, which is a unique feature of all salamanders. Wide head with three prominent bony ridges with pores, one along the centre and two along the lateral sides of the heads (the parietal ridge).
- Snout is short, there are no lobes on the lips and a strong fold is present on the chin.
- There is no crest running along the dorsal midrib. But, there is a prominent vertebral ridge with a series of knobs formed from the expansion of the neural processes of the dorsal vertebral bones.
- The legs are slightly flatenned, moderately long with the fingers and five toes with webs.
- The anal opening is a longitudinal slit and its borders are not raised.
- Maximum longevity is reported to be 11 years.

Distribution: Their present distribution range includes Bhutan, China, India, Myanmar, Nepal and Thailand. In India, it is reported from high altitudes and cold climate of the Eastern Himalaya and is found in the states of West Bengal and Sikkim along with smaller, isolated populations in Manipur and Arunachal Pradesh (Frost, 1985; van Dijk et al., 2009).

Population: Local abundance may be high, from 10 to 20 individuals per few acres of a lake. Reports from different sites in northern West Bengal varied from less than 10 salamanders to hundreds of individuals per site (Hedge and Deuti, 2007). Despite the fact that there is no data on population trend, scientists predict a gradual decline of the population.

Habitat: Himalayan salamanders live in various habitats, mostly around permanent and temporary pools, shallow ditches, marshes and slow-moving streams, from late April to early September (Roy and Mushahidunnabi, 2001). Besides they are also reported from rice fields, tea gardens, meadows covering the shores of mountain ponds and lakes, forest edges etc. situated between an altitude of 1255–2679 m. Reproduction occurs along small seasonal and perennial wetlands like streams, small rain puddles and permanent lakes. They generally prefer to inhabit shallow ponds of the hills which receive maximum sunlight. The ponds should have aquatic plants preferably *Acorus calamus, Polygorum* spp. These plants provide cover and shade to salamanders, as well as, attract smaller insects which serve as their food. During winter months they usually hide under stones or tree roots.

Behavioural Biology: Himalayan salamanders are predominantly terrestrial during their non-reproductive period and aquatic during their reproductive period (Dasgupta, 1996). They usually become active during night. After spending six to seven months in hibernation, they emerge from their hideouts with the first monsoon shower (Roy and Mushahidunnabi, 2001) and come out from the crevices and holes for breeding in the month of May. During this time they aggregate at shallow ponds and other water logged areas.

Food and Foraging Behaviour: Adult diet comprises mainly of spiders, worms, millipedes, scorpions, molluscs and a range of insects including larval forms of Diptera, Coleoptera, Lepidoptera, Odonata, adult dytiscid beetles etc. Larvae feed mainly on aquatic insects and adults feed on insects, earthworms etc. They also predate on eggs and larvae of other amphibian species. Cannibalism has also been reported. During breeding season, the diet of adult male and female salamanders comprise of both aquatic and terrestrial elements. Males start to become terrestrial in August/September, therefore had a more terrestrial diet than females which stayed longer in water (Dasgupta, 1996).

Breeding Behaviour: Reproduction starts soon after the newt emerges from hibernation. In a large part of its range, reproduction coincides with the start of the monsoon season (late March to early April). The animals show sexual dimorphism during the breeding season. Adults usually leave the water bodies and courtship occurs at night. The courtship behaviour is in the form of a nuptial dance which involves the male moving around the female while bending, pushing, curving its tail and the amplexus is ventral. According to Roy and Mushahidunnabi (2001), oviposition takes place in May and June amongst the permanent and temporary pools, shallow ditches, marshes and slow-moving streams. Under natural conditions, the eggs are laid singly onto submerged vegetation and on the bottom, rarely outside water. Salamanders need plants for egg laying. They first glue their eggs on the vegetation or to grass blades by the outer sticky jelly envelope and then by moving forward all the eggs easily come out from the body. In absence of such vegetation, it would be very difficult for a salamander to lay eggs only in water. The clutch size varies between the pairs and Roy and Mushahidunnabi (2001) reported a mean value of 116 and the clutch size is positively correlated to the length and weight of the female. The fertilized eggs are transparent. The developing embryos could be seen clearly in the jelly envelope. Female parental care has been observed. Metamorphosis occurs between summer and autumn. Larvae are known to overwinter. The age of sexual maturation is around 3-5 years.

Threats to Survival

- ***Anthropogenic pressures:*** Anthropogenic pressures like deforestation, draining of lentic-habitats, siltation in lentic-habitats and their conversion for agriculture and housing, introduction of exotic fishes, increase in the number of cattle and goats etc. lead to the decimation of the habitat of the Himalayan salamanders. These anthropogenic pressures along with sociological aspects related to local issues often pose as the chief threat to the conservation of salamander habitats.
- ***Housing and agriculture:*** The chief threat to the Himalayan salamander is destruction of lentic habitats as a result of great demand for flat-land for the purpose of agriculture and housing.
- ***Disposal of domestic wastes and pesticides and fertilizers pollution:*** In some habitats, wastes are directly discharged. Local people wash clothes in these habitats accompanied by direct urination and defaecation. Fertilizers, especially rock-phosphates are used in the tea-gardens along with pesticides, herbicides which are suspected to be detrimental to larval salamanders. Domestic wastes and phosphates result in growth of dense mats of aquatic weeds, which degrade and ultimately destroy these lentic-habitats.
- ***Demand for fresh water:*** Due to scarcity of fresh water, there is a tendency to overexploit mountainous wetlands in order to supply drinking water, as well as, to cater to the demand of water used in agriculture of these regions (like cardamom fields and winter cropping).

- ***Deforestation:*** Deforestation in the areas adjoining wetlands, especially in the catchment areas, often increases the rate of siltation in the wetlands where the salamanders thrive. Deforestation also leads to landslips and landslides which tend to fill up lake basins. Thus, deforestation indirectly leads to the destruction of the salamander habitats and threatens their survival.
- ***Introduction of exotic species:*** Another major threat comes from the introduction of exotic carps (Hedge and Deuti, 2007), catfishes etc. which voraciously feed on salamander eggs and small tadpoles.
- ***Pet trade:*** This species is harvested for use as traditional medicine in India. In addition, it is in demand in the domestic and international pet trade (Peter Paul et al., 2009).
- ***Climate changes:*** Instinctively salamanders come out from the crevices and holes after hibernation to the water points for mating. The timing of such events is very precise. But due to climate change, rainfall pattern is becoming very erratic. After the onset of monsoon, if there is a dearth of rain then a large number of eggs laid in shallow water pools are dessicated and destroyed as the water pools dry up.

Conservation Initiatives

The Himalayan salamander is an endangered species surviving in few isolated patches in the Himalayas. It is protected by legislation in Nepal, India, China and Thailand. But, there is no protected habitat for the salamander in the area after Jorephokri lost its relevance as Species Specific Wildlife Sanctuary. Darjeeling is endowed with plenty of natural ponds and marshy land where water logging occurs during the months of May to September. As salamander has to come to the water for mating and breeding, such ponds needs to be protected under planned conservation program during this period.

Besides, Padmaja Naidu Himalayan Zoological Park, Darjeeling, initiated 'Conservation Breeding Programme' of Himalayan salamander in the year 2000 under the guidance of State Wildlife Advisory Board. The Zoological Park is ideally situated within the natural distribution zone of the Himalayan Newt and the main objective of the project is to initiate conservation breeding and multiplication of this species in a well protected, undisturbed area to ensure their survival and to arouse public awareness about this unique species. Apart from Padmaja Naidu Himalayan Zoological Park in Darjeeling, amphibians are under represented in Indian zoos and no other zoo in this country maintains this amphibian. The Central Zoo Authority recognized the need to increase capacity for zoos for *ex-situ* conservation of *Tylototriton verrucosus*.

Conservation Actions Proposed for Himalayan Salamander Include

1. Protection and improvement of natural habitats like ponds, marshy lands.
2. Prevent damming, dragging and siltation of habitats.
3. Prevent deforestation and introduction of such vegetations that grow profusely in marshy land.
4. Complete ban on pesticides and herbicides use, especially in salamander rich areas.
5. Captive breeding program should be encouraged.
6. Nature Environment and Wildlife Society (NEWS) also carried out a project titled 'Estimation of population trends of Endangered Wildlife of West Bengal' sponsored by the Ministry of Environment and Forest, New Delhi in 2002. As an outcome of this project, Namthing Pokhri situated in Darjeeling, district of West Bengal was declared as 'Salamander Conservation Area' to ensure sustainable conservation of this species by an NGO along with the local people.

4.2 OLIVE RIDLEY TURTLES (*see* Plate I)

Order: Testudines
Family: Cheloniidae
Scientific Name: *Lepidochelys olivacea*

The olive ridley turtles are considered as the smallest and most abundant of all sea turtles found in the world, with an estimated 8,00,000 females nesting annually.

Present Status

Wildlife (Protection) Act, 1972	Schedule – I
IUCN	Vulnerable
CITES	Appendix – I
Population Trend	↓

Distinctive Features

- Olive ridley turtle is a small sea turtle with a mean weight of 40 kg. Females are heavier, but rarely weigh over 50 kg. The adult males are of significantly less body weight (about 33 kg).
- Carapace (top-shell) of an adult is 60–70 cm in length, heart shaped with more than five pairs (5–9 pairs) of costal (between the centre and outer margin of shell) scutes and four pairs of pore-bearing infra-marginal scutes. Each side of the

carapace has 12–14 marginal scutes. The carapace is olive/grayish-green in appearance.

- Although the upperparts are grayish green to olive in color, carapace sometimes appears to be reddish in colour due to presence of certain algae. The bridge and hinge less plastron of an adult varies from greenish white in younger individuals to a creamy yellow on older specimens.
- It has a medium sized, broad head with concave sides, which appears triangular from above. Presence of a short snout on the upper part of head is a striking feature.
- Forelimbs are modified into paddle-like flippers, each having two anterior claws.
- The hatchlings are blackish brown in appearance and weigh around 28 g with 4.1 cm long carapace.
- Both hatchlings and juveniles have serrated posterior margins, which become smooth with age. Juveniles also have three dorsal keels; the central longitudinal keel gives younger turtles a serrated profile, which remains until sexual maturity is reached.
- Adults are somewhat sexually dimorphic. As contrast to the females, mature males are lighter in weight and have longer and thicker tails, which are used for copulation. In males, the claw on the front flipper is also enlarged and hooked which help them to grasp the female carapace during copulation. Males also possess longer, more tapered, round, dome-like carapace and bear much concave and soft plastron than females.

Distribution

The olive ridley turtle is one of the most abundant sea turtles in the world with a circumtropical distribution. They inhabit tropical and subtropical warm waters of the Pacific, Indian and Atlantic oceans. In the Eastern Pacific, they occur from southern California to northern Chile; in Indian ocean they are found in tropical warm waters and coasts of India, Sri Lanka, while in the Atlantic ocean, they have been observed off the western coast of Africa and South America (in the coasts of northern Brazil, Suriname, Guyana, French Guiana, and Venezuela). Olive ridleys often migrate great distances between feeding and breeding grounds. Nesting occurs in nearly 60 countries, while they are believed to use the coastal waters of over 80 countries during migratory movements.

In India, they are reported from several places along the east and west coast, as well as, in the coasts of various islands in the Bay of Bengal and Arabian Sea. They are reported from several coastal areas in the state of West Bengal, Orissa, Andhra Pradesh, Tamil Nadu, Karnataka, Kerala, Maharashtra, Gujarat along with the Union Territories of Goa, Puducherry, Lakshadweep and Andaman and Nicobar Islands. *Gahirmatha*, *Devi River mouth*, and *Rushikulya* are three very important and spectacular nesting sites of the olive ridley turtles (called *Arribadas*) in the state of Orissa.

Population

Information on the exact population of these marine turtles is almost non-existent. Due to their vast area of occurrence, underwater presence and migratory nature, it is indeed difficult to make a population estimation of this species. However, wildlife biologists estimate that there are around 8,00,000 nesting females existing in the wild. Every year an average of 3,98,000 females are recorded in the *arribadas* of Gahirmatha, Orissa which is supposed to be the largest nesting population of these turtles in this country and is also one of the largest *arribada* nesting sites in the world. However, an indication of declining population trend is noticed in *Gahirmatha* beach in the recent past (Plotkin, 2007).

Habitat

Olive ridleys require a range of geographically separated localities and multiple habitats during their entire life cycle (Márquez, 1990) and have been recorded in both benthic and pelagic foraging habitats (Musick and Limpus, 1997). They primarily inhabit coastal waters, but captures far offshore indicate that at least some individuals may be pelagic. They exist in distinct populations and mostly breed annually. They usually migrate annually from pelagic foraging grounds to coastal breeding and nesting grounds and back. They are by and large found within 15 km of mainland shores in protected, relatively shallow (22–55 m deep) marine waters in coastal bays and estuaries, but occasionally occur in open waters over some parts of its range. They have been even observed in locations more than 4,000 km away from the shore. Juveniles are reported to share some of the adults' habitats (Kopitsky et al., 2000) until they attain sexual maturity (Musick and Limpus, 1997).

Behavioural Biology

Food and Foraging Behaviour: The olive ridley turtles, especially the immature ones, are predominantly carnivorous. Animal prey consists of protochordates or invertebrates, which can be caught in shallow marine waters or estuarine habitats. Common prey items include jellyfish, tunicates, sea urchins, bryozoans, bivalves, snails, shrimps, crabs, rock lobsters, sipunculid worms and a variety of fishes and their eggs. However, in areas devoid of other food sources, these turtles feed on filamentous algae. Juveniles are believed to occur in similar habitats as the adults (i.e. pelagic waters) where they forage on gelatinous prey such as jellyfish, salps and tunicates (Kopitsky et al., 2004). Studies on captive population have indicated some degree of cannibalism.

They typically forage off shore in surface waters or dive up to the depth of 500 feet (150 m) to feed on bottom dwelling crustaceans and other "benthic" invertebrates. Additionally, consumption of jellyfish and both adult fish (e.g. Sphoeroides) and fish eggs may be indicative of pelagic (open ocean) feeding. Foraging habitat can range from depths of several metres (Conway, 1994) to over 100 m (Whiting et al., 2005). Apart from one exception, they have not been recorded in coral reef habitat or shallow inshore sea grass flats (Limpus, 2008).

Breeding Behaviour: Olive ridley turtles display three modes of reproduction: arribada, dispersed nesting, and mixed strategy (Bernardo and Plotkin, 2007).

- **Arribadas:** Olive ridley turtles are best known for their behavior of synchronized community nesting in mass numbers, termed *arribadas*. Such mass nesting behaviour includes hundreds to thousands of females over a period of days and are reported from relatively few places worldwide. In the northern Indian ocean, *arribadas* occur on three different beaches along the coasts of India. Majority of the olive ridleys have been reported to nest in two or three large groups near *Gahirmatha* (35 km stretch) and a small stretch (3 to 4 km) of beach, 100 km south of *Gahirmatha* between Nandikhia and Akasia mohona (Kar and Bhaskar, 1982) in Orissa. Apart from *Gahirmatha*, two other mass nesting beaches have been located which are on the mouth of rivers Rushikulya and Devi. The other major nesting sites include Gorai, Kihim and Versova in Maharasthra (Tikadar and Sharma, 1985), a 50 km stretch beach south of Madras and Point Calimare in Tamil Nadu (Bhaskar, 1981), Andaman and Nicobar Island, Sundarban and Digha coast of West Bengal (Saha, 1984; 1986).
- **Dispersed nesting:** In addition to these mass nesting sites, minor dispersed nesting sites and solitary nests of the olive ridley turtles have been reported extensively in scattered locations throughout this species' range. Such minor and solitary nesting sites are found in the coasts of Goa, Kerala, Gulf of Manner, Andhra Pradesh, Lakshadweep islands and Gulf of Kutch (Whitaker, 1977). There are number of earlier reports on their nesting in coastal West Bengal extending from Sundarban region in the east to Digha-Shankarpur region in the west. Unlike mass nesting events, there is no apparent synchrony between individual solitary nesting events.
- **Mixed strategy:** Some females even employ a mixed nesting strategy. They lay some of their clutches in the *arribadas* while lay other clutches in solitary nest during the same nesting season.

Olive ridley turtles attain sexual maturity around 15 years. Reproductively mature turtles (both males and females) migrate toward coastal zones and concentrate near nesting beaches. Mating is often reported to occur in the vicinity of nesting beaches. However, some males remain in oceanic waters over 1,000 km from the nearest beach and mate with the receptive females enroute to their nesting beaches (Plotkin et al., 1996; Kopitsky et al., 2000). Mating takes place almost daily in swallow water at a distance ranging from 50 m to 5 km from the sea shore during October to December. Prior to peak mating period, large numbers of copulatory pairs swim passively along the surface current. In eastern India, turtle visit the coast in huge numbers from November for nesting and remain till first week of April. Nesting occurs throughout the year with peak nesting events (i.e. *arribadas*) occurring between September and December. They generally begin to aggregate near nesting beaches approximately two months before nesting season, although this may vary throughout its range. Mass nesting usually occurs in two batches, first major nesting in January to February and second minor nesting in March. They migrate from the Indian Ocean and adjacent areas, pass through Tamil Nadu and Andhra coast, reach the mass nesting beaches in Orissa and follow the same route during their downward migration from their breeding ground. These marine testudines usually prefer to nest in the mid zone of relatively flat beaches which are clean and free of debris. Interestingly, females tend to return to the very same beach from where they first hatched, to lay their eggs. Nesting events are usually nocturnal. But, in mass nesting sites diurnal nesting has also been reported (Ernst et al., 1994). Nesting is undertaken two to three times per nesting season (Spotila, 2004) and they exhibit an inter-nesting period of 17–30 days (Ackerman, 1997) during which the female remain near shore. During each nesting attempt, the females laboriously dig a 1.5 feet deep conical pit on the sandy beach with their hind flippers and then lay clutches of eggs. Females can lay up to three clutches per season, but most will only lay one or two clutches. Their mean clutch size is 109, which varies throughout its range and usually decreases with each nesting attempt. (Kalb, 1999) found that within a nesting season solitary nesters use multiple beaches for oviposition, but *arribada* nesters display nest site fidelity. In *arribadas* hundreds to thousands of females come ashore to lay their eggs. Hence, in many nesting beaches the nesting density is so high that the nesting females dig up the previously laid egg clutches of other females to lay their own eggs. The eggs remain under sand for a period of 45 and 51 days under natural conditions, which extend to as long as 70 days in poor weather conditions. Successful incubation of eggs requires the nesting sand temperature to be between 25–33ºC (Ackerman, 1997). Sex of the turtle is determined by temperature. It has been found that eggs incubated at 31–32°C will produce only females, while eggs incubated at 28°C or less will produce solely males and incubation temperatures of 29–30°C will produce a mixed sex clutch (Ernst et al., 1994). Olive ridley hatchlings generally emerge from the nest at night (Spotila, 2004). Hatchlings are dark grey with a pale yolk scar, but appear all black when wet. A thin, white line borders the carapace, as well as, the trailing edge of the fore and hind flippers. The serrated posterior marginal scutes and central longitudinal dorsal keels in hatchlings and juveniles give them a serrated profile. While the hatchlings synchronously emerge from their nest, then the beaches of the mass nesting sites are almost covered with numerous tiny turtles crawling over the beaches making their first trek towards the vast ocean.

Home Range

These turtles spend their entire lives in the ocean, and migrate thousands of kilometres between feeding and mating grounds in the course of a year. Whiting et al., (2005) estimated the home range for two adult females as 138 sq km and 1182 sq km respectively.

Social Organization

Very little is known about the social organization of this turtles. Thousands of females come together on the same beach to lay eggs in their mass roosting sites. In addition to that, many hatchlings and small juvenile turtles occur in the surface waters of the open ocean (Bjorndal, 1997).

Threats to Survival

- ***Commercial and recreational fishing:*** Accidental killing of adults through entanglement in trawl nets and gill nets due to uncontrolled fishing during the mating season around nesting beaches is considered to be the most severe threat for the turtles. Additionally, incidental captures of olive ridleys occur worldwide in trawl fisheries, long-line fisheries, purse seines, gill net and other net fisheries and hook and line fisheries (Frazier et al., 2007). These are serious ongoing sources of mortality that adversely affect the species' recovery. Since the early 1980s, many olive ridleys were found dead on the beaches of Orissa, presumably due to the expansion of the shrimp trawling fishery and subsequent incidental capture in shrimp trawls (Pandav, 2000) in the eastern Indian ocean. Gill net fisheries also operate in the region and contributes to their mortality along this coastline. Over 10,000 olive ridley carcasses per year have been counted on the Orissa coast since 1999 (Wright and Mohanty, 2006). Prior to the introduction of Turtle Excluder Devices (TEDs) hundreds of marine turtles were killed annually in trawling activities. Though not well quantified for olive ridley turtles, yet ghost nets (lost and discarded fishing nets) are also considered as a potential threat as they float in the ocean and coastal waters and many marine animals get entangled. Many olive ridley turtles are killed or injured due to commercial harvest and incidental capture (or bycatch). During 1993–2003, more than 1,00,000 turtles were reported dead in Orissa, India from fishery-related practices.
- ***Boat strike:*** Other major threats include mortality associated with boat collisions. Fast moving boats have the potential to cause marine turtle injury or death.
- ***Poaching:*** Olive ridley turtles are still extensively poached for their meat, shell and leather and their eggs have a significantly large demand around the coastal regions. Such illegal harvesting of adult olive ridleys and their eggs continues to be widespread in the Indian Ocean (Frazier et al., 2007). Large scale exploitation of turtle eggs were done along the beaches of the Indian ocean since remote past for personal consumption and to feed the domestic animals. Despite being legally prohibited at present, still exploitation of eggs continues, particularly in the nesting beaches of these marine turtles, leading to population decline (Cornelius et al., 2007).
- ***Predation:*** Predation pressure on the juvenile olive ridley turtles is very high throughout their distribution range. The juveniles are exposed to predators (like feral dogs, jackals, hyenas, predatory and scavenging birds, as well as, ghost crabs and fiddler crabs) prowling around their nesting sites. They are mainly killed in large numbers while they emerge from their nests and travel across the beaches to the sea water. Feral dogs, jackals and some other predators even dig up the nests of the olive ridley turtles to feed on the eggs. Due to very high density of nesting females in the *arribadas* the previously laid nests are inadvertently dug up and destroyed by other nesting females. Besides, developing eggs are often infested by fly and beetle larvae, which lead to significantly high mortality of embryos. However, adults have relatively few known predators. They are occasionally attacked by crocodiles in the estuaries and are predated upon

by the carnivores like sharks and killer whales in the open seas.

- *Diseases:* Very little information is available on the diseases and their effects on olive ridley abundance. Fibropapilloma, caused by a herpes-virus, is the only disease identified in these sea turtles almost throughout the world (Herbst, 1994). However, incidence of fibropapilloma is possibly not alarmingly high among these marine turtles.
- *Marine debris:* Death can occur when turtles become entangled in or ingest marine debris. Carr (1987) recorded that fishing line, rope and cord fragments, styrofoam beads, tar balls, plastic bags and balloons are all known to have killed marine turtles through ingestion or entanglement.
- *Habitat loss and degradation:* Olive ridleys face serious threats from the destruction and degradation of natural habitat along their nesting beaches. The increasing demands for developmental activities like building of shipyards and docks result in excessive release of oil and gas into these sensitive habitats. In power plants, juvenile and sub adult turtles get entrapped within the saltwater cooling intake systems. Some of the olive ridley's foraging grounds are also contaminated due to sewage, agricultural runoff, pesticides, solvents and industrial discharges. These contaminants have been shown to decline the productivity of the benthic community, which in turn negatively affect the turtles foraging on these communities. Beach erosion has also been cited as potential threat to their nesting grounds. In addition to these, coastal developments (including residential, industrial and tourism infrastructures, growth of existing coastal villages, construction of new aquaculture ponds etc.) and exploitation of nesting beaches for ports can directly destroy or degrade beach habitats used as nesting sites, particularly along the east coast of India (Pandav and Choudhury, 1999). All these impacts directly or indirectly change the thermal profiles of the beach and lead to increased light pollution (Witherington, 1992).
- *Light pollution:* Coastal development also threatens newly hatched turtles through the effects of light pollution (Karnad et al., 2009). Light pollution on nesting beaches alters nocturnal behaviors in sea turtles. During night, a barren shore is usually darker than the sea. The newly hatched turtles instinctively orient themselves towards the direction which is better illuminated in the night. But, with anthropocentric development and presence of electric lights, the coasts often become brighter than the sea even in the night. As a consequence, hatchlings which use light cues to orient themselves to the sea, get misled or wrongly oriented and instead of heading towards the sea they move in opposite direction. Subsequently, they die from exhaustion and dehydration, slaughtered on roads by speeding vehicles or get killed by its predators prowling on the beach.
- *Global warming and climate change:* Global warming and changing weather patterns associated with climate change has the potential to adversely impact the habitats and ecosystems of olive ridley populations worldwide (Hays et al., 2003; Weishampal et al., 2004). Cyclones and associated storm surges can alter hatchling production in particular seasons by washing away and/or inundating clutches or causing erosion of banks so females cannot emerge to nest (Hamann et al., 2007). Beach erosion, as a consequence of climate driven extreme events, has also been cited as potential threats to nesting grounds. Besides, the sex of marine turtle hatchlings is determined by the incubation temperature of the eggs. Warmer incubation temperatures lead to the production of female hatchlings and cooler incubation temperatures result in the production of male hatchlings (Spotila, 2004). Climate change may alter the temperature of nesting beaches, thereby affecting the male-female ratio.
- *Slow growth and delayed sexual reproduction:* Olive ridley turtles are also prone to population declines because of certain life history traits like slow intrinsic growth rate and delayed sexual reproduction. These hinder fast population recovery.

Conservation Initiatives: Olive ridley turtles are considered threatened as they have declined by-more than 30 percent (ranged between 31 and 36 percent) from historic levels and due to their few remaining nesting sites in the world. Hence, they are categorized as Vulnerable by IUCN. These marine turtles are protected by various international treaties and agreements, as well as, national laws. They have been listed in Appendix I of CITES, which prohibits international trade. This species is also listed in Appendices I and II of the Convention on Migratory Species. The highly migratory behaviour of sea turtles makes them shared resources among many nations. Thus, conservation efforts for sea turtle populations in one country may be jeopardized by activities in another. Protecting sea turtles on particular nesting beaches and in a particular ocean system alone, therefore, is not sufficient to ensure the continued existence of the species.

Conservation successes for the olive ridley turtles in India have relied on well-coordinated national programmes with cooperation from local communities and non-government organizations, which focused primarily on public outreach and education. *Arribada* management has also played a critical role in conserving olive ridleys (Plotkin, 2007). Lastly, enforcing the use of "Turtle Excluder Devices" (TEDs) in the shrimp trawling industry has also proved effective in some areas. The TEDs are specially designed nets with an exit cover which allows the turtles to escape while retaining the catch. Uses of such TEDs have been made mandatory for the trawlers in Orissa to reduce accidental killing of turtles. Initially the fishing communities strongly opposed this initiative as they thought that TEDs would result in loss of considerable amount of the catch. However, WWF-India, along with its partners, disproved this theory by conducting a study to measure the loss of catch through TEDs, revealing the loss to be a very small percentage of the total catch. This result, along with regular meetings with the fishing communities, is slowly helping to change their mindset and encouraging them to use TEDs, thereby aiding the conservation of olive ridley turtles. Another major project to preserve the olive ridley turtle population was carried out in Chennai, where the Chennai wildlife team collected close to 10,000 olive ridley turtle eggs along the Marina coast. Once the eggs hatched, the baby turtles were carried to the beach and released. In addition to these major initiatives, a substantial network of communities is working together to quantify the impact of ghost nets on turtle mortality, as well as removing ghost nets from beaches to reduce their negative impact on the survival of the turtles. Several organizations, like WWF-India, along with the fishermen community, are helping in various ways to ensure a safe passage for the hatchlings to the sea.

Gahirmatha coast serves as the natal nesting beach for millions of turtles and is regarded as the world's largest known rookery of these turtles. Thus, considering the ecological significance of diverse faunal and floral resources of *Gahirmatha* coast and its adjoining waters in turtle conservation, Government of Orissa has declared the beach and its adjoining waters as "Gahirmatha Marine Sanctuary" in September, 1997. The virgin beaches of Gahirmatha Marine Sanctuary stretch over a length of approximately 705 m. The marine sanctuary extends from Dhamra river mouth in the north to Mahanadi river mouth in south. It includes a width of approximately 20 km of the sea from the high tide line. The protected area includes 1408 sq km of seascape and 27 sq km of land mass comprising of mudflats, sea beach and mangroves. This is the first and the only Marine Sanctuary of Orissa.

Some other recommendations for threat abatement and proposed conservation initiatives for these marine turtles are as follows:

- More effort should be placed on understanding patterns of nest site selection and how nesting sites may change under different climate regimes. Efforts should be made to understand the ecological roles of olive ridley turtles and possible impacts of climate change to their important diet species (Hamann et al., 2007).
- National Recovery Plan for Marine Turtles need to be designed to outline actions for the protection, conservation and management of all marine turtles found in Indian coasts, including the olive ridley turtles.
- Specific guidelines for the Ecologically Sustainable Management of Fisheries need to be designed and implemented along with legislative initiatives and regulatory framework to reduce the threat which coastal fisheries pose to marine turtles by intentionally or accidentally catching them. Modification of fishing hooks should also be made.
- Specific actions to conserve the species need to be implemented through recovery plans, wildlife conservation plans and threat abatement plans.

4.3 GREAT INDIAN BUSTARD (*see* Plate I)

Order: Gruiformes
Family: Otididae
Scientific Name: *Ardeotis nigriceps* (Vigors, 1831)

Present Status

Wildlife (Protection) Act, 1972	Schedule – I
IUCN	Critically Endangered
CITES	Appendix – I
Population Trend	↓

Distinctive Features

- Great Indian bustard is a large, brown and white bird with a black cap which is in contrast with their pale head and neck. Their body is brownish with a black patch spotted in white. It resembles a young ostrich in appearance.
- The adult bird stands at about a metre high.
- Male bird is about 122 cm in length, weighing about 8–14.5 kg. It is deep sandy buff coloured and during the breeding season possess a black breast band. The crown of the head is black and crested and is puffed up by displaying males. Males also have well-developed gular pouches which are inflated when calling during display. These sacs help the males to produce the deep resonant calls.

- Females are smaller than the males measuring 92 cm in length weighing 3.5–6.75 kg and the head and neck are not pure white. Their breast band is either rudimentary, broken or absent.
- Their wingspan is around 210–250 cm.
- Both male and female possess long bare legs.

Distribution

The great Indian bustards were once widely spread across the Indian subcontinent, but the species has seen drastic fall in its population in last two decades. Currently, they are found in small pockets of India and Pakistan. A few of them are believed to be surviving in Sind of Pakistan. The major areas where they are known to breed are in central and western India and eastern Pakistan. Less than 100 individuals presently survive in Pakistan.

In India, earlier it was widely distributed in almost all arid and semi-arid plains of India, ranging from Uttar Pradesh in the north to Tamil Nadu in south and Rajasthan and Gujarat in west to Orissa in the east. But, it is now locally extinct from 90 percent of its former range. The current stronghold of the species is Thar desert in western India and Deccan peninsula in South. The dry semi-desert region where it was found in parts of Rajasthan has been altered by irrigation canals that have transformed the region into an intensively farmed area.

At present the occurence of bird is restricted to only six states of India namely Rajasthan, Karnataka, Maharashtra, Madhya Pradesh and Gujarat. Rajasthan alone holds more than half of the population, concentrating mainly in the western parts of the state adjoining the great Thar desert including the districts of Ajmer, Bikaner, Jodhpur, Jaisalmer and Kota. Large number of these birds congregate around the artificial waterholes present in the Desert National Park (Rajasthan) and strictly avoid hilly and forested region (Ali and Ripley, 1987; Rahmani, 1989). They are also present in several other protected areas in their distribution range, like Naliya Wildlife Sanctuary (Gujarat), Karera Wildlife Sanctuary (Madhya Pradesh); Nannaj Wildlife Sanctuary (Maharashtra), Shrigonda taluka (Maharashtra), Rollapadu Wildlife Sanctuary (Andhra Pradesh) and Ghatigaon Wildlife Sanctuary (Madhya Pradesh) It is mainly spotted in the Desert National Park (Rajasthan) and the Lala-Parjau Sanctuary in western Kutch (Gujarat).

Population

Although according to Rahmani (2001) perhaps 400–500 survive in India, yet Dutta et al., (2011) opined that the total Indian population consists of around 300 individuals in 2008, now principally confined to Rajasthan (175 birds), with smaller populations (fewer than 30 birds) in Gujarat, Maharashtra and Andhra Pradesh and Karnataka, and fewer than five birds in Madhya Pradesh, India (Bird Life International, 2013).

Habitat

Great Indian bustards inhabit open deserts, arid and semi-arid grasslands with tropical thorny scrublands. They are often found in open country with plenty of low bushes, scattered thorny scrubs and tall grasses interspersed with cultivation in flat or gently undulating terrains. They are sometimes reported from tropical dry deciduous forests present within their distribution range and they occasionally visit cultivated cotton fields. They generally prefer areas with low human population and less agricultural activities. They avoid irrigated areas.

Behavioural Biology

These are resident birds. But they often make local movements. These birds are seasonally nomadic and populations generally disperse after the monsoons. They are very shy and wary, and run at a great speed when alarmed. They usually hide under the bushes during noon to escape from the scorching sun.

Food and Foraging Behaviour: Great Indian bustard is an omnivorous bird. Their diet includes grass seeds, berries of *Zizyphus*, *Eruca*, insects, beetles, spiders, scorpions, lizards, snakes, small birds, rodents, etc. In cultivated areas, they feed on crops such as exposed groundnut, millets and pods of legumes. They prefer shoots of grasses, wheat, bajra and grains of barley.

These birds were seen to feed actively for 6–8 hours a day. They usually forage early in the morning and during late afternoon hours when the day temperature is relatively less and take refuge in cool shaded places in the hot hours. They drink water if it is available and will sometimes sit down to drink or suck water followed by raising up their heads at an angle.

Breeding Behaviour: These birds breed during monsoon, mostly between June to September. Males are polygamous and remain solitary during their breeding season. Their courtship display is prominent. During breeding season, the males inflate and display their fluffy white feathers. During courtship, males also display their gular sac which opens under the tongue, inflate it so that a large wobbly bag appears to hang down from the neck. The tail is held cocked up over the body. The male also raises the tail and folds it on its back. The male periodically produces a resonant deep, booming call that may be heard over nearly 500 m. Territorial fights between males may involve strutting next to each other, leaping against each other with legs facing each other and landing down to lock the opponents head under their neck.

The female lays single egg in an unlined scrape on the ground. Eggs are oval and pale olive brown in colour. The eggs are at risk of destruction by other animals, particularly ungulates and crows. Females may use a distraction technique that involves flying zig-zag with dangling legs. Incubation period is about 40 days and the fledging period is 30–35 days. Parental care is prominent, but only by the female parent. The females are involved in both incubation and subsequent rearing of the young. Males take no part in nourishing the young ones. Young stay with their mother for at least one year in the nest. When threatened, hens hide their young chicks under the wing. The first breeding occurs at 5–6 years in males and 2–3 years in females.

Social Organization: They usually stay alone or are found in flocks of three or more birds.

Threats to Survival

- ***Habitat loss:*** Large scale destruction, conversion and fragmentation of their habitat are mainly caused by widespread extension of agricultural activities, particularly through conversion of natural grasslands and scrublands of this country into intensive crop cultivation. Besides, increase in the construction of irrigation canals and use of pesticides are highlighted as on-going threats in Maharashtra state. In some places such as Rajasthan, increased irrigation by the Indira Gandhi canal has led to increased agriculture and the altered habitat has led to the disappearance of the species from these regions. Some habitats are also threatened by mining operations while some others are converted through plantations, urbanization and infrastructural development. Improved road communications and subsequent greater vehicular access to remote areas are leading towards collisions of bustards with vehicles. Many windmills around the Desert National Park are also posing a serious threat to the great Indian bustards. Wide stretches of habitat of the great Indian bustards throughout this country have been lost due to the conversion of grasslands and scrublands to agricultural fields. Presently they are locally extinct from almost 90 percent of its former range and have also ironically disappeared from two sanctuaries, which were specially made for their conservation. They are rapidly declining in other sanctuaries too.
- ***Hunting:*** In the past they were hunted in large numbers for sport, as well as, for their meat. Tribal *Bhils* used a unique technique for trapping females. They set fire on the twigs present around the nests of the great Indian bustards, which contained eggs or chicks. The female immediately ran towards the nest and the tribal people captured it.
- ***Poaching:*** Although not very widespread, yet some poaching of great Indian bustards still continues and has been reported from different parts of their present distribution range in this country (Sridhar 2005; Dutta et al., 2011). Current levels of hunting may result in the extinction of even the largest western Indian population in the next 15–20 years (Dutta et al., 2011).
- ***Retaliatory killing:*** One case of retaliatory killing of great Indian bustard was reported from Gwalior where mine-workers hunted bustards. Here the mine-workers lost their livelihoods when mines near Gwalior were closed for the creation of the Ghatigaon Bustard Sanctuary. Subsequently, they killed large number of great Indian bustards in order to undermine the criteria on which the area was designated as a sanctuary.
- ***Nest-trampling:*** High levels of livestock-grazing have led to disturbance for the great Indian bustard. Too many domestic animals and human beings in the existing bustard habitats are also leading to disturbances during the breeding season of these birds. As these birds construct nests on ground under scrubs, hence the nests often remain unnoticed and are trampled by cattle and also by the cattle-owners while moving through the bustard habitats.
- ***Egg-loss:*** Great Indian bustard share habitat with many small carnivores (like wolf, fox, jackal, wild cat etc.) which are reported to predate on their eggs. Increasing number of feral dogs from nearby villages is considered as another threat. They often destroy bustard eggs and feed on the chicks as well. In addition, certain nomadic tribes also collect bustard eggs. Such collection of the eggs of great Indian bustard, mainly for local consumption, was rampant in many states during early 19th century. But, this practice still prevails and has been sporadically reported from the states of Karnataka and Andhra Pradesh (Patil, 2011).
- ***Very low genetic diversity:*** A study in 2011 of the mitochondrial DNA (hypervariable control region II and cytochrome b) in 63 samples from 5 Indian states found very low genetic diversity (Ishtiaq et al., 2011). This is possibly because all the great Indian bustards existing in this country had descended from a flock of 10 to 100 birds. Attempts to breed them in captivity in the past have failed.

- ***Inappropriate conservation measures:*** At Ranibennur Blackbuck Sanctuary, habitat changes have affected the populations of blackbuck and bustards. In the 1950s the scrub forest was replaced with *Eucalyptus* plantations. These helped wildlife when the trees were short but after their extensive growth they made the adjoining grassland less favourable for bustards. Besides, conservation measures for the great Indian bustard resulted in increased numbers of blackbuck and nilgai. These herbivores often stray out of the protected areas and raid adjoining crop fields resulting in large scale crop damage and financial loss for the local farmers. This has led to resentment by villagers against conservation movement, as well as, apathy for the bustards. Moreover, policy on land use and domestic grazing is completely lacking in India.

Conservation Initiatives

IUCN categorized this species as critically endangered as very few individuals are presently remaining in wild. To protect this species from international trade, it has been included in the Appendix I of CITES. It is also listed in the CMS Convention.

In India, the great Indian bustard is legally protected and there are severe penalties for killing an individual. In the early 1980s, five states undertook conservation measures for the great Indian bustard and eight protected areas were declared. Since 1981, extensive fieldwork has investigated its status and distribution, yet some aspects of the basic biology of these birds are still unknown due to paucity of large scale and long-term researches on this species throughout its distribution range. In the year 1982 this species has been declared as the 'State Bird' of Rajasthan. It has also been identified as one of the species for the recovery programme under the Integrated Development of Wildlife Habitats of the Ministry of Environment and Forests, Government of India. The Indian government has provided financial support to conservation actions for this species in some regions (Anon, 2009).

'Project Great Indian Bustard', also known as Project Bustard, has been launched in Rajasthan. Under this project, enclosures for the species have been constructed and infrastructures have been developed to reduce human pressure on their habitats (Anon, 2013). The Ministry of Environment and Forests, Government of India has set up a Task Force to guide field implementation of bustard conservation actions.

Many NGOs of this country are playing a pivotal role in implementing various conservation initiatives to protect this critically endangered bird. The Bombay Natural History Society (BNHS) is a pioneer organization in promoting the conservation of the great Indian bustard and had conducted intensive campaigns to assist the Government of India in adopting appropriate measures to reverse the declining trend of the species. BNHS had extensively carried out meetings and processions with local communities to generate support for these birds among local people. WWF-India is assisting the Government of India in developing the 'Guidelines for the State Action Plan for Resident Bustard Recovery Programme'. The Great Indian Bustard Foundation held a two-day meeting with communities within and around the Great Indian Bustard Sanctuary at Nannaj in March 2011, where around 600 villagers participated and the problems of local people and threats to the species have been discussed (Patil, 2011). The Great Indian Bustard Foundaton along with Maharashtra Forest Department, is conducting a school awareness programme and large-scale community awareness programme (Birdlife International, 2013). WWF-India has also played a vital role in raising awareness at the national level about the declining populations and highlighting the need for implementing the bustard conservation programme.

Future Conservation Measures Proposed

- Investigate seasonal patterns of migration, habitat choice and breeding, perhaps using satellite tracking.
- Continue to survey all states within its range to clarify its current distribution and monitor population trends.
- Establish new protected areas at key sites, particularly community reserves, to promote sustainable utilization of grasslands, which ensure conservation of bustards (and other wildlife), along with providing benefits to the rural communities.
- Revise the design and management of bustard sanctuaries, in order to maintain core areas and promoting traditional agricultural practices in buffer zones.
- Campaign for realignment of the Indira Ghandi Nahar Canal Project in Rajasthan.
- Promote 'Project Bustards', which is a major conservation strategy for Indian bustards.
- Conduct research to control the predators, such as feral dogs and cats, jackals and foxes, at sites supporting small populations of *A. nigriceps*.
- Assess the strategy of supplementing small populations with captive-bred adults.

Text Box 4.1 Project Bustard

With an objective of conservation of the remaining population of critically endangered great Indian bustard (*Ardeotis nigriceps*), 'Project Great Indian Bustard,' was launched on 5th June 2013. Project Bustard is the dawn of a new era for the conservation of an earstwhile neglected species like great Indian bustard

The Aims of 'Project Bustard'

Conservation measures in India have shown that by identifying an indicator species and focusing attention on it and its habitat, a substantial part of the natural ecosystem can be protected, which benefits an array of threatened species. The aims of the **'Project Bustard'** thus include:

- to conserve all four bustard species (including the Great Indian Bustard), the associated species, as well as, their habitat types
- to establish, more bustard conservation areas with the cooperation of the state government and local people
- to supervise and coordinate management of bustard conservation areas
- to coordinate long-term studies on bustards and their habitats in different states
- to produce educational material for publicity, and for decision makers, stakeholders, students, and others;
- to integrate bustard habitat conservation with National grazing policy and overall land use pattern
- to make several publicity initiatives aimed at reducing poaching.

Conservation Actions

Aims of 'Project Bustard' have been proposed to be achieved through the following activities:

1. intensive patrolling by the field staff
2. developing intelligence network in the area
3. making of check posts and barriers at strategic locations
4. creation of a flying squad headed by not below the rank of a range officer
5. strengthening of existing wireless network
6. habitat protection through creation of some inviolate areas for the bird by making some closures of appropriate size and restricting anthropogenic pressures in such areas
7. habitat enrichment through planting grasses like *Lasiurus sindicus* (sewan grass) and providing water facilities
8. incentives to farmers and local people for giving information of the species and protecting it
9. involving local people in the eco-development and eco-tourism activities
10. generating mass awareness about the importance of this species
11. continuous monitoring of the species and its habitat

4.4 BENGAL FLORICAN (*see* Plate I)

Order: Gruiformes
Family: Otididae
Scientific Name: *Houbaropsis bengalensis* (Gmelin, 1789)

Present Status

Wildlife (Protection) Act, 1972	Schedule – I
IUCN	Critically Endangered
CITES	Appendix – I
Population Trend	↓

Distinctive Features

- Bengal florican is a medium sized ground bird ranging from 66–68 cm in length and about 60 cm tall while standing.
- Their plumage is mostly black with mottled buff-brown back and largely white wings. Wings appear completely white during flight except for black tips.
- They are also characterized by strong and well built muscular legs, big toes with sharp claws, a strong beak and majestic broad wings.
- These birds are sexually dimorphic. Head, neck and body of the adult males are almost black with buff-brown mottled back and contrasting white wings which are distinctly visible during flight. However, while standing the white wings are seen as a thin patch on either side of the body. A thick bunch of feathers hanging under the breasts of the males are noticed particularly during the breeding season. On the other hand, females had been found to be elusive and cryptically coloured.

The females and immature males are buff-brown to sandy-rufous in colour, molted on the back and have buffish-white wing-coverts with fine, dark barring.

- The females are slightly larger in size and also heavier than their male counterparts. Adult females weigh around 1.7–1.9 kg while the adult males weigh between 1.2–1.5 kg.
- Female Bengal floricans are less frequently noticed as compared to the conspicuous territorial males.
- These birds are normally silent but make shrill metallic *chik-chik-chik* when disturbed. But during display croaks and strange, deep humming sounds were made (Grimmett et al., 1998).
- Although the exact lifespan of the Bengal florican is not known, yet it is believed to survive around 20 years.

Distribution

The Bengal florican has two disjunct populations—one in the Indian subcontinent, the other in south-east Asia (Bird Life International, 2001). The south-east Asian population occurs in Cambodia and may be extant in southern Vietnam. The population of the Indian subcontinent was distributed in some alluvial plain grasslands in northern India, Nepal and Bangladesh. But, the species has possibly now gone extinct from Bangladesh and is presently restricted to few pockets of protected areas only in India and Nepal.

In India, Bengal florican was once widely distributed in the Gangetic and Brahmaputra plains south of the Himalayas from the Kumaon terai of Uttar Pradesh through Bihar and southern Nepal, to northern West Bengal and the foothills and plains of Assam and Arunachal Pradesh. However, this critically endangered bird has declined dramatically and presently survives only in small, highly fragmented populations. At present they are mostly restricted to the foothills of Bhutan Himalayas and in isolated forest pockets of north-east India, but are locally extinct in the wild elsewhere in the subcontinent. In recent times, the population is found to be mostly restricted only to Assam and Arunachal Pradesh. However, the most frequent and best observation of the species in the wild has been reported particularly from the state of Assam. The alluvial grassland of Assam is a unique habitat of Bengal florican. Protected areas of Himalayan foothills in the north bank of the river Brahmaputra in Assam has always been the stronghold for the species in India and are found mainly in Manas, Kaziranga, Orangand Dibru Saikhowa National Parks and in Burachapori and Laokhowa Wildlife Sanctuaries (WLS). A few birds are also found in river islands and sandbanks of Brahmaputra outside the protected area network in Tinsukia, Dibrugarh, Dhemaji, Lakhimpur and Sonitpur districts of the state. In Arunachal Pradesh, they are restricted around the D'Ering Memorial WLS, sand banks of Lohit River, grasslands in Dibang district and in Uttar Pradesh, they are mainly concentrated in the Dudhwa NP, north Pilibhit and Kishanpur WLS.

Population

The total global population of Bengal floricans is likely to fall in the range of 350–1,500 individuals. There are 432 individuals in Cambodia (Packman 2009) and 75–96 individuals in Nepal (Baral et al., 2012). There are no recent estimates from India. Possibly less than 350 birds presently thrive in India.

Habitat

Bengal florican is an extremely habitat specialist bird restricted to alluvial grasslands and is an indicator of grassland ecosystems. It inhabits lowland dry or seasonally inundated, natural and semi-natural grasslands, often interspersed with scattered scrubs or patchy open forests. Most Indian population appears to be resident and is restricted to the *Terai* grassland regions of the Indo-Gangetic and Brahmaputra floodplains. These grasslands are characterized by a high diversity of grasses (like *Imperata cylindrica, Saccharum munja, Saccharum narenga, Saccharum spontaneum, Themeda arundinaceum* and *Desmostachya bipinnata*) sedges, shrubs and sparsely scattered trees (such as *Acacia catechu*, *Phyllanthus emblica, Bombax ceiba* etc.). Bengal florican generally avoids very dense stands of tall grass and is seen in shorter grass dominated by *Imperata cylindrical* and *Narenga porphyrocoma* interspersed with patches of taller grasslands.

During the breeding season males preferably select habitats with low-intensity human activity, chiefly burned grasslands, whereas females primarily select unburned grasslands (Gray et al., 2009). It favours relatively open short grass (25–50 cm) for establishing territories, often within the expanse of tall grass (1–2 m) and scattered bushes. Although short grasslands appear to be favoured for foraging but the displaying birds seek shelter in tall grasses during the heat of the day, and females spend much of their time in these tall grasses.

Behavioural Biology

Bengal floricans are terrestrial species. In spite of being a capable flier, they are often seen walking or running along the ground. They walk slowly while foraging or moving from one site to another. Male floricans fly a lot during the breeding season and have one of the most spectacular flight displays among all bustard species. They are capable of sustained flights and take refuge in the trees for roosting and for security from ground predators.

Food and Foraging Behaviour: They are omnivorous and known to feed on various seeds, grains, tender shoots of grass and insects like grasshoppers, ants, beetles and even frogs. They have also been observed to feast on smaller mammals (rodents), frogs and toads, snakes, etc. Bengal floricans have been reported to forage on wild and cultivated sugarcanes, which provide them with energy and long-term nourishment.

Based on the availability, the proportion of various food substances varies. For example, invertebrate preys constitute a major portion of their diet during summer, while plant matter is their dominant food in winter and spring.

Breeding Behaviour: The breeding season of Bengal florican starts from February and lasts till early part of July. Adult males are territorial in the breeding season. But a few males remain non-territorial, probably due to lack of suitable habitat. The adult males usually establish individual territories in open areas in short grasslands and show a characteristic flight display within their respective territories to attract females for mating. Territorial aggression is also manifested by adult males against intruders into their territory, particularly to defend their harems of females from other contesting males. Contrary to the elaborate display by males, the females are far more secretive. They briefly visit a male territory only to breed and forage.

Text Box 4.2 Flight Display of Bengal florican males

Once the male is aroused, it fluffs up the head, neck and breast feathers. Just before taking the jump, it inflates the breast pouch even further, draws the head further back, and lowers the body by bending the legs partly. The bird springs up diagonally forward at an angle of about 45°. A loud and rapid wing-flapping sound is heard while ascending and on reaching a peak of 4–5 m high, the flapping stops and the wings are opened, displaying the glistening white wing feathers vividly against the jet black body. Then it delivers its sharp, whistle-like 'chip-chip' call. It subsequently glides down a metre or two, move forward on open wings, with the pouch drooping under their breast and the head is thrown back. Just 1–2 m above ground, it begins to flap its wings again to regain height and moves forward. On reaching the apogee, it stops flapping and floats down more or less vertically with partly open wings, drooping pouch, dangling and even paddling legs. During such display flight, the male covers about 20–40 m distance on ground and takes 6–8.5 seconds from take-off to landing. It calls 4–7 times while in the air.

Bengal florican does not prepare a proper nest. The females just lay 2–3 eggs after scratching the bare ground. The eggs are glossy and olive-green in colour with several tiny purple-brown freckles and blotches. The eggs are incubated for 25–28 days by the female. Males do not show any parental care and the hatchlings are raised by the female alone.

Social Organization: Bengal florican can fly well, but it is largely cursorial. It is normally solitary in the breeding season. However, up to six males may come together for a short period, fighting for suitable habitat or chasing each other. Sometimes two females are also seen in the same patch of grassland.

Threats to Survival

- ***Habitat loss:*** The extensive loss and modification of grasslands through drainage, conversion to agriculture and plantations, overgrazing, inappropriate cutting, burning and ploughing regimes, heavy flooding, invasion of alien species, scrub expansion, dam construction and inappropriate and illegal developments are considered as major threats in the survival of Bengal floricans (Evans et al., 2009; van Zalinge et al., 2009). The Bengal florican appears to have been almost completely eliminated from unprotected areas in its former Indian range. Huge areas of grasslands have been lost as a result of conversion to agriculture and forestry plantations. Some areas are altered as flooding regimes have been changed by dam and irrigation schemes. Many other grasslands are subject to high grazing pressure from domestic stock and intensive harvesting by local communities, often associated with grassland burning. This loss and degradation of habitat has resulted in huge declines in the population of this species and a contraction of its range (Rahmani, 2001). Small grasslands in Uttar Pradesh, which previously held Bengal floricans, have been rapidly replaced by sugarcane plantations either, legally or by encroachment (Rahmani 2001). The largest population of the species in India survives in Assam, and surprisingly, vast majority of them are restricted to protected areas only. Jaldapara Wildlife Sanctuary is heavily overgrazed. Likewise, grasslands have been degraded by grazing of domestic stock in Manas National Park, where park regulations are difficult to enforce because of insurgency problems.

Several other potentially suitable protected areas (like Laokhowa Wildlife Sanctuary in Assam) are also overrun by numerous grazing cattle and are being heavily used by fishermen and farmers. As a result, quality grasslands are highly disturbed and are rapidly getting degraded. Grasslands in Dibru-Saikhowa National Park are further threatened by the unusual annual floods in recent years, presumably because of greater run-off from the denuded Brahmaputra catchment. Erosion caused by these floods has already reduced the extent of grassland here. A similar problem is reported from Pobitora Wildlife Sanctuary, where floods in 1988 forced local people to increase their use of protected grasslands for thatch collection and grazing, subsequently forcing the Bengal florican population out of the reserve (Bird Life International, 2016).

Historically, the nature of terai grasslands was dependent on the changing river courses as well as by grazing and trampling from large wild herbivores such as rhinos, elephants, buffaloes and deers. Alterations of river courses thus contributed towards emergence of new areas that are subsequently colonised by grass and shrubs, whilst older grasslands and riverine forests have either eroded or submerged. However, due to radically increased human activities, newly formed lands are also being rapidly turned into agricultural pastures, instead of new grasslands.

Alluvial grasslands are also highly suitable for arable land and most of these have been converted. Thus, there has been a huge decline in the area and quality of grasslands across south and south-east Asia in recent past.

Most grassland patches are now small and isolated. Population of is species is thus susceptible to local extinction. Moreover, many regions within its range are prone to political instability, where long-term protection is not possible.

Illegal encroachments by humans in their wild habitats have drastically resulted in disturbing their wild habitats and fragmentation has negatively impacted their premier foraging grounds, as well as, affecting their courtship, breeding and nesting behaviour.

- ***Habitat degradation:*** Invasive species like *Mimosa, Mikenia* or *Eupatorium,* and colonising shrubs like *Lea* or like *Bombax* or *Dilenia*, have contributed to habitat degradation. Besides, many communities residing around protected areas collect thatch, wild herbs and fruits from grassland disturbing the bird and intensive collection cause habitat degradation. In Uttar Pradesh, collection of ripe *Grewia sapida* (phalsa) fruits by children and adults for eating and selling in the market is one of biggest threats. Although annual burning is important for maintaining suitable grassland habitat, yet frequent illegal or legal burning of grasses degrade the grasslands. This has undoubtedly altered the species composition of grasslands catastrophically, as well as, the survival of many small species including the Bengal florican. Indiscriminate dry season burning of grass every year by frontline staff as a traditional practice to clear dry grass, to promote fresh growth of grass or to improve visibility', eventually causes degradation of the grassland over a long period.
- ***Habitat disturbance:*** Direct human disturbance, especially in the breeding season, causes big problems throughout the range of this species. Birds might adapt to breed in certain crop fields, but chances of nest destruction during weeding or harvesting periods is very high. Sometimes, chicks are also trampled by increased number of people and cattle roaming around their breeding territory.
- ***Killing:*** Excessive hunting for sport and food might also have triggered its decline. During British colonial rule, sport-hunting was rampant. The relentless shooting of floricans drastically reduced their population. Several instances of birds being shot, snared or killed with long sticks were reported and were "among the best of table-birds", The Sahabad-Sayedabad tea estates in Darjeeling district, West Bengal, supported a small population of the species until recently. But, they were increasingly disturbed by people who killed adult floricans or robbed eggs from its nest. So the species apparently no longer exist there. However, this is no longer a serious threat as a result of long-term advocacy and strict enforcement of law.
- ***Destruction of eggs:*** Too many people or livestock in the Bengal florican habitat, leads to disturbance and trampling of nests. People come to grasslands mainly for thatch, edible plants and fruits or to graze livestock and sometimes collect the eggs of Bengal floricans.
- ***Inadequate protection:*** Presently, most of the Bengal floricans survive and breed in the protected areas. However, most of these PAs suffer from inadequate protection and management of habitat due to shortage of manpower, poor infrastructural facilities, lack of funding and personnel training. Management practices often fail to consider the

ecological requirements of the species and such oversight might lead to local extinctions in several cases.

- ***Small and isolated population:*** Populations of the Bengal floricans are small and isolated and are therefore, often vulnerable to local extirpation.
- ***Lack of scientific information:*** Information on their lifecycle, demography, sex ratio, food preferences, ecology and behaviour, as well as, their susceptibility to various avian diseases (like bird flu) and pesticide poisoning are almost nonexistent. Their dispersal pattern, local migration (if any) and the status of non-breeding habitat are largely unknown. Besides, no genetic study has been carried out so far on the species. Such dearth of scientific knowledge makes it very difficult to implement proper conservation initiatives for this species.

Conservation Initiatives

Bengal florican is listed as Critically Endangered in the IUCN categories of endangered species list and on Appendix I of the CITES. It is also listed under the CMS Convention.

This avian species is also listed in the Schedule I of the Indian Wildlife (Protection) Act, 1972. Conservation of Bengal floricans have been prioritized under Species Recovery Action Plan 1995 (Text Box 4.3). This species is also listed under the National Wildlife Action Plan 2002–2016. It has been identified as one of the species for recovery programme under Centrally Sponsored Scheme of Wildlife Habitats of the MoEF, Government of India. Several population of Bengal florican occur within protected areas in India, the most important being the Bengal Florican Conservation Area (BFCA) network which include Kaziranga National Park, Dibru-Saikhowa National Park and Dudwa National Park. Populations in these BFCAs and in adjacent areas have been monitored annually since 2008 and the data indicates that the population is probably stable at some BFCAs and possibly declining in others and in adjacent areas (Van Zalinge et al., 2009; 2010; Mahood et al., 2012). Some recent initiatives of breeding and reintroduction to the wild in the state of Assam have been successful. But, such initiatives need to be duplicated and multiplied across its range for the purpose of the resurgence of the species.

During World Conservation Congress in Thailand in 2004, the IUCN had passed a resolution to urge Government of India to protect all the bustard species and start **'Project Bustard'**. The project bustard is an Indian initiative for strengthening conservation of bustard species including threatened grassland habitat. It aims to promote a knowledge-based and adaptive conservation framework involving local communities in conservation efforts.

Looking at the precarious status and high probability of extinction of this species, the MoEF Government of India have identified the Bengal florican for taking initiatives for the recovery of this species involving state forest department, Wildlife Institute of India (WII), Bombay Natural History Society, WWF-India, Eco-Systems-India, Green Future Foundation under the Integrated Development of Wildlife Habitats Scheme in the year 2009.

Text Box 4.3 Species Recovery Action Plan (1995) of Bengal florican

Objectives

Objectives of the Species Recovery Action Plan of Bengal florican are to:

- ensure that Bengal florican and its existing habitats are well protected and scientifically managed.
- locate potentially suitable habitats outside their present distribution area.
- undertake research to fill up the knowledge gap about the species and its habitat for better management efforts and long-term conservation.
- raise awareness of the conservation issues about the species and its habitat and
- ensure that local communities and frontline forest staff have a positive impact on the conservation of Bengal florican

Proposed Outcomes

The Bengal Florican Species Recovery Action Plan is prepared to achieve the following proposed outcomes:

(i) Arresting the declining Bengal florican population trend
(ii) Immediate enforcement of existing provisions of the Protected Areas Action Plans
(iii) Restoration of Bengal florican

Through this Species Recovery Action Plan of Bengal florican, not only the species will be conserved, also the entire suite of species and the most threatened habitat, the grasslands, will be protected. To implement this, first a systematic, and centrally organized status and distribution survey has to be carried out at the landscape scale to obtain the baseline information. Satellite telemetry programme has to be scientifically undertaken to understand seasonal movement patterns and life history and habitat requirements. It is pertinent to mention here that a Darwin Initiative project was implemented in 2012 to assess the distribution and habitat requirements of this species in India and Nepal (Barber, 2013). Subsequently, three males were satellite tagged in 2014 in India (Barber, 2014).

- **Habitat level recovery:** Grasslands are the richest and unique ecosystem which support large number of endangered species. At the same time, grassland ecosystems are perhaps the most vulnerable ecosystems in the Indian subcontinent at present. Besides, grass is a vital resource for people who use it for fodder, thatch and to prepare rope, mats and other items, especially in the Indian *Terai*. Therefore, tall, moist and alluvial *Terai* grasslands on floodplains of river Ganges and Brahmaputra are considered as one of the highest priority regions for conservation action (CEPF, 2005). The remaining populations of Bengal floricans are largely confined to the protected areas. In some protected areas, efforts are underway to maintain valuable grasslands by uprooting woody vegetations and a schedule of controlled fires and collection of cut grass by locals for thatch in order to create more suitable habitats for the Bengal florican. Their breeding areas have to be excluded from all kinds of human disturbances.
- **Landscape level conservation plan:** Local people, especially those settled inside or near protected areas and reserve forests, are informed about the importance and legal status of the Bengal florican. Simultaneously, these communities are sensitized through popular lectures on the importance of grasslands and conservation of bustard in local languages. Also, attempts are to be made to generate interest and pride among locals about the existence of this species in their locality. Moreover, villagers are to be motivated and refrained from hunting, stealing or otherwise causing disturbance or damage to the birds, their nests or their young. For the awareness and capacity building of forest department officials and NGOs, training manuals should be published and workshops are to be arranged in different range states.

Further Recovery Actions

1. ***Status survey:*** Very little information is so far available on the status of Bengal florican of a few protected areas. But, their present status throughout distribution range, particularly in the areas outside the protected areas, is not available.
2. ***Intensive protection along the PA boundaries:*** As most of the Bengal florican habitats are situated along the protected area boundaries and their territories are prone to anthropogenic disturbances, hence, protection along the protected area boundaries needs to be strengthened.
3. ***Stop anthropogenic disturbances:*** Bengal florican is a habitat specialist of grasslands. This is also a very sensitive species and is unable to adapt to the disturbances in its habitat. There are evidences of disappearances of Bengal florican territories from highly disturbed grassland areas. Therefore, anthropogenic disturbances (like intensive grazing by livestock, collection of food plants and thatch etc.) in the grasslands having florican territories need to be completely stopped or at least largely curbed, to ensure protection of Bengal florican territories and its habitat.
4. ***Control repeated grass burning:*** Repeated grass burning results in habitat degradation and loss of suitable cover for Bengal floricans. Therefore, grass burning should be done once annually and burning should be completed in Bengal florican habitat within the third week of February.
5. ***Eradication of invasive species:*** In recent years, spread of invasive species in the grasslands is a major conservation issue in many protected areas. Some of the most important grassland habitats are affected by invasive species like *Eupatorium*, *Mimosa*, *Mikenia*. Hence, eradication of invasive species is the effective way to protect these habitats from their spread and further degradation of Bengal florican habitat.
6. ***Further research:*** Till date very little research has been carried out on habitat and breeding biology of Bengal floricans. Information on their sex ratio, life cycle, food preferences and food availability in its habitat is almost nonexistent. In addition to that, very little research is undertaken on non-breeding habitat of Bengal florican till date and almost no information is there about its non-breeding behaviour. Therefore, more research should be taken up to gather information on unrevealed biological information, behaviour and habitat use of Bengal florican.
7. ***Preparation of habitat reclamation plan:*** The potential grassland habitat in new areas especially in river islands should be identified and restored for species like Bengal florican. There should be

a proper action plan to protect such identified new grasslands along with their scientific management. There has to be an effort to reclaim the encroached Bengal florican habitat, at least in areas where human habitations (villages or crop fields) are absent or less. For this purpose a proper and effective habitat reclamation plan should be prepared.

8. ***Scientific management plan for grasslands:*** Proper management of *Terai* grasslands should be planned to protect grasslands. At the same time, the interest and benefit of the local people need to be ensured. So, a clear-cut policy on grassland management is of utmost importance. The most important methods to be considered in such a policy are rotational grazing, controlled burning, control of free-ranging livestock and protection of grassland plots to conserve seed banks. In most reserves sufficient grassland buffer zone will also be required to absorb the requirements of local people. In brief, the following actions are needed to conserve Bengal florican in India:
   - to regularly monitor the population of Bengal floricans in their natural habitats and protected areas.
   - to protect breeding areas from all kind of anthropogenic disturbances by restricting development and land use diversion.
   - to check grazing in the habitats of Bengal floricans as their eggs are often trampled by the livestock.
   - to check the repeated burning of grasses.
   - to strictly enforce the Wildlife Protection Act and CITES.
   - to showcase Bengal florican as one of the attractions and encourage eco-tourism as source of livelihood for local unemployed youth.

9. ***Increased awareness among the stakeholders:*** Many stakeholders of the Bengal florican habitat (like policy makers, PA managers, PA frontline staff and people living in the fringes of protected areas) are often not completely aware of the importance of Bengal florican. Therefore, target group based conservation education strategies on the species and its habitat need to be developed to enhance awareness amongst various stakeholders.

4.5 JERDON'S COURSER (*see* Plate I)

Order: Charadriiformes
Family: Glareolidae
Scientific Name: *Rhinoptilus bitorquatus* (Blyth, 1848)

Jerdon's courser was initially discovered in 1848 by British ornithologist and surgeon Thomas Jerdon and was again seen in 1871 and in 1900. Since then no single bird was seen for more than 85 years and was assumed to be extinct until its rediscovery around Lankamalai Wildlife Sanctuary in 1986 by ornithologist Bharat Bhushan. The last known sighting was in 2009 by researcher Rahul Chavan of Bombay Natural History Society (BNHS). This elusive species has been listed among the 50 rarest birds of the world.

Present Status

Wildlife (Protection) Act, 1972	Schedule-I
IUCN	Critically Endangered
CITES	Not listed
Population Trend	↓

Distinctive Features

- Jerdon's courser is a small bird, approximately 27 cm in size.
- This is a compact grey-brown courser with buffish body, two characteristic brown breast-bands, broad whitish supercilium, dark cheek patch and an orange-chestnut throat patch (gorget).
- Their bill is short and yellow with a black tip.
- Eyes are large with clear yellow iris.
- They possess a blackish crown and a narrow white crown stripe which runs on top of the blackish crown of the head.
- In flight, they show mostly black tail and a prominent white wing bar near the tips of their outermost black primaries.
- Sexes are thought to be alike.

Distribution

Jerdon's courser is endemic to India. The species was known from specimens collected at a few locations in eastern peninsular India. They were historically known from just a few locations of the Godavari valley near Sironcha and Bhadrachalam and from the Cuddapah and Anantpur areas in the valley of the Pennar river (Birdlife International, 2001). This species was also reported from extreme southern parts of Madhya Pradesh (Birdlife International, 2001).

But, presently they are extremely restricted in range and are endemic in the Eastern Ghat regions of Andhra Pradesh. Between 1986 and 1995, there were eight sightings of the species in the Lankamalai area with a maximum of six birds seen on a single night (Bhushan 1992; 1994). Two individuals were sighted in 2009 in the Cudaapah district of Andhra Pradesh, the first confirmed sightings in several years (Birdlife International, 2009). Jerdon's courser has been found at six other localities in the vicinity of the

Lankamalai, Palkonda and Velikonda ranges in the Pennar valley of Cuddapah district, Andhra Pradesh. Hence, it is now believed that a single population presently thrives within the Sri Lankamaleswara Wildlife Sanctuary.

Population

Birdlife International estimates the global population to be between 50 and 249 birds (Birdlife International, 2009). This population estimate is mainly based on camera trapping technique and carefully placed strips of fine sand to record footprints. The 2001 survey at the Sri Lankamalleswara Sanctuary revealed the existence of 32 pairs in the survey area.

Habitat

Jerdon's courser prefers to inhabit scrub forest of thorny (dominated by *Acacia*, *Zizyphus* and *Carissa*) and non-thorny (dominated by *Cassia*, *Hardwickia* and *Anogeissus*) plants, thin woodland and bushes, interspersed with bare grassless patches of ground in the gently undulating, rocky foothills of Eastern Ghats (Bhushan, 1990). They inhabit the dry deciduous forest regions of central Deccan Plateau, which represents the *Hardwickia* dominated woodlands (Sen and Lad, 2009). Some researchers spotted these elusive birds in narrow transitional patches between primary forest and degraded habitat or cultivated area. Studies using tracking strips have revealed the species has a strong preference for scrub-jungle habitats and favour areas where the density of large bushes is 300–700 per hectare and small bushes occur at less than 1000 per hectare (Jeganathan et al., 2004a). In Sri Lankamaleshwara Wildlife Sanctuary, the reported sightings between 1994–1995 were often close to small water bodies in undulating grasslands with thin thorny scrub (Samant and Elangovan, 1997). However, trappers in Sri Lankamaleshwara Wildlife Sanctuary have reported that the species inhabits hills during the monsoon and foothills for the rest of the year (Samant and Elangovan, 1997).

Behavioural Biology

Jerdon's courser is a nocturnal cursorial bird. They spend the day hiding under shade and are mostly active at dusk and during the night. Their distinctive calls are mostly heard at dawn and dusk. Their call is described as a series of staccato calls like '*Twick-too...Twick-too... Twick-too*' or '*yak-wak. yak-wak*'. The notes are repeated at the rate of about 1 per second and uttered 2 to 16 times and several birds in the vicinity may join in the calling (Jeganathan and Wotton, 2004; Jeganathan 2005a). Being a rare, elusive and nocturnal bird, very little knowledge is available so far about various aspects of their ecology and behaviour.

Food and Foraging Behaviour: Information on their diet and foraging behaviour is almost non-existent. But, these birds are presumed to be insectivorous and they hunt invertebrates by sight. They are also reported to partially forage on termites.

Breeding Behaviour: Almost nothing is known about their breeding behaviour. Birds obtained in March and May were not breeding, but a male collected in June had enlarged gonads and may have been breeding (Baker, 1922–1930). A clutch of two yellow eggs were once found laid on the ground in thin scrub jungle (Baker, 1922–1930; Ali and Ripley, 1968). In 2013, DNA analysis of a Jerdon's courser egg was done. This egg held at the Zoology Museum of the University of Aberdeen was supposedly collected from the vicinity of the Kolar Gold Fields, east of Bangalore, in 1917.

Threats to Survival

- ***Habitat loss:*** Their habitat is becoming increasingly scarce and fragmented. The scrub habitat preferred by this bird has declined due to increased agricultural practices. Scrub jungle clearance for farming, plantations and development projects in and around the protected areas are the main and well-documented threats to the Jerdon's courser. In addition to this, various anthropocentric developmental activities lead to the degradation and fragmentation of the remaining habitat of this critically endangered species.
  - (i) During the construction of Somasilla Dam, the residents of 57 villages were relocated in the very region in Lankamalai from where Jerdon's courser was rediscovered and lived. Subsequently, the area became overcrowded and increased disturbance, frequent livestock grazing, firewood extraction and clearing habitat for farmland ultimately threatened their habitat (Jeganathan et al., 2008).
  - (ii) The suitable habitat for the species lying outside Sri Lankamaleswara Wildlife Sanctuary was also threatened by the Telugu-Ganga Canal in Cuddapah District (Jeganathan and Rahmani, 2006), a scheme to supply water to the city of Chennai. However, considering the importance of this bird and on analyzing the possible threats to the survival of this species, in February 2006, India's Central Empowerment Committee suggested an alternative route for the Telegu-Ganga canal entirely avoiding the courser habitat (Jegannathan, 2005b; Jegannathan et al., 2005; Jeganathan and Rahmani, 2006). In 2008, the Supreme Court, halted the construction work and approved this new route avoiding important scrub forests to save the remaining habitat of these birds (BirdLife International, 2008).

(iii) Extensive quarrying of the hills in the distribution range of Jerdon's Courser also destroyed parts of their habitat (Bhushan 1992; 1994).

(iv) Project proposed to link the rivers of India might be disastrous for the Jerdon's courser as the construction of the canals would also lead to increased agricultural activity and would lead to the destruction of all the remaining scrub habitat of this critically endangered species.

- ***Accidental and opportunistic trapping:*** Accidental and opportunistic trapping has also been reported to be a threat to the survival of this avian species (Jeganathan et al., 2008).
- ***Lack of information:*** Ecology, distribution, habitat use and resource utilization pattern of this species is poorly known. Due to such lack of information, proper assessment of the threats and adopting appropriate conservation initiatives becomes difficult.

Conservation Initiatives

The Jerdon's courser is listed as Critically Endangered in the IUCN Red List (IUCN, 2010). Hunting or trapping of this species is prohibited in India, as it is listed under Schedule I of the Wildlife (Protection) Act 1972. It is also considered as a priority species under the National Wildlife Action Plan (2002–2016) of the Government of India.

According to Jegannathan et al. (2004a), some of the conservation efforts taken to conserve this species are:

(i) The Lankamalai (500 sq km) and the Veliconda (1,300 sq km) hill ranges have been respectively declared as Sri Lankamaleswara Wildlife Sanctuary and Sri Penusula Narasimha Wildlife Sanctuary as a result of its rediscovery in these areas.

(ii) Following the recommendation of the Central Empowerment Committee, the Telagu-Ganga canal was realigned by the Government of Andhra Pradesh entirely avoiding the courser habitat (Jeganathan and Rahmani, 2006) and 1,200 ha of land was given in compensation to expand the Sri Lankamaleswara Wildlife Sanctuary (Bird Life International, 2009).

(iii) This species has been included as one of twelve species to be included in the Integrated Development of Wildlife Habitats (IDWH) scheme of the Government of India and has been prioritized as animal that need immediate protection.

(iv) The local community, particularly the *Yanaadi* tribes, have been employed to locate this bird and also being encouraged to protect them.

Role of the Bombay Natural History Society (BNHS): Bombay Natural History Society (BNHS) along with the Royal Society for Protection of Birds (RSPB), Universities of Cambridge & Reading and Nature Conservation Foundation (NCF) with support from Andhra Pradesh Forest Department (APFD) have been carrying out intensive research programme since 2000 to save this species from extinction. This project has been funded by the Darwin Initiative and has played a vital role in developing the Species Recovery Plan (SRP) for the Jerdon's courser.

There has been considerable progress in developing the standard survey techniques to detect their presence and describe the broad habitat requirements. Up to 60 camera traps have been deployed since 2010, but these had not detected any birds by 2012 (Chavan and Barber, 2012). Therefore, a new method has been developed for detecting their presence by placing specially prepared natural tracking strips of fine sand to record their distinctive footprints (Jeganathan et al., 2002). The Jerdon's courser has a vestigial hind toe and this knowledge aids identification from tracks left on the tracking strips. An innovative survey method has been developed to conduct night-time call surveys for identifying new populations and studying existing ones (Jeganathan et al., 2004a; Jeganathan and Wotton, 2004; Jeganathan 2005a). Microchips with prerecorded call of Jerdon's courser were also used in the forest to confirm the presence of the bird in a precise location.

Capacity building of the forest staff: Forest department staffs are specially trained in survey techniques and habitat management. Moreover, an awareness-raising programme has been organized for the people from five villages present in the distribution range of Jerdon's courser.

Species recovery plan (SRP): Lack of information on the Jerdon's courser coupled with increasing pressure on its habitat, has prompted the policy makers to design a Species Recovery Plan (SRP) to ensure the long-term survival of the Jerdon's courser. In 2008, a workshop was held to draft the SRP, which was accepted by the State Forestry Department and Central Government. The final version was published in 2010 detailing priority conservation actions for the Jerdon's courser.

The SRP advocates a multi-pronged approach that includes elements of research, monitoring, advocacy, conservation education, habitat management, training and funding. It clearly outlines responsibilities and time-frames to facilitate regular monitoring and evaluation. The identified priorities are (i) to ensure protection of the species's habitat, (ii) to map potential habitat of the species within scrub forest using remote sensing, (iii) to capture and radio-tag individuals, (iv) to increase efforts to identify new sites that may host the species and (v) to raise awareness of the species (Chandrasekhar and Jeganathan, 2008).

This SRP is a result of inputs from a wide range of stakeholders including the government, NGOs, national and international scientists and civil society. It is, therefore, a very inclusive and realistic document. The document lays great stress on applying the 'precautionary principle' wherever possible considering the threatened status and restricted distribution of the species. This SRP will serve as a reference for conservation managers, policy-makers, researchers, decision-makers and form the basis of future conservation actions.

Proposed Conservation Action Plan

Identifying areas of suitable habitat within its putative range and conducting surveys of those are the major proposed conservation actions to establish its current distribution, to estimate population status and assess the potential threats. Hence, to ensure the survival of this critically endangered species, it is essential to:

1. Monitor the present status at all known locations at in'tervals of no more than five years.
2. Monitor the extent and condition of existing and potentially suitable habitats.
3. Carry out a radio-telemetry study and diet analysis using faecal samples to determine the ecological requirements of this species and enable more effective conservation recommendations to be formulated (Jeganathan et al., 2004b).
4. Employ call count techniques at night to locate undiscovered populations.
5. Make recommendations for its conservation based on survey findings, including the establishment of sites supporting population as strictly protected areas.
6. Ensure effective protection of all habitat within the courser's range and lobby against harmful activities such as quarrying and proposed mining activities that threaten existing habitat.
7. Take a precautionary approach regarding habitat management.
8. Expand conservation awareness programme and promote alternative livelihoods in and around areas supporting Jerdon's courser populations to minimise habitat alteration, disturbance and trapping.
9. Build capacity amongst forestry staff and local individuals in survey methods. Continue to train forest department staff, local communities and volunteers so that they can carry out surveys for the species.

The species is under great pressure from unsustainable development and management practices and more research is essential to understand the behaviour, range and potential threats to Jerdon's courser. But, due to the elusive and nocturnal habit of this bird, researchers often face difficulty in locating the birds to study. Besides, more and more staff of the Forest Department, as well as, various other stakeholders may also be trained with the sophisticated survey techniques and habitat management. Awareness of the plight of the species needs to be raised amongst local people to effectively save this species from being extinct in future.

4.6 WHITE-RUMPED VULTURE (*see* Plate I)

Order: Accipitriformes
Family: Accipitridae
Scientific Name: *Gyps bengalensis* (Gmelin, 1788)

Out of 22 vulture species found across the world, eight belong to genus *Gyps* (Mundy 1985). Of the nine species of vultures recorded from India, five belong to the genus *Gyps.*, white-rumped vulture (*G. bengalensis*), long-billed vulture (*G. indicus*) and slender-billed vulture (*G. tenuirostris*) are residents, and the remaining two, the Eurasian griffon (*G. fulvus*) and Himalayan griffon (*G. himalayensis*) are largely wintering species (Prakash et al., 2007).

The white-rumped vulture is an Old World vulture and until the 1990s were present in large numbers in southern and southeastern Asia. But, there has been reports of upto 95 percent decline in wild populations of three *Gyps* vultures-*G. bengaiensis, G. tenuirostris* and *G. indicus* (Prakash 1999; Gilbert et al., 2002, Prakash et al., 2003, Sarrazin et al., 2004).

Present Status

Wildlife (Protection) Act, 1972	Schedule – I
IUCN	Critically Endangered
CITES	Appendix – II
Population Trend	↓

Distinctive Features

- The white-rumped vulture is the smallest of the *Gyps* vultures weighing approximately 3.5–7.5 kg (average 4.4 kg) and measuring 75–85 cm in length. These medium-sized vultures have very broad wings (wingspan 180–210 cm) and short tail feathers.
- Their head and neck are devoid of feathers and are dark grayish brown in colour with a pinkish tinge upto neck. They also possess a unique white neck ruff. The whitish back, rump and underwing coverts, as well as, the silvery grey secondaries of the adult birds are in complete contrast with the dark blackish body plumage. Feathers under their tail are also black.
- Their beak is rather short, heavy, pale bluish gray with slit-like nostril openings and blackish cere at the base.

- In flight, the adults show a dark leading edge of the wing and have a white wing-lining on the underside.
- Vocalizations of the adult birds include croaks, grunts, hisses and squeals, which could be heard in their nest colonies, roosts and foraging stations (around carcasses).
- Juveniles are largely dark brown with prominent white shaft streaks, especially below. They possess white down feathers on head and neck and usually a brownish nape patch. The feathers of the ruff are longer, more lanceolate, less fluffy and more brownish in juvenile birds as compared to the adults. Sub-adults have a drab brown plumage. The juveniles acquire the adult plumage in about four to five years.
- Lifespan: A specimen in captivity lived for at least 12 years.

Distribution

Gyps bengalensis was earlier widely distributed from southeastern Iran, Afghanistan, Pakistan, India, Bangladesh, Nepal, Bhutan, Myanmar, south-central China (Yunnan), Indochina and the northern Malay Peninsula, Thailand, Laos, Cambodia and southern (BirdLife International, 2015).

Now they are extirpated from much of its former range, especially the portion in Southeast Asia and are possibly extinct from southern China and Malaysia (BirdLife International, 2001). Although reported earlier from south-east Afghanistan and Iran, yet their current status in these areas is unknown. This species has disappeared from most parts of Southeast Asia in the early twentieth century and the only viable populations in the region are found in Myanmar and Cambodia

In India, the white-rumped vultures were very common particularly in the Gangetic plains. They were often seen nesting on the avenue trees within large cities. However, since the early 1990s, this species has suffered a 99 percent population decline in India and nearby countries.

Population

Prior to 1985, the species was described as "possibly the most abundant large bird of prey in the world" (Houston, 1985) and their global population comprised of several million individuals. But after the catastrophic decline throughout its range since the 1990's, presently the population of the white-rumped vultures is estimated to lie between 3500 and 15000 birds. In India, Gujarat possibly holds the largest concentration of surviving *Gyps* vultures and these remaining populations are the best hope for the survival of this species (Pandey et al., 2010).

Habitat

The white-rumped vultures inhabit mostly in plains and light woodlands, and less frequently in hilly regions. They are commensal to human beings and are often associated with human habitations—villages, towns, cities and open areas. They were reported to build nest and form roost colonies on tall trees near or even amidst human habitations.

Behavioural Biology

These birds are mostly residents. Large numbers of these vultures were once visible in the late morning skies above Indian cities. They usually remain inactive in the morning and start flying as the temperature rises and warm air creates sufficient thermals to support their soaring flight. They circle and rise in altitude and glide to change thermals.

Food and Foraging Behaviour: Like other vultures this species is also a scavenger and feed mostly in large groups on putrid carrion as well as fresh carcasses of dead animals. They find their food by soaring high in thermals and spotting other scavengers. Once food is spotted they quickly descend, feed voraciously and sometimes swallow small pieces of bones. Large aggregations were noticed while foraging on carcasses. Some birds perch on adjacent trees and descend to feed on a carcass even after complete darkness sets in. A large flock of vulture can clean up the carcass of a large bullock within half an hour. These birds drink water regularly and also bathe when water is available.

Breeding Behaviour: Their breeding season commences in the third week of October (Pande et al., 2013) and continues upto March with eggs being laid mainly in January. They start building nests in November. They build large stick nests with a deep cup loosely lined with leafy twigs located in the main crown fork of tall trees (Wells, 1999), often near human habitation. During nest building, the male brings twigs to the nesting site and the female arranges them to form the nest. Several pairs may nest in the vicinity of each other, but usually one active nest is built on each tree (Pande et al., 2013). Younger birds usually construct solitary nests in isolated locations but such nests are not repeatedly used. Nests of white-rumped vultures are nearly 3 feet in diameter and half a foot in thickness. The nest is lined with green leaves prior to egg laying. The average height of the nesting trees are 27 m. Vultures prefer *Mangifera indica*, *Cocos nucifera*, *Terminalia cuneata*, *Terminalia bellirica*, *Alstonia scholaris*, *Calophyllum inophyllum*, *Tetramelis nudiflora*, *Thespesia populnea* and *Caryota urens* tree species for nest building (Pande et al., 2013).

During courtship the male bird of the breeding pair tenderly pecks the head, back and neck of the female with his beak. Once receptive, the female partner invites copulation while the male mounts over the female and holds the head of the female in his beak. The female usually lays single unmarked white egg with a tinge of bluish-green. If the egg is lost the female bird is reported to destroy the nest. After about 30–35 days of incubation, a young chick hatches which is covered with grey down feathers. The young birds remains for about three months at the nest while the parents feed them with bits of meat from carcasses.

Home Range: Although satellite-tagged vultures have shown that they forage over a vast range, yet precise information on the home range and the degree of connectivity of apparently separate populations of white-rumped vultures is still lacking.

Social Organization: These birds are usually found in conspecific flocks and are thought to be social to some extent.

Threats to Survival

The population of the white-rumped vultures declined rapidly in the last decade. There are multifarious causes behind such catastrophic decline of vultures.

- ***Diclofenac contamination:*** Several authorities (Oaks et al., 2004a; 2004b; Green et al., 2004, Swan et al., 2006) claim that contamination of livestock carcasses by a veterinary drug, diclofenac, is attributed to be the major reason behind the mass mortality of vultures. Diclofenac is used as veterinary non-steroidal anti-inflammatory drug to treat domestic livestock. Vultures feeding on the carcasses of the livestock treated with diclofenac often suffer from renal failure and visceral gout (Oaks et al., 2004a; 2004b). Such visceral gouts were often found to be male-biased, which might lead to problems in the future (Arshad et al., 2009). Ketoprofen is another veterinary drug used in India, which has also recently been identified to be lethal to the species and measurements of residue levels in ungulate carcasses in India indicates that they are present in sufficient concentrations to cause vulture mortalities (Naidoo et al., 2010).
- ***Habitat destruction:*** Destruction of the major roosting and nesting trees of vultures, particularly those situated in the private lands, are considered to be another major threat to white-rumped vultures. Sometimes, the landowners are not aware if the large trees within their premises are used as nesting and roosting sites by vultures. Some others consider those large trees as revenue generating resources. The ground beneath the nesting and roosting trees often becomes soiled with the excreta of these scavenging birds, which is not liked by many people. Some even consider vulture sitting on a tree in their premises as an omen and cut the trees once the presence of vultures is noticed. They often try to chase away vultures from their lands when these birds build nests there.
- ***Habitat disturbance:*** Destruction of nests and pelting stones on breeding pairs or roosting birds by local people are some major form of disturbances faced by vultures. Several anthropogenic activities close to the roosting site also scare vultures.
- ***Hunting:*** Pande et al., (2013) recorded few instances where vultures were killed by children with catapults for fun, as well as, collection of vulture egg by local people who believed that consumption of vulture eggs makes human bones stronger. Egg collection is an indirect form of killing, which adversely affect population dynamics. Archery is a famous sport among men in Manang and Mustang districts where people used vulture quills to make the tail of arrows (Pande et al., 2013).
- ***Food shortage:*** Earlier slaughtering of cattle was forbidden by the Hindu farmers in rural India and once dead, these cattle were thrown on the dumping grounds which were a good source of food for the white-rumped vultures. But, there has been a paradigm shift in this practice in the recent past. Now, farmers often sell their old cattle in exchange of money. These old cattle are then taken to the slaughter houses to satiate the demand for beef. Their bones and skins are also traded. On the other hand, carcasses were earlier left in open fields and vultures used to quickly feed on them. But, now the villages are growing fast leading to the paucity of dumping grounds. Besides, numbers of vultures have also declined. So, if a carcass is dumped, it remains for several days, putrefies and creates foul smell and abominable surroundings. Therefore, few farmers who still do not sell their cattle out of some religious beliefs now bury the dead cattle in the dumping grounds. All these social and economic changes have synergistically limited the food supply and led to serious food shortage to vultures in many parts of this country. Another major reason behind the food scarcity of white-rumped vultures in some the wilderness area in south-east Asia is thought to be the decrease of large ungulate populations and improved management of deceased animals (Clements et al., 2013).
- ***Diseases:*** Post mortem examination of dead vultures often reveals accumulation of uric acid crystals in their tissues in a lethal dose (known

as visceral gout), which is mainly caused due to inability to eliminate excretory substances as a result of kidney damage or tubular necrosis (Oaks et al., 2004a; 2004b; Shultz et al., 2004; Gilbert et al., 2006; Naidoo et al. 2010). Epidemic of avian malaria is also supposed to be affecting white-rumped vultures (Poharkar et al., 2009).

- ***Other reasons:*** Owls and crows have been reported to predate upon vulture eggs and chicks (Pande et al., 2013). Organochlorine pesticide residues were found from egg and tissue samples of white-rumped vultures in India in varying concentrations. Some vultures die due to catastrophic events like excessive rainfall, hailstorms and may be linked with long term climatic cycles such as the El Niño–Southern Oscillation.
- ***Lack of awareness:*** Many people of this country are not even aware of the important ecological roles played by these scavenging birds. In rural areas, many children either do not go to school or drop out of school to look after livestock. While grazing, if these children come across vulture colonies then some of them practice pelting stones on vultures with a catapult for fun and sometimes even kill vultures (Pande et al., 2013).

Conservation Initiatives

- ***Discontinuation of the use of diclofenac:*** Veterinary diclofenac is being removed from the veterinary market and campaigns to ban the use of diclofenac in veterinary practice have been underway in several South Asian countries. The Governments of India, Nepal and Pakistan passed a legislation in 2006 banning the manufacture and import of diclofenac as a veterinary drug. Subsequently, the Government of India passed further legislation in 2008 banning the manufacture, sale, distribution or use of veterinary diclofenac (BirdLife International, 2015). In the same year, the Drug Controller General of India also issued a letter to many manufacturing farms not to sell the veterinary form of diclofenac and to mark human diclofenac containers as 'not for veterinary use' (Bird Life International, 2008). However, veterinarians have initially refused to accept this ban and were illegally using human formulations of diclofenac to treat livestock as they were still widely available. Therefore, levels of diclofenac contamination still remained a high threat for the survival of vultures (Cuthbert et al., 2011). Consequently, efforts to completely eradicate diclofenac from the environment have so far been only partly successful. After long persuasion by several NGOs, raptor biologists and conservationists, the Union Ministry of Health has banned multi-dose vials of human formulations of diclofenac in 2015. This ban restricts diclofenac production to human formulations in a single 3ml dose.(vide Gazette notification no G.S.R 558 (E) dated 17th July, 2015).
- ***Introduction of 'vulture-safe' alternative veterinary drug:*** Efforts to replace diclofenac with a suitable and safe alternative are on-going and are showing signs of success (Cuthbert et al, 2011b). An alternative drug, meloxicam, has been tested on *Gyps* vultures with no ill-effects (Swan et al., 2006; Swarup et al., 2007) and necessary orders were issued to promote the use of meloxicam as an alternative drug with the same veterinary effect as diclofenac. Currently the vulture population of this country appears to be stabilizing with the substitution of toxic diclofenac with meloxicam (Richard et al., 2011).
- ***Vulture restaurants:*** 'Vulture restaurant' is a unique conservation initiative to combat the imminent threat of food shortage. Creation of such vulture restaurants are usually done involving the local communities. For instance, in Cambodia these vulture restaurants are used as ecotourism attractions to raise awareness and fund supplementary feeding programmes and research (Masphal and Vorsak, 2007). In Indian context, some incentives to leave the carcass of cattle in open fields particularly in areas with still good population of vultures might be a good proactive measure to combat food scarcity of vultures. Alternatively, old or unproductive livestock can be purchased from the owners and once they die, then their carcass might be fed to vultures (Pande et al., 2013).
- ***Vulture breeding centres:*** The report of the International South Asian Vulture Recovery Plan Workshop in 2004 (BNHS, 2004) gave a comprehensive list of recommendations including establishing a minimum of three "Conservation breeding and release centre" in this country. Accordingly, three captive breeding facilities (one at Pinjore, Haryana, second in Buxa, West Bengal and the third in Rani, Assam) have been established in India by the joint efforts of the respective state governments along with Bombay Natural History Society (BNHS), Royal Society for the Preservation of Birds (RSPB), Zoological Society of London (ZSL) and other ornithological organizations (Bowden, 2009). Successful attempts are being made to breed the *Gyps* vultures in these captive breeding centres (Lahkar et al., 2010).

1. **Jatayu Conservation Breeding Centre, Pinjore, Haryana:** This centre was established in September 2001 by BNHS in collaboration with the Haryana Forest Department at Pinjore, Haryana and funded by the Darwin Initiative for the Survival of Species Fund of the Government of UK and supported by Royal Society for Protection of Birds, Zoological Society of London and National Birds of Prey Trust, UK. The centre holds three species of *Gyps* vultures, viz. white-rumped vulture, long-billed vulture and slender-billed vulture. Adult and juvenile vultures have been captured from various states of the country and each bird is fitted with microchips for identification. In this centre, two chicks hatched in early 2007 and three more hatched in 2009 (Prakash et al., 2007; Bowden 2009). The main objective of this station is to establish a founder population of 25 pairs each of 3 species of vultures and produce a population of at least 200 birds of each species to be reintroduced in the wild.
2. **Vulture Conservation Breeding Centre, Rajabhat Khawa, West Bengal:** This centre was established in 2005 at Rajabhatkhawa in the Alipurduar district of West Bengal in collaboration with the Government of West Bengal and Bombay Natural History Society. This centre is situated right on the edge of Buxa Tiger Reserve in West Bengal and house a good number of white-rumped vultures.
3. **Vulture Conservation Breeding Centre, Rani, Assam:** Another centre was set up at Rani in the Kamrup district of Assam in 2007 by Bombay Natural History Society in collaboration with the Assam Forest Department. This centre was the first to be set up in Assam for carrying out a conservation breeding programme for two critically endangered species of vultures, white-rumped vulture and slender-billed vulture.

Few more breeding centres are planned to be set up in future with a vision to create reservoirs of birds to be reintroduced. Initial success of these vulture conservation breeding centres is encouraging. These centres probably represent the last hope to save these vultures from extinction. Nevertheless, naturally breeding populations of vultures are essential to ensure the effective, long term survival and genetic stability of captive bred birds, as well as, for their successful reintroduction in the wild so that these captive bred populations get an opportunity to mingle with wild populations and learn the essentials of survival from their wild kin.

- ***Research and monitoring of vultures:*** More ecological research on this species is essential as many aspects of their biology are still unknown. In many parts of the distribution range of white-rumped vulture, some birds have been tagged with ultra high frequency (satellite) transmitters to monitor their movements, foraging range and site fidelity in order to develop suitable conservation strategies (Ellis, 2004). State governments have been advised to set up state level committees to continuously monitor the vulture population and conservation efforts. Directives have also been issued to all the Chief Wildlife Wardens to conduct periodic population surveys till self sustaining populations of white-rumped vultures are established. Such monitoring of vulture populations have already been initiated in Assam, West Bengal, Madhya Pradesh, Himachal Pradesh, Gujarat, Rajasthan, Uttarakhand and Uttar Pradesh to assess the ranging patterns, foraging movements and identification and protection of the existing colonies of three species of vultures to ensure their breeding success in the wild. Bombay Natural History Society is carrying out the national level surveys on vultures. Identification of natural active nest sites and conserving the existing nest trees on private lands are the foremost requirement for safeguarding the breeding populations of the white-rumped vultures, which cannot be effectively implemented without active involvement of local people.
- ***Legal protection:*** White-rumped vultures have been included in the Appendix II of CITES and CMS Appendix II. It has been reported from many protected areas across the country where killing of these birds are prohibited under the Wildlife Protection Act. In 2004, the Wildlife (Protection) act was amended to include this species under Schedule I (Part III) to provide them with nationwide highest level of protection.
- ***Awareness programmes and peoples' attitude:*** Massive conservation awareness programs are required to make vulture conservation successful. The target groups (like farmers, members of forest user groups, vet professionals, students and teachers) need to be provided with booklets, pamphlets and other awareness generating resources to include them in the vulture conservation initiatives. Moreover, awareness camps targeting children and replacement of catapults with other playing gears (such as football or volleyball) can prevent fun hunting of vultures in certain areas (Pande et al., 2013).

4.7 HOOLOCK GIBBON (*see* Plate II)

Order: Primate
Family: Hylobatidae
Scientific Name: *Hoolock hoolock* (Harlan, 1834)

Earlier hoolock gibbons were placed under Genus *Bunopithecus*. However, recent investigations revealed that these primates are not closely related to the type species *Bunopithecus sericus*. Therefore, the previous generic name was changed to *Hoolock* (Mootnick and Groves, 2005).

Present Status

Wildlife (Protection) Act, 1972	Schedule–I
IUCN	Endangered
CITES	Appendix–I
Population Trend	↓

Distinctive Features

- Small arboreal creature and the only ape found in India.
- It has the distinctive build of an ape and is without a tail.
- Arms are longer, measuring almost double the length of its legs.
- The head and body length of an adult hoolock gibbon usually lies between 46–63 cm. Their mean body weight fall between 6–7 kg. A female generally weighs about 6.0–6.6 kg and a male about 6.1–7.9 kg.
- Sexual dimorphism present. Males have a distinct fully black coat with prominent characteristic white eye-brows, whereas females have a lighter coat of grayish brown or light brown colour. A newly born hoolock gibbon is with yellow-tinted greyish-white hair, which turns dark within a couple of weeks.
- Lifespan of the hoolock gibbons is about 25 years.

Distribution

Hoolock gibbons were formerly distributed widely across the eastern India, through Bangladesh to China and south to the Irawaddy River in Myanmar, northern Thailand and northern Laos. Presently, hoolock gibbons are native to north-eastern states of India, Chittagong Hill tracts in Bangladesh, as well as, in Myanmar. They are also reported from south Yunnan Provinces in China (northern Shan States).

In India, the distribution of hoolock gibbon is restricted to the regions between south of Brahmaputra and east of Dibang rivers (Choudhury, 2001a) and are found in the northeastern states of Arunachal Pradesh, Assam, Manipur, Meghalaya, Mizoram, Nagaland and Tripura. They presently thrive in isolated patches in the forests of lowland areas in Assam, in the southern and eastern part of the Brahmaputra river, in eastern side of Dibang river and also in Dibang Valley, Lohit, Tirap and Changlang districts of Arunachal Pradesh. Namdapha National Park in Arunachal Pradesh is a stronghold of this species in India (Chetry et al., 2003). Besides, they are also reported from Kaziranga and Manas National Parks.

Population

Population of hoolock gibbons in the north-eastern states has reduced to a few forest fragments, became isolated and is considered rare throughout their range (Choudhury 1991, 2001a). It has been estimated that there are about 2,600 gibbons in northeast India, of which majority (about 2,000 individuals) are present in Assam (Molur et al., 2005).

Habitat

Hoolock gibbons are forest dwellers and are found in areas with contiguous canopy of tropical rainforests, tropical evergreen forests, wet evergreen forests, semi-evergreen forests, tropical mixed deciduous forests and sub-tropical broad-leafed hill forests. They prefer the closed canopy or three-tiered forest vegetation with high, middle and low tier trees. Trees in the high tier provide space for sleeping, resting and sun-basking, whereas trees in the middle and low tiers provide food and paths for locomotion. They have also been occasionally reported from bamboo, *Terminalia myriocarpa* and *Largerstroemia flosreginae* plantations. Hoolock gibbons usually do not inhabit in monocultures. Altitude of their habitat ranges from two forest locations in the plains (Choudhury, 1991) up to 2,500 m above the sea level in Manipur (Choudhury, 2001a).

Behavioural Ecology

Hoolock gibbons are diurnal, arboreal species and spend almost its entire life on treetops. They usually move by specialized swing-arm type of locomotion by leaping or jumping between the trees and follow the same trail through treetops day after day. They come to the ground and walk bipedally only when the distance between the two trees large and not reachable. During bipedal movement on ground, they usually hold their long arms above the head, to maintain balance. Gibbons are also good swimmers.

***Food and Foraging Behaviour*:** Hoolock gibbons are mainly frugivorous and figs constitute a major portion of their diet. However, populations dwelling in small forest fragments experience a period of almost total lack of fruit in their diet at the end of the dry season (Kakati, 2004). A dominantly folivorous diet was reported during studies carried out in Assam and Tripura (Mukherjee, 1986; Kakati, 1997). Their diet also comprises of flowers, buds, shoots, as well as, a small amount of eggs, grubs, insects, spiders and small vertebrates, particularly during dry season with acute dearth of fruits. They also occasionally visit the adjoining cultivated lands to forage.

Breeding Behaviour: Hoolock gibbons (both male and female) attain sexual maturity between 6-7 years. Usually male choose a single female and the breeding pair usually mate in the early rainy season. Then after a gestation period of about seven months (ranging between 195–210 days), the female gives birth to single offspring, usually in winter between November and February. The newborn offspring is hairless, usually with a yellow tinged grayish white coat and within six months their fur changes to black. After birth, the newborn infant always holds around its mother's belly tightly with the help of its legs and totally dependent on her milk up to six months of age. After that the newborn spends most of times by playing and feeding with other group members. The newborn, always sleeps with its mother until another baby is born. The interval between two successive births is usually 2–3 years.

Home Range

Home ranges of hoolock gibbons usually lie within 0.08-0.63 sq km (Alfred, 1992; Ahsan, 2001). Nevertheless, unusually large home ranges of 2-4 sq km were reported from some populations in Tripura and Arunachal Pradesh (Mukherjee, 1982; Mukherjee et al., 1988), possibly due to low fruit availability.

Social Organization: Hoolock gibbons live in small, monogamous family groups ranging from 2-6 individuals, which mainly comprise of the mating pair and their offspring. Social interactions between the group members like grooming, playing and sun basking are quite common. Each group of gibbons is also reported to defend a territory, where it follows the same trail through treetops day after day. This territory size ranges from 0.15-0.3 sq km, depending mainly on the number of members in the group and on the quality of habitat. Each group hunts within its own territory, which they defend by making loud territorial songs. Gibbons' songs are the loudest of all calls in the northeastern forests and vocalized as "hookoo-hookoo-hookoo". With the ushering daylight and warmth, hoolocks begin to howl. Single group sings songs at a time, while other groups wait for their turn. They remain quiet during the hot hours of the day, when they take rest in the shaded branches of the trees beneath the canopy layer with a unique posture by keeping its head buried between its legs. They again start howling in the evening.

Threats to Survival

- ***Habitat loss:*** Destruction, degradation and fragmentation of forests in their distribution range is the most alarming threat in the survival of hoolock gibbons (Das et al., 2003; Dam, 2006). Legal and illegal logging, tree bark and fuel wood extraction, harvesting of bamboo for paper mills and domestic use, livestock grazing, conversion of rainforests to teak and other monoculture plantations significantly degrade their habitat. Littering by the tourists also has the potential to degrade their habitat. This has been viewed as collateral pollution of tourism by Ahsan (2001). Besides, the construction of roads, railway tracts, hydro-electric dam projects, high-tension electric wires, irrigation, oil drilling, coal mining, stone quarrying and ever encroaching human settlements also deplete the habitat of these primates by causing pollution and disturbance (Choudhury, 2001a). Forest clearance for tea and paddy cultivation and practice of 'slash and burn' (*Jhum*) cultivation also resulted in rapid rate of habitat loss for hoolock gibbons (Mukherjee et al., 1992; Gupta, 1994).
- ***Predation:*** In addition to its mortality by its natural predators, feral and domestic dogs occasionally kill hoolock gibbons, particularly when they come to ground to cross the gaps in discontinuous degraded forests (Chowdhury, 2000).
- ***Illegal poaching and gathering:*** Hunting, poaching and illegal trade are other serious threats to the hoolock gibbons. Several ethnic groups in northeast India hunt them for food using snares, muzzle-loading and automatic firearms (Mukherjee et al., 1992; Choudhury 1996a; 1996b; 2006). Some local tribal people in Assam are reported to hunt these primates. These apes are also hunted for their meat and bones, which are used in preparation of folk and oriental medicines. Hoolock meat has also been found to be sold in some local markets. Sub-adults are sometimes illegally traded live as pets (Choudhury, 2006).

Conservation Initiatives

Hoolock gibbon is designated as 'Endangered' by IUCN and is placed in the Schedule–I of Wildlife (Protection) Act, 1972, thus giving the animal a nationwide legal protection. Moreover, being listed in the Appendix–I of CITES, its use in international trade is also prohibited. In addition, several measures have been adopted to safeguard the only ape found in this country. Many parts of their distribution range have been declared as protected areas and presently they are found in about 30 protected areas of this country (Choudhury, 2001b). Besides, a prime habitat of hoolock gibbon in Jorhat district of Assam with semi-evergreen forests and evergreen patches amidst tea gardens and human settlements, measuring 20.98 sq km has recently been designated as 'Gibbon Wildlife Sanctuary' as a part of special conservation effort.

To facilitate research and conservation of this unique primate, the Gibbon Conservation Centre (GCC) was set up within the Gibbon Wildlife Sanctuary. This Centre is presently run by a trust in collaboration with the Assam Forest Department and *Aaranyak*, a leading NGO in the northeast India. GCC alone has reached more than 33,000 students through its education and awareness programmes. In addition to the students, this centre was also successful in improving awareness for conservation of hoolock gibbon and their habitat among the local communities to a great extent. Several organizations like *Aaranyak*, Primate Conservation Centre (PCC), Wildlife Areas Development and Welfare Trust (WADWT), the Zoo Outreach Organization (ZOO), Centre for Environment Education (CEE) also contributed significantly towards the conservation of hoolock gibbon by carrying out various education and awareness programmes. According to Molur et al., (2005), population and habitat viability assessment for western hoolock gibbons were conducted for the first time by the Zoo Outreach Organization (ZOO). In 2010, the Centre for Environment Education, Northeast also launched an education and awareness program for gibbon conservation. For the first time 'Hoolock Gibbon Conservation Action Plan' in Assam was developed by Das et al., (2005). In future, planned afforestation programmes need to be undertaken to bridge the gaps and to make a continuous corridor for the movement of these gibbons from one place to another in search of food. More and more areas with good numbers of hoolock gibbons should be declared as conservation areas.

4.8 GRAY SLENDER LORIS (VANGU) (*see* Plate II)

Order: Primate
Family: Loridae
Scientific Name: *Loris lydekkerianus* Cabrera, 1908

Formerly gray slender loris was considered a subspecies of *Loris tardigradus* and named as *Loris tardigradus lydekkerianus*. But, Groves (2001) regrouped them into 2 species—*Loris lydekkerianus* found in India and Sri Lanka and *Loris tardigradus* present only in Sri Lanka.

Loris lydekkerianus is a small nocturnal primate found in Sri Lanka and India and comprises of four geographically separated subspecies (Perera and Sandun, 2008). The Indian subspecies are Mysore gray slender loris (*Loris lydekkerianus* spp. *lydekkerianus*) and Malabar gray slender loris (*Loris lydekkerianus* spp. *malabaricus*) (Singh et al., 1999). On the other hand, the Sri Lankan subspecies include Northern Ceylonese slender loris (*Loris lydekkerianus* spp. *nordicus*) and Highland slender loris (*Loris lydekkerianus* spp. *grandis*).

Present Status

Wildlife (Protection) Act, 1972	Schedule–I
IUCN	Least Concern
CITES	Appendix–II
Population Trend	↓

Distinctive Features

- Gray slender loris is about the size of a chipmunk, measuring 15–25 cm in total body length. The body weight varies in different subspecies. Overall weight of the males range from 180 to 290 gm, while the weight of the females usually lies between 180 to 275 gm.
- Their head is large and round, body is banana-shaped and the limbs are long and extremely slim (pencil-thin). They walk on all four limbs and this type of locomotion is called *quadrupedalism*. Their great toe and thumb are opposable, which helps them grasp branches and twigs and also to hold prey. The digits have small finger nails.
- Their most prominent feature is the pair of two large, closely set, saucer-like dark brown and distinctly forward facing eyes. Eyes flank with a long nose, which ends in a heart-shaped knob. They have the closest orbital approximation of all primates. The eyes are surrounded by dark-brown to black circles of fur (circumocular patch), while the bridge of the nose is white.
- Ears are small and rounded.
- They have a small, vestigial tail.
- Second digit of both the hands and feet are characteristically very short.
- Lower jaw is small and narrow. Dental formula is 2:1:3:3.
- Body is covered by soft and woolly fur, while hands and feet have short fur. Colour of their pelage varies from dark-grey to red-brown on dorsal side with a darker medial stripe, with much paler underside (ventrum) and dirty white chest and belly.
- A patch with venom is reported to be present under their elbows. When faced with danger, they lick their elbow, cover their teeth with poison and bites the enemy to deliver the venom.
- They possess specialized digestive system for ingesting toxic prey and have an unusually low basal metabolic rate.
- Lifespan of grey slender loris in captivity is usually 15 years.

Above mentioned are some general characteristics of gray slender loris. However, it is to be noted that different subspecies markedly differ in terms of their pelage and size.

Distribution

Gray slender loris is endemic to the Indian subcontinent. They are found only in southern India and in central, north-central, and east-central Sri Lanka (Radhakrishna and Singh, 2002; Nekaris and Jayewardene, 2004a; Radhakrishna et al., 2011). Hence, gray slender loris is considered to be endemic to this region (Sasi and Kumara, 2014).

In India, gray slender loris is found below 15ºN latitude and is distributed south of Tapti and Godavari rivers along the Western Ghats in Kerala, Karnataka and western Tamil Nadu. They are found in forests of Dindigul district in Tamil Nadu, Eastern Ghats, southern Andhra Pradesh, eastern Indira Gandhi Wildlife Sanctuary in Tamil Nadu and Karnataka (Rao, 1994). Two subspecies of gray slender loris are reported to occur in India.

- **Mysore Gray Slender Loris (*Loris lydekkerianus lydekkerianus*):** Found in the drier forests of the Eastern Ghats, south of river Godavari (Groves, 2001). Their distribution is patchy and has been reported from the southern plains of Mysore, forested areas of Andhra Pradesh, Karnataka and Tamil Nadu and in the dry shrub jungles of the Eastern Ghats (Singh et al., 1999, 2000; Nekaris and Jayewardene, 2003). Singh et al., (1999) recorded this taxon most often in areas up to 1,000 m.
- **Malabar Gray Slender Loris (*Loris lydekkerianus malabaricus*):** Occurs as a contiguous population throughout wet forests of the Western Ghats in Karnataka, Kerala and Tamil Nadu south of river Tapti (Groves. 2001). It is also found from the coast up to 1,200 m in Karnataka, and lower elevations in Kerala (Nekaris et al., 2008).

Population

Very little research on population estimation of gray slender loris has so far been carried out. It is indeed very difficult to do an accurate census of these primates due to their small size and nocturnal habits. The greatest concentrations of *Loris lydekkerianus malabaricus* are present in the southeastern part of the Western Ghats with an encounter rate of 0.21 animals/km. On the other hand, population density of *Loris lydekkerianus lydekkerianus* was found to be highest in Dindigul district of Tamil Nadu, along with fairly high density in some localities of the Eastern Ghats, Karnataka and Andhra Pradesh (Singh et al., 2000).

Habitat

Gray slender loris thrives in a wide range of habitats which include tropical rainforest, montane forest, dry semi-deciduous forests, thorny shrubs, swamps etc. However, the ranges of two subspecies found in India usually do not overlap and they are reported to inhabit different kind of habitats. Malabar gray slender loris is often found in low, swampy areas or humid tropical rainforests. Mysore gray slender loris dwells in drier scrub jungle and semi-deciduous forests with low rainfall, including hedgerow plantations bordering farmlands of southern India. Both these subspecies are also found near plantations and cultivated areas near taller forests (Kumara et al., 2006). Mysore gray slender loris seems to rely heavily on undergrowth and are often found in secondary growth forest (Radhakrishna and Singh, 2002), where as Malabar gray slender loris is found to occur more in cardamom plantations and in degraded and stunted rainforests than in primary rainforests (Kumara et al., 2006; Radhakrishna et al., 2011).

They are often found to inhabit thick, thorny bushes and bamboo clumps, where they can evade their predators with relative ease. They also feed on the large assortment of insects present there. Singh et al., (1999) noticed that relatively open forest and adjoining croplands are their preferred habitat in the Dindigul Forests of Tamil Nadu and found that such habitat selection is to be associated with agricultural pest abundance. They are also found in a wide elevation gradient and are reported from plain land up to an elevation of about 1,850 m.

Behavioural Biology

Gray slender lorises are primarily arboreal animals and spend most of their life on trees. Their movement is slow, cryptic, non-saltatory and precise, which is considered characteristic of the family Lorisidae. Such slow and silent movements save them from being detected by their predators and also aids in food acquisition, particularly while catching insect prey. Slow movements are also used while moving across open ground between discontinuous forest stretches. However, they can move fast if alarmed and occasionally have also been observed moving quickly, running, as well as, performing short jumps. They generally climb trees by grasping branches strongly with their opposable thumbs and toes and prefer to move along the top branches. They have unique habit of swaying from side to side and make slow chattering noises and utter a low growl when disturbed. Slender loris is able to tolerate high environmental temperature largely due to their ability to increase evaporative cooling.

Gray slender loris is gregarious and maintains social networks with frequent calls throughout the night. Individuals communicate with a range of vocalizations like whistling, growling, screaming and a variety of other noises. They whistle in times of territorial warning, growl to express aggression and scream out of fear. If threatened, slender lorises usually freeze and remain motionless until the danger has passed. If this fails, they will stare at their attacker and growl while emitting an unpleasant odour from scent glands under their arms. Loud calls are also used when potential predators are detected. Rhythmic micturition and urine washing is another important method of social communication. Territorial olfactory marking has been observed as a stress response.

Studies on their daily activity budget revealed that they spend about 45 percent of the day just by sitting, vigilant watching, resting, and sleeping. Besides, a small percentage is spent grooming. During the remaining time they are quite active and spend in foraging or travelling.

Food and Foraging Behaviour: They are solitary, nocturnal feeders and sleep during day, remaining hidden among foliage or in a hole or crevice and start foraging at dusk. Their forward-looking eyes give them an owl like appearance. They have keen low-light vision because of their nocturnal mode of life.

They are omnivorous in nature and depend on insects as their primary food source. Majority of their diet is composed of ants, grasshoppers, and termites. They also consume large variety of noxious and bad smelling insects, beetles, orthopterans and spiders, as well as, hunt on molluscs, tree frogs, lizards, small birds and their eggs.

Prey is detected primarily by vision and a highly developed sense of smell. Once detected, they usually catch their prey using a 'sneak, spring, and grab' method and consume everything including feathers, scales, bones and exoskeleton of their prey. They stalk their prey along a branch, slowly approach and after getting sufficiently close they suddenly crouch and leap and grab prey with their nimble hands. They can stretch and twist their long arms and legs through the branches without alerting their prey. Consumption of toxic species is often accompanied by an elaborate behavioral repertoire including sneezing, head shaking, sucking of the hands and feet, and urine-washing.

They also feed on plant sap, young leaves, shoots, flowers and fruit and are particularly fond of berries of lantana bushes that grow profusely in scrub jungles.

Breeding Behaviour: Females become reproductively mature at 10 months and males at 18 months of age. Grey slender lorises have a polygynandrous mating system. Females mate with multiple males within a single estrous cycle and can mate with multiple males in a row. Males mate with multiple females throughout the year. An estrous female is often pursued by multiple males, who display their interest by increasing grooming frequency and more frequent vocalizations. Males interested in estrous females use more frequent vocalizations while following the desired female. Competition is often noticed between the males trailing a receptive female. These confrontations involve vocalizations such as growling, chittering and whistling. Male-male competition can also be physically violent involving chasing and grappling. Females emit the same noises when chasing away unwanted followers. At the end, the most successful male competitor normally gets the privilege to mate with the female. Depending on the outcomes of male-male competition, different males can mate with the same female consecutively. Studies of captive animals revealed that male ejaculation is associated with male pelvis wiggling and the insertion of a "copulatory plug" into the female that serves to block the mating success of other males. Females have been observed removing and consuming the copulatory plug. A complete sexual encounter often consists of several individual mating intromissions and can last for up to 12 hours (Nekaris, 2003; Radhakrishna and Singh, 2004).

Gray slender lorises were found to breed year round in captivity. But, two distinct mating seasons are noticed in wild—one from April to May and another from October to November. During these mating seasons, the females remain in estrus for a period of 29–40 days. During mating the female hangs from a branch by all four limbs and will completely support the male's weight, in addition to her own. After a gestation period of 166–169 days, the pregnant females give birth to single, occasionally two individuals in the months of May–June. Offspring are born pink, almost furless or with very thin fur and eyes do not open for several weeks. During this period they cling to their mothers. Pregnant females develop four teats, which start producing milk just before the infant is born. Mothers also provide unusually high-energy milk before weaning, which occurs at approximately 5 months of age. Females after giving birth are non-receptive to males and care for their young (Ramaswami, 1965).

Home Range: Adult males and females have individual home ranges, which varies from 11,200–36,000 sq m. Males hold larger home ranges than females. Besides, home ranges of females slightly overlap, while the males have highly overlapping home ranges. Any intrasex overlap in home ranges is usually limited to peripheral range areas, and core areas remain exclusive to one individual. On the other hand, overlapping of male and female home ranges (i.e. intersex range overlap) is common and can include core areas. A single male's home range can overlap with the home ranges of multiple females. Young grey slender lorises usually remain within their mother's home range till they are 10 months old (Radhakrishna and Singh, 2002; 2004).

They have a special way of marking their territory called urine washing. They rub urine over hands, feet and face, probably to soothe and defend against the sting of toxic insects, as well as, to mark their territory when walking.

Social Organization: Slender lorises are solitary nocturnal foragers, though amicable foraging pairs have also been reported. But during daytime they remain in tree branches by clutching nearby twigs with their limbs or sleep in the hollow of trees. They are often found to sleep in social groups of 2–7 individuals, often comprising of an adult female, her offspring and few adult or sub-adult males. A "sleeping ball" congregation is formed when the individuals sleeping together tangle the limbs of each other. The location and composition of these sleeping groups generally remain constant. Sleeping sites are typically located in the central position within the home range of the primary female, generally well protected within cacti or tangled branches. The lorises awaken at dusk groom one another of all ages and sexes and finally emerge from their roost cavities.

In general, social interactions occur between adult males and females, as well as between adults and juveniles, but rarely occur between adults of the same sex. Males and females have social contact within areas with overlapping home ranges. Social interactions are at the peak during dusk and dawn, while they have physical contact by playing, wrestling and grooming each other.

They demonstrate both female parental care and male allocare behaviours. Female parental investment is intensive, but they feed, carry, groom and protect exclusively their own infants. However, in captivity, females have been observed to care for the infants of other females as well. For the first three days after birth the infants are profoundly groomed by their mother. But after this period the infants are only groomed by their mother once it is sought by the infants through distinct vocalization. For the first 4 weeks of life, infants are carried all the time by their mother. Approximately 4 weeks after birth, mothers begin to 'park' her child on a branch at night before leaving to forage and licks it with mild allergenic saliva to discourage predators and rarely return to their infant before dawn (Nekaris, 2003; Radhakrishna and Singh, 2004). Parked infants emit "zic" sounds approximately thirty minutes before dawn to alert the mothers of their location. Adult and sub-adult males often visit parked infants, sometimes grooming or playing with the infants. Such male allocare is common among the gray slender loris. The genetic relationship between visiting males and parked infants is unknown, though the males observed playing with infants are always members of the infant's sleeping group. Males regularly groom both the mother and offspring during infancy. At first, babies move around carefully and by two months of age they manoeuvre around quite well.

Threats to Survival

- ***Poaching:*** Poaching is undoubtedly one of the major threats for the gray slender loris. Poachers, as well as, some native people kill these tiny creatures due to a wrong belief that these animals have magical and medicinal powers. Body parts are illegally sought for traditional medicine, with no proven efficacy (Nekaris and Jayewardene, 2004b).
- ***Pet-trade:*** Gray slender loris are also captured live from the wild and traded as pet to foreigners.
- ***Habitat Loss:*** Destruction and alteration of habitat are other major threats caused specifically by human encroachment. In India, this species is present in small, isolated populations and faces a persistent threat from deforestation. The destruction of primary and secondary forests, the reduction of forest cover, conversion of forests for agriculture and the formation of fragmented forest patches hinders the survival of grey slender loris. *Acacia* trees are often preferred by this loris species (Kumara et al., 2006) and loss of these trees in parts of their habitat is considered as another significant threat to their survival.
- ***Predators:*** Spotted owlets (*Athene brama*) have been noted as one of the potential natural predator of grey slender loris. In addition to this natural predator, domestic cats (*Felis* sp.) and human beings also kill fair number of these tiny primates.
- ***Parasitic infections:*** Some of the parasitic species discovered in *Loris lydekkerianus* include *Giardia wenyoni* in the duodenum, *Trichomonas tardigradi* in the intestine, *Physaloptera masoodi* in the stomach and *Subulura indica* in the appendix.
- ***Superstitious beliefs:*** In various parts of this country, gray slender loris are disliked and often killed due to some irrational beliefs. Some people in western India believe that sighting of these creatures bring bad luck and could lead to lifelong spinsterhood (Kanagavel et al., 2013). Similarly, locals in Karnataka even killed these primates as they were considered being an omen. None of these beliefs have any logical basis and are mere superstitions.
- ***Other threats:*** They are one of the least studied of all primates in India. Previously not much attention has been paid to the plight of this species. Besides, there is no confirmed estimate of the population size of grey slender loris, possibly because it has been difficult to do an accurate count due to their small size and nocturnal habits. Moreover, they have a very restricted distribution in this country and largely occur in private lands and commercial plantations outside designated protected areas.

Conservation Initiatives

Gray slender loris is designated as Least Concern on the IUCN Red List and is incorporated in the Appendix–II of CITES. Considering the high demand in illegal trade, the experts, however, suggested this species to be included in Appendix–I of CITES to prevent any exploitation through both international, as well as, domestic trade. Fortunately laws exist in India to protect this species and it is placed in the Schedule–I (Part 1) of Wildlife (Protection) Act, 1972, according them the highest level of legal protection. The Government of Andhra Pradesh has put in place afforestation schemes and people are encouraged to plant trees preferred by these tiny primates. Besides, WWF-India is working to protect the habitats of gray slender loris in the Western Ghats—Nilgiris landscape. Periodic census of this species is also necessary to evaluate their present status and population trend. A reduction in habitat loss, establishment of corridors between fragmented forest patches, maintaining contiguity of tree cover and greater anti-hunting efforts are essential for the continued survival of this species.

4.9 BROW-ANTLERED DEER (SANGAI)

(*see* Plate II)

Order: Cetartiodactyla
Family: Cervidae
Scientific Name: *Rucervus eldii eldii* (M'Clelland, 1842)

Present Status

Wildlife (Protection) Act, 1972	Schedule–I
IUCN	Endangered
CITES	Appendix–I
Population Trend	↓

Distinctive Features

- Brow-antlered deer is a medium-sized deer measuring 145–155 cm in length from the base of the ear up to the tail in both sexes. But the sexes are moderately dimorphic in body size and weight. The height and weight of a fully grown stag may be approximately 115–125 cm at shoulder and 95–110 kg in weight. The females are shorter and less heavy as compared to the male counterpart.
- *Sangai* males have very unique and distinctive antlers, which they attain in the second year and reach its prime at the age of seven years. The antlers at the base form an almost erect pedicle, thereby diverging from each other. The outline of their horn is almost circular and from the tip of the brow-line upto the antlers, form a continuous curve. This extremely long browline with uniquely set antlers signifies its name, brow-antlered deer. Their forward protruding beam appears to come out from the eyebrow. However, the antlers of the opposite sides are not identical always.
- The coat is coarse and sparse. The males are dark brown or nearly black and the females are lighter. The colour of male is dark brown in winter and fawn in summer, whereas the female is light fawn in colour and the young is spotted.
- It has distinct long hair on its neck.
- They had developed slightly sprayed out hooves and their pasterns are hairless and horny so that they can walk with them on reeds and grasses and not sink through the "*phumdi*".
- Their tail is short and rump patch is not pronounced.
- Their speed and sharp sight are their main defensive features.
- The *sangai* has a maximum lifespan in the wild of around 10 years.

Distribution

This species was once widely distributed across suitable habitats of south and southeast Asia, from the Manipur region of northeastern India through much of Myanmar, Thailand, Lao PDR, Cambodia, and Vietnam upto the island of Hainan (China) in the east (Grubb, 2005). However, presently the population of this deer species is much localized and is restricted to small areas within the species' former range. Taxonomic studies revealed that there are three subspecies of brow-antlered deer (Balakrishnan et al., 2003), of which *Rucervus eldii eldii* is found in India, *Rucervus eldii thamin* in the central plains of Myanmar and western most Thailand and *Rucervus eldii siamensis* are distributed in the lowlands of Cambodia, China, Lao PDR, Thailand (excepting southwestern most regions) and Vietnam (Bhumpakphan et al., 2004; Timmins and Duckworth, 2008).

The subspecies *Rucervus eldii eldii* are endemic to India. In the wild, now a single small population is found confined only in *Keibul Lamjao National Park* at the southern end of *Loktak Lake* in Manipur, India (Singh 2004). It's distribution is located between 24°27′ N and 24°31′ N latitude and 93°53′ E and 93°55′ E longitudes covering an area of only 40 sq km. Out of the 40 sq km in the Keibul Lamjao National Park, the *sangai* is reported to be present over an area of only 9 sq km.

Population

Sangai was thought to be extinct in the early 1950s. But, in 1953 E. P. Gee, the then Honorary Secretary Indian Board for Wildlife (Eastern Region), counted six *Sangai* in their natural habitat during a survey conducted under the auspices of the IUCN and thus was subsequently rediscovered (Gee, 1961). In 1975, only 14 animals were found to thrive in the swamps of Loktak Lake (Ranjitsinh, 1978). Recent census in 2013 revealed 204 brow-antlered deer including 90 stags,

86 hinds and 28 fawns in the Keibul Lamjao National Park. However, Wildlife Institute of India believes the number of deer to be much less.

Habitat

Earlier the subspecies *Rucervus eldii eldii* would also have occupied drier plains elsewhere in north-east India (Pocock, 1943). However, presently brow-antlered deer in India exclusively inhabits an area of floating vegetations of the Loktak Lake inside the Keibul Lamjao National Park (Singh, 2004). Such islands of the floating mass of entangled vegetations are locally called *"phumdi"*, which constitute the most important and unique part of the habitat of *Sangai*. *Phumdi* is usually formed by the accumulation of organic debris and biomass with soil. It floats with 4/5 part under water and the total thickness varies from few centimetre to around two metres. The humus of *phumdi* is black in colour and very spongy with large number of pores. The vegetation of *phumdi* also provides shelter to the deer, along with other wildlife in the park. They are thought to move from the *phumdi* to island hillocks only during periods of flooding.

Behavioural Biology

They are reported to be seen mostly in the early morning and late evening. They sometimes dance round and round with heads up and heads down. *Rucervus eldii eldii* is mainly nocturnal and crepuscular and are reported to have both daily and seasonal migrations. These movements are largely influenced by breeding seasons and on the availability of food and water in various seasons.

Food and Foraging Behaviour: *Rucervus eldii eldii* is herbivorous in nature and known to graze and browse opportunistically on a variety of aquatic plants, grasses, herbaceous plants, shoots and wild fruits. They feed mainly on the grasses sprouting on *phumdis*, leaves and fallen fruits. Their favourite food plants include *Zizania latifolia*, *Saccharum munja*, *S. bengalensis*, *S. latifolium*, *Erianthus procerus*, *E. ravernnae* etc. They also occasionally raid cultivated lands and feed on crops grown in the fields adjacent to their habitat in the fringes of the forest. A few commonly eaten crops are rice, lentils, maize, peas etc. Reportedly they can live without water for several days but regularly visit salt licks.

They exhibit a bimodial activity pattern. *Sangai* usually comes out for feeding in the dawn and generally continue grazing up to 8:00 am, which even extend up to 10:00 am on a cloudy morning. After feeding, it takes rest during the day time and again forage in the afternoon between 3:00 pm and 6:00 pm. There is no conflict among the deer population during foraging.

Breeding Behaviour: Brow-antlered deer breeds only once a year. Early spring months between February and May are reported to be their rutting season. During the rutting season, the stags (males) put grass on their antlers to impress the doe (females). Males get extremely restless at the onset of breeding season and compete with each other to gain control of a harem of females with whom they can mate. In the wild, the restlessness reaches such a degree that it can get into fight with anyone willing to compete with him for his chosen partner. This aggression can sometimes lead to fatal wounds. The gestation period lasts for around 240 days and calving occurs from mid-October to the end of December (Timmins and Duckworth, 2008). Usually one fawn is born. The young are spotted at birth and gradually fade as the animal grows. The young are weaned between five and seven months of age and becomes sexually mature from 18 months of age onwards (Wemmer and Grodinsky, 1988). Females become reproductively matured at the age of two years and may reproduce till the age of ten years. No unique parental care is recorded. However, the newly born fawns often latch on to their mothers for safety and comfort. The stags shed their antlers during late June.

Home Range: The home ranges of brow-antlered deers are reported to vary from 3.8–14.71 sq km. But, inside the Keibul Lamjao National Park their home ranges has been estimated to be within 15–20 sq km.

Social Organization: During most of the year, the males tend to lead a solitary life except during the rutting season in the spring and are not territorial in nature. Females, on the other hand, tend to remain in close association with their fawns. Such female-fawn pairs and even large groups consisting of two to twenty animals are often formed. Males only join this group of females with the onset of the breeding season.

Threats to Survival

- ***Habitat loss:*** Loss of habitat is one of the major threats for the brow-antlered deer. Large portion of the habitats of these deer have been encroached for grazing, cultivation and fish farming. Siltation, burning of grass and encroachment for human settlements are some other factors leading to their habitat loss.
- ***Habitat degradation:*** Their existing habitat is also degenerating steadily due to continuous high water level caused by the artificial reservoir of the Loktak hydroelectric power project and subsequently construction of Ithai Barrage in 1986. Thereafter, unnaturally high water level is maintained in the Loktak Lake which had not only changed the water quality, water flow patterns and hydrology of the lake (Singh, 2004), but has also disturbed the natural cycle of the vegetation growth of the *phumdis* upon which

the *sangai* thrives. *Phumdi* usually floats on the water surface during the season of high water (as in the monsoons), comes into contact with the lake bed as the water level reduces in the lean phase and again floats as the water level rise in the rainy season. While attached to the bottom of the lake the vegetation on the *phumdi* absorbs the required nutrient, increases in biomass and stores enough nutrients to live while afloat. But, with continuous high water level the *phumdis* cannot come in contact with the lake bed and thus, nutrient uptake process is discontinued. This results in the depletion of nutrient and biomass of the *phumdis* and they gradually become thinner and eventually break into pieces. A large chunk of the biomass in the northern part of national park had broken up into pieces and had drifted freely from the park area in January, 1999. As the *phumdis* become thin and brittle, they cannot sustain the weight of *Sangai.* So, the deer often drown while moving over certain parts of the *phumdis.* Within the park's 40 sq km, only 23 sq km of *phumdi* can sustain the weight of the deer (Banerjee, 2015). This has, in turn, restricted the mobility of the species over their preferred habitat patches, leading to high degree of inbreeding. As *Sangai* utilizes a limited area intensively, so the carrying capacity of the park is further reduced. In addition, local people are also reported to illegally collect fodder, fuel wood, vegetables and even cut the *phumdi* into sizable pieces and sell to fish culture owners. Pollution and deterioration of water quality of Loktak Lake is another problem leading to the degradation of these deer habitat.

- ***Frequent inundation:*** High water level also leads to flooding and inundation of the *phumdis.* Frequent floods could seriously affect the population of *Sangai*, as they often do not have any high ground to easily escape (Singh, 2004).
- ***Invasive species:*** Spread of invasive grass species is another threat for *Sangai.* Exotic para grass was introduced on a large scale in 1972–73 to support dairy development, which has spread widely and has become the dominant species in many parts of *phumdis*.
- ***Poaching and illegal wildlife trade:*** These animals were previously hunted as game animals and were used as a food source. They were prized as a game animal particularly because of their antlers and hides. The skin and antlers of brow-antlered deer is still reported in illegal wildlife trade. They have also been used as "traditional" medicinal products and are poached for this purpose.
- ***Human-sangai conflict:*** Brow-antlered deer are also reported to graze on the agricultural fields adjoining their habitat, which result in human-*sangai* conflicts. Although, their present populations seems to be too low for some serious conflict, yet this can be a potential threat in future if populations become large in areas close to agriculture (Timmins and Duckworth, 2008).
- ***Demographic threats:*** Small populations, such as this Manipur brow-antlered deer, are always vulnerable to both demographic and genetic problems. Genetic diversity of the present population is quite low as they have originated from a very small founder population (Balakrishnan, et al., 2003). Such single isolated population often inbreeds, which leads to further loss of genetic diversity of the animal affecting its vitality, vigor and survival of the newborn, as well as, the fertility of the individual animals.
- ***Disease:*** Tuberculosis, hepatic and enteric disorders, worms in the stomach and vitamin deficiencies are also noticed in brow-antlered deers. This small isolated population is also at greater risk to suffer from the diseases transferred from the domestic livestock.
- ***Other threats:*** Inadequate infrastructure, few trained wildlife staff, absence of proper veterinary care unit of the Keibul Lamjao National Park restrain the proper protection of brow-antlered deer inside this protected area. Confrontations between park staff and villagers on the issues of resource extraction, grazing and encroachment are frequently noticed as the Keibul Lamjao National Park is surrounded by several fish farms without clear demarcation of the park boundaries (Banerjee, 2015). Finally, lack of sense of pride for *sangai* among the local peoples and poor socio-economic condition of people living around the park get in the way of the present conservation initiatives.

Conservation Initiatives

This animal is presently categorized as Endangered by the IUCN, as very few individuals exist in the wild. The species has also been listed under Appendix–I of CITES which prevents any part of it being traded. Realizing the threats of extinction, these animals are accorded with the highest degree of legal protection in this country and are placed under Schedule–I under the Wildlife (Protection) Act, 1972. Hence, killing and harming this species is subject to stringent punishment in the form of imprisonment or fine or both.

Sangai is revered very dearly by the Manipur society and is deeply embedded into the legends and folklore of the Manipuris. *Sangai* is interpreted as the binding soul between humans and nature. Hence, slaying of the *sangai* is considered as an unpardonable sin. This love and reverence had helped these deer to survive in the past. Still, they became extinct in year 1951 and two years later this species was rediscovered by noted naturalist E. P Gee in 1953 (Gee, 1961).

Since then initiatives were taken to conserve this species in its natural habitat. Major habitat of *Sangai*, an area of 40 sq km in the southeastern part of the Loktak lake was declared as Keibul Lamjao National Park by the State Government of Manipur (vide notification No. 60/20/75-For dated 28/3/1977) to protect this flagship species and other associated wildlife under the provisions of Wildlife (Protection) Act, 1972. Status surveys of *R. eldii eldii* have been carried out annually in Keibul Lamjao National Park since 1975 (Singh, 2004). WWF-India has recently suggested the camera-trap method to monitor this deer species.

Loktak Lake has also been declared as a Ramsar site, a wetland of international significance and the Loktak Development Authority has been formed. Recently, reintroduction of wild *Sangai* to other suitable alternative sites was undertaken, but mostly within the state of Manipur. In the first phase of the programme, a rescue centre was constructed at KLNP to take care of injured deers. Subsequently, the captured *Sangai* will be observed in the rescue centre and finally reintroduce them in suitable sites. The proposed reintroduction sites for *Sangai* are—Langol reserve forest (Imphal West District), Sambei reserve forest (Imphal East District), Heingang reserve forest (Imphal West District), Pumlenpat and adjoining Thongam mondum hillock (Thoubal District), Kailam wildlife sanctuary (Churchandpur District), Yangoupokpi lokchao wildlife sanctuary (Chandel District), Ikoppat (Thoubal District) and Nongmaijing reserve forest (Imphal East District). Preliminary surveys have also been carried out in all the proposed sites except Kailam wildlife sanctuary and Yangoupokpi Lokchao wildlife sanctuary. *Ex-situ* Conservation of Manipur Brow-antlered Deer involves the practice of gene exchange of the wild and captive organisms by means of assisted reproduction. Captive population of *Rucervus eldii eldii* in this country comprised of 107 animals in 1994 (Sharma, 1994), which increased over the years and in 2003 there were 180 animals present in captivity (Timmins and Duckworth, 2008).

In addition to these, two national level consultative meetings and workshops have been organized, one by WWF-India in New Delhi and another by the Institute of Bioresources and Sustainable Development (IBSD) in Imphal, to discuss conservation and sustainable management of this species. At the Imphal workshop, experts proposed a *Sangai*-centric conservation programme, which should include formation of a task force, with various stakeholders, including local communities that live around the sanctuary.

Several other initiatives were taken at various administrative levels to increase mass awareness and to garner local support to conserve the endemic subspecies of brow-antlered deer in Manipur. As a part of such initiatives *sangai* was declared as the state animal of Manipur (Vide Govt. of Manipur order No 60/5/86-For (pt) Dated 21/3/89). In the Fifth National Game held at Imphal in 1999 *Sangai* was named as "Ningthem", which means "beloved son". Since 2010, the State Level Tourism Festival organized by the Tourism Department of Manipur has been named as "Sangai Festival". Despite of being such an integral part of the socio-cultural and economic life of the Manipuri people, the deer is still mired with various problems. It would rather be shameful for Manipur to lose its state emblem.

4.10 HIMALAYAN MUSK DEER (*see* Plate II)

Order: Cetartiodactyla
Family: Moschidae
Scientific Name: *Moschus* spp. (Hodgson, 1839)

There are two species of Musk deer found in India *viz. Moschus leucogaster* and *Moschus chrysogaster*, which are separated on the basis of different skull proportions and appearance of their throat (Groves and Grubb, 1987; Groves et al., 1995). Both these species are found in India, but they are distributed in different parts of Himalayan region. It is to be noted that, *Moschus leucogaster* was once considered the same species as *Moschus chrysogaster*, as both species have similar life history traits and characteristics (Plummer 2011). *Moschus leucogaster* is sometimes also treated as a Himalayan subspecies of Alpine Musk Deer *M. chrysogaster* (Grubb 1990).

Present Status

Wildlife (Protection) Act, 1972	Schedule–I
IUCN	Endangered
CITES	Appendix–I
Population Trend	↓

Distinctive Features

- Himalayan musk deer is a small deer, about 60 cm tall with a shoulder height of about 20 cm and weight between 13–18 kg. Distinct white stripes or a white patch is present in *Moschus chrysogaster*, while such white markings of throat (if at all present) is very much indistinct in *Moschus leucogaster* (Groves, et al., 1995; Wilson and Reeder, 2005). Nevertheless, it is very difficult to distinguish one species from another by sight in field conditions (Plummer 2011).

- The rear part of the body is more powerfully built and elevated than the forequarters. Hind legs are long and well muscled. Forelegs are shorter and weak and their rump is almost 10 cm higher than their shoulder. Hence, the body slopes forward and the back is curved. Therefore, musk deers show a distinctive jumping and galloping movement like kangaroo.
- Both sexes have well-developed characteristic upper canines. In males the upper canines are enlarged, 7-10 cm long, extend below the upper lip and are visible even when the mouth is closed. These sabre-like upper canines are used in displays and fights between rivals. These canines constantly grow, but due to their mobility and fragility, are also often broken. The dental formula is similar to that of true deer: $\dfrac{0-1-3-3}{3-1-3-3}$
- The musk pod is located only in males, which is an externally visible sac in between its reproductive organs (genitalia) and umbilicus (Shrestha, 1989). Musk pod exudes a strong smelling, dark brown semi fluid substance for attraction of females during the onset of rut. Fresh musk gland secretion has an unpleasant, pungent, urinary smell, but after becoming dry it acquires the scent of musk. The active chemical substance in musk is known as muscone and finds use in perfumes or in medicines or as aphrodisiacs and fertility drugs (Shrestha, 1997). The musk secreted from the musk pods is of highest quality during mating season (December-January).
- They are unique in having gall bladder, which no other deer possess.
- Body coat possesses long brittle hair, rich dark brown in colour and speckled with white on the flanks and white stocking legs. Age related changes in hair coats and colour could be noticed. Newborns possess dark brown coat with short and soft hair densely covered with yellowish or white spots. In winter, spots become less pronounced.
- A wide vertical whitish-yellow stripe on the chest extends till throat, even upto their chin. Several horizontal blotches of yellowish hair are present on the nape of the neck.
- Musk deers do not possess antlers.
- They have long and rounded "hare-like" ears, generally lined with whitish fur. The ears are tipped with yellow or orange hair.
- Tail is short (4–6 cm) and hairless, except for a small tuft of hair at the end. Tail is completely buried under the long hairs present in their anal region.
- The average lifespan of musk deer is 12–20 years in captivity.

Distribution

Himalayan musk deer range over a wide geographical area on the eastern and southern edge of Tibet and throughout the southern slope of Himalayas, particularly within the countries of Bhutan, India, Nepal, and a small part of China. This species is usually found at elevations of 2,000–5,000 m.

In India, musk deers are found in Jammu & Kashmir, Himachal Pradesh, Uttar Pradesh, Uttaranchal, Sikkim and Arunachal Pradesh. Its altitudinal range extends from about 2,400 m to above the tree line, which varies from about 3,200 m in the Western Himalaya to 4,200 m in the eastern Himalaya. The species is more common in the eastern Himalayas because the habitat of the animals is less disturbed there (Green, 1987).

Population

Due to solitary nature and nocturnal habits, population monitoring of Himalayan musk deer is very difficult in forest habitats and has rarely been done satisfactorily. Systematic counts have been carried out only in very few locations of their distribution range. Count data in selected areas is then extrapolated to larger distribution ranges of these deer to obtain a rough population estimate. The overall population of all musk deer species may be estimated to be between 4,00,000 and 8,00,000 individuals (Aryal, 2005).

Habitat

Himalayan musk deer are found in both alpine and forest belt and prefer rugged terrains with rocky outcrops in moderate to steep slopes (Green and Kattel, 1998). Such rock outcrops provide them shelter from predators. They primarily inhabit the dense, shrubby, forest undergrowth in middle altitudes of montane taiga (usually not found above 1,600 m). In winter, they are attracted to relatively steep slopes covered with coniferous forests. In summer, they spend most of their time in riverine forest valleys, around streams and near fields with good grassy vegetation. In the Himalaya, they prefer forest and scrubland at elevations of about 2,000–4,400 m (Whitehead, 1993) dominated by birch, rhododendron, blue pine, fir, oak, juniper, grass, lichens and shrubs (Green, 1987).

Behavioural Biology

Himalayan musk deer is a shy, secretive and nocturnal animal (Sathyakumar et al., 1993). They are sedentary and usually remain within a defined home range throughout the year. They alternately rest and forage throughout the period between dusk and dawn and are most active at twilight.

At night, musk deer can be seen in the open areas of their habitat as they graze, while during the day, they remain in dense cover.

Males have well developed musk glands, which releases a scent in their urine. They 'scent mark' their territory by rubbing the caudal gland (located at the base of their tail) and interdigital glands against plants, which leave a greasy smear on the plant (Green, 1985). Such scent marking is not only used for territorial marking by animals, but also expresses the status of the individual and most importantly used to attract a mate. This helps the females to know about their potential reproductive partners.

Neighbouring individuals of *M. chrysogaster* are reported to defecate (but never urinate) at a fixed spot, which consist of piles of droppings and is regarded as their "common latrine". As opposed to simple boundary markers, these are possibly the communication centers where information on neighbouring musk deer is available (Green and Kattel, 1998). Despite of their keen hearing and vision, mode of communication among musk deer is chiefly through olfaction. Such communication through olfaction and development of acute smell is quite unique amongst the small forest ruminants and is well suited to the dense nature of the habitat. Because, making too much of sound would directly compromise the predator avoidance strategy adopted by them. Therefore, Himalayan musk deer mostly remain silent in their habitat. However, they depend on its sense of hearing to locate sources of danger. They are wary of human beings and are easily alarmed. When frightened, they make broad leaps, make drastic changes in direction and usually stop and listen after every few jumps. They emit a loud double hiss when alarmed and scream plaintively if wounded.

Food and Foraging Behaviour: Himalayan musk deer is a ruminant herbivore (Sathyakumar et al., 1993). They feed on different types of herbs, woody plants, leaves, flowers, twigs and shoots of various trees and shrubs, as well as, grasses, herbs, mosses, ferns and lichens available in their habitat (Green and Kattel, 1998). Over 130 plant species are consumed by musk deer and easily digestible nutritious foods that are high in energy content, rich in protein and low in fibre are often preferred (Green, 1987). They usually consume a high quality diet during summer, which is an essential strategy to survive under extremely harsh climatic conditions in winter (Snider and Asplund, 1974). During winter most of their habitat is covered with snow. Hence, their winter diets mainly comprise of lichens *Usnea* spp. which, although are low in proteins, yet are easily digested and are also very high in energy (Negi, 1996). Terrestrial bushy lichens have been reported to constitute 70 percent of their diet in winter. Arboreal lichens and evergreen rhododendrons sometime serve as the only food available for musk deer, especially in areas where the snow is deep. Musk deer can climb into trees to graze on lichens and leaves otherwise out of reach. Although musk deer largely rely on wild plants, they are also reported to occasionally forage on high-altitude agricultural lands in their habitat. They also prefer juicy fruits like wild apple, pear, white melon, etc. They drink 2–6 times daily depending upon the season and take 50-60 ml water per intake (Joshi et al., 1993).

Breeding Behaviour: December to January has been reported to be the mating season of Himalayan musk deer which varies depending on area, altitude and region (Shrestha, 1989). The females remain in estrous for 3–4 weeks. Soon after the first snow fall in November, females start to exhibit the sign of heat. During the mating season, males secrete concentrated urine with musk, which appears dark pink or red on snow. Approximately at the age of 2.5 years the male is capable of performing more than three copulations a day, one cycle of copulation takes 5–10 minutes (Tewari and Singh, 2000). During the rutting season in winter, male deers fight each other for the receptive female and during the process inflict deep cuts on rivals with their long canines.

Gestation period is about 185–195 days. Musk deer usually gives birth to one offspring (Nowak, 1999) between May and June at selected places *viz.* beneath dense shrubs, under low branches of fir, around fallen trees etc. The young deers lie hidden in secluded areas concealed in the undergrowth for a period of one or two months and are 'nursed offspring' suckled by their mothers. At the age of about two months they begin to follow their mothers and are weaned. The young grow rapidly, become independent of their mothers by the age of six months. Female fawns are believed to grow quickly, become sexually mature at 18 months of age (Green and Kattel, 1998) and are capable of breeding in their first year (Green, 1989). But the males attain sexual maturity after 2–3 years of age.

Home Range: They are sedentary and usually remain within a defined home range throughout the year. However, size of their home ranges greatly vary (0.15–0.32 sq km). Studies in northern India revealed that in areas with low population density the home ranges did not overlap as much as when the densities were high (Green and Kattel, 1998).

Social Organization: Himalayan musk deer are solitary animals and hence their social organization is not very prominent. However, at times they are also seen in groups of 2–3 individuals, which are more often the females and calves moving together. The adult males usually move alone. Being highly territorial, the males actively defend a territory against intrusion by rival males and may allow the females within, whereas the female territories often overlap (Green and Kattel, 1998).

Threats to Survival

In the wild, musk deers also suffer from various natural threats. Some are killed by predators and some die in natural disasters like forest fires, landslides, etc. The main predators of musk deers are snow leopard (*Panthera uncia*), leopard cat (*Prionailurus bengalensis*), fox (*Vulpes vulpes*), wolf (*Canis lupus*), Lynx (*Lynx lynx*), yellow-throated marten (*Martes flavigula*), etc. (Rajchal, 2006). Despite the fact that their meat is not considered tasty and the skin is not valuable as the hairs fall out easily, still musk deer have been hunted for thousands of years (Homes, 1999). However, there are reports that their meat is considered as local delicacy in some parts of their distribution range (Timmins and Duckworth, 2015). The two major threats to populations of musk deer are: (i) loss of habitat (Green, 1986; Yang et al., 1989; Green and Kattel, 1997) and (ii) poaching (Wemmer, 1998; Green, 1986; Jackson, 1979) of musk deer for illegal trade of musk (Green, 1986; Homes, 1999). Himalayan musk deers are now confined to small fragmented populations due to large scale degradation of their forested habitats for timber trade, non-timber forest produce collection, as well as, due to expansion of agriculture and human settlements. Increased livestock grazing within their habitat deplete resources for these deers and put them in competition with existing resources, and also make them susceptible to the risk of disease transmission (Aryal et al., 2010). Sathyakumar et. al. (1993) have reported that increased livestock grazing and associated impacts have led to low musk deer densities in many areas in Kedarnath Wildlife Sanctuary, India. The musk secreted by the musk gland of the males has been used in the perfume industries for a long time for its intensity, persistence and fixative properties. Musk is highly valued for its cosmetic and suspected pharmaceutical properties and can fetch US $ 45,000 per kg in international market. Official trade figures of Japan indicated that 215-300 kg of raw musk were imported to Japan from China annually from 1981 to 1985 (Green, 1989). In addition, studies carried out by TRAFFIC-Japan revealed that 1154.4 kg of musk was illegally imported to Japan via Hong Kong between 1979 and 1985 (Sheng, 1992). Large scale poaching and illegal trade of musk has been recorded in Uttarakhand (Ilyas, 2014).

Conservation Initiatives

Due to high levels of international trade in parts and products derived from musk deer, all musk deer species (*Moschus* spp.) have been included in the Appendices of the CITES in 1979. Himalayan musk deer is listed on CITES Appendix II in China, and on Appendix I in the other countries within its range, thereby safeguarding this species from international trade. It is listed as Endangered (EN) by IUCN Red List of threatened species. Considering the degree of threats to its survival it is placed in the Schedule – I of Wildlife (Protection) Act, 1972. Several protected areas have also been declared within its distribution range. As a part of the ex-situ conservation of this species, captive populations are kept in Himachal Pradesh Musk Deer Farm (Kufri), Dachigram Sanctuary (Kashmir), Padmaja Naidu Himalayan Zoological Park (Darjeeling) and breeding enclosures at Kedarnath Wildlife Sanctuary. Breeding of Musk Deer and extraction of musk are done at Kufri. Sanctuaries and national parks on its distribution range protect its habitat. In order to conserve musk deer and its habitat, local people of musk deer distribution range also need to be encouraged for cash crop cultivation, scientific animal husbandry and tourism, so that they depend less on forest resources for their subsistence. Introduction of synthetic products allied to musk has reduced demand of natural product to a great extent. Finally, prohibition of international trade by increasing vigilance on smuggling, encouraging the in-situ conservation, promoting education and research on this dwindling species and above all mass awareness campaign may be a few initiatives for better conservation of this species.

4.11 BLACKBUCK OR INDIAN ANTILOPE (*see* Plate II)

Order: Cetartiodactyla
Family: Bovidae
Scientific Name: *Antilope cervicapra* (Linnaeus, 1758)

Blackbuck or Indian antelope (*Antelope cervicapra*) is endemic to the Indian subcontinent. Four subspecies of blackbuck are found in India *viz.* *Antelope cervicapra centralis* in central India, *Antelope cervicapra rajputani* in western India, *Antelope cervicapra rupicapra* in south India and *Antelope cervicapra cervicapra* in north India.

Present Status

Wildlife (Protection) Act, 1972	Schedule–I
IUCN	Near Threatened
CITES	Appendix–III (Nepal, Pakistan)
Population Trend	➡

Distinctive Features

- Blackbuck is a slender, medium sized antelope which stands about 80 cm at the shoulder. Their head and body length lies between 120–130 cm. and they weigh around 32–43 kg.
- Sexual dimorphism is prominent and the genders in the blackbuck are readily distinguishable. Although the coat colour of juvenile males are

brown and without horns, but the mature males have horns along with an almost elegant black (or blackish brown) coat. On the contrary, the young and females are without horns and the colour of the body coat is light yellow. Moreover, males also possess pronounced post orbital glands which exude a pungent sticky secretion. Males are often larger than females.

- Ventral region, belly, inside of the legs, the lower third of each flank, the chin, a patch around the eyes and inner side of the ears of both males and females are white or pale white.
- The horns in males are permanent, unbranched and never shed like deer's antler. The pair of cylindrical, ringed and spiral (corkscrew) horns is gracefully built and diverges on each side of head. Rings present on their horns are closely set near the skull and the turns of spiral vary from less than 3–5. The average length of the horns is 50 cm.
- They possess a short tail which is about 17–18 cm in length.
- Their average lifespan is about 12 years.

Distribution

Blackbucks are native species of India. They were earlier present throughout the Indian subcontinent. and were once found in India, Pakistan, Nepal and Bangladesh. At present, blackbucks are irregular vagrants in Pakistan and are reported to occur along the Indian border areas. In Nepal, the last surviving population of blackbuck is found inside the protected area south of the Bardia National Park. But, they are supposed to be extinct in Bangladesh and Pakistan (Mallon and Kingswood, 2001; Mallon, 2008). Besides, some introduced populations thrive in Argentina and United States (Mallon, 2008).

In India, blackbucks were widely distributed in the open plains from the foothills of the Himalayas in the north to Cape Comorin in south, and from Punjab in the west to lower Assam in the east at the beginning of the nineteenth century. Presently, blackbucks occur throughout the Indian plains (except the northeast and the Malabar coast) and their population is confined to some areas in Maharashtra, Orissa, Punjab, Rajasthan, Haryana, Gujarat, Andhra Pradesh, Tamil Nadu and Karnataka, with a few small pockets in central India. Chilika Lake in Orissa is their eastern limit of distribution and in the south they are distributed till Point Calimere, Tamil Nadu. They are distributed in several protected areas of India including: Velavadar National Park, Point Calimere Wildlife and Bird Sanctuary, Tal Chhapar Sanctuary, National Chambal Sanctuary, Keoladeo National Park, Ranebennur Wildlife Sanctuary, Great Indian Bustard Sanctuary, Kaimur Wildlife Sanctuary, Gir Forest National Park, Guindy National Park, Ranthambhore National Park, Sorsan Blackbuck Conservation Reserve, Shergarh Sanctuary, Vallanadu Blackbuck Sanctuary, (Mallon and Kingswood, 2001; Bagchi et al., 2003; Isvaran 2007; Singh and Gibson, 2011).

Population

Earlier the herds of blackbuck comprised of several thousand animals of both sexes and all ages. 22,500 to 24,500 blackbucks were reported to be thriving in this country in 1982 (Ranjitsinh, 1989). With conservation efforts, their number increased and is presently estimated to be around 50,000 individuals (Mallon, 2008). Velavadar National Park is considered to be a stronghold of blackbuck in this country where the population comprised of about 1,500 individuals in the mid-1990s (Jhala, 1997). The largest numbers are found in the states of Rajasthan, Punjab, Madhya Pradesh, Maharashtra and Gujurat (Rahmani, 2001).

Habitat

Blackbucks are often found in open plains and are less frequently noticed in dense jungles. They usually prefer open woodlands and flat open ground covered with intermittent tall grasses, bushes and scrubs. They avoid dense forests and hilly tracts. In such open plains, these animals are one of the fastest animals, can run over long distances and can often outrun most of their predators. They require water daily, which restricts their distribution to areas where surface water is available almost throughout the year.

Behavioural Ecology

Blackbucks are diurnal animals. During winter season they are noticed to be intermittently active throughout the hours of daylight. However, in summer months they restrict their foraging and other activities in the early morning and late afternoon and spend mostly under shade of trees and bushes during the hottest part of the day to avoid excessive heat and scorching sun. Blackbucks are primarily grazers and mainly sedentary. But, in summer they often move long distances in search of water and food (Rahmani, 2001).

Blackbucks are very shy, wary and are usually silent. Their sense of smell and hearing are not highly developed so they rely on eyesight in detecting danger. In the herd, the females are often more alert. Hence, once a potential threat is noticed the alert females usually first gives the alarm call by making a hissing noise that warns the herd of danger. Then one individual leaps into the air and it is soon followed by the rest of the herd. These animals move with great speed and exhibit high endurance. Blackbucks have been recorded to move at a speed of more than 80 km/h and can reach upto a speed of 100–140 km per hour. When alarmed, it moves off in a series of leaps and jumps. Once out of danger, the herd reduces its pace to a normal gallop.

Food and Foraging Behaviour: Blackbucks are primarily grazers. They largely feed on grasses, weak-stemmed plants, fruits, fresh tender leaves, buds, as well as, on various crops, cereals, vegetables and cultivated plants. In addition to these, they have occasionally been observed browsing on *Acacia* trees (Mallon and Kingswood, 2001), as well as, were observed feeding on pods of *Prosopis juliflora* (Jhala, 1997).

They particularly forage on succulent grasses, tender shoots of crops and plants. The fluid contained in these plant parts helps them to maintain water balance in their bodies. They consume very little amount of water and can survive without drinking water for a day to week. They do not drink water even when it is available and can recirculate the nitrogenous wastes in their bodies rather than immediately having to excrete them in their urine. This is a unique mode of conserving water through recirculation, which has helped them to adapt in the dry and xeric conditions of their habitat.

Breeding Behaviour: Blackbucks attain sexual maturity at the age of 1.5–2 years. They may breed throughout the year, but rutting mainly takes place between February to May. During the rut, the mature males establish a territory by regularly depositing faeces at particular points. Males are extremely aggressive during this time and drive all other males from their territory by a throaty grunt and an occasional horn fight. The gestation period is about six months after which the female usually give birth to single offspring. The newborn is able to run soon after birth.

Home Range: During the breeding season males become highly territorial, defending an area usually ranging in size from 0.01-0.17 sq.km. They vigorously protect their territories from rival males and attempt to keep the largest group of females within one's own territory for the longest period of time.

Social Organization: Blackbucks in the wild are usually seen in herds of 10–30 or even over 100 individuals. Four distinct types of herds are noticed among the blackbucks.

- **Mixed herd** formed with 5–50 animals, generally comprise of three or fewer males, many females of different age groups, as well as their offspring.
- **Harem herd** or **territorial herd** with one territorial male and a number of adult females of all age groups.
- **Bachelor herd** of all male members.
- **All female herd** comprising of only female blackbucks

Besides, there are lone wandering adult males too. Mixed herds and Harem herds usually have a master buck, which is the dominant male. Dominance among males within a herd is achieved primarily with posturing and threatening gestures. Fights with the sharp horns are rare and only take place if the dominance is not settled by such ritualized gestures.

Threats to Survival

- ***Hunting and poaching:*** Until independence in 1947, blackbucks were prized for their flesh and skin. Considered as a sporting trophy, blackbucks were then regularly hunted in many princely states with specially trained captive Asiatic cheetahs. But, even after the complete ban imposed on hunting of blackbuck through Wildlife (Protection) Act in 1972, occasional incidents of poaching still takes place in the arid region of Rajasthan. Hunting tribes (like *Bhils* or *Sanshi*, *Bawariya*, etc.) were occasionally involved in killing of blackbuck for their meat.
- ***Habitat loss:*** Large areas of the natural habitat of the blackbuck are regularly being encroached for various anthropogenic activities, *viz.* expansion of agriculture, construction of roads and other infrastructures, mining activities, as well as, increased grazing and introduction of exotic plants in the blackbuck habitat.

  1. **Developmental activities:** Decimation of its population has been accelerated due to rapid agro–industrial development in its preferred habitat throughout the country (Schaller, 1967). Besides, road expansion in their habitat are resulting in increased number of blackbuck deaths in road accidents.
  2. **Encroachment and overgrazing:** There has been a tremendous increase in agricultural activities in earlier uncultivated lands present in the arid blackbuck habitats of this country. Subsequently, human habitations have also spread far and wide. This has resulted in gradual encroachment on the natural habitats of blackbucks by human. Besides, arid region has a very high number of livestock populations including sheep, goat, cow and buffalo which are fully dependant on scrub land where blackbuck exists.
  3. **Mining:** Mining is another major threat that destroys many blackbuck habitats in this country.
  4. **Exotic plants:** Introduction of non-edible, exotic grass species and destruction of native wild plants, grass and herbs without realizing their role in sustaining a species like blackbuck is another major threat.

- ***Predation:*** Earlier Asiatic cheetah was the main predator of blackbucks. Besides, the blackbucks, particularly the fawns, are predated by wolf, hyena, jungle cat, jackal, pythons, etc. They also occasionally fall prey to large predators like leopards and tigers. But, in most of its distribution range the number of their natural predators is often very less. Presently feral dogs are the main predators of blackbuck. The feral dogs live in groups and encircle the blackbuck strategically to prey upon it.
- ***Water scarcity:*** Blackbucks regularly visit to water holes present in their habitat to drink, either once or twice depending on ambient temperature in Rajasthan. But no permanent water body is present in blackbuck habitats of *Thar* region. This lack of water was reported to result in death of many blackbucks in western Rajasthan, particularly during hot summer season.
- ***Diseases:*** Close association and frequent exposure to the livestock, also exposes blackbucks to various bovine diseases.
- ***Inbreeding:*** The remaining populations of blackbucks are small and fragmented. Such small populations, therefore, are always under threat of inbreeding.
- ***Blackbuck-Human Conflict:*** Blackbucks are in constant conflict with the farmers, as they wander out of the reserve and often enter croplands in search of food and water. Farmers of the expanding areas of cultivation consider blackbucks as crop-raiders. They sometimes set traps to catch blackbuck or drive them away from farms. Some agricultural lands (or orchards) use electrical fencing that restricts free movement of blackbucks. These electric fences either drive them away from crop fields or even sometimes kill them.

Conservation Initiatives

Though it is locally common, IUCN has listed this antelope as Near Threatened considering its global population status and present threats. It is also placed in the Schedule–I of Wildlife (Protection) Act, 1972. Thus, hunting of blackbucks is prohibited in India. Several protected areas have been declared within its habitat to protect this species as well as to safeguard its habitat. Blackbucks are protected in Abohar Wildlife Sanctuary (Punjab), Indian Wild Ass Sanctuary (Gujarat), Bagdara Wildlife Sanctuary (Madhya Pradesh), Kanha National Park (Madhya Pradesh), Karopani Black Buck Conservation Area (Madhya Pradesh), Jayamangali Blackbuck Reserve (Karnataka), Mahavir Harina Vanasthali National Park (Andhra Pradesh), Rehakuri Sanctuary (Maharashtra), Sathyamangalam Wildlife Sanctuary (Tamil Nadu), Vallanad Blackbuck Sanctuary (Tamil Nadu). Punjab and Haryana honour it as their state animal.

In Hindu mythology, blackbuck is considered as the vehicle (*vahana*) of the Moon-god *Chandrama* and according to the *Garuda Purana* these animals bestow prosperity in the areas where they live. Blackbucks, along with several other animals, find the *Bishnoi* villages as safe havens. The spirit of conservation has been deeply ingrained in every *Bishnoi* for over five centuries. It arises from the belief that every living organism on this earth has an equal right to live. Therefore, *Bishnoi* people actively protect the blackbucks from poachers around their villages. These people also allow blackbucks to graze freely in their farmlands and keep stone vessels always filled with water near their home from where these animals can drink. The protection afforded to blackbucks by the *Bishnoi* is undoubtedly laudable.

Some of the awareness campaigns and capacity building workshops have been organized in Rajasthan and several other parts of this country for better conservation of blackbucks. Besides, local communities were motivated through community level awareness meetings, workshops and conservation programmes to raise awareness, education and communication for better understanding of blackbuck conservation and its importance. Local youth, community leaders, farmers, teachers and students were actively involved in such activities.

4.12 GREATER ONE-HORNED RHINOCEROS (*see* Plate II)

Order: Perissodactyla
Family: Rhinocerotidae
Scientific Name: *Rhinoceros unicornis* Linnaeus, 1758

Present Status

Wildlife (Protection) Act, 1972	Schedule–I
IUCN	Vulnerable
CITES	Appendix–I
Population Trend	↑

Distinctive Features

- This species of rhinoceros have single grayish black medially placed horn on the snout. The horn is about 37–40 cm (rarely 60 cm) long and is composed of closely matted horny fiber and keratin. It is not connected with the skull bones. However, a slight enlargement of the nasal bone provides support to the horn.
- It has a pointed, prehensile lip.

- Skin is thick and blackish with characteristic folds (or shields), which give it an armor-plated appearance.
- Hair over the body is sparse. The only hair visible in the body is at the ends of the ears and at the tip of the tail.
- Greater one-horned rhinoceros is a huge animal and is the second largest among the rhino species. An adult male is about 300–380 cm long with a height of about 175–200 cm at shoulder and weighs 1,800–2,700 kg.
- Their vision is poor but the senses of hearing and smell are acute.
- Average lifespan of this animal is 30–35 years in the wild.

Distribution

Greater one-horned rhinoceros was once distributed in Pakistan, India, Nepal and Bangladesh. But, presently their distribution range includes *Terai* area of north and northeastern India extending upto Chitwan area in Nepal. Close to 85 percent of the total population occurs in India of which about 75 percent are present in the state of Assam. One protected area in particular, *Kaziranga National Park*, holds an estimated 70 percent of the world population. The other protected areas in Assam where this species occurs include Pobitora Wildlife Sanctuary, Orang National Park and Manas National Park. In India, this rhino species are also found in Dudwha National Park of Uttar Pradesh, as well as, in the Jaldapara Wildlife Sanctuary and Gorumara National Park in the state of West Bengal.

Population

Recent estimates indicate that there are approximately 3,270 individuals of greater one-horned rhinoceros in the wilderness of India and Nepal. According to the latest census, above 2,500 animals are present in India and little more than 500 individuals are thriving in Chitwan National Park, Bardiya National Park and the Suklaphanta Wildlife Sanctuary of Nepal.

Habitat

The greater one-horned rhinoceros inhabits dense jungles of tall elephant grass either on plains or in swampy areas near rivers. They also prefer to live in the dense riverine forests. However, due to habitat loss they have been forced into more cultivated land and even sometimes feed in cultivated fields and pastures.

Behavioural Ecology

Greater one-horned rhinoceros remain more or less solitary. They usually spent most of the day by resting, mostly wallowing in the mud. Rhinos often wallow and bathe in the muddy pools during the hot hours of the day; this helps them both for thermoregulation and avoiding flies. They follow the same walking paths while foraging and also use the same spots to defecate forming well-defined toilets. Urination spots and rubbing sticks seem to serve the function of territory marking. They usually seek to escape rather than combatting an enemy. When wounded or when with calf, they occasionally attack. In such defense charges, contrary to the popular belief, they use their sharp pointed tusks in the lower jaw, not the horn. They are also reported to be good swimmers.

Food and Foraging Behaviour: Greater one-horned rhinoceros feeds on grasses, reeds, twigs and shoots. They generally feed during morning and evening. When two rhinos meet, ritualized behaviour usually decides who is dominant and violence is thus avoided. Such behaviour includes a series of displays and postures, involving curling of lips and baring the sharp *tushes* accompanied by snarls and grunts. However, in certain occasions the dispute is settled by fierce battle between the two. These fights are noisy and sometimes lengthy affairs, can lead to serious injuries and in rare instances the losers are mortally wounded.

Breeding Behaviour: In the wild, February to April is the breeding season for greater one-horned rhinoceros. After a gestation period of about 16 months, a calf (exceptionally two) is born. At birth, the rhino calves are pink in colour and weighs about 60 kg. The mother and the calf stay together for three to four years. The female parent, meanwhile, mates again and get ready to produce another offspring.

Home Range: Males have loosely defined home ranges that are not well defended and often overlap. Normally they confine their movements to a small area of about 0.75–5 sq km, which act as their 'home range' and meet most of their requirements of food, water and shelter. Males wander further in search for their mates.

Social Organization: Greater one-horned rhinoceros are generally solitary. However, some loose aggregations between few individuals certainly occur at wallowing grounds and foraging areas. Territories of males are not well-defined and sometimes overlap. Sub-adults or adult males gather at wallows or to graze, as well as, the mothers are often found to be in close association with their offspring.

Threats to Survival

- ***Hunting and poaching:*** In the nineteenth and early twentieth century, the greater one-horned rhinoceros was hunted persistently for sport by the Europeans, as well as, by the Asians. They were also considered as agricultural pests, particularly in areas with tea plantations, and killed. Their populations severely depleted and the species were in the verge of extinction in the early 20th century. During 1975 there were only 600 individuals surviving in the wild. Despite protections and bans on hunting and international trade of rhino horn, poaching continues to be a major threat. Even today they are ruthlessly poached for their horns, which are used in traditional Chinese medicine and other oriental medicines for the treatment of a variety of ailments including epilepsy, fevers and strokes and are also used as an aphrodisiac. However, efficacy of rhino horn for none of these is scientifically proven and is more of a myth. Still the demand is large, particularly among Asia's growing middle class. As a consequence, extensive illegal trade of rhino horn persists throughout Asia and the price of a processed horn may reach up to US $30,000 per kg. *Rhino horns* are being smuggled to places like China, Myanmar and other southeast Asian nations through the northeast India. Rhino skin, blood, urine and dung have also been reported to have certain economic value.

- ***Habitat loss:*** Habitat loss is another major threat to the survival of this species. Disappearance of alluvial plain grasslands driven by the need for land by the growing human population is considered to be the driving force behind habitat loss. Habitat destruction is also caused due to expansion of agricultural lands and grazing by domestic livestock inside rhino habitats. Frequent flood in Kaziranga regularly inundate a large portion of rhino habitat. Spread of invasive weed (like *Mimosa*) are also known to degrade some of the rhino habitat of this country.
- ***Human-rhino conflicts:*** Populations of rhinoceros in many protected areas have now reached the carrying capacity. On the other hand, agricultural lands and tea gardens are often present just outside the boundary of these protected areas. Therefore, rhinos tend to come out of the boundaries of the protected areas to forage in the surrounding landscapes leading to human-rhino conflicts. Rhinos, mainly females with juveniles, are reported to kill several people each year in India and Nepal.
- ***Diseases:*** Domesticated cattle often enter and graze inside rhino habitat. This makes the rhino population susceptible to diseases, like hoof and mouth disease, from these livestock.
- ***Other threats:*** Large cats sometimes predate on young rhinos. Besides, loss and subsequent extermination of rhino by poachers were witnessed in Laokhowa-Burachapori Wildlife Sanctuary during the social unrest in early 1980's and in Manas National Park during the civil conflict in 1990's.

Conservation Initiatives

This species is listed as 'Vulnerable' by the IUCN. Trade in any of the rhino part (including horns) is illegal as it is listed on the Appendix–I of CITES since 1975. One population in Nepal is protected with 700 armed troops and rangers, almost two guards per rhino. Rhinos are also being radio-collared in recent times. In Nepal, such collaring expedition was led by the Department of National Parks and Wildlife Conservation and Department of Forests, Government. of Nepal with active support from WWF Nepal, National Trust for Nature Conservation and the local communities.

In India, this species is provided with highest degree of legal protection by enlisting this species under Schedule-I of the Wildlife (Protection) Act. Special forces are working in these natural strongholds of greater one-horned rhinoceros under project "Operation Rhino" to protect them from the poachers. Initiatives have also been taken to safeguard this species in its natural habitat within several protected areas (Kaziranga National Park in Assam, Gorumara National Park and Jaldapara Wildlife Sanctuary in West Bengal). Forest departments are now involving communities around these protected areas in their anti-poaching efforts. Such efforts to control poaching and illegal wildlife trade will help in the recovery of the Indian rhino populations.

Besides, Indian Rhino Vision (IRV) 2020 and Nepal Rhino Action Plan have been developed with the support of the IUCN SSC Asian Rhino Specialist Group. IRV 2020 is a major initiative in rhino conservation, which is achieved through partnership among the Government of Assam, the International Rhino Foundation, the World Wide Fund for Nature, the Bodoland Territorial Council and the US Fish & Wildlife Service. The aim of IRV 2020 is to attain a population of 3,000 wild rhinos in seven protected areas of Assam from the present population of more than 2,000 in three of its protected areas by the year 2020. The goal is to reduce risks to India's rhino population by ensuring that the animals are spread throughout multiple parks with enough habitats to encourage population growth. Wild to wild translocation is the backbone of IRV 2020 programme. Other objective is to reintroduce populations in areas where they have been extirpated. The action plan is to reintroduce rhinos in the potential habitats of Manas National Park, Dibru Saikhowa Wildlife Sanctuary, and Laokhowa-Bura Chapori Wildlife Sanctuary from Kaziranga and Pobitora. Several rhinos have so far been translocated to Manas and are regularly monitored using radio telemetry and visual sightings. Patrolling staff in Manas now uses cameras and devices enabled with global positioning system to locate and monitor the movements of many wild animals including rhinos. Post-release behaviour and ranging patterns of the rhinos are also being monitored to find out areas used by these translocated rhinos. Data thus obtained are then integrated into GIS platform and mapped using remote sensing and GIS for better management decisions.

Under the IRV 2020, several programmes are, therefore, being taken up to spread awareness, build partnerships and promote livelihood options among the local communities living around the rhino habitat to ensure their participation in rhino conservation.

Several NGOs undoubtedly play a crucial role as well. WWF-India supports national park staff and rangers with equipment and training. Centre for Wildlife Rehabilitation and Conservation (CWRC) is a joint facility of the Wildlife Trust of India (WTI), International Fund for Animal Welfare (IFAW) and the Assam Forest Department near Kaziranga National Park that rehabilitates rescued animals before releasing them back in the wild. Over the years, this centre had played an important role in rescuing many greater one-horned rhinoceros. WWF-India, WTI and TRAFFIC strive to stop trafficking of rhino horn by funding antipoaching patrols and also support intelligence networks in strategic locations to prevent rhinos from entering black markets in Asia. As a consequence of these continuous conservation measures over the past few years, the rhino populations have increased to a large extent.

4.13 ASIAN ELEPHANT (*see* Plate III)

Order: Proboscidea
Family: Elephantidae
Scientific Name: *Elephas maximus* Linnaeus, 1758

Present Status

Wildlife (Protection) Act, 1972	Schedule–I
IUCN	Endangered
CITES	Appendix–I
Population Trend	↓

Distinctive Features

- Asian elephants are the largest land mammals found in India. The adults are up to 6.4 m in length, stand 245–275 cm at shoulder and weigh around 3000 kg.
- These animals usually have dark grey to brown wrinkled skins and sometimes have light pink blotches over the body, particularly on the forehead, ears, as well as, on the base of the trunk and chest.
- Asian elephants have small eyes, long flapping ears, two-domed forehead and a curved back.
- The long trunk (proboscis) is a combination of nose and upper lip and has a single finger like projection at the tip. This is the most striking feature of an Asian elephant.
- Few long, stiff hair are present all over their body and a tuft of hair is present at the tip of their tail that is used for batting away insects.
- In contrast to its African counterparts, Asian elephants have smaller ears, four nails in each hind foot instead of three and only the males bear tusks. Tusks of males are actually the elongation of incisors of the upper jaw. The females have very small dental protrusion, extend only few inches outside their lip and are known as 'tushes'. Some males called 'makhnas' are tuskless too and can be distinguished from the females by the presence of penis bulging below their tail.
- The life span of Asian elephants is 60–70 years.

Distribution

Asian elephants presently occur in isolated populations over an approximate total range area of 4,86,800 sq km (Sukumar, 2003) and is distributed in Bangladesh, Bhutan, India, Nepal, and Sri Lanka in south Asia and Cambodia, China, Indonesia (Kalimantan and Sumatra) Lao PDR, Malaysia (Peninsular Malaysia and Sabah), Myanmar, Thailand and Vietnam in south-east Asia.

In India, the range of Asian elephant is highly fragmented and are found in four isolated regions *viz.* northeastern India, central India, northern India, and southern India. These animals are present in the states of Assam, Meghalaya, Manipur, Mizoram and Arunachal Pradesh in northeastern India; West Bengal and Orissa in eastern India; Jharkhand and few parts of Bihar and Chattisgarh in central India; Uttar Pradesh and Uttarakhand in northern India and Tamil Nadu, Kerala, Karnataka and Andhra Pradesh in the southern India. Once widespread in India, the species is now found along the Himalayan foothills as far as the Mishmi Hills, the plains of upper Assam, Khasi and Garo Hills, parts of the lower Brahmaputra plains and Karbi Plateau, Terai forest regions, as well as, in the hilly terrain and forests of the Western Ghats and in parts of the Eastern Ghats. Feral populations are reported to be present on some of the Andaman Islands as well.

Population

Global population size of the Asian elephants has been estimated to be comprising of 41,410–52,345 animals, of which 2,400–3,400 are present in Indonesia, 2,500–3,200 in Thailand, 2,100–3,100 in Malaysia, 500–1,000 in Lao

PDR, 250–600 in Cambodia, 70–50 in Viet Nam, 200–250 in China, 4,000–5,000 in Myanmar, 150–250 in Bangladesh, 250–500 in Bhutan, 100–125 in Nepal, 2,500–4,000 in Sri Lanka, while 57 percent of the global population of Asian elephants (comprising of 26,390–30,770 individuals) occur in India (Sukumar, 2003; Choudhury et al., 2008).

Habitat

Asian elephants are generalists and usually prefer mixed deciduous and evergreen forests interspersed with scrub jungles and grasslands, as well as, tall forests with hilly and undulating grounds. Habitat of Asian elephant thus includes grasslands, tropical evergreen forest, semi-evergreen forest, moist deciduous forest, dry deciduous forested and dry thorn forest. In addition to these, they also occur in secondary forests, scrublands, cultivated lands and also frequent areas with dense bamboo vegetations. They are found in steamy humid jungles, forest at higher altitude and colder climates too. In few areas of eastern Himalaya in northeast India they are reported to regularly move up to above 3,000 m in summer (Choudhury, 1999).

Behavioural Biology

Asian elephants are terrestrial animals and generally lead a diurnal mode of life. They generally keep to the denser forests during hot and dry seasons. However, during rains they come out into open stretches and enter the cultivations. They are extremely sociable, forming groups of 6–7 related females that are led by the oldest female, the 'matriarch'. These groups occasionally join others to form large herds. However, these associations are relatively transient. They migrate over long distances in pursuit of food, water and in search of security. They traditionally use same pathway, known as '*corridor*', to migrate from one place to another. Once these corridors are destroyed or blocked by human habitations then they enter human settlement, which often leads to human-elephant conflict. In pursuit of food they also raid crop fields close to their original habitat or nearby their corridor. Most frequently, they are attracted to the human habitation by the smell of country liquor.

Their eyesight is not that keen which is compensated by their acute sense of smell and hearing. They communicate between the members of a herd by means of various sounds *viz.* growls, roars, grunts, trumpeting and snorts for specific type of communications. Loud trumpeting noise is used to gather a herd. A hollow resonant sound made by tapping the trunk on a hard surface with the tip turned upward while snorting appears to be an alarm signal. During the hot hours of the day they rest standing or stretched on its side and flap ears to cool the blood inside the vessel running beneath the surface of their pina. They love to bathe and shower themselves with water and afterward with dusts to repel insects.

Food and Foraging Behaviour: Asian elephants are strictly herbivorous in nature and their diet consists of various kinds of grasses, leaves and barks of specific kinds of trees. Cultivated crops such as bananas, rice and sugarcane are favoured foods. The proportions of the different plant types in their diet vary depending upon the habitat and season. More than two thirds (14–19 hr) of the day may be spent feeding. A full grown adult consumes around 270–320 kg of green fodder and drinks 30 gallons of water daily. Baskaran (2002) recorded that elephants fed on 82 species of plants (59 woody plant species and 23 grass species). They defecate about 16–18 times a day, producing about 100 kg of dung. They feed early in the morning and evening and come out to raid crop or to feed in the open forests after darkness sets in. During the dry seasons, the larger herds break into smaller groups to explore different habitats and again reunite once the condition is favourable. The tuskers feed keeping a distance from the main herd. The herd generally follows a regular and synchronized routine of drinking and feeding at specific places. However, succulent crops like sugarcane, banana etc. and distilleries of country liquor allure these large animals and they frequently raid those places.

Breeding Behaviour: The exact breeding season of Asian elephants in different parts of this country is still uncertain. But, breeding season is believed to be during summer till the commencement of rainy season. Females reach sexual maturity between 9–15 years of age, while males reach sexual maturity at 15 years. Male elephants (rarely females) show peculiar periodical signs of excitement on attaining sexual maturity, mostly during the cold season, which is known as '*musth*'. An elephant in *musth* usually shows some erratic behaviour and generally seeks for a mate.

After completion of the gestation period of 18–22 months generally single offspring is born, mostly during late autumn. However, they seldom give birth to the twins. Once, a calf is born, the female members of the herd provide good care for both the mother and her baby. They assist the female parent to take care of her calf, as well as, they themselves act as guardians to the newborn calf. The calves weigh about 90–100 kg at birth.

Home Range: As a matter of fact, Asian elephants have a larger home range as compared to other terrestrial mammals and practice seasonal migration. They usually roam over large areas. Home ranges of more than 600 sq km have been recorded for females in south India (Baskaran et al., 1995). In north India, female home ranges of 184–326 sq km and male home ranges of 188–407 sq km have been recorded (Williams, 2002).

Social Organization: Asian elephants are social animals and have a wide complex of community laws, rules and regulations. They are very much disciplined and follow many well-established customs. They live in a matriarchal society. Each herd consists of 15–30 individuals led by an old female. Herds are believed to be composed of single families and consist of chiefly females, immature elephants and one or few old tuskers. However, stray females and young males may migrate from one herd to another.

Threats to Survival

In India, the survival of Asian elephants in the wild is threatened mainly by fragmentation and degradation of natural habitat, poaching for ivory, human-elephant conflict and accidents.

- ❒ ***Habitat loss:*** All Asian elephants range countries are currently experiencing rapid human population growth. This growth in population expedites the destruction of the forests, which serve as the principal habitat of these animals. Large-scale logging practices and clearing of forest for agriculture and infrastructure development are the main underlying causes. Besides, loss of elephant corridors due to construction of industries, railway tracks and highways are other major threats for these herbivores.
- ❒ ***Poaching:*** Asian elephants have a long history of being hunted by people, originally for food, later for domestic stock, ivory, leather and other products. Poaching for ivory continues to devastate wild populations and is considered to be a serious problem in some parts of Asia (Menon et al., 1997). Tuskers are frequently killed for their tusks, which are smuggled to feed into the ivory market of the Far East, subsequently affecting sex ratios which become highly female biased, genetic variation is reduced, fecundity is influenced and ultimately the entire population may decline (Sukumar, 2003).
- ❒ ***Human-elephant conflicts:*** Human-elephant conflict refers to negative interaction between wild elephants and human beings such as crop raiding by elephants, human death and injury caused by elephants and humans killing elephants. As the natural habitat of Asian elephants shrinks, hungry elephants are forced to locate food sources outside the forest. Often, these food sources are local villager's subsistence crops, such as banana, rice, and cassava plantations. As a result, human-elephant conflicts occur. Such conflicts are considered as one of the main threats to Asian elephants as angry villagers frequently retaliate against elephants by harming or killing elephants. During such conflicts, sometimes people also got injured or killed, which aggravate the scenario further.
- ❒ ***Removal of live elephants:*** Live elephants were earlier removed from the wild and used in forestry operations or for ceremonial purposes.
- ❒ ***Mortality due to railway accident:*** Fair number of Asian elephants are killed every year by the speeding trains running through railway tracts passing through some of the elephant habitats in this country.
- ❒ ***Diseases:*** Anthrax, Endotheliotropic Elephant Herpes Virus (EEHV) and tuberculosis are some of the diseases identified from Asian elephants.

Conservation Initiatives

Elephants are an important cultural icon in India. According to Indian mythology, elephant is one of the nine jewels (*navratnas*) that surfaced as the gods (*deva*) and the demons (*asura*) churned the oceans in a search for the elixir of life (*Amrit*). The Asian elephants are often considered as the flagship for conservation in south and southeast Asia. Asian elephants have been legally protected throughout the country being placed under Schedule–I of the Indian Wildlife (Protection) Act, 1972. Killing or harming Asian elephant and causing destruction of its habitat is prohibited and is punishable under law. They are also included in Appendix–I of the CITES, thereby preventing any trade in elephant parts and ivory. Hence, trade in any part of an Asian elephants is illegal and is subject to strict punishments.

In 1991, the Ministry of Environment and Forests, Government of India had launched "Project Elephant" to protect the Asian elephants existing in India. At that time such an initiative was the need of the hour as this species was then critically mired with several natural and anthropogenic problems. This project has helped considerably to revive the population of the Asian elephants and has pulled them back from the verge of extinction.

Over 25 Elephant Reserves (ER) have been established throughout the traditional range of Asian elephants covering a total area of 58,000 sq km. Besides, Project Elephant has initiated several research projects in collaboration with many leading institutions of this country to understand and mitigate several conservation issues of wild elephants. Project Elephant Directorate along with Wildlife Trust of India and Asian Nature Conservation Foundation has published a report titled "Right of Passage: elephant corridors of India" which identified 88 elephant corridors in India (Menon et al., 2005). Initiatives are being taken by the government and several NGOs to secure these corridors either by voluntary relocation of people, through community intervention or by purchasing the land (Rangarajan et al., 2010).

Since January 2004, the Project Elephant has also formally implemented the MIKE (Monitoring of Illegal

Killing of Elephants) programme of CITES in 10 Elephant Reserves (viz. Shiwalik (Uttarakhand), Eastern Dooars (West Bengal), Mayurbhanj (Orissa), Ripu-Chirang (Assam), Dehing-Patkai (Assam), Garo Hills (Meghalaya), Deomali (Arunchal Pradesh), Wayanad (Kerala), Mysore (Karnataka) and Nilgiri (Tamil Nadu). The main aim of MIKE programme is to measure levels and trends in illegal hunting of elephants, determine changes in these trends over the years and to identify the causal factors.

"Wildlife without Borders" is working to mitigate human-elephant conflicts and to stop poaching, to increase law enforcement capacity and conduct community outreach and awareness to inspire pride and optimistic views among the local communities in elephant ranges. The United States Congress also passed the Asian Elephant Conservation Act in 1997, which established a fund for the protection of the Asian elephants and conservation of its habitat. WWF invests into anti-poaching operations through the Asian Rhinos and Elephants Action Strategy (AREAS) programme each year to develop successful anti-poaching strategy. Other conservation initiatives of WWF include limiting human impacts on elephant populations in the western Terai, as well as, prevent further habitat loss in some of the priority landscapes like Nilgiris-Eastern Ghats, Terai Arc and North Bank landscapes. Due to improved conservation effectiveness there is indication of increasing population in the Western Ghats in recent years.

4.14 FISHING CAT (*see* Plate III)

Order: Carnivora
Family: Felidae
Scientific Name: *Prionailurus viverrinus* (Bennett, 1833)
Present Status

Wildlife (Protection) Act, 1972	Schedule–I
IUCN	Endangered
CITES	Appendix–II
Population Trend	↓

Distinctive Features

- Fishing cat is a medium sized, stout animal with characteristic medium to short limbs. They are about twice the size of a domestic cat and are considered as one of the largest among the lesser cats.
- Their head-body length is typically about 65–85 cm and the tail is short measuring about 30 cm in length. Their height at shoulder is 35 cm while their weight lies within 6–12 kg depending on gender (Sunquist and Sunquist, 2002). The body size and the whiskers are considerably larger in males and the males are also heavier than the females.
- Their coat is short, coarse and is brownish-grey in colour with distinctive dark markings combining of both spots and stripes. There is a pair of dark stripes around the throat, six to eight black lines run down from the forehead to the neck. These lines gradually break up into shorter bars and spots on the shoulders. Blackish brown cheek stripes are also present. The tail also has a number of incomplete black rings and a black tip.
- Their face is elongated and spotted with a distinctly flat nose. Ears are short and blunt and are present on either side far back on the head. Outer side of the each ear is black with a central white spot.
- The ventral side of the body is paler with longer fur and is often overlaid with spots.
- Their claws are not fully retractable and the tips of the claws slightly protrude out from the protective sheath of skin on their toes.
- Fishing cats are found to live upto 12 years in captivity.

Distribution

Fishing cats are found in many places scattered throughout the Oriental region. In south-east Asia, these lesser cats are discontinuously distributed (Duckworth, 2016) in a number of countries including Bangladesh, Bhutan, Cambodia, India, Lao People's Democratic Republic, Malaysia, Myanmar, Nepal, Sri Lanka, Thailand along with the Indonesian Islands of Java (Mukherjee et al., 2016). However, there are no recent records from Pakistan, Peninsular Malaysia and Vietnam (Mukherjee et al., 2010; 2016). In India, it is primarily found in the *Terai* region of the Himalayan foothills, particularly in the eastern India up to Bangladesh, where it is widely distributed and locally common (Khan, 2004). It is reported to be distributed in some states of northeastern India along with some prime habitats in eastern India (Kolipaka, 2006), West Bengal, Uttar Pradesh, Keonjhar district and vicinity of Chilika Lake in Orissa, from Mangalore to Kanyakumari in the west coast and few other scattered areas in the rest of India. It has perhaps also been obliterated from the southern Western Ghats (Nowell and Jackson, 1996).

Population

There is no information available on the population of fishing cats surviving in the wild. But, the present population is small, fragmented and are believed to be declining in the wilderness areas of southeast Asia (Mukherjee et al., 2016).

Habitat

Fishing cats are strongly associated with water bodies and ideally inhabits wetland areas with plenty of densely vegetated areas to ensure cover both from predators and also to hide from their potential prey. They are often found in a variety of wetlands such as swamps, marshes, oxbow lakes, reed beds, tidal creeks and mangroves. However, their occurrence tends to be highly localized and show strong habitat preferences (Nowell and Jackson, 1996). In certain areas fishing cats are even known to live around city suburbs with little vegetation and close to human settlements. They are also noticed around large aquaculture ponds (*bheri*) with sparse vegetation nearby. They even inhabit heavily forested regions adjacent to rivers, streams or other water bodies and have been reported in Himalayan forests at an elevation of 1,525 m (Phillips, 1984).

Behavioural Biology

Fishing cats are highly elusive and primarily nocturnal predators. During daytime, they spent most of their time amongst dense vegetation and in dense tall and short grasslands, sometimes well away from water. They prefer to remain hidden in the dark and shaded places. They become active in the night and generally come out from their refuge in the late afternoon or in the evening and then move towards the wetland to find food. They are excellent swimmers and have been known to swim long distances, even under water.

Food and Foraging Behaviour: Fishing cats are carnivorous animals and feed on the freshly killed animals and fishes. However, they are possibly best designated as 'piscivores' as fishes are favourite food of these animals. Scat analysis of fishing cats in Keoladeo National Park, India revealed that fish comprises 76 percent of the diet, followed by birds (27 percent), insects (13 percent) and small rodents (9 percent) as reported by Haque and Vijayan (1993). Molluscs, amphibians and reptiles found in or adjoining the water are also taken. During this study Haque and Vijayan (1993) observed fishing cats entering the water and scooping out their prey during moonlit nights. They even witnessed fishing cats eating grass and gerbils.

They usually hunt along the edges of wetlands, streams and rivers. Instead of entering the water, they frequently adopt hunting strategy that involves crouching on a rock or overhanging bank, lightly tapping the water surface with its paw mimicking insect movements to attract fish and once the fish is close enough, then they scoop up the fish out of the water with a blow of its paw and flicks it onto dry land before eating it. But, if required they also dive into the water to catch the fish. They have also been observed playing with fish in shallow water before killing it (Breeden, 1989). They can even swim underwater to catch ducks and other aquatic birds. They are powerful enough to predate upon large mammalian prey, like small fawns of *Axis axis* in the wild, as well as, civets, small domestic cattle and dogs in areas close to settlements (Nowell and Jackson, 1996; Sunquist and Sunquist, 2002). These animals have even been observed to scavenge on livestock carcasses (Haque, 1988) and tiger kills (Nowell and Jackson, 1996). They start feeding from the head of its prey. The amount of food consumed by a fishing cat is 1–1.5 kg of fish daily. In captivity, while fishing cats were provided with cow flesh, they have been observed to take the piece of meat, drop it in the water, retrieve it and then eat it. Such 'washing behaviour' was noticed even when they were offered live quail (Iwaniuk et al., 2001).

Breeding Behaviour: Research on fishing cats in the wild is scanty. Hence, information on many aspects of the breeding biology of these elusive nocturnal cats is based on the observation of captive population. Wild fishing cats are reported to breed once every year, most likely during the months of January and February. During March and April most kittens were observed. However, there are also reports of these cats breeding in June (Cat Specialist Group 1996). The estrous cycle lasts for 21–25 days approximately. It has been found that the females become receptive at the middle of the estrous cycle. Then they become restless and are occasionally found to roll on the ground. Frequent micturition is also found during this period. A receptive female usually makes characteristic calls to attract the males and to initiate mating. They also display "flehmen behaviour" (Mellen, 1993).

In captivity, the gestation period lasts for 60–70 days, after which the female usually gives birth to two or three offspring (Mellen, 1993). The kittens generally weigh around 170 g at birth and are born blind. Their eyes open on the 16th day. They are able to actively move around by the age of one month, take meat around two months of age and are weaned once they are six months old. Females take care for their young. Although, the males help the females to rear the young in captivity, yet it is rather doubtful if such parental care is shown by the males in the wild. At eight and a half months of age, they attain the size of adult and are able to breed. They become completely independent of their mother at 10 months and leave to establish their own territory (Sunquist and Sunquist, 2002). They become sexually mature when they are approximately 15 months old.

Home Range: Fishing cats are largely territorial animals that occupy home ranges. The size of home ranges depend on the availability of various resources and is usually larger in male (22 sq km) as compared to the females (4–8 sq km).

Social Organization: There is little available information on social behaviour of fishing cats. They are usually solitary in nature and do not lead a social life. Adult males mark their territory using cheek-rubbing, head rubbing, chin rubbing, neck rubbing, and urine-spraying to leave scent marks. The adult males only copulate with the receptive females at the time of breeding. The females play a major role in caring the young and are accompanied by their mother until they become completely mature and independent.

Threats to Survival

- ***Habitat loss:*** Wetlands are the favoured habitats of fishing cats, which are under serious anthropogenic threat due to increasing levels of industrial and commercial activity. Destruction and degradation of wetlands is considered as a primary threat faced by this species (Nowell and Jackson, 1996). Over 45 percent of protected wetlands and 94 percent of globally significant wetlands in southeast Asia are under threat and disappearing (Dugan, 1993).
- ***Overfishing:*** Fishing cats are in danger due to destructive fishing practices that greatly lead to the over-exploitation of local fish stocks. Such overfishing in the lakes and rivers often deplete the available food of the fishing cats. Fisherman communities even consider these lesser cats as pests and incessantly kill them to save fish stocks (Kolipaka, 2006).
- ***Poaching:*** Poaching of these animals is another major threat. They are often hunted for their hide, skin and other body parts (CAMP-BCPP, 1997). Earlier skins of fishing cats were often found in illegal trade in India (Anon, 2005). Frequent seizures in various markets of the Far East indicate that illegal trade in skin and other body parts of these lesser cats is still thriving and poachers are continuing to decimate their populations. Widespread and indiscriminate snaring, trapping and poisoning are possibly responsible for the recent declines of this small carnivore in southeast Asia (Mukherjee et al., 2016).
- ***Parasitic disease:*** Parasitic diseases are also reported to kill some of these animals.

Conservation Initiatives

Fishing cat is included under CITES Appendix–II, which indicates that hunting and trade in the body parts of this species is legally prohibited in most of its range countries. Although hunting is prohibited in Bangladesh, Cambodia, China, India, Indonesia, Myanmar, Nepal, Pakistan, Sri Lanka and Thailand, yet the species is still not protected outside protected areas in Bhutan and Vietnam (Nowell and Jackson, 1996). In the IUCN Red List of Threatened Species, fishing cats are categorized as Endangered considering their dwindling population. Perceiving the paramount threat in their natural environment, fishing cats are also placed under Schedule–I of the Wildlife (Protection) Act, 1972, which provide them nationwide legal protection. Therefore, hunting and killing of this species is prohibited and such activities might invite stringent punishment in the form of imprisonment and/or fine. In India, the fishing cat is reported to occur in some of the protected areas of this country like Sundarbans, Corbett, Dudwha, Dalma and Kaziranga (Datye, 1993), where they are protected along with all other species. But, areas with healthy populations outside the protected areas need to be identified and conserved on a priority basis through awareness generation and community participation. Therefore, initially extensive field surveys need to be planned to identify the habitat and breeding grounds of the fishing cats. Once identified, these habitats need to be protected from poaching, destruction due to several anthropogenic activities and from other conservation threats. Wetlands supporting a sizable population of these threatened species may also be declared as 'conservation reserve' or 'community reserve' under the recent provisions of the Wildlife (Protection) Act. There are reports that the species is to some extent benefited by improved protection in the conservation areas of Rajasthan and Gujarat. Recently the European and American Associations of Zoos and Aquariums have jointly initiated captive breeding programmes for the fishing cats. As an initial step of this *ex-situ* conservation programme, fishing cats kept in zoos around the world are listed in the International Studbook of the World Association of Zoos and Aquariums.

In addition to these, conservation projects need to be initiated in a number of wetlands within the present distribution range of fishing cats where their presence is already known. Finally, adequate protection of remaining wild wetlands in Asia, and prevention of indiscriminate trapping, snaring and poisoning can ensure continued survival of this species in this country.

4.15 INDIAN TIGER (*see* Plate III)

Order: Carnivora
Family: Felidae
Scientific Name: *Panthera tigris tigris* (Linnaeus, 1758)

Present Status

Wildlife (Protection) Act, 1972	Schedule–I
IUCN	Endangered
CITES	Appendix–I
Population Trend	↓

Distinctive Features

- Indian tigers are warm-blooded mammals and have a majestic look, graceful built and is second-largest of the surviving subspecies of tigers.
- Adult tigers are normally 90–110 cm in height at shoulders. Adult males are 270–310 cm in length from nose to tail and weigh between 180–250 kg. Females are slightly smaller, range from 240–265 cm in length and weigh between 100–160 kg. The smallest and lightest Indian tigers are reported from Bangladesh Sundarbans, where adult females are 75–80 kg in weight (Sunquist and Sunquist, 2002).
- Coat color varies from light yellow to reddish yellow, with a pale and whitish underside. Stripes, ranging from dark brown to black, are present all over the body. Stripes act as camouflage and help tigers to hide from their prey.
- The ears are black, each with a prominent round white spot on the outer side of pinna.
- The black ringed tail is another unique characteristic feature of this animal. Length of their tail varies within 85–110 cm. Tigers use their tails to communicate with other tigers, as well as, for balance when they take fast turns while running.
- Tigers have prominent whiskers, which are much bigger in males than the females.
- There are 30 teeth in tigers. The canines are long (7.5–10 cm), powerful and are used to kill and grab their prey.
- Hairs often act as tactile receptors, helping them to assess immediate surroundings. The length of hair, density of fur and their coat colour varies depending on their geographical location and seasonal factors.
- Tigers have round pupils and yellow irises. The night vision of tigers is six times better than that of humans due to a special retinal adaptation that reflects light back to the retina.
- Their forefeet consist of five toes and the hind feet have four toes, all with sickle shaped retractile claws. The claws are retracted during walking and extended during attack.
- Paw prints of tigers are called pugmarks, which are individualistic (like human finger prints) and no two tigers have same pugmarks.
- During breeding season, conspicuous mammary gland is evident in the females. The tits are present along the ventro-lateral side of the body from the axilla to the groin.
- The average life span of tigers in the wild is around 8–15 years.

Distribution

Tigers are believed to have evolved over one million years ago in Asia, from where they have spread north to the Amur region of eastern Russia, south to the islands of Indonesia and southwest to Indochina and the Indian subcontinent, eastern Turkey and the Caspian Sea. The tiger populations in these regions have distinct traits and are, therefore, grouped as separate sub species. Six different subspecies of tigers presently survive in different parts of the globe.

Indian tiger (*Panthera tigris tigris*) is the most common subspecies and is distributed in Nepal, Bhutan, Bangladesh, Myanmar and India. India holds over half the world's tiger population. Indian tigers are widely distributed over the forests of 17 states of this country ranging from the sub-alpine Himalayas to down south and across east-west, except in the Kashmir valley and the deserts of Rajasthan and arid regions of Punjab, Kutch and in the Sind.

Population

Indian tiger population in Bangladesh is around 440, somewhere between 163–253 in Nepal and 67–81 individuals in Bhutan (Global Tiger Initiative 2011, NTNC 2013). Populations of tigers in India have been estimated to range within 1,706–1,909 in 2010 (Jhala et al., 2011). As of 2014, they have increased to an estimated 2,226 individuals (Mohan, 2015; George, 2015). Out of these, 406 tigers are estimated to be present in Karnataka, 340 in Uttarakhand, 308 in Madhya Pradesh, 229 in Tamil Nadu, 190 in Maharashtra, 167 in Assam, 136 in Kerala, 117 in Uttar Pradesh, 79 in West Bengal, 68 in Andhra Pradesh, 46 in Rajasthan, 45 in Chhattisgarh, 28 each in Odisha, Bihar and Arunachal Pradesh, 5 in Goa and 3 tigers each were reported from Jharkhand and Mizoram (George, 2015).

Habitat

Dense vegetation cover (shelter), healthy prey base (food), pools of water (for drinking and bathing) and minimum human interference are some of the essential components of a good tiger habitat. Tiger density and range size has been closely tied to prey availability. Kaziranga, Nagrahole, Bandipur and Kanha National Parks in India are home to some of the highest densities of tigers in the world because of high prey abundance. Tigers require shelter to remain concealed from potential prey as they stalk their victim and for protection from threats (usually from human), particularly when the female has cubs. Tigers usually prefer to live in areas with dense vegetation as they can camouflage better in these areas.

Indian tigers are found in a wide range of habitats, including dry open scrub forests, dry and wet deciduous forests, the humid evergreen forests, subtropical and tropical rainforests, semi-evergreen and wet forests, high-altitude, cold, coniferous Himalayan forests, alluvial grasslands, grassy swamps, and mangroves. In India, tiger tracks have also been recorded from the winter snows of the Himalayas at an altitude of 3,050 m. On the other hand, the tiger leads an almost amphibious life in a terrain with mangrove trees, mud and water in Sundarbans.

Behavioural Biology

Tigers are mainly active at night and less active during the mid-day heat. On a hot day, they are commonly seen in the shade or wading in pools. They may even stroll to a stream or a water hole for a refreshing drink. They usually hunt late in the evening. However, this pattern may vary depending on season and prey activity. Grooming is an important part of their daily activity. They spend long periods of day by licking its paws, chest and back. Grooming process keep their coat in good condition by removing loose hair and dirt from their fur. While grooming they use their rasping tongue for cleaning fur and spread oils secreted from their glands.

Their sense of hearing is most acute of all its senses and is mainly used for hunting. In general, they are more sensitive to high-pitched sounds (up to 60 kHz) emitted by prey and their movements. They are also capable of hearing infrasound below the range of normally audible sound (20 hertz) for humans. Tigers use infrasound to communicate over long distances or dense forests because the waves of these sounds can pass through a variety of mediums such as trees and mountains. Their sense of smell is not as highly developed as some of its other senses. They have small amount of odour-detecting cells in their nose and an olfactory region in the brain that identifies various scents. They have a Jacobson's organ (also called vomero-nasal organ or VNO) in the roof of their mouth. Tigers often exhibit a behavior called flehman, in which they pick up an odour particle on their upper lip and curl it upwards towards VNO to detect scents. Hence, during flehmen behaviour, tigers appear to be snarling but without making any sound. Tigers are good swimmers and take to water readily. They are capable of traversing lakes and rivers and often enter water in pursuit of prey. Though not arboreal in nature, but they can climb trees as and when necessary.

Food and Foraging Behaviour: Tigers are strictly carnivorous in nature and hunt medium-sized and large-sized animals. They prefer to predate upon large ungulates like gaur, sambar, chital, barasingha, nilgai, water buffalo etc. Besides, they also often kill medium-sized prey species like wild boar, hog deer, muntjac and gray langur. Smaller animals like hares, porcupines and peafowls are seldom killed and form a very small part in their diet. They have also been reported to kill elephant and rhino calves in rare cases. Indian tigers have also been known to take other predators such as leopards, wolves, jackals, foxes, crocodiles and wild dog as prey, although these predators are not typically a part of their diet. Due to the encroachment of humans and presence of domestic livestock into their habitat, some tigers opportunistically take to cattle killing (Andheria et al., 2007; Wegge et al., 2009). However, when driven by hunger, tigers feed almost anything, such as fowl, fish, reptiles or even carrion.

Tigers hunt mostly at dusk and dawn. As they are not able to chase their prey up to a long distance, they hide in the undergrowths or tall grasses, stalk and suddenly pounce upon its unwary prey. Excellent camouflage combined with its excellent stalking techniques, enables the tiger to approach its prey within striking distance without being noticed. In most cases, tigers approach their victim from the side or behind upto as close as possible. They kill prey species with a single bite—usually applying a suffocating bite on the throat in the case of large animals or at the back of the neck of smaller prey severing their spinal cord. Then they often drag their prey into thick cover preferably near water, occasionally over several hundred metres to protect it from vultures, scavengers or even other tigers. A tiger can consume as much as 40 kg of meat in one feeding (Mazak, 1981) and then can survive up to three weeks without food.

Breeding Behaviour: Females achieve sexual maturity at the age of 3–4 years, whereas males become sexually mature at 4–5 years of age. Tigers are polyestrous animals and are found to breed throughout the year. The tiger in India has no definite mating and birth seasons. Female comes into heat at intervals of about 3–9 weeks and is receptive for 3–6 days. A receptive female shows different signs like restlessness, frequent micturation, unusual posture with legs directed upwards, occasional rolling on the ground and snores loudly. Mating follows a definite courtship period. The gestation period is about 100 days, after which usually 2–4 cubs are born. But sometimes, as many as six cubs are born at a time. Most young are born in December and April (Panwar, 1987). Association of male and female appears to end when the cubs are born. It is not known whether the tigers are strictly monogamous in nature.

The tigress usually gives birth in a shelter of tall grass, thick bush or in caves. Newborn cubs weigh about 780–1,600 g at birth. Their eyes and ears are closed and they have thick wooly fur with more stripes than an adult tiger. The female parent provides maximum parental care. Tiger cubs are completely dependent of their mother for nutrition until one year of age. They usually suckle for 3–6 months and begin to eat small amounts of solid food from 2 months of age. At this time, they follow their mother on her hunting expeditions and begin to take part in hunting once they are 5–6 months old. Scent glands between a tigress's toes leave behind an individualized scent that enables a cub to follow its mother's footsteps. At the age of one year, they are able to kill smaller prey, but are still very vulnerable to larger predators. Thereafter, they slowly start to separate from the family group in search of an area, where one can establish its own territory. Male cubs leave their birthplace and move further away from their mother's territory, as compared to the female cubs. Female cubs generally stay in the same area as their mother. Once the family group split, the mother comes into heat again (Mazák, 1981). Male tigers are generally intolerant of cubs and are not known to play any part in rearing of their young.

Home Range and Territory: The size of tiger territories greatly vary depending on the locality, season and prey density. Males usually have larger territories than females. In Ranthambhore Tiger Reserve, territories of male tigers range from 5–150 sq km where the prey concentrations are high. In Panna Tiger Reserve an adult radio-collared male tiger was reported to move 1.7–10.5 km between different locations in winter, and 1–13.9 km in summer. Home range of this radio-collared tiger was 110 sq km in winter, whereas about 200 sq km in summer (Chundawat et al., 1999).

Social Organization: Adult animals congregate only on an *adhoc* and transitory basis under special circumstances (during mating or in conditions with plentiful supply of food etc.). Otherwise they lead solitary lives. However, there are reports that a group of females within an area are mutually tolerant, meet frequently and even share their kill. Only one male is usually associated with each such group of females. Their social system is connected through visual signals, scent marks and vocalizations.

These solitary predators hunt individually and are strongly territorial. They usually establish and maintain their control over their territories by continuously patrolling them. Territorial marking is a very powerful but silent communication system to convey the other individuals about its movement and announcing the territorial claim. They usually mark the boundary of their territory with spray-marking of a strong musky smelling fluid (mixture of urine and secretion from anal glands) on a tree, bush or a big stone or pole. Droppings along with the raked marks, scratch marks on trees and clawing are some other tools for communication. All these activities, including spray-marking are found with higher frequency and intensity usually on the animal paths, *nallahs,* streams, specific trees, poles and stones etc. The adult males are intolerant to each other. The home ranges occupied by adult male residents tend to be mutually exclusive. Sometimes, one of these residents may tolerate a transient or sub-adult male at least for a time. But, the territory of adult male usually overlaps with smaller territories of two or more females. The females share their area with single male without showing any hostility. Hence, it is believed that the male tiger keeps a large territory in order to include the home ranges of several females within its limits, so that he may maintain mating rights with them. The spacing of territories among females is less complete and often there is partial overlap of the territories of the neighboring female residents. Tigresses usually occupy territories adjacent to or take over parts of their mother's territory. Territories of the females although smaller than that of males, but contain vital resources required for rearing young. However, home range and territories of both males and females are not stable and shift or alteration of a home range by one animal leads to the shift of another.

Threats to Survival

- ***Poaching and illegal trade:*** Tiger populations were being decimated by poaching and illegal trade as there is high demands for tiger skins as status symbols and decorative items. Poaching of the animals for their hide and skin, nails and other body parts driven by the international illegal wildlife trade between India, Nepal and China is the largest immediate threat to the remaining tiger population. There are well-organized gangs of professional poachers, who smuggle tiger skin and other body parts to markets outside India, mainly in China, through a complex interlinking network. Besides, various tiger parts are believed to have certain curative properties in certain traditional medicinal practices. Tiger bones have been an ingredient of traditional Chinese medicines prescribed as a muscle strengthener and treatment for rheumatism and body pain (Hemley and Mills, 1999). Wildlife Crime Database of the Wildlife Protection Society of India (WPSI) shows 893 cases of tiger poaching in India between 1994 and 2009, which is just a fraction of the actual poaching activity in India (WPSI, 2009).
- ***Habitat loss:*** Exploding human populations have resulted in major loss of tiger habitat. Illegal logging, indiscriminate felling of trees and excessive fire wood extraction has resulted into shrinkage of cover for tigers. Tiger habitats are further fragmented due to clearing of forests for agriculture and large development projects, like mining, hydroelectric dams, thermal power plants, as well as, construction of highways and road networks. As a consequence, tigers are forced to thrive in small and scattered habitat patches.
- ***Loss of prey:*** Tigers suffer from a severe loss of natural prey due to large scale poaching of these herbivores for meat and trade. Competition with livestock over food and habitat degradation has also reduced natural prey of tigers.

- ❒ ***Human-tiger conflict:*** Tigers stray out of their natural habitat in the adjoining human habitations, attack domestic animals and sometimes people. On the other hand, tigers are also killed by angry villagers in retaliation. Possibly most of the tiger attacks on people occur in Sundarbans, where people were attacked while collecting honey, fuel wood, timber or other raw materials or while fishing (Azad et al., 2005).
- ❒ ***Natural disasters*** like floods, super cyclones, forest fires etc. destroy many tiger habitats.
- ❒ ***Infighting*** between the adult tigers for protecting territory and for mate selection often lead to fatal injury and death of the loser.

Conservation Initiatives

Tiger is included in Schedule–I of the Wildlife (Protection) Act, 1972 to impose a countrywide ban on tiger hunting. Launched on 1 April 1973, Project Tiger aimed to ensure the existence of a viable population of tigers in India. This is one of the most intensive conservation efforts in India and over the years, it has become one of the most successful conservation ventures in India. This conservation project advocates for setting up of tiger reserves in order to help maintaining the population of tigers. In 1974, a nationwide programme for the conservation of tigers was launched and subsequently 19 tiger reserves have been established throughout the country.

Over the years, the numbers of tiger reserves have also increased and 18 tiger States have notified 50 reserves under section 38V of the Wild Life (Protection) Act, 1972 (as amended in 2006) covering an area of 71,207.10 sq km (Project Tiger, 2016). Based on advisories of Project Tiger National Tiger Conservation Authority, with inputs from Wildlife Crime Control Bureau, State officials and tiger experts have designed Standard Operating Procedures to meet the present challenges of tiger conservation (viz. for dealing with straying tigers in human dominated landscapes, as well as, for dealing with tiger deaths),

A dedicated anti-poaching force composed of experts from Indian police, forest officials and various other environmental agencies has been formed in January 2008. Stringent laws and their successful implementation, intense patrolling, community based anti-poaching operations and scientific management of the tiger reserves, have made a significant increase in the tiger population of India. As an international initiative of tiger conservation, India has bilateral understanding with several neighbouring countries (for instance, understanding with Nepal and China to control trans-boundary illegal trade in wildlife and with Bangladesh for conservation of the Royal Bengal Tiger of Sundarbans). Moreover, international ban on tiger trade since 1993 and inclusion of tiger under Appendix–I of CITES has considerably reduced the killing of tigers and trade of its body parts. A sub-group on tiger/leopard conservation has also been established with cooperation of the Russian Federation,

Many NGOs, like WWF, TRAFFIC, Wildlife Protection Society of India (WPSI) has also taken significant measures to ensure the survival of Indian tigers. With the ambitious goal to double the wild tiger population by 2022, WWF initiated a global campaign 'Save Tigers Now' since May 2010. Thus, adequate funding and international pressure, along with sincere participation of different NGOs will further enhance the tiger conservation initiatives in India to a large extent. An online tiger crime data base has been launched and Guidelines for preparation of reserve specific Security Plan has been evolved with technical input and collaboration from TRAFFIC-India.

Recent initiatives involve continuous monitoring of tigers using camera traps, building up data on photo captures of individual tigers and setting up of a national repository of camera trap photo IDs of individual tigers. At present, country level status assessment of tiger, co-predators, prey and habitat using scientific methodologies is being carried out in collaboration with tiger States and the Wildlife Institute of India. Independent Management Effectiveness Evaluation of Tiger Reserves has also been initiated.

4.16 ASIATIC LION (*see* Plate III)

Order: Carnivora
Family: Felidae
Scientific Name: *Panthera leo persica* (Meyer, 1826)

Present Status

Wildlife (Protection) Act, 1972	Schedule–I
IUCN	Endangered
CITES	Appendix–I
Population Trend	➔

Distinctive Features

- ❒ Asiatic lions are significantly smaller than African lions, about 2.75 meter in length and weighs between 150–250 kg with a shoulder height of about 1–1.23 meter. The males (150–250 kg) are much heavier than the females (120–182 kg).
- ❒ The coat of adult Asiatic lion is pale yellowish or sandy gray in colour without any marking. The cubs are marked with spots and stripes.
- ❒ The most conspicuous physical characteristic feature in all Asian lion is the presence of longitudinal fold of skin running along their belly. They also bear prominent tufts of hair on their elbows.

- Asiatic lions bear scanty mane, which is absent in the lioness.
- Both male and female have a long naked tail (70–105 cm) with a tuft of hair at the tip.
- They have powerful retractable claws and long sharp canine teeth.
- Asiatic lions have a potential life span of 20–30 years in captivity. But, in wild their average life span is more or less 15 years.

Distribution

Asiatic lion had a wide historic distribution across southwest Asia and once ranged from Syria through India and Iran to as far west as Greece until the middle of the 19th century. However, at present it is found only in India. In India, majority of the lions are restricted inside the Gir National Park of Gujarat (Nowell and Jackson, 1996). However, recent reports indicate the presence of Girnar coastal and Bali Tana subpopulations, which thrive outside the Gir forests.

Population

Asiatic lion presently exists as single isolated population in Gujarat comprising of 411 animals in 2010 consisting of 97 adult males, 162 adult females, 75 sub-adults and 77 cubs (Singh and Gibson, 2011). Out of this dwindling population, at least 100 animals exist outside the protected area boundary of Gir National Park.

Habitat

Habitat of Asiatic lion in India is a mixture of dry savanna forest and dry deciduous scrub forest. Presently Asiatic lion lives in the rugged terrain of Gir forests, which is dominated by dry teak in the western and by *Acacia* in the eastern parts (Khoshoo, 1997). Besides, *palas*, *jambul*, *ber* along with patches of bamboo grooves with undergrowth of thorny shrubs and bushes are also present within their habitat.

Behavioural Biology

Asiatic lions are predatory nocturnal animals with keen sense of hearing. They rest during daytime under the shade of the trees, go in search of food at dusk and usually hunt at night in areas with sparse vegetation. Their activities include periods of socializing, grooming, and defecating. During rest, the most common peaceful tactile gestures are head rubbing and social licking (Schaller, 1972). Males tend to rub other males and cubs and females rub females, while social licking is generally mutual and often occurs in tandem with head rubbing. Head rubbing is reported to be a form of greeting, manifested by nuzzling one's forehead, face and neck against another lion (Joslin, 1973). They also show a wide array of facial expressions and body postures that serve as visual gestures (Schaller, 1972), as well as, a large repertoire of sounds include snarling, purring, hissing, coughing, miaowing, woofing and roaring. Lions tend to roar in a very characteristic manner, starting with a few deep, long roars that trail off into a series of shorter ones. Their roars are heard throughout the night, most noticeably during dusk and dawn. They have developed a strong sense of hearing. They were also recorded to hunt during daytime, particularly in areas with thick growth of vegetation. They spend an average of two hours a day walking and 50 minutes eating (Schaller, 1972). They generally do not attack humans unless it is threatened, troubled, injured or diseased.

Food and Foraging Behaviour: Asiatic lion is a carnivore and mainly feeds on the cattle (domesticated cow, buffalo, goat etc.) and game animals (deer, antelope, wild boar etc.) present within their habitat. Interestingly, a study revealed that 75 percent of Asiatic lion's diet was livestock, while wild ungulates made up only 25 percent (Joslin, 1985). Among the wild ungulates, chital, sambar and chinkara are preferred by the Asiatic lions (Paulson, 1999).

Inside the forests of Gir National Park they stalk their prey, stealthily approach their prey and then make a short chase with a speed up to 80 km per hour. The prey is grabbed with one paw on the back and the other on the flank or chest to drag it down. Then they bite the throat of its prey until the victim dies of suffocation. Hunting in Asiatic lion is also a cooperative event. The lionesses do most of the hunting in a lion pride. Adult males rarely participate in hunting, but they join the group once the kill is made. They feed on the meat picking them clean without crushing the bones, usually leaving enough for the scavengers. Lions generally eat until they are fully satiated and after having a full-meal they may not hunt for several days. During this phase they completely ignore the presence of prey in their vicinity. Amount of food consumed by a full-grown Asiatic lion is about 10–12 kg per day on average.

Breeding Behaviour: Asiatic lions are polyestrous animals. Females become sexually mature within 2–3 years whereas a male attains maturity at around five years of age. Sexually mature female forms the breeding pair with a sexually mature male. There is severe competition among the males for mate selection. The successful male follows the female in heat and mates. Mating is not seasonal and takes place all year round. However, October and November have been reported to be the peak mating period and most of the offspring are produced between January and February. Gestation period lasts for 100–119 days after which the lioness gives birth to a litter of 1–6 cubs in a secluded den, usually away from the rest of the pride. Interval between two successive birth events is found to be 18–24 months.

Cubs are born blind and their dentition appears after 15 days. During this period they are very much vulnerable and fall prey to leopard and other predators. The lioness moves her cubs one by one by holding the nape of their neck in her mouth and cleans them by licking with her tongue. Lionesses in a pride often synchronize their reproductive cycles and cooperate in suckling of the young. Lactation continues for about 6 months. The cubs start eating meat at about 3 months of age while continuing to suckle for up to 6 months. Lioness trains her cubs with all hunting strategies till they are 9 months of age. At one year of age the cubs start living an independent life. During this time cub mortality is fairly high. Upto 80 percent cubs might die before 2 years of age, either due to lack of food or being hunted by other predators (Macdonald, 1983). The surviving individuals reach maturity at 3–4 years of age. Male cubs are excluded from their maternal pride when they reach maturity. The males mark their territory by spraying urine into the tree trunks and several other prominent stationary posts.

Home Range: Each full-grown male require about 100 sq km of space which varies with the habitat condition and prey availability of the area.

Social Organization: Asian lions are highly sociable animals living in loosely knit groups known as 'prides'. The pride is usually small, typically consisting of single male, 2–5 related females and their young. As compared to the African lions, male Asiatic lions are reported to be less social and only associate with the pride when mating or on a large kill. Adult males are temporary members of the pride living for few months to years. There are fierce battles among the males to take possession of a pride and the winner dominates the entire pride. He then gets the privilege to mate with any and every receptive female of that pride. When this dominant male becomes old or shows signs of weakness, he is again forcefully replaced by a younger and more vigorous male.

Threats to Survival

- ***Habitat loss:*** Destruction of the habitats of these animals due to extension of human settlements and agricultural lands, construction of roads and illegal logging had presently restricted them to a single population. Moreover, lopping of tree branches for firewood is widespread and is having a devastating effect, especially upon riverine forest, which is prime habitat for lionesses with cubs during the dry season (Chellam and Johnsingh, 1993).
- ***Human-lion conflict:*** Close proximity of predators, livestock and humans in the Gir Forest often gives rise to human-lion conflicts. Inhabitants of the Gir forest frequently enter in different parts of the forest to collect topsoil, fruit and firewood and to visit temples present inside the protected area. On the other hand, populations of Asiatic lions inside Gir have become quite dense and there is fierce competition for the prime habitats inside forests. As a result, some individuals (predominantly sub-adults, old, injured and diseased individuals) stray outside the protected area and establish their territories in the edges with less competition. They mainly subsist on the domestic cattle and other feral animals, which are easy to predate. In 1995, as many as 1,650 livestock were killed by Asiatic lions in and around the protected areas. Even more alarming is the fact that the lions, which have long been famed for their docility toward humans, have recently begun to attack people mainly outside the sanctuary. Saberwal (1990) has documented 81 attacks resulting in 16 deaths from January, 1988 to April, 1990.
- ***Hunting and poaching:*** Previously Asiatic lions were hunted for sport in large numbers by the *maharajas* who collected them as the trophy for pride. In recent times some of these animals are still illegally killed by the poachers for their hide and skin. There are reports that organized gangs of illegal wildlife traders have switched their attention from tigers to these lions. According to Jackson (2008) 34 animals were killed in 2007.
- ***Diseases:*** Several bacterial, viral and helminthic diseases have been reported to occur in this species. Bacterial disease like feline infectious anaemia is caused by *Hemobartenella felis* and plague is caused by *Yersinia pestis*. Viral diseases caused by feline parvo virus and feline herpes virus-I leading to kerato-conjunctivitis affects the cubs. Helminthes such as round worm (*Ancylostoma braziliensis*) and Tape worm (*Dipylidium* sp.) also infect the cubs and the adults. On the other hand, captive lions have been reported to be vulnerable to the canine distemper virus, feline immunodeficiency virus and feline infectious peritonitis (Jack, 2001).
- ***Demographic factors:*** Only a single population of Asiatic lion is present in India. Such geographically isolated, small population often inbreeds and consequently, their genetic diversity reduces which threatens their survival.
- ***Reduced tolerance by the local communities:*** *Maldharis* community living inside the Gir forests have often lost their cattle to lion ever since they moved into the area, which has resulted in

dramatic alteration of their perspective towards lions. Cumbersome and unrealistic compensation scheme of the Government for livestock loss and confusing bureaucratic procedures are the major cause for such change in the attitude of the local communities (Chellam and Johnsingh, 1993). Subsequently the illegal killing of lions, by weapon or by poisoning, has increased (Saberwal et al., 1994).

- ***Climatic factors:*** Extreme climactic events and increased incidences of natural calamities like drought, flood and fire in the recent past have further jeopardized the scenario of coexistence between humans and Asiatic lions in Gir (Srivastav, 1997). As a result of unnatural drought, water holes within the reserve dried, native ungulates dispersed and the dearth of prey inside the forest compelled the lions to venture outside in the adjoining human habitations. This has further aggravated the human-lion conflicts in this region.

Conservation Initiatives

The first significant effort toward protection for the Asiatic lion was initiated in 1900 when the Nawab of Junagadh banned lion hunting on his private land holdings (Meegama, 1979). Presently, Asiatic lions are listed as Endangered on the IUCN Red List. It is also listed under Appendix-I of CITES and is in the Schedule–I of the Indian Wildlife (Protection) Act. Thus, they have been accorded the nationwide highest level of legal protection along with global prevention in trade of any of its body parts. This subspecies is legally protected in India (Nowell and Jackson, 1996). Gujarat Forest Department employs some 300 rangers and guards to protect the Gir National Park and its lions (Chellam and Johnsingh, 1993). Conservation initiatives in this protected area involved relocation and proper rehabilitation of *Maldharis*, creating and restoring water holes inside habitat, introducing native plant species and conducting census every five years since 1986. Besides, Gujarat Forest Department initiated several management plans to minimize the human-lion conflicts.

Despite of all these efforts, the Asiatic lion in India still exists as a single population and is thus vulnerable to extinction from unpredictable events, such as epidemic or natural calamities like drought, flood and large forest fire etc. Hence, establishment of at least an alternative wild stock is advisable for population safety, as well as, to maximize genetic diversity and to reestablish lion in some of its former range. However, there are various problems in such attempts. It is risky to introduce lions into an area where people have had no experience of them historically. Moreover, unplanned translocation of such mega carnivores might not only threaten the very existence of lions in these areas, but also might generate considerable hostility towards wildlife, which in turn might jeopardise the larger cause of big cat conservation. A previous attempt to establish a second subpopulation in the Chandraprabha Wildlife Sanctuary in eastern Uttar Pradesh initially appeared to be succeeding. But, as the population grew from 3 to 11 animals, the lions suddenly disappeared and were presumably shot or poisoned (Nowell and Jackson, 1996). Presently, the Asiatic lion Reintroduction Project plans to establish a second independent population of Asiatic lions at the Palpur-Kuno Wildlife Sanctuary in northern Madhya Pradesh (Johnsingh et al. 2007). However, this proposed translocation plan has been bitterly contested by the Gujarat Government. There are other major concerns regarding the level of poaching in this area, altogether different climatic conditions and insufficient prey base within the sanctuary to support a viable lion population. Resettlement of the communities will also be required to make available room for the lions. But this time greater care is being taken to make the translocation process participatory by satisfying local needs, ensuring that there is no hostility among the local communities toward lion conservation.

In addition to these *in-situ* conservation efforts, the captive (*ex-situ*) population of Asiatic lions can be theoretically considered to represent a second population. The total global captive population of pure Asiatic lions is believed to be 82, of which 23 are held outside of India (Walker, 1994).

Recently, a collaborative effort 'Asiatic Lion Project' has been developed jointly by Gujarat Forest Department, Government of Gujarat, Wildlife Institute of India and the Zoological Society of London (ZSL) with aims to strengthen conservation efforts in India to safeguard the future of the Asiatic lion in both captivity and in the wild (Armond, 2015). This project also involves strengthening conservation breeding, improve the wildlife health protocols and support conservation education.

4.17 HIMALAYAN BLACK BEAR (*see* Plate III)

Order: Carnivora
Family: Ursidae
Scientific Name: *Ursus thibetanus laniger* (Pocock, 1932)
[Himalayan black bears (*Ursus thibetanus laniger*) is a rare subspecies of the Asiatic black bears (*Ursus thibetanus*)]

Present Status

Wildlife (Protection) Act, 1972	Schedule–I
IUCN	Vulnerable
CITES	Appendix–I
Population Trend	↓

Distinctive Features

- Himalayan black bear is a medium sized species of bear. Males weigh between 110–150 kg, while females are smaller in size weighing about 65–90 kg. Their head and body length is 120–180 cm.
- They usually have a coat of long and smooth black fur with a ruff of longer fur around their neck. A characteristic and distinct pale yellow or whitish "V" shaped breast marking is present on their chest. Their muzzle is light brown in colour.
- Head of Himalayan black bear is large and round, eyes are small and ears are large and are set wide apart.
- Their legs are thick and strong, paws are broad and all the digits in fore and hind limbs are fitted with long razor sharp claws.
- They often stand up and even walk on their strong hind limbs in a plantigrade posture. Such bipedal movement is particularly seen when they feel threatened or are competing for territory with other individuals in order to make themselves appear larger in size than they actually are.
- Their tail is short and is barely visible under a long, coarse coat.
- Life span of the Himalayan black bear is over 30 years in captivity, but they rarely exceed the age of 25 years in wild.

Distribution

The range of Asiatic black bear extends from Pakistan through Nepal and Sikkim to Bhutan and in to China, Southeast Asia and the Amur region of the USSR (FAO, 2006). But, Himalayan black bears occupy a narrow band mostly in the northern part of the Indian subcontinent, which is contiguous with Nepal and Bhutan. In India, the Himalayan black bears are distributed throughout the Himalayan ranges (from Jammu & Kashmir in the west to Arunachal Pradesh in the east) and also possibly in some hills of other northeastern states and probably support one of the largest populations of black bears (Sathyakumar, 2001).

Population

There is no authenticated or definitive population estimate of Himalayan black bears throughout its distribution range. However, available data suggested that there are approximately 7,000–9,000 individuals in India (Sathyakumar, 2006).

Habitat

Himalayan black bears primarily inhabit forested hills and gorges ranging from 1,200–3,300 m (Prater, 1980). They are found in a variety of forested habitats in the Himalayas including upper subtropical, lower moist temperate, broad leaved and coniferous forests. However, their exact habitats depend on the geographical and climatic factors of the region. Likewise, individual bears also move to different habitats and elevations seasonally (Izumiyama and Shiraishi, 2004). For example, they range up to the tree line in the Himalayas at an altitude of about 3,700 m above sea level in summer. Himalayan black bears have also been reported from an elevation of 4,300 m, but they usually do not spend much time in the open meadows of alpine zones. During winter, most of them descend down to the valleys at an altitude of 1,525 m and even lower. During this time they are also found in *Shorea, Castanopsis* and *Rhododendron* forests, as well as, in forests with bamboo groves. They have also been encountered in the *Terai* jungles. In the Assam hill ranges, they are found to live at even lower altitudes. These bears also use regenerating forests, having a high production of berries or young bamboo shoots (Garshelis and Steinmetz, 2008).

Behavioural Biology

Himalayan black bears mostly lead a nocturnal mode of life in most of their range, particularly to avoid contact with humans. They are primarily nocturnal feeders and their nocturnal activity increases during autumn. They usually come out at dusk to collect food and retire after sunrise. Sometimes, they are found to be active in the late afternoon or early morning. In areas with minimal human interference they even forage diurnally. Otherwise during daytime they mostly spend sleeping in caves, rock crevices, tree hollows or thick undergrowths.

Their exact mode of communication is still less explored. However, they are gifted with exceptional good senses of sight, hearing and smell and they mostly communicate vocally. Bear cubs are noticed to make crying calls while away from their mother. Visual communication is adopted to express dominance as and when two bears are in close vicinity. One individual walks or runs towards its rival to express dominance, while the subordinate status is shown by either moving away, or by sitting or lie down postures. They also use 'scent-marking' as a mode of communication with other members, where they use their acute sense of smell. In this mode of communication, a bear urinates or defecates and rubs against trees or other persistent structures thereby pronouncing their presence through scent for other bears to detect.

They typically walk on four feet placing their full paw on ground and therefore, are considered as *plantigrades*.

While fighting they stand up on their two hind feet and attack their enemy with their forepaws and often injure by their razor sharp long claws. They usually avoid man and only attack when they are wounded or trying to protect their cubs. They are also very efficient climbers and are often noticed to climb trees to forage, rest, elude enemies and to hibernate. Himalayan black bears were noticed to hibernate through the winter months within dug out hollow on trees, hollow logs, caves or holes in the ground or steep, mountainous and sunny slopes. Hibernation is particularly noticed in the northern most part of their natural range where harsh cold climate prevails in winter,

Food and Foraging Behaviour: Himalayan black bears are omnivorous animals. Their diet varies seasonally depending upon the availability of food. In summer, they largely feed on wild fruits and berries and raid orchards for pears, apricots and nuts of various kinds. During autumn, they usually shift on a diet of acorns, beechnuts and walnuts that have a high fat content in order to build up a good layer of fat which sustain them throughout the winter. Again in spring, they forage mostly on bamboo, raspberry, hydrangea and other plants. They also feed in plantations and cultivated areas, especially corn and oat fields and fruit orchards (Gong and Harris, 2006; Vinitpornsawan et al., 2006). They are known to damage trees by stripping the bark and eating cambium in order to supplement their nutritionally deficient diet. In addition to this predominately herbivorous diet, they also eat insects, termites, larvae of beetles and other invertebrates, small mammals and eggs, bees and honey. During scarcity of food, they sometimes attack and kill domestic livestock (such as sheep, goat, larger cattle etc.) and even feed on carrion. Being an efficient climber, they can also collect food from the treetops.

Breeding Behaviour: Himalayan black bears are reported to mate in late autumn, particularly in the month of October. During this time they copulate many times. Then after a gestation period of 200–240 days, normally 1 or 2 cubs are born between November and March. However, timing of reproduction is not precisely known for all portions of their range and possibly varies with locality.

They give birth to their cubs and raise them in the shelter of maternal den, which are present usually in thick undergrowth or in the hollow of a tree. The newborn cubs are hairless and blind and therefore, rely mostly on their mother. Eyes open three days after birth and since then they begin to walk. Cubs are weaned when they are six months old and begin to eat solid foods and gradually stop suckling mother's milk. However, cubs were usually seen to stay with their mothers for two years or until her next breeding cycle. They attain sexual maturity at around three or four years of age.

Home Range: In a habitat with sufficient food, Himalayan black bears tend to be less mobile and may remain in a small fixed area for a long time. Therefore, the size of their home range is also relatively small ranging from 10–20 sq km.

Social Organization: Himalayan black bears are solitary animals and usually do not have proper social organization. They only come together to mate or when competing for more desirable territories. Even the pair stays together for only a few days during the breeding season. However, relatively longer association is noticed between the mother and her cubs. At the best they are found to live in family groups consisting of two adults and two successive litters of young. In such associations the individuals often walk in a procession of largest to smallest.

Threats to Survival

- ***Habitat loss:*** Large scale and rapid deforestation often caused by extension of human settlements and agricultural lands, construction of roads, hydro-power stations and illegal logging results in the destruction of the habitats of these animals. In India, more than 90 percent of their distribution range is present outside the protected areas and those areas are particularly threatened by various development projects and extraction of wood for fuel and livestock fodder (Sathyakumar, 2006). Political unrest and associated activity prevent effective habitat protection in Jammu and Kashmir, extensive livestock grazing is considered to be the major threat in Himachal Pradesh and Uttarakhand, while jhum cultivation has led to serious impacts on Asiatic black bear habitat in the northeast states (Sathyakumar, 2001).
- ***Poaching and illegal trade:*** Hunting of the Himalayan black bear has been legally prohibited and forbidden since 1977. Still the threat of poaching looms large on these animals and many bears are illegally killed for their body parts, specifically for gall bladder, hide, skin and paws. Bear bile is widely used in the traditional Chinese medicine. Besides, demand for bear paws also appears to be increasing, which is considered as a very expensive delicacy and are craved by increasing number of wealthy people of Far East (Garshelis and Steinmetz, 2008). Some indigenous people in northeastern states also hunt black bear for its skin, which is merely used as trophy or for ornamental purposes. The scenario became even worse as many of these subsistence hunters have now become commercial poachers (Garshelis and Steinmetz, 2008).

In addition, the "Dancing Bear Trade" is also reducing their number. Once the adult bears are killed or trapped, the cubs often captured and sold to the *madaris*. They train the cubs to dance adopting some cruel methods. As a consequence, these dancing bears often die at a very young age due to malnutrition, mishandling and several diseases.

- ***Human-bear conflict:*** Livestock predation and crop damage by the Himalayan black bears have resulted in an antagonistic relationship with the farmers and shepherds of the Himalayan region, who consider them as pests. Bears were found to raid crop fields frequently during summer and autumn, resulting in high crop damage and during this time the livestock predation was also highest (Sangay and Vernes, 2008). Besides, they frequently attack human beings, which often turn out to be fatal for the victim. It is estimated that livestock predation, crop damage, as well as, attacks on humans have increased considerably since recent past.
- ***Predators:*** They have very few predators in the wild. However, sometimes leopards, tigers, packs of wolves and other predators kill bears, especially the cubs. Despite of fierce protection by mother bear, the small cubs are still vulnerable to predation.
- ***Natural calamities:*** Natural calamities like drought, earthquake and fire also affect bear population in the wild.

Conservation Initiatives

Considering the threats, Himalayan black bears is listed as vulnerable in IUCN Red List of Threatened Species. It has also been included on CITES Appendix–I since 1979. Thus, trade in live bear or bear parts is illegal and are subject to stringent punishment and penalties. Although Himalayan black bears are protected under both international and national laws, yet these laws are often not properly enforced (Garshelis and Steinmetz, 2008).

In India, this species is provided with nationwide legal protection as a Schedule–I species under Indian Wildlife (Protection) Act. Conservation initiatives to increase the number and/or area of protected areas and reduce habitat degradation outside the protected areas would be highly beneficial. In 1999, 'Status and management of the Asiatic black bear in India' was published in the Status Survey and Conservation Action Plan of IUCN (Sathyakumar 1999). A short term research project on 'Behavioural study of Asiatic black bear' was carried out in Padmaja Naidu Himalayan Zoological Park, Darjeeling funded by Central Zoo Authority, India for their conservation breeding (Jha, 2009). Recently, National Bear Conservation and Welfare Action Plan (NBCWAP) was released in the year 2012, which is an outcome of the collaborative efforts of Ministry of Environment and Forests (MoEF), Wildlife Institute of India (WII), and several non-government organizations including Wildlife Trust of India (WTI) and International Fund for Animal Welfare (IFAW). This Action Plan documents the threats faced by bears in India and outlines management actions to be undertaken for their conservation and welfare. Besides, several NGOs like WWF–India, TRAFFIC and others are working relentlessly to conserve habitat, stop illegal hunting and protect this species involving local communities.

4.18 GANGES RIVER DOLPHIN (*see* Plate III)

Order: Cetacea
Family: Platanistidae
Scientific Name: *Platanista gangetica* (Roxburgh, 1801)

Present Status

Wildlife (Protection) Act, 1972	Schedule–I
IUCN	Endangered
CITES	Appendix–I
Population Trend	? Unknown

Distinctive Features

- The colour of Ganges river dolphin varies from dark grey or grey-brown to black dorsal surface and their ventral surface is lighter in colour.
- Body is fairly stocky, fusiform, measures 1.7–2.5 m in total length and weighs between 70 and 85 kg. Females are larger than males and may have longer rostrums.
- The skull is highly asymmetrical and has a distinctly steep forehead and a longitudinal ridge The forehead rises abruptly from the base of the snout.
- Ganges river dolphin has a characteristic prolonged snout forming a long narrow slender beak that thickens at the tip. Their elongated snout can reach 20 percent of total body length. Unlike other dolphins, *Platanista gangetica* lacks snout hair. The beak is proportionally longer in females than in males and is designed for quick snapping action to capture fast moving prey. Both jaws contain a row of sharp pointed interlocking teeth, which are visible even when the mouth is closed. On the upper jaw, there are between 26 and 39 teeth on each side while the lower jaw bears 26–35 teeth on each side. The teeth on lower jaws are typically longer than the teeth on upper jaw.

- Their blowhole is a longitudinal slit. This is unique in comparison to the horizontally positioned blowholes in most other toothed whales. The local name '*susu*' is said to refer to the noise this dolphin makes when it breathes.
- These river dolphins are unique in having long visibly constricted necks with unfused vertebrae.
- The flippers are large and can be up to 18 percent of total body length. Ends of the pectoral fins are squared instead of tapered. Similarly, the tail fluke is also quite broad and large, reaching 46 cm in width on average with pointed tips. But the dorsal fin is undeveloped, rudimentary, triangular ridge-like. This is usually just a few centimetres in height and resembles a fleshy hump on its back.
- The eyes and optic nerves of this species are degenerated. The eyes lack crystalline lenses and are, therefore, incapable of forming images on the retina. It is believed that the lack of a true visual apparatus in the river dolphin is due to its habitat. Because, vision in basically useless in the muddy water where they live. However, their eyes may be able to sense light intensity and direction but not distinct shapes.
- Very little is known about the lifespan and longevity of Ganges river dolphin. Some opine that the lifespan of these freshwater species lies between 18–22 years.

Distribution

Ganges river dolphin is the sole survivor of once a diverse cetacean group. According to Kasuya and Haque (1972), presently there are two subspecies of *Platanista gangetica* viz. (i) Ganges river dolphin (*Platanista gangetica gangetica*) found in the Ganges-Brahmaputra-Meghna and the Karnaphuli-Sangu river systems and their tributaries in Nepal, Bhutan, India and Bangladesh and (ii) Indus river dolphin (*Platanista gangetica minor*) found in the Indus River in Pakistan.

In India, the distribution range of Ganges river dolphin covers seven states namely, Assam, Uttar Pradesh, Madhya Pradesh, Rajasthan, Bihar, Jharkhand and West Bengal. They are found in Ganges river from Varanasi (Uttar Pradesh) to Patna (Bihar), in Ghaghra and Gandak rivers (Bihar and Uttar Pradesh), in Chambal river (Madhya Pradesh and Uttar Pradesh), in Sone and Kosi rivers (Bihar), in Brahmaputra river from Sadia (foothills in Arunachal Pradesh) up to Dhubri (Bangladesh border) and in Kulsi river, a tributary of the Brahmaputra. These animals are best seen at Kaziranga National Park (Assam) and Vikramshila Wildlife Sanctuary (Bihar) within their distribution range.

Population

Surveys in certain portion of the distribution range of Ganges river dolphin collectively accounted for 1,200–1,800 animals. However, the true population is believed to be larger because some potentially important areas, like the Indian Sundarbans, are yet to be surveyed (Smith and Braulik, 2012).

Habitat

They are restricted to freshwater habitats, sometimes occur in the tidal limits, even found along the coast of the Bay of Bengal, but they never enter the sea. In India, they inhabit the stretches of slow-moving muddy water of some of the major river systems and their tributaries, streams, as well as, in connecting lakes in riverine flood plains. They usually migrate locally to tributaries of main river systems during monsoon and come back to larger river channels in the dry, winter season. They are reported to tolerate a wide range of temperature (i.e. 8°C to more than 33°C). They prefer areas of deep waters and reduced flow and generally occupy depths from 3–9 m. However, they must come to the surface every few minutes to breathe. They often congregate in counter-current pools below channel convergences and sharp meanders (Kasuya and Haque, 1972; Smith et al., 1998). They have been also found to concentrate around small mid-channel islands, bridge pilings and other structures as these areas are often rich in prey availability.

Behavioural Biology

Ganges river dolphins are very active and continuously make vocal sounds. They use echolocation to navigate, as well as, to detect food (Perrin et al., 2002). They are very elusive, fast moving and shy of boats. They usually swim few centimetres above the river-bed, tilted on their sides with one flipper trailing along the substratum making roughly a 10 degree angle with the substratum. While swimming their tails are always positioned higher than the head. They occasionally come to the surface at a steep angle with its beak and head sticking out of the water, jump partly or completely clear of the water and landing on the side of the body (Nowak, 2003). During monsoon, their migratory behaviour is prominent. They spend the dry season in deep pools or the main channels of the river systems and tend to migrate to tributaries of the main river systems in monsoon (Nowak, 1999). During rainy season they also descend to tidal waters and sometimes get trapped in the fishing nets.

Food and Foraging Behaviour: Ganges river dolphins are strictly carnivorous and frequently forage on prawns, molluscs, catfishes and several other smaller freshwater fishes. Their side swimming mode and flexible neck allows them to search river bottoms. Mostly they forage in shallow areas or near the bottom substratum. As their vision is poor, hence, the individuals usually rely on echolocation to detect food in the murky water, as well as, to locate preys hidden in the mud of the river bottom. They probe and stir up the bottom with their long beak and thus, detect the hiding shrimp, fish and other prey upon which they feed (Perrin et al., 2002). They also chase and catch schools of small fishes by swimming in shallow water with formidable speed and agility. Once the prey is within reach, they grab them with their long snouts (Reeves and Brownell Jr., 1989). Their teeth and long snouts are designed to catch and hold fish. Particularly while foraging on the fishes, they have been noticed to shake the captured fish in their jaws in order to position it properly and finally swallow 'head first' so that the scales and fin rays of the fish do not injure their oesophagus.

Breeding Behaviour: Very little is known about the breeding behaviour of this animal. They are believed to breed throughout the year. But most births appear to be concentrated between October to March, with a significant birth peak noticed in December and January, just before the beginning of the dry season. Gestation period is typically about 10 months, after which generally one or two offspring are born. The newborn dolphins are usually 70–90 cm long. Interval between two successive births is two years.

Lactation by the mother dolphin to her offspring until weaning is the main form of parental care and the juveniles are normally weaned at around 9 months of age. Once weaned, they disperse and lead an independent life (MacDonald and Norris, 2001). Males and females usually reach sexual maturity at the age of 10 years and are reported to remain sexually active even at the age of twenty-six.

Home Range: There are some indications of territoriality, as male possess chasing behaviors. However, very little information is available regarding the size of their home ranges. Nevertheless, it is believed that these animals have large home ranges as they were found to travel extensively throughout river ecosystems, and in monsoons they move from mainland channels to coastlines and tributaries.

Social Organization: Ganges river dolphins are believed to be solitary animals (Nowak, 1999). But they are often found in pairs and occasionally in small groups of 3–10 individuals in certain parts of the rivers. Groups of up to 30 animals have also been reported. It is believed that they assemble in loose aggregations in areas where the water current is relatively weak with large congregations of their prey. Therefore, they are considered as semi-gregarious. But the young dolphins usually remain solitary before they are one year old.

Threats to Survival

- ***Construction of dams, barrages and water development projects:*** Ganges river dolphins live in one of the most densely populated areas in the world, where extensive damming of rivers for irrigation and electricity generation is a major threat. At least 50 dams have been constructed within the known or historical range of the subspecies (Smith et al., 2000). Since 1956 alone, more than twenty barrages (low-gated diversion dams) and eighteen high dams have been constructed in the Ganges-Brahmaputra-Megna and Karnaphuli-Sangu river systems. More dams and barrages are either under construction or in advanced planning stages. Such structures degrade their foraging and spawning habitats, subsequently leading to food scarcity, as well as, resulting in significant changes in breeding. All these changes also prevent their seasonal migration leading to isolation of populations, elevate chronic/acute exposure to toxins, and thus, make many portions of the rivers less habitable for these freshwater cetaceans (Perrin et al., 2002). In addition to fragmenting populations, dams and barrages have degraded downstream habitat and created impoundments with high sedimentation and altered assemblages of fish and invertebrate species. Moreover, the insufficiency of water released downstream of many barrages have eliminated dry-season habitat for more than 300 km (Smith et al., 1998). This has also allowed salt water to intrude an additional 160 km into the Sundarbans delta (Rahman, 1986), further decreasing the amount of suitable habitat for this obligate freshwater dolphin (Reeves et al., 1993). Long-term implications of reduced dry-season flows in the Ganges are catastrophic, both for the survival of river dolphins and also for a major portion of human population, inhabiting around the Ganges basin.
- ***Pollution:*** Pollution of the rivers in their distribution areas is another major threat to their survival. The pollution of river Ganges severely affects this species. Extensive use of fertilizers and pesticides in the adjoining agricultural fields come as run-off and pollute the riverine ecosystem. Besides, untreated industrial and domestic effluents are also responsible for the death of many fishes and are likely to have a negative effect on dolphin populations. In certain population, the accumulation of heavy metal and organochlorine is posing serious health

hazards. Concentrations of organochlorine and butyltin were found to be alarmingly high in the tissues of Ganges river dolphins (Senthilkumar et al., 1999).

- ***Poaching and accidental deaths:*** Fishing nets and harpoons are used to capture these animals for their meat and fat. They were reported to be killed by tribal people in the upper Brahmaputra for their meat and by the fishermen in middle reaches of the Ganges for their fat. Oil extracted from fat is used for burning lamps, as an ingredient in traditional medicines and several other purposes, whereas the meat was used as 'catfish bait' by the fishermen and food by local people. Poaching of this species was once extensively done throughout its range. With increased awareness among the fishermen communities such deliberate killing of river dolphins is believed to have declined in most areas, but some amount of poaching is still thriving (Sinha, 2002). At present, accidental entanglement of dolphins in fishing gears, especially gillnets and subsequent drowning is causing considerable fatalities for Ganges river dolphins throughout their range (Sinha, 2002).
- ***Parasites:*** *Platanista gangetica* acts as a host for *Cyclorchis campula*, *Echinochasumus andersoni*, *Anisakis simplex* and *Contracaecum lobulatum* (Moreno, 2003).
- ***Other threats:*** Bull sharks entering the south Asian river systems are highly aggressive and they often attack waders and fishermen. These sharks are very similar in size and color with Ganges river dolphins, for which many of these attacks on local peoples are wrongly blamed on these cetaceans. As a result, these dolphins are often persecuted by local people out of retaliation (Kannan et al., 1993; Perrin et al., 2002).

Conservation Initiatives

The animal is listed in the Appendix–I of CITES. Hence, trade of any part of this species is prohibited. It is also listed in the Agreement on the Conservation of Small Cetaceans of the Baltic and North Sea (ASCOBANS) and Appendix–I of the Convention on Migratory Species (CMS or the Bonn Convention). Being placed in the Schedule–I of the Wildlife (Protection) Act, 1972, this aquatic mammal is provided with the highest degree of legal protection and legally protected from hunting in all range states of this country. The National Ganga River Basin Authority chaired by the Prime Minister declared Ganges river dolphin as the National Aquatic Animal of India. Recent proceedings of the Patna High Court directed the state and federal Governments to allocate funds for supporting efforts to conserve and monitor dolphins in the Ganges.

The upper Ganga river from Brijghat to Narora, in the state of Uttar Pradesh has been declared as a Ramsar site and WWF–India, along with the local communities, has taken significant efforts there to protect this species. Due to such conservation initiatives over the decade, the population of Ganges river dolphins have almost doubled in this stretch. The area between Sultanganj and Kahalgaon in Patna, Bihar was also declared as The Vikramshila Gangetic Dolphin Sanctuary (VGDS) in August 1991. This is the first dolphin research centre and protected area for dolphins in this country. Moreover, dolphins present inside the existing national parks and sanctuaries receive protection by virtue of being located within a protected area. It has been recently found that fish oils can be used as an efficient alternative of dolphin oil for the preparation of bait or fish attractant. Thus, further awareness generation among the fishermen, better availability of these alternative fish attractants and strict vigil on use of dolphin oil will reduce the threat of poaching on these animals.

Several research projects on Ganges river dolphins are now being undertaken by various Government departments, non-government organizations and academic institutions to promote further research. Status surveys are conducted throughout the present and historical distribution range of Ganges river dolphins to assess the current distribution and abundance of *Platanista gangetica* and to assess the suitable habitat availability. Some of the projects also aim to increase awareness. Outcome of all these projects ultimately strive to develop conservation strategy and subsequent conservation action plan for this elusive river-dweller. WWF–India has been engaged in various activities to conserve the habitat of the Ganges river dolphin and secure a future for the endangered species. The Action Plan prepared by WWF–India in 1997, has been implemented to bring about a sustainable improvement in their habitat and thereby increase their population. Moreover, *Platanista gangetica*, serve as key indicators of water and environmental quality. They are also important in controlling and maintaining healthy fish and crustacean population. Therefore, plight of Ganges river dolphins should be considered before clearing any development projects (such as construction of dams and barrages) on rivers within their distribution range.

REVIEW QUESTIONS

1. Name one endemic species of Eastern Himalaya. Give an idea on the habitat of Indian salamander. Identify the threats to the survival of Indian salamander. Suggest measures to save this animal from extinction.
2. What do you mean by "Aribadha"? Give an account on the mass nesting behaviour of olive ridley turtle. What are the challenges against successful Aribadha? Elaborate different management interventions to save the species.
3. Why great Indian bustard is called a keystone species of Indian grassland? Comment on its present conservation status. State the distribution of great Indian bustard. Why their population are declining? Elaborate "Project Bustard".
4. How does great Indian bustard differ morphologically from Bengal florican? Comment on the present distribution pattern of Bengal florican. Enumerate the threats to the survival of Bengal florican. Explain different conservation initiatives to save this animal from extinction.
5. State the objectives of habitat level recovery. How does it differ from landscape level conservation plan? Comment on proposed recovery action plans of Bengal florican.
6. Mention the current population trend of Jerdon's courser. Discuss the role of BNHS in the special recovery plan for this species. State their recommendation.
7. Enumerate different causes for recent disappearance of white-rumped vulture. What do you mean by "Vulture restaurant". Discuss in detail the conservation management of vultures.
8. Comment on the systematic status of hoolock gibbon. How they are distributed presently? Elaborate food and feeding habit of hoolock gibbon. Explain the phenomenon of social organization among gibbons. Identify the reasons for their possible extinction. Give a brief account on the conservation management undertaken to save this animal from extinctions.
9. Point out the unique features of slender loris with special reference to their food and feeding behaviour, breeding behaviour and social organization. Why they are vulnerable to extinctions?
10. Enumerate the present status of Manipur brow-antlered dear. Comment on the habitat preference of this animal. Identify the threats to the survival of this unique species. Elaborate the conservation initiatives taken to save this animal from extinction.
11. Mention the present status of Himalayan musk dear. Why they should get conservation priority? Enumerate the threats to the survival of this species. Suggest measures to conserve the species.
12. Mention the home range and territoriality of royal Bengal tiger. Give an idea regarding food and foraging strategies of tiger. Identify different threats to their survival.
13. Give an impression on the social organization of Asiatic lion. Comment on the current distribution pattern of Asiatic lion in India. Identify different threats in their existing distribution range. Suggest measures to overcome this problems.
14. State the distinctive features of Himalayan black bear. How they are distributed along the Himalayan range? Comment on their habitat preference.
15. How does Asian elephant differ morphologically from African counterpart? Comment on their distribution range. Name the Indian states devoid of elephant population.
16. Highlight the nature of parental care observed among dolphin community. Mention the anthropogenic threat responsible for its population decline in Indian rivers.

REFERENCES

Ackerman, R.A., The Nest Environment and the Embryonic Development of Sea Turtles, In: Lutz, P.L. and Musick, J.A. (eds.), *The Biology of Sea Turtles*, CRC Press Inc., Boca Raton, Florida, 1997.

Ahsan, M., Socio-ecology of the hoolock gibbon (*Hylobates hoolock*) in two forests of Bangladesh. In: Chicago Zoological Society (ed.), *The apes: challenges for the 21st century, Brookfield Zoo, 2000*, Chicago Zoological Society, Brookfield, Illinois, USA, 2001.

Alfred, J., The hoolock gibbon – *Hylobates hoolock*, *Primate Report*, **34**, 65–69, 1992.

Ali, S. and Ripley, S.D., *Compact Handbook of the Birds of India and Pakistan*, Oxford University Press, Bombay, 1987.

Ali, S. and Ripley, S.D., *Handbook of the Birds of India and Pakistan, Together with Those of Nepal, Sikkim, Bhutan and Ceylon, Volume 2: Megapodes to Crab Plover*, Oxford University Press, Bombay, 1968.

Andheria, A.P., Karanth, K.U. and Kumar, N.S., Diet and prey profiles of three sympatric large carnivores in Bandipur Tiger Reserve, India, *Journal of Zoology*, **273**, 2, 169–17, 2007.

Anon, Rajasthan launches 'Project GIB', *Protected Area Update*, **19**, 4, 17, 2013.

Anon, Recovery programme for the Great Indian Bustard, *Buceros*, **14**, 2, 4, 2009.

Anon, Fishing cat found dead in central India, *Cat News,* **43**, 33, 2005.

Armond, R., *A Step Forward for Asiatic Lion Conservation*, The Zoological Society of London, London, England, 2015. Retrieved from: https://www.zsl.org/blogs/a-step-forward-for-asiatic-lion-conservation

Arshad, M., Chaudhary, M.J.I. and Wink, M., High mortality and sex ratio imbalance in a critically declining Oriental Whitebacked Vulture population (*Gyps bengalensis*), *Journal of Ornithology*, **150**, 2, 495-503, 2009.

Aryal, A., *Status and distribution of Himalayan Musk deer 'Moschus chrysogaster' in Annapurna Conservation Area of Manang District, Nepal,* Institute of Forestry Pokhara, Nepal, 2005.

Azad, M.A.K., Hashem, M.A. and Hossain, M.M., Study on Human-Royal Bengal Tiger Interaction of *in situ* and *ex situ* in Bangladesh. *Journal of Biological Sciences*, **5**, 3, 250–252, 2005.

Bagchi, S., Goyal, S.P. and Sankar, K., Habitat separation among ungulates in dry tropical forests of Ranthambhore National Park Rajasthan, *Tropical Ecology*, **44**, 2, 175–182, 2003.

Baker, E.C.S., *The Fauna of British India including Ceylon and Burma, Birds*, 2nd ed., Taylor and Francis, London, 1922–1930.

Balakrishnan, C.N., Monfort, S.L., Gaur, A., Singh, L., Sorenson, M.D., Phylogeography and conservation genetics of Eld's deer (*Cervus eldi*), *Molecular Ecology,* **12,** 1, 1-10, 2003.

Banerjee, A., Keibul Lamjao: The world's only floating national park: Up close with the endangered brow-antlered deer floating on Manipur's Loktak Lake, *Livemint E-Paper*, 2015. Retrieved from. http://www.livemint.com/Leisure/FvDmxWW6IamPeFQMw7TrVI/The-sangai-struggles-to-live.html

Baral, H.S., Ram, A.K., Chaudhary, B., Basnet, S., Chaudhary, H., Giri, T.R. and Chaudhary, D., Conservation Status of Bengal Florican *Houbaropsis bengalensis bengalensis* (Gmelin, 1789) (Gruiformes: Otididae) in Koshi Tappu Wildlife Reserve and adjoining areas, eastern Nepal, *Journal of Threatened Taxa*, **4**, 3, 2464-2469, 2012.

Barber, I. *Bengal florican—tag-teamed and a first for the Indian Subcontinent,* Royal Society for the Protection of Birds, 2013. Retrieved from: http://www.rspb.org.uk/community/ourwork/b/biodiversity/archive/2013/05/01/bengal-florican-tag-teamed-and a-first-for-the-indian-subcontinent.aspx.

Barber, I., *Conserving the Critically Endangered Bengal Florican—a Terai Flagship Species. Half Year Report* (1st April 2014 to 30th September 2014). Darwin Initiative, UK, 2014. Retrieved from: http://www.darwininitiative.org.uk/documents/19011/23267/19-011%20HR2%20-%20Edited.pdf.

Baskaran, N., *Ranging and resource utilization of Asian Elephants (Elephas maximus) in Nilgiri Biosphere Reserve, South India* (Ph.D Thesis), Bharathidasan University, Tamil Nadu, India, 2002.

Baskaran, N., Balasubramaniam, M., Swaminathan, S. and Desai, A. A., Home range of elephants in the Nilgiri Biosphere Reserve, South India. pp. 296–313. In: J. C. Daniel and H. S. Datye (Eds), *A Week with Elephants*, Bombay Natural History Society and Oxford University Press, Bombay and New Delhi, 1995.

Bernardo, J. and Plotkin, P.T., An evolutionary perspective on the Arribada phenomenon and reproductive behavioral polymorphism of olive ridley sea turtles (*Lepidochelys olivacea*). In: P.T. Plotkin (ed.), *Biology and Conservation of Ridley Sea Turtles*. Johns Hopkins University Press, Baltimore, MD, 2007.

Bhaskar, S., Preliminary report on the status and distribution of sea turtles in Indian waters. *Indian Forester*, **107**, 11, 707–711, 1981.

Bhumpakphan, N., Sukmasuang, R. and Chaiyarat, R., Thailand: The crossroad where two Eld's deer subspecies existed. In: B. Pukazhenthi (Ed.), *Workshop on Eld's deer conservation and restoration*, pp. 10–14, Khao Kheow Open Zoo, Chonburi, Thailand, 2004.

Bhushan, B., *Ornithology of the Eastern Ghats* (Ph.D. Thesis), Bombay University, Bombay, 1994.

Bhushan, B., Jerdon's Courser—rediscovery and survey. In: *BNHS Bombay, Final Report: Endangered Bird Project*. pp. 127–134, 1990.

Bhushan, B., Jerdon's Courser at Cuddapah. *Newsletters for Birdwatchers*, **32,** (5 and 6), 20, 1992.

BirdLife International, *Ardeotis nigriceps*. The IUCN Red List of Threatened Species, Ver. 2015.2, 2013. Retrieved from: www.iucnredlist.org

BirdLife International, *Canal diverted to save Jerdon's Courser*, 2008. Retrieved from: http://www.birdlife.org/news/news/2008/08/jerdons_courser.html.

BirdLife International, *Houbaropsis bengalensis*. The IUCN Red List of Threatened Species 2016: e.T22692015A93333629, IUCN, 2016. Retrieved from: http://dx.doi.org/10.2305/IUCN.UK.2016-3.RLTS.T22692015A93333629.en.

BirdLife International, *Rhinoptilus bitorquatus*, IUCN Red List of Threatened Species. Version 2009.1., IUCN, 2009.

BirdLife International, Species factsheet: *Gyps bengalensis*, 2015. Retrieved from: http://www.birdlife.org

BirdLife International, *Threatened Birds of Asia: the Birdlife International Red Data Book*, Birdlife International, Cambridge, UK, 2001.

BirdLife International, Triple helping of good news for Jerdon's Courser, 2009. Retrieved from: http://www.birdlife.org/news/news/2009/09/jerdons_courser.html.

BirdLife International, 2008, Drugs firms told to do more to prevent vulture extinctions. Retrieved from: http://www.birdlife.org/news/news/2008/08/indian_drug_announcement.html#.

Bjorndal, K.A., Foraging ecology and nutrition of sea turtles. In: Lutz, P., J.A. Musick, Ed. *The Biology of Sea Turtles*. pp. 199–231. BCRC Press Inc., Boca Raton, 1997.

Bombay Natural History Society (BNHS), Report of the International South Asian Vulture Recovery Plan Workshop. *Buceros*, 1–48, 2004.

Bowden, C., The Asian *Gyps* vulture crisis: the role of captive breeding in India to prevent total extinction, *Birding Asia,* **12**, 121–123, 2009.

Breeden, S., The Happy Fisher. *BBC Wildlife Magazine*, **7**, 238–241, 1989.

CAMP-BCPP, *Conservation Assessment Management Plan of Biodiversity Conservation Prioritization Project Workshop on Freshwater Fishes of India*, National Bureau of Fish Genetic Resources, Lucknow, 1997.

Carr, A., New perspectives on the pelagic stage of sea turtle development, *Conservation Biology*, **1**, 103-121, 1987.

Cat Specialist Group, Fishing Cat *Prionailurus viverrinus* (On-line), 1996. Retrieved from: http://lynx.uio.no/catfolk/viver01.htm.

Chandrasekhar, A. and Jeganathan, P., A glimmer of hope for the critically endangered Jerdon's Courser. *Mistnet*, **9**, 4, 19, 2008.

Chavan, R. and Barber, I., In search of the elusive Jerdon's Courser: what future for one of the most endangered birds on earth? *Birding ASIA,* **18**, 102–104, 2012.

Chellam, R. and Johnsingh, A.J.T., *Management of Asiatic lions in the Gir Forest, India.* In N. Dunstone and M. L. Gorman (Eds.) *Mammals as predators.* The Zoological Society of London and the Mammal Society, London, **65**, 409–423, 1993.

Chetry, D., Medhi, R., Biswas, J., Das, D. and Bhattacharjee, P.C., Nonhuman primates in the Namdapha National Park, Arunachal Pradesh, India, *International Journal of Primatology,* **24**, 2, 383–388, 2003.

Choudhury, A., Ecology of the hoolock gibbon (*Hylobates hoolock*), a lesser ape in the tropical forests of north-eastern India, *Journal of Tropical Ecology,* **7**, 1, 147–153, 1991.

Choudhury, A., A survey of hoolock gibbon (*Hylobates hoolock*) in southern Assam, India, *Primate Report,* **44**, 77-85, 1996a.

Choudhury, A., Primates in Bherjan, Borajan and Podumoni Reserved Forests of Assam, India, *Asian Primates,* **5**, (3-4), 10–11, 1996b.

Choudhury, A., A survey of hoolock gibbon (*Hylobates hoolock*) in Dibru-Saikhowa National Park, Assam, India. *Primate Report,* **56**, 61–66, 2000.

Choudhury, A., Primates in Northeast India: An overview of their distribution and conservation, *ENVIS Bulletin: Wildlife and Protected Areas,* **1**, 1, 92–101, 2001a.

Choudhury, A., New primate sanctuary in Assam, India. *Asian Primates,* **7**, (3–4),18–19, 2001b.

Choudhury, A., Status and Conservation of the Asian elephant *Elephas maximus*in north-eastern India, *Mammal Review*, **29**, 141–173, 1999.

Choudhury, A., Lahiri Choudhury, D.K., Desai, A., Duckworth, J.W., Easa, P.S., Johnsingh, A.J.T., Fernando, P., Hedges, S., Gunawardena, M., Kurt, F., Karanth, U., Lister, A., Menon, V., Riddle, H., Rübel, A. and Wikramanayake, E., (IUCN SSC Asian Elephant Specialist Group). *Elephas maximus, The IUCN Red List of Threatened Species*, 2008. e.T7140A12828813. Retrieved from: http://dx.doi.org/10.2305/IUCN.UK.2008.RLTS.T7140A12828813.en.

Choudhury, A., The distribution and status of hoolock gibbon, Hoolock hoolock, in Manipur, Meghalaya, Mizoram, and Nagaland in northeast India, *Primate Conservation*, **20**, 79–87, 2006.

Chundawat, T.S., Gogate, N., Johnsingh, A.J.T., Tigers in Panna: preliminary results from an Indian tropical dry forest, pp. 123–129 In: Seidensticker, J., Christie, S., Jackson, P., (Eds.). *Riding the Tiger: Tiger Conservation in human-dominated landscapes*, Cambridge University Press, Cambridge, 1999.

CITES, *CITES-listed Species Database: Fauna* (On-line), 2001. Retrieved from: http://cites.org/eng/resources/fauna.shtml

Clements, T., Gilbert, M., Rainey, H.J., Cuthbert, R., Eames, J.C., Bunnat, P., Teak, S., Chansocheat, S. and Setha, T., Vultures in Cambodia: population, threats and conservation, *Bird Conservation International*, **23**, 724, 2013.

Conway, S., *Diets and feeding biology of adult olive ridley* (Lepidochelys olivacea) *and loggerhead* (Caretta caretta) *sea turtles in Fog Bay, Northern Territory.* (Hons. Thesis), Northern Territory University, Darwin, 1994.

Cornelius, S.E., Arauz, R., Fretey, J., Godfrey, M.H., Márquez, M.R. and Shanker, K., Effect of land-based harvest of *Lepidochelys*. In: Plotkin PT (Ed.), *Biology and Conservation of Ridley Sea Turtles*, Johns Hopkins University Press, Baltimore, MD, 2007.

Critical Ecosystem Partnership Fund (CEPF), *Ecosystem Profile: Eastern Himalayan Region*, WWF, US-Asian Programme/CEPF, Kathmandu, Nepal, 2005.

Cuthbert, R.J., Dave, R., Chakraborty, S. S., Kumar, S., Prakash, S., Ranade, S. P. and Prakash, V., Assessing the ongoing threat from veterinary NSAIDs to critically endangered Gyps vultures in India, *Oryx,* **45**, 420–426, 2011a.

Cuthbert, R., Taggart, M.A., Prakash, V., Saini, M., Swarup, D., Mateo, R., Chakraborty, S.S., Deori, P. and Green, R., Effectiveness of Action in India to Reduce Exposure of Gyps Vultures to the Toxic Veterinary Drug Diclofenac, *PLoS One,* **6**, 5, e19069, 2011b.

Cuthbert, R.J., Prakash, V., Saini, M., Upreti, S., Swarup, D., Sharma, A.K., Das, A., Green, R.E. and Taggart, M., Are conservation actions reducing the threat to India's vulture populations? *Current Science,* **101**, 1480–1481, 2011c.

Dam, S., A short study on wild hoolock gibbons (*Hoolock hoolock*) in Assam and Bangladesh. *Gibbon Journa,l* **2,** 40-47, 2006.

Das, I., Natural history of the Indian Salamander, *Herpetofauna News,* **9**, 3, 1987.

Das, J., Bhattacharjee, P.C., Biswas. J. and Chetry, D., *Western hoolock gibbon: Socioecology, threats and conservation action plan*, Department of Zoology, Gauhati University, and Primate Research Centre, Northeast Centre, Guwahati, India, 2005.

Das, J., Feeroz, M., Islam, M., Biswas, J., Burjarborua, P., Chetry, D., Medhi, R. and Bose, J., Distribution of hoolock gibbon (*Bunopithecus hoolock hoolock*) in India and Bangladesh, *Zoos' Print Journal,* **18**, 1, 969–976, 2003.

Dasgupta, R., Feeding ecology of the adult Himalayan Salamander *Tylototriton verrucosus* Anderson, 1871 (Caudata: Salamandridae), *Herpetozoa*, **9**, 1/2, 19 – 29, 1996.

Datye, H., First record of the fishing cat Felis Viverrina Bennet in Dalma Wildlife Sanctuary and Chhotanagpur Plateau of Bihar, *Journal of Bombay Natural Historical Society*, **90**, 90. 1993.

Duckworth, J.W., Fishing Cat in Southeast Asia: speculations on status. In: A. Appel and J.W. Duckworth (Eds.), *Proceedings of the First International Fishing Cat Conservation Symposium*, 25–29 November 2015, Nepal, pp. 19–23, Fishing Cat Working Group, Bad Marienberg, Germany and Saltford, Bristol, United Kingdom, 2016.

Dugan, P., *Wetlands in Danger: Conservation Atlas*. Mitchell Beazley and IUCN, London, UK. 1993.

Dutta, S., Rahmani, A.R., Jhala, Y.V., Running out of time? The Great Indian Bustard*Ardeotis nigriceps*—status, viability, and conservation strategies. *European Journal of Wildlife Research*, **57**, 3, 615–625, 2011.

Ellis, C., Of *Gyps* vultures, gypsies and satellite technology, *Peregrine Fund Newsletter,* **35**, 14–15. 2004.

Ernst, C.H., Barbour, R.W. and Lovich, J.E., *Turtles of the United States and Canada*, Smithsonian Inst. Press, Washington, 1994.

Evans, T., van Zalinge, R., Chamnan, H., Borie, R., Kimhout, S. and Packman, C., *Bengal Floricans in the Tonle Sap floodplain: 2007/8 monitoring report (unpublished report to the Tonle Sap Conservation Project)*, Wildlife Conservation Society Cambodia Program, Phnom Penh, 2009.

FAO, Global forest resources 2005. *Progress towards sustainable forest management*, Food and Agriculture Organization of the United Nations, Rome, Italy, 2006.

Frazier, J., Arauz, R., Chevalier, J., Formia, A., Fretey, J., Godfrey, M.H., Márquez, M.R., Pandav, B. and Shanker, K., Human-turtle interactions at sea. In: Plotkin PT. (Ed.), *Biology and Conservation of Ridley Sea Turtles*, Johns Hopkins University Press, Baltimore, MD, 2007.

Frost, D.R., *Amphibian Species of The World. A Taxonomic and Geographic Reference*. Allen Press, Inc., and Associations of Systematic Collections, Lawrence, 1985.

Garshelis, D. L. and Steinmetz, R., *Ursus thibetanus. IUCN Red List of Threatened Species, Version 2015.2*, IUCN Bear Specialist Group, International Union for Conservation of Nature, 2008.

Gee, E.P., The brow antlered deer of Manipur, *Oryx*, **6**, 103–115, 1961.

George, N., *India counts more wild tigers, credits conservation* [Online], Associated Press, 2015. Retrieved from: http://bigstory.ap.org/article/fe18af60d7fd428ab3

5f993d5a57107f/india-counts-more-wild-tigers-2014-credits-conservation

Gilbert, M., Virani M. Z., Watson R. T., Oaks, J.L., Benson P.C., Khan A.A., Ahmed S., Chaudhry J., Arshad M., Mahamood S. and Shah, Q. A., Breeding and mortality of oriental white-backed vulture Gyps bengalensis in Punjab Province, Pakistan. *Bird Conservation International*, **12**, 311–326, 2002.

Gilbert, M., Watson, R.T., Virani, M.Z., Oaks, J.L., Ahmed, S., Chaudhry, M.J.I., Arshad, M., Mahmood, S., Ali, A., Khan, A.A., Rapid population declines and mortality clusters in three Oriental Whitebacked Vulture *Gyps bengalensis* colonies in Pakistan due to diclofenac poisoning, *Oryx*, **40**, 4, 388–399, 2006.

Global Tiger Initiative, *Global Tiger Recovery Program 2010–2022*. Global Tiger Initiative Secretariat, Washington, 2011.

Gong, J. and Harris, R. B., The status of bears in China. *Understanding Asian bears to secure their future*, pp. 50–56, Japan Bear Network, Ibaraki, Japan, 2006.

Gray, T.N.E., Hong, C., Collar, N.J. and Dolman, P.M., Sex-specific habitat use by a lekking bustard: conservation implications for the critically endangered Bengal Florican (*Houbaropsis bengalensis*) in an intensifying agroecosystem, *The Auk*, **126**, 1, 112–122, 2009.

Green, M.J.B. and Kattel, B., Musk Deer: Little Understood, Even its Scent *In: Proceedings of the First International Symposium on Endangered Species Used in Traditional East Asian Medicine: Substitutes for Tiger Bone and Musk*, TRAFFIC/IUCN, Hong Kong, 1998.

Green, M.J.B., Musk Production from Musk Deer. *Traffic Bulletin*, **8**, 59-61, 1989.

Green, M.J.B., Some ecological aspects of a Himalayan population of musk deer. In: C.M. Wemmer (Ed.), *The Biology and Management of Cervidae*, pp. 307–319, Smithsonian Institution Press, Washington, D. C., USA, 1987.

Green, M.J.B. *Aspects of the ecology of the Himalayan Musk deer* (Ph.D. Thesis), University of Cambridge, Cambridge, UK, 1985.

Green, R.E., Newton, I., Shultz, S., Cunningham, A. A., Gilbert, M., Pain, D.J., Prakash, V., Diclofenac poisoning as a cause of vulture population declines across the Indian subcontinent. *Journal of Applied Ecology,* **41**, 793–800, 2004.

Grimmett, R., Inskipp, C. and Inskipp, T., *Birds of the Indian Subcontinent*, Christopher Helm, London, 1998.

Groves, C, P., *Primate Taxonomy*, Smithsonian Institution Press, Washington DC, 2001.

Groves, C.P. and Grubb, P., Relationships of Living Deer. In: C.M. Wemmer (Ed.), *Biology and Management of the Cervidae*, Smithsonian Institution Press, Washington, DC, USA. 21–59, 1987.

Groves, C.P., Yingxiang, W. and Grubb, P., Taxonomy of Musk-Deer, Genus*Moschus* (Moschidae, Mammalia). *Acta Theriologica Sinica,* **15**, 3, 181–197, 1995.

Grubb, P., List of deer species and subspecies. *Deer, Journal of the British Deer Society,* **8**, 153–155, 1990.

Grubb, P., Artiodactyla, In: D. E. Wilson and D. M. Reeder (Eds), *Mammal Species of the World. A Taxonomic and Geographic Reference* (3rd ed.), pp. 637–722, Johns Hopkins University Press, Baltimore, USA, 2005.

Gupta, A.K., Status and conservation of non-human primates in Tripura, India. In: Thierry B, Anderson JR, Roeder JJ, Herrenschmidt N, editors. *Current Primatology, Volume I: Ecology and Evolution,* pp. 101–111, Universite Louis Pasteur, Strasbourg, France, 1994.

Hamann. M., Limpus, C. and Read, M., Vulnerability of marine reptiles in the Great Barrier Reef to climate change. In: Johnson J, & Marshall P. (Eds.) *Climate Change and the Great Barrier Reef: A Vulnerability Assessment*, pp. 465–496, Great Barrier Reef Marine Park Authority and Australia Greenhouse Office, Hobart, 2007.

Haque, N.M., Scavenging habit of fishing cat (*Felis viverrina*) in Keoladeo National Park, Bharatpur. *Journal of Bombay Natural History*, **85**, 1, 183–184, 1988.

Haque, N.M. and Vijayan, V., Food habits of the fishing cat *Felis viverrina* in Keoladeo National Park, Bharatpur, Rajasthan. *Journal of the Bombay Natural History Society*, **90**, 3, 498–500, 1993.

Hays, G.C., Broderick, A.C., Glen, F. and Godley, B.J., Climate change and sea turtles: a 150-year reconstruction of incubation temperatures at a major marine turtle rookery. *Global Change Biology,* **9**, 4, 642–646, 2003.

Hedge, V.D. and Deuti, K., Distribution sites of the Himalayan Salamander (*Tylotrotriton verrucosus*) Anderson in the Darjeeling Hills of Northern West Bengal, India. *Cobra*, **1**, 2, 29–36, 2007.

Hemley, G. and Mills, J. A., The beginning of the end of tigers in trade?" in: Seidensticker, J., Christie, S. nand Jackson, P. (Eds.) *Riding the Tiger. Tiger Conservation in human-dominated landscapes*. Cambridge University Press, Cambridge, 1999.

Herbst, L.H., Fibropapillomatosis of marine turtles, *Annual Review of Fish Diseases,* **4**, 389–425, 1994.

Houston, D.C., Indian Whitebacked Vulture (*Gyps bengalensis*), pp. 456-466. In: Newton I, & Chancellor RD (Ed.), *Conservation Studies of Raptors*, International Council for Bird Preservation, Cambridge, UK, 1985.

Ishtiaq, F., Dutta, S., Yumnam, B., and Jhala, Y.V., Low genetic diversity in the endangered great Indian bustard (*Ardeotis nigriceps*) across India and implications for conservation. *Conservation Genetics*, **12**, 3, 857–863, 2011.

Isvaran, K. Intraspecific variation in group size in the blackbuck antelope: the roles of habitat structure and forage at different spatial scales, *Oecologia*, **154** , 2, 435–44, 2007.

IUCN. *IUCN Red List of Threatened Species, Version* 4, International Union for Conservation of Nature, 2010. Retrieved from: http://www.iucnredlist.org/

Iwaniuk, A.N., Blankstein, W.G., and Whishaw, I.Q., Observations of the feeding behaviour of fishing cats (*Prionailurus viverrinus*). *Mammalia*, **65**, 1, 89–91, 2001.

Izumiyama, S. and Shiraishi, T., Seasonal changes in elevation and habitat use of the Asiatic black bear (*Ursus thibetanus*) in the Northern Japan Alps, *Mammal Studies,* **29**, 1–18, 2004.

Jackson, P., Nearly one-tenth of last Asiatic lions died this year, *Cat News,* **47**, 36–37, 2008.

Jeganathan, P., Green, R. E., Norris, K., Vogiatzakis, I. N., Bartsch, A., Wotton, S. R, Bowden, C. G.R., Griffiths, G. H., Pain, D. and Rahmani, A. R., Modelling habitat selection and distribution of the critically endangered Jerdon's courser *Rhinoptilus bitorquatus* in scrub jungle: an application of a new tracking method, *Ecology*, **41**, 2, 224–237, 2004a.

Jeganathan, P., Rahmani, A.R., Green, R.E., Norris, K., Bowder, C., Wotton, S.R. and Pain, D, *Conservation of the Critically Endangered Jerdon's Courser Rhinoptilus bitorquatus in India [Final Report]*, Bombay Natural History Society, Mumbai, 2004b.

Jeganathan, P., Call of the Jerdon's Courser, *Hornbill*, Jan-Mar. 2005, 14–19, 2005a.

Jeganathan, P., Telugu-Ganga canal construction in Jerdon's Courser habitat, *Mistnet,* **6**, 4, 12–13, 2005b.

Jeganathan, P. and Rahmani, A.R., Digging a grave for the Jerdon's Courser, *Sanctuary Asia*, **XXVI**, 2, 34–37, 2006.

Jeganathan, P., and Wotton, S. R. The First Recordings Of Calls Of The Jerdon's Courser *Rhinoptilus bitorquatus* (Blyth), Family Glareolidae. *Journal of Bombay Natural History Society*, **101**, 1, 26–28, 2004.

Jeganathan, P., Green, R.E., Bowden, C.G.R., Norris, K., Pain, D. and Rahmani, A., Use of tracking strips and automatic cameras for detecting critically endangered Jerdon's coursers *Rhinoptilus bitorquatus* in scrub jungle in Andhra Pradesh, India, *Oryx*, **36**, 182–188, 2002.

Jeganathan, P., Rahmani, A.R. and Green, R.E., *Construction of Telugu-Ganga Canal in and Around Two Protected Areas in Cuddapah District, Andhra Pradesh, India. Immediate Threat to the World Population of the Critically Endangered Jerdon's Courser Rhinoptilus Bitorquatus. Survey Report*. Bombay Natural History Society, Mumbai, India, 2005.

Jeganathan, P., Rahmani, A.R., Green, R.E., Norris, K., Vogiatzakis, I.N., Bowden, C. and Pain, D. Quantification of threats and suggested ameliorative measures for the conservation of the critically endangered Jerdon's Courser *Rhinoptilus bitorquatus* and its habitat, *Journal of the Bombay Natural History Society*, **105**, 1, 73–83, 2008.

Jha, A.K., *Behavioural study for the conservation breeding of Asiatic black bear (Ursus thibetanus) in Padmaja Naidu Himalayan Zoological Park, Darjeeling (Final Report)*, Padmaja Naidu Himalayan Zoological Park, Darjeeling, 152p, 2009.

Jhala, Y.V., Seasonal effects on the nutritional ecology of blackbuck *Antilope cervicapra*. *Journal of Applied Ecology*, **34**, 6, 1348–58, 1997.

Jhala, Y.V., Qureshi, Q. and Sinha, P.R. (Eds.), *Status of tigers, co-predators and prey in India, 2010 (TR 2011/003)*. National Tiger Conservation Authority, Govt. of India, New Delhi, and Wildlife Institute of India, Dehradun, India, 2011. Retrieved from: http://projecttiger.nic.in/WriteReadData/PublicationFile/Tiger_Status_oct_2010.pdf

Johnsingh, A.J.T., Goyal, S.P., and Qureshi, Q., Preparations for the reintroduction of Asiatic lion Panthera leo persica into Kuno Wildlife Sanctuary, Madhya Pradesh, India. *Oryx*, **41**, 01, 93–96, 2007.

Joshi, G.C., Tiwari, K.C., Tiwari, R.N. and Pandey, G., Conervation Strategy and Some Studies on Habitat Ecology of Musk Deer (*Moschus moschiferous*) – A Vanishing Species. *Indian Forester*, **199**, 10**,** 798–903, 1993.

Joslin, P., The environmental limitations and future of the Asiatic Lion. *Journal of the Bombay Natural History Society*, **81**, 3, 648–664, 1985.

Joslin P., *The Asiatic Lion: a study of ecology and behaviour* (Ph.D Thesis), University of Edinburgh, Edinburgh, U.K, 1973.

Kakati, K., *Impact on forest fragmentation on the hoolock gibbon in Assam, India* (Ph.D. Thesis), University of Cambridge, Cambridge, 2004.

Kakati, K., *Food selection and ranging in hoolock gibbon (Hylobates hoolock Harlan* 1834*) in Borajan Reserved Forest, Assam* (M.Sc Thesis), Wildlife Institute of India, Saurashtra University, Rajkot, India, 1997.

Kalb, H.J., *Behavior and physiology of solitary and arribada nesting olive ridley sea turtles (Lepidochelys olivacea) during the internesting period* (Ph.D. Thesis), Texas A&M University, College Station, Texas, 1999.

Kanagavel, A., Sinclair, C., Sekar, R. and Raghavan, R., Moolah, misfortune or spinsterhood? The plight of Slender Loris Loris lydekkerianusin southern India, *Journal of Threatened Taxa*, **5**, 1, 3585–3588, 2013.

Kannan, K., Sinha, R.K., Tanabe, S., Ichihashi, H. and Tatsukawa, R., Heavy metals and organochlorine residues in Ganges River Dolphins from India. *Marine Pollution Bulletin,* **26**, 159–162, 1993.

Kar, C.S, and Bhaskar, S., Status of sea turtles in the eastern Indian Ocean. In: Bjorndal, K. (Ed.), *Biology and conservation of sea turtles*, pp. 365–372, Smithsonian Institution Press, Washington D.C., 1982.

Karnad, D., Isvaran, K., Kar, C.S. and Shanker, K., Lighting the way: Towards reducing misorientation of olive ridley hatchlings due to artificial lighting at Rushikulya, India, *Biological Conservation*, **142**, 10, 2083–2088, 2009.

Kasuya, T. and Haque, A.K.M., Some informations on the distribution and seasonable movement of the Ganges dolphin, *Scientific Reports of the Whales Research Institute (Tokyo)*, **24**, 109–115, 1972.

Khan, M.M.H., *Ecology and Conservation of the Bengal Tiger in the Sundarbans Mangrove Forest of Bangladesh.* University of Cambridge, Cambridge. 2004.

Khoshoo, T.N., Conservation of India's endangered mega animals: Tiger and lion. *Current Science*, **73,** 10, 830–842, 1997.

Kolipaka, S., Fishing cat on India's east coast, *Cat News,* **44**, 22, 2006.

Kopitsky KL, Pitman, R.L. and Dutton, P.H., Aspects of olive ridley feeding ecology in the eastern tropical Pacific. In: Coyne, M.S., & Clark, R.D. (Eds.), *Proceedings of the 21st Annual Sea Turtle Symposium on Sea Turtle Biology and Conservation*, NOAA Technical Memorandum, NMFS-SEFSC-528, 2004.

Kopitsky, K., Pitman, R.L. and Plotkin, P.T., Investigations on at-sea mating and reproductive status of olive ridleys, *Lepidochelys olivacea*, captured in the eastern tropical Pacific. In: Kalb, H.J. and Wibbels, T. (Eds), *Proceedings of the Nineteenth Annual Symposium on Sea Turtle Biology and Conservation*, pp. 160–162. NOAA Technical Memorandum, NMFS-SEFSC-443, 2000.

Kumara, H. N., Singh, M. and Kumar, S., Distribution, Habitat Correlates, and Conservation of *Loris lydekkerianus* in Karnataka, India. *International Journal of Primatology,* **27**, 4, 941-969. 2006.

Lahkar, D., Prakash, V., Sahu, H.K., Raut, S.D., Datta, S.K. and Prakash N., Feeding ecology of Gyps species of vultures in captivity, *Newsletter for Birdwatchers*, **50**, 5, 65–69, 2010.

Leyhausen, P., *Verhaltensstudien an Katzen* (2nd ed.), Paul Parey, Berlin, 1960.

Limpus, C.J., *A biological review of Australian marine turtle species. 6, Olive Ridley Turtle, Lepidochelys olivacea (Eschscholtz)* [Online]. Queensland Environment Protection Agency, 2008. Retrieved from: http://www.epa.qld.gov.au/publications/p02836aa.pdf/A_Biological_Review_Of_Australian_Marine_Turtles_4_Olive_Ridley_Turtle_emLepidochelys_olivacea/em_Escholtz.pdf.

MacDonald, D., Norris, S., *The New Encyclopedia of Mammals,* (Vol. I, 1st edn.), Oxford University Press, New York. 2001.

Macdonald, D.W., The ecology of carnivore social behaviour, *Nature*, **301**, 379–384, 1983.

Mahood, S., Virak, S., Chamnan, H. and Evans, T., *The status of Bengal Florican in the Bengal Florican Conservation Areas (2010/11 monitoring report)*, Wildlife Conservation Society Cambodia Program, Phnom Penh, 2012.

Mallon, D.P. and Kingswood S.C. (Eds), Antelopes. Part 4: North Africa, the Middle East, and Asia. *Global Survey and Regional Action Plans*, pp. 178–187, IUCN, Gland, Switzerland, 2001.

Mallon, D.P., *Antilope cervicapra. The IUCN Red List of Threatened Species. Version 2014.3.* Retrieved from: www.iucnredlist.org, 2008.

Márquez M.R., Sea turtles of the world. An annotated and illustrated catalogue of sea turtle species known to date. *FAO Species Catalog, FAO Fisheries Synopsis*, **11**, 125, 81, 1990.

Masphal, K., and Vorsak, B., Vulture restaurants across Cambodia. *The Babbler: BirdLife in Indochina*: 24. 2007.

Mazák, V., *Panthera tigris*, *Mammalian Species*, **152**, 1–8, 1981. doi:10.2307/3504004.

Meegama, N.C., The Asiatic lion–the last refuge. *Loris,* **15**, 1, 35–36, 1979.

Mellen, J.D., A Comparative Analysis of Scent-Marking, Social and Reproductive Behavior in 20 Species of Small Cats (*Felis*). *American Zoologist*, **33**, 2, 151–166, 1993.

Menon, V., Tiwari, S.K., Easa, P.S. and Sukumar, R., *Right of Passage: Elephant Corridors of India. Conservation Reference Series 3*, Wildlife Trust of India, New Delhi, 2005.

Menon, V., Sukumar, R. and Kumar, A., *A God in Distress: Threats of Poaching and the Ivory Trade to the Asian Elephant in India*. Wildlife Protection Society of India, New Delhi, India, 1997.

Mohan, V., India's tiger population increases by 30% in past three years; country now has 2,226 tigers. *The Times of India*, Delhi, 2015.

Molur, S., Walker, S., Islam, A., Miller, P., Srinivasulu, C., Nameer, P., Daniel, B. and Ravikumar, L., *Conservation of western hoolock gibbon (Hoolock hoolock hoolock) in India and Bangladesh*, Coimbatore, India, 2005.

Mootnick, A. and Groves, C., A new generic name for the hoolock gibbon (Hylobatidae), *International Journal of Primatology*, **26**, 4, 971–976, 2005.

Moreno, P., Ganges and Indus Dolphins. In: M. Hutchins, D. Kleiman, V. Geist, J. Murphy, D. Thoney, (Eds.), *Grzimek's Animal Life Encyclopedia* (*Vol. 15, 2nd edn.*), pp. 13–17, Gale Group, Farmington Hills, 2003.

Mukherjee, R., Survey of non-human primates of Tripura, India. *Journal of the Zoological Society of India,* **34**, 1–2, 70–81, 1982.

Mukherjee, R., The ecology of the hoolock gibbon, *H. hoolock*, in Tripura, India. In: J. G. Else and P, C. Lee (Eds), *Primate ecology and conservation*, Cambridge, UK and London, UK. 1986.

Mukherjee, R., Chaudhuri, S. and Murmu, A., Hoolock gibbons in Arunachal Pradesh, northeast India: Lohit District, *Primate Conservation,* **9**, 121–123, 1988.

Mukherjee, R., Chaudhuri, S. and Murmu, A., Status and conservation problems of hoolock gibbon (*Hylobates hoolock*) in some of its range of distribution in north-eastern India, *Primate Report,* **34**, 133–138, 1992.

Mukherjee, S., Sanderson, J., Duckworth, W., Melisch, R., Khan, J., Wilting, A., Sunarto, S. and Howard, J.G., *Prionailurus viverrinus. IUCN Red List of Threatened Species. Version 2015.2*, International Union for Conservation of Nature, 2010.

Mukherjee, S., Appel, A., Duckworth, J.W., Sanderson, J., Dahal, S., Willcox, D.H.A., Herranz Muñoz, V., Malla, G., Ratnayaka, A., Kantimahanti, M., Thudugala, A., Thaung R., and Rahman, H., *Prionailurus viverrinus. The IUCN Red List of Threatened Species 2016: e.T18150A50662615*, 2016. Retrieved from: http://dx.doi.org/10.2305/IUCN.UK.2016-2.RLTS.T18150A50662615.en.

Mundy, P.J., The biology of vultures: a summary of the workshop proceedings, *ICBP Technical Publication* **5**, 457–482, 1985.

Musick, J.A. and Limpus, C.J., Habitat utilization and migration in juvenile sea turtles, pp. 137–164. In: Lutz PL, & Musick JA (Eds.), *The Biology of Sea Turtles*, CRC Press, Boca Raton, Florida, 1997.

Naidoo, V., Wolter, K., Cromarty, D., Diekmann, M., Duncan, N., Meharg, A.A., Taggart, M.A., Venter, L. and Cuthbert, R., Toxicity of nonsteroidal anti-inflammatory drugs to Gyps vultures: a new threat from ketoprofen, *Biology Letters*, **6**, 3, 339–341, 2010.

National Trust for Nature Conservation (NTNC), *NTNC Chairman Released the Recent Tiger Number in Nepal*, National Trust for Nature Conservation, Kathmandu, 2013.

Negi, H.R., *Usnea longissima*—the Winter Staple Food of Musk Deer: A Case Study of Kanchulakharak Musk Deer Breeding Center in Garhwal Himalayas. *Tigerpaper,* **23**, 1, 30–32, 1996.

Nekaris, A., Singh, M. and Kumar Chhangani, A. 2008. *Loris lydekkerianus*. *The IUCN Red List of Threatened Species 2008: e.T44722A10942453.* Retrived from: http://dx.doi.org/10.2305/IUCN.UK.2008.RLTS.T44722A10942453.en.

Nekaris, K.A.I., Rediscovery of the slender loris in Horton Plains National Park, Sri Lanka. *Asian Primates,* **8,** 3, 1–7, 2003.

Nekaris, K.A.I. and Jayewardene, J., Pilot study and conservation status of the slender loris (*Loris tardigradus* and *L. lydekkerianus*) in Sri Lanka, *Primate Conservation,* **19**, 83–90, 2003.

Nekaris, K.A.I. and Jayewardene, J. Distribution of slender lorises in four ecological zones in Sri Lanka, *Journal of Zoology,* **262**, 1–12, 2004a.

Nekaris, K.A.I. and Jayewardene, J. Survey of the slender loris (primates: Lorisidae Gray, 1821: *Loris tardigradus* Linnaeus, 1758 and *Loris lydekkerianus* Cabrera, 1908) in Sri Lanka, *Journal of Zoology,* **262**, 4, 327–338, 2004b.

Nowak, R., *Walker's Mammals of the World* (*Vol. 2, 6th edn.*). The Johns Hopkins University Press, Baltimore, 1999.

Nowak, R., Ganges and Indus Dolphins, or Susus,. In: *Walker's Marine Mammals of the World* (*Vol. 2, 1st edn.*), pp. 128–130, The Johns Hopkins Univesity Press, Baltimore, 2003.

Nowell, K. and Jackson, P., *Wild Cats. Status Survey and Conservation Action Plan*, IUCN/SSC Cat Specialist Group, Gland, Switzerland and Cambridge, UK., 1996.

Oaks, J. L., Gilbert, M., Virani, M. Z., Watson, R. T., Meteyer, C. U., Rideout, B. A., Shivaprasad, H. L., Ahmed, S., Chaudhry, M.J. I., Arshad, M., Mahmood, S., Ali, A., Khan, A. A., Diclofenac residues as the cause of vulture population decline in Pakistan, *Nature,* **427**, 6975, 630–633, 2004a.

Oaks, J. L., Meteyer, C. U., Rideout, B. A., Shivaprasad, H. L., Gilbert, M., Virani, M. Z., Watson, R. T., Khan, A. A., Diagnostic investigation of vulture mortality: the anti-inflammatory drug diclofenac is associated with visceral gout, *Falco*, 13-14, 2004b.

Packman, C., Conservation ecology of Bengal Florican in Cambodia: update October 2009, *The Babbler: BirdLife in Indochina*, **29**, 2009.

Pandav, B. and Choudhury, B.C., An update on mortality of Olive ridley sea turtle in Orissa, India, *Marine Turtle Newsletter,* **83**, 10–12, 1999.

Pandav, B., *Conservation and Management of Olive Ridley Sea Turtles on the Orissa Coast* (Ph.D. Thesis), Utkal University, Bhubaneshwar, India, 2000.

Pande, S., Mestri, P., Deshpande, P., Warange, A. and Mahabal, A., Promising trend of *in situ* breeding of Oriental White-rumped Vulture *Gyps bengalensis* in Raigad District, Maharashtra, India: Conservation implications for re-introduction of ex situ populations, *Journal of Threatened Taxa*, 5, 7, 4106–4109, 2013.

Pandey, C.N., Tatu, K.S. and Vyas, V.R., *Report on status of Gyps vultures in Gujarat*, GEER Foundation, 2010.

Panwar, H. S., Project Tiger: The reserves, the tigers, and their future. In: Tilson, R. L., and Seal, U.S., *Tigers of the world: the biology, biopolitics, management, and conservation of an endangered species*. pp. 10–117, Noyes Publications, Park Ridge, N.J., 1987.

Patil, P., Joint meeting to discuss conservation of Great Indian Bustard Sanctuary, *Protected Area Update*, **17**, 3, 13, 2011.

Paulson, M., Pride in Place: Reintroduction of Asiatic Lions in Gir Forest, India. *Restoration and Reclamation Review*, **4**, 3, 1–5, 1999. Retrieved from: http://conservancy.umn.edu/bitstream/handle/11299/59294/1/4.3.Paulson.pdf

Perera, M. and Sandun, J., A Review of the Distribution of Grey Slender Loris (*Loris lydekkerianus*) in Sri Lanka, *Primate Conservation*, **23**, 89–96, 2008.

Perrin, W.F., Wursig, B., and Thewissen, J.G.M., *Encyclopedia of Marine Mammals*, Academic Press, San Diego, 2002.

Phillips, W., *Manual of the Mammals of Sri Lanka*, Wildlife and Nature Protection Society of Sri Lanka, Colombo, Sri Lanka, 1984.

Plotkin, P.T. (Ed.), *Biology and Conservation of Ridley Sea Turtles*, Johns Hopkins University Press, Baltimore, 2007.

Plotkin, P.T., Owens, D.W., Byles, R.A., and Patterson, R., Departure of male olive ridley turtles (*Lepidochelys olivacea*) from a nearshore breeding ground. *Herpetologica*, **52**, 1, 1–7, 1996.

Plummer, J. "*Moschus leucogaster*" (On-line), *Animal Diversity Web*. 2011. Retrieved from: http://animaldiversity.org/accounts/Moschus_leucogaster/

Pocock, R.I., The larger deer of British India. Part II. *Journal of the Bombay Natural History Society*, **43**, 553–572, 1943.

Poharkar, A., Reddy, P.A., Gadge, V.A., Kolte, S., Nurkure, N. and Shivaji, S., Is malaria the cause for decline of the Indian Whitebacked Vulture (*Gyps bengalensis*)? *Current Science*, **96**, 4, 553–558, 2009.

Prakash, V. Status of vultures in Keoladeo National Park, Bharatpur, Rajasthan, with special reference to population crash in Gyps species. *Journal of Bombay Natural History Society*, **96**, 3, 365–378, 1999.

Prakash, V., Green, R.E., Pain, D.J., Ranade, S.P., Saravanan, S., Prakash, N., Venkitachalam, R., Cuthbert, R., Rahmani, A.R. and Cunningham, A.A., Recent changes in populations of resident Gyps vultures in India. *Journal of the Bombay Natural History Society*, **104**, 2, 127–133, 2007.

Prakash, V., Pain, D. J., Cunningham, A. A., Donald, P. F., Prakash, N., Verma, A., Gargi, R., Sivakumar, S. and Rahmani, A. R., Catastrophic collapse of Indian white-backed *Gyps bengalensis* and long-billed *Gyps indicus* vulture populations. *Biological Conservation,* **109**, 381–390, 2003.

Prater, S.H., *The Book of Indian Animals*. Bombay Natural History Society, Mumbai, India, 1980.

Project Tiger, List of Core and Buffer Areas of Tiger Reserves of India (Online), 2016. Retrieved from: http://projecttiger.nic.in/content/109_1_ListofTigerReservesCoreBufferAreas.aspx

Radhakrishna, S. and Singh, M., Activity schedule and habitat use of the slender loris (*Loris tardigradus lydekkerianus*). *Journal of the Bombay Natural History Society,* **99**, 400–407, 2002.

Radhakrishna, S. and Singh, M., Reproductive biology of the slender loris (*Loris lydekkerianus lydekkerianus*), *Folia Primatologica,* **75**, 1, 1–13. 2004.

Radhakrishna, S., Kumara H.N. and Sasi, R., Distribution patterns of slender loris subspecies (*Loris lydekkerianus*) in Kerala, southern India, *Int. J. Primatol*, **32**, 4, 1007–1019, 2011.

Rahman, M.G., Reducing the flow of the Ganges: the consequences for agriculture in Bangladesh, In: Goldsmith E., and Hilyard N. (Eds.) *The Social and Environmental Effects of Large Dams*, pp. 267–275, Wadebridge Ecological Centre, Cornwall, UK., 1986.

Rahmani, A.R., The great Indian bustard. *Final report in the study of ecology of certain endangered species of wildlife and their habitats*. Bombay Natural History Society, Mumbai, 1989.

Rahmani, A.R., India. In: Mallon, D.P., and Kingswood, S.C. (Eds.), *Antelopes. Part 4: North Africa, the Middle East, and Asia, Global Survey and Rgeional Action Plans*, pp. 178–187, IUCN, Gland, Switzerland, 2001.

Ramaswami, L. S., Some Aspects of Reproduction of the Female Slender Loris, Loris tardigradus lydekkerianus Cabr.". *Acta Zoologica*, **46**, 257–273, 1965.

Rangarajan, M., Desai, A., Sukumar, R., Easa, P.S., Menon, V., Vincent, S., Ganguly S., Talukdar, B.K., Singh, B., Mudappa, D., Chowdhary, S. and Prasad, A.N., *Gajah: Securing the Future for Elephants in India. The Report of the Elephant Task Force*, Ministry of Environment and Forests, New Delhi, India, 2010.

Ranjitsinh, M. K., *The Indian Blackbuck*. Natraj Publishers, Dehradun., 1989.

Ranjitsinh, S., The Manipur brow-antlered deer (*Cervus eldi eldi*) – a case history, *Proceedings of the IUCN Threatened Deer Programme*, International Union for Conservation of Nature and Natural Resources, Morges, Switzerland, 1978.

Rao, P., Occurrence of the slender loris *Loris tardigradus* in south coastal Andhra Pradesh, India. *Journal of the Bombay Natural History Society,* **91**, 2, 303, 1994.

Reeves, R.R., and Brownell, Jr. R.L., *Susu Platanista Gangetica (*Roxburgh, 1801) and *Platanista minor* Owen, 1853. In: Ridgway SH, Harrison SR, Eds., *Handbook of Marine Mammals* (Vol. 4), Academic Press, London, 1989.

Reeves, R.R., Leatherwood, S. and Lal Mohan, R.S., *A Future for Asian River Dolphins: Report from a Seminar on the Conservation of River Dolphins in the Indian Subcontinent, 1992, New Delhi, India,* Whale and Dolphin Conservation Society, Avon, England, 1993.

Richard, C.J., Prakash, V., Saini, M., Upreti, S., Swarup, D., Das, A., Green, R.E. and Tagart, M., Are conservation actions reducing the threat to India vulture populations? *Current Science*, **101**, 11, 1480–1484, 2011.

Roy, D. and Mushahidunnabi, Md., Courtship, mating and egg-laying in *Tylototriton verrucosus* from the Darjeeling District of the Eastern Himalaya, *Current Science*, **81**, 6, 693–695, 2001.

Saberwal, V.K., Lion-human conflict around Gir, *Bulletin of Wildlife Institute of India*, **5**, 3, 28–30, 1990.

Saberwal, V.K., Gibbs, J.P., Chellam, R. and Johnsingh, A.J.T., Lion-human conflict in the Gir Forest, India, *Conservation Biology,* **8**, 2, 501–507, 1994.

Saha, D., Olive ridley turtle, *Lepidochelys olivacea* of the Sunderbans, West Bengal, *Environment and Ecology,* **4**, 1, 172–174, 1986.

Saha, D., Olive ridley marine turtle from the Sunderbans, West Bengal. *Environment and Ecology*, **2**, **3**, 236–237, 1984.

Samant, J.S. and Elangovan, V., *Avifauna of the Eastern Ghats with special reference to the Jerdon's Courser Cursorius bitorquatus* (*Final report*), Bombay Natural History Society, 1997.

Sangay, T. and Vernes, K., Human-wildlife conflict in the Kingdom of Bhutan: Patterns of livestock predation by large mammalian carnivores, *Biological Conservation*, **141**, 5, 1272, 2008.

Sarrazin, F., Virani, M.Z., Gilbert, M. and Khan, A.A., Preliminary population viability analyses for oriental White-backed Vulture *Gyps bengalansis* in Punjab province, Pakistan. In: Chancellor, R.D and B.U. Meyburg, Eds., *Raptors Worldwide. Proceedings of the VI world conference on birds of prey and owls*, pp. 257–261, World Working Group on Birds of Prey and Owls, MME BirdLife Hungary, Budapest, 2004.

Sasi, R. and Kumara, H.N., Distribution and Relative Abundance of the Slender Loris *Loris lydekkerianus* in Southern Kerala, India, *Primate Conservation*, **28**, 165–170, 2014.

Sathyakumar, S., The status of Asiatic black bears in India, In: *Understanding Asian bears to secure their future*, pp. 12–19, Japan Bear Network, Ibaraki, Japan, 2006.

Sathyakumar, S., Asiatic Black Bear Conservation Action Plan: Status and management of the Asiatic black bear in India. In: Servheen C., Herrero, S., and Peyton, B. (Eds.). *Bears: Status Survey and Conservation Action Plan*, pp. 202–206, IUCN, Gland, Switzerland, 1999.

Sathyakumar, S., Prasad S.N., and Walker, S., Status of captive Himalayan Forest musk deer *Moschus chrysogaster* in India, International Zoo Yearbook, **32**, 32–38, 1993.

Sathyakumar, S., Status and management of Asiatic black bear and Himalayan brown bear in India, *Ursus*, **12**, 21–29, 2001.

Schaller, G.B, *The Serengeti lion: a study of predator–prey relations*. University of Chicago Press, Chicago, Illinois, 1972.

Schaller, G.B., *The deer and the tiger*, University of Chicago Press, Chicago, 1967.

Sen, S., and Lad, N., *Birds of India: Notes on Jerdon's Courser Rhinoptilus bitorquatus* (Online), Kolkata Birds, Kolkata, India, 2009. Retrieved from: http://www.kolkatabirds.com/jerdonscourser.htm

Senthilkumar, K., Kannan, K., Sinha, R.K., Tanabe, S. and Giesy, J.P., Bioaccumulation profiles of polychlorinated biphenyl congeners and organochlorine pesticides in Ganges River dolphins, *Environmental Toxicology and Chemistry*, **18**, 7, 1511–1520, 1999.

Sharma, S.C., Listing of Sangai in Indian zoos as of March 1994. In: Anonymous (Ed.), *Manipur brow-antlered deer (Cervus eldi eldi), Report on the population and habitat viability assessment*, Chamarajendra Zoological Gardens, Forest Dept. of Manipur, Indian Zoo Directors' Association, Zoo Outreach Organization, Captive Breeding Specialist Group, Sangai, 1994.

Shrestha, M., Musk deer *Moschus chrysogaster*: musk extraction from live deer, *Journal of the Bombay Natural History Society*, **86**, 438–440, 1989.

Shrestha, T.K., *Mammals of Nepal: With reference to those of India*, Bangladesh, Bhutan and Pakistan, Tribhuvan University, Kathmandu, 1997.

Shultz, S., Baral, H.S., Charman, S., Cunningham, A.A., Das, D., Ghalsasi, D.R., Goudar, M.S., Green, R.E., Jones, A., Nighot, P., Pain, D.J. and Prakash, V., Diclofenac poisoning is widespread in declining vulture populations across the Indian subcontinent. *Proceedings of the Royal Society of London B: Biological Sciences*, **271**, Suppl. 6, S458–S460, 2004.

Singh, H.S. and Gibson, L.A., A conservation success story in the otherwise dire megafauna extinction crisis: the Asiatic lion (*Panthera leo persica*) of Gir forest, *Biological Conservation*, **144**, 5, 1753–1757, 2011.

Singh, M., Kumar, M.A., Kumara, H.N. and Mohnot, S.M., Distribution and conservation of slender lorises (*Loris tardigradus lydekkerianus*) in southern Andhra Pradesh, South India. *International Journal of Primatology,* **21**, 4, 721–730, 2000.

Singh, M., Lindburg, D.G., Udhayan, A., Kumar, M. A. and Kumara, H.N., Status survey of slender loris *Loris tardigradus lydekkerianus* in Dindigul, Tamil Nadu, India, *Oryx,* **33**, 1, 31–37, 1999.

Singh, S. Brow antlered deer (*Cervus eldi eldi*) in Keibul Lamjao National Park, Manipur, India. In: B. Pukazhenthi (Ed.), *Workshop on Eld's Deer Conservation and Restoration,* pp. 19–23, Khao Kheow Open Zoo, Chonburi, Thailand, 2004.

Sinha, R.K., An alternative to dolphin oil as a fish attractant in the Ganges River system: conservation of the Ganges River Dolphin, *Biological Conservation,* **107**, 253–257, 2002.

Smith, B.D. and Braulik, G.T., *Platanista gangetica. IUCN Red List of Threatened Species. IUCN. 2012: e.T41758A17355810*, 2012 Retrieved from: http://www.iucnredlist.org/details/41758/0

Smith, B.D., Aminul Haque A.K.M., Hossain, M.S. and Khan, A., River dolphins in Bangladesh: conservation and the effects of water development, *Environmental Management*, **22**, 323–335, 1998.

Smith, B.D., Sinha, R.K., Zhou, K., Chaudhry, A.A., Renjun, L., Wang, D., Ahmed, B., Haque, A.K.M. and Sapkota, K., Register of water development projects affecting Asian river cetaceans, In: Reeves, R.R., Smith, B.D., and Kasuya, T. (Eds.), *Biology and Conservation of Freshwater Cetaceans in Asia, IUCN/SSC Occasional Paper No. 23*, pp. 22–39, IUCN, Gland, Switzerland and Cambridge, UK, 2000.

Snider, C. C. and Asplund, J. M., In Vitro Digestibility of Deer Foods from the Missouri Ozarks, *Journal of Wildlife Management*, **38**, 20–31, 1974.

Spotila, J.R., *Sea Turtles: a Complete Guide to their Biology, Behavior, and Conservation*. Johns Hopkins University Press, Baltimore, 2004.

Sridhar, S., Bustards are wearing thin in Ghatigaon Sanctuary, *Newsletter for Birdwatchers,* **45**, 1, 4, 2005.

Srivastav, A., Livestock predation by Gir lions and ecodevelopement. *Tigerpaper*, **24**, 2, 1–5, 1997.

Sukumar, R., *The Living Elephants: Evolutionary Ecology, Behavior, and Conservation*. Oxford University Press, Oxford, UK, 2003.

Sunquist, M. and Sunquist, F., *Wild Cats of the World,* Chicago, University of Chicago Press, 2002.

Swan, G., Naidoo, V., Cuthbert, R., Green, R.E., Pain, D.J., Swarup, D., Prakash, V., Taggart, M., Bekker, L., Das, D., Diekmann, J., Diekmann, M., Killian, E., Meharg, A., Chandra Patra, R., Saini, M. and Wolter, K. Removing the threat of diclofenac to critically endangered Asian vultures, *PLoS Biology,* **4**, 3, 395–402, 2006.

Swarup, D., Patra, R.C., Prakash, V., Cuthbert, R., Das, D., Avari, P., Pain, D.J., Green, R.E., Sharma, A.K., Saini, M., Das, D. and Taggart, M., Safety of meloxicam to critically endangered *Gyps* vultures and other scavenging birds in India, *Animal Conservation*, **10**, 2, 192–198, 2007.

Tewari, I. and Singh, R.P., Conserving the endangered, but economically potential, musk deer in the Himalayas through captive farming, *Tiger Paper*, **27**, 1, 6–13, 2000.

Tikader, B.K. and Sharma, R.C., *Handbook: Indian Testudines*, Zoological Survey of India, Kolkata, 1985.

Timmins, R.J. and Duckworth, J.W., *IUCN Red List of Threatened Species (Version 2010.4)*. International Union for Conservation of Nature, 2008. Retrieved from: www.iucnredlist.org

van Dijk, P.P., Wogan, G., Lau, M.W.N., Dutta, S., Shrestha, T.K., Roy, D., and Truong, N.Q., *Tylototriton verrucosus. The IUCN Red List of Threatened Species 2009: e.T59487A11934912*, 2009. Retrieved from: http://dx.doi.org/10.2305/IUCN.UK.2004.RLTS.T59487A11934912.en

van Zalinge, R., Evans, T., Hong, C., Ro, B. and Packman, C., Bengal Floricans in the integrated farming and biodiversity areas, *The Babbler: BirdLife in Indochina*, 27–28, 2009.

van Zalinge, R., Virak, S., Evans, T. and Chamnan, H., *The status of Bengal Floricans in the Bengal Florican Conservation Areas, 2009/10 monitoring report*, Wildlife Conservation Society Cambodia Program, Phnom Penh, 2010.

Vinitpornsawan, S., Steinmetz, R. and Kanchanasakha, B., *The status of bears in Thailand*. Japan Bear Network, Ibaraki, Japan, 2006.

Walker, S., Executive summary of the Asiatic lion PHVA. First draft report. *Zoo's Print*, Jan./Feb., 2–22, 1994.

Wegge, P., Odden, M., Pokharel, C.P., and Storaas, T. Predator–prey relationships and responses of ungulates and their predators to the establishment of protected areas: A case study of tigers, leopards and their prey in Bardia National Park, Nepal, *Biological Conservation*, **142**, 189–202, 2009.

Weishampel, J.F., Bagley, D.A. and Ehrhart, L.M., Earlier nesting by loggerhead sea turtles following sea surface warming, *Global Change Biology*, **10**, 8, 1424–1427, 2004.

Wells, D., *The Birds of the Thai-Malay Peninsula*, Academic Press, San Diego, 1999.

Wemmer, C. and Grodinsky, C., Reproduction in captive female brow-antlered deer (*Cervus eldi thamin*), *Journal of Mammalogy*, **69**, 2, 389–393, 1988.

Whitaker, R., Sea Turtles in Indian Waters, *Cheetal*, **16**, 1, 1977.

Whitehead, K.G., *The Whitehead Encyclopedia of Deer*, Voyageur Press, Inc., Stillwater, MN, 1993.

Whiting, S.D., Long, J., Hadden, K. and Lauder, A., *Identifying the links between nesting and foraging grounds for the Olive Ridley (Lepidochelys olivacea) sea turtles in northern Australia (Final Report)*, Department of the Environment and Water Resources, Government of Australia, 2005. Retrieved from: http://www.environment.gov.au/system/files/resources/a9aab5e7-8726-4478-afaa-517966c45344/files/olive-ridley-grounds.pdf

Wildlife Protection Society of India (WPSI), *WPSI's Tiger Poaching Statistics*. Wildlife Protection Society of India, Delhi, 2009, Retrieved from: http://www.wpsi-india.org/statistics/index.php

Williams, A.C., *Elephants, their habitats in Rajaji-Corbett National Parks* (Ph.D Thesis), Saurashtra University, Rajkot, India, 2002.

Wilson, D.E. and Reeder, D.M. (Eds.), *Mammal Species of the World. A Taxonomic and Geographic Reference* (3rd edn.), Johns Hopkins University Press, Baltimore, USA, 2005.

Witherington, B.E., Behavioral responses of nesting sea turtles to artificial lighting, *Herpetologica,* **48**, 31–39, 1992.

Wright, B. and Mohanty, B., Operation Kachhapa: An NGO initiative for Sea Turtle Conservation in Orissa, In: Shanker K, and Choudhury BC (Eds.), *Sea Turtles of the Indian Subcontinent*, pp. 290–302, Universities Press, Hyderabad, India, 2006.

5

BEHAVIOURAL ECOLOGY OF WILD ANIMALS

5.1 COMMUNICATIONS AND SIGNALING

Communication is generally referred to as the transfer of information through the use of specially evolved traits, known as *signals*, between one individual (*signaler or sender*) to another (*signal receiver*). Such information transfer generally occurs with the help of different sensory modalities—either singly or several signals may be sent through different sensory channels simultaneously. Senders produce signals in order to increase the chances that the receiver will manifest an appropriate reaction which is beneficial and productive to the sender. On the other hand, the receiver responds to the signal in such a way so that the chance of getting a beneficial effect for both the sender and receiver increases. However, the receivers are not altruistic as both the parties have common interests or they have different interests and have reached equilibrium in view of their responses. Though, the signals are often beneficial for the receivers, but the sender primarily provides this information in an attempt to manipulate a receiver's behaviour to its own advantage. Signals can be either directed at conspecifics or at members of other species. Thus, classically communication is the cue given by the sender and perceived by the receiver in order to alter the pattern of behaviour of the receiver in such a fashion that is adaptive to either one or both of the participants (Wilson, 1975). Moreover, the signals used by the animals to attract mates also play a significant role in the reproduction of two distantly located and isolated populations. Individuals are able to select mates only from their own population due to the distinct differences in critical communication signals.

Definition: Krebs and Davies (1993) defined communication as the process in which the actors use specially designed signals or displays to modify the behaviour of reactors. According to Bradbury and Vehrencamp (1998), true communication is an exchange of a signal between a sender and receiver to the benefit of both parties.

5.1.1 Why Do Animal Communicate?

The ability to communicate effectively with other individuals plays a critical role in the lives of all animals. Studying communication, therefore, not only gives insight into the inner worlds of animals, but also allows a better understanding of several important evolutionary questions. The main reasons for the animals to communicate include transfer of environmental information such as:

- Alarming and warning the con-specifics about the presence of predators
- Sexual advertisement to attract mates
- Maintenance of social grouping, alerting the kin and social integration through diversification of calls
- Convey messages to the members of the same group about the location and presence of the food resources
- Parental care through appreciation and pleading,
- Territory defense and conflict resolution by deterring rivals
- An important source of additional information in the decision-making process

5.1.2 Modes of Communications

Though the animals might not be able to speak, but they have several ways of communication. Whales sing, wolfs howl, frogs croak, birds chirp, waggle dance of honeybees or even the waving of a dog's tail — are some of the common instances where animals perform to transmit information between themselves and also to other members of the animal kingdom. Various morphological, physiological, biochemical and behavioural traits in animals such as olfactory (or chemical), tactile (or touch), visual and acoustic signals are being used for communication. Each of those modalities have certain degree of advantages and disadvantages, and they are used either alone or in different combinations with each other.

Olfactory and other Chemical Signals

Signaling through olfactory mode of communication is one of the primitive ways of transferring information that operates at the cellular level and is also responsible for a wide array of complex social organization. This mode of signal transmission follows the same pattern as the mechanism of action of hormones and is considered to be the main way for chemical recognition of signals. Olfactory communication is widespread across various taxa. The social insects and mammals extensively rely on olfaction as their chief mode of communication. But, there is no concrete evidence on the use of olfaction for social communication in birds.

Olfactory and other chemical signals are transmitted by the process of diffusion through a medium and the rate of such transmission differs on the viscosity of the medium. Olfactory signals can be passed on over very short range (as in localized signals *viz.* urine marking in mammals) or can travel substantial distances (pheromones in moths). Although the primary decoding of the chemical signals is much easy as compared to decoding auditory or visual cues, yet tracking the location of a distant source of such olfactory signals is often very difficult. However, this problem can be mitigated if the animals can sense the (i) variations in the density of released chemical, (ii) wind velocity and (iii) direction of wind flow.

Text Box 5.1 Pheromones—A Common Mode of Olfactory Communication

'Pheromones' are a class of species-specific chemical compounds or molecules that are produced to communicate between members of the same species. The pheromones are secreted as liquids and transmitted as liquids or gases. They are often transmitted as gaseous elements and are sensitized through smell over great distances, but can also operate locally. Use of pheromones is noticed across faunal taxa like insects, fish, amphibians, reptiles and mammals. The pheromones play a potent role in building the societies of ants, bees and termites. Mammals use pheromones (or scents) to proclaim their readiness to mate, to mark out territorial boundaries, to deter intruders and predators or, in some cases, to attract prey. More than 100 mammalian species are reported to have anal glands for adding characteristic pheromones to faeces. Many of them also possess a number of specialized scent glands. In both mammals and insects, pheromones are deposited as trail markers. In this case, even if the individual who transmits the signal is in distant from the receiver (in space and time), yet the airborne dispersal of chemical attractants provide an efficient mechanism for bringing together the dispersed individuals of opposite sex. For instance, deers transmit scents from glands located on the legs and head through the air, can also mark trees and twigs from the same glands, and has other glands on the feet for leaving scent trials on the ground. Although pheromones certainly influence sexual behaviour in many terrestrial mammalian species, but there is a distinct lack of specialized glands in higher primates, thus, scent-marking behaviours is fairly low.

Tactile Signal — Mechanoreception

Mechanoreception is possibly the most widely adopted mode of communication that occurs among animals. It is inevitably a part of close-contact social and emotional interactions between individuals. Physical contact is an important element of the social bonding between offspring and parent in most mammals. Mutual grooming is a particular case of tactile stimulation associated with sociality. Such grooming or preening of one animal by another is often interpreted as a ritualized form of appeasement or social bonding. Studies on the distribution between individuals placed in dominance hierarchies and other social sub-groupings, as well as, the time of grooming also suggest that the motivation for grooming is inversely related to aggression. Monkeys and apes spend most of their time scrupulously picking parasites and dirt from each other's hair (called co-operative cleaning). Such behaviour enable them to clean parts of the body which the recipient would have difficulty to reach (Figure 5.1).

Evidence of social grooming between adults is also witnessed in many rodents and in several bird species as well. Tactile signals are also manifested by many carnivores. The most common instance is the tendency of the domesticated dogs and cats licking the hands and faces of their masters. Hugging, kissing, embracing and biting are specialized forms of tactile signals of sexual behaviour which elicit specific responses. In many mammals (except primates) ovulation and pregnancy related hormonal changes are also initiated by the tactile stimulations during copulation.

FIGURE 5.1 Physical contact as social bonding between offspring and parent Hanuman Langurs (Photograph: Dr. Subhendu Mazumdar)

Tactile signal or mechanoreception is advantageous as it leads to instantaneous feedback on individual recipient and is effective in absence of light (in the caves, wood galleries etc.). Communication by tactile signals between animals is extremely short-ranged, and does not perform well over distances. This mode of signalling is ineffective unless there is direct contact between the participants. Moreover, repetitive touches are required for a recipient to decipher the encoded message within tactile signals and there are always risks of the interception of tactile signals by the predators.

The Visual Signals

There is a wide variety of visual signals that are used in animal communication. These visual signals are extremely remarkable (e.g. the bright plumage coloration of many birds) and often take conspicuous shapes and forms (e.g. the eyespots and enlarged fins of some fish). Diurnal animals (like birds and humans) often use visual signals because they are active and awake during the day and can easily see these signals being communicated. In addition to morphological traits, visual displays also make use of some other unfamiliar artifacts and structures. A study in Spain suggested that black kites (*Milvus migrans*) decorate their nests with bright materials (such as white plastics), which may have a role in signaling to keep away other kites (Sergio et al., 2011). The emission of light in dark environments (as seen in fireflies, several invertebrates and deep sea fishes) provides a clear example of specialized communicative means.

Movements are also used in visual displays, which perhaps increases the chance of being perceived over relatively short distances. This combination of movement with visual signals is generally considered as 'behavioural displays', which also incorporates signals from other sensory modalities.

There are a good number of examples in favour of visual communication across different taxa. Such behavioural responses are often termed as *displays*. In fish, reptiles and cephalopods (octopus and squid) there are noted and rapid changes in skin colour or markings. In mammals, particularly carnivores and primates, visual displays include changes in facial expressions accompanied by vocalization. In lizards, changes in the appearance of the head by extensions and colourings of dewlaps, crests and frills are quite frequent. Other parts of the body may also take part in visual displays. Posture, gait and gestures via movements of the extremities can be identified as social signals in a wide range of vertebrate and invertebrate species, which have the ecological and perceptual opportunities for the detection of visual messages. For instance, lizards have back arching, tail lashing, head bobbing and circular forelimb waving for aggressive and submissive gestures. Apart from primates, mammals have little or no colour vision and no retinal fovea for high visual acuity. Therefore, they have little opportunity to use colour signals and some limitation on very detailed visual display or markings. Colour is in fact of little importance even in primate social signaling, apart from one or two species of monkeys.

The major constraint of visual communication is that the visual signals are only operative in well lit conditions when animals can easily see each other and only last as long as the sender is signaling. Therefore, visual signals are most often used during the day as they simply cannot be seen in the darkness of night. Even in sufficient daylight, one can identify each other by appearance and gesture only within a limited distance with uninterrupted direct line of sight. Operational range of visual signals although better than the tactile signals, but is much shorter as compared to the chemical and acoustic cues. However, the studies of communication have overemphasized visual communication, most likely because humans and primates are much more dependent on this type of communication than non-primate animals.

Visual signal is also a deceptive channel of communication as it allows for a certain amount of cheating. It can lure receivers to respond in such a fashion so that the sender is benefited and the receiver is harmed. This is noticed in *Photuris* fireflies, which are the only predatory species of firefly. *Photuris* female lures the males by mimicking the female response of their prey species and then preys upon them. As a consequence, the wary males of the prey species are suspicious in responding even to the female displays of their own species out of the fear of being preyed upon by the *Photuris* females. In this way, the prey males experience conflicting pressures from natural selection, which demands both individual survival and mating for species survival. This example reveals that the visual signals are not receiver specific.

The Acoustic or Vibrational Signals

Sound serves as a very effective communication modality. Acoustic signals and similar other vibrational signals (grouped under mechanical stimuli) are transmitted through a medium such as air, water or a variety of solid materials. Depending upon the medium through which the signal is sent, these signals may be used for various ranges of communications — very short range (vibrations in a plant stem by spiders), medium range (bird song) and very long range (underwater sounds and songs of whales). It may also vary in frequency (high pitch vs. low pitch), amplitude (loudness) and periodicity (the temporal pattern of frequency and amplitude). These three variables, in combination, can create an extremely wide and complex range of signals.

Though very complicated to determine, this highly organized form of communication is typically associated with social behaviour. Many animals produce sounds to impart different information. Vocalizations in higher vertebrates and songbirds, as well as, many courtship noises produced by fishes and insects are quite obviously specialized ways of sending social signals. Insects (such as crickets and cicadas) produce large amount of noise in relation to their size, whereas among amphibians and reptiles, acoustic communication appears to be highly related with nocturnal environment. In higher vertebrates though the peripheral hearing apparatus is used exclusively for general auditory purpose, but the central nervous system is clearly able to selectively process sounds with species-specific characteristics. Nocturnal predators (like cats and owls) have highly developed sense of hearing which is used for detecting sounds produced by prey.

Following are some prominent examples of acoustic communication across different taxa:

Insect Sounds: The sounds of insect flight and other noises of locomotion are the unavoidable outcome of the wing-movements. Among insects, diurnal sound production is evident in grasshoppers and cicadas. Crickets also emit auditory signals for social communication. Though in general these sounds are not usually detectable by flying con-specifics, but surprisingly, the male mosquito has a sense organ on its antennae tuned precisely to the species-specific distinctive buzz of the female and insensitive to the higher pitched flight sounds of males belonging to other species. This provides an excellent example of an entire perceptual mechanism being specialized for social communication.

Vocalization in Amphibians: Some of the complexities which may be carried by the acoustic channel are apparent in the courtship calls of male frogs (particularly in sub-tropical species), which breed opportunistically after heavy rains. Frogs are modern amphibians, and their vocalization has evolved in context of nocturnal surroundings and time-limited breeding (after rains). In many of these species, the male members assemble to make simple sounds in choirs. Such chorus is highly coordinated, rather than being the result of the inadvertent closeness of individuals. There are species in which individuals within chorus alternate calls within duos, trios, and quartets, at precise intervals. The females too have specific mechanism to differentiate the auditory signals of different species, thereby discriminating between the males of different species occupying the same areas. The males produce a biphasic call in tree frogs, where a low frequency, "co" is followed by a high-frequency "qui". The inner ears of the males being tuned to the "co", which serves as a territorial signal maintaining their dispersal, while the inner ears of the females are tune to the "qui", as a sexual attractant.

Vocalization in Reptiles: There is a greater level of similarity in the neural organization of the auditory pathways in the reptilian brain to that of higher vertebrates. Therefore, the acoustic mode of communication in many reptiles is almost negligible. Instead they prefer the visual or olfactory methods of communications. However, a limited range of vocalizations occur during the courtship and mating of several species of tortoises and turtles. Use of the acoustic channel as extensive as that of frogs is mostly confined to the geckos, which have an external auditory meatus and highly developed cochlea. Vocalization in geckos is characterized as chirruping or multiple chirruping, but very little is known about their behavioural functions. Loud continuous chirruping during a "dusk chorus" is heard in the gecko *Ptenopus garrulus garrulus*, when individuals emerge from their burrows. Most species are territorial and some vocalization probably functions as an assertion display for territorial defense.

Bird Songs: Vocal signals play an important role in the life of birds in a variety of aspects like pair maintenance, parent-offspring interactions, cohesiveness among flock or family members, and in threat situations. Birds use a variety of acoustic signals in their communication. These signals may be long and complex or short and simple, and they may occur in particular contexts. Owls vocalize at night and the most intensive singing in song-birds takes place at dawn and dusk. However, nocturnality is not the only factor favouring the use of the acoustic channel as enough avian vocalization also takes place during the hours of daylight. In most birds vision and hearing are both well developed, while olfaction is of lesser importance. It has been suggested that male courtship singing is less elaborate in highly coloured species. There may also be a negative correlation between size and complexity of vocalization. The song birds are relatively small and have very detailed control of the sound producing organ (the syrinx), while larger and more conspicuous birds tend to produce a narrower range of sounds. For example, storks are almost mute and the cries of geese and cranes being notable for volume rather than variety.

Vocalization in Mammals: In addition to making considerable use of the visual channel for facial expression, gestural and postural displays, social primates (such as rhesus monkeys, chimpanzees and gibbons) also have a wide range of vocalizations. Many species of whales and dolphins also use auditory channels for communication. Olfactory bulbs are reduced or completely absent in baleen whales (humpback, sei and rorqual) and toothed whales (sperm, killer and all dolphins). Many cetacean species usually have poor vision (as they feed in deep water or under ice, or are nocturnal). Evidences also suggest that their sense of taste functions to detect water-borne chemicals are also lacking. Therefore, most whales should essentially rely heavily on audition for any form of distant social communication. The study of mammalian vocal production provides a crucial context for understanding the evolution of human speech and singing. Conversely, from an acoustical and physiological viewpoint, the best understood mammalian vocalization is human speech. So theories and techniques from speech science have played an important role in increasing our understanding of the vocal production system of other mammals.

The advantages of acoustic signaling includes higher degree of freedom over environmental barriers, as these types of signals are transmitted over considerable distances and are available in the dark or when lines of sight are interrupted. These signals have high information content and have greater superficial similarity to human speech. Like olfaction, acoustic signals are also transmitted over considerable distances. Thus, advantages of the acoustic channel include its rapid transmission, as well as, swift and accurate source localization. But, the production of acoustic signals in animals is often energetically costly. For instance, a cicada may need to increase its resting metabolic rate by 20 folds in order to sing and some small frogs increase their metabolic rate 5 times expending more than 80 percent of their total calorific intake while calling during their breeding season. This may also be contrasted with the use of chemical signals, where, since the recipient can be sensitive to just a molecule and air-borne transmission is free, minute amounts of *pheromones* are sufficient to produce dramatic effects. Other constraints of auditory signals are that the production of sound may reveal the location of the sender to a potential predator, it is less effective in disturbed environments (like sea shore). Moreover, the intensity of sounds fall rapidly, so the signals degrade with increasing distance from source.

Text Box 5.2 Some Special Modes of Auditory Communication

Echolocation: *Echolocation* is the use of ultra-high frequency sounds emitted by an animal for its own navigation and to locate prey. In *echolocation* the animal produces sound pulses at very high frequencies that are not audible to humans. Distance is then measured (ranging) by the animal by measuring the time delay between the animal's own sound emission and any reflected sound waves (echoes) that return from the environment.

Echolocation is noticed among mammals, particularly in microchiropteran bats and odontocetes like toothed whales and dolphins (Figure 5.2). For echolocation bats generate sound waves at an impressive rate of 200 pulses per second. Also, two cave-dwelling avian species belonging to genus *Aerodramus* and another *Steatornis caripensis* are a few birds that perform echolocation. It is to be noted that the distinctive animal noises have evolved particularly for intraspecific communication. So, the production of sounds for the purposes of echolocation is basically a specialized kind of auditory communication and thus an exception to the general rule.

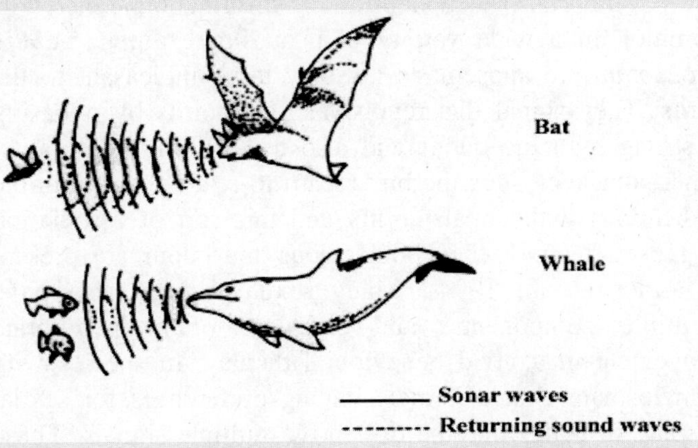

Figure 5.2 Illustrations of echolocation in bats and whales.

Whale Songs: Apart from locating the prey, sound production and reception by many toothed cetacean species is usually assumed to play a part in their social communication. However, detailed evidence of the precise functions of particular sounds is sparse for species other than the bottle-nosed dolphins. Scientists have drawn a distinction between pure tone whistles (or squeals) and pulsed clicks. Squeals serve individual identification and other social purposes while the pulsed clicks are primarily for echolocation. Many different categories of pulsed sounds have been identified, whose behavioural function is unclear. An extremely wide range of sounds other than clicks or whistles have been recorded in other species, such as the baleen humpback. These odontocete beluga, or "sea canary" travel vast distances and are commonly referred to as "whale songs".

Multi-modal Signaling

Complex signals may be defined as signals consisting of multiple components and are prevalent in the animals for various modes of communication, which allow more effective transfer of information or convey more information as compared to the single component signals. Multimodal communication is defined as communication via composite signals received through more than one sensory channels. Multi component signals can be *unimodal* where it is perceived in only a single sensory modality by the receiver or *multimodal* where it is produced in more than one sensory modality. Multimodal signals differ from unimodal composite signals in that the additional channels afford new constraints and opportunities for communication (Table 5.1).

Table 5.1 Benefits and Costs Associated with Multimodal Signals for Communication

Benefits	*Costs*
Multiple redundant signal components provide insurance that the message will be received, and they correct for possible errors of signal detection and identification.	Production, coordination, reception, and cognitive and neural integration of multiple signals may have high energy costs and require extensive anatomical and physiological equipment.
Multiple nonredundant signal components provide increased information content; each nonredundant components may play a different functional role (e.g., one may attract attention, and another may transmit more specific information).	The use of multiple channels can increase risk of predation: senders may be more conspicuous to eavesdroppers because of signaling in more channels, or they may attract a new predator by signaling in an additional channel; receivers may be more vulnerable to predation by devoting more senses to detecting conspecific signals and leaving fewer free to detect predators.

Multimodal communication, whereby individuals use several sensory modalities for information transfer, is common in a wide variety of taxa. For example, *Adelia bipunctata* are aposematic i.e. they taste unpleasant to the birds. They signal this repulsiveness to birds by releasing a strong pyrazine odour and also use striking colouration when attacked. Thus the birds learn to relate these multiple indications with unpalatability and this sort of association is most effective when both colour and odour are present (Marples et al., 1994). Many sexual signals also have multiple components, and signalers often incorporate movement in a vivid behavioural display. In species with female mate choice, female mating preferences for sexual display in males may be driven by multiple signals. These signals indicate the benefits of mate choice by revealing different aspects of the male's phenotypic and genetic quality (multiple messages hypothesis) or alternatively, by signifying the overall quality of the signaler (back-up hypothesis or redundant signal hypothesis).

In multimodal signaling, long-term signals are determined over a long period of life and would reflect past condition, whereas short-term signals depend on current nutritional condition and are highly sensitive to short-term changes in the environment.

5.1.3 Biological Significance of Signaling

Sexual Signaling: The purpose of sexual signaling is either to attract mates of the opposite sex or to deter rivals of the same sex. They use different modalities of communication (either singly or in combination with each other) to perform the functions of sexual signaling. Sexual signals evolve in response to a variety of factors. Some of the most important selective factors are: presence of conspecifics, transmission efficiency in a particular environment, detection by predators, and phylogenetic constraints.

A classical example of sexual signal is the biological ornament. They are basically the secondary sexual characteristics of an animal that appears to serve a decorative function and are morphological traits used to attract mates of opposite sex. This includes the plumage feather ornaments and beautiful songs of many birds, the colour markings of some lizards and fish and the leg tufts of spiders (Andersson, 1994). An animal may shake, lengthen, or spread out its ornament in order to get the attention of the opposite sex, which will in turn choose the most attractive one in order to sexually reproduce. These traits are also often used in aggressive displays in competition for mates or for other resources, and many of these ornaments have been shown to convey information about the fighting ability of their bearer. Ornaments are most often observed in males and choosing an extravagantly ornamented male benefits females because the ornament displays "good genes" will be passed on to her offspring, increasing their own reproductive fitness.

Vocalizations or auditory signals are also used to attract mates. Bird song and the calls of crickets and frogs are examples of such signaling. For example, in *Hyla versicolor* (gray tree frog), the male produces a call to attract females. But the female chooses its mate based on a specific style of male calling. The signal can be the call itself or the intensity of a call, its variation in style or its repetition rate. Various hypotheses were postulated to explain why females would select for one call over the other. The *sensory exploitation hypothesis* proposes that pre-existing preferences in female receivers can drive the evolution of signal innovation in male senders, while the *hidden preference hypothesis* proposes that successful calls are better able to match some 'hidden preference' in the female. Olfactory signals are also common, especially in insects. Other morphological traits and signals evolve in response to competition between members of one sex for access to mates in the other. These are used in contests between individuals where ornaments and threat signals are produced to deter rivals, such as horns of some beetle species and the antlers of many ungulates.

Social Signaling: Social signals are used by conspecifics living in close groups. These signals generally disclose the supremacy and ranking of an individual living in a group and also its pecking order. Cooperative nature of social behaviour can be viewed when both the signaler and receiver are benefitted by the transfer of relevant information. For example, small passerine birds use alarm calls to inform individuals within the same flock of an approaching predator. Alarm calls benefit receivers as it provides them with an opportunity to flee, but also protects the signaler as it is less likely to be attacked in the flock than if it was to flee on its own.

Warning Signaling: It is unwise to think that all communication occurs between conspecifics; signals can also be directed at interspecific receivers (like predators). '*Aposematism*' (commonly known as warning colouration) is one such example which describes certain anti-predator adaptations where warning signals inform the predator that there is a cost of attacking the signaler (such as unprofitability of the prey). The warning signal may take the form of conspicuous animal coloration, sounds, odours or other perceivable characteristics. Usually the function of signals that are directed towards predators is to escape predation by warning potential predators that the prey animal has defenses such as being unpalatable or poisonous. Warning signals are honest indications of noxious prey, because conspicuousness evolves in tandem with noxiousness. Grossly it is associated with the unprofitability of a prey item to potential predators. Thus, this type of signals are beneficial for both the predator and prey, since both avoid potential harm. The easily detected warning is a primary defense mechanism and the non-visible defenses are secondary.

Aposematic signals involve advertising signals that are primarily visual, using bright colours and high-contrast patterns such as stripes and spots. The most common and the best-studied warning signals are colour patterns. Some animals with warning colours (such as the yellow, red and black coral snakes or the redback spiders *Latrodectus* spp.) are deadly poisonous and it is therefore the predator's interest to avoid these species. A classic example of warning colouration is the black and yellow pattern of monarch butterfly where the black and orange coloration of adult butterflies warn the predators about the cardiac glycosides in their body. These chemicals are emetic for most predators and the recovery time after eating an adult butterfly may be up to half an hour. Nevertheless, *aposematism* is less observed in vertebrates and are mostly confined to a smaller number of reptiles, amphibians and fish species. Perhaps the most numerous aposematic vertebrates are the poison dart frogs.

Multicomponent warning signals are also emitted by aposematic species (Rowe, 1999). For a long time, the different components of these multi-component signals, such as odours, colours and behaviour, were thought to be directed at different groups of predators. For example, visual signals were thought to be effective against birds, while odours warned nocturnally hunting mammals. Recent studies of multi component signaling have, however, revealed that in fact more than one signal may be directed at a single predator (Marples et al., 1994), and having more than one warning signal increase the chance of survival of the prey species (Marples et al., 1994; Rowe and Guilford, 1996).

The underlying defense mechanism of warning signaling relies on the memory. An individual (predator) which had a previous experience of inedible another individual (prey) will endeavour to avoid the repetition of the experience. Aposematic species are often gregarious organisms and often move in a languid fashion, as they have little need for speed and agility. Instead, their morphology is frequently tough and resistant to injury, thereby allowing them to escape once the predator is warned off. They usually do not need to hide or stay still as cryptic organisms do. So aposematic individuals also benefit from more freedom in exposed areas and can spend more time foraging, allowing them to find more and better quality food and can similarly make use of conspicuous mating displays.

5.1.4 Honesty of Signals: Handicap Principle

Honest signaling assumes a correlation between an observable signal and a non-observable quality. There are many mutually nonexclusive mechanisms that can achieve such a correlation. However, for a long time the handicap principle has been identified as the main solution to this problem. Maintenance of honesty in the signal is a fundamental component of signaling systems where there is a conflict of interest between the signaler and the receiver. The *handicap principle* was introduced in the context of sexual selection and mate choice, but it is also applicable to many other signaling systems like signals from prey to predators, from offspring to parents and between opponents in agonistic contests. This principle first appreciated the signal honesty (Zahavi, 1975; Johnstone, 1995) and proposed that signals are intended for a receiver as they convey honest information about the signaler. However, signal honesty can only be maintained if two conditions are fulfilled.

- First, the signals must be expensive for the signaler to be produced or maintained, and
- Second, the cost must be dependent on the condition of the signaler, as because the signaler in good condition can withstand the cost of signaling at a given level better than a signaler in poor condition (Johnstone, 1995).

Differentiation between high-quality and poor-quality individuals is vital. According to the handicap principle, honest signals are generally produced by good quality individuals who can afford this extra cost of an honest signal. In brief, this theory claims that signals need to be costly to be honest and that honest signalers have to pay this extra cost. Honesty, however, is not maintained by the realized cost paid by honest signalers at the equilibrium, but by the potential cost of cheating. Due to such extra costs, the honest signals are in one sense handicap for the signalers.

Honesty, however, is not maintained always. Thus, the honest signalers also face the potential risk of cheating. But in cases, where there is no conflict of interest between the signaler and the receiver and the communication is cooperative, the signal may convey reliable information even if signaling is cost-free.

5.1.5 Deceptive Signals

Not always each and every signal is honest; some signals are deceptive too. Such deceptive signals are transmitted by the signaler who propagates untrue information and eventually causes the receiver (belonging to the same or different species) to behave in such a way that is beneficial only to the signaler. Deceptive signals are emitted when the outcome of transmission of a signal is more beneficial for the signaler than the cost of producing such signals. Presence of deceptive signals in a signaling system is problematic and confusing for the receivers to respond to the signalers who are actually transmitting the same signals honestly. In such cases, the receivers may completely ignore or question the truthfulness of the honest signal. Deceptive signals may further complicate the signaling system for receivers and honest signalers if they incur the cost of maintaining a signal's reliability through sanctioning, policing and punishing. As a final consequence, such deception may erode the meaning of the signal altogether.

Text Box 5.3 ***Batesian mimicry: an example of a dishonest signal***

Batesian mimicry is a form of dishonest signaling where a harmless species has evolved to imitate the warning signals of a harmful species directed at a common predator. Harmful prey sends warning signals to inform predators that they are inedible. It is advantageous for both predators and harmful prey to use these signals, as the prey avoids being eaten. The benefit of avoiding such prey is potentially very high for predators as eating such deadly poisonous prey could lead to detrimental fitness effects for them. But some other species despite not being unpalatable or dangerous exploit this scenario to their own advantage by displaying dishonest signals.

The harmful species (referred to as *model*) might have spines or toxic substances, while the mimicking species (referred to as *mimic*) has no defense against the predator, other than resembling the harmful species. Batesian mimics are palatable individuals that avoid predation by using their resemblance to unpalatable or dangerous models for deceiving potential predators. By copying the same colourful warning patterns of unpalatable species, the palatable 'Batesian mimics' escape predation. The predators cannot discriminate between the models and the mimics and often associate such resemblance of the mimics with a bad experience encountered earlier while catching the actual harmful species (the model). So they avoid the mimicking species too.

But, if the mimics become too abundant, then the predators are likely to sample both edible and inedible species and might be able to distinguish the mimics from the models by some specialized features. Then the deceptive signal produced by the mimics will lose its meaning to receivers. So, Batesian mimics should always be rare as compared to the abundance of their models.

5.1.6 Eavesdropping

Eavesdropping is the situation where the signal is received neither by the signaler nor the intended receiver, rather a third animal receives the signal and acquires information from it. Eavesdroppers are more commonly predators or parasites belonging to other species who exploit the signals generated by their prey or hosts respectively to locate their victims. A good example of this has been found in studies of field crickets and their parasitoids. Male field crickets produce acoustic signals by stroking their modified forewings together, which serve as sexual signals to attract females. Parasitoid flies (*Ormia* spp.) find these field cricket hosts by acoustically orienting towards their song (Zuk et al.,1998). Thus, the parasitoid flies are eavesdropping on the male sexual signals which were actually intended for the female crickets. Signalers also evolve adaptations to minimize the chance of signal detection by eavesdroppers. Such signals are altogether prevented, if the cost of eavesdropping is very high for the signaler. One good way to do this is to use a signal that their predators cannot perceive. For example, nestlings of bird species those are prone to nest predation use pecking calls of higher frequency and lower amplitude. These acoustic features make finding the nest much more difficult for the predator.

5.1.7 Signal Design and Receiver Psychology

One more important aspect of transferring information through signaling in an efficient way is the straightforward and effortless distinction and recognition of the signal. This is dependent on – (i) how the signal is designed to transfer its message, (ii) the environment in which a signal is emitted, (iii) the sensory systems of receivers and (iv) receiver's psychology. Among these, 'receiver psychology' is important in selecting those signals that are easier to detect, recognize, discriminate, learn and remember. 'Strategic design' is concerned with how a signal is constructed by natural selection so that it is good in displaying underlying quality, and also provides necessary information to make a receiver respond. On the other hand, 'efficacy' is concerned with how a signal is designed to get that information across to the receiver. Therefore, the three aspects of receiver psychology (viz. better detectability, uncomplicated discrimination and easy remembrance) constitute powerful selective forces in signal design of which greatest emphasis is given to the ability to memorize. Learning and memory are involved in a wide range of signals. The perceptual abilities of receivers have a significant impact on signal design.

- First, the signal has to be sent within the sensory limits of the receiver. The sensory systems of animals vary. For example, birds can perceive ultraviolet wavelengths of light to which humans, and most other mammals, are blind. In fact, avian visual systems are more sensitive to colour than those of many mammals, which may explain why birds often use colourful signals, whereas many mammals use olfactory or acoustic signals.
- Second, signals have to be detected by the receiver against background noise (like acoustic signals need to be heard over other sounds), and
- Finally, once the signal has been detected, the receiver has to recognize the signal and discriminate between signals that are similar. So, the receiver needs to learn and remember the meaning of various signals. Then, features of a signal that are easily remembered will be selected for by receivers.

Receivers exert strong selection pressures on signalers to produce signals that they can readily perceive and signalers benefit from their signals being more effective at producing the desired response from receivers. However, as mentioned above, it is not only the intended receivers that affect signal design, but also those animals that eavesdrop.

5.1.8 Classical Example of Communication: Bee Dance

The honey bees are highly responsive to colours, odours, tastes, and learn them through classical and operant conditioning and retain this information for several days to communicate about the location and nature of sources of food. They fine-tune their foraging nature depending on the specific timings when the food is available and form cognitive maps of their surroundings. Forager honey bees after returning to the bee-hive precisely communicate the direction and distance of the nectar and pollen source through two distinct modes of dance language (the *round dance* and the *waggle dance*), so that the other worker bees are also recruited to search in the same area. Honey bees also heavily rely on smell to communicate with one another. Olfactory organs of the honey bees are located in the antennae. Using their antennae, workers in a hive can smell the scent of a flower on a returning forager and also use this information to locate the flower. The returning forager may even offer a sample of nectar from the flower. Thus, "*dance language theory*" and "*odour plume theory*" are the two main hypotheses that explain how foragers recruit other workers. Due to several experimental evidences and empirical support, the *dance language theory* is more widely accepted. Karl von Frisch, an Austrian ethologist and Professor of Zoology at the University of Munich in Germany, was credited with Nobel Prize in Medicine in the year 1973 for interpreting the meaning of honey bee dance (Frisch, 1967).

A few bees, called scout bees, fly around searching for new sources of food. When a scout finds a good patch of flowers, she flies back to the hive. She walks into the hive onto one of the combs, where other workers are grouped. There she performs a dance by running in a precise pattern that communicates the direction and distance of the flowers to the other bees. She is greeted by the bees present in the hive, and start dancing on the vertical comb surface within the dark nest to communicate the direction and distance of the food source. When food is within 50 – 75 meters of the hive, the scouts perform "*round dance*" on the surface of the comb; but when the food is farther than 75 m from the hive, the scouts perform "*waggle dance*".

Dance Proper

Waggle Dance: Waggle dance is performed by the foragers when the pollen or nectar sources are more than 75 m away from the colony. The waggle dance consists of two phases: the *waggle phase* and the *return phase*. In the *waggle phase,* the bee first runs straight ahead for a precise distance waggling her abdomen from side to side. This is also called "*waggle run*". During such *waggle run* the bee vigorously waggles her abdomen from side to side in a pendulum motion at about 13 times per second while moving forward in a straight line. After the *waggle phase*, without any interruption the bee moves in a semicircular trajectory and returns to the starting point of the last *waggle-run*. This is called the *return phase.* After the *waggle run* she turns left and circles back in a counter-clockwise direction to the starting point. The outer loops are simply walked during *return phases*. Then she again waggles her abdomen moving forward, stop waggling after reaching the same distance as before, turns right and circles back in a clockwise direction to the starting point. In this fashion the dancer tends to alternate clockwise and counter clockwise directions throughout successive *return-phases* intermitted by straight *waggle phases* (or *waggle runs*). Thus, *waggle dance* usually denotes a specific figure-eight pattern and, therefore, it is also called "Figure of eight dance" (Figure 5.3).

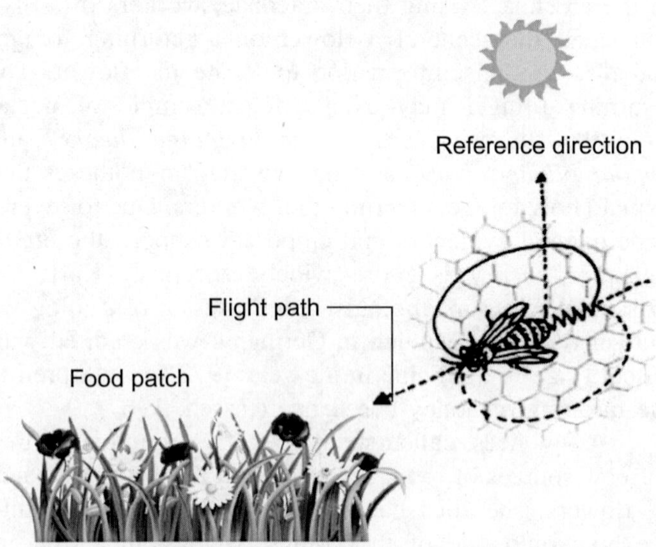

FIGURE 5.3 Illustration of the waggle dance in honey bees.

The bee will continue this until other bees pay attention. Depending on how plentiful the nectar is, the figure-eight may be repeated a number of times. Usually the number of circuits in a *waggle dance* range from 1–100 or more.

Distance is conveyed by the distance of a *waggle run* and the speed of the waggling movement. If the shaking of abdomen is fast and vigorous or the distance of waggle run is short, then the food source is not very far. On the other hand, if the distance of the *waggle run* is more or waggling of abdomen is less then it is to be understood that the food source is farther away.

Direction is communicated with respect to the position of the sun when the bee dances on the vertical face of the comb. It was noted that for cavity-nesting honey bees, floral resources that are located directly in line with the sun are represented by waggle runs in an upward direction on the vertical combs and any angle to the right or left of the sun is coded by a corresponding angle to the right or left of the upward direction. For example a bee that runs straight down when the sun is in the west indicates the food directly east. But if the bees carry out their dances inside dark inner chambers of the wax comb from where sun is not visible, then the gravitational force is used as an important cue to communicate the direction of food source. In such a scenario, bees waggle moving straight upwards against gravity indicate flying towards the sun while waggle run straight downwards in the direction of gravitational force denotes that the food source is in the opposite direction of the sun.

There can be more than one scout returning from different locations and performing the waggle dance, each trying to convince the observing bees to follow her lead. Then there may be competition between the members and these bees may even fight with each other. In such a scenario somehow the swarm of bees in the hive evaluates the alternatives and chooses which one to follow.

The bees can get some information about what type of flower the scout bee visited by the odour of the nectar. Using SPME sampling and GC/MS analysis it was revealed that waggle-dancing bees produce and release into the air two alkanes (Tricosane and Pentacosane) and two alkenes (Z(9)–Tricosene and Pentacosene) in minute quantities.

Efficiency of Waggle Dance

Honey bee colonies routinely perform the *waggle dance.* In some cases, unsuccessful foraging may result even after more than 50 *waggle runs*, while in other instances bees can successfully forage after observing only five runs. Therefore, it seems that the degree of functional efficiency of the *waggle dance* varies and may be dependent on immediate environment. Temperate environments resources are relatively homogeneous. So even if the dance is experimentally obscured, honey bees can still successfully forage. But in the tropical regions, sources of the food can come from sparsely scattered flowering trees, rich in nectar and have specific periodic bloom timings. Thus, information about forage location is more valuable in tropical zones than in temperate zones and without a *waggle dance* the foraging attempts of honey bees might well be unsuccessful due to patchiness of resources in these tropical habitats.

Round Dance: When food is less than 75 m away, then the tail wagging portion of the waggle dance (i.e. the *waggle* *phase*) is omitted and the bees merely circle around. This form of dance is known as *round dance* (Figure 5.4).

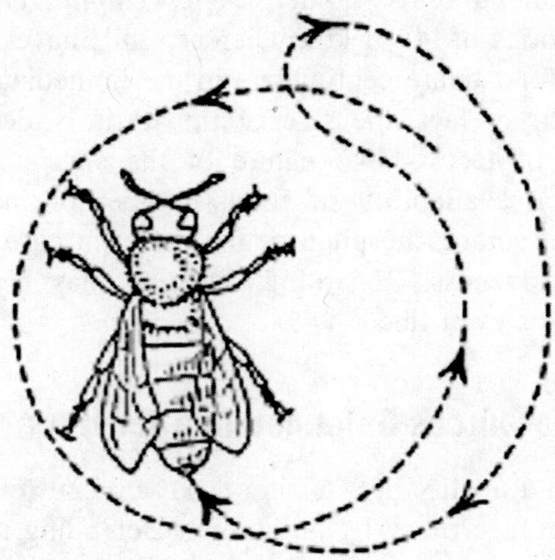

FIGURE 5.4 Illustration of the round dance in honey bees.

It is important to note that the inside of a hive is very dark. So, the honey bees use touch to help them feel, rather than see, the dances. While dancing, the bees also make buzzing sounds with their wings. The entire motion pattern is strongly linked to the dancer's recent navigation experience. Honeybees congregate an electric charge either through movement or rubbing their body parts or also during their flight. It was also observed that they also produce constant and modulated electric fields during the waggle dance and induce passive antennal movements in stationary bees. Greggers et al., (2013) reported that electric fields emanating from the surface charge of bees stimulate mechanoreceptors and may play a role in social communication during the waggle dance.

The Dance Language vs. Other Modes of Communication in Honey Bees

In a recent experiment, *Apis mellifera* was reported to communicate the location of a profitable food source through dance and the type of the plant through the odour of flowers. In situations where the dancers indicate an unfamiliar location but carry the scent of a known flower species, then the scents often overrule and reactivate bees to collect food from previously visited food patches. But, these are often different from the locations indicated through dance language. Here the information communicated through dance and odour of the flower creates a conflict between the 'social vector information' and the 'private navigational information' of the follower honeybees. In such situations, the followers often ignore the spatial information encoded by the waggle dance even if they have followed a dance thoroughly. Instead, in most (>90 percent) cases, they relied on private information about food source locations in the above experiment with *Apis mellifera*. So, the dances indicating an unfamiliar location are of little interest to experienced foragers.

Thus, honey bees can independently forage successfully without even decoding the dance language information in the following ways:

- They may use the olfactory information (scent of flower) from the dancer and use that in finding the same resource or even a different one with a similar odour.
- Following a dance may simply instigate foraging behaviour and thereafter the bees commence random searching of resources.
- A dance may also reactivate secretive knowledge of a honey bee about a resource. So, instead of visiting the location deciphered through dance language, the forager may simply return to her known resource.
- The information communicated in the waggle dance is more functional to foragers only when private information about resources is lacking.

5.2 HOME RANGE AND TERRITORY

Animals travel through various places within their habitat to obtain food, seek shelter or find mates. Competition for food and other resources ultimately determines the distribution patterns of animals in space. The actual physical area covered in the course of these regular movements is the animal's ***home range***. An animal's familiarity with the features of its home range allows it to forage efficiently and escape predators in emergency. Even when animals do not interact, clumped resources may cause individuals to aggregate.

Definition: The region that ensures all the basic needs of an animal to stay alive and reproduce, which is not necessarily defended but is habitually utilized by an individual or a group of animals and the region where an animal spends its time comfortably and at ease, is called the home range of the animal. The home ranges of different groups of animals often overlap. In such overlap areas, the groups will tend to avoid each other instead of seeking to expel each other. Within the home range there may be a *core area* that no other individual group uses. But, this is as a result of avoidance rather than defense. Presuming that home range behaviour is the product of decision-making processes shaped by natural selection to increase the contributions of spatially distributed resources to fitness. Thus it can be said that a home range represents an interplay between the environment and an animal's understanding of that environment, in other words its cognitive map. Home ranges differ among animals of different species, among individuals within a species, and even within individuals over time. Nonetheless, all animals use their home ranges to procure food and other resources, including avoiding predators.

On the contrary, a territory provides a safe place for the young to be raised and usually contains a breeding / nesting site at its centre. Most vertebrates and some invertebrates (such as arthropods, including insects) exhibit aggressive behaviour in defending its own territory. Thus, territory of an animal strikingly differs from its home range. Territories may be held by an individual, a mated or unmated pair, or a group. Territoriality is not always a fixed behavioural characteristic of a species. Territories may vary with time (season). For example, robins defend territories as pairs during the breeding season, while as individuals during the winter. Resource availability may cause changes in territoriality. For instance, some nectarivores defend territories only during morning hours, when plants are richest in nectar. In species that do not form pair bonds, male and female territories are often independent, i.e. males defend territories only against other males and females only against other females. In this case, if the species is polygynous, one male territory will probably contain several female territories, while in some polyandrous species (such as the bronze-winged jacana *Metopidius indicus*) this situation is reversed.

Definition: Territory may be defined as the socio-graphical area that the territorial animal of a particular species consistently defends against conspecifics or occasionally, animals of other species.

The home range and territory is illustrated in Figure 5.5 below:

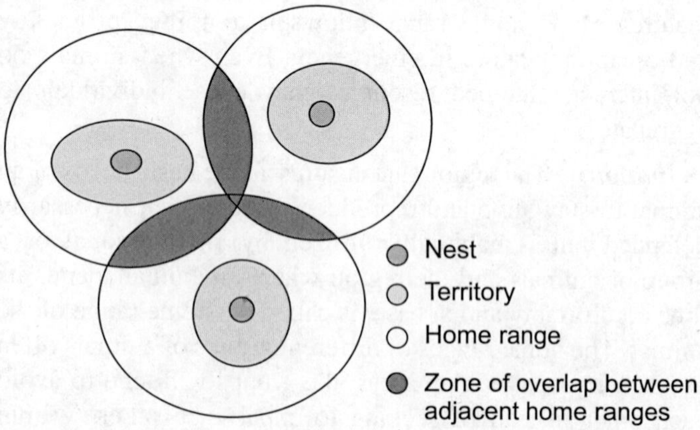

FIGURE 5.5 Illustration of the home range and territories.

5.2.1 Size of Territory

The size and shape of a territory can vary according to its purpose, season, the quantity and quality of resources present within and is also based on the geography. The size of a territory is usually determined by the resource base, defense costs, predation pressure and reproductive needs. On average, a territory may be approximately 0.5 sq km. But, in very poor habitat, the territory may be as large as 3 sq km. Size of territory also varies between different species. Among birds, golden eagles (*Aquila chrysaetos*) have territories of 90 sq km, whereas, gulls have territories of only a few square centimeters in the immediate vicinity of the nest. In fact, the size of the territory depends on a number of factors like nature of the species (colonial or solitary), availability of food, number of individuals, their age structure, the pitch of the song (in case of birds) and aggressiveness. Regarding shape, it may be circular, hexagonal or even linear.

5.2.2 Resources Defended in a Territory

The size and quality of a territory play crucial roles during selection of a territory by an animal. Defending a territory incurs large amount of energy, time and risk of injury costs. Therefore, territory is usually not larger than the size which the organism requires for optimum survival.

On the other hand, the quality of the territory is the most important aspect of territoriality for some animals, than territory size. Food distribution primarily determines the nature of territoriality. However, several other types of resources including partners, potential mates, offspring, nests or lairs, display areas or *leks* may also play crucial roles in selecting and defending a territory. Territoriality is most strongly manifested in case of the conspecific intruders, as they share exactly the same set of resources as the owner of the territory.

Types of resources usually defended within a territory are as follows:

- ***Food:*** Large solitary or paired carnivores, such as bears and large raptors, often require an extensive area to be guarded to ensure their food supply. But such territorial defense is only interrupted when there is excess food. Food related territoriality is least likely with insectivorous birds, where the food supply is plentiful but unpredictably distributed. Swifts rarely defend an area larger than the nest. Conversely, other insectivorous birds occupy more constrained territories. The ground-nesting blacksmith lapwing, may be very much territorial, especially in the breeding season. During breeding season they not only threaten or attack many kinds of intruders, but have stereotyped display behaviour to deter conspecifics sharing neighbouring nesting spots.
- ***Nests and offspring:*** Many birds, particularly seabirds, colonially nest in dense communities. Nonetheless, they are territorial in defending their nesting site up to the distance where they can reach while brooding. This is necessary to

prevent attacks on their own chicks, as well as, to safeguard the nesting material being stolen by their neighbours. Some species of penguin also defend their nest from intruders who often try to steal the pebbles by which the nest is constructed.

- ***Mating opportunities:*** The striped mouse (*Rhabdomys pumilio*) is a group-living rodent. Single breeding male and up to four communally breeding females are present per group. Groups typically contain several *philopatric* adult sons (and daughters) that are believed not to breed in their natal group and all group members participate in territorial defense. Males defend their territory using 'nasty neighbour strategy'. Male breeders living in a particular group are nearly five times more aggressive towards their neighbouring males than towards strangers. As the male neighbours are the major competitors for paternity (28 percent of offspring by neighbouring males and only 7 percent by strangers).

5.2.3 Strategies for Territory Defense

To advertise and retain a territory animals create "sign-posts" through olfactory, auditory or visual signals or a combination of these. These sign-posts may be located on the boundary thereby demarcating the territory of an individual with others. But such sign-posts may also be scattered throughout the territory, sending a message to other animals that the territory is occupied along with additional information such as the sex, reproductive status or dominance status of the territory-holder. If an intruder progresses further into the territory beyond the sign-posts and encounters the territory-holder, then both animals manifest "ritualized aggression" toward each other. Territorial fight is the last resort and only occurs if the dispute regarding the ownership of the territory is not solved by 'ritualized aggressions'. Such territorial fights often result in fatal injuries. Strategies for territory defense depend on which intruder poses greatest threat to the territory owner and are explained through following theoretical models:

- ***Hawk Dove game strategy:*** The *Hawk-Dove game* is the most accepted game theory model of territory defense. The principle objective of the hawk strategy is to always try and injure its opponent and only withdraw from the contest immediately after receiving an injury, while a dove strategy always use a non-injurious display if the rival is another dove and always withdraw if the rival is a hawk.
- ***War of attrition strategy:*** In this model of territory defense, two contestants aggressively compete for single resource by persisting, thus, constantly accumulate costs over the time till the contest lasts. Strategically, the game is an auction in which the prize goes to the player with the highest bid and each player pays the loser's low bid.
- ***Dear enemy effect strategy:*** In this strategy two neighbouring territorial animals become less aggressive towards one another once territorial borders are well-established and they are familiar to each other, but aggression towards unfamiliar animals remains high. This strategy is generally adopted by the resident territory-holder if the resource requirements of the neighbouring territorial animals are different. In this case the territory-holder perceives lesser amount of threat from the familiar neighbours, as compared to the unfamiliar intruders.
- ***Nasty neighbour effect strategy:*** The *nasty neighbour effect* is opposite to the *Dear enemy effect*. In this strategy of territory defense, a territory-holder shows higher aggression towards neighbouring territory-holders, but not so much aggression to unfamiliar animals or distant territory-holders. This strategy is adopted when the territory holder perceives greatest threat from the familiar intruder of the adjacent territory seeking for similar resources.
- ***Reciprocal altruism strategy:*** In territory defense by groups of animals, *reciprocal altruism* can operate whereby the cost to the benefactor in helping defend the territory is less than the gains to the beneficiary.

5.2.4 Modes of Advertising the Territory

Olfactory Stimuli — Scent Marking

Scent marking, also known as *territorial marking* or *spraying*, is used by many animals to mark and advertise their territory. This is commonly done by releasing strong-smelling substances contained in the urine, faeces or from specialized scent glands located on various parts of the body. The odour mostly contains pheromones and other carrier proteins (urinary proteins), which stabilize and maintain the smell for longer duration. To understand the communicated information, the animal sniffing the scent mark often displays a 'flehmen response' (Figure 5.6).

FIGURE 5.6 'Flehmen response' in Indian tiger. (Photo: Dr. Subhendu Mazumdar)

Pre-orbital, forehead, tarsal, metatarsal and interdigital glands are mainly involved in the production of scent. The location and function of these glands are summarized in Table 5.2.

Table 5.2 Major Glands Responsible for Scent Production

Gland	*Location*	*Function*
Pre-orbital	In front of the eye	Usually rubbed on tree branches
Forehead or sudoriferous	Found on the forehead region, usually between the antlers and eyes	Used to deposit scent on branches that overhang the areas which is initially scraped by the deer's front hooves prior to rub-urination.
Tarsal	Found on the upper inside of the hock (middle joint) on each hind leg.	Used as an alarm scent.
Metatarsal	Found on the outside of each hind leg, between the ankle and hooves	Used as an alarm scent.
Interdigital	Located in between the hooves of each foot	Emit a yellow waxy substance having an offensive odour

Scent Marking – Both Art and Science

Territorial scent marking sometimes may involve specific behavioural response. Felids (such as common leopard *Panthera pardus*) mark territories by rubbing themselves against vegetation. Prosimians and New World monkeys also use scent marking to communicate. This includes urine washing where one individual put its own urine over the body. Many ungulates use scent marking from two glands, the pre orbital gland and a scent gland in the hoof.

When a wolf marks its territory, it lifts a hind leg and usually urinates on an elevated position like a tree, rock or bush. Such urination on 'scent posts' is altogether different from normal urination which they performed during squatting. Usually, this urine marking posture is exclusively performed by females and also by the alpha male. The alpha female usually urinates on a scent post that her breeding partner has just urinated on. But, during mating season the female may first urinate on the ground.

Indian muntjac (*Muntiacus muntjak*) is a solitary animal and they use olfactory stimuli to communicate. Adult males mark grass and bushes at several places within their territory with secretions from their pre orbital glands located on their face, just below the eyes. Often they rub their pre orbital glands on the ground and on trees (Figure 5.7), scraping their hooves against the ground, and scraping the bark of trees with their lower incisors. Scent-marking is prominent in males than females and more in dominant males than subordinates.

FIGURE 5.7 Illustration of scent marking in Indian muntjac.

White-tailed deer possess number of glands for the production of scents. Perceiving any danger through sight, sound or smell, the deer stomp their hooves, which results an excess secretion of odour to warn other members against possible danger. This deer also 'rub-urinate' throughout the year. This is a process during which a deer squats while urinating, so that urine will run down the insides of the deer's legs, over the tarsal glands, and onto the hair covering these glands. Bucks (males) rub-urinate more frequently during the breeding season. Secretions from the tarsal gland mix with the urine and bacteria to produce a strong smelling odour. During the breeding season females release hormones and pheromones, which signify that they are in heat and are able to breed. Bucks (males) also rub trees and shrubs with their antlers and head during the breeding season, possibly transferring scent from the forehead glands to the tree, so that other deers can detect.

In rhinoceros, the dominant bulls mark their territory with faeces and urine (olfactory marking). After defecating, they scratch their hind feet in the dung and through walking, they disseminates their own smell around the paths, thus establishing a scent-marked trail.

Many animals have scent glands in their paws. The male ring-tailed lemur has a specialized adaptation which assist them in leaving visual/olfactory territorial marks. On their inner forearm a scent gland is present, which is covered by a spur. In a behaviour called "spur marking", they grasp the substrate, usually a small sapling, and drag the spur over it, cutting into the wood and spreading the gland's secretions. When on the ground, they preferentially mark small saplings and when high in the trees, they usually mark small vertical branches.

Visual Stimuli

Visual sign-posts are another prominent mode of advertising a territory. Coloration or behaviour of the animal is a short-term mode of communication and is only effective when the resident is present. Other animals may use more long-term visual signals such as faecal deposits or marks on the vegetation or ground. Such signals are effective even when the animal is not present on the actual site. Visual marking of territory is often combined with other modes of animal communication.

Some animals have prominent visual displays to advertise their territory, often in combination with scent marking or auditory signals. Male Oriental magpie robins (*Copsychus saularis*) show highly aggressive territorial behaviour. They often attack other males and other small birds that stray into their territories without apparent provocation. In some instances, such attacks often lead to fatal consequences.

One-horned rhinoceros (*Rhinoceros unicornis*) have poor vision but may use visual marking. They defecate in specific locations resulting in well defined piles (20 – 30 in numbers) to alert trespassers that it is an occupied territory. Other males may deposit dung over the piles of another and subsequently the sign-post grows larger and larger and may become up to five meters wide and 1 m high. Another method of visually marking their territory is wiping their horns on bushes or the ground and scraping with the feet, in combination with the smell of the marking animal.

Several species of bear (*Ursus* spp.) scratch or chew trees in order to leave visual mark of their territory. Indian tigers (*Panthera tigris tigris*) scratch the trunks of large trees within their territory with their sharp claws. Such claw marks act as visual signals of territoriality (Figure 5.8). Many other animals also deposit fur during tree-marking. They sometimes also rub their bodies against tree trunks leaving tufts of fur. In addition to such tree marking, olfactory signals are also given to advertise the territory.

FIGURE 5.8 Claw mark of Indian tiger (*Panthera tigris tigris*) on a tree trunk. (Photo: Dr. Subhendu Mazumdar)

Auditory Stimuli

Many animals including birds, frogs and canids use vocalization to advertise their territory. These are short-term signals transmitted only when the animal is present, but can travel long distances over varied habitats surpassing several physical barriers.

In addition to scent marking, Indian wolf (*Canis lupus pallipes*) and Indian jackal (*Canis aureus indicus*) also advertise their territories to other packs through howling. Such howls can be heard over wide areas. When howling together, the individuals often harmonize their calls rather than chorusing on the same note, thus creating the illusion of presence of more wolves than they actually are. Territorial calls are also generated by many avian species. Calling by the male birds in Asian koel (*Eudynamys scolopaceus*) and Oriental magpie robin (*Copsychus saularis*) are also some of the most common examples of auditory signals advertising territoriality.

Ritualized Aggression

An individual exhibits a series of behaviours to frighten intruders in order to defend its own territory, thereby avoiding actual fights which are expensive in terms of energy and the risk of injury. It includes a series of displays including aggressive gestures like vocalizations, spreading of wings or gill covers, lifting and presentation of claws, head bobbing, tail and body beating and finally, direct attack. Ritualized aggression often ends by one of the animals fleeing (usually the intruder). Only in extreme cases actual fighting takes place. Some of the interesting examples of ritualized aggression are:

(i) Domestic cats (*Felis catus*) defend their territories with ritualized body posturing, stalking, staring, spitting, yowling and howling.
(ii) Spider monkeys (*Ateles* spp.) defend their territory by screams, barks, rattling or dropping branches and urinating and defecating on intruders below.
(iii) Oscar cichlids (*Astronotus ocellatus*) are able to alter their colouration rapidly, a trait which facilitates ritualized territorial and combat behaviours amongst conspecifics.
(iv) Individuals of blunt-head cichlid (*Tropheus moorii*) defend their feeding territory with a display through quivering the tail and fins to terrorize the intruder or even attack by darting at the intruders and chasing them away.
(v) Male ring-tailed lemurs have scent glands on their wrists, chests and in the genital area. During encounters with rival males they may perform "stink fight", in which the males massage their tails by rubbing the ends of their tails on the inside of their wrists and on their chests. Now, they bend their tails over their bodies and wave them at their opponent. The intruder either responds with a display of his own, shows physical aggression or else flees.

5.2.5 Costs and Benefits of Territorial Defense

Defending a territory requires time and energy and there are high risks of injuries or even death. So, time, energy and risk of injury are the 'costs' of territory defense, while the improved access to resources (food, mate, nest sites or roost sites) represents the 'benefits' of territory defense. Animals usually defend territories only if the benefits of defense outweigh the costs. The *optimum territory size* is the area where the difference between the benefits derived from the territory and the costs of defending the territory is maximum as shown in Figure 5.9.

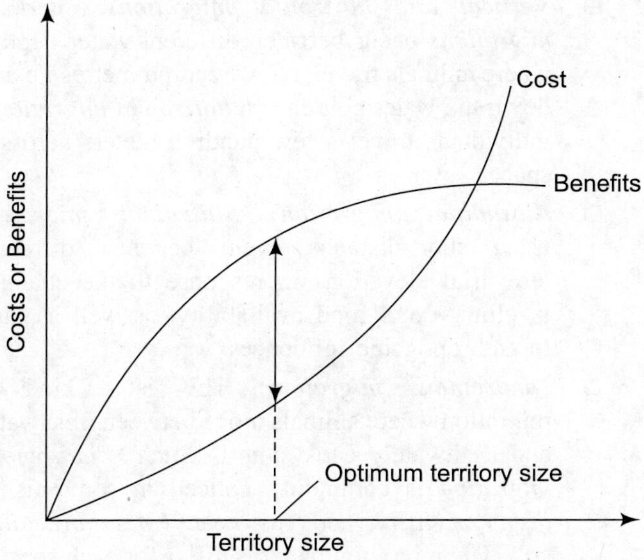

FIGURE 5.9 Graph depicting the relationship of territory size with the costs of defending the territory and the benefits arising out of it.

The proximate functions of territory defense may vary from acquiring and protecting food sources, nesting sites, mating grounds or attracting a mate. But, the ultimate objective of animals inhabiting and defending a territory is to increase the individual fitness or inclusive fitness of the individuals (group) expressing the behaviour. Thus, *territory* plays an important role as a mechanism of population regulation.

5.3 ANIMAL MIGRATION

Movement is an integral part of the behavioural ecology of many animals. Animals move across different spatial and temporal scales either as part of their daily life or seasonally to exploit resources in the environment. Animals usually disperse from one place to another through a variety of media (rivers, oceans, land and skies) and the animals move by swimming, drifting, walking, running or flying. It can affect individual fitness and population persistence by enabling foraging and predation, behavioural interactions and migration. Migration is relatively long distance seasonal movement of individuals and a wide-spread phenomenon in the animal kingdom, occurring in diverse taxonomic groups, particularly among insects, fishes, reptiles, birds and mammals. In other words, true migration is not just a local dispersal or a rapid increase in number beyond the normal limit, rather it is the annual or seasonal movement of animals (*viz.* birds migrate from colder region to warmer climatic regimes during winter and return during spring) or a major change in habitat as a part of their life history (for example, young Atlantic salmon leave rivers immediately after birth). The primary reasons for the migration may be local climate, availability of food, the season of the year or for mating purposes. Animals use predictable environmental cues for the timing and navigation of migration and a change in these cues will affect the phenology and extent of migration. Migration is a central part in the life history of many animals, where migrants can benefit from temporal variation in the profitability of different habitats.

The conceptual migration model incorporates aspects of the environment in which migration occurs (the "migration arena"), the spatiotemporal population demography that results from migration (the "population trajectory"), the traits that implement migration and determine the fitness of the migrants (the "migration syndrome") and the genetic complex underlying the migration syndrome. However, the phenomenon of migration precisely involves four related basic concepts (Dingle and Drake, 2007):

1. A type of locomotory activity that is notably persistent, undistracted, and straightened out.
2. Relocation of the animal that is on a much greater scale, and involves movement of much longer duration, than those arising in its normal daily activities.
3. Seasonal to-and-fro movement of populations between regions where conditions are alternately favourable or unfavourable (including one region in which breeding occurs).
4. Movements leading to redistribution within a spatially extended population.

5.3.1 Types of Migration

Migration can take a number of forms and has been described by the scientists in various ways (Table 5.3), by classifying based on the organisms, the spatial or temporal attributes or the medium in which migration takes place.

Table 5.3. Basis of the Classification of Different Types of Migration

Category	*Pattern*
Organism	Obligate, facultative, partial, differential
Space	To-and-fro, round-trip (loop), one-way, vertical, horizontal, altitudinal, nomadic
Time	Seasonal, irruptive (irregular)
Medium	Diadromic, drift (including devices)

Some of the important types are described below following Dingle and Drake, (2007):

- ❒ ***Obligate migration:*** In a situation where migration is a compulsion for all the individuals in a population, then such type of migration is termed as *obligate migration.*

- ***Facultative migration:*** In a situation where migration is a matter of choice for the individuals who can choose to migrate or not, then such type of migration is termed as *facultative migration* Facultative migration usually takes place as a proximate response to the deterioration of local conditions.
- ***Complete and partial migration:*** It is usually observed that within a migratory species or even within a single population, all individuals do not migrate always. *Complete migration* refers to the situation where all individuals migrate, while *partial migration* is the migration of some individuals of a population, but not all. In *partial migration*, a fraction of the population remains either in its breeding or its non-breeding area while the remainder moves away.
- ***Differential migration:*** In case of *differential migration* there are differences in migration patterns of older and younger individuals or of the two sexes i.e. the difference between migratory and non-migratory individuals is based on age or sex.
- ***'To-and-fro' migration:*** Space is a determining factor in *'To-and-fro' migration* where animals migrate between two different habitats.
- ***Round-trip migration:*** *Round-trip migration* is a variant of 'to-and-fro' migration, in which the animals return to the general breeding area from which they originated, but may stage their movements through a succession of non-breeding areas. If the animals follow different paths during the outward and return journeys then such migration is termed as *loop migration*.
- ***One-way migration:*** In case of *one-way migration*, animals move from a location where they breed and produce the next generation (or generations) in a different place before dying. However, a succession of such one-way movements through a series of breeding areas may form a *multiple-generation round trip*. Such type of migration is found mainly in insects and marine invertebrates.
- ***Annual and seasonal migrations:*** *Annual migrations* are round trips synchronized with the annual cycle and *seasonal migrations* are particular stages of these annual journeys. Though most migratory movements occur on an annual or seasonal cycle, yet there are also some degrees of daily movements of animals. But, such diurnal movements are not considered as true migration, rather are more appropriately called as *diurnal dispersions*.
- ***Vertical and horizontal migrations:*** *Vertical migrations* occur between different water depths, where animals travel a few hundred metres up and down the water column. In *horizontal migrations*, individuals travel a few hundred meters across a space.
- ***Altitudinal migration*:** *Altitudinal migration* is a short-distance event between different terrestrial elevations in response to the changes in climate and food availability, as well as, due to anthropogenic influences.
- ***Diadromous migration:*** This is a kind of migration where animals move between freshwater and saltwater ecosystems. Such *diadromous migration* is commonly noticed in some fishes (*Tenulosa ilisha*) and crustaceans (*Macrobrachium* sp.). The migration patterns differ for each species and have seasonal and lifecycle variations.
- ***Drift migration:*** In *drift migration*, individuals are blown off by the winds or water currents essentially during their locomotion through a medium. Drift is assisted by disorientating conditions such as mist or drizzle and can result in large numbers of individuals (*viz.* birds) arriving together in an area in which they are not normally seen. Specially evolved devices, such as the ballooning threads of spiders and some larval insects, are sometimes employed to promote drift.
- ***Nomadism:*** In *nomadism*, migration does not follow any regular pattern or route but links temporary breeding sites that have ephemerally favorable conditions.
- ***Irruptions:*** *Irruptions* are non-cyclical, occasional, irregular movements of a significant proportion of a population beyond its usual breeding or non-breeding area that occurs under pressure of famine, overpopulation of a locality or some more obscure influence.

5.3.2 Navigation During Migration

Navigation is the ability of many animals to accurately find their way of return to their original location after displacement to a site in altogether unfamiliar territory, without access of any maps or instruments or even information about the displacement route. Vertebrates have multiple compass systems such as sun, star, polarized light and magnetic compasses that are used for navigation. Several factors (like weather conditions, time of day and past experience) determine which of these compass systems to be used at a given time. Each of these compass systems requires different sensory processing and coordinating methods. For instance, time compensation mechanism is necessary for the sun compass, an ability to relate the alignments of star patterns to the axis of celestial rotation is essential for the star compass, specialized sensory receptors capable of detecting the plane of polarized light is indispensible to use polarized light as a navigational tool and alignment of the geomagnetic field is needed for the magnetic compass. In addition, incorporation of varying degrees of both innate and learned components is also vital for aptly using those compasses during navigation. However, in order to avoid systematic errors in the direction of orientation when switching between compasses, each of these systems must be standardized with respect to a common reference system. In birds, the primary compass calibration reference appears to be derived from celestial cues, polarized patterns present during sunset and sunrise. Animals use an amazing diversity of senses and strategies in order to navigate in the natural environment. The Arctic tern, monarch butterfly and salmon regularly migrate thousands of miles to and from their breeding grounds. Similarly, many other species also accurately navigate over shorter distances.

Text Box 5.4 Animal Navigation – Fact File

- Charles Darwin (1873) suggested that the mechanism of navigation from a known position using only information about one's own speed and direction (Dead reckoning).
- Karl von Frisch (1967) showed that the honey bees use the sun, polarization pattern of the blue sky and the earth's magnetic field for its navigational movements. He showed that the sun is the preferred or main compass. The other mechanisms are only used under cloudy skies or inside a dark beehive.
- Homing pigeons were able to navigate using the earth's magnetic field, the sun, as well as both olfactory and visual cues (Sherry and Duff, 1996).
- Bats used echolocation to detect and track prey and to "see" and thus navigate through the world around them (Kalko and Schnitzler, 1993).
- Insects and birds are able to form internal 'map' of a location using vision along with other senses including olfaction and echolocation. Then they sense their direction from the earth's magnetic field or from the position of the sun or star in the sky and also use the existing landmarks to navigate.

Mechanisms

Mechanism of navigation in migratory animals over an apparently trackless country, through pathless forests, across bare deserts, over and under the oceans without any visible compass, sextant, chronometer or chart is one of the most debated aspects of animal migration. Scientists believe that during migration different animal taxa use one or more different external and internal cues to navigate (Table 5.4).

Table 5.4 Different Navigational Cues used by Different Animal Groups during Migration

Navigational cues	*Animal group*
Smell	Moths, Salmon
Vibrations	Spiders, Mole rats
Electric fields	Electric fish
Temperature	Snakes
Sound	Bats, Elephants
Visual	Ants, Bees, Birds (food storing, migration)
Magnetic	Sea turtles, Birds

- ***Landmarks:*** Many animals including mammals, birds and insects (such as bees and wasps) are capable of memorizing distinct landmarks present in their environment and meticulously use them in navigation (Thomas and Paul, 2004). Certain wasps recognize landmarks around their nest. If their nest is removed, they will still return to its original location. If the nest remains and the landmarks are placed at a different location, then the wasps will look for their nests in this new location. Likewise, birds often follow the topography (shape) of a coastline to their nesting sites.
- ***Orientation by the sun:*** There are evidences that animals can navigate using celestial cues, like the position of sun. As the sun moves across the sky, so using the position of the sun as a compass for navigation also requires a sense of timing (an internal clock). The migrant need to constantly adjust its path accordingly with the changing position of sun throughout the day. Polarized light at sunrise and sunset may play an important role especially in calibrating organisms' compasses. Many animals depend on such internal clocks to maintain their 'circadian rhythm' (Dunlap et al., 2003).
- ***Orientation by the night sky:*** In a pioneering experiment inside planetarium, warblers initially oriented themselves towards the south seeing the night sky, and then they subsequently changed their position to maintain proper orientation as the position of the stars were slowly rotated inside the planetarium (Lockley, 1967). To navigate

by the stars, birds would need both a "sextant and chronometer", i.e. an inherent ability to read patterns of stars and to navigate by them accordingly. This involves using the position of the stars as a compass. The position of stars also changes throughout the night and accordingly the organism needs to be able to adjust its path. Therefore, an accurate internal clock and a sense of timing is also necessary for proper navigation.

- ***Orientation by polarized light:*** Some animals, particularly insects, are sensitive to the polarization of light. Honey bees orient themselves using polarized light on overcast days to estimate the position of the sun in the sky relative to the compass direction they intend to travel and subsequently fly towards the direction and distance of a food source accurately. Compound eyes of insects are possibly better suited to perceive polarized light than the vertebrate eyes. Nevertheless, pioneering research of Able (1982) revealed the importance of polarized lights in migratory orientation of birds.
- ***Olfaction:*** Olfaction has been suggested as a possible mechanism of navigation in some animal groups. According to Papi's 'mosaic' model, pigeons build and remember a mental map of the odours in their area and recognize their location by the smelling the odour of the area. Such olfactory cues are also reported to be important in salmon, which are known to return to the exact position of the river where they hatched. Salmon may use their magnetic sense to navigate from oceans upto the position of the river where they were born. Then they switch to olfaction cues to identify their birth place in the river at close range.
- ***Chemical navigation:*** Chemical navigation is sensitivity to a chemical or chemical gradient that allows an organism to find its way back to nesting sites. It often requires a heightened sense of smell toward a chemical pheromone. Ants leave a pheromone trail for other ants to follow. This also helps them to find their way back to the nest. This is why ants are often seen to move in a line, following each other to a feeding site. The pheromone secreted by an ant only lasts for about 2 minutes. This ensures that only fresh trails to nearby food sources will be detected by other ants. Once a suitable food source has been found, the increased number of ants walking along a trail means that pheromone is repeatedly secreted by every ant and then the trail lasts longer. Ants can also use an alternative pheromone to mark out territories and more permanent trails to reliable food sources.
- ***Magnetoreception:*** Some animals, including mammals (such as blind mole rats) and birds (such as pigeons), are sensitive to the earth's magnetic field (Lindauer and Martin, 1972). Homing pigeons use the information on magnetic field along with other navigational cues. Pioneering research by Keeton (1971) showed that time-shifted homing pigeons preferably rely on the direction of sun and only depend on the magnetic field if sun is not visible. This was confirmed by the experimental evidence that the pigeons could not orient themselves correctly on an overcast day when the magnetic field was disrupted using magnets.
- ***Other senses:*** Other senses may also contribute to animal navigation. Many marine animals (such as seals) are capable of hydrodynamic reception, enabling them to track and catch prey such as fish by sensing the disturbances left behind in the water of their passage (Schulte-Pelkum et al., 2007). Mammals (such as Cetaceans and Chiropterans) are capable of echolocation, which they use both for detecting prey and for orientation by sensing their environment (Schevill and McBridge, 1956).

Case Study: Migration in Birds

Bird migration is the regular seasonal movement between breeding and wintering grounds in response to changes in food availability, habitat, or weather conditions and often occurs in north and southward along a flyway. Migration is critical in the life cycle of more than half of the world's bird species, and without this annual journey many species would not even be able to raise their young. Birds migrate to find the richest, most abundant food sources that will provide them adequate energy to nurture their offspring. If no birds take part in migration, competition for adequate food during breeding seasons would be fierce and many birds would starve. Thus, migration is essential to stay alive and birds move to an area to improve their chances of survival, usually because its climate provides a better environment for feeding or rearing young. There is a corresponding return movement at the end of the breeding season.

Types of Bird Migration

Long-distance Migration: Long-distance migrants are those which perform a complete shift between the breeding and wintering areas. Out of estimated 10,000 bird species, about 1,800 species usually migrate long distances along different flyways. The most common pattern involves flying northward in the spring to breed in the temperate or Arctic summer and returning in the autumn to wintering grounds in warmer regions to the south. Most birds, particularly the larger ones, migrate in flocks to reduce their energy costs.

Such migration is primarily, but not entirely, a phenomenon common in the Northern Hemisphere. Since food becomes scarce in winter at high northern latitudes, the land birds leave for areas further south (even in the Southern Hemisphere) during winter. In addition to that, the continental landmass is much larger in the Northern Hemisphere. In contrast, pelagic seabird species are more likely to migrate in the Southern Hemisphere. This is because there are large stretches of oceans and many islands are present in the Southern Hemisphere, which provide suitable nesting sites for these seabirds. Birds fly at varying altitudes during migration, mostly in the range of 150 m – 600 m.

During migration, birds usually prefer mountain ranges, coastlines, or sometimes rivers as their route and these preferred routes are termed as 'flyways'. To avoid or surpass geographical barriers (such as large stretches of open water, desert, mountains etc.) they often take advantage of updrafts and other wind patterns. The specific routes may be genetically programmed or learned to varying degrees. Interestingly, the flyways during forward and return journey are often different.

Studies on the flyways of migratory bird passing over India are very few. Available information reveal that the long distance migratory birds from Europe and west Asia (including western Siberian region) cross the trans-Himalayan region and the western regions of high ranges of the mighty greater Himalayas to enter India and finally leave towards Sri Lanka and Africa during the winters (Figure 5.10). Other long-distance migrants from east Asia (which includes eastern Siberia, Mongolia, and Tibet) follow a different flyway where they enter India crossing the eastern and north eastern Himalayan ranges. Then they usually fly along the eastern coast line of India towards the south. Then some species pass the coastline between Point Calimer and Ramesvaram and arrive in Sri Lanka from India, while some other species (like Amur falcons) cross over the Western Ghats and southern parts of India, leave India from the west coast and fly to Africa (Figure 5.10).

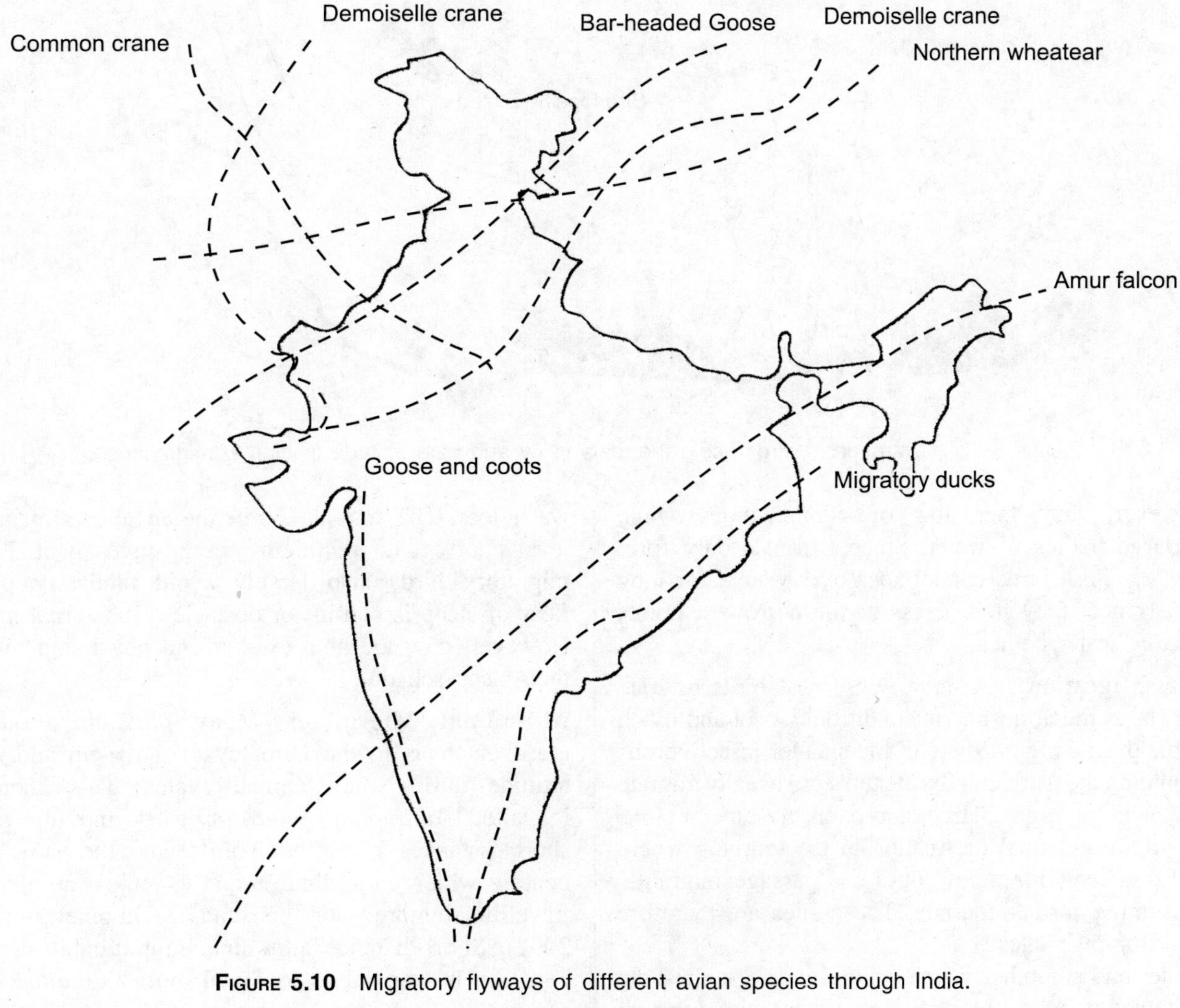

FIGURE 5.10 Migratory flyways of different avian species through India.

Other than flight, migration may also take place through walking (Emus undertake long-distance movements on foot during droughts) and swimming (penguins can migrate over 1000 km).

Short-distance Migration: Short-distance migrants usually make shorter trips in response to local weather conditions, such as up and downward movement along the side of a mountain. Thus, mountain and moorland breeders, move only altitudinally to avoid extreme cold at higher ground. Other species like merlin, Eurasian skylark etc. also show short-distance migration and move towards south or to the coasts.

Diurnal Migration: Diurnal migrants (like eagles, hawks, kites, vultures etc.) depend heavily on rising air currents called 'thermals'. As these air currents heat up during the day and rise in the atmosphere, birds take advantage of this lift. Many species perform thermal hop – they rise to the top of one thermal set their wings in the direction they want to travel, move to the next thermal, and then repeat the process (Figure 5.11). Some large and broad-winged birds of prey such as vultures, eagles and buzzards rely on thermal columns of rising hot air which enable them to soar and migrate in the daytime. Other thermal riding or soaring birds include storks, pelicans, cranes and some Neotropical songbirds (like swallows and blackbirds).

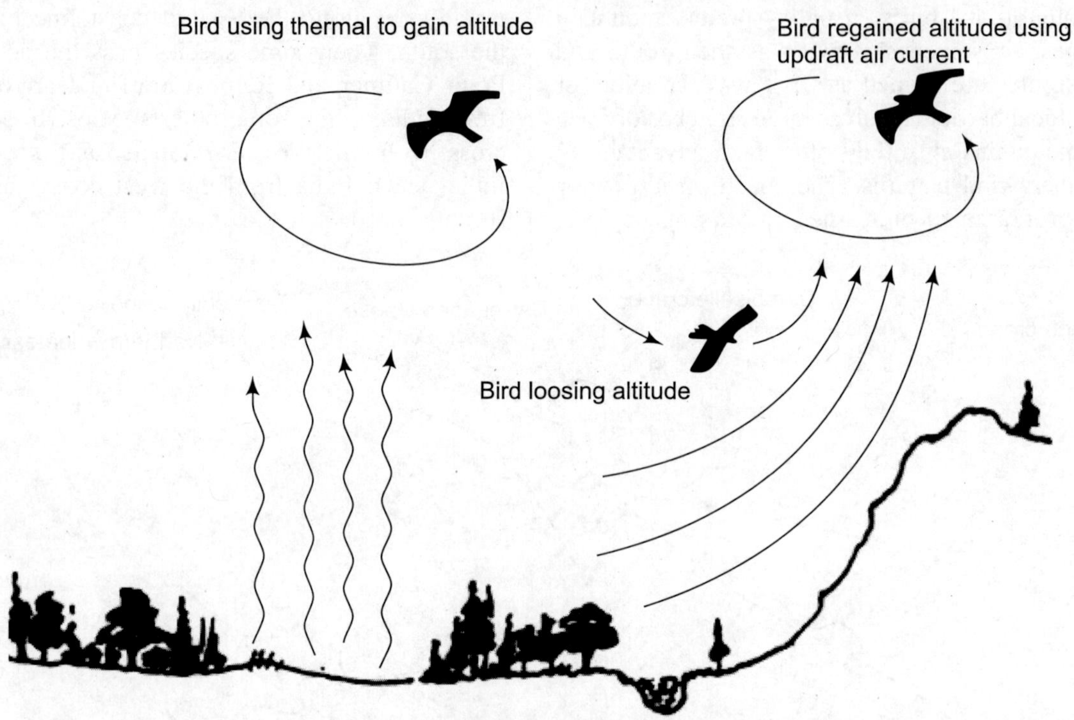

FIGURE 5.11 Illustration of birds using thermals to fly and gain altitude in diurnal migrations.

However, they face lots of complications while crossing large bodies of water. Since thermals only form over land, so these birds cannot soar over waters for long distances. Hence, they must cross at the narrowest points of such large water bodies.

Nocturnal Migration: A large number of birds migrate only at night as the atmospheric condition is cool and much more stable during night. Many of the smaller insectivorous birds (including the warblers, flycatchers etc.) usually migrate large distances at night. They stop-over in some regions between origin and final destination in the morning where they stay and feed for a few days as 'passage migrants' before resuming further journey. These sites are therefore called as 'stop-over sites'.

Cooler and smoother weather conditions of night help the birds to maintain healthy body temperature without much water loss. The smoothness of the air allows for a straight level course with minimum energy investment. Nocturnal migratory birds also largely avoid predatory pressures. Loss of sleep is one major obstacle of nocturnal migration. However, they are able to alter and physiologically adjust their sleep schedule.

Altitudinal Migration: Many birds in mountainous areas (such as in the Himalayas) move up and down in altitude during their annual cycles. This phenomenon is called '*altitudinal migration*'. By moving relatively short distances in altitude, birds gain the same climatic benefit which latitudinal migrants enjoy at the cost of travelling hundreds or thousands of kilometres (Newton, 2008). Short-distance altitudinal migration is particularly common in tropical regions and most altitudinal migrants are primarily frugivores or nectarivores. On the alpine region of Himalaya, many breeding bird species exhibit altitudinal migration.

Irruptions: Irruption is a dramatic, highly unpredictable and irregular but spectacular migration of large number of birds into unusual areas, far outside their expected ranges in search of suitable food and water resources, mostly during winter. Irruptions are noticed under unusual circumstances where a good breeding season is followed by a food source failure in the following year. In such conditions large numbers of a species move in areas far beyond their normal range. This type of population shift may occur in cycles from 2-10 years. Irruptions in birds might also be much more unpredictable depending on the species.

Dispersal: Bird dispersal is relatively predictable seasonal movements of birds and occurs at least once a year. This is not always considered as true migration. Here the juvenile birds are forced away from their hatching grounds and must seek out their own territories, where as their parents continue to use the same range. Dispersal is relatively more common among birds that are resident throughout the year in a same range and defend their territories throughout the year.

Adaptations for Migration in Birds

Migratory birds undergo considerable physical, physiological and behavioural changes prior to their migratory flights.

(i) Physical Adaptations

- Old, ragged feathers create more wind drag and require more energy investment during flight. Therefore, many birds molt to a new plumage just prior to migration. These newly molted and more aerodynamic feathers reduce air resistance and make their flight easier. They increase flight muscles at the expense of leg muscles. But, during long flights mass of the flight muscle also declines as sustained flight causes damage to the flight muscles.
- Body size and wing morphology are easily interpreted in terms of aerodynamic efficiency and migration speed. Adaptations are also noticed in the flight apparatus, i.e. wings and musculo-skeletal systems, to reduce the costs of sustained flight. Migrants generally have wings of higher aspect ratio and more pointed wing tips as compared to the resident birds. Their tails tend to be short and square rather than long and graduated.
- The forebrain is smaller in migrants as compared to the rather enlarged brain in residents.

(ii) Physiological Adaptations

- Migratory birds ensure greater fat supply to provide extra energy for their travels. Ruby-throated hummingbird deposits nearly double amount of fat just a week or two before migration. To ensure greater fat supply, great variations occur in nutritional organs and flight muscles during the fuelling–flight cycle.
- Before actual initiation of migration, most birds partly change the composition of their bodies. They show atrophy of digestive and metabolic organs. Enlarged gizzard, stomach, intestine and liver may serve to increase the metabolic capacity and energy assimilation rate, thus, the rate of fuelling.
- Shortly before departure on long flights, parts of the nutritional organs may be discarded to reduce the payload and thereby the flight cost in order to ensure increased flight range.
- It has been suggested that some proteins breakdown to serve as intermediates of the citric acid cycle and for maintenance and repair of organs.
- In many species, the reproductive system actually develops during migration, while in others gonadal development may commence at far later stages. The degree of overlap of migration and reproductive functions is mainly influenced by the migratory distance and length of their breeding season, which tends to be shorter at higher latitudes and altitudes.

(iii) Behavioural Adaptations

- A number of remarkable changes in avian behaviour have been noticed during migration which ensure their safe and risk free journey.
- Many birds fly at comparatively higher altitudes during migration than they usually follow during shorter flights, because wind patterns higher up help to push them along and cooler air and prevent overheating due to exertion.
- Many diurnal birds, such as most songbirds, change their flight time during migration and fly at night to minimize their risk of being predated by migrating raptors.

Navigation during Flight

Navigation by the birds is one of the greatest mysteries in migration phenomenon. Their ability to fly home from a totally strange and distant location indicates that the birds have both an internal compass and an internal map.

Magnetic Sensing: Birds use the geomagnetic fields of the Earth to obtain at least a partial map of horizontal space and to assess its position. The intensity (declination) of the magnetic field changes with latitude providing a reliable cue about geographic position. A bird might be able to estimate its latitude based on the strength of the magnetic field and can detect even tiny changes in the strength of the magnetic field. Many birds have special chemicals or compounds in their brains, eyes or bills that help them sense the Earth's magnetic field and help them to orient themselves for long journeys. Magnetic compass helps to explain how birds can maintain direction under total cloud cover or in situations where both celestial and visual cues are obscured. This is evidenced by an experiment where birds oriented them properly even when placed in large cemented cages without any environmental cues (Merkel and Wiltschko, 1965). But, they could not orient properly and were rather random in orientation when they were put in a large steel cage which affected the magnetic lines around the cages.

Migratory birds may use two electromagnetic tools to find their destinations – one that is entirely innate and another that is attained through experience. A young bird on its first migration flies in the correct direction according to the Earth's magnetic field, although they do not have any idea regarding the distance to be covered. Over the years it becomes accustomed to the journey and learns various landmarks present in their flyways. This "mapping" is done by magnetite in the trigeminal system, which gives the bird fair idea about the strength of the field. As the birds migrate between northern and southern regions, so the varying strength of magnetic fields at different latitudes let the bird know when it has reached its destination. There is a neural connection between the eye and "cluster N", the part of the forebrain that is active during migrational orientation, suggesting that birds may actually be able to '*see*' the magnetic field of the earth. Research indicates this magneto-receptor may be based on pigment proteins in the retina known as cryptochromes. The Earth's magnetic field seems to induce a chemical reaction in these proteins when certain light wavelengths (mostly blue) strike the retina. This results in signals being sent from the eye to the brain via optic nerve.

The Sun Compass: In 1951, Gustav Kramer discovered the sun compass. He performed his experiments by placing European starlings in orientation cages and then used mirrors to shift the apparent location of the sun. In response, the birds shifted their migratory restlessness to match the compass direction indicated by the apparent new position of the sun. Probably all birds determine their direction by the position of sun when there is good visibility. Sun compass of a bird is tied to its circadian rhythm and works in conjunction with the bird's own sense of time. It seems the birds using sun compass are aware of the sun's position over the course of the day. So, at 8 a.m. the bird knows where the sun should be.

It is also believed that the birds use polarized light (the light that occurs in an arc about 90 degrees form the sun's position). Patterns of polarized light also appear to play a key role in navigation. Birds apparently use the polarized light patterns to provide information on initial migratory flight directions.

Thus, diurnal migrants can use the sun in cloudier conditions or just after sunset and many of the nocturnal migrants start their flights at sunset or a little after.

Star Compass: For nocturnal migratory birds, star positions and the orientation of constellations can provide necessary navigation directions. Use of star compass by birds was first demonstrated by Sauer (1957). Experiments in planetarium proved that birds can navigate using stars. When night skies with actual position of stars are presented birds exhibited *zugunruhe* (migratory restlessness) facing the correct direction. But, when the positions of the key stars were rotated to incorrect positions, they simultaneously oriented themselves in wrong direction. However, the very use of star as compass is not innate. The birds have to observe the starry sky and learn its rotation during early stages of their life to develop the skill to use this compass as a navigational tool.

Geographic Mapping: Birds follow the same migration routes over the years and use their keen eyesight to map their journey across different landforms and geographic features such as rivers, coastlines and mountain ranges. Both diurnal and nocturnal migrants rely on landmarks to determine location.

Learned Routes: Some bird species (like cranes and geese) learn migration routes from their parents and other adult birds in the flock. Once learned, younger birds can travel the route successfully themselves.

The ability of birds to navigate during migrations cannot be fully explained by endogenous programming, even with the help of responses to environmental cues, rather it can probably be fully explained with an accounting for the cognitive ability of the birds to recognize habitats and form mental maps. Navigation is based on a variety of senses, either alone or in combination of other attributes including their ability to detect magnetic fields, using visual landmarks as well as olfactory cues. Long distance migrants are believed to disperse as young birds and over time they establish attachments to potential breeding sites and favourite wintering sites. Once such site attachment is made, they show high site-fidelity and visit the same wintering sites year after year unless the sites are drastically degraded due to some climatic or anthropogenic events.

Threats Encountered during Migration

Migration is a hazardous journey and the birds encounter many threats while migrating between their breeding and wintering grounds each year. The phenomenon involves high energy budget, higher level of stress, physical exertion costs and other risks of the migration like predation pressure, higher chances of pathogenic and parasitic infections at stopover sites. It is estimated that more than 60 percent of a migratory bird species peril and never complete a full roundtrip migration.

Following are the threats encountered by many of the migratory avifauna:

- Loss of habitat in the stopover sites due to ongoing development or increasing pollution is one of the major obstacles for successful migration. Polluted habitats often reduce food supplies and suitable other resources. Besides, ingestion of potential toxins also causes several health hazards which reduce their migratory efficiency.
- Inadequate food supplies cause starvation among migrating birds every year. This may be caused due to large scale habitat destruction along their migratory route. It may also be a result of greater feeding competition among large numbers of migratory birds.
- Exhaustion can make the birds less wary of potential threats and tired birds are more apt to collide with obstacles or falter in flight.
- Collisions with windows, buildings and wind farms along migration routes is common for thousands of migrating birds in mid-flight and the majority of these collisions cause fatal injuries. Tall buildings, electrical wires and poles, wind turbines and similar structures are the commonest obstacles to migrating birds. Even if the birds are not killed, but such injured and staggered birds are very much susceptible to predators.
- Predators (including wild animals, along with feral cats and dogs) may kill migratory birds in their wintering grounds. Predatory species of the stopover sites pose greatest threats and kill many birds each year in various sites as the migrating birds are often unaware of local predators of these temporary sites.
- Hunting (both legal regulated hunting and poaching) are also a threat during migration. Even the expert hunters may make mistakes and inadvertently shoot protected birds as a result of misidentification in flight.
- Light pollutions in cities have recently been realized as serious threats that disorient bird navigation.
- Poor weather, storms and other natural disasters (like hurricanes, blizzards, wildfires, etc.) may cause injury, disorientation, debilitation or even death of many individuals and can also destroy their crucial stopover sites and final destinations.

5.4 COURTSHIP DISPLAYS

Courtship behaviour is of great biological significance for the survival of many sexually reproducing species and often includes one or more of the following *viz.* ritualized movements, vocalizations, mechanical sound production, or morphological displays. Displays of beauty, strength or agonistic ability are manifested through several ornamentations such as elaborate plumage, brilliant and striking colours, etc. Such behaviour particularly helps in proper identification of the animal species performing the display and thus prevents biologically wasteful mating between different species. In some animals courtship is short and brief, while in others the acts of mating lasts long and involve vigorous and elaborate displays. The males often play active role during courtship and eventually display to attract a receptive female in his vicinity for the purpose of reproduction.

Definition: *Courtship* refers to the heterosexual behavioural interaction occurring between male and female before, during and after the act of mating. When one individual moves or creates postures in a way that transmits signals to another individual of the same species, then the first individual is said to be performing a *display*. So, *courtship display* may be defined as a particular, ritualized set of behaviours which some animals perform as a part of courtship to attract a partner and advertise their desire to mate.

5.4.1 Stages Involved in Successful Courtship

Successful courtship requires finding appropriate partner from the same species, persuade the individuals of opposite sex through various displays, selection of mate, synchronization of courtship behaviour and finally isolation of the mating pair. Thus, the courtship behaviour of an animal can be broadly discussed under following major stages:

Finding a Mate: Finding a mate is not random, but a highly organized process. This requires discovery and recognition of a receptive partner belonging to the same species. Reproductive state of a potential mate is assessed through visual, auditory, olfactory or tactile signals.

Persuasion (Courtship Display): After finding a suitable mate, animals perform various behaviour patterns in order to stimulate and convince the other partner for mating. To bring the desired mate in close proximity is really challenging task as various other potential competitors are also performing similar displays. So, the individuals must manifest various ritualized displays to communicate its reproductive vigour in order to persuade its desired mate. Such courtship displays consist of species specific 'fixed action patterns' (FAP) which are accompanied by various signals (visual, auditory, olfactory or tactile) and orientation movements.

Types of courtship displays are briefly discussed below:

- *Male display:* In this form of courtship display male manifests his traits or perform various acts in order to impress the receptive female with his ability, vigour and biological fitness and mate choice is made by the females. Such displays are made by the male expressing his willingness to mate, in order to convince the female to choose him amongst other displaying males. These particular forms of display by the males also discourage other rival males. Displays by males thus help the females to assess and select the strongest male, who would be a pleasant mate, a potentially good father and an efficient protector of the family.
- *Female display:* In this form of courtship display, the responsibility to attract a mate for copulation lies on the females and the females compete with each other to claim the desired male for mating. Therefore, sex-role reversal is noticed in female display and mate choice is made by the male amongst the competing females. In this form of courtship display, females need to invest energy for the improvement and maintenance of sexually dimorphic traits, development of gametes, as well as, for reproduction. As a result, the investment of energy by the females becomes exceedingly high. Therefore, female displays are less common in the animal kingdom.
- *Mutual display:* In this form of courtship display, the pair bonds between two sexes strengthen as males and females perform mutually synchronized and responsive courtship gestures (gestures like calling and head bobbing or one partner repeating the motion of the other) during the breeding season. Birds such as albatrosses, penguins and grebes, are well known for this type of behaviour. Among fishes, the dragonets exhibit mutual display. Some species of *Nereis* perform nuptial dance in which the males and females swim rapidly in a circle. The females produce 'fertilium' which attracts the males and stimulates them to release sperm, which again excite the females to release eggs.

Mate Selection: Convinced by the courtship display, mate selection usually takes place (elaborately discussed in section 5.5).

Synchronization of Courtship Behaviour: Synchronization is a phenomenon where the same behaviour takes place in two different individuals of the mating pair at a given time. In many species, particularly those sexually reproduce through external fertilization, successful mating depends on proper synchronization of complex mating behaviour of male and female partner. External cues (like day length, lunar cycle, tidal pattern etc.) play vital role in such synchronization of courtship behaviour.

Isolation of the Mating Pair: Once a mating pair is formed, they move to a place where they can perform the act of copulation in seclusion and raise their offspring. Even in social animals, the breeding pair usually moves away from the other members in a suitable locality within their home range having ample resources. On the other hand, in solitary animals the pair moves to a secluded place with optimum resource usually within the central position of their territory.

5.4.2 Courtship Behaviour among Birds

The phenomenon of courtship display is quite complex in birds. Elaborate courtship dance and/or distinct sounds are used to attract the compatible and potential mates to form breeding pair. Individual birds select the best partner based on the type of behaviour, reactivity during courtship, advertisement of strength, health and mating desirability. Close contact between male and female birds is an integral part of the courtship rituals that help to diffuse their normal spatial boundaries and aggression. While forming of a breeding pair, the birds stand in close body contact. One bird may even lean on another to show it is not intending to harm its partner and may lightly preen one another. After pair formation they proceed to nest building followed by successful mating, egg-laying, hatching and parental care to ensure successful fledging of offspring.

Different Modes of Avian Courtship Displays

Courtship may either be simple (involving a small number of visual, chemical or auditory stimuli) or may be a highly complex (with series of acts involving several types of communication). Various types of courtship rituals are performed throughout the breeding season by most of the bird species, in order to either strengthen the existing pair-bonds or to create a new one. Displays are usually more intense while forming new pairs. In such situations where the male needs to attract and impress a new female through different types of postures, movements and actions.

Singing: Singing is one of the most common modes adopted by the birds to attract a mate. The complexities of the songs advertise the desirable characteristics for a healthy mate such as maturity, vigour and intelligence. In most avian species, males often emit vocalizations (calls and songs) from above the territory during the breeding season, in order to attract the female mates and also to warn-off other rival male intruders (Andersson, 1994). Rate, duration of calling, pitch, as well as, phrase, syllable and elements are some of the important acoustic aspects of vocalizations in male birds which influence female mating decisions (Andersson, 1994). In some species, male birds get hormonal cues that keep them singing longer during mating season and express his mating desirability. Males can also emit copulation calls immediately before, during, or after copulation (Alatalo et al., 1987; Hohmann, 1989). Small passerines make use of a number of calls and songs. Sparrows have very simple songs while warblers are known for their intricate songs. During breeding season, Indian peafowl (*Pavo cristatus*) form exploded leks and the peacocks emit loud courtship vocalizations (Takahashi and Hasegawa, 2008). Sometimes other partner also sings 'duet' as part of the bonding ritual. Initially melodious and loud songs are emitted for advertising. But, communication between mates and young are made through softer calls. Birds also produce non-vocal sounds such as bill-clapping (in herons), wing-whirring or wing-flapping (in many songbirds), hisses, and grunts which usually occur on the ground, branches or at places close to the nest-site within their territory.

Courtship songs/calls benefit the males by attracting females and advertising their quality (Andersson, 1994). In dense habitats where the mates are difficult to detect, females can locate the males by listening to their song (Hedrick, 1986). However, singing can also be costly as production of large vocalizations are often energetically expensive (Vehrencamp et al., 1989), incite aggression between rivals (Searcy and Andersson, 1986) and may even attract predators (Zuk and Kolluru, 1998).

Displays: Courtship displays amongst the birds may include dancing, aerial acrobatics, fancy preening or posturing to show off the individual's best features. The male often use several postures and flights in order to appear stronger and larger than usual. Some display brighter colours, others exhibit strong bill and claws to hunt. Some birds also bring food at nest. Once impressed by the displaying male, the female stands motionless in a bowing posture to indicate that she is ready to mate.

Some birds form mating flocks (called *leks*) where the males show off their plumage in an attempt to attract a mate. Performing courtship display in flocks is beneficial as here the males can show off its best features to more females than if they were in small groups, which also increase their chances of finding a mate from the females present in the *lek*.

- ***Terrestrial displays:*** In *terrestrial displays*, different postures are used by males to advertise the plumage colours. They exhibit elaborate displays to increase glistening of specific areas such as wing-bars and head. This is mainly performed by the Galliform birds, such as pheasants, grouses, partridges and others similar species. The male pheasants and peacocks shake their long tails while turning around the females. The males also uses the bright plumage colours and elaborate displays of its body contour, skin sacs to advertise his suitability as a mate, as well as, a testimony of his physical fitness. In common pheasant (*Phasianus colchicus*) feathers are ruffled. The huge beaks of hornbills, toucans and pelicans also play important roles in displays.
- ***Aerial displays:*** *Aerial displays* during flight are performed by either males or both mates. More often male performs such displays in the air, while the female looks at him and occasionally join him. Spectacular aerial displays are often seen in raptors, where the birds fly close together over their territory in the vicinity of the nest-site. Acrobatic aerial displays called 'claw-catching' behaviour (Figure 5.12A) are performed by numerous birds of prey like eagles, hawks, buzzards, kites, falcons where one member of the pair turns onto its back and grab the feet of the other, fall down together in a cartwheel fashion and then rise again separately. Such behaviour is repeated several times in the same way.

(A) (B)

FIGURE 5.12 Illustration of (A) claw-catching flight display and (B) Fly in tandem in birds of preys.

On the other hand, some of the heaviest vultures of the genus *Gyps* perform more simple flights, both mates circling, soaring and gliding together. They can fly one above the other for long time and this flight is named "*Fly in tandem*" (Figure 5.12B). Seabirds and shorebirds also perform aerial displays and courtship feeding where both fly together above their colonies or nest-site or sometimes the females fly with a fish in their bill. Some of the birds perform flight displays accompanied by calls. However, flight displays by females are relatively uncommon.

- ***Dancing:*** Several physical movements (such as bold jumps, wing flaps, head dips or different dancing steps) form integral part of a courtship dance. Mistakes in such courtship dances reveal inexperience or indecision of the dancer and often lead to unsuccessful mating. In some species (like Indian Peafowl), male dances to attract a receptive female and she carefully observes his actions, while in other species (like sarus crane) both partners take part in the dancing.

Text Box 5.5 Dancing Birds

Some of the most spectacular courtship dance is performed by the **great crested grebe (*Podoceps crestatus*).** Their courtship dance consists of head shaking ceremony, dive and cat display, mutual greeting and penguin dance. In head shaking ceremony, the mating pair raise their conspicuous crest, face each other and empathically shake their heads sidewise. During cat displays one partner dives and the other waits in a cat posture. The diver then emerges with its back facing the other bird and settles close to it. This cat attitude might be the part of mutual display during which alternatively one bird shows the display and the other dives and rises out of the water in front of its partner. During penguin dance both birds dive under water, emerge with bunches of weeds in their bills, swim towards each other, then stand on water in an upright posture and move together shaking their heads.

Another fascinating dance is performed by the **sarus crane (*Grus antigone*)** which are large non-migratory cranes found in parts of the Indian subcontinent. They usually form long-lasting pair-bonds and breed in wet marshes or paddy fields. Their courtship displays include flying in harmony, along with a spectacular series of territorial leaps, posturing and dance-like movements. These "dancing" movements involve a short series of jumping and bowing movements as one of the pair circles around the other (Mukherjee, 2002). Besides, loud trumpeting calls are made together by both partners. These birds are considered symbols of marital fidelity and are believed to form the mating pair for life.

Birds of paradise also perform elaborated and spectacular displays. Here the males perform the mating dance in front of the females to expose their fabulous plumage. They ruffle their feathers and fan tail and wings, to produce vibrations that enhance the bright coloured feathers and the beautiful plumage pattern. During these displays the male often hangs upside down on a branch or perches on shrub or bush. It calls loudly while displaying alone or in groups at *lek*.

One of the most popular and fascinating courtship display is manifested by **Indian peafowls (*Pavo cristatus*)**. Peacocks are polygamous and several males usually congregate at a *lek* site (mating arena). Males at *lek* appear to maintain small territories next to each other and they allow females to visit them. During the breeding season, the peacock raise their upper-tail coverts into an arched fan and periodically vibrates the long feathers producing a ruffling sound. The wings are held half open and drooped to maintain balance. Initially the dancing peacock faces the peahen and then he turns to display the tail (Ali and Ripley, 1983). Initially the females do not appear to show any interest (Johnsingh and Murali, 1978). Once persuaded by the dancing peacock, the receptive peahen quickly runs around the tail and comes in front of the displaying male. The peacock responds by shaking his upper-tail coverts. Then the peacock turns back again and the dance continues. Finally the peahen sits down on the ground in front of the peacock in a unique posture and copulation takes place.

- ***Preening:*** In birds, preening is a way of grooming feathers to keep them in the best condition. Preening is also seen to be a part of courtship display in some avian species. In avocetes male and female both preen their feathers in hasty fashion during courtship. The pied avocet (*Recurvirostra avosetta*)**,** is a large black and white wader which show preening and "bill-dipping" as a part of their highly ritualized courtship displays (Figure 5.13). The female extends her head forwards with stiff neck parallel to the water, immerse up to eye-level and utters a soft piping call. The male then moves by her side and rubs his head against the female's body. Then the male repeatedly swipes his bill across the back of the female before beginning the exaggerated preening. During such *sexual preening*, the male stands close to the female and extends his neck so that his bill tip can preen his breast, usually the side closest to her. The male also places his bill in the water, vigorously stirs the water by splashing his bill in the water and then brings the water in his bill to his breast. Such displays are also called "dip-shake-preen display". These displays become more intense just before copulation. Finally, the female assumes a soliciting posture in which the head is lowered and the bill is almost horizontal. The male moves from side to side in semi-circle behind her several times and finally climb sideways up to the back of the female with her both wings raised, quickly copulate and then climb sideways off her again. In the mounting posture, the male places his bill on the side of her neck, either as a part of the ritual to stimulate her or to stabilize himself while mounting over the female. Immediately after copulation, both birds rub heads and necks, briefly cross bills, the male places his wing over the female and finally both partners perform a brief bowing dance.

FIGURE 5.13 Illustration of the preening display in avocets.

- *Gifting:* Courtship displays also involve some "gifts" (such as petals of flower, twigs, rootlets, grasses etc.) from male to female. Great-crested grebes (*Podiceps cristatus*), perform mutual offering of vegetation after an elaborated dance during which male and female face each other and alternately move head and neck (Figure 5.14).

FIGURE 5.14 Illustration of mutual gifting in great-crested grebes (*Podiceps cristatus*).

Offering such gifts often prove the ability of an individual to find nest materials and to ensure food supply to the young.

- *Feeding:* In many birds, the male feeds the female during courtship or incubation. So, offering food is another common part of the courtship behaviour for many avian species. In species where female incubates alone, the male often brings her food at nest. In some birds, males even place a seed or insect directly in the mouth of his female partner just as he is expected to do during feeding his hungry nestlings. For some species the male may just bring food and transfer it to the female to feed. In some other species, the male calls the female close to the nest or in the surroundings or food transfer takes place in mid-air, as in northern harrier (*Circus cyaneus*). This type of courtship feeding often involves spectacular aerial movements.

The male offers selected prey species such as insect, caterpillar, small mammal, fish, snake or other food according to the choice of his mate. Such courtship display demonstrates that the male is not only able to find food, but can also share it and is able to provide food for his partner during breeding period.

Apart from a ceremonial or pair-bonding function, such courtship feeding also provides the female with considerable nutritional benefit before the laying and helps in increasing the clutch size as the number of eggs laid by the female is partly determined by the female's nutritional status. Feeding by male usually continue during the incubation phase.

Text Box 5.6 Food Gifting in Hornbills

Hornbills are unable to excavate their own nest and are therefore, compelled to rely on natural tree cavities or tree cavities created by other fauna. In many species of hornbills (like **Oriental pied hornbill** ***Anthracoceros albirostris***), the males place fruits inside such cavities to entice the females. Once a cavity is selected by a female, both partners enlarge the cavity to make sufficient room for the female. Then after successful copulation, the female stays inside the cavity and the male makes regular trips (about once every 10–15 minutes), to bring lumps of mud in his bill for the female. The female puts this mud at the entrance of the cavity and slowly seals herself inside the cavity. This procedure leads to the accumulation of debris inside the cavity that the female has to shovel out. At times, males swallow this mud and then again regurgitate it to the female in a softened wet form. In between bringing lumps of mud, the male also brings fruits for his partner. Once the nest is built, the male hornbill regularly makes foraging trips, store fruits in his gullet, regurgitate and position the fruits at the tip of his bill before passing them to the female. Depending on size of the fruit, male hornbills usually collects and delivers 10–50 fruits after one foraging trip. Beetles, praying mantis and lizards are some other food items gifted to the females (Figure 5.15).

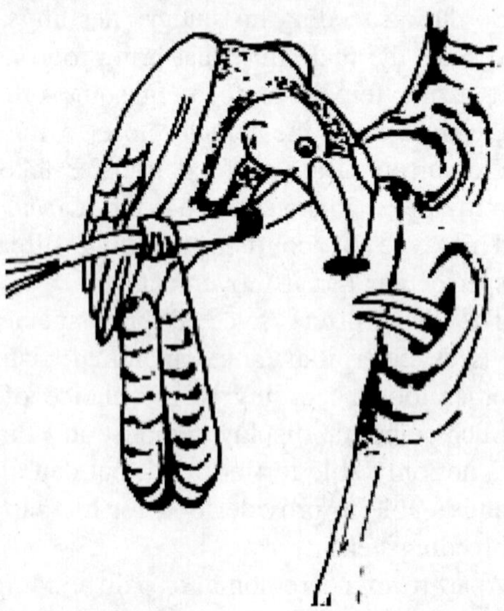

FIGURE 5.15 Illustration of food gifting in Hornbills.

- ***Nest building:*** Some birds try to attract a mate by exhibiting their architectural skills. Male constructs several nests before the female arrives and shows his ability to defend suitable nesting areas. They may also decorate the nest with pebbles, moss, flowers or even litter to make it more attractive for the females. The female may then choose her preferred nest, form pair with the nest owner and breed.

Such nest building form a part of the courtship display in baya weavers (*Ploceus philippinus*), which are sparrow-sized (15 cm), social and gregarious birds found across the Indian subcontinent. These weaver birds are best known for their elaborately woven pendulous nests. The nests are constructed by the males consisting of a long vertical tube leading to the side entrance to a central nesting chamber (Figure 5.16).

FIGURE 5.16 Illustration of nest building by baya weaver.

They use their strong beaks to strip-off 20 and 60 cm long fibres from paddy leaves, rough grasses and other plants. They also weave and knot them while building their nests. A male weaver bird makes around 500 trips to collect nest materials. The males partially construct the nest and then display by calling and flapping their wings hanging from their nests. The females in the vicinity visit and inspect the nest. It was earlier believed that the females select the nest based on the intricacy of the nest architecture. But, a recent study found that nest location is more important than nest structure and the females prefer nests built high in trees, over dry land and on thin branches (Quader, 2003). Once a nest is selected, the females signal their acceptance and the pair is formed. Then the male solely completes the nest, while his partner slightly modifies the interiors or adds lumps of mud inside.

5.4.3 Biological Significance of Courtship Displays

Modes and rituals of courtship behaviour vary widely across different taxa and plays crucial role in the survival of almost all species. By advertising such behaviour, an animal attracts mate and exhibits its desire to copulate. Each courtship behaviour also has its own threshold of firing. Some of the common significances of courtship behaviour are as follows:

- Locating and bringing the potential mates together in a particular place.
- Manifest the strength, health condition and mating desirability of the displaying individuals, which in turn help receptive individuals of the opposite sex to choose best partners (mate selection).
- Play crucial roles in reproduction and ensure viable offspring.
- Help to strengthen pair bond that may last till the raising of their nestlings or even longer.
- Synchronize the reproductive physiology of a pair. The males often initiate the courtship behaviour by orienting towards the female and emit important mating stimuli for the females. The stimuli delivered by males raise the receptivity of the females until a certain threshold is attained and the female accepts the courtship. Thus, it prepares the females of same species for mating. On the other hand, the inhibitory and excitatory stimuli received by the males from the females during courtship interact with internal factors of the males to produce a common excitation and lead to the output of certain types of behaviour.
- Genes associated with successful courtship displays pass from generation to generation and thus might lead to unique and further brilliant courtship displays.
- Lead to the reduction of hostility between potential partners in territorial animals.
- Plays an important role in species recognition. Because, the signals generated during courtship are only recognized by the potential mate belonging to same species.
- Interspecific courtship is avoided and also the sexual isolation between species is maintained (i.e., interbreeding is prevented) as other species either does not recognize the courtship signals or avoid them.

5.5 MATE CHOICE OR MATE SELECTION

Sexual conflict for selection of an appropriate mate is a widespread phenomenon across animal taxa. Mate choice is a phenomenon where effects of traits expressed in one sex lead to non-random mating and reproductive investment with specific individuals of the opposite sex (Kokko et al., 2003).

During mate choice, one sex is competitive with members of the same-sex while the other sex is choosy (selective when it comes to pick individuals to mate with). In most species, females are the choosy sex that discriminates amongst competitive males. But, reverse situations are not uncommon.

Definition: Mate choice (or intersexual selection or mating preferences) can be defined as an evolutionary process where the sensory and behavioural properties influence the propensity of individuals to mate with certain phenotypes depending on the attractiveness of his or her traits (Jennions and Petrie, 1997).

5.5.1 Historical Perspective

The term 'sexual selection' was coined by Charles Darwin in 1871, where he tried to find out why males of many species possess elaborate ornamentations and other conspicuous traits, which are apparently detrimental to the survival of the individual. He explained the phenomenal existence of the elaborate sexual traits in two different ways: (i) these traits are useful in male-male combat or (ii) they are preferred by females. He treated natural selection and sexual selection as two different topics, but other school of thought advocates that sexual selection is a form of natural selection. Fisher (1915) advocated his ideas on the evolution of female preference through *runaway selection*. Later, he described a scenario where feedback between mate preference and a trait results in elaborate characters such as long tail of peacock. Experiments using *Drosophila* as a model revealed that male reproductive success is limited by the number of mates while female reproductive success is limited by the number of pregnancies that she can have in her lifetime (Bateman, 1948). Trivers and Willard (1973) presented their *parental investment theory*, which envisage that investments are made by the parent to benefit his or her current offspring (like the costs of producing gametes, parental care etc.) and often comes at the cost of investment in future offspring. The differences in levels of parental investment create the condition that favours mating biases. According to this theory, the sex exhibiting less parental investment will have to compete for mating opportunities with the sex that invests more. Thus *parental investment theory* explains why the sexual selection is generally strongest in the sex that invests least resources in offspring, usually males (Andersson and Iwasa, 1996).

5.5.2 Direct and Indirect Benefits of Mate Choice

The evolutionary mechanisms of mate choice are driven by two types of fitness benefits – direct or indirect.

- ❒ ***Direct benefits:*** Direct benefits occur when the fitness of the choosing individual is increased by choosing a mate who is either more fecund or provide greater parental care to offspring (Edward and Chapman, 2011). Such benefits, therefore, include direct material advantages (such as better territory quality, nutrition, avoidance of disease transmission, reduced inbreeding, efficient parental care, increased protection from predators etc.). Direct benefits are least controversial and are often used to explain mate choice.
- ❒ ***Indirect benefits:*** Indirect (genetic) benefits are gained when choice of a particular individual enhances the genetic quality of their offspring (Kokko et al., 2003). Thus, indirect benefits may be the payoff for being selective and increase genetic fitness of the offspring when the 'choosy sex' does not receive direct benefits from his or her mate.

The relative importance of the direct versus indirect benefits accrued by each sex during mate choice are not very much clear (Servedio, 2007). However, mate selection arising from direct benefits of choice will generally be stronger than selection arising from indirect benefits of choice (Kirkpatrick and Barton, 1997).

5.5.3 Factors Influencing Mate Selection

Mate selection is often difficult as it require assessment of potential mates through acquisition and processing of a wide variety of information about mate quality (White, 2004). Static traits of potential mates (such as colouration, body size, song quality or scent) are evaluated based on innate preferences, degree of choosiness or both (Andersson and Iwasa, 1996). Behavioural cues (such as courtship vigor, winning intrasexual contests, acquiring territory, nuptial gifts, or engaging in parental care) also play important role in mate choice (Schwagmeyer and Mock, 2003). Several demographic and life history factors (such as number of potential mates, the costs of searching for a mate, past mating history and age of the chooser) significantly, influence the mate selection (Kodric-Brown and Nicoletto, 2001). Besides, social factors from infancy into adulthood (White, 2004) and environmental factors like ambient colour, temperature and light conditions, seasonalily and other climatic events (Badyaev and Martin, 2000) may also significantly modify and shape mate choices. Animals usually acquire mate preferences by observing the mating behaviour of others. Females acquire preferences for a particular male by learning about his traits (White and Galef, 2000) or behavioural characteristics (Ophir and Galef, 2003) or even after previously seen him mating (White and Galef, 1999). Males, in comparison, use similar information to determine the likelihood of fertilization of a potential mate (White and Galef, 1999). In a particular area, all the above mentioned factors interact and thus influence the selection of the best potential mate.

5.5.4 Evolution of Mate Selection

Several hypotheses have been put forward to explain the evolution of mate choice.

Direct Phenotypic Benefits: Choosy individuals select mates based on certain ornamentation which usually reflect the ability of the individual to deliver direct benefits, ultimately resulting in increased fecundity or the number of offspring produced (Andersson and Simmons, 2006). Having such a mating preference is advantageous as it directly affects reproductive fitness.

In some birds males have conspicuous red bright plumage while the females are more cryptic in coloration. In such cases, the females are the choosy sex and will use male plumage brightness as a signal during mate choice. The males with bright plumage are considered to be more caring for their young (than males with duller plumage) and are expected to share the parental responsibilities efficiently, so that the female can concentrate more on raising offspring. There are many empirical evidences for this mechanism (Moller and Jennions, 2001).

Sensory Bias Hypothesis: According to the *sensory bias hypothesis*, preference for a trait initially evolves for non-mating purpose. One sex subsequently exploits this trait for better mating opportunities. As a result, such traits gradually evolve amongst the competitive sex to get benefit from a pre-existing bias of the other sex for such trait. Studies using neural network models support that the possibility of sensory bias is caused by the developmental process of sensory organs, rather than by adaptation through selection (Enquist and Arak 1994; Johnstone 1994). Some male ornaments have also been found to initially evolve through female sensory biases (Ryan 1998; Boughman 2002).

Sensory bias has been well-demonstrated in some species of freshwater guppy fishes. Some orange fruits occasionally fall into the streams and are preferred by these guppies. So, the affinity for orange objects initially arose in both sexes and evolved under non-mating and foraging context. Later the male guppies exploited preference by incorporating large orange spots to attract females and female guppies also started preferring to mate with males with such orange body colouration.

Fisherian Runaway Selection or 'Sexy Sons' Hypothesis: According to *Fisherian runaway selection*, a trait expressing better genetic quality arises in a population through natural selection and is subsequently carried to the offspring resulting in greater expression of the trait in their phenotypes. So, there will be a tendency to select individuals of the opposite sex with such exaggerated trait who enjoy more fitness from both natural, as well as, sexual selection perspective. Subsequently, there will be an ever increasing selective force favouring stronger preferences for such traits. This is referred to as *Fisher's runaway process*. In this process, development of the trait will continue due to advantages associated with its sexual selection, even after the point beyond which further development is no more advantageous for the animal. The process only stops when natural selection is eventually strong enough to counteract sexual selection, i.e. when the costs of possessing sexually selected traits (such as increased visibility to predators and other energetic costs to maintain the evolved traits) are much higher than the benefits.

Female choice could give rise to extreme sexual traits through '*Fisherian runaway selection*'. For instance, in female preference some females show an underlying preference for males with certain exaggerated trait. Sons of these choosy mothers have the exaggerated trait (sexy sons), while her daughters also tend to be choosy for the same exaggerated male trait.

Indicator Trait Hypothesis: *Indicator traits* are honest signals which indicate better genetic quality, overall quality of the individual and are selected and preferred in evolution. So, the 'choosy sex' enjoys indirect genetic benefits. Because, mating with individuals having indicator traits often result in high quality offspring through inheritance of favourable alleles.

The patch of red feathers around the face and shoulders of male house finch is an indicator trait, which varies in brightness among individuals. Pigments that produce the red colour (carotenoids) are sparse in the environment and the males with brighter patch supposedly subsist on a high-quality diet rich in carotenoids. So, the males with brighter patches are selected by the females with an anticipation that he will provide better food to her and her offspring. In a manipulation experiment with house finches, females indeed preferred males with brighter red patches as compared to relatively dull males. The males with naturally brighter patches and better feathers, in turn, exhibited higher offspring feeding rates.

The indicator traits hypothesis is further explained under following three theories:

- ***Handicap theory of sexual selection:*** Indicator traits bear associated costs (*handicap*). So individuals possessing such traits are expected to be of superior genetic quality as they are able to bear the additional costs and are therefore, often selected by the 'choosy sex'.
- ***Good genes hypothesis:*** Individuals possessing traits which indicate overall genetic quality are selected by the 'choosy sex' in order to ensure better genetic fitness for their offspring.
- ***Hamilton-Zuk hypothesis:*** Individuals with exaggerated sexual ornaments indicate better resistance against parasites and diseases. So individuals possessing such exaggerated sexual ornaments are selected by the 'choosy sex' in order to ensure better protection from parasites and diseases.

Genetic Compatibility Hypothesis: According to this hypothesis choosing a mate with alleles that complement the genome of the chooser is very crucial and might render non-additive benefits (Mays and Hill 2004; Neff and Pitcher 2005) through producing optimally fit offspring with notably improved reproductive fitness. In order to select the appropriate partner, the choosy sex must know their own genotype, as well as, the genotypes of their potential mates. Some animals, such as mice, assess the genetic compatibility through the body odour of their respective mate, as well as, through the scent of the urine.

Due to complex genetic interactions, the genetic compatibility model is applicable to only a few specific traits (like Major Histocompatibility Complex or MHC in humans and mice). This makes testing of this hypothesis difficult and controversial. In three-spine sticklebacks, the females prefer to mate with males that share a greater diversity of MHC genes.

5.5.5 Types of Mate Selection

Mate choice is noticed in both males and females (Andersson, 1994) and competition over mates is the common aspect in both forms of sexual selection (Andersson and Iwasa, 1996), Sex differences in the evolution of mate choice (i.e. male mate choice and female mate choice) were originally attributed to variation in parental investment between males and females (Trivers, 1972). Differences between two distinct types of mate choice are reflected in the operational sex ratio (OSR, the ratio of sexually active males to females; Emlen and Oring, 1977) and the potential reproductive rate (PRR) of each sex (Clutton-Brock and Parker, 1992). Females often maximize reproductive fitness by providing greater parental care, while males invest more in mating effort (Clutton–Brock, 1991).

Female Choice

Female mate choice is prevalent in nature which is viewed as the first step in the process of paternity choice (Andersson and Simmons, 2006). Females usually prefer males emitting more conspicuous, stronger visual and acoustic signals given at higher rates, which are better than their mean trait size and such deviations elicit greater sensory stimulation (Ryan and Keddy-Hector, 1992).

Pre-copulatory Mechanisms

(a) **Acoustic signaling:** Acoustic signals are widespread and most prominent forms of communication in avian species to attract mates. Song repertoire is positively correlated with the size of the brain's song control nucleus (HVC) and large HVC indicates developmental success. Song repertoires are therefore, considered as 'honest signals' of the male quality. Hence, large song repertoires are preferred by females of many avian species. Direct benefits to the female include superior parental care or territory defense, and indirect benefits are provisioning of good genes for their offspring. Song repertoire size varies with HVC volume and is indicative of male quality in song sparrows (*Melospiza melodia*) (Pfaff et al., 2007). Therefore, song sparrows with large song repertoires have better lifetime fitness. Frequency of a song also influences the reproductive success in some avian species.

Bird calls continue even after pair formation in several socially monogamous bird species. In an experimental study, an increased singing activity by the male zebra finches after breeding was found to be positively correlated with the reproductive investment of his partner.

(b) **Olfactory signaling:** Some avian species discriminate sex using olfactory cues alone. Composition of the uropygial gland secretion is known to differ among individuals of spotless starlings. By smelling the scent individuals are able to identify the sex and quality of members belonging to the same species. Specific odours in crested auklets are also related directly to courtship behaviour. Birds belonging to this species preferentially orient themselves to a specific tangerine-scented plumage odour emitted from their scented neck region.

(c) **Visual signaling:** Birds often use visual stimuli (such as bright colours or large ornamentation) for socio-sexual communication, as well as, species recognition. Various such visual signals are used and often act in combination of other signals to attract a mate and female choice usually shifts toward phenotypically exaggerated traits. These ornaments are often costly and serve as "honest" signals of fitness indicating that the individual is healthy enough to mate. A significant decline in mating success was noticed when eyespots were removed from the tail feathers of male Indian peafowls (*Pavo christatus*). Apart from such plumage ornamentation, nest building is another way of advertising the fitness of breeding birds as seen in Baya weaver. Here, female birds inspect multiple nests constructed by a male within his territory and finally select the males based on the architectures and location of the nests.

Post-copulatory Mechanism: Post-copulatory sexual selection drives the evolution of sperm morphology which results in the efficiency of sperms to fertilize an egg after successful copulation.

(a) **Sperm competition:** Sperm competition occurs when a female is inseminated by multiple males in one breeding season. In birds, the last male who inseminates the female usually fertilizes the highest proportion of eggs and this phenomenon is known as *last male sperm precedence*. Because the oldest spermatozoa are lost by the time fertilization occurs. In many species of avifauna (e.g. black kite *Milvus migrans*), it has also been noticed that the male bird copulates with its partner immediately after returning to nest from a foraging trip to prevent any extra pair fertilization. The best strategy for increasing the parenthood of males is to time the copulation close to the onset of female oviposition. Some adaptations include variable sperm morphology, testes size, as well as, strategies to evade mate guarding in a variety of avian species. Morphological sperm traits (such as flagellum, head and mid-piece length) have been studied in several species of birds to determine phenotypic correlations across species. Sperms with longer flagella, despite their ability to swim faster do not increase fertilization success in some passerine species who store sperm up to several weeks between insemination and fertilization. Because such sperms with longer tails though better at outcompeting previously stored sperm, but require more energy and have shorter sperm lifespan. On the other hand, shorter sperm with large heads are more able to withstand long durations of storage. So, amount of extra-pair paternity was greater in individuals having sperm with a shorter flagellum and a larger head, whereas the sperms with longer flagella and smaller heads had higher within-pair paternity.

Fertilization chances for an individual male are also proportional to the amount of sperm simultaneously transferred into a female. So, the size of the testes and production of sperm increases in situations with high intrasexual competition. On the other hand, testis size is negatively correlated with mate guarding behaviour.

Male Mate Choice (Sex Role Reversal)

Females in different taxa are typically found to be the 'choosy sex' as they provide greater parental investment than males. However, there are instances of 'sex role reversals' where females compete with each other to mate with their desired males, particularly in species where parental investment of males is greater than that of females (Andersson 1994, Buchan et al., 2003).

Production of single sperm is energetically less expensive than production of single egg. But in ejaculate, millions of spermatozoa are delivered and also contains potentially costly accessory-gland secretions (Dewsbury, 1982). So, production of sperms, secretion of accessory-glands during ejaculation, along with the costs of mate searching, courtship, nuptial gifts, mating, mate guarding, and parental care cumulatively makes the male reproduction costlier (Bonduriansky, 2001). Male-mate choice is particularly beneficial if male reproductive success is limited by several factors and the females differ in the quality of their reproductive potential (Altmann, 1997). As the male contributes a higher level of parental investment (i.e. invest much more time and energy in raising the offspring), so in 'male mate choice' the normal role of the male is reversed (sex reversal) and the males get the privilege to choose one female out of many competing females.

Some of the unique examples of male mate choice (sex role reversal) across several taxa are given below:

- ❐ ***Fish:*** In some species of fishes (like pipe fish, sea-horses etc), males display high levels of parental care. Here, the females deposit their eggs in a special brooding pouch of the male and, thereafter, the female does not participate in parental care. Male alone performs all the responsibilities of raising the offspring. Thus, males in these species choose among competitive females for mating. Mating systems (monogamy and polygamy) are also responsible for male mate choice in some other species of fishes.
- ❐ ***Amphibia:*** In some species of frogs (like *Dendrobates auratus*), males perform very efficient parenting role. Male first lures the females to arrive at the rearing sites and deposit eggs. The male then fertilizes these eggs, defends and provides care to the young until they are independent.
- ❐ ***Birds:*** in some species of jacanas females just lay eggs. Males then defend the nest for an extended period and provide complete parental care to the hatchlings until they fledge successfully.

5.5.6 Other Behavioural Aspects Associated with Mate Choice

Territorial Behaviour: Before and after social pairing and mating, animals often show territorial defense and performance level of such territory defense is very important in the context of sexual selection. Most courtship songs were performed at relatively low amplitudes, whereas territorial songs or "broadcast songs" were performed at high amplitudes. So, defending a territory demands for higher energy to produce high amplitude calls, as compared to producing low amplitude courtship songs to attract a mate. Hence, this behaviour is a sexually selected trait because it ensures defense of the female who is rearing offspring. Such vocal amplitude influences male-male competition as in great tits.

Dominance: Intense visual signals by displaying several sexually selected traits (ornaments) and acoustic signals are often used to show dominance status between males. Such visual and acoustic signals requiring high amount of energy are often used in male-male competition (intrasexual competition) and mate choice. At times these displays escalate into physical fights, where the less dominant male is severely injured or killed.

Female galliforms prefer males with well developed ornaments (such as combs and wattles) presumably because they are reliable indicators of dominance of the males (Holder and Montgomerie, 1993). Dominance status of males in both domestic roosters and jungle fowls are found to be positively correlated with the size and colour of his comb (Graves et al., 1985; Ligon et al., 1990).

Mate Guarding: Mate guarding is a common defensive post-copulatory behaviour in male birds to prevent extra-pair mating. Males that exhibit higher levels of mate guarding behaviour usually have a higher chance of paternity after copulation. Increase in the number of males in an environment leads to subsequent rise in mate guarding behaviour. But, mate guarding behaviour is energetically costly and is inversely related with foraging behaviour and body condition. In mate guarding strategy, either the male follows the copulated female, or increase the frequency of 'in-pair' copulations, which increase the proportion his own sperm stored by his female partner and thus increasing his likelihood of paternity.

5.5.7 Costs Associated with Mate Choice

Expression of traits related to mate choice can often be costly. Fights over territories (or females) are regularly noticed between the males leading to serious injury or death of the loser. Emitting signals and searching for the mates are energetically costly and may also attract predators. Hence, males of some species face higher rate of predation during the breeding season. Males with larger body size are often sexually selected by the females in many species of birds and mammals. Such large body size makes males more prone to starve during the scarcity of resources.

Secondary sexual traits can also impose energetic and foraging costs and are, therefore, often limited by several types of natural selection forces. Besides, the sexual selection trait can also be self-limiting. For example, large male body size is advantageous in male contests, but larger males spend more time foraging and have less time to defend their territory and attract female (Andersson and Iwasa, 1996).

5.5.8 Evolutionary Significance of Mate Choice

For many years it has been suggested that sexual isolation caused by mate choice is a precursor for reproductive isolation in nature, consequent lack of gene flow and ultimately leading to speciation. Sexually selected traits often evolve to become more pronounced in competitive breeding situations unless the trait itself begins to limit the individual's fitness. Conflicts during mate choice also ensure that sexually selected ornaments are "honest" traits. Signals must be costly to ensure that only good-quality individuals can present these exaggerated sexual ornaments and behaviours. Therefore, selection of attractive traits is often very strong during mate choice. Speciation by this method occurs when the preference for some sexual trait shifts and produces a 'prezygotic barrier' preventing fertilization. These processes have been difficult to test until recently. With advances in genetic modelling, speciation by sexual selection is gaining popularity in the literature with increasing theoretical and empirical studies. Jennions and Petrie (1997) summarized that variation in mating preferences and costs of choosiness could:

- ❐ Influence the rate and direction of evolution by sexual selection.
- ❐ Provide information about the evolutionary history of female preferences.
- ❐ Help explain inter-specific differences in the evolution of secondary sexual characteristics.
- ❐ Provide information about the level of benefits gained from mate choice.
- ❐ Provide information about the underlying mechanisms of mate choice.

REVIEW QUESTIONS

1. Define animal communication. Why do animals communicate? Elaborate different modes communications encountered among wild animals Mention different purposes of signaling among wild animals.
2. Elaborate "Handicap Principle". Justify the statement "Batesian mimicry is an example of dishonest signal". What is deceptive signal? Define eavesdropping?
3. What do you mean by aposematism? Elaborate the phenomenon citing suitable example.
4. Explain the mechanism of waggle dance. Comment on its functional efficiency.
5. What do you mean by home range? How does it differ from territoriality of animals? Elaborate different modes of advertizing the territory. How the *optimum territory size* is determined?
6. What is ritualized aggression? Elaborate its objectives. Explain various strategies of territory defense.
7. What is territorial marking? Explain various strategies of territorial defense. Elaborate the phenomenon of scent-marking with suitable example. Mention the location and functions of two major glands responsible for scent production. What is spur marking?
8. What is migration? How does it differ from irruptions and dispersal? Elaborate the conceptual model of migration. Write short note on Types of Migration.
9. Mention different morphological and physiological adaptations during bird migration. Enumerate different threats they encounter during migration.
10. Why birds undergo migration? Distinguish between complete and partial migration. How do they navigate during migration? What do you mean by 'migratory flyways'?
11. Define courtship display. Mention the stages involved in successful courtship. Briefly narrate different types of displays encountered among bird community for courtship. What are the biological significances of courtship displays?
12. Define mate selection. What are the advantages of apparently detrimental elaborate ornamentations and other conspicuous traits present in males of many species?
13. Give an account on different mechanisms of mate selection. What do you mean by sex role reversal? Explain how mate selection leads to speciation.
14. Elaborate different pre-copulatory mechanism for female choice among birds.
15. Write a comparative account on the direct and indirect benefits of mate choice. What are the evolutionary significance of mate choice?
16. Write short note on : (a) Sperm competition, (b) Mate Guarding, (c) Male-Male competition, (d) Scent marking in big cats.

REFERENCES

Able, K.P., Skylight polarization patterns at dusk influence migratory orientation in birds. *Nature*, **299**, 550–51, 1982.

Alatalo, R.V., Gottlander, K. and Lundberg, A., Extra-pair copulations and mate guarding in the polyterritorial pied flycatcher, *Ficedula hypoleuca*. *Behaviour*, **101**, 139–155, 1987.

Ali, S. and Ripley, S.D., *Handbook of Birds of India and Pakistan* (Compact. Ed.), Oxford University Press, New Delhi, 1983.

Altmann, J., Mate choice and intrasexual reproductive competition: Contributions to reproduction that go beyond acquiring more mates, p. 320–333. In: Gowaty PA, Ed., *Feminism and Evolutionary Biology*, Chapman & Hall, New York, 1997.

Andersson, M., *Sexual Selection*. Princeton University Press, Princeton, 1994.

Andersson, M. and Simmons, L.W., Sexual selection and mate choice, *Trends in Ecology and Evolution*, **21,** 296–302, 2006.

Andersson, M. and Iwasa, Y., Sexual selection, *Trends in Ecology and Evolution*, **11**, 53-58, 1996.

Badyaev, A.V. and Martin, T.E., Sexual dimorphism in relation to current selection in the house finch. *Evolution*, **54**, 987–997, 2000.

Bateman, A.J., Intra-sexual Selection in Drosophila, *Heredity*, **2**, 349–368, 1948.

Bonduriansky, R., The evolution of male mate choice in insects: a synthesis of ideas and evidence, *Biological Reviews*, **76**, 305–339, 2001.

Boughman, J.W., How sensory drive can promote speciation, *Trends in Ecology and Evolution*, **17**, 571–577, 2002.

Bradbury, J.W. and Vehrencamp, S.L., *Principles of Animal Communication*, Sunderland, Massachusetts, Sinauer, 1998.

Buchan, J.C., Alberts, S.C., Silk, J.B. and Altmann, J., True paternal care in a multi-male primate society, *Nature*, **425**, 179–181, 2003.

Clutton–Brock, T.H., *The Evolution of Parental Care*, Princeton University Press, 1991.

Clutton-Brock, T.H. and Parker, G.A., Potential reproductive rates and the operation of sexual selection. *Q. Rev. Biol.* **67**, 437–456, 1992.

Darwin, C., Origin of certain insects, *Nature*, **7**, 417–418, 1873.

Darwin, C., *The Descent of Man, and Selection in Relation to Sex*, John Murray, London, 1871.

Dewsbury, D.A., Ejaculate cost and male choice, *American Naturalist*, **119**, 601–610, 1982.

Dingle, H. and Drake, V. A., What is migration? *BioScience,* **57**, 113–121, 2007.

Dunlap, J.C., Loros, J. and DeCoursey, P.J., *Chronobiology: Biological Timekeeping*, Sinauer, Sunderland, 2003.

Edward, D.A. and Chapman, T., The evolution and significance of male mate choice, *Trends in Ecology and Evolution*, **26**, 647–654, 2011.

Emlen, S.T. and Oring, L.W., Ecology, sexual selection, and evolution of mating systems. *Science*, **197**, 215–223, 1977.

Enquist, M. and Arak, A., Symmetry, beauty and evolution, *Nature*, **372**, 169–172, 1994.

Fisher, R.A., The evolution of sexual preference, *Eugenics Rev*, **7**, 184–191, 1915.

Frisch, Karl von, *The Dance Language and Orientation of Bees*, The Belknap Press of Harvard University Press, Cambridge, Mass, 1967.

Graves, H. B., Hable, C.P. and Jenkins, T.H., Sexual selection in Gallus: Effects of morphology and dominance on female spatial behaviour. *Behavioural Processes*, **11**, 189–197, 1985.

Greggers, U., Koch, G., Schmidt, V., Du¨rr, A., Floriou-Servou, A., Piepenbrock, D., Go¨pfert, M.C. and Menzel, R., Reception and learning of electric fields in bees. *Proc. R. Soc. B*, **280**, 20130528, 2013.

Hedrick, A.V., Female preference for male calling bout duration in a field cricket. *Behav. Ecol. Sociobiol.*, **19**, 73–77, 1986.

Hohmann, G., Vocal communication of wild bonnet macaques. *Primates*, **30**, 325–345, 1989.

Holder, K. and Montgomerie, R., Context and consequences of comb displays by male rock ptarmigan, *Animal Behaviour*, **45**, 457–470, 1993.

Jennions, M.D. and Petrie, M., Variation in mate choice and mating preferences: A review of causes and consequences. *American Naturalist*, **72**, 283–327, 1997.

Johnsingh, A.J.T. and Murali, S., The ecology and behaviour of the Indian Peafowl (*Pavo cristatus*) Linn. of Injar., *J. Bombay Nat. Hist. Soc.* **75**, 1069–1079, 1978.

Johnstone, R.A., Sexual selection, honest advertisement and the handicap principle: reviewing the evidence, *Biological Review*, **70**, 1–65, 1995.

Johnstone, R.A., Female preference for symmetrical males as a by-product of selection for mate recognition, *Nature*, **372**, 172–175, 1994.

Kalko, E.K.V. and Schnitzler, H.U., Plasticity in echolocation signals of European pipistrelle bats in search flight: Implications for habitat use and prey detection, *Behav. Ecol. Sociobiol*, **33**, 415–428, 1993.

Keeton, W.T., Magnets interfere with pigeon homing. *Proceedings of the National Academy of Sciences of the United States of America*, **68**, 102–106, 1971.

Kirkpatrick, M. and Barton, N.H., The strength of indirect selection on female mating preferences, *Proc. Nat. Acad. Sci. U.S.A.*, **94**, 1282–1286, 1997.

Kodric-Brown, A. and Nicoletto, P.F. Age and experience affect female choice in the guppy (*Poecilia reticulata*), *American Naturalist*, **157**, 316–323, 2001.

Kokko, H., Brooks, R., Jennions, M.D. and Morley, J., The evolution of mate choice and mating biases, *Proc. R. Soc. Lond., B*–**270**, 653–664, 2003.

Kramer G., Eine neue Methode zur Erforschung der Zugorientierung und die bisher damit erzielten Ergebnisse. *Proc. X Ornithol. Congr.*, Uppsala, pp. 269–280, 1951.

Krebs, J.R. and Davies, N.B., *An Introduction to Behavioural Ecology,* Blackwell, Oxford, 1993.

Ligon, J.D., Thornhill, R., Zuk, M. and Johnson, K., Male–male competition, ornamentation, and the role of testosterone in sexual selection in red junglefowl. *Animal Behaviour*, **40**, 367–373, 1990.

Lindauer, M. and Martin, H., Magnetic effects on dancing bees. In: *Animal Orientation and Navigation*, S.R. Galler, K. Schmidt-Kienig, G.J. Jacobs, and R.E. Belleville, Eds., NASA SP–262, U.S. Government Printing Office, Washington, 1972.

Lockley, RM., *Animal Navigation*, Hart Publishing Co., New York, 1967.

Marples, N.M., van Veelen, W. and Brakefield, P.M., The relative importance of color, taste and smell in the protection of an aposematic insect *Coccinella septempunctata. Animal Behaviour*, **48**, 967–974, 1994.

Mays, H.L. and Hill, G.E., Choosing mates: good genes versus genes that are a good fit. *Trends in Ecology and Evolution*, **19**, 554–559, 2004.

Merkel, R.W. and Wiltschko, W., Magnetismus und Richtungsfiden Zugunruhiger Rotkehlchen (*Erithacus rabecula*), *Vogelwarte*, **23**, 71–77, 1965.

Møller, A.P. and Jennions, M.D., How important are direct fitness benefits of sexual selection? *Naturwissenschaften*, **88**, 401–415, 2001.

Mukherjee, A., Observations on the mating behaviour of the Indian Sarus Crane *Grus antigone* in the wild., *J. Bombay Nat. Hist. Soc.*, **99**, 108–113, 2002.

Neff, B.D. and Pitcher, T.E., Genetic quality and sexual selection: an integrated framework for good genes and compatible genes, *Molecular Ecology*, **14**, 19–38, 2005.

Newton, I., *The Migration Ecology of Birds*, Academic Press, Oxford, 2008.

Ophir, A.G. and Galef, B.G. Jr., Female Japanese quail affiliate with live males they have seen mate on video. *Animal Behaviour*, **66**, 369–375, 2003.

Pfaff, J.A., Zanette, L., MacDougall-Shackleton, S.A. and MacDougall-Shackleton, E.A., Song repertoire size varies with HVC volume and is indicative of male quality in song sparrows (*Melospiza Melodia*), *Proc. Biol. Sci.*, **274**, 2035–2040, 2007.

Quader, S., *Nesting and mating decisions and their consequences in the Baya Weaver bird Ploceus philippinus. (Ph.D. dissertation)*, University of Florida, Gainesville, 2003.

Rowe, C., Receiver psychology and the evolution of multicomponent signal, *Animal Behaviour*, **58**, 921–931, 1999.

Rowe, C. and Guilford, T., Hidden colour aversion in domestic chicks triggered by pyrazine odours of insect warning displays, *Nature*, **383**, 520–522, 1996.

Ryan, M.J., Sexual selection, receiver biases, and the evolution of sex differences, *Science*, **281**, 1999–2003, 1998.

Ryan, M.J. and Keddy-Hector, A., Directional pattems of female mate choice and the role of sensory biases, *Am. Nat.,* **139**, s4–s35, 1992.

Sauer, F., Die Sternenorientierung nachtlich ziehender Grasmiicken (Sylvia atricapilla, borin und curruca), *Zeit. f. Tierpsych.*, **14**, 29–70, 1957.

Schevill, W.E. and McBride, A.F., Evidence for echolocation by cetaceans, *Deep Sea Research*, **3**, 153–154, 1956.

Schulte-Pelkum, N., Wieskotten, S., Hanke, W., Dehnhardt, G. and Mauck, B., Tracking of biogenic hydrodynamic trails in harbour seals (*Phoca vitulina*), *Journal of Experimental Biology,* **210**, 5, 781–787, 2007.

Schwagmeyer, P.L. and Mock, D.W., How consistently are good parents good parents? Repeatability of parental care in the house sparrow, *Passer domesticus*, *Ethology*, **109**, 303–313, 2003.

Searcy, W.A. and Andersson, M., Sexual selection and the evolution of song, *Annual Review of Ecology and Systematics*, **17**, 507–533, 1986.

Sergio, F., Blas, J., Blanco, G., Tanferna, A., Lopez, L., Lemus, J.A. and Hiraldo, F., Raptor Nest Decorations Are a Reliable Threat Against Conspecifics, *Science*, **331**, 327–330, 2011.

Servedio, M.R., Male versus female mate choice: sexual selection and the evolution of species recognition via reinforcement, *Evolution*, **61**, 2772–2789, 2007.

Sherry D.F. and Duff, S.J., Behavioural and neural bases of orientation in food-storing birds, *Journal of Experimental Biology*, **199**, 165–172, 1996.

Takahashi, M. and Hasegawa, T., Seasonal and diurnal use of eight different call types by Indian peafowl (*Pavo cristatus*). *J. Ethol.*, **26**, 375–381, 2008.

Thomas, S.C. and Paul, G., Animal Navigation: Path Integration, Visual Landmarks and Cognitive Maps, *Current Biology*, **14**, 12, R475–R477, 2004.

Trivers, R.L. and Willard, D.E., Natural selection of parental ability to vary the sex ratio of offspring, *Science*, **179**, 90–92, 1973.

Trivers, R.L., Parental investment and sexual selection, pp. 136–179, In: *Sexual selection and the descent of man*, Campbell, B., ed., Aldine, Chicago, IL, 1972.

Vehrencamp, S.L., Bradbury, J.W. and Gibson, R.M., The energetic cost of display in male sage grouse, *Animal Behaviour*, **38**, 885–896, 1989.

White, D.J., Influences of social learning on mate-choice decisions, *Learning & Behaviour*, **32**1, 105–113, 2004.

White, D.J. and Galef, B.G. Jr., Mate choice copying and conspecific cueing in Japanese quail, *Coturnix coturnix japonica*, *Animal Behaviour*, **57**, 465–473, 1999.

White, D.J. and Galef, B.G. Jr., 'Culture' in quail: social influences on mate choices of female *Coturnix japonica*, *Animal Behaviour*, **59**, 975–979, 2000.

Wilson, E.O., *Sociobiology*: *The New Synthesis*. Belknap Press (Museum of Comparative Zoology. Harvard University), Cambridge, MA, 1975.

Zahavi, A., Mate selection: A Selection for Handicap, *Journal of Theoretical Biology*, **53**, 205–214, 1975.

Zuk, M., Kolluru, G.R., Exploitation of sexual signals by predators and parasitoids, *The Quarterly Review of Biology*, **73**, 415–438, 1998.

Zuk, M., Rotenberry, J.T. and Simmons, L.W., Calling songs of field crickets (*Teleogryllus oceanicus*) with and without phonotactic parasitoid infection, *Evolution*, **52**, 166–171, 1998.

6

WILDLIFE TOOLS, TECHNIQUES AND PRACTICES

6.1 WILDLIFE CENSUS TECHNIQUES

Many wildlife studies are carried out to record the presence or absence of certain species in a particular area and are used to prepare the distribution list of a particular species. Sometimes the presence of certain threatened species is also located through these studies. These studies are also helpful to prepare checklist of flora and fauna of a study area. Despite being simple, there are certain drawbacks of the species lists prepared in such a way. These studies just record the presence or absence of a particular flora and fauna in an area and do not assess their abundance. Therefore, the data cannot be statistically analysed in temporal or spatial scale. Such species richness can neither be compared between various surveys, nor between two or more different wilderness areas as the amount of effort is not recorded.

Estimating the population size or density of flora and fauna is one of the fundamental aspects to understand their status and demography of a species. This, in turn, is essential in designing appropriate management and/or conservation strategies. So wildlife population studies often demand for considerable investment of time and other resources such as money, equipment, labour etc. Therefore, it is very important that the wildlife studies are properly designed with a set of study objectives. The personnel carrying out the research also need to be well versed with various wildlife tools and techniques and should be able to aptly apply the appropriate ones on field.

6.1.1 Objective of Census

The abundance of any species does not necessarily mean any absolute number, rather often the abundance is expressed as an estimated value. Such values are then compared to determine trends of the population fluctuations in order to find out whether the population is increasing, decreasing or stable. Indices of population change with time, thus, enable the wildlife researcher to compare between areas, seasons and treatment. Similarly, to find out the effectiveness of certain management practices, abundance is measured before and after the management intervention.

6.1.2 Important Considerations

In practice, no population survey or census is completely bias free (Ross and Reeve, 2003). Therefore, selection of appropriate technique largely depends on study area and species to be surveyed. It also depends on where (i.e. habitat) and when (i.e. season) the study is being carried out. Finally, before initiating any wildlife study it is to be carefully considered that how much resource (both in terms of money and manpower) are going to be utilized. There is always a trade-off between the depth of the data gathered and the number of the replicate samples that can be obtained (Ross and Reeve, 2003).

Several alternative techniques are available to achieve a particular research goal. Hence, adequate background information is necessary to select appropriate technique for a particular wildlife research (Table 6.1).

Table 6.1 Prerequisites for Wildlife Census

- ❒ Covering letter seeking permission from the appropriate authorities/landowners.
- ❒ Map or toposheets of the area with the boundaries and topographic features.
- ❒ Climatic, geological and vegetation features of the study area.
- ❒ Identification manual of the focal species.
- ❒ Detailed and clear instructions for the field worker regarding collection of data.

It is very important to learn about the study site and target species. In most wildlife studies it is often very wise to initially carry out a brief pilot survey when different tools, techniques and methods are alternatively tried out. Finally, the most appropriate one is selected through trial and error basis. It is to be noted that once a method is selected, it should be carried out for the entire study period with the same surveyor(s) in order to obtain best results.

Species those require management intervention, internationally and locally endangered species, species of local and national importance, species of high economic importance, important prey species in a particular ecosystem and species having tourist attraction are usually selected for census. Proper timing for any kind of animal study is another very crucial aspect as the visibility of habitat varies with season. Therefore, the timing of census (or survey) largely depends on the objectives of the study and the type of census being undertaken. For example, water-hole census are often performed in dry season, breeding bird census is usually done in spring while census of migratory birds is done in winter. It is to be noted that census should never be carried out in areas and during the period of disturbance (*viz.* tourist season, fire, timber work etc.) as the result might be erroneous. The most important criteria to obtain authentic and reliable data are largely dependent on the sincerity, patience and honesty of the observer. Thus, trained and dependable staff is the prime requisite for any wildlife study.

6.1.3 Abundance / Density Estimation in Wildlife Studies

Total Count (Complete Census)

Complete census is usually done to count the total number of animals present over a specified area to obtain correct and unbiased estimate of their abundance without any statistical inferences or underlying assumptions. This technique is often very much labour intensive and is suitable only for conspicuous species, usually present in open, discrete and well-defined habitats. This technique, therefore, can be adopted to count large mammals and birds in a small area.

However, it is usually almost impossible to count all plants and animals present in a given area. Besides, there are some inherent difficulties to implement total count in some of the wilderness areas. The method is expensive, often leads to high amount of errors and the statistical analysis of data is very difficult.

Sample Count

Complete census of the organisms in the area of interest can rarely be done because of limitations of time or research funds. Moreover, if the study area is too large to carry out a complete census within a reasonable amount of time, then sample counts are usually preferred. Therefore, wildlife biologists often rely on various *sample census techniques* (commonly referred to as *sample count*) to estimate the relative abundance, dominance and diversity of wild populations.

Sample is a portion or segment that is representative of the whole and *sampling* is a procedure, wherein a fraction of the data is taken from a large set of data and the inference drawn from the sample is extended to the entire group (Raj, 1972).

So, the basic principle involved is the wildlife numbers are estimated from a smaller known area (*sample*). The sample areas surveyed need to be representative of the larger habitat with various *replicates*. Then total population size can be estimated by extrapolating the outcome of the sample count and readily subjected to statistical treatment. Another positive aspect is that a range of minimum and maximum can be obtained. Sample count is considered to be a basis of wildlife monitoring and sample plots can provide fairly accurate data on species diversity, as well as, abundance of each species within the study area.

6.1.4 Sampling Methods – At a Glance

All sampling methods should be non-destructive, and include the collection of *quantitative* and *qualitative* data. First, the study area is divided into various grids and numbers are assigned to each grid (Figure 6.1).

Various types of sampling methods are used in wildlife research, of which some important ones are briefly described below:

Random Sampling

Random sampling is often used when the area being studied is very large with fairly uniform habitat and there is a limited amount of time available. Thus, random sampling theoretically assumes that all areas within a site have an equal opportunity of being sampled as any other sites. Samples are taken from different positions within a habitat and those positions are chosen randomly (Figure 6.2).

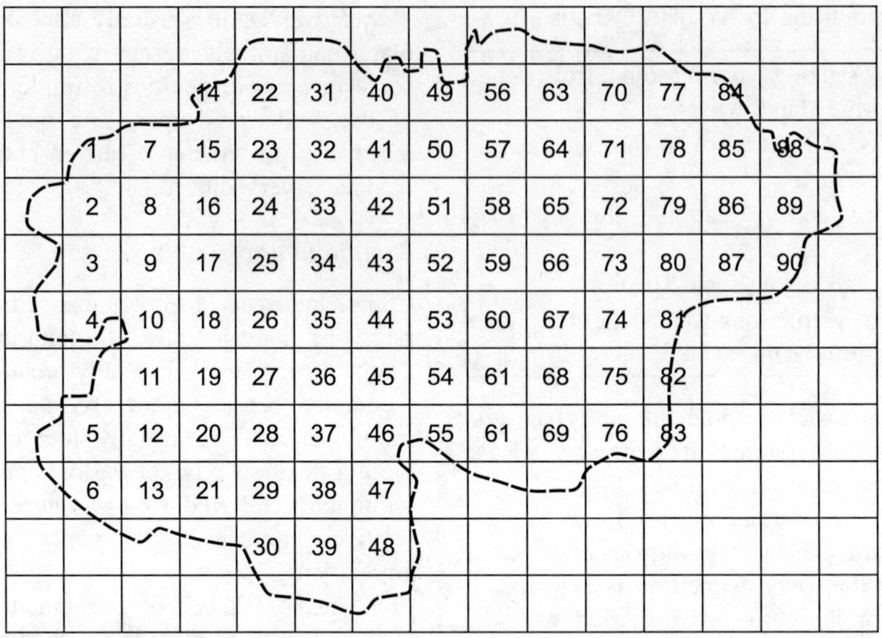

FIGURE 6.1 Study area divided into uniform grids and grids are assigned with numbers.

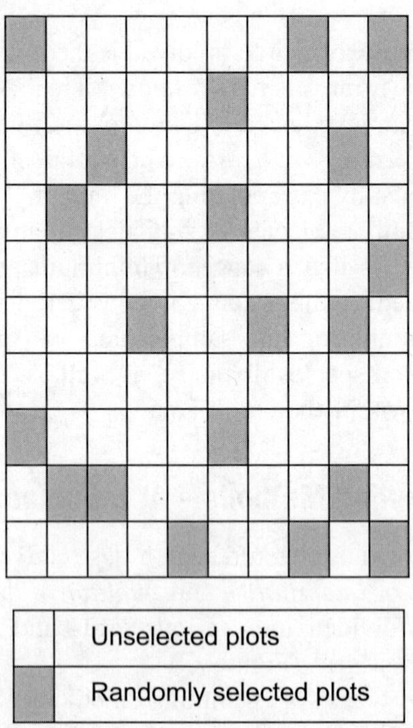

FIGURE 6.2 Diagram of randomly selected sampling units in a study area.

There are many strategies available for selecting a random sample. For large populations, this often involves generating random numbers with a computer and for small populations it might involve using a table of random numbers, by flipping book pages or even writing a unique identifier for every sample unit in the population on a scrap of paper, placing those numbers in a jar, shaking it, and then selecting them from the jar blindly. The approach used for selecting the sample removes potential bias by the researcher during selection of samples.

Systematic Sampling

Systematic sampling is another statistical sampling method. In this method, one number (n) is randomly selected and then all samples are selected by adding that number to the initial one. Usually every (n+1)th element is selected as the sample. Estimators for systematic sampling and simple random sampling are identical; only the method of sample selected differs. Therefore, systematic sampling is used to simplify the process of selecting a sample or to ensure ideal dispersion of sample units. So in brief it is implemented by choosing a starting point at random and selecting samples at uniform intervals thereafter. For example if a researcher randomly select number 7, then he would carry out his field observations in grid number 8, 16, 24, 32 .... and so on, until the last grid number is reached (Figure 6.3). It is to be noted that the sample size drawn will vary and depends on the location of the first unit drawn.

Systematic sampling is convenient, easy to implement, and ensures maximum dispersion of sample units throughout the study area. This method also requires minimum knowledge of the habitat. As compared to random sampling, systematic sampling provides less protection against introducing biases. If the study area is heterogeneous then this method is inefficient and can also be imprecise. Moreover, adequate care must be taken to ensure that the initial number has not been ordered in a way that introduces any non-random factors into the sampling. A comparative account of the random and systematic sampling is given in Table 6.2:

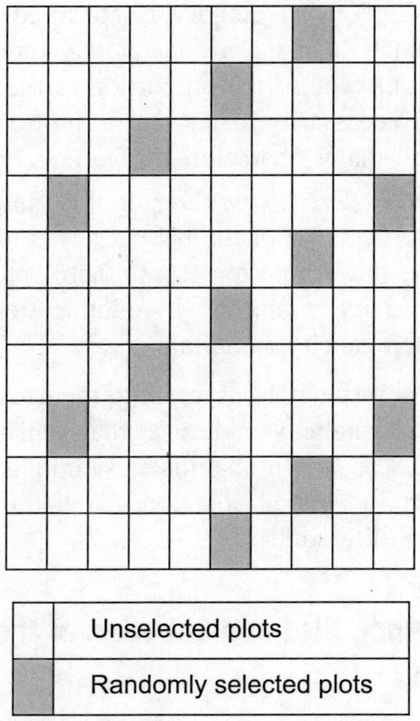

FIGURE 6.3 Diagram of randomly selected sampling units in a study area.

Table 6.2 Comparative Account of Random Sampling and Systemic Sampling

Random Sampling	*Systematic Sampling*
❒ This is used where the habitat being sampled is fairly uniform. ❒ Where a large area needs to be covered quickly. ❒ To remove observer bias in the selection of samples. ❒ Where statistical tests are to be used which require randomly collected data. ❒ If time is very limited.	❒ To show zonation of species along some environmental gradient. (e.g. down a sea shore, across a woodland edge). ❒ Where there is some kind of continuous variation along a line. ❒ To sample linear habitats, e.g. a roadside verge. ❒ Where physical conditions demand it (e.g. sampling a vertical rock face, using a rope to climb it).

Stratified Sampling

A large area is rarely uniform throughout their extent and often there are smaller identifiable areas within a habitat which are substantially different from the main part of the habitat. For example, grasslands and wetlands may exist within a forested habitat. Applying random sampling in such a situation might be problematic as the random samples may not cover all areas of a habitat equally. If the forest habitat mentioned in the above example is randomly sampled, then there lies a possibility that none of the samples might fall within the wetland or grassland patches. If so happens then the random samples would clearly not be an accurate reflection of the entire habitat. In such a situation, stratified sampling would be used to avoid missing out on important areas of the habitat.

Stratified sampling usually takes into account the different areas present in a particular habitat. These different areas need to be sampled separately. Each individual area separately sampled within the overall habitat is then called a *stratum*. The name 'stratified sampling' originates from the term *stratum* (singular) or '*strata*' (plural). In this context it is to be mentioned that although different *strata* need to be taken into account, yet it is also important to avoid overemphasising its significance within the habitat as a whole. Therefore, number of sampling units placed in a particular *stratum* should be proportional of the total number of sampling units. This proportion is determined by the area of the *stratum* in relation to the overall area of the habitat. For example, if a forest expands over 1000 sq km area, encompassing 200 sq km of grasslands and 100 sq km of wetland, then grassland stratum accounts for 20 percent and wetland stratum encompasses 10 percent of the entire forest habitat. Say, if a total of 20 samples need to be taken in order to accurately reflect the composition of the whole habitat, then 4 (20 percent) sampling units need to be placed on the grasslands, 2 (10 percent) sampling units on the wetlands and remaining 14 sampling units are to be located over the forest habitats.

The first step in stratified sampling is, therefore, to divide the population into subgroups (*strata*) based on mutually exclusive criteria. Then random or systematic samples are taken from each strata in the same proportion as the stratum represents in the entire habitat. The standard formula for calculating the number of samples to be placed in each stratum in case of carrying out stratified sampling is as follows:

The number of sampling unit in a particular *stratum*

$$= \frac{\text{the area of the } stratum \times \text{Total number of the sampling unit}}{\text{Total area of the complete habitat}}$$

The stratified sampling is redundant and usually not performed if the habitat of the study area is fairly homogeneous.

Cluster Sampling

Another kind of statistical sampling method is called cluster sampling or block sampling. If random sampling is adopted to sample a population distributed across a wide geographic region, then to reach all the sampling units the researcher needs to travel extensively in and cover a lot of ground geographically. This geographic trotting to collect data from all the sampling units demands for large manpower, thus, is often an expensive affair. In such situations cluster sampling is often conducted to reduce the cost of the survey. In this sampling method the study area is divided into various heterogeneous groups, which are called *clusters*. Samples are then randomly selected from the clusters.

Cluster sampling can tell us a lot about the particular cluster from where the samples are taken. But, unless a lot of samples are randomly selected from all the clusters, it is very difficult to make statistically valid generalization. This method is not commonly practiced in wildlife studies.

Non-statistical (or Non-probabilistic) Sampling Methods

There are many other types of non-statistical (also termed as non-probabilistic) sampling methods which do not depend upon the rationale of probability theory and *random* selection is not usually performed while selecting these sampling units. So by adopting these sampling methods, information obtained from the sample cannot be extrapolated to the entire population. However, in certain circumstances statistical sampling methods (random sampling) may not be feasible, practical or theoretically sensible. In such situations a wide range of non-statistical sampling methods serve as useful alternatives. Some of these are:

- ***Accidental, haphazard or convenience sampling:*** As the name indicates, in this method the selection of sampling units is by chance (accidental), or haphazard or based on a matter of convenience. Therefore, these samples are often not representative of the population.
- ***Purposive sampling:*** Purposive sampling is done with a purpose in mind.
- ***Modal instance sampling:*** The most frequently occurring value in a statistical distribution is regarded as the mode. In modal instance sampling, the most frequent or the most typical case is usually sampled. But the incidence which appear to be the most frequent or the most typical case, need not be the actual mode of the statistical distribution.
- ***Expert sampling or judgmental sampling:*** In these non-statistical sampling methods, the samples are selected based on the judgments of persons with known or demonstrable experience and expertise in the relevant area. But, the judgments of the experts can be wrong and then the samples are not representative of the entire population.
- ***Quota sampling:*** In this method the samples are non-randomly selected according to some fixed quota. Quota sampling is again of two types—proportional and non-proportional. In proportional quota sampling, the samples should represent the proportional amount of each major characteristics of the habitat. On the other hand, in non-proportional quota sampling the minimum number of sampling unit of each category is specified assuring that smaller habitats are adequately represented. But, in this type of the proportion of the samples may not necessarily match the proportional amount of each major characteristic features of the habitat.
- ***Heterogeneity sampling:*** In this sampling method, heterogeneity of the habitat needs to be included, but may not represent them proportionately. Diversity sampling is another term used for heterogeneity sampling.

These non-statistical sampling methods are usually quicker and use smaller sample sizes than statistical sampling techniques. These non-probabilistic sampling methods are often adopted in applied social research, but not usually adopted in wildlife studies.

6.1.5 Number, Size and Location of the Sampling Units

For all the sampling methods it is to be remembered that they must have adequate sample size with sufficient replicates. Samples must also have adequate spatial, as well as, temporal dispersion and should avoid any correlation between transect orientation and particular features of the landscape (such as ridges or valleys). The researchers need to bring randomization into the design process at some point, in order to avoid observer bias. Location and number of sampling plots can strongly influence the population estimates. Therefore, appropriate number of sample plots should be carefully placed when designing a study. The size and number of sample plots will depend on the effort required to detect individuals of the target species. It is necessary to take enough samples so that an accurate representation of the entire study site is obtained.

Therefore, the next obvious questions are *'How many samples are required for the study?'* and *'What should be the size of the sampling plots so that most species are accounted for.'* Species Discovery Curves and Species Area Curves are often used to optimize the effective sampling effort with limitation of time and other resources (Javed and Kaul, 2002).

Appropriate size of the sampling unit depends on (i) size of the habitat *viz.* small habitats (e.g. small patch of bush) require smaller sized samples and large habitats (eg. forests) require larger sized samples and (ii) size and density of organisms *viz.* small and dense organisms (e.g. grass) require smaller samples while large and scattered organisms (e.g. trees) require larger samples. Although sample plots may be of varied shape, yet regularly shaped plots (e.g. square or circular) are frequently used as these are usually easier to demarcate and analyse. Boundaries of the sampling plots should be marked and coordinates recorded with a GPS unit for carrying out repeat surveys.

6.1.6 Census Techniques Used in Wildlife Survey — At a Glance

Number of techniques have been suggested from time to time to census different group of animals in variety of habitats. Techniques also vary according to aims and objectives of the survey. Ironically no method is elastic enough to cover all groups or all habitats.

The census techniques used in wildlife surveys are broadly classified as (i) direct census techniques and (ii) indirect census techniques.

1. Direct Census Techniques

In direct census techniques the animals are counted through direct sighting and are usually adopted for species with relatively high densities, especially medium to large sized mammals, birds etc. Outlined below are some of the direct census techniques, which are often used to count animals, estimate density and characterize an area:

(i) Capture-Mark-Recapture (CMR) Technique: Capture-mark-recapture (CMR) technique has been used since long back in wildlife studies to estimate population abundance. Let us assume that within a closed population of animals (N) two samples (n_1 and n_2) are captured, marked and released at time 1 (m_1) and again the number of marked animals recaptured at time 2 (m_2), The CMR techniques estimating abundance assume that the proportion of marked animals recaptured in the second sample (m_2/n_2) should equal to the proportion of the total animals captured at time 1 in the total population (n_1/N),

This can be then mathematically expressed as:

$$m_2/n_2 = n_1/N \text{ or, } N = n_1\, n_2/m_2$$

The merits and limitations of Capture-Mark-Recapture (CMR) Technique are briefly outlined in Table 6.3.

Table 6.3 Merits and Limitations of Capture-Mark-Recapture (CMR) Technique

Merits	*Limitations*
❒ Estimate population abundance of the focal species. ❒ Useful in monitoring changes in population size. ❒ Temporary or permanent markings can be used on the captured animals. ❒ Practiced to assess population of diverse animal taxa.	❒ Time consuming. ❒ Requires specialized equipment and training for handling the captured animals, as well as, careful analysis of data. ❒ Handling of the captured animals during marking might influence their behaviour.

(ii) *Drive Count:* Drive count is used to get a fair estimation of the population of certain species, especially deer, and usually involves less manpower. This method requires only two observers—one who drive through the area and the other one count the individuals leaving or entering the area. To yield the net count, the sum of animals passing forward along the drive line is subtracted from the sum of animals entering the area ahead of the driving crew. This method is very popular to count the number of game animals present in open habitats. Nevertheless, drive count is also used to count raptors and many other species of mega fauna. But this method is unsuitable for small, secretive and nocturnal animals, as well as, those inhabit dense forested habitat where visibility is hindered by trees and undergrowths. This method is often not feasible to be adopted in large protected areas of this country due to the dense vegetation and uneven visibility (Tak and Lamba, 1978).

(iii) Roadside Count: Roadside counts are performed by walking or cycling along narrow paths or driving vehicles on motorable roads and counting the number of individuals of a focal species encountered while travelling. These surveys are usually done in the morning. Then the relative density of the species being censused is simply expressed as number of individuals recorded per kilometre. Each trip along these tracts serves as a sample. The number of tracts should be determined considering the availability of manpower and other resources, so that each tract can be monitored repeatedly at regular intervals. These tracts should be placed in a way so that they represent all habitats within the study area. For roadside counts, maximum distance that could be traversed in two hours should be chosen (Rodgers, 1991).

The roadside counts are influenced by condition of road-side cover (habitat, visibility, etc.) and the activity of the animals influenced by the hour of day, weather condition, seasonal, food-supply along the road side etc. (Newman, 1959). So a researcher needs to select specific tracts and should choose a particular mode to traverse them (walking/ cycling/driving) in order to minimize bias. Vehicles should be driven at a slow speed (say 20 km per hour) for proper observation and same observer should perform the survey repeatedly.

Roadside count is a simple and widespread method to get indices of relative density and population abundance measures of the focal species spread over very large geographical areas. It is opined that the road side counts can be usefully applied for estimation of total or relative densities of animal populations in sanctuaries and national parks, in India, where the well-maintained roads present inside those protected areas can be taken as transects (Tak and Lamba, 1978). Roadside-surveys are also considered as one of the most popular survey methods for diurnal raptors, which has been frequently used to study distribution and abundance of raptors in a locality (Ferguson, 2004). Johnson and Enderson (1972) used road survey data to compare wintering raptor populations in similar areas between years.

Besides, surveys from roads have also been used to locate nests in natural and urban landscapes (Goldstein, 2000).

(iv) Transect Method: Surveys using transect methods are fairly common in published literatures and can be conducted from the ground (McLeod and Andersen, 1998) which generally involves traversing a specified route along roads or trails (Vinuela, 1997). Transects are usually set up along environmental gradients (*viz.* along the slope of a hillside, outward from a source of pollution etc.). Each transect is considered a sample unit. Summarized data from several transects are required for statistical analysis to compare differences between years or sites. Transects are randomly located, often within stratified sub-areas of the total study area, to obtain representative samples of the species and numbers of each species present.

Transects can be broadly categorised as (i) Line Transect (Transect with fixed length but zero width) and (ii) Strip transect or Belt transect (transects with fixed length and width)

(a) Line transect method: In line transect method, a measured line is placed across an area and the observer counts while travelling along a fixed transect line instead of searching over an entire plot (Text Box 6.1). The species touching the line is either recorded along the entire length of the line (continuous sampling) or at specific points situated along the line (systematic sampling). There are certain merits and limitations of 'Line-Transect Methods' (Table 6.4).

Table 6.4 Merits and Limitations of Line-transect Method

Merits	*Limitations*
❒ More economical, require less technology and practical method. ❒ Efficient but simple and at the same time inexpensive. ❒ Data analysis simple. ❒ Applicable throughout the year for all habitat types; larger area may be covered in relatively shorter time. ❒ User friendly, particularly for monitoring purposes. ❒ Greater turnover of species.	❒ Distance often not measured correctly. ❒ Movement of observer may cause disturbances. ❒ Skulking, cryptic and shy animals may be missed.

Text Box 6.1: Line Transect Method Protocol

In line transect method a researcher walks along a predetermined route at regular interval to record the objects on or near the line.

Study Design: Line transects are placed either in random, stratified or systematic manner based on research goal and objective of the study.

Habitat Type: Applicable in almost all habitats such as open habitat, forests, plainlands, as well as, hilly terrains.

Placement of Transect: Transects are laid on selected habitats, usually in straight line, often placed along roads, streams or along contour of hilly terrains. Transects should be well spaced out. Distance between two parallel transect should not be less than 200 m.

Permanent or Temporary: Depending on objective of the study, transects might be permanent or temporary. Permanent line transects are monitored round the year. Both permanent or temporary monitoring lines should be marked (with stone, boulder or big trees) on field and always recorded as tracks on GPS.

Transect Length: Depending on habitat and focal species of study (single species or several species in community), the transect lengths vary and are usually determined through 'species discovery curves'.

(b) Belt transect method (or strip transect method): Belt Transect Method is similar to line transect but the sampling area is wider than a line, and the counts are limited to objects within a fixed distance of the transect line. As a defined distance from the line is measured, thus the sampled plot becomes a rectangular strip extending a specified distance on either side of the transect line. Such rectangular shaped plots are called 'belt transect' or 'strip transect'. In this method, samples can be taken all the way along the line, at specific intervals or even randomly.

Strip transects are one of the most commonly used survey techniques for determining species composition and density. Strip transects can be conducted by observers on the ground, in boats or in aircraft. This method is usually adapted for a variety of species and habitats where density estimates are desired. Aerial and boat-based strip transect methodologies have been specifically developed for conspicuous aquatic species and these techniques have become the preferred survey method in large open water habitats. Aerial strip transects can be established to assess the distribution and abundance of waterfowl over broad geographic areas.

The density from a strip transect plot can be extrapolated over the study area to obtain an abundance estimate as shown in Figure 6.4.

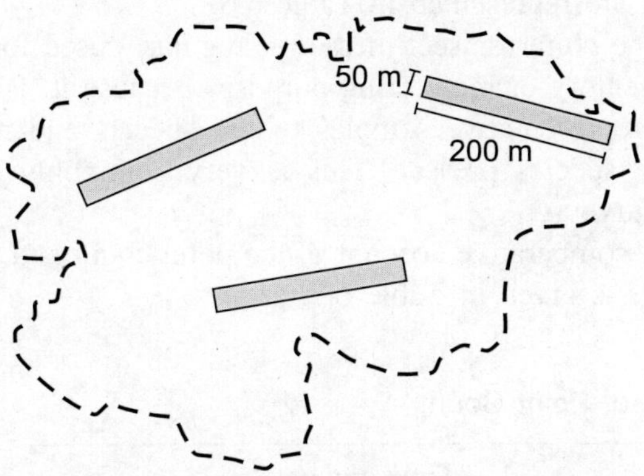

FIGURE 6.4 Diagram of strip transects used to estimate species abundance and diversity.

Several factors must be considered before strip transect methodology is adopted. Carefully choosing the appropriate strip transect width is very important if density estimates are desirable. In practice, often a compromise is noticed between maximising detection probability for the target species and surveying as large an area as possible. Intuitively, detection probability (and strip transect width) increases for large, conspicuous species in more open habitats. Moreover, it is assumed that all animals within the plot are detected while calculating the density of a species from the belt transects. The observer does not usually leave the transect line to search the plot, rather visual-aids, like binoculars, are commonly used during ground and boat-based strip transect surveys to aid detection and species identification. Strip transects are, therefore, best conducted in open habitats where visibility is unobstructed.

Determining Transect Length

Species Discovery Curve is a commonly used method to determine the optimum length of transects. This curve is generated by graphically plotting the number of species discovered, with increasing transect length. Amidst such different lengths of transects the minimum transect length is determined by the point from where the curve starts flattening as shown in Figure 6.5.

There are certain merits and limitations of 'Species Discovery Curves' (Table 6.5)

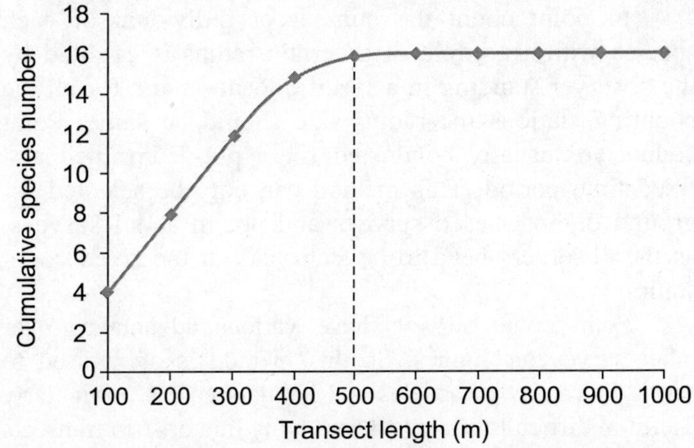

FIGURE 6.5 Species discovery Curves to determine transect length.

Table 6.5 Merits and Limitations of Species Discovery Curves.

Merits	*Limitations*
❐ Assess the total number of different species present in the study area.	❐ Does not assess abundance of individual species within the study area.
❐ Useful in comparing the species richness between different sites.	❐ Requires careful analysis of data.

(v) Point Count Method: The point count is another most commonly used survey techniques for determining species composition and abundance. Point counts are also considered as 'transects of zero length and width.

In this technique, survey stations (points) are placed throughout the study area either randomly or systematically and around each of those fixed survey stations the observer performs the count in a 360° arc. If density estimates are desired from point counts, the counts are limited to objects within a fixed radius from the survey point and thus the sampled area becomes a circular plot of specified radius from the survey point as shown in Figure 6.6.

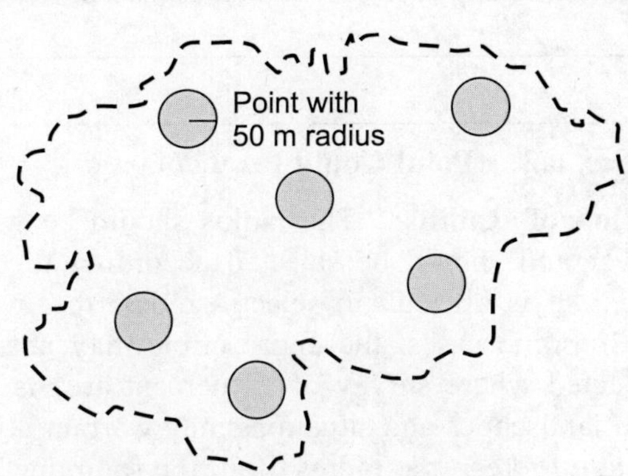

FIGURE 6.6 Diagram of point count method used to estimate species abundance and diversity.

In point count the number of individual of each species within a circle of a certain radius is counted by the observer standing in a specific location and for all the counting stations the radius size should be same. Point counts are usually conducted for a pre-determined and fixed time period. This method can only be selected for ground or boat-based surveys and not in aerial surveys, as the observers need to be stationary at the fixed count station.

Point count surveys have various advantages over other survey techniques. So this method is often used to survey a variety of species and habitats and is particularly useful in difficult terrains where laying line or strip transects or performing counts while travelling along the transect line may not be possible. In addition to that, shy and secretive species are more likely detected during point counts as the observers are sedentary, These individuals often hide and escape detection of the mobile and conspicuous observers carrying out the transect methods. Moreover, in nocturnal surveys or in densely vegetated habitats point counts are based on vocal cues as in these situations visual cues are limited. However, distances from the point count station are often difficult to determine from vocal cues, making density estimates problematic. Merits and limitations of point count method are represented in Table 6.6.

The point transect method is regularly used for rangel and inventory or monitoring purposes because it is easy to obtain representative samples of the species and numbers of each species present. This is very commonly used in avian surveys.

A comparative account of the point count and transect methods is given in Table 6.7.

Table 6.6 Merits and Limitations of Point Count

Merits	*Limitations*
❐ Time to spot and identify shy and cryptic birds. ❐ Adaptable to species and habitats. ❐ Good for habitat studies.	❐ Double counting is a concern. ❐ Time is ''lost'' moving between points.

Table 6.7 Comparative Account of Point Count and Transect Methods

Point Count Method	*Transect Method*
❐ Observer walk to predefined spots, allow time for the animals therein to settle and then record all the animals around the spot for a defined time (usually for 5–10 minutes).	❐ Observer walk along predefined routes and record all the animals along the line (*line transect*) or within a fixed distance on either side of the route (*belt transect*).
❐ Ground covering is less as the observer need to spend the defined duration of time at every point and time is also lost to move between points.	❐ Quite a good amount of ground is covered relatively quickly.
❐ Better method to spot, identify and assess the abundance of shy and cryptic birds.	❐ Better method to spot, identify and assess the abundance of conspicuous birds.
❐ Double counting is a concern.	❐ Double counting is a minor problem.
❐ Good for density estimates, as well as, habitat studies.	❐ Good for density estimates, but not usually adopted in habitat studies.

Text Box 6.2: Point Count Protocol

Selection of Radius: The radius should be within the limit for proper sighting and auditory perception of the observer and should be selected according to the nature of landscapes as it may vary from one survey site to the next. It is difficult to select a radius that works for every situation. For most situations, a radius of 20 m is used. In some cases, the entire circle may not be possible to survey due to obstacles. Therefore, points should be selected where survey of 90 percent area is possible. Since situations are different from one area to the next, certain landscapes and situations may warrant utilizing a larger or smaller radius of the survey points. But it is very important to keep the radius of all the sampling points same. Otherwise the final data would lead to biased results.

Time of Counts: As with the survey area, the time devoted to point counts at each point must be consistent. In most cases, the recommended time is 5–10 minutes, preferably 1–3 counts per month, for every alternate months or for four distinct seasons of the year. Counting should be done within three hours after sunrise, as birds are most active during this time.

Weather: As the climatic variables are known to affect animal activity, so the climatic conditions like wind intensity (no wind, slight/gusty/ strong wind), temperature and percent of cloud cover (no cloud, <50 percent cloud cover, >50 percent cloud cover, overcast) are to be recorded while conducting the point count. Usually it is customary to carry out point counts in clear days and counting birds should preferably be avoided in rainy, stormy or extremely windy days.

Set-up and Practice: Before conducting the point count, the boundaries of the area need to be marked with some identifiable object (e.g., corner of building, a large tree, etc.). One should also mark the spot from where the count is to be carried out and should return to this exact point during each subsequent count. Results thus obtained from one point can then be compared to the results of other similar point counts carried in other places or over different seasons or years.

Clothing Colour: While carrying out the point count, the observer should avoid wearing bright coloured clothes. Because such bright coloured clothing often makes the presence of the observer prominent and animals tend to disperse away.

Counting: One should quietly approach the survey location. Then after reaching the centre of the survey circle, he/she should wait a little before starting the count. This is necessary in order to get oriented, and to allow the animals to adjust the presence of observer. After starting the point count, individuals of the focal species that are seen or heard within the sampling area (i.e. within the circle of defined radius from the observer) are to be recorded on a data sheet. One can use own codes to mark the individuals during the survey. After a count is completed, transcribe the codes to the full common name and prepare the checklist for the day.

Counting Fly-Thrus (FT): All birds that fly through a point count area but do not land on any structure should be counted as FT. and be recorded under the FT column of the data sheet. However, if the observer is sure that the flying bird came from somewhere in the point count, it should not be not counted as an FT.

Counting Fly-Overs (FO): All higher-flying birds (above the tallest structure in a census area) should also be noted in the FO column of the data sheet, if they are within the boundaries of the point count area.

Unidentified Individuals: Unidentified individuals of any species are listed as such with the closest taxonomic affiliation that can be determined (for example, unidentified snipe, unidentified butterfly etc). Attempts should be made to identify all individuals using a field guide.

Abundance Estimate: In a situation where multiple sightings of a species occur within a point count, then only different individuals of a given species should be counted. Hence, multiple entries should only be made if the observer is reasonably certain that they are different individuals. Thus numbers assigned in the data sheets are assumed to be separate individuals (for example: 5 house sparrows means that 5 different house sparrows were sighted).

Additional Notes: Record anything unusual or interesting (like bird behaviours, dramatic changes in the habitat etc.) in the Additional Notes section at the bottom of the data sheet.

(vi) Distance Sampling Method: During transects and point count methods, all animals cannot be detected over all distances. Often animals present at a distance from the transect line or the survey points are overlooked. Such decline in detection varies with different species and habitats. Distance sampling takes this decreasing detectability of animals with increasing distance from the observer into account and does not assume that all individuals present in a particular area are counted. Rather, distance sampling can only be used if the following assumptions are satisfied:

- Transects or observation points are placed in a manner so that they are representative of the habitat.
- All animals, which are present on the transect line or on the observation point are detected.
- Perpendicular distance from the transect line or radial distance from the observer point to every individual animal (or group of animals) must be accurately measured as shown in Figure 6.7.

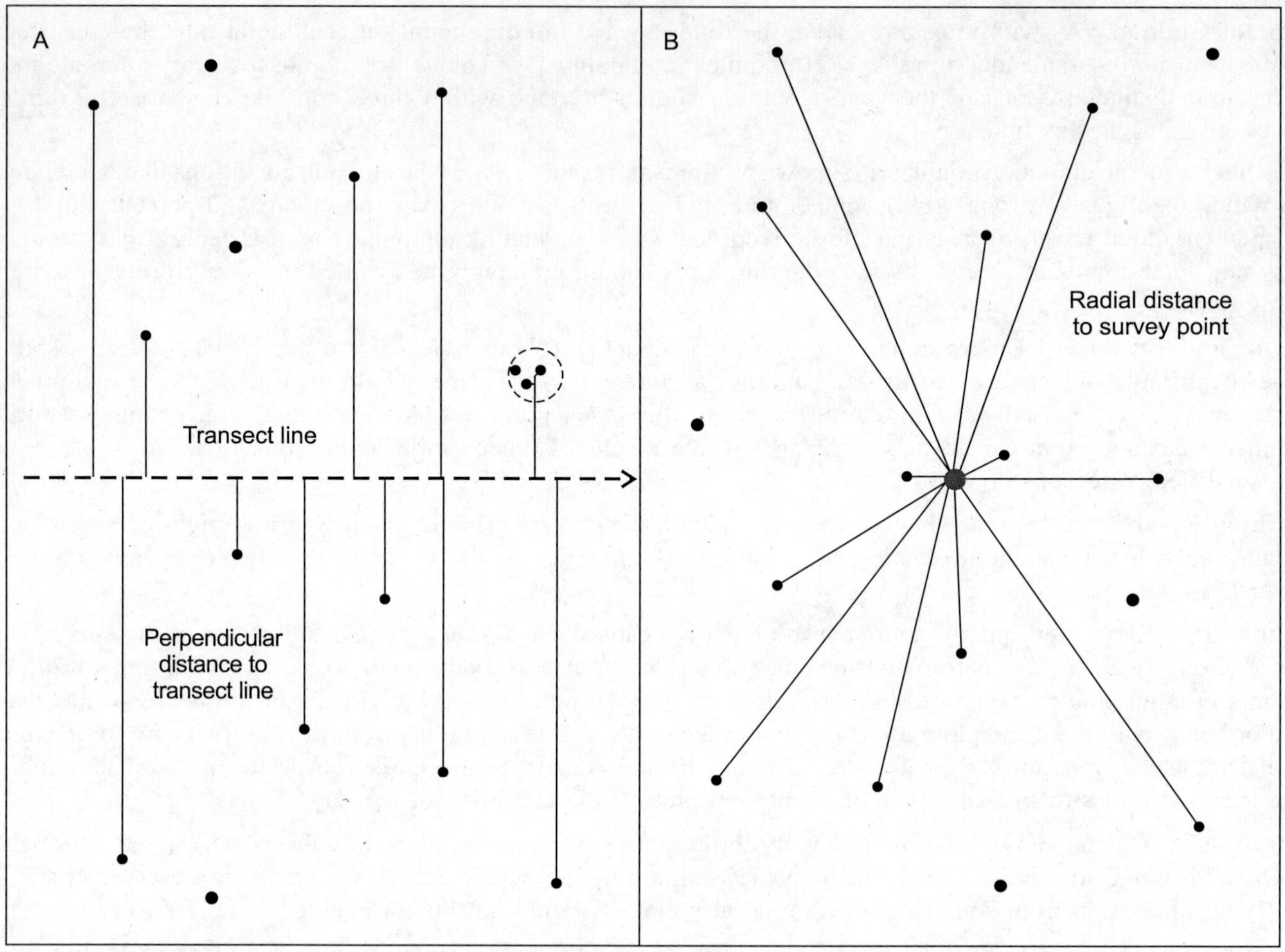

FIGURE 6.7 Use of distance sampling method to estimate species abundance and diversity during (A) point surveys and (B) transect surveys.

However, accurate measurement of distance from the observer to every individual is often difficult in certain field conditions and in such cases, distance bands are used.

- ❒ Animals need to be detected in their initial position and the distance is measured before they move in response to the observer's presence.
- ❒ There should be no double counting of animals.

If all the above assumptions are met and a sufficient number of observations are acquired, then theoretically, this method is expected to yield more reliable estimates than transect or point counts. Distance sampling method is usually adopted when the wildlife survey aim to generate absolute density or abundance estimate of a focal species.

Unique feature of distance sampling, as compared to transect or point count, is that in this method distance data from the observer to the animals (or group of animals) in the form of either perpendicular distance from the transect line or radial distance from the point count station is measured. Then the collected data is analysed using the computer software 'DISTANCE' (Thomas et al., 1998, 2002). This software is quite user-friendly and offers a wide range of analysis options.

The merits and limitations of distance sampling technique are mentioned in Table 6.8:

Table 6.8 Benefits and Limitations of Distance Sampling Method

Merits	*Limitations*
❒ Efficient way to estimate absolute density or abundance.	❒ Require accurate measurement of the distance of focal animal (or group of animals) from the observer.

(Contd...)

Table 6.8 Benefits and Limitations of Distance Sampling Method (*Contd...*)

Merits	*Limitations*
❐ Considers the fact that species detect ability varies over distance and with habitat. ❐ Some species are observed from greater distance, and in some habitats animals are more detectable than others. This method accounts for differences in levels of 'conspicuousness' or 'detect ability' between habitats and species. ❐ Allows for comparisons between species, and within species, across different habitats.	❐ Expertise is essential to measure the distance of many animals accurately before they move from their initial position. ❐ Large amount of data need to be generated for reliable analysis of abundance. ❐ Prior knowledge of the DISTANCE software is necessary.

(vii) Waterhole Census Method: Water hole census is a direct census method, which is used to count large animals (herbivores, carnivores and omnivores) visiting the waterholes present within the study area. This method is well suited for the habitats where the water holes are not numerous, but widely distributed throughout the study area. This method is often implemented in arid and semi arid wilderness region of this country to count various mega fauna. In other areas, dry season is the appropriate time to conduct water hole census, as during this period water is the main limiting factor and most animal present in the area visit these natural or artificial source of water to quench their thirst. In brief, water hole census should be done during the period of minimum water availability in the study area. It has also been recommended that this census should be carried out continuously for a period of 24 hours, preferably during full moon so that every individual animal of different species visiting the water hole during day and moonlit night could be properly recorded. This exercise must be repeated for 3 – 4 consecutive days to obtain a mean value for each species. The population estimation from this data is based on the assumption that a linear relationship exists between the number of animals visiting the water hole per unit time and the population size of this species in the area. Despite the fact that some animals may visit the water holes more than once in a 24 hour span, it is obvious that animals with a higher abundance will have more animals drinking than animals with small population.

Operational Procedure

First an extensive survey should be carried out to locate all the water holes present in the study area. Then certain water holes should be selected (either randomly or systematically) from different habitat types of the study area and preferably be located wide apart from one another. If the water hole selected for census is being closely situated then some individuals may visit both the water holes in different times of the day and result in double counting. On the other hand, if the water hole is not selected from a particular area, then the animals present in that particular habitat will not be represented in the final analysis and result in biased estimation of diversity and abundance. Once the water holes are selected, a *machaan* needs to be constructed in a suitable position adjacent to the waterholes, preferably on natural vantage points (like blinds on trees, large rocks etc.). At least two observers should be able to sit on the *machaan* to observe the animals visiting the site to drink. Census can also be carried from tourist watchtowers, wherever available. Out of the two observers, one is usually expert in animal identification and the other person is usually helper. One forest guard is usually present on every *machaan* for safety purposes. Observers should have a clear and uninterrupted view of the waterholes from their vantage hides to keep score of every animal visiting the waterhole. A pair of binoculars is used to identify species during times of poor visibility.

Species of the animal, total number per group, time of arrival at the waterhole, time when the first member of the group starts drinking water, time when the last member of the group would finish drinking and the time when all the members of the group would disappear from the waterhole are the information commonly collected during waterhole census. Data is then tabulated to specify the abundance of different animals in the study area. Waterhole counts are also suited to obtain data on population demographics (sex and age ratios) of various species, which are not as easily obtained by the other census techniques. The data generated from waterhole census also helps to understand the number of animals depending on a particular water hole and to explore the extent to which different species overlap in the use of water resources. Moreover, if studied for several years, then data of a particular water hole for successive years can be compared to determine species diversity variations at waterholes, as well as, to comment on the fluctuation in population trend of a particular species provided geo-climatic and other habitat features remain constant.

Precautions

The following precautions need to be taken to make the waterhole census more accurate:

- Personnel should be alert and carry out the census continuously for 24 hour period to ensure that no animal visiting the water hole during the survey period is missed and remains unrecorded. To ensure this, waterhole census usually begins in the evening, so that the survey personnel can have adequate rest and sleep during the day and remain awake in the night.
- Personnel should be adequately trained to properly identify the animals coming to waterholes not only in day times but also in the dim moon light at night hours. If fund is available then night vision cameras may be used to complement the data and reduce the chance of misidentification of animals, as well as, missing any animal visiting the water hole.
- The *machaan* preferably be located at a distance between 200 m – 500 m from the water hole and should be constructed in such a way so that their presence does not hinder the animals to visit the waterhole.
- Personnel present on the *machaan* should be absolutely quiet and avoid using any perfume, smoking or drinking alcohol. They should also avoid lighting fires at the base or on the *machaan* (to cook or to make a cup of tea) and not even light up a flash light during the entire span of survey. Because, unnatural smell, light or any other unusual activities often deter the animals to visit the waterholes.
- While data analysis, prior knowledge about the habit and frequency of drinking of different animals is essential. However, this information largely varies with the age, sex and body condition of the individuals of even same species, based on the habitat or the study area, as well as, depending on the season and weather conditions (temperature, humidity, cloud cover, etc.) of the day when the survey is being conducted.

Merits and Limitations

The merits and limitations of waterhole census are briefly mentioned in the following table (Table 6.9):

Table 6.9 Merits and Limitations of Waterhole Census

Merits	*Limitations*
❒ Simple direct census method to assess the abundance of mega fauna. ❒ Give a crude idea of abundance and diversity. ❒ Population trend can be estimated if regular, simultaneous and continuous (24 – 48 hour) counts are performed (usually at full moon) from hides overlooking a permanent waterhole. ❒ Waterhole census help to assess the spatial overlap of different wild species in the use of waterholes located at different habitat within the study area. ❒ Waterhole censuses also throw light on the sex-ratio of adult male to female of a species.	❒ Waterhole counts are only feasible during the dry season and in the absence of other nearby waterholes and/or constant flowing rivers; but are useless in the raining season, or in areas with constant running rivers. ❒ Not suitable for small animals. ❒ Very time and labour intensive. ❒ Require dedicated, reliable and knowledgeable people doing the counts to prevent the same herds concentrating around water holes being counted more than once. ❒ Knowledge about the habit and frequency of drinking of different animals is often unavailable.

(viii) Quadrat Sampling Method: Quadrat sampling is a technique generally used to study the presence or absence of species, numbers of organisms, or the percentage cover of each species within square sampling units.

Size, shape, number and location of the quadrats: If the study site is large enough, then quadrats are randomly placed. In most cases quadrats are generally square in shape. However, the shape of the sampling units may vary (such as rectangular areas) based on the topography and vegetation pattern of the study area. An animal or plant present at the edge of a quadrat creates a dilemma for the researcher, as whether it should be counted or not, and often tends to be counted. This might lead to an overestimation of the abundance. Therefore, edge is a major criterion and needs to be carefully considered while determining the shape of the quadrat. The shape showing minimum ratio of edge length to inner area should preferably be selected. The ratio of edge length to inner area changes as follows: circle < square < rectangle. Therefore, theoretically using a circular sampling plot would minimize edge effects, but the area of a circle is more difficult to calculate than the area of a square. On some occasions the shape of the quadrat may be a long, thin rectangle in order to maintain habitat homogeneity (i.e. to ensure that the habitat type within the quadrat remains constant). In some other studies, quadrat may even be of some other unique shape as this shape has been used in previous studies. So, by keeping the shape of the quadrat intact, some comparative analysis could be made. The shape of a quadrat, thus, can vary depending on what is being sampled and where. But, once the shape of the quadrat is determined, the same shape should be used throughout the study.

Apart from shape, appropriate size of the quadrat is another very important parameter for any survey. The size of a quadrat can vary from 0.25 cm × 0.25 cm to 100 m × 100 m. Small quadrats can be surveyed relatively quickly, but yield a smaller individual sample of habitat. Therefore, larger numbers of quadrats are necessary to cover the entire habitat. On the other hand, larger quadrats provide a larger amount of data and usually require a smaller number of samples to represent the habitat, but require more time and effort to conduct a survey. Size of the quadrat is determined to suit the objective of the sampling taking the practical constraints (such as, habitat of the study area, the focal organism, time and effort limitations etc.) into consideration. The minimum size for each quadrat can be determined using the 'Species-Area Curve' method. This involves beginning with a small quadrat and counting the number of different species within the quadrat. The size of the quadrat is slowly increased and the count is repeated. Then a graph of quadrat size vs. species number is drawn and the point where the curve flattens out indicates the minimum quadrat size.

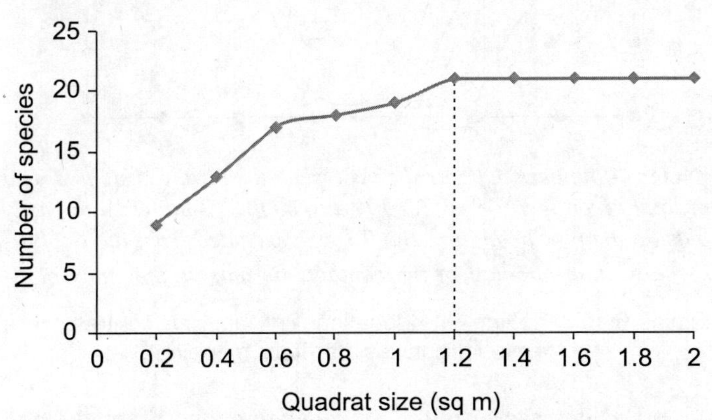

FIGURE 6.8 Species-Area Curve to determine the size of a quadrat.

The line in the hypothetical Species-Area Curve (shown in Figure 6.8) levels off after 1.2 m, which means that for this particular study the minimum size of the quadrat to be used has to be of 1.2 m ×1.2 m. It is very essential to keep the size and shape of the quadrat consistent, in order to compare samples from different places and/or times.

It is obvious, that more quadrats would be more representative but there are some constraints of time, manpower and other resources. So the next question comes *how many quadrats are enough for a particular study area?* Generally the number of quadrats should ensure that approximately 20 percent of the total area of the study site is sampled. The number of quadrat is usually determined by the following formula:

$$\text{Number of quadrat} = \frac{20\% \text{ area of the total study area}}{\text{Area of each quadrat}}$$

For instance, if the study area is of 1000 sq m, then the quadrats should cover at least 200 sq m area (i.e., 20 percent of 1000 sq m). Now, if the size of each quadrat determined by the Species-Area curve for this particular study area is found to be 5 m × 5 m (i.e. 25 sq m), then eight quadrat (i.e. 200/25 = 8) need to be placed in this entire study area.

Commonly the quadrats are positioned at random (see *random sampling*) in the study area (Figure 6.9), which means that every potential point in the study area has an equal chance of being selected for the sample. But, quadrat may also be placed within the study area following other statistical and even non-statistical sampling methods.

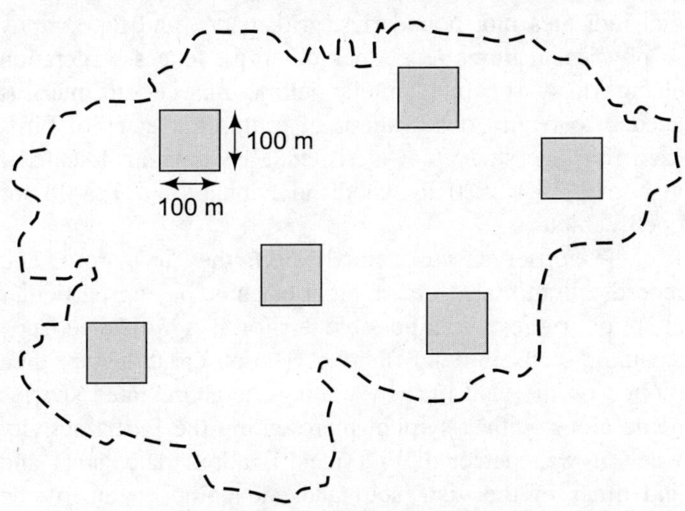

FIGURE 6.9 Use of randomly placed quadrats to determine the species abundance and diversity.

Quadrat sampling methods are generally used to record the abundance or density of a particular species of plants and other slow moving animals. For each quadrat sampling plot, following data can be recorded (Whitworth et al., 2007):

- ❒ ***Vegetation cover:*** the most common data generated from any quadrat is the vegetation cover. It is estimated by measuring the percentage of the quadrat covered by each plant type. This also gives a measurement of plant abundance.
- ❒ ***Species density:*** Species density is assessed by counting the number of different species found within the quadrat. The mean value for all quadrats is then calculated giving a total number of a particular species per unit area.
- ❒ ***Species frequency:*** Species frequency is determined by calculating the percentage of quadrats where a particular species is present. Such

species frequency can be separately calculated for every species found in all the quadrats present within the study area.

- ***Species diversity:*** The total numbers of species found in all the quadrats present within the study area are then used to measure the diversity of the study site.

(ix) Territory Mapping: Territory mapping involves repeated visits to a nearly square gridded study plot (usually 0.01–1 sq. km). Square plots minimize the length of its perimeter and reduce the number of borderline territories that are partly in and partly outside the plot. By using larger plots, the investigator can detect more species, obtain more accurate density estimates for the less common species and reduce the length of the perimeter per unit of plot area. But, the plot should be as large as the investigator can handle efficiently. A base map of the study plot should be prepared that indicates plot boundaries, grid marks, and topography or physical features (e.g., rock outcrops, fences, vegetation changes). A separate simple outline map (visit map) is needed to record observations of multiple species of birds each time the study plot is visited. Recommended scale of visit map is 1:2500 in woodland habitats and 1:5000 for open habitats.

The observer walks slowly along the survey route and records all animals through sight or calls, paying particular attention to those with possible territorial significance, such as singing, chasing and fighting. The observations are then plotted on the visit map by writing the abbreviated species name along with a symbol representing the bird's activity when it was detected. Plot identification, date, start and end times of the visit, start and end points, name of the observer, weather conditions, the time of the sighting and a symbol for sex or age should also be mentioned on those visit maps.

Individual visits should be made in the morning, preferably in the first 3 – 4 hours after sunrise, as during this time territorial behaviour is normally at its peak and most animals are relatively easy to detect. Moreover, surveys should preferably be done on clear and calm days with no rain. It is also recommended that not more than one visit should be made to a particular study site in a day. Several visits (10 visits to a closed habitat and 8 visits to an open habitat) at regular intervals are required to gather sufficient data. Such visits are usually carried out during the breeding season, when most terrestrial species within the study area establish and defend territories and manifest peak of territorial activity. Therefore, territory mapping method should be accomplished in the shortest period that includes the breeding times of the majority of species.

Data thus accumulated over a period of days or weeks and plotting them on visit maps eventually result in clusters of plotted locations of each species, which are then interpreted as distinct coveys and activity centres of territorial individuals of the focal species. A cluster should be counted as a territory if it consists of at least 3 observations of which 2 have territorial significance. Population density of these terrestrial species is determined by counting the number of occupied territories in a circumscribed area. For example, territories of an avian species as indicated by sight and sound contacts accumulated during five visits to study plot is shown in Figure 6.10.

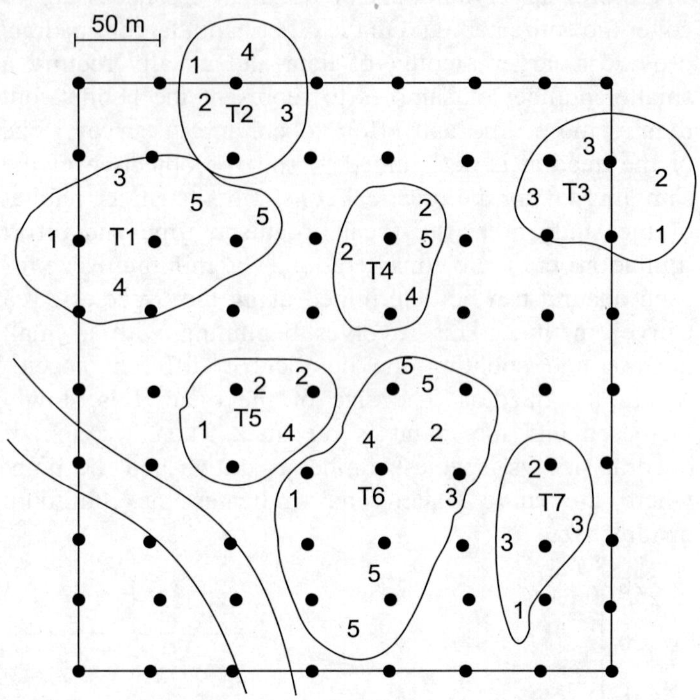

[**Note:** *Numbers indicate the visit when the bird was sighted. Out of total seven territories (T1–T7), three (T1, T2 and T3) lie partly outside the plot boundary. But T3 was excluded from the analysis as more than one-half of the contacts lie outside the study plot.*]

FIGURE 6.10 Plotting the locations of activity centres of a territorial species (territory mapping).

Besides, description of vegetation on the study plot is another important aspect of territory-mapping studies. Vegetation structure of the habitat is determined by random (or stratified random) sample plots. Descriptions of vegetation include information on ground cover, canopy cover, shrub density, canopy height, and the density, basal area, and frequency of trees. Then the territory boundaries were superimposed over the vegetation map of the sampling sites. Thus, characteristics of individual territories were determined (Figure 6.10).

Applications

This method is often costly and demands substantial effort and is, therefore, suitable only for intensive surveys in small study areas. Besides, territory mapping works best with species that are highly detectable. This technique is widely used to estimate the abundance of songbirds, woodpeckers, and owls, but is not suitable for counting waterfowl, seabirds, or colonial species. In most applications only the number of territorial males is determined. Rosene (1957) advocated this method for assessing the abundance of game birds by territorial morning and noon calls of the males. Saharia (1978) opined that the number of highly territorial animals (like tiger and leopard) can be better ascertained by territory-mapping method using cooperation census techniques, which can provide fairly accurate information if properly done. According to him, this is most suited for tiger census as the tigers are mostly solitary and highly territorial animals. Noon (1981) opined that this sampling method is quite useful in direct comparison between structural habitats of the species if sufficient data are generated, and is amenable to studies in both non-forest (< 25 percent cover by trees) and forest habitats. Presently, remote sensing, GIS and wildlife telemetry, play very important role in territory mapping in many wild fauna.

Precautions

A pilot study on a small area is recommended before anyone adopts territory mapping method. Because researchers without any experience of territory mapping procedure may face problems to determine the location of birds that are heard but not seen, as well as, to differentiate the simultaneously calling individuals of same species. They also may face difficulties to complete visits in a reasonable period of time. Therefore, experience of a pilot survey is indispensable to reduce confusion and increase sampling efficiency. It is also essential to be thoroughly familiar with the procedure of recording data in territory mapping method before adopting this method in any wildlife study.

Limitations

The major limitation of this method is that only males of most territorial species are recorded and can only be carried out in the breeding season when the manifestation of territorial behaviour is optimum. Females, juveniles and non-territorial birds are not detected consistently enough to map their activity centres. Changes in territory boundaries during the period of implementation of this method and the territorial behaviour of migrants are two other major events which make the territory mapping method even more complicated (Oelke, 1981). Migrants may still be passing through southern India while the breeding activities of many resident territorial species reach a peak. In such scenario, song and territorial behaviour of the passing migrants make territory mapping complicated. Data interpretation and plotting of territories can be a highly subjective exercise as territory mapping of one person may vary with another using the same dataset.

(x) Arial Survey: Arial survey technique was propounded by Erickson and Siniff and first implemented to study brown bears (Erickson and Siniff, 1963). They counted the focal animals thrice a day for nine consecutive days. Population size of brown bear was then determined by the formula:

$$N = 2n_K - n_{K-1}$$

where, N = total number of individuals in a population; n_K is the highest count and n_{K-1} is the next highest count.

Aerial surveys are usually done from small aircrafts flying low over a particular habitat and are usually adopted to count animals in open habitats. For example, this method can be used to count large mammals (like deers, antelopes or other large animals) in open grasslands as they can easily be seen from the aircraft flying over the habitat. Literature reveals that nest counts of large raptors have also been carried out using aerial surveys.

In India, aerial surveys can be adopted to observe and estimate abundance of several medium and large sized animals present in the open and dry wilderness areas of western India, open floodplains of the Ganges and Brahmaputra valleys, alpine regions and cold deserts in the trans-Himalayas. However, this method is unsuitable for wilderness areas having high tree density and close canopy cover and dense undergrowth as in case of tropical evergreen forests in Himalayas and Western Ghats (Rodgers, 1991). Besides, most of the protected areas of this country are with thick and close canopy cover of forests, for which animals present inside those dense habitats are often not viewed by the observer sitting in a moving aircraft and thus making this method unsuitable for many Indian forests (Tak and Lamba, 1978). Furthermore, this method cannot be used to survey small and secretive fauna as they are difficult to locate and identify from a moving aircraft. Above all, the permission and cost of flight of small aircrafts are other limiting factors to adopt this method.

2. Indirect Census Techniques

Indirect census techniques are suitable for species with very low densities, which are difficult to see due to poor habitat visibility or cryptic behaviour of the animals. These methods are suitable for obtaining relative indices of population and are often used to study carnivores, small and nocturnal mammals, large mammals in dense habitats. However, these methods rarely yield a good estimate of actual population. Most popular indirect census methods are: call count, dung, pellet, nests, burrows or pugmark counts.

(i) Track Count: Track count is one of the most ancient animal census techniques, where the animal abundance is assessed just by seeing the number of marks along their tracks on ground. The tracks of animals were often used by the erstwhile hunters to follow the herds for hunting. In addition to the numbers, tracks of many animals also convey information on the age (adult, juvenile or newborn) and sex (male or female) of the individual. Pugmark census is one kind of track count and was extensively used to count tigers in India. Track count can only be carried out in grounds which are impressionable enough to permit the marking of tracks. So, this method is inoperative in areas of thick forest, undergrowths, long grasses or hard grounds. Besides, interpretations of the result are also difficult and require well-trained experts.

(ii) Dung Surveys: Droppings are considered as one of the most confirmatory parameters of the animal's presence within a particular habitat. Therefore, 'dung count' (also termed as pellet count) is an indirect census method which is frequently being used to assess animal abundance. This method is often useful for the secretive species which are difficult to see. The collected droppings during this census method may later be subjected to further analysis in the laboratory to comment on the diet, health condition and also the genetic make-up of the animal.

According to Rodgers (1991), dung count can give a fairly reliable population estimate if the following assumptions are met:

- ***Dung or droppings of different species need to be identified properly.*** The best way to identify is to actually collect the dung in a transparent bag when the animal is actually seen to defecate. Droppings thus collected should be preserved for future reference in field when the droppings are found, but the animal is not seen. Size (large or small)), shape (round or elongated), pattern of indentations or protuberances at the end of each pellets are the key features of differentiation.
- ***Different groups of droppings should be properly recognized and separated.*** Animals usually defecate in a stationary position and dung is deposited at one spot. But, if the animal moves while defecating, then dung may be found to be present over a few metres in the direction where the animal moved. So, if droppings found in a small area are similar in size, shape, colour or condition, then they might be assumed to be from same individual. Hence, separating dung of same species in different groups requires a fair bit of experience.
- ***Sampling units (transects/quadrats) should run across diverse micro habitats.*** The sample plots should be designed to allow easy searching of all representative habitat of the study area.
- ***Sampling units (transects/quadrats) need to be adequately large so*** that at least one or two dung groups are present. Too large plots demand for excessive time or large number of field personnel to cover it, while if the sampling plots are too small then dung may not be present in many of them resulting in inadequate data for analysis.
- ***Entire area of the sampling unit should be thoroughly searched.*** Prior information on the estimated defecation rate of the focal species and knowledge on the rate of dung degradation in the study area are two important parameters for these surveys.

Dung surveys through pellet count is often carried out in cold and dry regions where the dung does not degrade quickly, remains in actual shape and are often found in proper condition for further analysis. Therefore, dung surveys are often used in wildlife surveys to assess the abundance of many species of herbivores and carnivores of temperate regions. On the contrary, this method is seldom adopted in wildlife studies of the tropical countries. Because, (i) dung degrades quickly in tropical humid conditions, where many other creatures (like dung beetles) expedite the process and (ii) forest floors in tropical region are often covered with dense undergrowths. So, in these tropical conditions, finding dung of a particular species is quite difficult and time consuming, unless the animal defecates in the open fields or muddy stretches present within the forests. As a consequence, dung is often unsuitable when they are found from the wilderness areas in the tropics. This method is also suitable for Rabbits and Gallinaceous birds.

(iii) Total Capture or Extermination: Total capture or Extermination is a method where capturing or killing of total population is usually done. This is practiced to eliminate the old or diseased population before introducing the fresh one in the shooting preserves of some of the countries where hunting is legally permitted (Tak and Lamba, 1978). As hunting is not permitted in this country, so this technique cannot be used in India.

6.2 BIRD CENSUS METHODS

Birds live in a variety of habitats. Density and diversity are two crucial aspects of many avian surveys and serve as important indicators of habitat quality (Javed, 1996). Birds are easily seen in open habitats like open grasslands or agricultural fields, while direct sighting is poor for birds living under dense vegetation cover inside the forest. They also have varied social structure. Some may be gregarious and live in flocks, whereas others may be solitary or may form pairs. Behaviour of different species of avifauna also varies strikingly. Certain birds are very bold while others are shy and skulking. Therefore, employing a particular method to count such a wild variety of birds is neither feasible nor recommended.

The important considerations during bird surveys are summarised below:

1. Selection of Proper Method: Proper method most suitable to achieve the research goal and appropriate for individual bird species and its habitat is to be selected first. This is usually done through review of existing literatures.

2. Selection of Time: As per objective of the study seasonality and timing of count is important. Often short surveys suffer from seasonal or temporal bias. For example, water bird surveys are to be carried out during breeding season along with the wintering season to document waterbird diversity of the site.

3. Selection of Site: Sites often selected to carry out ornithological studies fall under four broad categories, which include (i) known site of ornithological importance (such as Important Bird Areas or IBAs); (ii) areas within the flyway zone of migratory birds; (iii) potentially good sites which are not yet surveyed; and (iv) sites under great anthropological interferences.

The bird census techniques are largely diverse and need to be properly selected. Various types of direct and indirect methods are adopted in avifaunal surveys depending on the species, habitat, terrain type and other ecological parameters (Javed and Kaul, 2002). In single species survey, knowledge and good understanding of the bird behaviour, as well as, biology of the focal species is essential to adopt the best method (Javed and Kaul, 2002).

Some popular methods like distance sampling, line transect, point count, territory mapping are also frequently used for survey of birds. In addition to those, some other methods like call count, artificial call playback survey, Encounter rate survey, McKinnon's species richness method, timed species count, mist netting are used to study species richness and nest counts are adopted during breeding bird surveys. Some of these methods particularly suitable for avian surveys are elaborated below:

1. Call Count

In many species of birds, the males consistently produce large calls during the early part of the breeding season to advertise their presence and attract mate, as well as, for the purpose of territorial defence. The existing population at a particular area can be estimated by counting the numbers of calling males. This technique is popularly known as call count (see Text Box 6.3).

Call count is an easy, simple and non-invasive indirect census method to get a fair estimate of bird population by listening to the calls of different individuals, at a particular time of the year. This method is particularly useful for the species which are relatively easily heard than seen. Call counts are widely used on a variety of species, particularly in the survey of Galliformes (Kaul and Howman 1992; Khaling et al., 1999), where the males produce distinct loud calls audible from about 300 m away. Call count surveys is usually most successful when surveyors are familiar with the calls of all species, likely to be found in a study area.

Text Box 6.3: Call Count Protocol

Data Collection: Call counts are usually carried out simultaneously by a number of observers from strategic points, which are selected before the survey begins and should be spread throughout the study area. Observers first synchronize their watches and reach these predetermined strategic points well before dawn. The distance between two observers is decided by the intensity, as well as, based on the maximum audible distance of the call.

As the birds start calling, soon the observers note the time, assess the approximate distance and direction of each calling individual and accordingly mark the relative position on a datasheet. Call counts are usually done for a span of 15–20 minutes after the listening the first call so that double counting of bird and subsequent overestimation of abundance could be avoided. Such call counts should be done repeatedly for about a week in the successive dawn hours.

Analysis: Calling locations have to be noted down and corrections are to be made with the help of information provided by distance, direction and time of the call by different observers to avoid over counting. Thus, suspected double counts are removed by summarizing information from all observers and subsequently the minimum number of calling birds in a given area on a particular day is obtained. Now using mathematical model an index of density for that particular site can be worked out.

The area within which calls are heard is usually estimated in two ways. The common one represent the use of fixed radius (generally of 300 m) and any calling bird believed to be outside this circular plot should not be considered for analysis. The other method include variable radius and the distance to the furthest bird heard calling forms the radius of the circle within which all calling birds are recorded. The density index of a point is calculated by dividing the number of callers heard calling by the area of the circular plot. The total number of birds heard calling in the total area monitored by a series of observers becomes the index of density for that site.

Like many other survey methods, call counts also have certain merits and limitations, which are briefly mentioned in Table 6.10:

Table 6.10 Merits and Limitations of Call Count

Merits	*Limitations*
❐ Quick, non-invasive and indirect census technique. ❐ Very useful for species those are highly vocal and make loud and distinct calls, but are very difficult to see (pheasants, owlets etc). ❐ Provides fairly accurate abundance estimates. ❐ Does not require much instruments. ❐ If performed at same location over the years, then might reflect the trend of the abundance of breeding birds.	❐ This survey method can only be used for the species which make distinct and loud calls. ❐ Call counts cannot be executed in the non-breeding period of the focal species, as the males usually emit loud and frequent mating calls during the breeding season. ❐ This method demands for a well-trained observer who can properly identify different types of calls of single species (viz. normal call, mating call or alarm calls) and also distinguish between the calls of different species. ❐ Calling birds may not necessarily be always in monogamous pairs. In case of solitary calling males or in polygamous species (where one male is accompanied by many females), the population cannot be accurately measured and the estimate may reflect only density indices of calling groups. ❐ The calling male often shift his position after initial calling and might call from a different location within his own territory, which might lead to double counting for the same birds, if the call count session is prolonged. ❐ Inexperience observer may find it difficult to get used to the calls and properly judge the direction and distance, in order to accurately mark the location of the calling males.

2. Artificial Call Playback Method

The primary method of call count has been modified in certain field conditions and is termed as 'artificial call back' or 'play back method'. In this modified method, the vocalizations of the species of interest are broadcasted and the responses were noted. Hence, to implement this method, first the calls are recorded using a hand held tape recorder with a microphone closely placed to the calling individual of the focal species. Recordings of the calls and songs of many species are now also available commercially. Then the call is played back within the study area through an audio device (a simple hand-held loudspeaker). A short length of call can be repeated continuously in a loop for as long as is required. After an initial play back for one minute, the observer needss to wait for 30 seconds for a response either through listening a call back or through sighting. If no response is received, then the artificial call should be broadcasted once more. If no response is received after broadcasting two such playbacks, then it may be inferred that the bird is absent up to certain range of particular point station where the artificial playback was distinctly audible. But, it is very important to keep disturbance to a minimum, so that observers' presence and call playback does not affect the natural behaviour of the animal. The males usually respond to these broadcasted artificial calls and thus counted during the surveys. This method has been used to increase the number of detections per unit effort for elusive species which are known to respond to such a stimulus.

Such playback of vocalisations has been widely used to survey birds. Some species of birds are difficult to see or hear, particularly those that have skulking behaviour, live in dense habitats, are nocturnal or crepuscular or nest in burrows. The probability of detecting these species can be increased by broadcasting their vocalization and listening to their responses. For instance, this method was used in the survey of forest owlets to confirm the presence of these birds in a forested habitat.

Merits and limitations of 'Artificial Call Playback' technique are described in Table 6.11 below:

Table 6.11 Merits and Limitations of Artificial Call Playback Technique

Merits	*Limitations*
❐ Simple use of tape playback to detect the focal species. ❐ Practiced to assess population of elusive birds with loud vocalization along with other animal taxa (like amphibians etc.). ❐ Useful in monitoring changes in population size.	❐ Time consuming. ❐ Requires specialized equipment and training for handling the captured animals, as well as, careful analysis of data. ❐ Frequent and regular artificial call playback might interfere with their communication process and also degrade the value of this auditory signal for the species.

3. Encounter Rate Survey

This is a very simple method to obtain a quick list of birds and a basic idea about their abundance. Encounter rate surveys are often done in hills, dense forests and other difficult terrains where the existing trails or paths are used for data collection (Javed and Kaul, 2002). 'Encounter rate' is assessed by calculating the number of species recorded per unit effort. The 'encounter rate' is often expressed as number of individual observed per unit effort (Burnham et al., 1980). Transects laid on roads from where encounter rate is calculated is also termed as 'encounter transects' by Fuller and Mosher (1987). The effort is expressed in terms of either spatial distance traversed (as in case of encounter transects) or time spent by the observer. Distance is measured using a pedometer and total time spent can be determined by careful recording of start and end time. Encounter rate data is often analysed in SPECDIR.BAS software (Ludwig and Reynolds, 1988).

Encounter rates are very useful method to quickly generate a preliminary index of species abundance. In single species surveys, encounter rate are compared between different sites to stratify the abundance of the focal species within the study area. Ethier (1993) opined that such encounter rates provide an insight on the general distribution of raptors and are suitable for single species survey. Encounter rate has been used as an index of population density of spotted owlets (Forsman et al., 1977) and western tragopan (Javed and Kaul, 2002). Ghosh (2003) measured the encounter rates in terms of number of birds per km to measure the relative abundance of three species of tragopans in parts of North-East India. Similarly, Mazumdar (2013) assessed 'encounter rate' to stratify the distribution and relative abundance of black kites (*Milvus migrans govinda*) in urban areas of Kolkata, India.

In multispecies survey, the number of individuals of different species encountered can be used to assess species richness and diversity of a particular area. But in multispecies surveys, some additional information like visibility, weather parameters, habitat conditions etc., should also be recorded. Moreover, encounter rate obtained in multispecies studies can also be used to compare species richness and diversity between different sites, as well as, for the same site over the years provided the amount of effort remains constant.

4. McKinnon's Species Richness Method

McKinnon and Phillips (1993) developed this method to quickly estimate the species richness and composition in an area. In this method, the observer walks along a trail and counts the number of individual birds belonging to each species, until a specific number of species (say 20 species) are obtained. How many species are to be recorded at one go are to be decided at the beginning of the survey based on the overall richness of avifauna in the study area and this number has to be maintained for every list prepared throughout the study period. Once the predetermined number of species is recorded, the observer records the time taken to prepare the list. In this method the observer should be able to quickly detect and identify the birds. After one such list is complete, the observer should move further away from the position where the list was completed. This is very crucial to ensure that all lists are independent and the same birds are not recorded repeatedly. This process is repeated unless 10–15 such lists are prepared for a particular area. In heterogeneous habitats, all habitats should be covered and separate lists should be prepared for each habitat type. Number of lists in each habitat type must be proportional to their respective proportion of land cover in the study area. Commonly occurring species will be recorded on several lists (Javed and Kaul, 2002).

Frequency of occurrence of a particular species is determined by the number of times it reappears in subsequent lists. This gives a preliminary idea about the relative abundance of different species within the study area. The average time required to prepare one list (i.e. to record say 20 species of birds) and the number of individual for each species are used to measure the richness of avifauna in the area. This method is simple, quick, does not require sophisticated instruments and can be easily adopted in varied habitats (like grasslands, forests etc.) including difficult terrains.

5. Timed Species Count

Timed Species Count is a relatively simple method which considers the time taken to detect a species as a measure of its abundance and depends on the hypothesis that rare birds require more time for detection while the common birds are detected relatively quickly (Javed and Kaul, 2002). During Timed Species Counts, the observation period is subdivided into six equal time periods. The duration of each visit is usually one-hour, but may be longer or shorter based on the availability of time. Whatever be the duration of the visit, it has to be divided into six equal time periods. The observer slowly moves through the study area. In the first time period all the species observed are recorded. Then for the subsequent time periods of the survey observer records only the species not seen earlier. Therefore, a species may be seen more than once but, is recorded only once in the time period when it was first noticed. Therefore, species once recorded, should be ignored even it is noticed afterwards. The observer should visit different parts of the study area at least 10–15 times and should cover at least 1 sq km area during every visit (Pomeroy and Tengecho, 1986).

For analysis of the Timed Species Count data, all the recorded species are ranked according to their respective time-period lists. For example, species ranks for one-hour observation period are accorded in the following way:

Time-period when the Species was first seen	*Rank of the Species in TSC analysis*
Observed between 01–10 minute	6
Observed between 11–20 minute	5
Observed between 21–30 minute	4
Observed between 31–40 minute	3
Observed between 41–50 minute	2
Observed between 51–60 minute	1
Species not seen	0

The mean value of ranks given to a species given during all visits provides an index of its relative abundance in the study area. Collection and analysis of data in the Timed Species Count has been illustrated below with an imaginary data set (Table 6.12):

Table 6.12 Providing Rank to Bird Species in a Hypothetical Dataset using Timed Species Count Method

Common Name of Birds	*Visit 1*	*Visit 2*	*Visit 3*	*Total Rank Score*	*Mean Rank Score*	*Species Rank*
Small Green Bee-eater	6	6	5	17	5.666667	2
Rose-ringed Parakeet	3	0	1	4	1.333333	13
Pied Myna	6	3	4	13	4.333333	6
Purple Sunbird	6	3	3	12	4	7
Spotbill	3	5	6	14	4.666667	5
Little Cormorant	1	1	2	4	1.333333	13
Grey Heron	2	1	3	6	2	11
Purple Heron	2	3	6	11	3.666667	8
Red Wattled Lapwing	6	6	5	17	5.666667	2
Red vented Bulbul	3	2	6	11	3.666667	8
Hoopoe	1	1	1	3	1	14
Intermediate Egret	1	2	2	5	1.666667	12
Rufous Turtled Dove	2	3	4	9	3	10
Ring Dove	5	3	2	10	3.333333	9
Black Drongo	6	6	6	18	6	1
House Sparrow	1	0	0	1	0.333333	15
Pond Heron	5	5	4	14	4.666667	5
Ashy Prinia	6	4	5	15	5	4
Hume's Warbler	1	0	0	1	0.333333	15
Common Myna	6	5	5	16	5.333333	3

Timed Species Counts are often done initially in large areas to efficiently identify few intensive study sites with high avian diversity and richness. Merits and limitations of Timed Species Count are given below (Table 6.13):

Table 6.13 Merits and Limitations of Timed Species Count

Merits	*Limitations*
❐ This is quick, simple and non-invasive method. ❐ Relative abundance of different species within an area can be measured. ❐ Richness and diversity of species between two different areas can be compared.	❐ Provides very crude relative indices of species richness and abundance. ❐ Analysis and interpretation of data generated through Timed Species Counts require special care as the detectability of different species varies in different habitats. ❐ Abundance of a species assessed through Timed Species Counts is often influenced by the behaviour of the bird species. For example, skulking species may not be noticed quickly even if they are present in large numbers; flocking species may result in lower relative indices of abundance than widely dispersed bird species.

6. Mist-netting

Mist-netting is a specialized technique for avian survey and is frequently used to survey small to medium size birds. This method is generally used to survey birds in a forested habitat with dense undergrowth where other direct census methods are often unsuitable due to poor visibility and fast moving nature of the small feathered creatures. 'Mist-nets' are thin and almost invisible nylon nets which are strategically set up (usually up to a height of 3 m) between two small habitat patches where regular and frequent bird movements are noticed. Once the mist-net is being set up, the observer leaves the area and return after a certain time period. The birds entangled in the mist-net are then carefully removed, identified, measurements of their several physical traits are taken and often ringed before releasing them back in the wild in their original habitat. Ringing is done by putting light aluminum rings or coloured plastic bands with specific codes imprinted on them. Subsequently, mist-netting of bird in a particular area and carefully observing the ringed and unringed individuals among the captured birds can yield the abundance of a particular avian species following the principles of capture-mark-recapture method (Rodger, 1991).

The merits and limitations of mist-netting are briefly mentioned in the following table (Table 6.14):

Table 6.14 Merits and Limitations of Mist-Netting

Merits	*Limitations*
❒ Suitable to study small and fast moving birds in forests with dense undergrowth, where other direct census methods are unsuitable. ❒ This method is most suitable for identifying and counting the cryptic/skulking species. ❒ Captured birds may be ringed for further individual identification and to avoid repeat counts. ❒ Provide indices of abundance expressed in terms of capture rate (i.e. number of birds of a particular species caught per mist-net per hour). ❒ Many physical traits (like length, wing span, feather condition, number of primary feather etc.) of the captured bird can be measured accurately.	❒ Require skill and experience of the surveyor to set up and use the mist-nets, as well as, for proper handling of the birds captured in the mist-nets. ❒ Removing the birds from the mist-net and handling the small birds (while taking body measurement or ringing) should be carefully done without inflicting any damage to the birds. ❒ Require permission from the competent authorities. ❒ Frequent mist-netting of birds should be avoided as it may pose threat to the entire population and the birds may leave the habitat. ❒ Often expensive and require large amount of effort to survey the entire area as only a few species of a small vegetated area is sampled in a single mist-net.

7. Nest Count

Nest count is performed for many species of birds, particularly those who nest in colonies. The breeding population of a colonial species is easily estimated using this method. The nests situated in the outer most part of the breeding colony are mapped to calculate the total area. Then the total number of breeding birds and estimated area of the breeding colony might be used to calculate the density of the breeding population using the following formula:

Density of the breeding colony

$$= \frac{\text{Total number of individual in the breeding colony}}{\text{Total area of the breeding colony}}$$

It is to be noted that the birds are very sensitive during the breeding season and might abandon their nest if disturbed. So, during nest counts adequate care should be taken to minimize the disturbance to the breeding pair at nest. Therefore, individuals present on the nests should always be counted from a suitable distance and preferably from nearby vantage points so that the breeding pairs are not disturbed. For cliff nesting birds (like raptors), nest counts are made from other cliffs present on the opposite side using a spotting scope or binocular. In case of tree nesting colonial species (like herons, pelicans, storks, etc), as well as, for ground nesting colonial species (like gulls, terns, flamingos etc.) the observer may easily count the conspicuous nests and incubating parent birds from ground (Javed and Kaul, 2002).

In case of small colonies, usually all birds present in the nest or within the breeding colony are counted. But, if the colony is very large, then transect or quadrat method is used to count the nests present therein. In fact a systematic and well planned survey provide valuable feedback on the presence/absence status, relative abundance and population trend of avifauna, as well as, help to formulate appropriate conservation measures.

The precautions and suggestions for successful bird surveys are mentioned in Text Box 6.4:

Text Box 6.4: Precautions and Suggestions for Avifaunal Surveys

Counting birds using both direct census techniques by visual observations (like transect sampling, point count, distance sampling etc.) and other indirect method (call count, nest count etc.) are fascinating, as well as, challenging too.

- Bird survey teams should be small in size, usually with two to four members in each team.
- Speak and move quietly and avoid sudden movements.
- Bird counts should be conducted at the start of first light which is before sunrise. This is the time when birds vocalise most, which is known as 'dawn chorus'. It is also a time of maximum bird movements as birds move through the bushes to begin feeding.
- All surveys should be finished within 3 – 4 hours after first light.
- On cold mornings keep binoculars inside clothing when not in use to reduce fogging.
- Always check where you are standing when you stop to view a bird, as ants have little respect for busy bird watchers.
- Data entry should be done as quickly as possible, as the dawn chorus is short.
- Do not conduct survey in bad weather condition such as wind, heavy rain, mist, fog, haze and electrical storms.
- When point counts are to be done in dense habitats with poor visibility, then fix smaller radius of the circle at each sample point.
- It may be difficult to identify some species in dull light. In poor lighted areas that is still in darkness after sunrise, like a steep gully, then this transect should be surveyed later in the morning as the light in the sky increases.

6.3 PUGMARK CENSUS

Pugmark denotes paw prints of most feline animals (like tiger, leopard), where as foot prints of herbivores (such as deer, antelope) are called *hoofmark*. Every species has distinct morphology of limbs. Therefore impressions of foot of different species vary. Moreover, individual also has its own distinct pugmark and hence, this is used for identification purposes. Thus, pugmark plays a major role in identifying a specific animal in terms of sex, age or size. So, pugmark census is used to assess the total number of individuals of a particular species. Pugmark is also helpful in tracking animals that stray away from the wilderness areas into the human-dominated habitats leading to human-animal conflicts.

Among all field methods of animal census, especially in tiger counting, pugmarks are the most common and the earliest method to get reliable information and a fair estimate of tiger populations. Pugmark census was invented in 1966 by Indian forester S.R. Choudhury. First 'All India Census of Tigers' was conducted in summer, 1972 using the method of Pugmark Census Technique along with the Tiger Tracer. This effort revealed that, if practiced well, the pugmark technique can be useful to identify species, sex, major age classes, as well as, link male-female or mother-cub. It could develop a map showing terrestrial distribution and areas of tiger movement. For 30 years, this method has been exclusively used to derive tiger numbers in individual protected areas and larger regions on a country-wide basis. It is claimed that the pugmark census yields accurate results in a cost-effective and practical manner (Panwar, 1980; Singh, 1999).

The method is simple and easy to count the animal in a very special manner. In this census method thousands of forestry department personnel simultaneously search for tiger tracks across India for a period of 1–2 weeks. They are expected to locate tiger tracks and obtain plaster casts (or tracings) of the imprints of the left hind paws of nearly all the tigers in the entire country. The pugmarks collected are later compared to identify individual tigers based on perceived differences in shape and other measurements obtained through ancillary local knowledge. These 'individual tiger identifications' are then refined through cross-comparisons among census blocks, reserves and larger regions to obtain 'reliable estimates' of wild tiger numbers in India.

6.3.1 Tiger Pugmark

Prior to the implementation of pugmark census in counting tiger numbers, it is very important to know the design of the tiger paw (Figure 6.11), which actually generates pugmarks. The paw of a tiger consists of a pad and four toes. A fifth toe, commonly called the dew claw, is placed high on the front limbs only. These dew claws are retractable, do not touch the ground and usually serve as a part of the tiger's weaponry. Ordinarily, the pad is 3-lobed at the rear end.

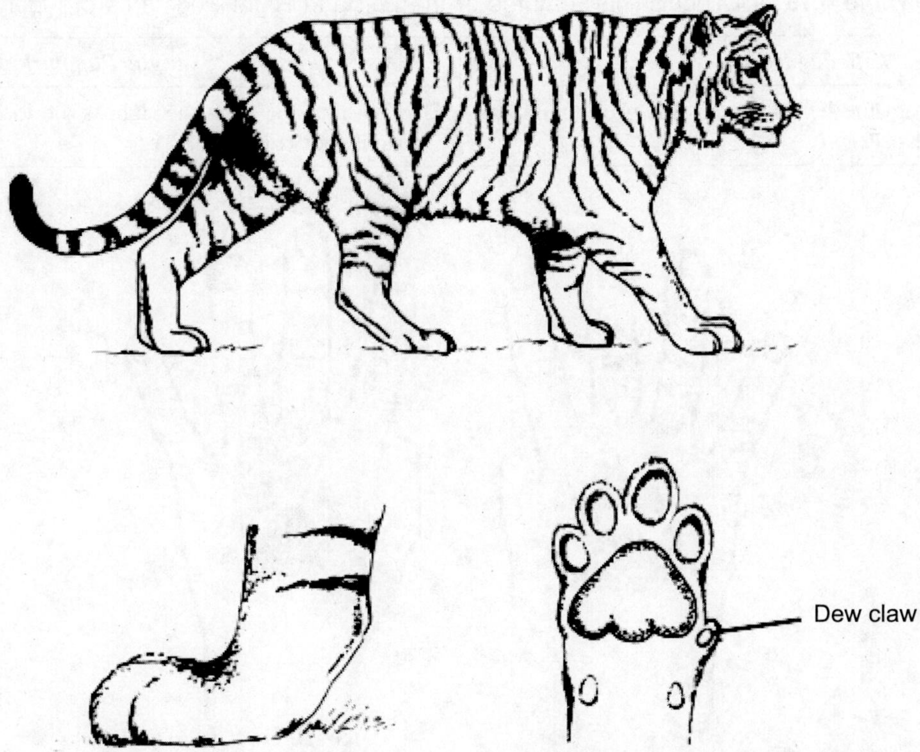

Placement of paw on ground   Design of a tiger claw

FIGURE 6.11 Design of a tiger's paw and placement of tiger's paw on ground.

The differences between pugmarks of front and hind foot, as well as, between the hind pugmark of tiger and tigress are mentioned below in separate tables (Table 6.15; 6.16 and 6.17).

Design of a Tiger Paw

Table 6.15 Distinguishing Features of the Front and Hind Pugmarks of Tiger

Pugmark of forelimb	*Pugmark of hind limb*
❒ Pugmarks of forelimbs are larger than the hind limbs. ❒ In front paws, the forward most points of the two middle toes are almost at the same level.	❒ Pugmarks of hind limbs are smaller than the fore limbs. ❒ In hind paws, the forward most points of the two middle toes are distinctly at different levels.
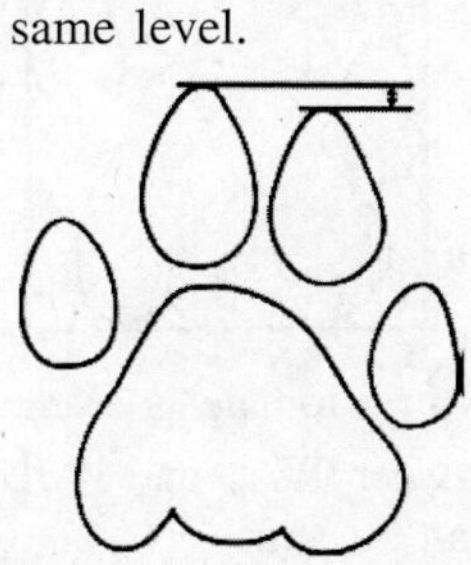	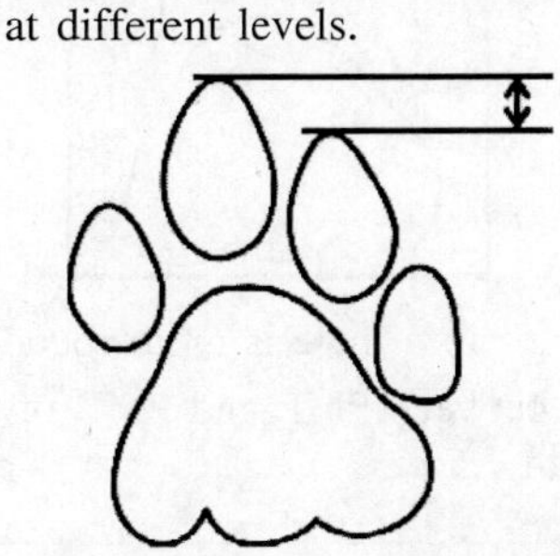
❒ In male tigers, the pugmark breadth (PMB) of the front pug is mostly greater than its pugmark length (PML). ❒ Front pugs are used for killing prey. Therefore, injuries (including human induced injuries) are sustained on front paws. Hence pugmarks of front paws often manifest injuries. Wherever existing, these may serve as a conclusive identification feature of a specific animal.	❒ In male tigers, the PMB of the hind pug is similar or lesser than its PML. ❒ Hind paws are less susceptible to injuries (except the human-induced ones) and, therefore, in very less occasions pugmarks of hind paws manifest injuries.

Note: Front pugmark is selected only if the front pugmark stands out distinctly due to an injury or deformity. Even in such cases, the hind left pugmark must also be traced and submitted attached to the tracing of the deformed pugmark.

Table 6.16 Distinguishing Features of the Left and Right Pugmarks of Tiger

Left Pugmark	*Right Pugmark*
❒ The third finger from the left is the longest in the pugmark of left foot (Figure 6.12).	❒ The third toe from the right is the longest in the pugmark of right foot (Figure 6.12).

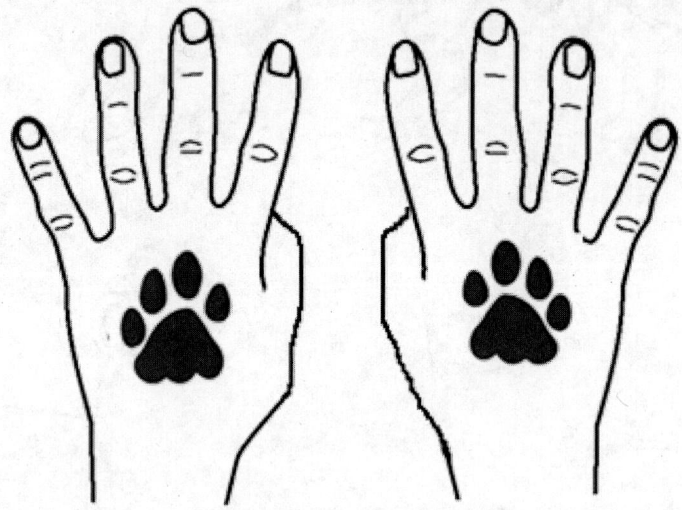

FIGURE 6.12 Distinguishing features of the right and left pugmarks of tiger.

Note: For uniformity, the hind left pugmark is always selected for estimation of tiger population, unless right hind is specified by the CWLW for the entire state.

Table 6.17 Distinguishing Features of the Hind Pugmark of Tiger and Tigress

Hind Pugmark of Tiger	*Hind Pugmark of Tigress*
❒ Paws of males are larger than the females. ❒ A box drawn around the pugmark of the male is almost square. 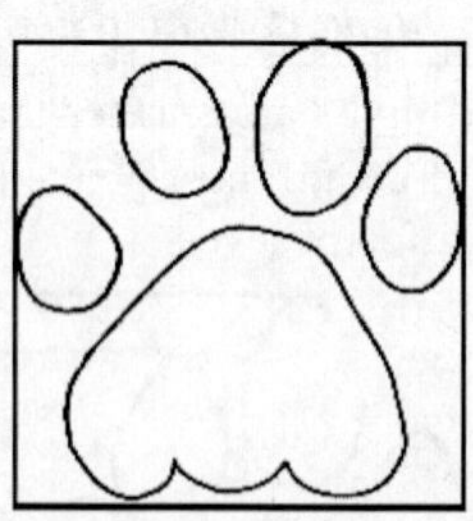 ❒ The shape of toes in a male is more rounded. ❒ The difference between PML and PMB of the pugmark of a tiger is less than 1.5 cm.	❒ Paws of females are smaller than the males. ❒ A box drawn around the pugmark of the female appears almost rectangular. 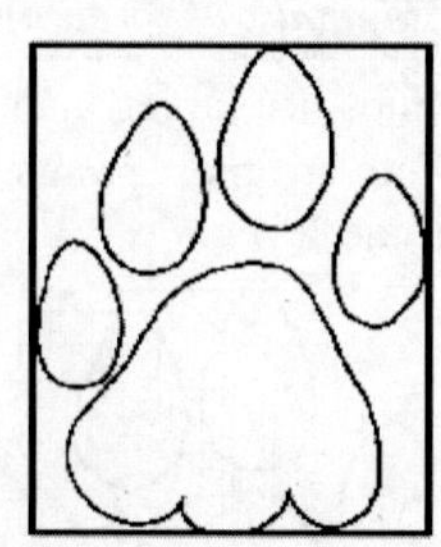 ❒ The shape of toes in a female is elongated. ❒ The difference between PML and PMB of the pugmark of a tigress is more than 1.5 cm.

Note: Only the hind pugmark is different in male and female, particularly in shape and size of toes. Therefore, above distinctions are not applicable to the front pugmarks.

6.3.2 Measurements of a Pugmark

Pugmark Length (or PML) is the measurement from the tip of the farthest toe to the base of the pad along the line of walk and Pugmark Breadth (or PMB) is the measurement between the outer edges of the first and last toe. PML and PMB are measured by drawing a box (all corners at 90 degrees) touching the extreme ends of the pugmark as shown in Figure 6.13.

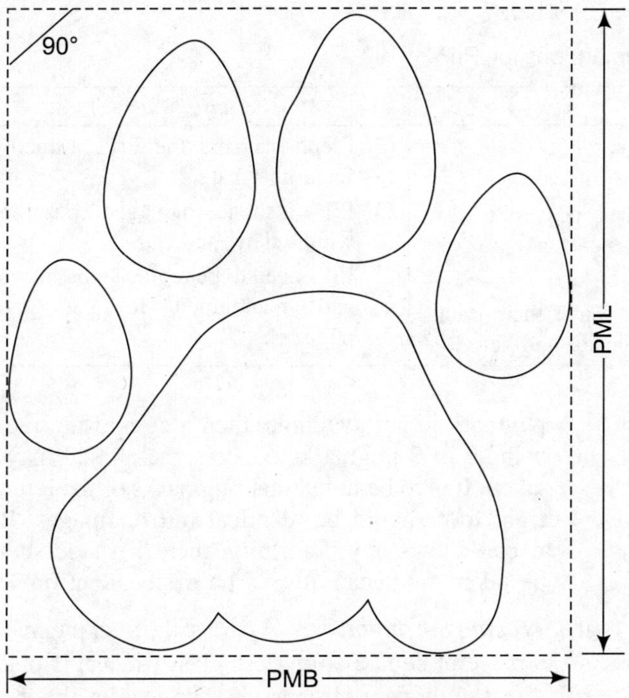

FIGURE 6.13 Measuring PML and PMB in a pugmark.

6.3.3 Timing of the Survey

Surveys should be carried out over a period of several weeks during the time when tiger tracks can be most conveniently located if the study aims to estimate the population size and structure. But in order to determine home range and utilization of different habitats within a given area, the survey should be extended through a full seasonal cycle.

The pugmark records obtained are compared everyday and individual locations should be entered in a map. Within a few weeks this will lead to identification of all individuals present in the area, as well as, their movement pattern in the habitat.

6.3.4 Searching for Pugmarks

Pugmarks are usually searched along – (i) dusty or damp ground, (ii) forest paths and roads, (iii) animal trails, (iv) river and stream banks, (v) in the vicinity of water holes, (vi) dry *nala* beds inside forest and (vii) area adjacent to natural salt licks.

6.3.5 How to Get Good Impressions?

The quality of pugmarks formed often depends on the soil conditions and ideally pugmarks made in similar soil conditions should be taken for further analysis to reduce error. But, this is never possible under natural circumstances as the soil conditions vary substantially in different parts of the same forest. Therefore, Pugmark Impression Pads (PIPs) are laid down to overcome this problem.

Pugmark Impression Pads (PIP)

Pugmark Impression Pads (PIPs) consist of an area approximately 6 m long and as wide as the road (~2.5 m), where the soil is finely pulverized to an optimal soil depth of 0.5 – 1 cm, to provide the best possible surface for recording pugmark impressions. PIPs are manually created preferably by using the soil from the same surrounding area, usually laid on routes along which the tiger and leopard are known to move frequently and are large enough to allow the registration of 3 – 4 pugmarks. Animals are sometimes weary of stepping on PIPs that are freshly prepared. So PIPs should be prepared well before the enumeration process begins. Some barriers (like large tree trunks or spiny branches etc) should be laid down in the vicinity so that the animal cannot bypass and is somewhat compelled to walk over the PIP. PIPs are widely used in India for the census of tigers. The procedure of laying down a PIP is illustrated in Figure 6.14.

FIGURE 6.14 Illustration of preparation and laying of a Pugmark Impression Pad (PIP).

The PIPs need to be properly maintained to get good pug impressions on them. Pugmarks are disturbed by many factors. The movement of vehicles over the PIPs might destroy any pugmark on it. So the drivers should be asked to avoid driving vehicles along main tracks near PIPs during counting operations. Inspection of all PIPs should be completed by 10 a.m. in the morning after which vehicles may ply on these routes up to 3 p.m., if necessary. After every check, the PIP must be thoroughly wiped and all debris like leaf litter, sticks etc. must be removed to make it ready to receive fresh pugmarks again.

Merits and limitations of PIP are briefly mentioned in Table 6.18 below:

Table 6.18 Merits and Limitations of PIP

Merit	*Limitations*
❐ PIPs can be created in large numbers and are available continuously. ❐ Low equipment cost. ❐ Provides employment to people living in and around tiger habitats who possess skill in laying PIPs and participating in animal tracking. ❐ Can be used for round-the-year monitoring of tigers. ❐ Nocturnal animals, which are difficult to see during the day, also leave their tracks on PIPs and information can be gathered about their distribution, density and activity.	❐ Elephants find the PIPs attractive for a dust bath. ❐ PIPs also get damaged by strong winds, dew, and rain. ❐ PIPs need to be regularly monitored and maintained to get good pugmarks.

6.3.6 Methods of Pugmark Census

Traditionally tiger censuses in India have been carried out by collecting plaster of Paris casts and hand tracings of pugmarks (usually of a tiger's left hind foot) found in an area during a specified time. These are then analysed, along with movement and other data, to estimate the tiger population.

1. Pugmark Census using Plaster Casts

Preparation of plaster cast: Plaster of Paris, water, plastic container, a thin stick for stirring and strip of thick paper or flexible aluminium are the basic requirements for the preparation of plaster casts. Plaster of Paris is taken in a plastic container. Then required amount of water is mixed to it and stirred constantly to make a homogeneous suspension. Aluminium strip or thick papers or sticks are then placed around the selected pugmark to create a temporary frame. The suspension of plaster of Paris is poured inside the area of this frame and allowed to dry to form a hard plaster cast. Before complete drying some basic information like date, place, reference number for tracing and the signature of the observer are to be written on the back of the plaster cast by using a thin stick. Once completely dry, the plaster cast is carefully removed and the surface facing the pugmark is cleaned properly.

2. Pugmark Census using Tiger Tracer

(i) ***Selection of track for tracing:*** A well formed impression of the hind foot, preferably from a series of tracks along a road, sandy stream bed, soft mud etc. should be selected at first. If a perfect pugmark is not available, then a composite tracing using 2 or 3 pugmarks of the same animal may be taken. It is to be noted that pugmarks of the left and right foot should be identical mirror images. But, if one shows any deformity, then that side should be taken, as it can always be easily identifiable.

(ii) ***Tracing the pugmark:*** To trace the tiger pugmarks, a piece of square colourless glass (tracer) is placed directly above a clear track. The legs of the tracer are then pushed into the soil until the glass pane is just above the track surface. If that ground is too hard, then the glass pane is lowered by adjusting the wing nuts which hold it in place. The 'tracer' should always be kept as close to the pugmark as possible and should be parallel to the pugmark. After properly placing the tracer, the researcher kneels down near the pugmark with both knees on the ground on either side of the tracer to position himself/herself. Then the researcher rest elbows on the ground, hold the glass marker pen on his/her writing hand, keeps eyes directly above the pugmark and looking straight down to start tracing the pugmark on the piece of glass by a glass marker (Figure 6.15 A). The researcher then trace the outline of the pad and all four toes on to the glass surface of tracer. By moving the head while drawing, researcher should always keep his/her eyes vertically above the tip of the panes and the portion of the mark under tracing to avoid the parallax error and make an accurate tracing. Skills and proficiency of tracing comes with practice.

A B

FIGURE 6.15 (A) Researcher tracing the pugmark on 'tiger tracer'; (B) Pugmark drawn on the glass of the tiger tracer is transferred to paper.

Then the pugmark drawn on the glass of the tiger tracer is transferred to paper. For this step tracing paper is attached to the glass using rubber bands and holding it up against the light. Then just the outline of the pugmark is redrawn on the paper as shown in Figure 6.15 B. In this step also adequate care need to be taken to avoid parallax error.

Documentation: It must be noted that the size of the pugmark of same individual may vary according to the texture and consistency of the ground surface. Hence, additional information like name of the recorder, date and time of tracking, location, direction of movement, surface type (sand/earth) and conditions (dry/wet/muddy etc.) and freshness of the track (fresh/probably last night/yesterday/old etc.) need to be recorded on the tracing sheet (or on a separate form attached to it. This additional information might be of utmost importance during analysis of the pugmarks and calculating the abundance.

The possible measurements in a tracing of tiger pugmark are illustrated in Figure 6.16.

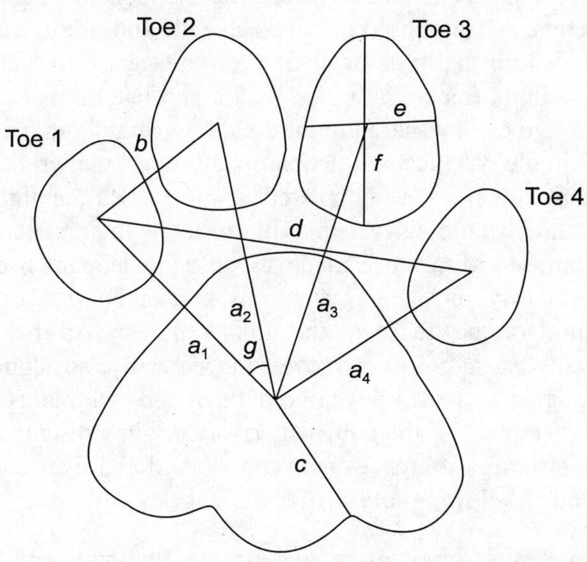

FIGURE 6.16 Parameters of a tiger pugmark [a_{1-4} = distance from centre of the pad to the centre of toe1, toe2, toe3 and toe4 respectively; b = distance between the centres of toe 1 and toe 2; c = distance between centre of the paw to notch; d = distance between the centres of toe 1 and toe 4; e = maximum toe width; f = maximum toe length; g = angle].

3. Digital Pugmark Census Technique

Digital pugmark technology (DPT) is another new method based on the theory of pugmark census technique (i.e. each tiger leaves a distinctive set of pugmarks) with some modifications. This method is used for identifying the specific individual of a species using statistical approach.

According to Sharma and Wright (2005), digital photographs of a series of fresh good quality pugmarks on PIPs and on trails are taken from the first sight along with the stride and straddle measurements where a tiger has walked in a normal gait. Besides, GPS (Global Positioning System) location of the site is also recorded. This data is then entered in a computer which calculates the values of several variables from the photographs. Twelve predictor variables (Figure 6.17) are used to accurately identify individual tigers from their pugmark impressions.

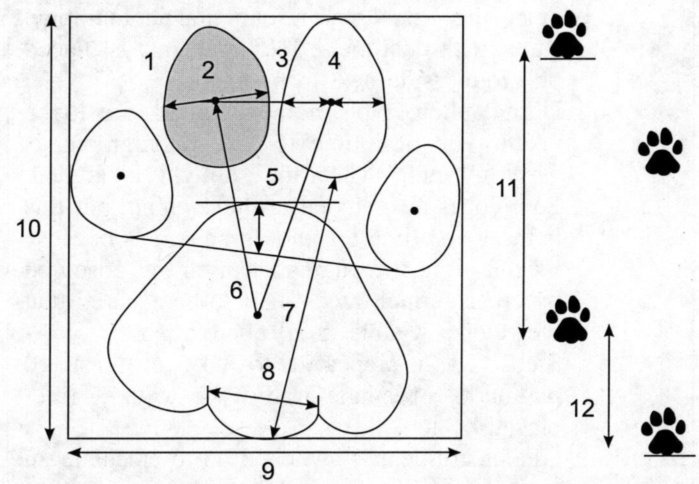

Note: 1 = Area of Toe3 (AT3); 2 = Length of minor axis of Toe3 (MiT3); 3 = Distance between Toe2 and Toe3 (DT2T3); 4 = Length of minor axis of Toe2 (LT2); 5 = Distance between top of base pad to base of toe (H); 6 = Angle between Toe2 and Toe3 (QT2T3); 7 = Length between base of the lead toe to heel (HLTL); 8 = Distance between notch1 and notch2 on paw (DN1N2); 9 = Width of pugmark (Wpg); 10 = Length of pugmark (Lpg); 11 = Stride; 12 = Straddle

FIGURE 6.17 Twelve predictor variables used in digital pugmark census technique to identify individual tigers from their pugmark impressions (Sharma and Wright, 2005).

It is important to note that an entire pugmark set (a series of continuous pugmarks made by the same tiger) provides the identity of a tiger, i.e., the accuracy depends on data from a set of pugmarks, and not an individual pugmark. Moreover, at least 10 good hind pugmarks (left as well as right) are required to be photographed from a set of tracks for Digital Pugmark technique. Similarly, 10 measurements of gait variables i.e. stride (i.e. the distance between two successive pugmarks on the same side) and straddle (i.e. the distance between the left and right hind pugmarks), must also be recorded from the same pugmark trail. The data is then analyzed with the help of software PUGMARK 1.0 (Sharma, 2001). The basic premise for this new approach for tiger population estimation is extracting quantitative information from sets of pugmarks using the software PUGMARK 1.0 (Sharma and Wright, 2005). Such analysis of the data creates a 'profile' of the tiger, which can then be used to estimate the tiger population using specific statistical approach. In this method, use of digital camera to photograph the pugmark along with the use of PUGMARK 1.0 software for the image analysis completely eliminates human error.

Text Box 6.5: Implementation of Digital Pugmark Census Technique

Sharma and Wright (2005) suggested following steps for successful implementation of tiger census through Digital Pugmark Census Technique:

1. Reach the study site.
2. Select the best pugmarks for digital photography.
3. Ruler with centimetre measurements is placed on ground side next to pugmark.
4. Digital photograph of the pugmark are to be taken. The best time to take photographs is early morning when the sunlight is angled. Sunlight is also angled in the evening, but this is the worst time for photographing as because by this time the pugmarks often get obscured by other animal tracks. It is to be ensured that the ruler is visible in all photographs.
5. Steps 2-4 is repeated to take at least 10 pugmarks of single trail, each with a ruler placed by its side.
6. GPS instrument is switched on to calculate an accurate position of each pugmark.
7. A ruler is inserted into soil to measure depth, and note the texture and moisture of soil.
8. Stride is measured by placing a steel measuring tape on the base of the pad of the pugmarks.
9. Straddle is also measured by placing the tape on its edge and pressing it into the soil to make a straight line between the outer edges of the trail of the hind pugmarks.
10. Steps 8 and 9 are repeated for successive pugmarks on both sides, to obtain series of stride and straddle measurements (10 each).

Digital Pugmark technique had been used for the first time to monitor and estimate a single tiger population in Ranthambhore (Sharma and Wright, 2005).

6.3.7 Distinguishing Tiger Pugmarks from other Animals

The interesting fact is that tiger cub pugmark (TCP) is much similar with the pugmarks of leopard or wild dogs. The overall difference between a cat and a dog footprint (Figure 6.18) are stated below:

(i) Claw marks are visible in a dog's pugmark, but not in the pugmarks of cats unless they are startled or walking over slippery or very steep ground.

(ii) In the dog family (excepting the hyenas), the gap between the top of the pad and the two middle toes is distinctly more than what is found in cats.

(iii) Careful comparison the ratio of toe to pad size in dogs and cats reveal that toes are comparatively larger in dogs, while pad is comparatively larger in cats.

FIGURE 6.18 Difference between the pugmark of a dog and a cat.

In tiger, toes are smaller with non visible, retractile claws and relatively larger pads. Contrastingly in wild dogs toes are larger with visible claws and pads are relatively smaller. Pugmarks with PML less than 6 cm are likely to belong to lesser cats. On the other hand, linear factor is the common methods for identifying the leopard pugmarks. Different age groups (i.e. cub, subadult and adult) can be classified on the basis of distinct differences in the relative track length, track width, pad width, pad length, pad curve, stride size etc. measured in the field by using digital caliper. For simple verification, leopard pads are smaller in size with narrow toes as compared to tigers. But, a three to four months old tiger cub will make pugmarks that can be confused with those made by an adult leopard because of similarity in size. This confusion can be resolved by looking for the tracks of the mother tigress. As the, tiger cubs of that age do not move independently, so alongside the pugmark of a 3-4 year old tiger cub, pugmarks of a tigress (mother of the cub) will invariably be present. Some other striking differences between leopard and tiger cub are appended below (Table 6.19):

Table 6.19 Comparative Account of Pugmarks of Tiger Cub and Leopard

Pugmark of Tiger Cub	*Pugmark of Leopard*
❒ Pugmarks of tiger cubs are larger and wider. ❒ The pugmark of a tiger cub is more splayed out. The pad and the toes are held more loosely. ❒ The stride of a tiger cub is about ten times its PML. ❒ PML of pugmarks falling between 7 – 10 cm and 9 – 17 could respectively belong to tiger cubs and adult tigers.	❒ Pugmarks of leopards are smaller and narrower. ❒ The pugmark of an adult leopard is compact. The pad and the toes are held closer together. ❒ The stride of an adult leopard is about 13 – 14 times its PML. ❒ PML of pugmarks falling between 5 – 7 cm and 7 – 9.5 cm could respectively belong to leopard cubs and adult leopards.

6.3.8 Precautions

Tigers lead solitary lives except mother and their offspring. However, when males join the "family" for a short period and because of simultaneous movement distortion of tracks occurs as marks of one individual get superimposed by another. Great care should be taken in identifying of an individual in the series of multiple tracks.

6.3.9 Criticism of the Pugmark Census Method

Though the technique is a very sound one and also help to generate employment opportunities among the local people, still there are some valid reasons of criticism. Pugmarks vary considerably with substratum and gait, as well as, based on the personal skill of individual tracers. Interpretations of the pugmarks also vary from person to person. So there are reasonable doubts regarding the efficiency of pugmark technique to identify individual tigers. Moreover, the objective of this method is 'censusing' and not 'sampling' tiger populations. So, the field effort invested often goes unrecorded and it is also not possible to obtain pugmarks from all 'Tiger Occupied Landscapes'. In this census method the numbers of tiger cubs are always underestimated possibly because tracks of tiger cub are often misidentified as pugmarks of leopard adult. Despite of high level of dedication and rigor among the Forest personnel in carrying out the protocols of tiger census, yet most of them are unaware of the significance of the exercise and take this as a part of their routine duties. Hence, the awareness about the significance attached to population figure often remains inadequate. To overcome all these constrains, the method is improved since 1990 to make it more clear and transparent, simplified, standardized, verifiable and easily available.

6.4 CAMERA TRAPS IN WILDLIFE RESEARCH

Camera traps are used as a non-invasive sampling tool in wildlife research and are particularly well suited to animals that are elusive, often occur at low densities and are difficult to capture or detect. Over the last two decades, the use of various non-invasive techniques for the sampling of animal populations has increased significantly. Technological advances have allowed practitioners to sample and monitor animal population without ever physically capturing or handling animals, and to feel confident that the equipment will operate acceptably under a variety of environmental conditions. Being highly sensitive in terms of animal welfare, reduction of time, effort, and expenses in the collection of scientific data, this non-invasive surveying technique using remote triggered photographic units (cameras) has become very popular and often used in wildlife studies. Camera trap method is used to capture images of wild creatures in the wild with as little human interference as possible. This method has been used in variety of ecological research including studies of nest ecology, detection of rare species, estimation of population size and species richness, as well as, researches on habitat use of various wild fauna.

Definition: Camera trap is a non-invasive technique of wildlife monitoring comprising of remotely activated camera that is equipped with a motion sensor or an infrared sensor, or uses a light beam as a trigger to take the photograph of an animal when it is present in its vicinity.

Camera traps are initially costly. But once a camera trap is being set up, it has the unique ability to sample animals remotely without involving any human volunteer to manually operate the equipment (except for occasional equipment checks and to retrieve images or film) and also does not require the constant presence of the experienced field personnel (Rappole et al., 1985). Therefore, in long-run the use of a camera trap becomes cost-efficient as well. Besides, the costs of the camera traps have also reduced with the improving technology and with increasing number of manufacturers. In addition to that, camera traps are relatively easy to use and is not much dependent on the environment to be sampled or the field condition. Such reduction in costs, advancements in technology, improvement of the quality of camera equipment and easy operational procedures have eventually made this method of field observation very popular and a preferred tool for sampling animal populations among researchers.

Camera traps allow us to make undisturbed observations on a wide variety of wildlife, in a wide variety of habitats, at all hours, and under the most challenging conditions. In recent years, the use of camera traps in the study of wild animals has undeniably improved our understanding of their ecological relationships, as well as, population dynamics. There are now literally hundreds of studies and surveys being conducted that involve camera traps, from urban parks to the most remote jungles.

6.4.1 A Brief History and Genesis of Camera Trapping

Desire to observe wild animals without disturbing them were noticed since the time of hunter-gatherers, who used to construct blinds. But, George Shiras in the year 1890s was the first to develop a method using a trip wire and a flash system in which wild animals photographed themselves. Shiras was successful in photographing so many wild species in part because of the variety of methods he developed to induce the animal to pull the trip wire. In the early decades of the 20th century, there were several other successful attempts around the world to have animals to take their own pictures. The German sportsman and photographer

Carl Georg Schillings adapted Shiras' methods to study the wildlife of east Africa in 1903 and 1904. Using bait such as a live donkey, and photographing at waterholes, Schillings produced spectacular photographs of many wildlife species, all taken by the subjects themselves. In India, the photograph of the first wild tiger (*P. tigris*) was taken with this apparatus, by F.W. Champion of the Indian Forest Service.

Methods for capturing animals on film when researchers are not present have been used in ecological research for decades. But use of "remote photography," also called camera trapping, dramatically increased with the advent of commercial wildlife camera traps in the early 1990s. By the mid 20th century, smaller photographic equipments and the replacement of the clumsy and dangerous magnesium flash powder with flash bulbs allowed further refinement of remote wildlife photography. These advancements have enabled practitioners to use camera traps more efficiently and to sample a variety of species under diverse environmental conditions.

This method is now preferred over track surveys and direct counts in conducting rapid faunal assessments of mammals for conservation purposes. For example, camera traps have been extensively used in the population studies of tigers (Karanth and Nichols, 1998) and bears (Mace et al., 1994) in the last two decades. This is also considered as an efficient technique to prepare inventory of small and medium sized animals in different habitats. Remote photography is now being used in an increasing variety of studies like nest predation, feeding ecology, nesting behaviour, activity patterns and evaluation of habitat use. Literatures reveal that wide arrays of topics are recently being investigated using camera traps in a truly impressive variety of habitats and locations. Presently, camera traps serve as an important non-invasive tool for assessing patterns of abundance through space and time, activity patterns, habitat use and reproductive behaviour, which are considered as vital parameters for any wildlife conservation programme (Silveira et al., 2003).

6.4.2 The Equipment

While there are several types of camera-traps, all models have the same basic principle. The equipments include a still (and/or video) camera protected by some sort of weatherproof housing, coupled to a mechanism that allows the camera to be triggered automatically when an animal moves in front of it. There are two main types of camera-traps: analogue and digital. Digital camera-traps are becoming increasingly popular over film ones. Modern digital camera-traps usually do not have photographic films but record the photographs digitally onto a memory card. In addition, some camera-traps have the ability to record video. Camera traps can be passive (heat in motion sensor) or active (infra-red beam established across a potential animal path). In short, camera-traps are a system or device with a trigger or sensor that activates a camera to take a photograph when an animal is present within its range.

6.4.3 Application

One of the most important things to consider when setting up camera traps is choosing the location in order to get the best results. The areas near mineral licks or along game trails, where the animals would visit frequently and congregate, are normally selected for camera traps. Species such as small birds and insects may be too small to trigger the camera, while reptiles and amphibians will not be able to trip the infrared or heat differential-based sensors. Nevertheless, methods have been developed to detect these species by utilizing a reflector based sensor system. Otherwise, camera traps have proven to be a successful tool for studying most of the medium and large-bodied terrestrial species.

Many factors influence the performance of camera traps. Poor performance is usually caused by a combination of weather, user experience, user skill, unique field conditions and poorly engineered equipment. In addition, there are great differences among types of camera traps in terms of their sensitivity, zones of detection, and performance under different environmental conditions. Some of these factors can be alleviated, whereas others (such as weather) are beyond a researcher's immediate control. It is, therefore, important to know the problems of potential equipment and select traps suitable for local application. These different applications may have very different requirements. For example, a trap to detect rare species in a remote area needs to be rugged, reliable, and capable of taking photographs for several weeks after it is set, while a trap used to observe feeding behaviour of hatchling birds in a nest must be quiet, unobtrusive, and capable of taking a large number of images in succession.

6.4.4 Types of Camera-Traps

Camera traps can be categorized in various ways, but the major types are (i) non-triggered camera traps and (ii) triggered camera-traps.

(i) Non-Triggered Camera-Traps

Non-triggered systems include cameras that are programmed to record images either continuously or at regular, pre-set time intervals. Such non-triggered (time-lapse or continuous recording) camera-traps usually consist of a camera unit (a still camera with a time lapse timer, or a digital video camera), a power source, and a wire or wireless connection between them. In general, non-triggered camera-traps are most appropriate when the event of interest occurs frequently (such as feeding behaviour), or when a continuous record is required. Therefore, these systems are most commonly used to study animal behaviour and nest ecology. Prior to the widespread use of commercial triggered camera-traps, time-lapse cameras were used in studies conducted at specific locations, such as to record wildlife at water catchments.

Advantages: Continuous recording by the non-triggered camera-traps can be advantageous (over the triggered camera trap. But, it is important to know how long an animal is absent from a location (e.g. nest) during a given time period. Sometimes a rare animal may also appear, but fail to trigger the camera trap. In such situation the non-triggered type is also better than the other type. Moreover, due to less number of parts and more compactness of the instruments, the non-triggered cameras usually fail less frequently in the field than triggered camera-traps.

Disadvantages: The great disadvantage of non-triggered camera traps is that, excepting some time-lapse systems, most of these camera-traps tend to require more power, which makes them less useful for remote situations. This may not be a problem in studies of nesting birds, where a long cord can connect to a direct power source. But, use of these traps in remote field locations are difficult unless solar power is used. As these non-triggered camera-traps continuously record data, so longer amount of time is required to review images to find target animals or focal events during analysis.

(ii) Triggered Camera-Traps

Triggered camera-traps are inactive until they are triggered by an event of some kind, usually the arrival of an animal. The trigger may be *mechanical*, such as the animal stepping on a pressure plate that fires the camera, but more typically the trigger is an *infra-red light source.*

- *Mechanically triggered camera-traps* use either pressure pads or bait lines in which a line connects the trigger of a camera and the bait, decoy, or egg. A modification of the bait line works in a similar way as the pressure pad does whereby a micro-switch triggers a camera when bait is removed from a platform and completes the circuit. Mechanically triggered camera-traps have become less common in recent years due to improvements in light-triggered technology, but are appropriate for studies where an animal might closely inspect a small area or moves within an area of interest. They are often used in nest predation studies.
- *Light-triggered camera-traps* use a light beam (typically, an infrared beam) as a trigger and can be either "*active*" or "*passive*".

  Active infra-red-triggered traps emit a continuous beam from a transmitter to a receiver that is like an invisible string; when the beam is broken, a message is sent to the camera to record an image. Active traps consist of a separate receiver and transmitter, as well as a camera and a connection (usually a cord) between the camera and the receiver.

  Passive camera-traps consist of two separate sensors placed side by side. When an animal passes in front of the sensors, both of them sense the movement and detect the temperature change from the background temperature signature due to the presence of the animal. This different temperature signature of the animal then triggers the camera trap to record an image. Passive camera traps are more compact and are more frequently used than active systems.

Table 6.20 Comparative Account of Active and Passive Camera Traps

Active (infra-red-triggered) Camera-Traps	*Passive Camera-Traps*
Active infrared traps tend to have a much higher rate of false triggers than passive traps, as events can be triggered whenever objects that are not animals (including not only blowing or growing vegetation, but even rain or snow) move through the infra-red beam.	Passive units are usually not as prone to being triggered by non-animals, but false triggers do occur, particularly when the zone of detection is very large.
Very small animals moving below the infra-red beam cannot be detected by this type of camera-trap.	As the passive traps usually sense the thermal difference, so they often have a wider "zone" of detection and can detect animals of varied sizes. However, detection zone and sizes vary among different passive units.
Active traps consist of a separate receiver and transmitter, as well as a camera and a connection (usually a cord) between the camera and the receiver.	Most commercial passive camera traps come in a single unit.
As the components are separate, so the active traps are sometimes difficult to set up in field.	Passive camera-traps are easier to set up in the field as all the components are bundled into a single box. As a result, the number of commercial passive camera traps has proliferated in recent years.

Advantages: Triggered camera traps are more appropriate when the event of interest is infrequent or discontinuous, such as when it is important to record the presence of a species or individual at a site. Their great advantage for wildlife studies, particularly studies of rare animals, is that they use little power and can be easily utilized for long periods in remote settings.

Disadvantages: The greatest disadvantage of triggered camera traps in comparison to non-triggered traps, in addition to false triggers, is that sensors sometimes fail due to environmental conditions or operator error.

The differences among triggered and non-triggered camera traps are significant, and it is important to think carefully before choosing one instead of the other. Bird studies often use non-triggered systems, while nearly all large mammal studies use triggered traps, although this difference may be partially cultural among biologists. Some commercial camera-traps can be programmed both for non-triggered time-lapse and infrared-triggered operation (Table 6.21).

Table 6.21 Different Types of Camera Trap Systems and their Field of Application

System	*Most Applicable*	*Least Applicable*
Non-triggered	When animals are resident, occur in the open, or have high rates of visit or when recording continuous data (e.g., to establish absence) is important.	For rare species or infrequent events (as power requirement is large and photo analysis can be time-consuming).
Triggered – general	When camera traps need to be left in the field for a long period of time, but events are infrequent.	When events of interest are frequent or continuous (triggered systems may be more complicated and less reliable than non-triggered systems for recording continuous or frequent events).
Triggered – mechanical	When activity of interest requires an animal to physically step in a specific location or pull on a bait or object of interest.	When activity of interest may not be recorded by a physical trigger.
Triggered – infrared – general	When activity of interest does not require animal to physically step in a specific location or pull on an object; when animal is too light or fast for a mechanical trigger.	When the activity of interest involves a physical activity by animals (triggered traps may be more complicated and less reliable than mechanical ones).
Triggered – infrared – active	When it is important that non- target species (e.g., those below certain height) do not trigger the trap, especially if film or digital images are limited. In general, when activity of interest is in a precise location but would not be detected by a mechanical trigger.	In areas where vegetation growth is so fast that it will obscure the beam between maintenance visits. In areas where wind, rain, or snow frequently breaks the light trigger or blows vegetation or other objects across it.
Triggered – infrared – passive	When a larger zone of detection of target species is desirable. In areas where wind, rain, and snow are common.	In hot environments where equipment may fail to detect the differential temperature of target species.

6.4.5 Technological and Analytical Advancement and Camera Traps

Technological advances have actually improved all attributes of modern camera traps substantially due to automation of system components, miniaturization and networked systems. These advances have enabled practitioners to use camera traps more efficiently and to sample a variety of species under vastly different environmental conditions. Finally, as camera trap systems have become more efficient and reliable, the costs of purchase, operation, and maintenance have also decreased significantly. The development and use of powerful analytical techniques to make appropriate inferences from camera trap data have undergone a similar evolution.

Making valid inferences about population requires addressing two important sources of variation:

(i) detect ability, and
(ii) spatial variability.

Addressing spatial variability requires some consideration of probabilistic sampling, where data from the sampled sites allow for inferences to the larger area of interest (i.e., study area). The sampling design must also be efficient (in terms of precision) in estimating the parameters of interest. Use of indices requires strong assumptions about detect ability and the relationship between the count and the parameter of interest (e.g., abundance, density). However, without information about the validity of such assumptions, an index is of little value in making inferences to populations.

(i) Camera Trap External Hardware Options

Housing for camera traps varies by colour, weight, size, shape, weather-proofing, and durability. Different colour options are often desirable in order to reduce the visibility of the trap to wildlife or humans by camouflaging it with the surrounding.

The most durable camera traps are made of sturdy metal and are larger and heavier. But, if the units need to be carried for long distances then smaller and lighter (plastic) hardware are preferred. Besides, weather-proof housing is essential for the equipments in areas of extreme weather, and it is important to carefully check manufacturer's specifications for different field situations. For example, tropical field conditions require units that are water-proof, with components that can all be kept dry during regular exposure to high heat and humidity. Moisture damages computer components, causes sensors to malfunction, oxidizes metal parts, and causes film to stick inside of the camera. If the covering of the camera trap is not air-tight, then ants and termites might nest inside. Termites may well eat the interior parts (cables and other components), and ants can be hazardous to the operators. Lastly, moisture from human perspiration can easily build up in non-waterproofed camera traps when being transported in a backpack. Vandal-proof housing and locks may not be necessary in some areas, but are absolutely critical in others.

In addition to these, proper housing to protect camera traps from animals is another important prerequisite in most field situations. Exposed cables and cords often chewed by animals (like rodents). So, these hardware components need to be reinforced in the field with tinfoil or covered with some toxic substance. Armoured systems have also been designed to protect the camera from possible attack by large mammals (such as bears, elephants etc.).

Thus, external hardware of many camera traps largely vary based on the focal species and habitat type, vegetation pattern and terrain features of the study area, as well as, based on the objective of the study (Table 6.22).

Table 6.22 Housing and External Hardware Options Available for Camera Traps

Feature	*Purpose*
Camouflage colour	Lowers visibility of traps to animals and people.
Water proofing	Essential in rainy or humid environments to prevent equipment malfunction.
Tree cables and locks	Reduces risk of vandalism and theft.
Compact unit size	Smaller camera traps designed for nest boxes where little room is available.
Noiseless housing	Reduces noise produced by unit, such as by camera shutter click, so that animals are not alarmed.
Sound recording	Allows recording of sound of animal with images.
Armouring of housing	Reduces risk of damage by animals, vandalism and theft.
Armouring of connective cables	Reduces risk of damage by animals, like rodents.
Extra-length connective cables (for non-triggered systems)	Allows >100 m connectivity of cameras with other hardware for viewing, power, or transmission.

(ii) Software Options

Most commercial camera traps now contain software that can assist in system operation and increase functional efficiency, many of which are very helpful for ecological studies (Table 6.23). Typical software features include following options set by the user:

- ❒ ***Record additional data***: Recording of additional data of triggered events (such as time and date or even temperature) may be important for many studies.
- ❒ ***Recording images at pre-determined times***: Some software is programmed in such a way that the device only record images at predefined time. In other times, the software pause the camera so that multiple images of the same individual are not recorded. This not only reduces the recurrence of same images of similar events, but also efficiently save power or film. This option is very useful if a camera with photographic film is being used where the film needs to be conserved, but is less significant for digital cameras.

Many camera traps also come with power options that reduce battery use and increase battery longevity, which is essential in remote field situations. Increasingly, camera trap features can be programmed directly from a laptop or personal computer.

Table 6.23 Software Options Available for Camera Traps

Feature	*Purpose*
Event data recording	To record time and date of event as data that can be downloaded
Event recording options	To record events 24 h per day, or only at specific intervals to record events of interest, in order to conserve battery and reduce film use
Image recording options	Camera delay; to prevent capture of too many images, which may use up film and power
Speed options	To reduce time between triggering of animal event and recording of photographic images
Power options	Sleep mode, used to reduce battery use and increase battery longevity
Sensitivity settings	Allow sensitivity to be set to detect target species; more sensitive settings will detect smaller, lighter species such as birds
Password protection	Software anti-theft devices, to prevent theft of data
Audio devices for target animals	Features such as “whistle stop,” to cause target species to stop in front of camera for better photograph
Data loggers	To record environmental variables, such as temperature, while camera is operating

6.4.6 Use of Camera Trap Data

Earlier camera traps were only used by nature photographers and natural historians to obtain snapshot observations of secretive animals. But, over the years the application of camera trap data has become very important in wildlife studies. In various parts of the world, camera traps are being used to monitor animal populations. Some isolated estimates of abundance have low inherent value. Likewise, series of such estimates across time and/or space are also of limited utility when viewed alone. Nevertheless, these estimates are most useful when the monitoring programme is embedded within a larger programme of science or management. In India, Karanth made pioneering efforts to use camera trap data in drawing inferences about population size of tigers in India. He used the natural markings on tiger skin (i.e. stripe pattern) to estimate tiger abundance using formal capture-recapture (CR) methods. Currently, scientists and managers employ camera traps to investigate animal behaviour and to estimate variables and parameters that characterize populations and communities of animals.

Many of the investigations using camera traps over the last decade have focused on estimation methodology and subsequently the statistical methods for drawing inferences from camera trap data have also evolved rapidly. Initial uses of camera trap data for statistical inference were focussed on abundance of individually identifiable animals. Over the past 20 years there has been some development of new models for abundance estimation and a great deal of development in the companion problem of translating abundance estimates into inferences about density. Recent work has also moved from time-specific snapshots of abundance and/or density to dynamics of these state variables over time. The last decade has brought recognition that camera trap data for animals that are not individually identifiable can also be used for inference about two additional variables, occupancy and species richness. Occupancy models permit inference about the occurrence of a species over space and habitat types, and dynamic models permit inference about changes in distribution over time. Species richness within a specified taxonomic group is a community-level state variable, and its dynamics can also be studied with camera trap data.

In future, camera traps could be integrated into conservation programmes which aim to assess and subsequently increase animal numbers through establishment of corridors to connect isolated animal populations. As with other areas of conservation and wildlife management, biologists and managers can incorporate information generated from camera traps for monitoring and scientific evaluation of various management decisions. Camera trap investigations have frequently focused on species of high conservation value, and these investigations can properly be integrated into serious programmes of management and conservation.

6.4.7 Advantages of using Camera Traps

Camera traps have revolutionized wildlife research and conservation, enabling collection of photographic evidence of rarely seen and often globally endangered species, with little expense, relative ease and minimal disturbance to wildlife. These are also helpful in quantifying the number of different species in an area. Working day and night, camera traps are ideally suited for detecting rare and cryptic species, which an observer may rarely, if ever, encounter.

These cost effective monitoring tools have received wide coverage in both scientific and popular literature because of the following advantages:

- operate continually and silently
- work independently of an observer once they have been set up – at least as long as their batteries and picture storage medium (either film or digital SD cards) permit
- possible to simultaneously sample large areas for extended periods of time with relatively low manpower and thus provide opportunities to gather large amount of data
- record very accurate data without the animal being captured and with minimum disturbance
- provide proof of the presence of a species, particularly the elusive ones, in an area
- helpful in determining behavioural and activity patterns of animals
- the well-being and survival rate of animals can be observed over time
- document wildlife presence, abundance and population changes, particularly in the face of deforestation and habitat destruction
- an ideal tool for remote areas, since they do not need to be accessed daily

For these reasons, the uses of camera traps have enormous potential for the surveying and consequent management of wildlife. Camera traps are, therefore, increasingly being used to raise conservation awareness worldwide. Many NGOs are embracing the tool as a powerful way of reaching out to the public through electronic media. Camera trapped videos and photos of wildlife serve to be an important part of campaigns to save threatened or endangered species.

6.4.8 Limitations of using Camera Traps

There are certain limitations of camera traps which have been broadly categorized as *biological constrains* and *non-biological constrains* and are briefly discussed below:

Biological Constraints

- Camera traps can only gather information in a small area where their sensors are positioned. Hence, some animals can easily go undetected. Otherwise, a large number of camera traps are to be set up to cover all animals present in the survey area.
- Camera traps are ideally suited to sample medium to large sized, ground-dwelling mammals and some terrestrial birds (such as pheasants).
- Small mammals, such as rodents, are often too small to be detected reliably by the cameras.
- Predominantly arboreal species, such as most primates or squirrels, will rarely, if ever, be detected by ground based camera traps.
- The habitat can impact the usefulness of camera traps in several ways. Open habitats such as grasslands or wetlands may present few obvious landscape features along which animals could predictably move. In the absence of predicted travel routes the optimal choice of camera location is unclear.
- Camera traps work well under dry conditions and in areas of low humidity and are not an effective or a suitable choice in the humid tropics.

Non-biological Constraints

- The high initial costs of purchasing camera traps is often a major constrain to adopt this methodology in wildlife surveys, particularly in developing countries. The recurring costs (such as batteries, memory cards or film, processing and printing of images, external hard drives and card readers) also need to be considered before opting for this methodology in research.
- Transportation of the equipment to the survey sites along with other logistic support may be costlier than for other survey methods.
- The camera, cable, cord or other integral components may be damaged by certain animals. For instance, tigers, elephants and other big mammals have been known to attack and break the camera, while rodents often damage the cables and cords.
- There is always a risk of the loss of data due to equipment failure. These instruments operate on their own and do not require the presence of researcher. Therefore, malfunctioning of the instrument, is not immediately noticed by the researcher until the he/she visits the site to change the power source (*battery*) or data storage device (*film or data card*). As a result no data is recorded during this period.
- In spite of being fairly easy to operate, each model of camera traps has its own specifications. Thus, all team members need special training in order to be familiar with the model deployed.
- Camera traps usually collect a large amount of data. So, involvement of several trained people is necessary to process all the primary data and come up with a meaningful interpretation.

6.5 WILDLIFE TELEMETRY

The primary objective of wildlife telemetry is to acquire information about the behaviour of animals in their natural habitat. The oldest known method of identifying the presence of an animal in a particular area is by following their tracks of footprints in dust, mud, sand or snow. Even in the mid 20th century, the study of the animal movement and dispersion largely depended upon physically following the animal tracks (such as footprints, distribution of faeces, claw marks etc.) and live-trapping of the animal. Thereafter, the captured animal is marked (with bright and contrasting colours) or tagged (with brightly colour coded ear tags, collars and rings) and then is released with a hope to recapture them somewhere else. Despite the low costs, these earlier tracking methods are greatly influenced by field conditions, behaviour of the animal and also relied heavily on the efficiency of the trained personnel (Smallwood and Fitzhugh, 1995). Following this method the researcher needs to identify the marked animal from a distance, which might also lead to some degree of observer bias. Besides, tracking of movements of an animal are often not possible with simpler mark-recapture or mark-resight studies. Hence, these methods are not very effective and often end up with very little scientific information for the researchers. Such crudeness and inherent biases of this method are quite obvious.

Modern remote tracking methods like radio tracking, camera and video trapping etc. (Burghardt et al., 2007) and acoustic telemetry (Hu et al., 2005) evolved to track and identify animals overcome the drawbacks of earlier methods. In spite of being a relatively expensive technique compared to mark-recapture studies, radio-tracking led to some advantages to wildlife research *viz.*, ability to locate each animal when desired, as well as, to identify individual animals. Hence, radio telemetry is now widely applied for various scientific and conservation purposes.

6.5.1 Radio Telemetry or Very-High-Frequency (VHF) Radio Tracking

The VHF radio tracking was first used in 1963 (Cochran and Lord, 1963). Radio telemetry has revolutionized the wildlife research and has been used to study local movements, dispersal and migration routes, estimate home ranges, habitat use and selection, estimate population abundance, examine intra and interspecific relationships and estimate survival.

Radio Tracking vs Radio Telemetry

Radio tracking is the technique of locating an animal through the use of very-high frequency radio waves generated from a transmitting device borne by the animal to another receiving unit carried by the researcher. On the other hand, **radio telemetry** refers to the recording of data that can be used to infer the activity of the animal in a specific time.

Radio tracking is the primary form of information on the location of an animal at a particular time. In addition to the location of the animal, if any other forms of information such as heart rate, body temperature, vaginal temperature, foraging, defecation etc. are acquired, then the method is referred to as **radio telemetry** (Moll et al., 2007). Thus, radio-tracking involves telemetry. Due to such overlap between the two concepts and for the similarities in obtaining the information, both the terms (i.e. radio tracking and radio telemetry) are frequently used interchangeably.

Working Principle of Radio Telemetry

In radio telemetry initially the animal needs to be trapped and sedated for the initial deployment of the tracking device. This can be difficult in case of elusive or cryptic species. Once found, the animal has to be immobilized for long enough to attach the tracking device. Then a device is firmly placed on the animal, which emits a very high frequency (VHF) radio signal. For selecting an ideal transmitter, the device and its attachment need to have a few basic criteria (such as minimum weight, minimum effect on the animal, maximum protection for the transmitter and permanence of the attachment). To obtain better data, protection of the radio collared animal from various mortality factors (such as predation and accident) are also to be taken into consideration. Once the transmitting subunit is attached, the animal is released in the wild. Then the animal is tracked by the researcher once the VHF radio signals are 'picked up' by the receiving subunit. Frequencies of radio waves generated by different tracking systems are unique, which allow individual identification of the animals fitted with a transmitter.

Essential Instruments for Radio Telemetry

(i) Transmitting Subsystem: Transmitting subsystems include a transmitter with propagating antenna, a power source, protective cover for the electronic components and attachments to fix the system to the animal. It is advisable that the weight of the tracking device should not exceed 5 percent of the host's bodyweight in order to prevent detrimental effects on it's behaviour. Besides, tag shape is also important, particularly in case of flying and aquatic creatures. Because, the device attached on the animal's back might result in a drag, so animal would require greater amount of energy to move, resulting in increased traversing times and other deleterious effects.

(a) ***Radio transmitter:*** Radio transmitters considerably vary in terms of their size, mass and life of the unit. Complete transmitter packages can weigh as little as 0.8. Range of VHF transmitters typically lies within 5–10 km on ground, which is increased to 15–25 km aerially (Rodgers et al., 1996). Signals can be either continuous (which sounds through a speaker like a high-pitched whine) or pulsed (which sounds like a series of "beeps"). Pulsed signals are usually used at rates of 30–120 per minute. Lower and narrower pulse rates yield longer transmitter life. Frequencies used in wildlife telemetry usually range from 27 MHz to 401 MHz. But the commonest frequency ranges used for VHF tracking are 148–152 MHz, 163–165 MHz, and 216–220 MHz.

While setting the frequency of the radio-transmitters it is crucial to coordinate among researchers working in adjacent areas or in similar landscape to avoid possible interference and overlapping.

(b) ***Transmitting antennas:*** Transmitting antennas are one of the most important and integral components of any radio-transmitter package, since they project the signal for capture by receiving antennas. Transmitting antennas are basically of two types:

- *Whip antennas* consist of a wire with one end attached to the transmitter and the other end remaining free. Whip antennas incorporated into a collar are often used on large mammals.
- *Loop antennas* are connected on both ends to the transmitter, fits around the animal's neck and the diameter of the loop is adjusted to tune the antenna to match the frequency of the transmitter. Loop antennas are usually used on small mammals.

Orientation, construction, and length of a transmitting antenna (along with the power source) determine the effective power radiated (EPR) which determine the range of signal reception.

Transmitting antenna ideally should be oriented perpendicularly and away from the animal's body. But, their range is often compromised as these antennas are often embedded between layers of a collar, so that they are not entangled in vegetation or damaged.

(c) ***Power source:*** The total weight as well as the life of the transmitter is mainly determined by the battery used in any transmitting subunit. There is a proportional relationship between the weight of the battery and its lifetime. Also there are species-specific limits to the weight of a transmitter device, which an animal can carry without significantly affecting its survival or behaviour. Therefore, proper selection of the power source is critical.

Most tracking devices are powered mainly by three lithium batteries, as they provide the highest energy to weight ratio, operate over a wide temperature range, serve as a good energy source and have a long shelf life. Alternatively, solar powered tags are also used for some animals (Snyder et al., 1989) and are particularly well suited in tracking birds (Bamford et al., 2007). Such solar powered tracking devices are only suitable for species which are regularly in bright sunlight and are unlikely to damage or obscure the panel. Battery life in VHF telemetry could also be extended through duty-cycling wherein the transmitter is turned on and off at regular intervals (e.g., on 8 hr, off 16 hr). This feature minimizes the number of times a radio-tagged animal must be recaptured to replace a battery.

(d) ***Protective cover:*** There are various types of protective covers for the transmitting subunits which have different degrees of shock-resistance. These protective covers minimize damage done both by the animal (chewing, scratching, etc.) and by the environment (moisture, mechanical damage etc.). Many types of coating are commercially available such as bees wax, dental acrylic, epoxy resin, electrical resin, silastic and Plasti-Dip etc. In case of animals with aggressive lifestyles (like wolves), high-shock resistant crystals are often used to built the protective cover of radio transmitters. Various sealing materials are used to seal the transmitting subunits and selecting appropriate sealant is important while studying aquatic organisms.

(e) ***Attachments for radio transmitters:*** Selection of proper attachments for the radio transmitters is also very important. An unsuitable attachment can result in death or injury to the host animal, as well as, destruction or poor performance of the tracking tag.

- *Neck collar:* Collars have traditionally been used to fit radio transmitters on mammals with prominent narrow neck region, large ears, horns or antlers since these structures help to prevent the collar from slipping over and off the head of the animal (Markham, 2008). Collars are made from a variety of materials such as nylon, leather or brass depending on the host species. The radio tag is fastened around the neck of the animal using screw attachments or cable ties. In some highly social carnivores (such as wolves), the collar needs to be reinforced or armoured to prevent removal or destruction of the transmitter, antenna, or the entire collar (Thiel and Fritts, 1983).
- *Expandable collar:* Expandable collars remain fitted on the animal as the young

animals grow. Sewn pleats or foam-rubber inserts within the collar allows the collar to expand as the animal grows. Such expandable collars have been successfully applied in number of animals like mountain lions (Garcelon, 1977), black bears (Strathearn et al., 1984) and white-tailed deer fawns (Kunkel and Mech, 1994).

- *Ear-tag transmitters:* Some alternatives to applying collars or harnesses on mammals include ear-tag transmitters (Servheen et al., 1981).
- *Backpack harness:* Transmitters with whip antennas are fitted to backpacks with attachment loops under the wings (Fuller et al., 1998). Sea turtles have also been radio-tagged using transmitting harnesses (Ireland, 1980).
- *Leg band:* Transmitters are also fitted to the birds through loops under their legs (Rappole and Tipton, 1991) and leg-band transmitters.
- *Direct attachment:* Sometimes radio transmitters are attached directly to the body of an animal through adhesives. Direct attachment of tracking devices has been successfully attached to bats, hedgehogs and in bears. In birds, hip antennas are also adhered directly to tail feathers (Giroux et al., 1990).
- *Surgically implanted transmitters:* Radio transmitters are sometimes surgically implanted within different bodyparts of the focal animal such as subcutaneous transmitters, abdominal transmitters, or rumen transmitters. Such surgical implantation of transmitters are often practised in case of mammals (like beavers, otters, yellow-bellied marmots, lions, black bears), as well as, in various species of birds and snakes. Both internal and external radio-tags have been applied to fish also. However, surgical implantations are made only when external attachment is either not suitable or absolutely impossible. In case of implanted transmitters, the transmission range reduces significantly (sometimes < 50 percent) and there are also risks of post-operative infection and pathological complications. Invasiveness of the surgery and subsequent veterinary care may also result in biased data.

(ii) Receiving Subsystem: The receiving subsystems detect and identify signals from transmitters and usually comprise of a battery-powered receiver, a receiving antenna, cables, an amplifier and a detector (a mechanical or human recorder). Finally a human, with a speaker or headphones, interprets the signals received through this subunit (Samuel and Fuller, 1996).

Receiving Antennas: A typical receiver should be able to detect and distinguish signals of specific frequencies. Antennas increase the gain (signal gathering capacity) of a receiver and also assist the operator to determine the direction from which a signal is coming. Size of receiving antennas are inversely related with the frequency of the receiving waves (i.e. smaller antenna receives higher frequency waves). Larger antennas (receiving lower frequencies) generally yield greater gain and better directionality.

In spite of being larger in size and complicated, the **multi-element *Yagi* antenna** is very popular and commonly used for its greater range and precise directionality (Kuechle, 1982). It consists of a horizontal length of metal (usually aluminum) with 3–17 vertical lengths attached in one plane. The length of the vertical elements and their spacing depend on signal frequency. Origin of a signal can be received by swinging the antenna and determining the direction of the strongest signal when the tip of the *Yagi* is farthest from the user (Mech, 1983). Other antennas include omni-directional **dipole antennas**, bi-directional **Loop antennas,** small sized **Adcock or H–antennas** and large, stationary **Mounting antennas**.

- ***Cables:*** The signal is transferred from the antenna by coaxial cables to the receiver. These specialized cables shield the electronic signal against extraneous noise and minimize loss of signal strength (Samuel and Fuller, 1996).
- ***Power source:*** Most portable receivers are powered by standard alkaline batteries (i.e., 8 AA, 1.5 V penlight cells) and will function for 8–12 hours.
- ***Receiver:*** Standard receiver controls include a power switch, dials for gain and channel, band, and fine frequency adjustments, as well as, jacks for an external antenna, headphones, a recorder, and external power. Some receivers also have a volume control. With technological advancements, small hand-held receivers are now available which can store up to 999 frequencies and weigh only about 350 g.
- ***Recorders, counters and decoders:*** Recorders are of various types ranging from simple to complex. Finally the detector can be a researcher listening to the demodulated radio signal (this is called **manual tracking**) or a data-logger (this is termed **automatic tracking**). Counters and decoders are used in automatic recording systems primarily to count and decode signal pulses associated with telemetry. Such automated

devices are very useful for presence/absence, activity, or physiological studies and help the researcher by performing a majority of the recording, counting, and decoding necessary for data analysis.

Tracking Methods

Researchers track animals in the field mainly through **homing** or **triangulation**. Besides, passive remote tracking is done through automatic tracking systems.

(i) Homing: Homing is a tracking method of moving in the direction of the signal (toward its greatest strength) until the animal is physically sighted or detected (Figure 6.19). The signal increases as the researcher closes in on the animal.

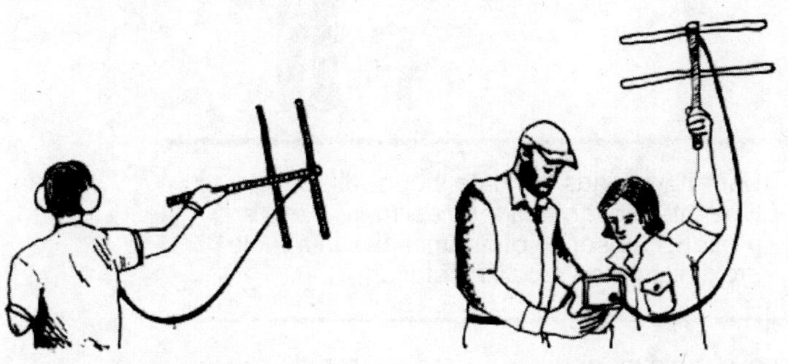

FIGURE 6.19 Illustration of tracking method 'Homing' in VHF tracking.

Then the gain of the receiver is continually decreasing to precisely identify the direction of the signal until the researcher either sees the animal or estimates its location when sufficiently near. However, this tracking method can introduce bias to the data as the animal may be disturbed due to the presence of the researcher in the close vicinity resulting in altered behaviour (White and Garrott, 1990).

(ii) Triangulation: Triangulation is the process of tracking animals where the position of an animal is determined by obtaining signal bearings from two different locations (preferably at angles of about 90° to one another). The position of the animal is determined by the intersection of these bearings. When more than two bearings are plotted, the bearings form a polygon on a map, which theoretically indicate the location of the animal as shown in Figure 6.20 (White and Garrott, 1990). Ideally several researchers should simultaneously record the bearing of an animal from different locations during triangulation. Alternatively, once a bearing is recorded, the researcher quickly moves to another location to take a second bearing (Kenward, 2001) and determine the position of the animal from the intersection of the bearings. But, if the animal also moves between the short time periods of two successive bearings, then the location of the animal would be inaccurate. As opposed to homing, in triangulation the animal is located with minimal disturbance since the researcher is usually far from the animal while recording a bearing, therefore, there is no alteration in the animal behaviour.

FIGURE 6.20 Illustration of animals tracking through VHF triangulation.

(iii) Automatic Tracking: In automatic radio-tracking researcher is not required to be in the field to obtain the animal's location as the bearings of an animal are recorded automatically by automated tracking systems (Figure 6.21). The researcher later downloads the data to know when and which animal with a radio tag was present within the radio range of the receiving station.

FIGURE 6.21 Illustration of automatic tracking of animals by a fixed radio station.

Advantages of VHF Radio-telemetry

- This simple method of tracking animals is the most useful and versatile type of radio-tracking with reasonable accuracy.
- VHF tags are light weighed with long (battery) life.
- The VHF tags available in market are relatively inexpensive.
- Suitable for monitoring a wide range of species from very small animals (even insects) to large mammals. The lightest tag currently available is 0.2 g. If funding is low or if a large number of animals are to be studied for long periods, VHF telemetry is the only option.

Disadvantages of VHF Radio-telemetry

- The tracking process through VHF radio tags are labour intensive and sometimes also weather-dependent.
- Possibility of bias through habitat disturbance as the researcher needs to be in the field to obtain tracking data.
- Homing also has the possibility of distorting locations through disturbance to the animal's habitat.
- Limited coverage. A researcher needs to be within radio range of an animal in order to determine its location (50–300 sq km). Thus conventional VHF is not used for tracking wide ranging species.
- Interpretation of location data is also complicated by the non-uniform error distribution.

6.5.2 Satellite Telemetry or Ultra-High-Frequency (UHF) Radio Tracking

Satellite telemetry utilizes a platform transmitter terminal (PTT) attached to an animal which sends an ultra-high frequency (UHF; e.g., 401.650 MHz) signal to satellites. Then the location of the PTTs (i.e., latitude and longitude) is relayed to receiving stations where researchers record and interpret the data. The procedure of satellite tracking has been illustrated in Figure 6.22.

If the aims of the study includes only to locate the animal, their movements, dispersal path and pattern, then satellite tracking is employed. Once a tracking device is placed on the focal animal, the researcher need not spend time on field to track the animal. Thus, satellite tracking saves a lot of field effort and is especially useful for monitoring dispersal pattern of long-ranging and migratory animals.

PTT of animal emits signal and it is received by satellite	Animal moves to a different location and signal from its PTT is again received by satellite.	The position of the animal is assessed from the known position of satellite at a particular time.

FIGURE 6.22 Illustration of satellite tracking of animals.

Advantages of UHF Radiotelemetry

- UHF radiotelemetry renders continuous and global coverage through ARGOS satellite. Thus, tracking a species is possible even in remote and nearly inaccessible terrain.
- Satellite telemetry is extremely useful for tracking organisms that are difficult to track through VHF-radio telemetry (like elusive and far-ranging species, penguins in Antarctic, off shore marine animals, etc.).
- Satellite telemetry is the only choice to document long-distance movements across formidable geographic terrains (like mountains and oceans), trans-border movements and easily identify the stopover and staging sites of migratory animals.
- Minimize travel time and field effort of the researcher.
- One-time handling of the animal is required until the battery of PTT expires. So the risk of disturbing the habitat and the focal species is greatly reduced.
- Near real-time updates of position of the animal is available. Such satellite-tracking locations can be superimposed on habitat information gathered via remote sensing and can serve as very useful scientific document in management (or conservation) of the species.

Disadvantages of UHF Radio-telemetry

- UHF radio telemetry devices are very expensive (10–20 times more than a conventional VHF transmitter) and data acquisition and processing cost is also too expensive.
- Satellite tracking devices and UHF radio tags are larger than VHF tags and are, therefore, often unsuitable for smaller animals.
- Apart from presence and dispersal data, satellite tracking does not provide any much other information. For example, information about size and trend of the population of focal species, the number of companions of a tagged animal, productivity and behaviour of the individual, rate of predation of a carnivore, as well as, the location, species, age, sex and condition of the kills made by these predators cannot be obtained by satellite tracking.
- Relatively less accurate (mean accuracy = 480 metres)
- Often need an additional VHF transmitter, to facilitate recapturing the animal and retrieving the expired PTT for re-use.

Reduction in the costs of satellite transmitters and allied equipments along with elevated accuracy level of satellite tracking in future would allow biologists to make greater use of those technologies in wildlife research.

6.5.3 GPS Telemetry

Since the implementation of the Global Positioning System (GPS) in 1993, a new era ushered in wildlife tracking (Tomkiewicz, 1996). A constellation of 24 artificial satellites are orbiting the earth in precise 12 hour orbits which broadcast signals and at least four GPS satellites are always in view from any position on Earth. Any GPS receiver needs to acquire signals from at least four such satellites in order to determine its three dimensional position and provides excellent spatial accuracy of a location (typically < 5 m) throughout the day anywhere in the world (Kaplan, 1996).

This GPS tracking revolutionized the field of wildlife telemetry and was first used to track animals in 1994. In this telemetry technique, GPS receiver is attached to the collar of an animal which receives signals from three or more satellites and records the time, date and location of the animal at programmed intervals (like once per hour, once per day etc.). The information is then either stored in the telemetry unit or remotely downloaded.

Unlike prior two telemetry methods (VHF radio telemetry and UHF satellite telemetry); GPS tracking is based on a radio receiver (rather than a transmitter) which is placed in the animal's collar. Here the GPS unit attached to the animal acts as receiver and the satellites function as transmitters. Therefore, the locations calculated and stored in the GPS unit (attached to the animal's collar) have to be transferred to the end-user (researcher). This procedure is illustrated through Figure 6.23.

GPS receiver on the animal continuously record the latitude and longitude of its position from the satellites	Researcher track the animal with GPS receiver through VHF or UHF tracking methods and collect the GPS device	Researcher conneets the GPS device to a computer to download data

Figure 6.23 Illustration of GPS tracking of animals.

Data Retrieval for GPS Tracking

The data is stored in the telemetry unit and three main methods of data retrieval are used. There are advantages and disadvantages to each type of data storage and retrieval.

(i) On-board Storage for Later Collar Retrieval and Subsequent Downloading: This is the simplest option of data retrieval but also with highest risk of complete data loss. GPS instruments attached to the collars store data and drop off the animal when expired after an automatic or remotely triggered drop-off mechanism. At the end of the study, the collar is retrieved and the locations are downloaded all at once from the collar (Merrill et al., 1998).

This reduces researcher effort on one hand and also minimizes invasiveness to the animal (only one handling required). Store-on-board collars are relatively smaller in size, less complex, contain comparatively smaller circuitry, require less hardware and are less expensive. However, in store-on-board method the risk of data loss is higher due to the risk of malfunction, loss or destruction of the collar. The unit may not collect data at all, may collect data at the wrong intervals and if the collar is not retrieved after the end of the study then all the data are lost (Merrill et al., 1998). Therefore, sometimes VHF transmitters with separate power source are attached to the GPS collars so that the collar can be located after the study. If the collar is still attached to the animal, then the animal must be re-sedated/captured to retrieve the collar. Some collars are equipped with automatic break-away mechanisms which physically break the collar and it slips off the animal's neck. The retrieved collar can then be reused after refurbishing with minimum cost (Merrill et al., 1998).

(ii) Remote Downloading to a Portable Receiver: In this process, the collar is programmed to transmit data through a VHF signal (some systems use FM-relay devices or a UHF modem) to the researcher's receiver. On a programmed schedule (e.g. weekly, daily, up to 5 times per day etc.) the reports are send to biologists who must then be in field to receive them.

In this method, intermittent retrieval of data is valuable in allowing data analysis throughout the study which allows the researcher to assess and, if required, supplement the location information with field data. However, the telemetry unit and the receiving equipment is relatively more complex, heavier and of higher cost. It also requires additional effort to retrieve data through VHF receiver on field and analyze the data.

(iii) Remote Relaying Through the ARGOS Satellite System: This method of data retrieval and storage uses the ARGOS satellite system to relay the intermittent data reports to the researcher. Therefore, the researcher gets data reports without being in the field. But, transmitting data to satellites requires high power for which, the telemetry unit with such data retrieval unit is very bulky. Therefore, such GPS telemetry units cannot be used for smaller animals. The cost of data retrieval through satellite is also very high as the researcher need to pay ARGOS for relaying data through its satellites.

Advantages of GPS Telemetry

- Global tracking system enables the acquisition of detailed location information anywhere in the world
- Generally do not require frequent field visits, which reduce in-field tracking time of an animal by biologists
- Data obtained through GPS telemetry is highly accurate (accuracy <5 m)
- GPS telemetry is especially suited to studies where intensive and frequent data is needed
- Obtain data on animal location anywhere in the world, 24 hours a day, in all weather and as frequently as every minute or as infrequently as once per week
- Possibility of disturbing the habitat of the focal species is greatly reduced

Disadvantages of GPS Telemetry

- Longevity of GPS receivers is also much less than conventional VHF units due to fairly high power consumption. Thus, precluding continual operation for long term studies.
- GPS receivers are heavy and are, therefore, suited only for monitoring larger animals.
- GPS tracking is expensive. A single GPS collar usually ranges from $3,000 to $4,500, about 10 times that of a VHF collar for mid-sized mammals (Merrill et al., 1998). Hence, fewer individual animals could be tracked because of such huge expense per GPS unit resulting in small sample size. But, for studying large areas GPS collars can be economical alternative to VHF radio tracking when cost per location is considered, as opposed to cost per animal. Being less labour intensive, the expenses of field visits and field personnel are also saved and more location data are obtained.
- Biases in the data must be considered because of differential interference of various habitat types on the receivability of GPS signals.
- High risk of data loss is possible due to loss of the GPS collar.

Solar powered GPS transmitters are now available for birds. GPS collars need to be made lighter so that it could be used on smaller species. More efficient antenna would reduce power requirements.

6.5.4 GPS–GSM Tracking

Data stored in the GPS receiver can also be uploaded to a cellular network and send to the researcher through SMS texting. The tag acquires GPS locations, and buffers them up until it is in range of a GSM tower. Once within the range of such tower, the data stored in GPS are transmitted through SMS. Many wilderness areas usually do not have cellular coverage. So, GPS–GSM tracking cannot be adopted to track and monitor wildlife in those remote areas. GPS-GSM collars are heavier than GPS data loggers, as they contain the GSM modem, its antenna and also a larger battery for increased power requirements.

6.5.5 Selection of Appropriate Telemetry Method

Each telemetry system has its advantages and disadvantages. None of the radio-tracking technology can simultaneously satisfy all of the following parameters: (i) small size, (ii) low weight, (iii) long lifetime, (iv) global coverage, (v) real time access to data anywhere in the world, (vi) excellent spatial accuracy, (vii) high sampling frequency and (viii) generate high resolution data from multiple sensors (ix) at low cost. So while deciding which type of tracking system is most appropriate for a particular wildlife telemetry study, the following three questions need to be carefully considered and addressed beforehand:

Focus of the Study

(a) ***Dispersal patterns:*** For animals moving over shorter distances conventional VHF transmitters and ground-based tracking could be adopted and cost effective. Satellite telemetry will be appropriate for animals with large home range or dispersal.

(b) ***Habitat selection*** (den or roost-site use): Ground-based triangulation methods are most appropriate.

Biological Characteristics of the Target Species

A number of biological parameters are often decisive on which telemetry type need to be used for their telemetry studies.

(a) ***Size:*** As per the 5 percent rule, very small animals can carry only small transmitters. So, for these animals VHF transmitters are the only option. But in large mammals UHF and GPS telemetry will be appropriate.
(b) ***Habitat:*** Aerial telemetry is appropriate in rugged or inaccessible terrains. But, animals inhabiting thick vegetation may not be suitable for satellite-based methods.
(c) ***Activity:*** For nocturnal animals aerial tracking may be less suitable because of possible flight restrictions.
(d) ***Movements:*** Satellite telemetry is suitable for very long distance migration and dispersal, especially those across national boundaries, over large topographical barriers or through inaccessible terrains. Local animal movements could be tracked through VHF radio telemetry.

Available Budget

As the costs of various telemetry type largely vary from one another, so the appropriate telemetry method should be selected based on the available fund and must be appropriate to fulfill the aims of the study.

6.5.6 Improvements Required in the Radio Tracking Systems

For VHF, satellite and GPS radio tracking, the primary refinement and essential improvements involve making the equipment more energy efficient by using more efficient, lighter and smaller batteries. This improvement would eventually result in lighter transmitters with longer life and greater range, which could then be used to track smaller animals. Such improvements would greatly facilitate radio-tracking and enhance its acceptance.

6.5.7 Applications of Wildlife Telemetry

Conventional radio telemetry has been used in numerous studies in different regions. In addition to the analysis of movements and home ranges, radio telemetry has been successfully used to study diverse topics including disease transmission, scent marking, predation, co-evolution, vocalizations, socio-ecology and breeding behaviours, sleep characteristics, as well as, physiological studies of heart rate, respiration rate, body temperature and nest egg condition.

Out of all telemetry techniques, VHF telemetry is the oldest and are extensively used by the researchers throughout the globe mainly due to the availability of smaller and relatively cheaper VHF tags. VHF telemetry is often adopted in studying animals that are sedentary, slow moving and are known to disperse short distance within a known distribution range. This VHF radio telemetry for wildlife was introduced in India in 1976 by Dr. LD Mech. After this initial study there was a rise in the radio telemetry studies in this country. Between 1976 to 1980 two sambars (*Rusa unicolor*), three nilgai (*Boselaphus tragocamelus*), two chitals (*Axis axis*) and one wild boar (*Sus scrofa*) were collared and tracked under the auspices of Project Tiger. Again in 1980, one Asiatic elephant (*Elephas maximus*), one tiger (*Panthera tigris*) and one Asiatic lion (*Panthera leo persica*) were radio-collared and tracked. Among the avian species, white crested kalij (*Lophura leucomelanos hamiltoni*) became the first bird species to be monitored using VHF telemetry in 1987. In the very next year (1988), swamp francolin (*Francolinus gularis*) was studied using radio telemetry. In India, first wildlife radio-tracking study on reptiles was carried out on gharial (*Gavialis gangeticus*) in the year 1985.

On the other hand, satellite telemetry is best applicable for studying far ranging species that are almost impossible to track with conventional VHF radio telemetry. Satellite telemetry offers a powerful tool in the conservation efforts, especially when it is combined with Landsat image analysis of habitats utilized by the wildlife species that are tagged. Thus, satellite telemetry emerged as an important tool in wildlife studies. Although satellite telemetry is more expensive than VHF tracking, it may be the only option in case of far ranging species (such as transoceanic migratory birds or offshore marine mammals). Satellite tracking of long-distance migrants has allowed scientists to identify migration routes and important staging and stopover sites. Such information is critical for implementing conservation activities along flyways that include many countries with various political challenges. Satellite telemetry has also been useful in tracking the marine mammals like dugongs, dolphins, hooded seals, humpback whales, as well as, other aquatic animals like sea turtles, basking sharks. Terrestrial animals such as African wild dogs, muskoxen, camels, wolves and elephants have also been tracked by satellite telemetry. Over the globe, satellite telemetry studies have been carried out in many long-migrating avian species, like, bald eagles (*Haliaeetus leucocephalus*), Eurasian cranes, white-naped cranes (*Grus vipio*), hooded cranes (*Grus monacha*), demoiselle cranes (*Grus virgo*), Japanese red-crowned cranes (*Grus japonensis*), white storks (*Ciconia ciconia*), lesser spotted eagles (*Clanga pomarina*) and several seabirds. Smaller species like shorebirds, cormorants, rails, coots, grebes, corvids, sparrows, smaller ducks, gulls, raptors, herons and egrets, are not usually suitable for satellite telemetry studies, as because they are either diving birds or are too small (<500 g) to accommodate PTTs. However, some studies were carried out on smaller species like northern pintail (*Anas acuta*) and the eastern curlew (*Numenius madagascariensis*). Satellite transmitters have been useful to mark important locations, find the den or nest and also to mark fawning sites. Besides, implanted transmitters can also help authorities to catch the poachers (Samuel and Fuller 1996). In spite of such wide potential and despite of being extensively used to study migratory birds in different part of the globe, the use of this technology is rather limited in the Indian subcontinent. Very few satellite tracking studies have been conducted in India. Satellite tags were first used to track the migratory Eurasian crane (*Grus grus*) from Keoladeo National Park to their breeding grounds in Siberia between 1993 and 1994. In 2001, four olive-ridley turtles (*Lepidochelys olivacea*) were tracked using satellite telemetry which had thrown light on many of the unknown facets of the life history of these marine turtles. In the winter of 1999–2000, two bar-headed geese (*Anser indicus*) were fitted with PTTs and one of them was tracked to its probable breeding grounds in Tibet (Javed et al., 2000).

GPS telemetry for wildlife study is relatively new and the first animal-based GPS location system was introduced in 1994. GPS telemetry is the most accurate form of tracking and can be used with reasonable confidence for relatively fine-scale habitat studies (Rodgers et al., 1996). Reliability and accuracy of GPS collars have been tested for moose (Moen et al., 1996; Dussault et al., 1999), white-tailed deer (Bowman et al., 2000), and wolves (Merrill, 2002).

6.6 REMOTE SENSING, GEOGRAPHIC INFORMATION SYSTEM AND GPS IN WILDLIFE RESEARCH

Remote sensing technologies largely deal with satellite imageries generated by means of various types of electromagnetic waves to analyze many aspects of geospatial data. According to Dr. Nicholas Short "remote sensing is a technology for sampling electromagnetic radiation to acquire and interpret non-immediate geospatial data from which to extract information about features, objects, and classes on the Earth's land surface, oceans, and atmosphere." American Society for Programmetry and Remote Sensing (ASPRS) defined remote sensing as "the measurement or acquisition of information of some property of an object or phenomenon, by a recording device that is not in physical or intimate contact with the object or phenomenon under study" (Colwell, 1983). Alternatively, Jensen (2005) defined it as "the art and science of obtaining information about an object without being in direct contact with the object". The technology of remote sensing has undergone immense advancement over last several decades and their application has also increased across various disciplines. The electromagnetic waves reflected from the Earth's surface is recorded by sensors mounted in various instruments and the data received by those sensors are then interpreted though various software to produce final output.

6.6.1 Fundamentals of Remote Sensing

Remote sensing deals with the detection and measurement of phenomena with devices sensitive to electromagnetic energy such as *light* (cameras and scanners), *heat* (thermal scanners), *radio waves* (radar) etc. Camera is one of the most popular instruments used in remote sensing. Remote sensing science mainly deals with electromagnetic energy as this is the only form of energy which can transfer through vacuum (present between the sun and the earth). In space electromagnetic waves travel at the speed of light (i.e., 3 $\times 10^8$ m/s).

Two major steps in remote sensing are: "(i) *data collection* and (ii) *data analysis*. Data collection process involves an energy source, propagation of energy through atmosphere and finally capturing the waves to produce data in either digital or pictorial form. Thus, recorder, medium of transmission and receiver of data are three essential components for data collection for any remote sensing studies.

Sun acts as the primary energy source used in most of the remote sensing systems. The wavelength of the electromagnetic spectrum present in sunlight range from 0.3 μm to 1000000 μm (Figure 6.24). Human eye can perceive a very small portion of this electromagnetic spectrum (from 0.4 μm to 0.7 μm) and are regarded as 'visible spectrum'. Ultraviolet (UV) and infrared (IR) wavelengths respectively adjoin the violet end and red end of the visible spectrum. The part of electromagnetic spectrum having wavelengths of 1 mm to 1 m, is known as microwaves. Remote sensing systems usually use visible, infrared, thermal infrared or microwave regions of the solar radiation which is reflected, emitted or scattered by the objects depending on its physical and chemical properties.

Electromagnetic waves coming as incident radiation from the sun are reflected, absorbed or transmitted from various objects on Earth (like the top of the clouds, water surfaces, build-up areas, vegetation covers or the uncovered terrestrial earthen areas like rocks and soils). Such electromagnetic waves reflected or emitted from Earth's surface once again enter the atmosphere and are finally radiated back to space. While passing through the atmosphere and after hitting the Earth surfaces their wavelengths alter, directions change and the electromagnetic waves scatter due to reflection and refraction. The proportion of such reflected, absorbed or transmitted energy also varies depending on the condition and material type of the Earth's surface. Such reradiated electromagnetic waves are finally recorded by the airborne or satellite borne sensors. These remote sensing images are used to differentiate between different features of a particular geographical area. The general process and elements involved in data collection by remote sensing is illustrated in Figure 6.25.

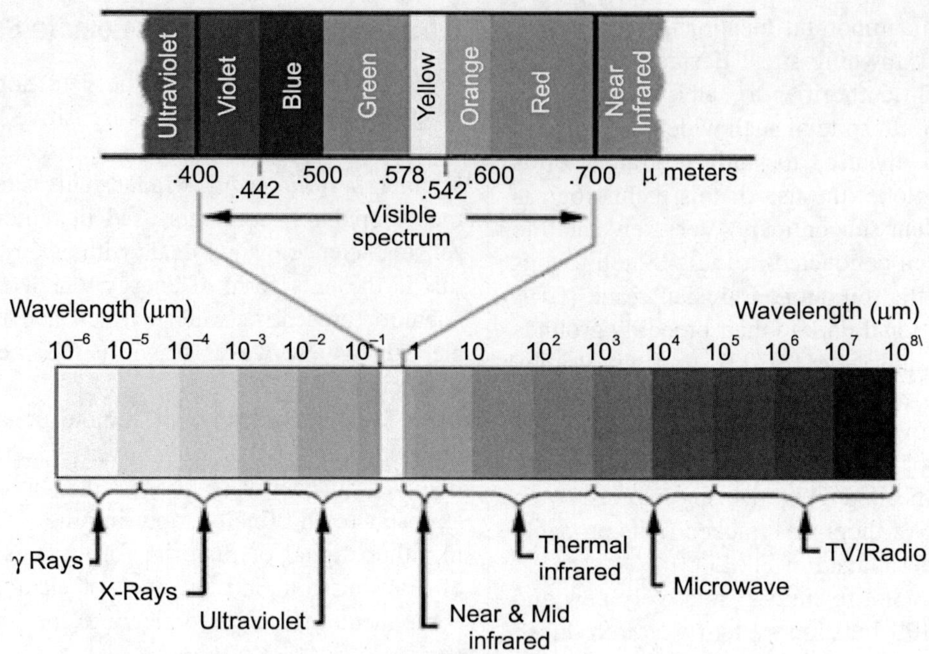

FIGURE 6.24 Different types of electromagnetic waves

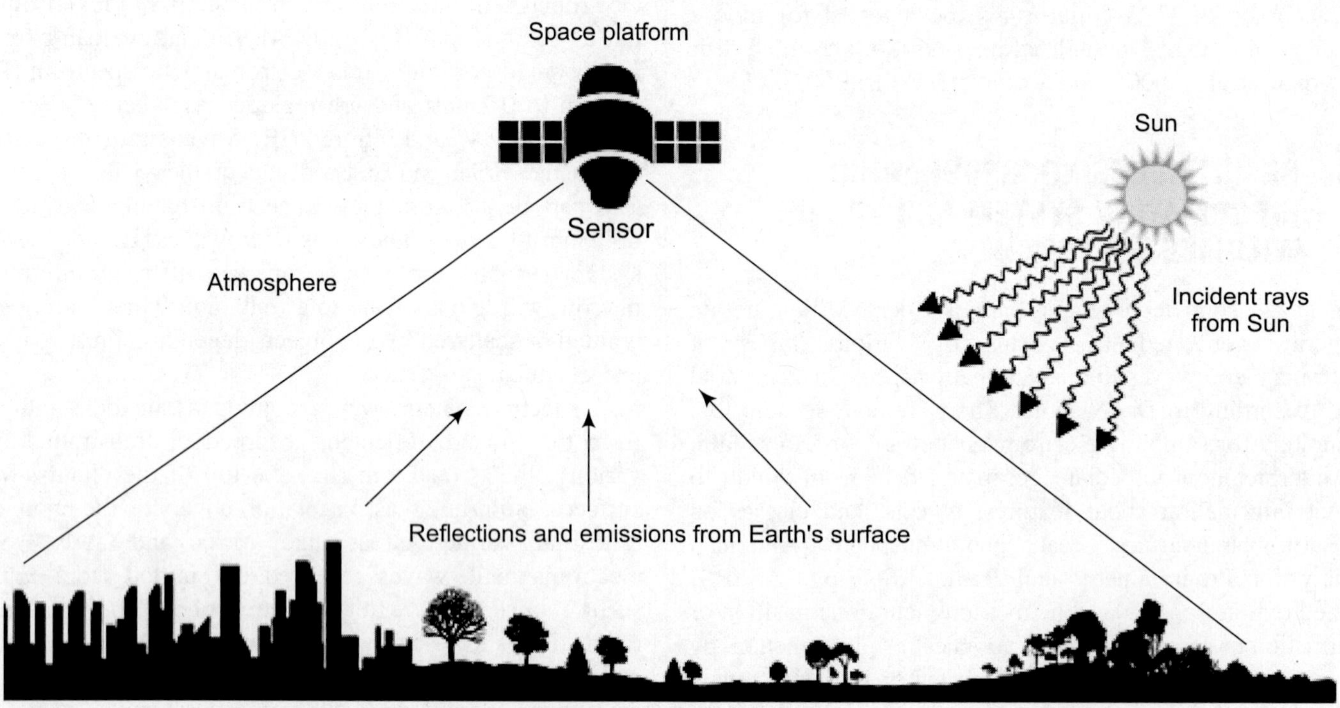

FIGURE 6.25 Processes and elements involved in data collection by remote sensing.

On the other hand, *data analysis* process involves – collection of field data to complement remote sensing data, visual interpretation of aerial pictures or satellite imageries, computer-aided interpretation of digital data (through software) and lastly preparation of maps as final output.

6.6.2 Components of Remote Sensing Systems

(i) Remote Sensing Platforms

Any remote sensing sensor need to be mounted on a carrier and are usually placed on a stable platform away from the target. The level where such sensors are mounted are known as remote sensing platforms. Distance of the sensors from ground range from 1 m to 36,000 km. Based on the level at which the sensors are mounted, the remote sensing platforms are of three types:

(a) ***Ground platform***: Ground platform is the level where the scanner operates from few meters above ground. Example: Ladder, Towers, etc.

(b) ***Aerial platform:*** Aerial platform is the level where the scanner usually operates from a height of about 100 m to 10 km. Aerial platforms provide images of much wider geographic area. These images allow the scientists to identify objects and understand the land-use pattern in a much better way, which would otherwise never be possible from any earth-bound vantage point. But, these aerial platforms remain airborne for a limited period for which data cannot be collected continually. Example: Balloon, Aircraft etc.

(c) ***Space Platform:*** In case of space platforms, the sensors are mounted at varying altitudes ranging from 200–40,000 km and truly provide the scope of continuous monitoring and repetitive coverage of Earth's surface. Space platforms are mounted on satellites. Moon is the natural satellite of this planet. In addition to that there are several artificial satellites revolving around the Earth. These artificial satellites are the commonest and widely used vehicles for mounting the sensors in space platforms.

Following are some advantages and disadvantages of a sensor being mounted on satellites in space platforms (Table 6.24):

Table 6.24 Advantages and Disadvantages of Space Platforms

Advantages	*Disadvantages*
❒ Synoptic view, which provide information about very large area	❒ Needs ground verification
❒ Repetitive coverage	❒ Does not offer minute details
❒ Time efficient and cost effective	❒ Often expensive
❒ Overcomes inaccessibility and collects information about areas not easily accessible in ground survey	❒ Not the best tool for small areas
❒ Faster extraction of GIS-ready data	❒ Needs experts to extract data
❒ Multi-spectral—Sensors can measure energy at wavelengths beyond human vision range (UV, IR, microwave)	
❒ Global monitoring is possible from nearly any site on earth	
❒ Multi-temporal	
❒ Multi-sensor	

(ii) Remote Sensing Sensors

The instruments that record electromagnetic radiations are called 'sensors'. Depending on the energy source used to illuminate the object under study, the sensors are of two types:

(a) ***Passive sensors:*** In passive remote sensing sensor systems, the naturally radiated or reflected energy (like sunrays) from the Earth's surface features are utilized and measured by the sensors. They usually operate in different spectral bands from the aerial or space platforms. Passive sensors do not have their own source of energy.
Example: Photographic camera, optical scanners etc.

(b) ***Active sensors:*** An active remote sensing sensor system supplies its own energy to illuminate the object and then measures the reflected energy returned to it. The source of energy is often man-made.
Example: Microwave radar, laser etc.

Passive remote sensing sensor system is quite similar to taking a photograph on a bright sunny day, while active remote sensing sensor system is like photographing an object in complete darkness using the flash bulb.

Depending on the end product, the sensors are also classified into two types:

(a) ***Imaging sensors:*** In imaging sensors the radiation is received from specific points of the area being studied through an image producing device (like camera). Here the reflected or emitted wavelengths from various features of Earth's surface are recorded either digitally or on photographic films of a camera and produce the images of the required part of the terrain. Subsequently aerial photographs are produced. Therefore, imaging sensors are also called photographic sensors. Photographic sensors record the reflected solar energy from Earth surface within a range of 0.38–1.1 μm (visible and near IR spectrum).

(b) ***Non-imaging sensors:*** Non-imaging sensors, also called non-photographic sensor or multi spectral scanners (MSS), measure the radiation received from all points within the focal area. Then they integrate this radiation and produce the results in the form of electrical signals of varying strength. MSS usually record energy over a wide spectral range (0.3–14 μm) and (1mm-1m). They can operate from aircrafts, as well as, from satellites. MSS perpendicularly scans the ground line-by-line. Therefore, they view only a small area of the ground at a particular moment.

6.6.3 Resolution of Sensors

Data obtained in a sensor should be spectrally separable, spatially discernible and be frequently recorded. *Resolution* is defined as the ability to distinguish and discriminate between two (or more) spatially near or spectrally similar objects. Each remote sensing system has four major types of resolutions associated to it *viz.* spectral resolution, spatial resolution, radiometric resolution and temporal resolution.

(a) **Spectral resolution:** Spectral resolution may be defined as the number and dimension of wavelengths of the electromagnetic spectrum measured through the sensors. Based on the objective of a particular study, the remote sensing system may be configured to collect data of a specific band or multiple wavelengths of the electromagnetic spectrum.

(b) **Spatial resolution:** Spatial resolution refers to the smallest unit-area measured by the sensor of a remote sensing system. Therefore, this refers to the ability of a particular sensor to resolve the smallest angular or linear separation between two objects.

(c) **Radiometric resolution:** Radiometric resolution is the ability of a sensor to quantify the radiance reflected or emitted by a target and to measure the smallest differences in energy in terms of brightness values (digital numbers) for each pixel. This is the sensitivity of a sensor to differentiate in signal strength while recording the radiant flux reflected or emitted from the terrain.

(d) **Temporal resolution:** Temporal resolution of a remote sensing system refers to the revisit time between two successive image acquisitions over the same area. This refers to how often a particular sensor records imagery of a particular area.

6.6.4 Advantages of Remote Sensing

- Remote sensing can provide large amount of data in a shorter amount of time and also dramatically reduces the field work of a researcher or surveyor.
- Remote sensing devices are often programmed to collect data systematically, which can remove the sampling bias that might otherwise be encountered in case of on-field data collection. This advanced technology thus leads to increased land coverage and systematic data collection over very large geographical areas than just some point observations (Jensen, 2005).
- Regions difficult or impossible to reach (like hazardous terrains, open oceans, hot and cold deserts, high mountains, extreme weather areas etc.) can be monitored using remote sensing data.
- Increased ground resolution of a digital imagery produced through GIS can directly serve as a visual aid for many policy implementations. Remote sensing images also indirectly serves as a source to derive information and allows retrieval of data for various other aspects such as land use pattern, land cover, atmospheric emissions, vegetation cover, location and distribution of water bodies, cloud cover etc.
- Remote sensing plays vital role in predictive modelling and simulation. Comparing a present image with a historical one also help to identify if any subtle, dramatic or marked change occurred over certain period of time (Colwell and Jensen, 1998).

6.6.5 Geographic Information System or GIS

Geographic Information System (GIS) is comprised of powerful set of tools and is used to collect, store, retrieve, transform, analyze and present spatially referenced data for the real world (Burrough and McDonnell, 1998) in order to support decision making for planning and management of land use, natural resources, environment, transportation, urban facilities, and other administrative records. Grimshaw (1993) simply defines GIS as 'a technology that enables decision-makers to explore the geographical dimension of data'.

Components of GIS

GIS is an advanced and complex technology which comprises of the following components:

- *Hardware:* The hardware of GIS primarily includes desktop or laptop computers with sufficient disc drive capacity (preferably over 80 GB). Besides, digitizers and scanners are data capture hardware and printers and plotters are the required output devices.
- *Software:* The software of GIS are ArcGIS, DIVA GIS, Q GIS, GeoMedia, GRASS, MapInfo etc.
- *Data:* GIS utilizes both geographic data and related tabular information. Data models are the schemes for organizing the geospatial data.

- *People:* People in a GIS platform are broadly of two types – one group comprise of GIS experts who vectorize the map objects and prepare GIS based maps and the other group mainly include mostly researchers along with other end users who use the maps and data in the GIS platform to represent their research findings.

How does GIS Work?

The series of layers of information or data can be added over a base map or image. Each data layer is called a 'theme' and can be turned on or off depending on the viewer's interest. The themes can overlap and have specific data associated with them. Thus, functions of any GIS include capturing, storage, querying of data; subsequent analysis and display of data, as well as, producing a need based final output.

Advantages of GIS

Geospatial data and information are better maintained in a standard format of GIS. They are relatively easier to revise and update. GIS data are also easier to search, analyse and represent and can be shared and exchanged freely. Moreover, the geospatial data help to generate more value added products. Subsequently, more efficient and better decisions could be made.

6.6.6 Geographic Positioning System or GPS—A Brief Account

Satellite-based navigation and surveying system for accurately determining the geo-coordinates of any location on Earth utilizing the radio signals from the satellites is known as Global Positioning System or GPS. First operational GPS satellite was launched by the US Military in the year 1978. To make the Global Positioning System functional and operative, there is a constellation of 24 satellites operating in 6 different orbital planes (i.e. 4 satellites in each plane) in space and all 24 GPS satellites became operative since 1993 (Guha, 2008). On the other hand, precise position of a particular area (latitude and longitude) on earth is determined by the 'GPS receiver' which receive signal from 3 or more satellites present on space. There are two types of GPS receiver *viz.* Handheld GPS receiver and Differential GPS receiver. GPS instruments are used for:

- ***Positioning:*** GPS receivers provide accurate and precise information of a location of any place at any time irrespective of weather conditions.
- ***Navigation:*** GPS instruments assist to move from one location to another and in most instruments there are scope of display and storage of navigation paths.
- ***Time dissemination:*** GPS instruments are used to display precise time of a particular location across the globe.
- ***Mapping:*** GPS instruments are used for creating maps by recording a series of locations and plotting them in the remote sensing image through GIS software.
- ***Tracking:*** Once GPS receivers are tagged to any object (or living being), then the object or living being carrying the GPS can easily be tracked from satellite using wireless communications. This method is used to track people, vehicles, and is frequently used to monitor the migration of far ranging animals.

6.6.7 Data Analysis in Remote Sensing and GIS

Remotely sensed data are entered in the GIS database and are very much useful in monitoring large areas. Data analysis is very important to draw inferences. This can be carried out through visual interpretation of aerial images or analysis of satellite imageries by software, subsequent statistical computation and GIS modeling. Remote sensing images (aerial photo or a satellite image) contain information on many objects present on Earth but do not define them. It is the onus on the expert of remote sensing and GIS to analyze and interpret an image. Such image analysis is not only a time taking process, but also require extensive and specialized training. It is pertinent to mention here that remote sensing yields fundamental scientific information and is therefore, different from other mapping sciences (such as cartography) which often rely on data produced elsewhere (Jensen, 2005).

Processing of Satellite Imagery

The images of Earth surface features from a multispectral scanner (MSS) consisting of a number of black and white images for each spectral band. Therefore, for data interpretation the image needs to be processed properly. A colour composite is the pictorial representation of the satellite imagery in a combination of colours, which is produced when any three spectral bands are passed through red, green and blue (primary colours) filters respectively and ultimately projected on a screen. Such colour composites are of two types:

(i) ***True colour composite*:** In a True Colour Composite (TCC) the image is generated by displaying the red band as red, green band as green and blue band as blue (Figure 6.26 A). As the displayed colour in the colour composite correspond to the spectral bands in which the data are acquired, so the end-product looks 'natural'. Hence, this colour composite is termed as True Colour Composite or TCC. However, TCC often restricts the EMR band only within the visible range and not beyond it (like infrared, ultraviolet or microwaves). Therefore, TCC are rarely used in scientific studies.

(ii) ***False colour composite:*** In a False Colour Composite (FCC) the image is generated by displaying the near infrared band as red, red band as green and green band as blue (Figure 6.26 B). Portrayal of a scene as FCC by combining at least 3 bands enhances the interpretability of the scene. Therefore, FCCs are most commonly used in scientific studies. The plants reflect infrared rays, so any area with dense vegetation cover appears red in a standard FCC.

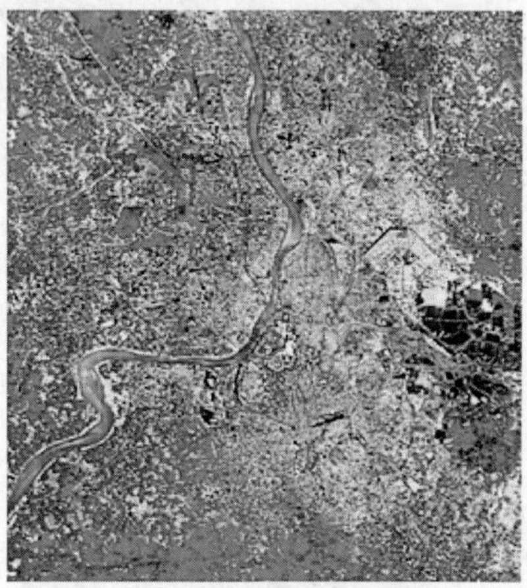

(A) Standard True Colour Composite of Kolkata
(Source: Google Earth)

(B) Standard False Colour Composite of Kolkata
(Source: http://fas.org/irp/imint/docs/rst/Sect16/Sect16_10.html)

Figure 6.26 (A) True-colour Composite; (B) False Colour Composite. (*see* Colour Plate I)

Interpretation of Remote Sensing Imagery

Image interpretation is the identification of various objects present within an image and to judge their significance (Phillipson, 1997). **Photogrammetry** is the art and science of making accurate measurements of various objects in an aerial imagery. Orthophotographs are very important for photogrammetry. An **orthophotograph** is an aerial photograph that has been corrected to remove distortions caused by camera optics, tilt of the device and elevation differences of the terrain. Human perform ***analog photogrammetry*** to visually interpret an image and is usually applied when the data is in hardcopy (like 9″×9″ photographic print or as positive transparency). On the other hand, ***digital (or analytical) photogrammetry*** is performed to analyze digital images using appropriate GIS software. The method of photogrammetry is selected based on the type of remote sensing data, as well as, being driven by the objective of the study and available resources. Nevertheless, sophisticated analysis of satellite imageries (like the extraction of quantitative information from remote sensor data) is usually done using appropriate GIS software.

Most fundamental elements that are routinely used in interpretation of any aerial photograph or a satellite image include *shape*, *size*, *tone and colour*, *texture*, *pattern*, *height and depth*, *site and association*, etc. But it is difficult to identify any object in an image if one has never seen that particular object in real world.

Some other information (like political boundary, property line, socio-economic data, transportation, hazard information, geological data, topographic and bathymetric data, soil taxonomy, terrain features, forest stand, surface and subsurface hydrological data, wetland information etc.) are parallally collected. These are termed as **collateral or ancillary information**. These ancillary information are stored in GIS database for easy retrieval and overlay on the remotely sensed data (Jensen, 2005). For better interpretation, remote sensing data should always be analyzed taking these collateral or ancillary information into account (Ramsay et al., 1995).

Scale of Remote Sensing Imagery

The scale of a photograph is defined as the ratio of a distance on the photograph to the distance corresponding to it on the ground. Images with a scale of 1:500000 or 1: 250000 is selected when the area of study is large, while studying small or medium area images with scales of 1:100000 or 1: 50000 or even 1:25000 are preferred.

Geo-referencing

Geo-referencing is the process of providing the precise geographic positions of the known data points (at least three) on a digitized image. Images obtained through remote sensing need to be geo-referenced for further analysis.

Synergy between remote sensing and GIS can be useful for both the techniques. Remote sensing provides timely and accurate updation of spatially distributed variables in the GIS database, while remote sensing itself is benefitted through the access to accurate ancillary data of the GIS database for improved image classification and precision in other type of modelling (Jensen et al., 1994; Jensen, 2005).

6.6.8 Applications of Remote Sensing and Geographical Information System

Application of remote sensing in India dates back to as early as 1920 when black and white aerial photographs were used for geological surveys. Aerial photographs were also used in 1926 to assess the flood in Indus River. In 1970, Indian Space Research Organization (ISRO) used sophisticated sensors on a helicopter to obtain high quality aerial images, which were then used for remote detection of root-wilt disease in the coconut plantations in Kerala. This is possibly the first application of remote sensing technology in agriculture in India. In recent times there is a sharp increase in the application of these technologies and are applied in diverse branches of study. Among different areas where remote sensing and GIS are applicable include:

- *National security:* Over the years, these technologies played crucial role in maintaining national security of many countries; very useful in weapons monitoring, navigation, targeting the risk zones etc. and thus help in adopting better policy measures for homeland security.
- *Land information system:* Useful in updating road maps, evaluating asphalt conditions and for wetland delineation of a region; often used to identify rural, sub urban and urban areas, as well as, to maintain administrative and legal records of a particular region. Particularly helpful in urban planning which include the assessment of urban sprawl, fringe area development, developing land-use policy, utility services, public works etc.
- *Geological studies:* For assessment of mineral deposition and mining, geomorphological studies, petroleum exploration etc.
- *Disaster management:* Often applied to predict floods, storms and cyclones. These are also useful to assess the impact of natural hazards like earthquake, landslides etc. and are vital in the management of the same.
- *Natural resource management:* Remote sensing also plays an important role in the management of natural resources; used for habitat analysis, land use and land cover monitoring, environmental assessment and also mountain, ocean and coastal zone management etc. These technologies are also used to monitor pest and disease outbreaks in an area, mapping impervious surface, as well as, in hydrological, geomorphological and geological assessment of a particular terrain.
- *Agricultural sector:* Application of remote sensing and GIS is growing rapidly in agricultural practices like in soil management, planning of irrigation, monitoring and evaluation of plantations, crop health analysis, nutrient deficiency, insect damage, weed infestation, herbicide damage etc. They are also crucial for compliance mapping and to estimate the yield in order to bring better precision in adopting agricultural policies.
- *Management of water resources:* Identification of precise groundwater location helps in selecting potential areas for ground water exploration. In addition to ground water, quality and distribution of wetlands and other surface water bodies can be plotted on satellite images with relative ease. Satellite imageries are also used for the assessment of flood and drought, map the areas inundated by flood, duration of flood, identify the areas with flood deposits, areas vulnerable to bank erosion, glacier inventory, detection of water pollution etc.

6.6.9 Applications in Wildlife Studies

Human-caused disruptions, such as habitat loss, pollution, invasive species introduction, and climate change, are some major threats to wildlife health and biodiversity. Understanding the specific needs of wildlife populations is the key in preventing local or global extinctions, rehabilitating populations and restoring habitat. Accurate and real time information of a region is very essential for wildlife management (Kushwaha et al., 2000). Remote sensing and GIS technologies are effective tools for managing, analyzing and visualizing wildlife data in order to identify target areas where conservation and/or management practices are needed. It is also useful to monitor the impact and effectiveness of a particular wildlife management strategy. Wildlife biologists, managers and professionals use these advanced technologies to explore various aspects of habitat and ecology of wild flora and fauna like habitat assessment, identification of population patches and linkages between them, monitoring corridors, habitat suitability and carrying capacity analysis, assess the density and distribution of a species over time (historical and present record) etc. Aerial and satellite imageries are often useful in monitoring the high risk zones of deforestation, disease outbreaks, forest fire and human-animal conflicts. These technologies are also used in the preparation of Management Plans, as well as, to scrutinize the implementation and progress of certain management activities and to evaluate its impact.

Generally following procedure is followed for the application of remote sensing and GIS in various wildlife studies:

1. Topographic maps (toposheets) of the study are collected which usually indicate the administrative boundaries, transportation network, drainage, canal, settlement locations, etc.
2. Such toposheets are then scanned and digitized.
3. The digitized toposheets are then 'geo-referenced' and common ground control points (GCP) are plotted on it.
4. The forest and wildlife administrative boundaries (like division, range, beat, compartment etc.) are extracted from the working plans and/or wildlife management plan of the Forest Department and transferred to the geo-referenced digitized toposheets.
5. Satellite images obtained through remote sensing are processed in GIS platform.
6. Different thematic maps (*viz.* land use, land cover, forest type, vegetation mapping, risk zone etc.) are produced and are usually displayed as False Colour Composite (FCC).
7. Field work is carried out and sample plots are located using Global Positioning System (GPS).
8. Plotting the GPS locations on the FCC of the thematic maps help to identify and/or prioritize the key area in a particular wildlife study.
9. The outcome of the study (distribution and pattern, habitat use and suitability, risk zones etc.) is often plotted on the remote sensing image of the study area and pictorially represented for better comprehension.

Remote sensing and GIS are now extensively used in wildlife studies and detail account of them is beyond the scope of this textbook. So, few key areas of wildlife studies with wide application of remote sensing and GIS are discussed below:

- ***Mapping forest cover and vegetation status:*** Statistics of forest cover, forest types, deforestation rate etc. are essential data for forest management and forestry science. These data are now being obtained applying remote sensing and GIS. Remote sensing and GIS technologies are very often used in the forest-resource survey, monitoring forest cover, evaluating forest ecosystem, assessing plant diseases, and insect manifestations. Although it is very difficult to interpret the species composition of an understorey from remote sensing images, but the deteriorating forest areas and deforestation can easily be monitored. Nationwide Forest Cover Mapping was carried out by National Remote Sensing Association (NRSA) using remote sensing technology resulting in 1:1 million scale map of the then forest cover of India. This first remote sensing effort by NRSA revealed that actual tree cover of this country is much lower than 'legal' forest cover and created concern amongst the policy makers. Chauhan et al., (2012) also applied remote sensing method to know the status of forest cover conditions of protected areas like Great Himalayan National Park (GHNP), Sainj Wildlife Sanctuary and Tirthan Wildlife Sanctuary located in Kullu district of Himachal Pradesh in India. Forest cover map generated from Landsat TM satellite data using digital image processing revealed that the Ecozone had maximum forest cover followed by Tirthan Wildlife Sanctuary, Sainj Wildlife Sanctuary and least forest cover was found in GHNP core area. Subsequently, they came up with nice conservation recommendations.

- ***Monitoring wildlife corridors:*** The forest connectivity and corridors are critical for biodiversity conservation. Wildlife corridor is a narrow strip of forest cover, connecting two larger forest areas. These corridors help in dispersal and movement of individuals between different habitats for food, fodder, shelter, breeding and other activities. Corridors connect habitat patches for the exchange of materials and energy in the form of food web and dispersal and play very important role in genetic exchange (Vogt et al., 2007). Degradation of forest connectivity in between landscapes occurs due to fragmentation and anthropogenic activity, which causes biodiversity decline. Yadav et al., (2012) studied the change detection and conflict analysis of Nagzira-Navegaon Corridor in central India. They found that although the forest cover in both these protected areas did not change over the years, yet the habitat changes in the corridor areas were extensive and the density of forest in the corridor region reduced very much. From this study they concluded that the overall forest cover and water bodies are decreasing continuously in the corridor. If present scenario of deforestation and degradation of water bodies continue, then the corridor existence would be severely threatened, thereby threatening the survival of many faunal species in both the protected areas, as well as, those who thrive primarily on the corridors.

- ***Managing human-animal conflicts:*** Man-animal conflicts in different parts of the country have increased particularly due to habitat degradation and human encroachments in forest areas, In such scenario, geospatial technologies (remote sensing and GIS) have been widely used and played a crucial role in understanding the causes of such conflicts in relation to habitat characteristics. Agarwal et al., (2011) studied human-leopard conflicts in areas of Pauri Garhwal in Uttarakhand, India using remote sensing and GIS and identified the high conflict zones. This information is very useful to implement better conservation measures in these areas to protect both human and leopards and also to alleviate this treat efficiently. Similar studies may also help to mitigate other human-animal conflicts (like human-elephant conflict, human-tiger conflict, human-lion conflict etc.) in different corners of the country.
- ***Habitat suitability modelling:*** Various studies indicate that geospatial technology play vital role in the field of habitat evaluation and management (Khanna et al., 2001; Nandy et al., 2007). Remote sensing and GIS can be applied in the modelling of habitat suitability index. Many authors are now studying habitat suitability of various wild faunal species in wilderness areas present different corners of this country. Few such studies are mentioned here. WWF-India in collaboration with Arunachal Pradesh Forest Department prepared the tiger habitat suitability map and recommended the potential sites for watch tower using the satellite imagery of the Namdapha National Park in Arunachal Pradesh. In the state of Maharashtra, geoinformatics approach using remote sensing and GIS technologies for modelling habitat-suitability of Great Indian Bustard was done in Solapur district (Yedage et al., 2011). Similar studies have been carried out for Muntjac (*Muntiacus muntjak*) in Chandoli Tiger Reserve (Ekwal et al., 2012) and for elephant habitat in Kolhapur district (Tikhile et al., 2013).
- ***Monitoring forest fire:*** Satellite remote sensing is very efficient and practical means of monitoring and acquiring information about the spatial distribution of fire scars and fire activity. Hence, Sowmya and Somasekhar (2010) studied the forest fire patterns of Bhadra WLS in Karnataka using satellite imageries from 1989 to 2006. They mapped the burnt areas and four categories of fire risk regions (low, moderate, high and very high) were identified and predicted that around 10.31 percent of the protected area falls under moderate risk zone. This study was useful in the forest fire management of this PA.
- ***Preparation of management plans of the protected areas:*** Management Plans of many Protected Areas of this country are now being created using the remote sensing and GIS technologies.

REVIEW QUESTIONS

1. Why census is necessary? Differentiate between total count and sample count. What is quadrat sampling?
2. State the principle of line transect method. Elaborate line transect method. Why this method is well accepted by the scientific community? Mention its limitations.
3. Distinguish between pug mark and hoof mark. Give an account on the pug mark census technique for tiger census using tiger tracer. State the advantage of using Pug Impression Pad (PIP).
4. State the basic criteria for the measurement of pugs of tiger. Differentiate hind pugmark from that of front ones. How could you distinguish between (a) Male and female and (b) tiger cub and leopard?
5. Comment on the recent controversies regarding the acceptance of Pug marking technique for wild tiger census.
6. State the principle of Call count of birds with a note on its merits and demerits. Distinguish between song and call.
7. Mention basic principle of Point Count method of bird counting. How the radius is being determined in point count? Elaborate the method of point count. Comment on the merits and demerits of point count.

8. Enumerate the advantages of using Camera Traps in wildlife research. How does non-triggered camera trap differ from triggered one? Discuss in brief the biological and non-biological constrains of using camera traps.
9. Establish the importance of telemetry in wildlife research. Mention the working principle of radio telemetry. Give an account on different Very-high Frequency (VHF) radio telemetry instruments along with their functional mechanisms. Point out advantages and limitations of VHF radio telemetry.
10. Elaborate the homing and triangulation methods of animal tracking.
11. What is satellite telemetry? How does satellite telemetry work? Explain its mechanism of action. Add notes on advantages and disadvantages of satellite telemetry.
12. What is GPS? Why GPS instruments are used?
13. Define GPS telemetry. Mention the working principle of GPS telemetry. How does it differ from satellite telemetry? Explain different mechanisms of data retrieval in GPS tracking. Add notes on advantages and disadvantages of GPS telemetry.
14. What are the important parameters considered to select appropriate telemetry method? Briefly discuss the applications of wildlife telemetry in Indian context.
15. Define remote sensing. Mention the working principle of remote sensing. What do you mean by resolution of sensors? Elaborate different types of resolutions of remote sensing sensors.
16. What do you mean by remote sensing platforms? Give an account on different types of remote sensing platforms. Briefly narrate the advantages and disadvantages of space platforms in remote sensing.
17. Define Geographical Information System (GIS). What are the essential components of GIS? Distinguish between 'True Colour Composite' and 'False Colour Composite'. Define 'scale' of a remote sensing imagery.
18. Briefly discuss different applications of remote sensing and GIS in Indian context. In India, how remote sensing and GIS technologies are used in (i) forest survey, (ii) monitoring wildlife corridors, (iii) managing human-wildlife conflicts, (iv) habitat suitability modelling, (v) management of forest fires and (vi) preparation of management plans of protected areas.

REFERENCES

Agarwal, M., Chauhan, D.S., Goyal, S.P. and Qureshi, Q., Managing Human-Leopard Conflicts in Pauri Garhwal, Uttaranchal, India using Geographical Information System and Remote Sensing, *International Journal of Scientific and Engineering Research*, **2**, 9, 1–8, 2011.

Bamford, A.J., Diekmann, M., Monadjem, A. and Mendelsohn, J., Ranging behaviour of cape vultures *Gyps coprotheres* from an endangered population in Namibia. *Bird Conservation International*, **17**, 331–339, 2007.

Bowman, J.L., Kochanny, C.O., Demarais, S. and Leopold, B.D., Evaluation of a GPS collar for white-tailed deer, *Wildlife Society Bulletin*, **28**, 1, 131–140, 2000.

Burghardt, T., Barham, P.J., Campbell, N., Cuthill, I.C., Sherley, R.B. and Leshoro, T.M., A fully automated computer vision system for the biometric identification of african penguins (*Spheniscus demersus*) on robben island. In: *6th International Penguin Conference (IPC07)* (E.J. Woehler, Ed.), Hobart, Tasmania, Australia, 2007.

Burnham, K.P., Anderson, D.R. and Laake, J.L., Estimation of density from line transect sampling of biological populations, *Wildlife Monographs*, **72**, 1–202, 1980.

Burrough, P.A. and McDonnell, R.A., *Principles of Geographical Information Systems*, Oxford University Press, Oxford, 1998.

Chauhan, V.K., Acharya, R., Kumar, A. and Singh, R.D., Application of Remote Sensing in studying forest cover conditions of protected areas in Himachal Pradesh, India. In: *Proceedings of 14th Annual International Conference and Exhibition on Geospatial Information Technology and Applications, 7-9th February 2012*, 2012. Retrieved from: http://indiageospatialforum.org/2012/proceedings/ppt/vandana.pdf

Cochran, W.W. and Lord, R.D. Jr, A radio-tracking system for wild animals, *Journal of Wildlife Management*, **27**, 9–24, 1963.

Colwell, R.N. and Jensen, J.R., Extraction and modelling of urban attributes using remote sensing technology, p 164–188, In: *People and Pixels* (Liverman, D., Ed.), National Academy Press, Washington DC, 1998.

Colwell, R.N., *Manual of Remote Sensing* (2nd Edn.), American Society of Programmetry, Falls Church, VA., 1983.

Dussault, C., Courtois, R., Ouellet, J-P and Huot, J., Evaluation of GPS telemetry collar performance for habitat studies in the boreal forest. *Wildlife Society Bulletin*, **27**, 4, 959–964, 1999.

Ekwal, I., Tahir, H. and Tahir, M., Modelling of habitat suitability index for Muntjac (*Muntiacus muntjak)* using remote sensing. *Journal of Settlements and Spatial Planning*, **3**, 2, 93–102, 2012.

Erickson, A.W. and Siniff, D.B., A statistical evaluation of factors influencing aerial survey results on brown bears, *Transactions of the North American Wildlife and Natural Resources Conference*, **28**, 391–409, 1963.

Ethier, T., *Survey Methods for Raptors in British Columbia*, British Columbia Resource Inventory Committee, Victoria, British Columbia, 1993.

Ferguson, H.L., Relative abundance and diversity of winter raptors in Spokane County, eastern Washington. *Journal of Raptor Research*, **38**, 181–186, 2004.

Forsman, E.D., Meslow, E.C. and Strub, M.J., Spotted owl abundance in young versus old-growth forests, Oregon. *Wildlife Society Bulletin*, **5**, 43–47, 1977.

Fuller, M.R. and Mosher, J.A., Raptor survey techniques, In: *Raptor Management Techniques Manual* (Pendleton, G., Millsap, B.A., Cline, K.W. and Bird, D.M. Eds.), National Wildlife Federation, Washington DC, 1987.

Fuller, M.R., Seegar, W.S. and Schueck, L.S., Routes and travel rates of migrating Peregrine Falcons *Falco peregrinus* and Swainson's Hawks *Buteo swainsoni* in the Western Hemisphere. *Journal of Avian Biology*, **29**, 4, 433–440, 1998.

Garcelon, D.K., An expandable drop-off transmitter collar for young mountain lions. *California Department of Fish and Wildlife*, **63**, 185–189, 1977.

Ghosh, D., *Distribution and habitat preference of Tragopan satyra (Linnaeus, 1758), Tragopan blythii (Jerdon, 1870) and Tragopan temminckii (Gray, 1831) in northeast India* (Ph.D. Thesis), University of Calcutta, Kolkata, India, 2003.

Giroux, J.F., Bell, D.V., Percival, S. and Summers R.W., Tail-mounted radio transmitters for waterfowl. *Journal of Field Ornithology*, **61**, 303–309, 1990.

Goldstein, M.I., Nest-site characteristics of crested caracaras in La Pampa, Argentina. *Journal of Raptor Research*, **34,** 330–333, 2000.

Grimshaw, D.J., *Bringing GIS into Business Geoinformation*, Longman, London, 1993.

Guha, P.K., *Remote Sensing for the Beginners* (3rd Ed.), East-West Press, New Delhi, 2008.

Hu, W., Tran, V.N., Bulusu, N., Chou, C.T., Jha, S. and Taylor, A, The design and evaluation of a hybrid sensor network for cane-toad monitoring. In: *IPSN' 05: Proceedings of the 4th international symposium on Information Processing in Sensor Networks*, IEEE Press, Piscataway, New Jersey, USA, 2005.

Ireland, L.C., Homing behavior of juvenile green turtles, *Chelonia mydas*. In: *A Handbook on Biotelemetry and Radio Tracking* (Amlaner, C.J. Jr. and MacDonald, D.W., Eds.,), pp. 761–764, Permagon Press, Oxford, U.K., 1980.

Javed, S., *Study on Bird Community Structures of Terai Forest in Dudwa National Park* (Ph.D. Thesis), Aligarh Muslim University, Aligarh, India, 1996.

Javed, S. and Kaul, R., *Field Methods for Bird Surveys*, Bombay Natural History Society, Mumbai, India, 2002.

Javed, S., Takekawa, J.Y., Douglas, D.C., Rahmani, A.R., Kanai, Y., Nagendran, M., Choudhury, B.C. and Sharma, S., Tracking the spring migration of a bar-headed goose (*Anser indicus*) across the Himalaya with satellite telemetry, *Global Journal of Environmental Research,* **4**, 2, 195–205, 2000.

Jensen, J.R., *Remote Sensing of the Environment—An Earth Resource Perspective*, Pearson Education Inc., Delhi, India, 2005.

Jensen, J.R., Cowen, D.J., Halls, J., Narumalani, S., Schmidt, N., Davis, B.A. and Burgess, B., Improved urban infrastructure mapping and forecasting for Bell South using remote sensing and geographic information system technology, *Photographic Engineering and Remote Sensing*, **60**, 3, 339–346, 1994.

Johnson, D. and Enderson, J.H., Roadside raptor census in Colorado—winter 1971–72, *The Wilson Bulletin*, **84**, 489–490, 1972.

Kaplan, E. (Ed.), *Understanding GPS: Principles and Applications*, Artech House, 1996.

Karanth, K.U. and Nichols, J.D., Estimation of tiger densities in India using photographic captures and recaptures, *Ecology*, **79**, 2852–2862, 1998.

Kaul, R. and Howman, S., Distribution and habitat requirements of the northern painted francolin Francolinus pictus pallidus in Jamnagar, India, *Gibier Faune Sauvage*, **9**, 483–492, 1992.

Kenward, R.E. *A Manual for Wildlife Radio Tagging*, Academic Press, San Diego, California, 2001.

Khaling, S., Kaul, R. and Saha, G.K., Surveys of the Satyr Tragopan *Tragopan satyra* in the Singhalila National Park, Darjeeling, India using spring call counts, *Bird Conservation International*, **9**, 361–371, 1999.

Khanna, V., Ravichandran, M.S. and Kushwaha, S.P.S., Corridor analysis in Rajaji–Corbett Elephant Reserve—a remote sensing and GIS approach, *Journal of the Indian Society of Remote Sensing*, **29**, 1, 41–46, 2001.

Kuechle, V.B., State of the art of biotelemetry in North America. In: *Telemetric Studies of Vertebrates*, Cheeseman, C.L. and Mitson, R.B. Eds., Academic Press, London, U.K., 1982.

Kunkel, K.E. and Mech, L.D., Wolf and bear predation on white-tailed deer fawns. *Canadian Journal of Zoology*, **72,** 1557–1565, 1994.

Kushwaha, P.S., Roy, P.S., Azeem, A., Boruah, P. and Lahan, P., Land area change and habitat suitability analysis in Kaziranga. *Tiger Paper*, **27**, 9–17, 2000.

Ludwig, J.A. and Reynolds, J.F., *Statistical Ecology: A Primer on Methods and Computing*, John Wiley & Sons, New York, 1988.

Mace, R.D., Minta, S.C., Manley, T.L. and Aune, K.A., Estimating grizzly bear population size using camera sightings. *Wildlife Society Bulletin*, **22**, 74–83, 1994.

Markham, A., *On a wildlife tracking and telemetry system: a wireless network approach* (Ph.D. Thesis), Department of Electrical Engineering, University of Cape Town, Cape Town, South Africa, 2008.

Mazumdar, S., *Ecology and Conservation Issues of Black Kite Milvus migrans govinda (sykes) In Kolkata Municipal Corporation Area* (Ph.D. Thesis), University of Calcutta, Kolkata, India, 2013.

McKinnon, S. and K. Phillipps, *A Field Guide to the Birds of Borneo, Sumatra, Java and Bali*, Oxford University Press, Oxford, UK, 1993.

McLeod, M.A. and Andersen, D.E., Red-shouldered Hawk broadcast surveys: factors affecting detection of responses and population trends. *The Journal of Wildlife Management,* **62**, 1385–1397, 1998.

Mech, L.D., *A Handbook of Animal Radio-tracking*. University of Minnesota Press, Minneapolis, 1983.

Merrill, S.B., *An evaluation of the use of global position system telemetry in studying wolf biology* (Ph.D. Thesis), University of Minnesota, Minnesota, 2002.

Merrill, S.B., Adams, L.G., Nelson, M.E. and Mech, L.D., Testing releasable GPS collars on wolves and white-tailed deer. *Wildlife Society Bulletin,* **26**, 4, 830–835, 1998.

Moen, R., Pastor, J., Cohen, Y., and Schwartz, C.C., Effects of moose movement and habitat use on GPS collar performance. *Journal of Wildlife Management*, **60**, 659–668, 1998.

Moll, R.J., Millspaugh, J.J., Beringer, J., Sartwell, J., He, Z., A new 'view' of ecology and conservation through animal-borne video systems. *Trends in Ecology and Evolution*, **22**, 12, 660–668, 2007.

Nandy, S., Kushwaha, S.P.S. and Mukhopadhyay, S., Monitoring the Chilla-Motichur wildlife corridor using geospatial tools. *Journal for Nature Conservation*, **15**, 237–244, 2007.

Newman, D.E., Factors influencing the winter roadside counts of cottontails. *Journal of Wildlife Management*, **23**, 290–294, 1959.

Noon, B.R., Techniques for sampling avian habitats. *The Use of Multivariate Statistics in Studies of Wildlife Habitat* USDA Forest Service General Technical Report RM-87, (Capen, D.E., Ed.), U.S. Department of Agriculture, 1981.

Oelke, H., Limitations of the mapping method, pp. 114–118 In: *Estimating numbers of terrestrial birds. Studies in Avian Biology (Issue 6)* (Ralph, C.J. and Scott, J.M. Eds.), Cooper Ornithological Society, Camarillo, California, 1981.

Panwar, H.S., A note on tiger census technique based on pugmark tracings. *Cheetal,* **22**, 40–46, 1980.

Phillipson, W., *Manual of Photographic Interpretation* (2nd Edn.), American Society for Programmetry and Remote Sensing, Bethesda, MD, 555 p, 1997.

Pomeroy, D. and and Tengecho, B., 1986, A method for analysing bird distribution. *African Journal of Ecology,* **24**, 243–253, 1986.

Raj, D., *The Design of Sample Surveys*. McGraw-Hill, New York, 390 p, 1972.

Ramsay, R.D., Falconer, A. and Jensen, J.R., The relationship between NOAA-AVHRR normalized difference vegetation index and ecoregions of Utah. *Remote Sensing of Environment*, **53**, 188–198, 1995.

Rappole, J.H. and Tipton, A.R., New harness design for attachment of radio transmitters to small passerines. *Journal of Field Ornithology*, **62**, 335–337, 1991.

Rappole, J.H., Lopez, D.N., Tewes, M. and Everett, D., Remote trip cameras as a means for surveying for nocturnal felids, pp. 45–49. In: *Nocturnal Mammals: Techniques for Study. School of Forest Resources* (Brooks, R.P., Ed.), Pennsylvania State University Park Press, University Park, Pennsylvania, 1985.

Rodgers, W.A., *Techniques for Wildlife Census in India: A Field Manual*, Wildlife Institute of India, Dehradun, 1991.

Rodgers, A.R., Rempel R.S. and Abraham K.F., A GPS-based telemetry system. *Wildlife Society Bulletin*, **24**, 3, 559–566, 1996.

Rosene, W.J., A summer whistling cock count of bob white as an index to wintering population. *Journal of Wildlife Management*, **21**, 153–158, 1957.

Ross, C. and Reeve, N., Survey and census methods: population distribution and density, In: *Field and*

Laboratory Methods in Primatology: A Practical Guide. (Setchell, J.M. and Curtis, D.J., Eds.), Cambridge University Press, Cambridge, 2003.

Saharia, V.B., Wildlife census and monitoring in India: a review, pp. 159–172. In: *Proceedings of The Workshop On Wild Life Ecology*, Zoological Survey of India, Dehra Dun, India, 1978.

Samuel, M.D. and Fuller M.R., Wildlife Radiotelemetry. In: *Research and Management Techniques for Wildlife and Habitats,* 5th ed. (Bookhout, T.A., Ed.), The Wildlife Society, Bethesda, MD, 1996.

Servheen, C., Their T.T., Jonkel, C.J. and D. Beaty. An ear-mounted transmitter for bears. *Wildlife Society Bulletin*, **9**, 56–57, 1981.

Sharma, S. and Wright, B., *Monitoring Tigers in Ranthambhore using the Digital Pugmark Technique*, Wildlife Protection Society of India, New Delhi, 2005. Retrieved from: http://www.wpsi-india.org/images/ranthambore_census_report.pdf

Sharma, S., *Evaluation of Pugmark Mark Census Technique* (MSc. Thesis), Saurashtra University, Rajkot and Wildlife Institute of India, Dehra Dun, 2001.

Silveira L., Jácomo, A.T.A. and Diniz-Filho, J.A.F., Camera trap, line transect census and track surveys: a comparative evaluation. *Biological Conservation*, **114**, 351–355, 2003.

Singh, L.A.K., *Tracking tigers: Guidelines for Estimating Wild Tiger Populations Using the Pugmark Technique*, WWF Tiger Conservation Program, New Delhi. India, 1999.

Smallwood, K.S. and Fitzhugh, E.L., A track count for estimating mountain lion (*Felis concolor californica*) population trend. *Biological Conservation*, **71**, 251–259. 1995.

Snyder, N.F.R., Beissinger, S.R. and Fuller, M.R., Solar radio-transmitters on snail kites in Florida, *Journal of Field Ornithology*, **60**, 171–177, 1989.

Sowmya, S.V. and Somashekar, R.K., Application of remote sensing and geographical information system in mapping forest fire risk zone at Bhadra wildlife sanctuary, India. *Journal of Environmental Biology*, **31**, 969–974, 2010.

Strathearn, S.M., Lotimer J.S., Kolenosky G.B. and Lintack W.M., An expanding break-away radio collar for black bear, *Journal of Wildlife Management*, **48**, 939–942, 1984.

Tak P.C. and Lamba B.S., A review of census and monitoring techniques of wild life populations and observations on relative abundance of some mammals in Corbett National Park, pp. 185–197, In: *Proceedings of The Workshop on Wild Life Ecology*, Zoological Survey of India, Dehra Dun, India, 1978.

Thiel, R.P. and Fritts S.H., Chewing-removal of radio collars by gray wolves in Wisconsin, *Journal of Wildlife Management,* **47**, 851–852, 1983.

Thomas, L., Laake, J.L., Derry, J.F., Buckland, S.T., Borchers, D.L., Anderson, D.R., Burnham, K.P., Strindberg, S., Hedley, S.L., Burt, M.L., Marques, F.F.C., Pollard, J.H. and Fewster, R.M., Distance 3.5, Research Unit for Wildlife Population Assessment, University of St. Andrews, UK., 1998. Retrieved from: http://www.ruwpa.st-and.ac.uk/distance/

Thomas, L., Buckland, S.T., Burnham, K.P., Anderson, D.R., Laake, J.L., Borchers, D.L. and Strindberg, S., Distance sampling, In: *Encyclopaedia of Environmetrics* (El-Shaarawi, A.H. and Piegorsch, W.W., Eds.), John Wiley, Chichester, 2002.

Tikhile, P., Gavade, V.V., Patil, R.R. and Palkar, J.M., Elephant habitat suitability in southern part of Kolhapur district with geoinformatics approach, *International Journal of Science and Nature*, **4**, 304–310, 2013.

Tomkiewicz, S., GPS Application for Wildlife: A Review, *Telonics Quarterly*, **9**, 1–12, 1996.

Vinuela, J., Road transects as a large-scale census method for raptors: the case of the Red Kite *Milvus milvus* in Spain, *Bird Study*, **44**, 155–165, 1997.

Vogt, P., Riitters, K.H., Iwanowski, M., Estreguil, C., Kozak, J. and Soille, P., Mapping landscape Corridors. *Ecological Indicators*, **7**, 481–488, 2007.

White, G.C. and Garrott, R.A., *Analysis of Wildlife Radio-Tracking Data*, Academic Press, Inc., San Diego, 1990.

Whitworth, D., Newman, S.H., Mundkur, T., and Harris, P. *Wild Birds and Avian Influenza: an introduction to applied field research and disease sampling techniques (FAO Animal Production and Health Manual,* No. 5*)*, Food and Agriculture Organization of the United Nations, Rome, 2007.

Yadav, P.K., Kapoor, M. and Sarma, K., Land use land cover mapping, change detection and conflict analysis of Nagzira-Navegaon Corridor, Central India using Geospatial Technology, *International Journal of Remote Sensing and GIS*, **1**, 90–98, 2012.

Yedage, A.S., Patekar, P.R., Gavali, R.S., and Gavade, V.V., Habitat suitability modeling for Great Indian Bustard (GIB), in Solapur district; A geoinformatics approach, pp. 1–8, In: *Proceedings of 12th Esri India User Conference 2011*, 2011. Retrieved from: http://www. esri.in/~/media/esri-india/files/pdfs/events/uc2011/papers/NRM_UCP0011.pdf

7

CAPTURE, HANDLING AND RESCUE OPERATIONS OF WILD ANIMALS AND THEIR MANAGEMENT

7.1 CAPTURING OF WILD ANIMALS

Capturing of wild animals is an age old practice. Over the years, many animals have been trapped for a variety of reasons—to procure food, clothing, for recreation and hunting etc. Capturing of animals also has connection with pest and disease control programmes, population regulation activities, wildlife management issues and research. Although setting traps require time and energy, yet using various traps to capture animals is found to be relatively safe, inexpensive and very efficient. But, due to the injuries suffered by the animals and cruelty of some trapping procedure, use of traps is very much controversial in Indian context. Regardless of the reasons for capture, scientists univocally agree that animal welfare and safety are two most important concerns during capture, handling and rescue operations of wild animals. Therefore, capture methods should be employed ensuring minimum distress or pain to the animal during capture procedure.

Capturing of animals involves both art and science. For instance, most wildlife managers deploy professional game capture teams as successful game capture requires both practical and scientific skills, experience and the use of appropriate method with proper equipments. Individuals of a wild species in captivity are under greater stress than domestic species. Suffering from continuous and higher stress during capture and even after capture during transportation, wild animals are more susceptible to injury and serious infirmity during capture, handling and transportation. So, any successful capture operation includes effective handling, transportation and subsequent care of animals in captivity where enough cautions have been taken to minimize stress. In addition to the welfare of captured animal, human safety must also be given top most priority as many wild fauna are potentially dangerous to the handler. Therefore, every capture procedure must also ensure maximum safety of the handler. Important aspects to be considered while planning a capture operation are summarized in Table 7.1.

7.2 CAPTURE METHODS

Several new techniques to capture animals of varying sizes have been developed in recent times. Several traps are broadly classified as **(i) live traps** (where the animal is captured live without sustaining much injury) and **(ii) lethal or kill traps** (where the animal is killed or suffers severe injuries). Among lethal traps, snap traps, scissor traps, harpoon traps, choker loop traps and pincher traps are useful for capturing mice, rats, moles and voles. These traps can be baited or left un-baited and are lethal to the animal captured. Another kill or lethal trap, conibear traps are useful for capturing beavers.

In both these forms, some traps are meant to be left unbaited, whereas others will never successfully capture an animal without bait. Many household food items like peanut butter, nuts and seeds, cat food and sardines are attractive to a variety of wildlife species and are often used to allure the targeted animal in baited traps. However, baits used to allure the target animal often varies depending on the target species.

Table 7.1 Important Considerations while Planning a Capture Operation

Any capture operation should be thoroughly planned and the following aspects must be considered beforehand:

- **Selection of Proper Animal:** The physical condition including health, sexes and ages of the animals, number of young and possible advanced and expected pregnancy of the targeted animal for capture need to be thoroughly assessed.
- **Selection of Proper Timing:** Capturing should not be done during extreme climatic conditions (such as very hot summers or very cold winters) as health condition of animals deteriorate during harsh weather. It is advisable to start capture operations early in the morning during pleasant or slightly warm days.
- **Selection of Proper Capture Method:** Safest and most effective capture method should be selected based on the specific type of animal to be captured. For instance, mist netting may be useful to capture songbirds, but are often a wrong method to capture birds of prey. As compared to other animals, capturing of mammals often becomes more difficult because of their varying size (small rodents to large carnivores) and aggressive attitude in many species., Certain game animals (such as elephant, rhino, hippopotamus, giraffe etc.), however, require specialized capture techniques.
- Every person involved in the operation should be briefed in detail about their specific task.
- Necessary permissions required for the capture, holding and transport of animals should be taken.

7.2.1 Capture of Wild Amphibians, Reptiles and Mammals

Different types of specially designed traps are used to capture small mammals, reptiles and amphibians. Most animals are captured by hand, using mechanical devices, remote injection of drugs or drugs administered orally in bait. Some of the most popular capture methods are briefly discussed below:

(i) ***Hand capture:*** Hand capture of animals is the simplest technique and is deployed in a variety of situations like monitoring and research activities and the removal of nuisance, derelict or displaced fauna. There are numerous methods suitable for capturing wildlife by hand, some by grasping it with the bare hands before it is able to escape while others require the use of specific tools. All species can potentially be collected in this manner, but it is mostly applied during the capture of amphibians, reptiles and sick or injured animals of different other taxa. Care should be taken while applying force to capture an animal, because excessive force might break the limbs or even suffocate the animal. Hand capture of the target animal should also be done efficiently but quickly so that the animals suffers minimal stress and injury. Gloves or other personal protective measures (e.g. glasses, long sleeve clothing, boots etc.) need to be used to avoid scratches and bites.

(ii) ***Hand netting:*** Hand netting is a technique most commonly used to capture medium-sized ground dwelling mammals in open terrain. But, it can also be used for birds, reptiles, frogs and some invertebrates using typical long hand nets (Figure 7.1). The rate of success of this capture method depends on many factors, like the speed of the animal and its proximity to cover, as well as, the skill of the operator. Merit of this technique is that it is quick and inflicts only short-term stress to the animals.

FIGURE 7.1 Illustration of a hand net and capture of an animal through hand capture method.

(iii) ***Noosing:*** Noosing is a technique used to catch larger reptiles (e.g. monitors and crocodiles) and some mammals in rare occasion. Noosing involves the use of a rope or nylon slip loop usually attached to a solid cylindrical rod. The loop is then placed around the neck of the animal and pulled tight so that the animal cannot escape before it is restrained.

(iv) ***Tonging:*** Usually used to capture snakes (snake tongs) or to retrieve invertebrates from pit fall traps. In this technique, padded metal tongs are used to grasp the animal gently but tightly enough so that the animal cannot escape before it is restrained (Figure 7.2).

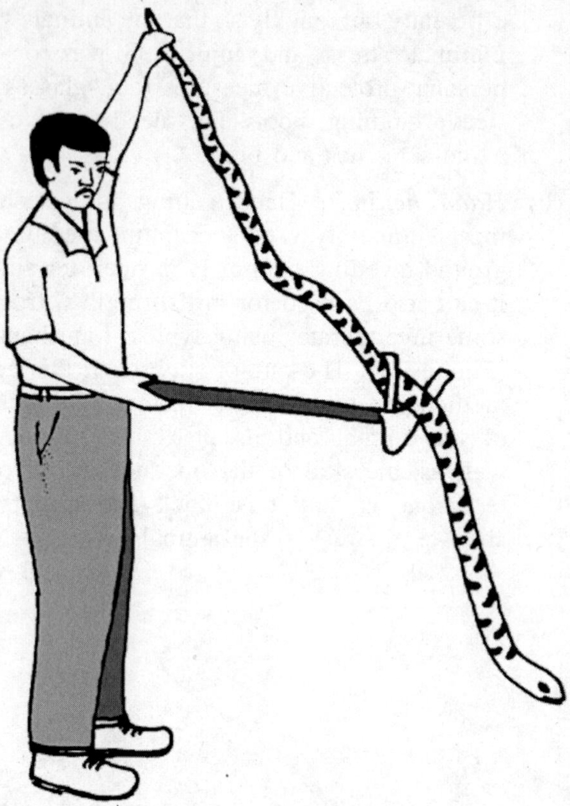

FIGURE 7.2 Illustration of a standard snake-tong instrument and the procedure of tonging.

(v) ***Raking:*** Raking is used to detect burrowing species by disturbing substrate under rocks and other habitats usually to catch small reptiles by active searches through leaf litter and topsoil. It is very successful during winter and early spring, when most small reptiles are generally inactive and are relatively easier to catch.

(vi) ***Cover boards:*** Many ground dwelling species of wildlife (amphibians, reptiles, small mammals, insects etc.) habitually seek shelter under surfaces such as rocks, boards, sheets of iron and other flat material. Cover boards made of either metal or wood can be laid intentionally and left undisturbed over the months to attract wildlife to those artificial shelters. Then these cover boards are removed and the animals taking shelter beneath are easily captured.

(vii) ***Fish net:*** Aquatic invertebrates, tadpoles and fish may be captured using a fish net dragged through the water (Figure 7.3). Such nets are often made up of nylon threads and are robust, light weighed and simple to use.

FIGURE 7.3 Illustration of capture of fish and other aquatic organisms by using fish nets.

(viii) ***Cage traps:*** Cage traps are designed to catch live animals in a baited cage. With slightest pecking on the bait by an inquisitive member of the target species, the door of the cage closes. Subsequently, the animal is captured live inside the cage. The type of the bait varies depending on the species to be captured. Wire cage traps are available in various sizes, making them appropriate for catching a wide variety of wildlife species. These traps are frequently used to capture small to medium sized animals (such as squirrels, rodents, feral cats, rabbits etc.).

(ix) ***Pitfall traps:*** In this capture method, deep pits are dug into the ground (or built from stone) in order to trap animals (Figure 7.4). Like cage traps, they are usually employed for catching live animals without harming them.

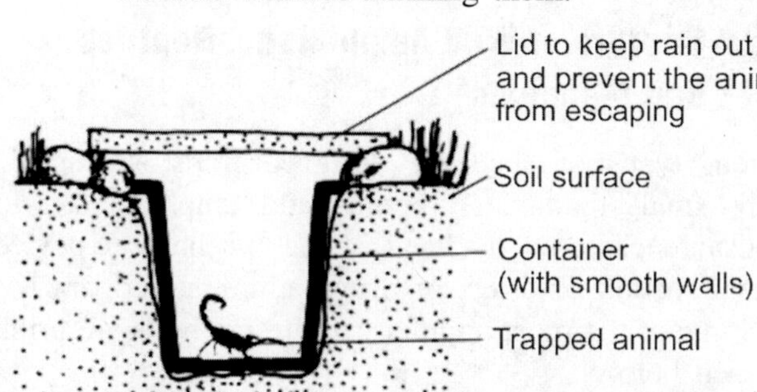

FIGURE 7.4 Schematic representation of a pitfall trap.

(x) ***Glue traps:*** Glue traps are made using natural or synthetic adhesive applied to cardboard or similar material and baits are usually placed in the central position of the board surrounded by adhesives. Scents that attract the target species are often added to the adhesive as well. Glue boards are primarily used for capturing indoor rats or mice, but are also appropriate for snakes and other smaller ground dwelling species.

(xi) ***Chemical immobilization:*** Wildlife capture through chemical immobilization is widely accepted and increasingly dynamic field. This cutting-edge technique is the most effective and safest method to capture rare and valuable animals. Animals may be captured by injecting either immobilizing drugs or tranquilising drugs with the use of dart by a dart gun in to the muscle of the target animal. It requires great skill, scientific knowledge and experience to immobilize wild animals. Immobilizing drugs are used to immobilize the animal completely, where the animal become completely unconscious. On the other hand, tranquilising drugs are used to sedate the animal, where the animal is conscious of its surroundings, but it remains in a relaxed state with limited movement. Large and aggressive animals are manageable with great ease and can be loaded and transported while immobilized. However, overdosage of these drugs could be fatal if an antidote is not administered in time.

7.2.2 CAPTURE OF WILD BIRDS

A number of trapping techniques and devices have been developed over the time, mostly with the use of bait, decoys, recorded calls or lures to attract birds to trapping sites and ultimately capture them. Nevertheless, live capture of wild birds is often challenging due to great mobility and diverse habitat conditions of avian species along with their wariness of human beings. So, the health and well-being of the birds is of primary concern in all capture methods.

Following are some of the conditions to ensure that birds are captured correctly, safely and with minimum disturbance:

- The volunteers engaged in capture activities should always be aware of and comply with local and national laws during wild bird capture and need to obtain all the required local, state, provincial and federal permits well in advance.
- Capture techniques and equipments used should not put the birds to foreseeable risk of injury.
- Necessary precautions should be taken to avoid disturbing nesting birds at breeding sites.
- Capture operation should not be conducted during extreme climatic conditions to avoid increased risk of hypothermia or hyperthermia.
- Deploy sufficient number of experienced personnel (at least four) available before undertaking any capture operation.
- Check operative traps and nets at regular intervals as birds should not remain in traps or nets any longer than is necessary.

Capture techniques for diverse avian taxa (such as wetland species, passerines, raptors etc.) are different from one another and has been elaborately reviewed by (Schemnitz, 2005) and Whitworth et al., (2007). Some of the most common and important capture techniques are discussed below:

(i) ***Corral traps:*** This mode of trapping is carried out mostly for waterfowl, grebes and coots. Basic drive trap design used by the Wildfowl & Wetlands Trust (WWT) consists of a capture pen or "corral" with two long barriers or "wings" extending some distance from the mouth of the corral as shown in Figure 7.5.

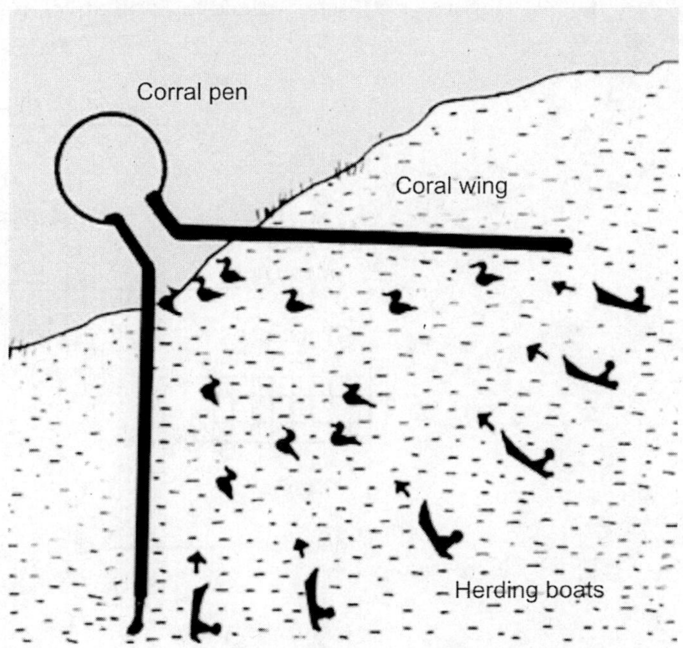

Figure 7.5 Illustration of the basic set-up of a corral trap.

The appropriate time for capturing these species is during 2–3 weeks after breeding when the target species of avifauna moults all their flight feathers. During this flightless period, birds are "rounded up" by herding or driving them between barriers which funnel the birds into capture pens constructed near the moulting grounds.

(ii) ***Baited traps:*** Baited trap is an effective technique for capturing wide array of wild birds, including waterfowl and many ground-feeding terrestrial species. Many of the baited trap used self-contained wire cages or enclosures supported by posts and are baited with appropriate food stuffs for the target species. For most waterfowl, typical baits include wheat, corn kernels, whole rice or other grains. Among various designs available, two designs are mostly accepted for capturing waterfowl namely, *baited funnel traps* and *baited dive-in traps.*

(a) *Baited funnel traps:* A baited funnel trap (Figure 7.6) can be deployed on land or in shallow water (usually <25–30 cm deep) to capture foraging dabbling ducks, coots and waders. The basic funnel trap design consists of a wire cage or enclosure with one or more funnel shaped entrances through which the birds can readily enter, but cannot exit easily. Fine mesh netting are usually placed over the traps to prevent birds escaping over the wire fence when the handlers approach.

(b) *Baited dive-in traps:* Baited dive-in traps (Figure 7.7) are effective primarily for capturing diving ducks and are constructed in aquatic habitats less than 1.25 m deep. The basic dive-in trap design is similar to the funnel trap enclosure, except the wire fence is slightly raised (0.3–0.5 m) off the wetland bottom allowing the birds to dive under and into the enclosure. Dive-in traps are only effective in wetland habitat. It may also be used in permanent water bodies of adequate depth, as well as, shallow or tidally influenced wetlands.

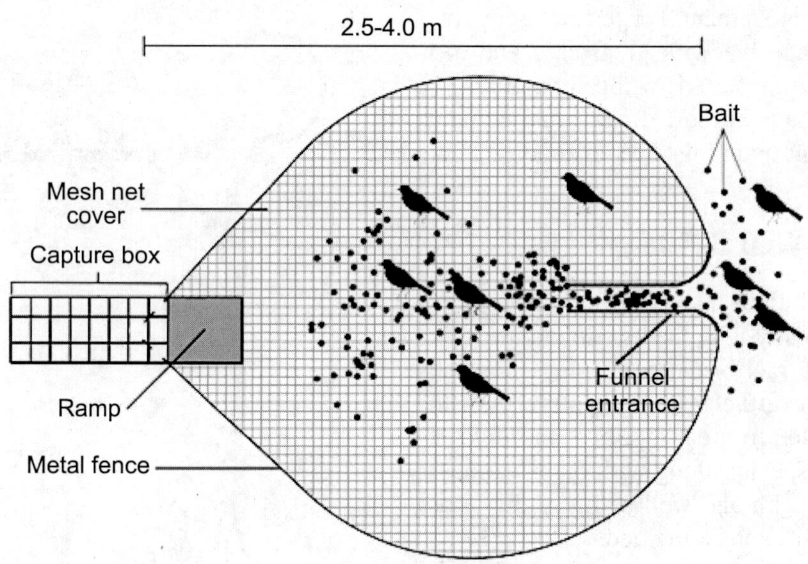

Figure 7.6 Illustration of the basic set-up of a baited funnel trap.

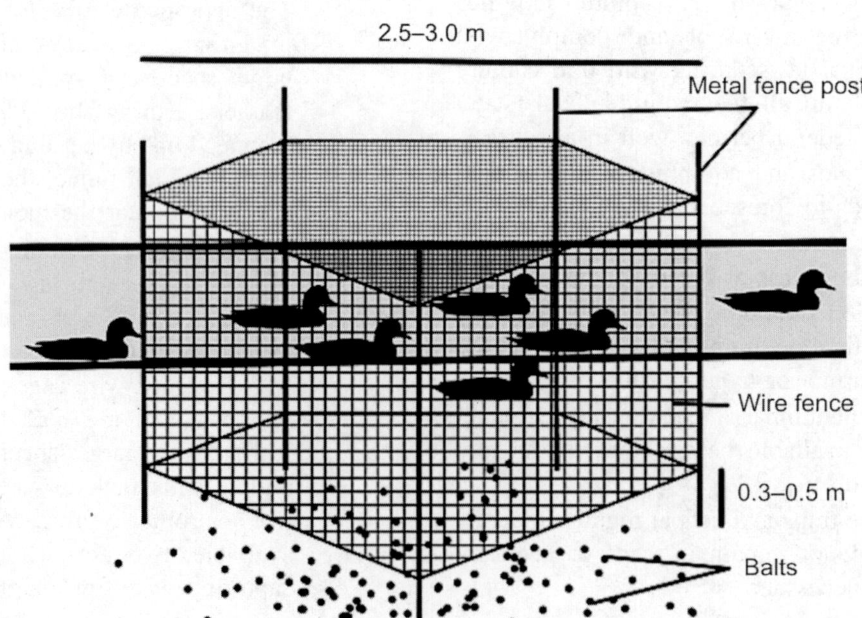

Figure 7.7 Illustration of the basic set-up of a baited dive-in trap.

Since, hunting often occurs where waterfowl and other game birds aggregate, it is advisable to deploy bait traps under constant vigilence within protected areas to avoid possible hunting.

(iii) ***Cannon nets:*** In this capture method, large flocks of roosting or feeding birds can be captured with large mesh nets attached to projectiles that are propelled over the flocks by explosive charges (Figure 7.8). Cannon nets have been used to capture many species of waterfowl, wading birds, upland game birds, gulls and shorebirds which congregate in large numbers at roosting or feeding sites. It must be performed under technical supervision of experienced personnel since this technique often leads to significant risk of injury or mortality to large congregation of wild birds. Bait and decoys can also be used to attract waterfowl and other target species to suitable capture sites.

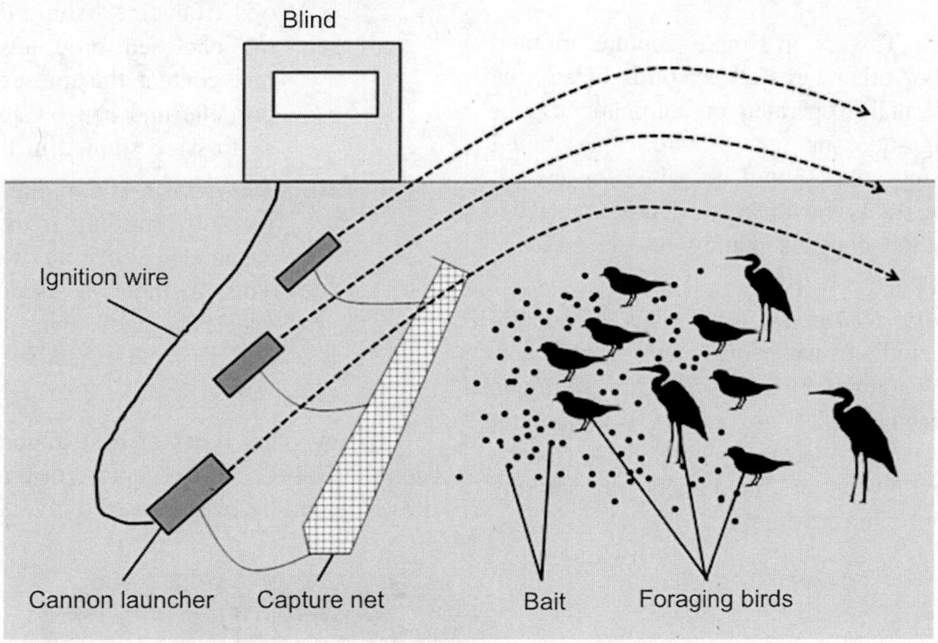

Figure 7.8 Illustration of the basic set-up of a cannon net.

(iv) ***Mist net:*** Mist-netting is perhaps the most versatile and widely used method for catching small to medium-sized wild birds (such as passerines and shorebirds). In this technique, an inconspicuous mesh (mist net) is erected vertically on poles and deployed in areas of high activity to intercept birds flying from one patch to another following their normal daily routines (Figure 7.9).

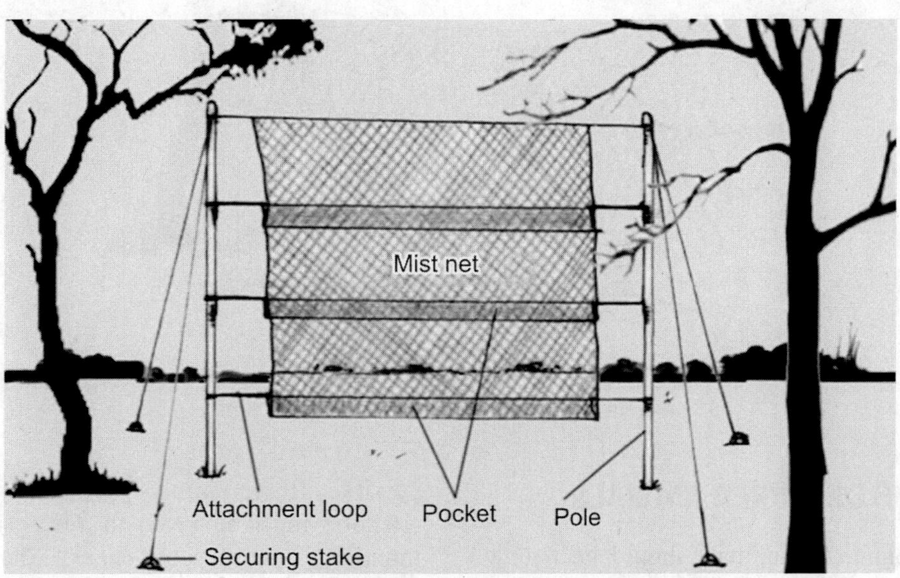

Figure 7.9 Illustration of the basic setup of mist net.

Mist nets are available in many different measures, materials, mesh sizes, colours and strand thickness. Dark-coloured nylon nets are most commonly used. However, selection of net colour will depend on the target species and habitat characteristics at the netting site and the mesh size is directly related to the size of the target species. Nets with finer strands are less visible but more fragile than nets with coarser strands.

(v) ***Drop trap:*** This is a simple capture method where bait or other lures attract birds to an area where a manually operated or automatic trigger drops a cage-door or net. As with other baited traps, trapping areas should be baited for several days before traps are deployed and set. Success of this method depends mainly on the patience of the trapper.

(vi) ***Night-lighting technique:*** A variety of aquatic species including waterfowl and cormorants have been captured by night-lighting technique utilizing bright lights to attract or disorient nocturnally active species which then can be captured passively in fixed nets or actively pursued with hand-held nets.

(vii) ***Raptor Capture Methods*** Raptors require specifically designed capture and trapping techniques (Bloom et al. 2007). In most cases, capture technique for raptor is used to trap individual birds rather than large groups.

(a) *Bal-chatri traps* consist of small wire cages of various sizes and shapes containing live bait (a rodent or small bird) and covered with numerous small nooses or slip knots tied from fine fishing line. Raptors attacking the enclosed prey are ensnared when the feet contact the nooses. Bal-chatri traps are portable and can be quickly deployed when raptors are sighted in the vicinity.

(b) *Dho-gaza nets* exploit the tendency of raptors to mob intruding owls. A fine mesh net is suspended above an owl decoy (Figure 7.10). This method is used for capturing these species as they dive on the perceived threat and is most effective when placed near a raptor nest.

Many other types of nest trapping methods have also been developed, but the capture of breeding birds from nest sites is generally discouraged to avoid possible nest failure.

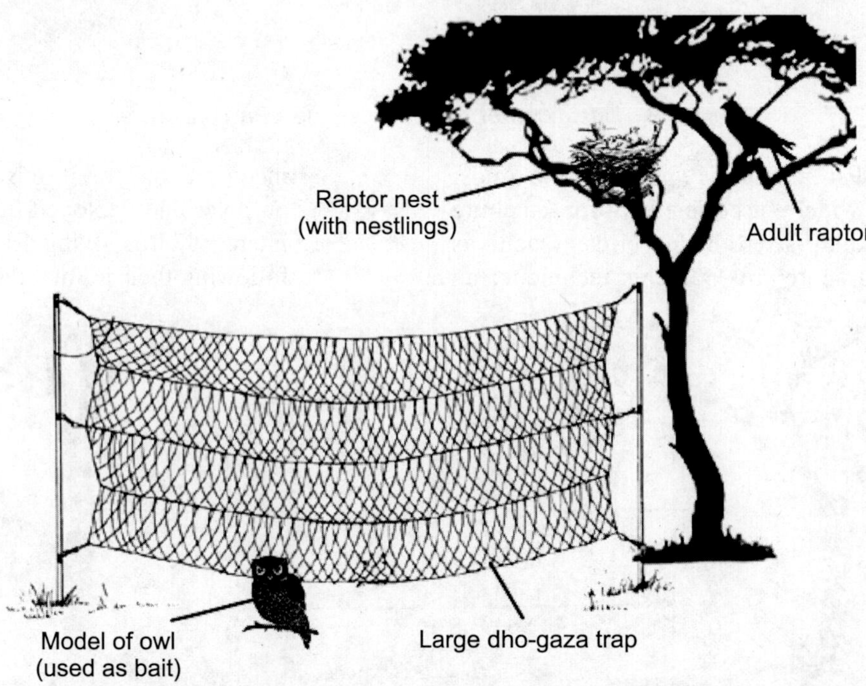

FIGURE 7.10 Illustration of Dho-gaza nets

7.3 HANDLING OF CAPTURED ANIMALS

Immediately after capture, the animals should be handled properly under less disturbed conditions and as little as possible. If the animals are temporarily kept in captivity, attention must be given to ensure that they do not injure themselves inside the cages. Enclosures must be high enough so that the captive animals do not escape by jumping over them. In addition to that, aggressive animals should be kept separately to avoid any mutual conflict and subsequent injuries. Animals within the enclosures need to be provided with sufficient food, water and adequate protection against sun, cold and rain.

An immobilized carnivore could suffer from considerable injury and collapse, if kept in an unnatural and inappropriate position. The animal should be placed on its side, with its head extended. The tongue should be kept wet and immobilized animal should be turned from side to side after every 20 minutes. Regurgitation during immobilization is life-threatening to a carnivore. So, regurgitated materials should be removed from the mouth as soon as possible to avoid suffocation. To prevent overheating the animal should be cooled down after capture and should never be kept in the sun. An immobilized animal is still able to perceive loud noises, so every effort should be made to reduce the noise level around the animal. Vital signs like respiration rate, pulse rate, blood pressure and temperature should be checked periodically. Handling and restraint of great majority of wild animals in captivity is more difficult and dangerous than it would be with domestic species and, hence, need more specialised procedure requiring particular skills and experience. Some of the important considerations are listed below:

- Rehabilitation units should have suitable, well maintained equipments for capture, restraint, first-aid and transportation of the species likely to be encountered and all personnel need to be properly trained to attend wildlife casualties in the field.
- Care must always be taken to ensure that any additional stress is minimized. Adequate attention is to be given so that no further injury is sustained by the animal.
- It is to be looked after that the animal is secured and prevented from escaping out of the enclosures.
- Containers used for transportation to a rehabilitation centre or veterinary unit must be secured, preferably darkened, adequately ventilated and designed to ensure that neither further casualties exacerbate the existing injuries, nor sustain further damage.
- All equipment used in handling the wild animal should be thoroughly cleaned and disinfected or destroyed after use. If cardboard pet carriers are used, these should be incinerated.

7.4 TRANSPORTATION OF CAPTURED ANIMALS

The transport of an animal is an unnatural situation for the animal and is most likely to put them under some degree of stress. High levels of stress may increase metabolic rates and hazardous behaviour, which in turn increases chances of further injuries and susceptibility to diseases.

Injured animal or animal with physiological weaknesses or pathological problems should not be considered fit for transport. If unavoidable, such transportation should be done under special veterinary supervision. Sedatives are not usually used on animals to be transported, unless absolutely necessary. If anesthesia has been given during capture, then prior to commencement of transportation the animal must be completely awake, alert and able to balance itself. Weather conditions, condition of transport routes, potential causes for delays (such as waiting times at border check posts) and other issues (like commercial licenses, passport requirements, visas, truck scales, chase vehicles, locations of fuel and repair services etc.) must be taken into account prior to the onset of transport. National and international laws and regulations as applicable in the countries of origin, transit, and destination must be checked and complied with. Before transportation, full information and other legal documents concerning import and/or export of the live animal (like in-transit permits, veterinary health certificates, veterinary import/export permits, CITES import/export/re-export permits etc.) should be obtained well in advance.

Means of Transport

Modes of transport, containers and their fittings should be designed, constructed, maintained and operated in such a way so that optimum safety of the animal is ensured. From the point of animal welfare, transportation of live animals must be well planned, quick and efficiently executed in order to avoid as much stress as possible to the animal. Therefore, air passage should be the first choice for long distance transportations. The animal during transport needs to be protected from inclement weather and adverse changes in climatic conditions. Further, unnecessary fear, injury, damage to health and cruel treatments are to be avoided. Severe jerks or shaking during transportation should preferably be minimized. Containers must be secured throughout the transport and the vehicle should be equipped with fire-extinguisher.

Marking and Labeling

Detailed information must be clearly noted on the container and relevant papers (permission, license etc.) should accompany. Vehicles should be clearly marked indicating the presence of live animals and with a sign indicating the top of the container. All markings and labels must be legible, durable and printed or otherwise marked on the external surface of the container or vehicle. Containers carrying animals which can inflict poisonous or venomous bites and stings must be boldly marked "POISONOUS" or "VENOMOUS". Special care must be taken during transport of such poisonous or venomous animals.

Accompanying Persons

Personnel accompanying and handling animals should be properly trained and competent for this purpose. Individuals deemed competent to accompany a shipment of live animals must have very good knowledge of animal health and welfare regulations and also be able to handle emergency situations.

Loading and Unloading

Loading and unloading facilities should be adequately designed and operated ensuring safety of the animal. All necessary facilities and equipment for crating, hoisting of containers, loading and unloading should be readily available to minimize the time for loading and unloading. Arrangements should be made well in advance with appropriate equipments and relevant personnel at the destination prior to the estimated time of arrival of the transported animal to ensure quick and safe unloading.

Precautions during Transportation

- Transporters must take into account the species and number of animals transported, expected weather conditions during the transport, anticipated duration of the transport and the possibility of unforeseen delay.
- In case of a delay during transport, all necessary actions required to safeguard the welfare of the animals and reducing the risk of unnecessary fear, injury and suffering should be taken on emergency basis.
- Containers must always be kept upright, well ventilated and should be stored in a way so that ambient conditions are stable and appropriate and that does not impede ventilation. Inside temperatures of the container should also be monitored at regular basis during transportation.
- Adequate protection must be provided at all times during the transport to ensure that the needs of the animals are fully met.
- The container should be large enough (with sufficient floor area and height based on the size and number of animals) to accommodate the animal and partitions and compartments must be sufficiently strong to withstand the weight of the animal.
- The animal inside the containers should be provided with a non-slip flooring surface and appropriate bedding or equivalent material which ensures their best comfort. Such materials need to also have adequate capacity to absorb urine and faeces and can be properly cleaned and disinfected with relative ease. Other organic materials such as remains of animal feed or bedding material, must be collected and properly disposed.
- Food and water provided for animals should be appropriate and adequate for the species as per their size and age and should be made easily accessible. The food must be protected from the weather and various other contaminants such as dust, fuel, exhaust gases and animal excrements. If specific feeding equipment is used for feeding the animals, then that equipment should be transported in the conveyance.
- Food and water should always be offered in a way that is familiar to the animal and that also minimizes contamination.
- Animals should be offered a rest period at suitable intervals depending on the species and length of transport.
- Conditions of the animals must be checked regularly and properly maintained by competent personnel. Hence, there must be sufficient lighting arrangements inside the containers for inspection and care of the animal during transport. If the animals fall ill or are injured during transport, then immediate and appropriate veterinary treatment should be provided.
- Birds should not be shipped together in groups if they are unfamiliar with each other or display aggression in close quarters. Also birds of different sizes, ages and sexually mature males should not be transported in same groups.

CASE STUDY: Capture, Collection and Rescue of Injured or Dead Wildlife during Oil Spills

During an oil spill, birds and marine mammals are often injured or killed by oil that pollutes their habitat. Without direct human intervention, such distressed animals have no chance to survive. During such unnatural situation the first and foremost important thing is immediate intervention by properly trained staff to rescue the affected birds and marine mammals. Rehabilitation of such oiled wildlife is a complex medical and technical procedure.

First, all dead animals should immediately be removed to avoid further contamination amongst scavenging animals, domestic pets etc. Bodies should be collected into labeled plastic bags, sealed and transported to the nearest incinerator. Simultaneously, immediate measures should be taken at source of oil spill to stop further release and spread of oil. Efforts are also to be made to keep other animals away from the site of contamination. Depending on the situation and species involved, capture operations may be shore-based, boat-based or both. Since animal welfare is a priority, particular care should be taken while restraining individual birds during capture. Birds are then individually transported in suitable cardboard or plastic cartons with adequate ventilation and soft absorbent padding on the floor.

Cleaning and Drying

Immediately after reaching rescue centre, efficient cleaning process (washing, rinsing and drying) should be conducted in a quick and professional manner to minimize stress. In the cleaning process, plumage of the affected birds must be thoroughly rinsed to remove all traces of oil. Once the feathers are washed, they are allowed to dry properly.

Rehabilitation

The objective of rehabilitation is to release the birds into the wild as soon as possible to lessen complications rendered through captivity. But after cleaning and drying, restoration of waterproofing is the main precondition for such rehabilitation and birds should not be released until their plumage is fully waterproof. However, restoration of waterproofing is a time taking process and is achieved through preening and physical restoration of correct feather structure. Preening is stimulated by allowing the bird to swim preferably in moving water. Hygiene and quarantine are other important aspects during rehabilitation. In case of seabirds which are mostly affected by oilspills, a gradual transition from freshwater to a 3 percent salt solution is necessary prior to release.

- ❒ ***Pre-release Assessment:*** Prior to the release, each individual must pass through a waterproofing test. A veterinary assessment should be done to find out if the animals are normal (both biologically and behaviourally) and whether they are capable of competing with conspecifics in the wild.
- ❒ ***Post-release Monitoring:*** Post release response and behaviour of wildlife affected by oil spill need to be closely monitored, as well as, their survival rates should be assessed meticulously. Because these are considered to be vital parameters to assess the success of rehabilitation. However, such post-release monitoring is quite difficult and expensive and, therefore, depends mostly on the availability of funds and research interest.

REVIEW QUESTIONS

1. Give an account on different methods of capturing wild Amphibians and Reptiles. What is chemical immobilization?
2. Give an account of different types of traps commonly used to capture wild birds.
3. What are the precautions to be taken during transportation of captured wild animals?
4. Elaborate different steps of capture and rescue of injured or dead wild life.

REFERENCES

Bloom, P.H., Clark, W.S. and Kidd, J.W., Capture Techniques. In: Bird D.M., and Bildstein K.L. (Eds.), *Raptor Research and Management Techniques*, Hancock House, British Columbia, Canada, 2007.

Schemnitz, S.D., Capturing and handling wild animals, In: Braun CE. (Ed.), *Techniques for wildlife investigations and management*, pp. 239–285, The Wildlife Society, Bethesda, USA, 2005.

Whitworth, D., Newman, S.H., Mundkur,. T. and Harris, P., (Eds.) Wild Birds and Avian Influenza: an introduction to applied field research and disease sampling techniques (FAO Animal Production and Health Manual, No. 5), Food and Agriculture Organization of the United Nations, Rome, 2007. Retrieved from: http://www.fao.org/3/a-a1521e.pdf

8

CAPTIVE BREEDING OF WILD ANIMALS

8.1 CONCEPT OF CAPTIVE BREEDING

The process of reproducing animals in human controlled environments with restricted settings (such as wildlife reserves, zoos and other conservation facilities) is termed as 'captive breeding'. Sometimes the process is followed by the release of individual organisms to the wild after thorough feasibility studies for safe and conducive habitat. In spite of the fact that the genetic diversity and thus fitness of the species is sometimes reduced, still such programmes are adopted to save a threatened species from extinction and to safeguard the overall biodiversity of a region. Thus, captive breeding programmes act as 'insurance policy' against species extinction and biodiversity loss. In addition to intensive habitat conservation efforts, many species in the past were saved by the combination of captive breeding and release programmes. Loss of genetic diversity is another issue which many endangered species are facing today. Many fragmented populations thus require human intervention to maintain a viable and genetically diverse population. Introduction of new genes into a small and isolated genetic pool through captive breeding programmes can be a useful solution to this problem. On the other hand, in most cases it is very difficult to study the reproductive biology of a species in nature. But, a thorough knowledge on their reproductive biology is vital in assisting conservation efforts. Captive breeding, in this context, is also useful as it provides us the opportunity to observe and study the breeding behaviour of a particular animal in captivity. Captive breeding also provides a safe and reliable source for the animals used in zoological institutions and greatly reduces the need to harvest them from the wild. Finally, one of the biggest benefits of captive breeding is public education. Since, one can be able to see live animals in zoos, it inspires people to have a greater understanding and appreciation for their surroundings. In fact, the majority of animals that are used in public display and educational presentations are of captive source and they are not subjected to unnecessary stress while exposed to public as they are habituated to see large crowds since their birth.

8.2 REINTRODUCTION OF CAPTIVE BREEDS — CONTROVERSIES AND REALITIES

Humans have a long history of translocation of animals from one place to other primarily for the purpose of replenishing native game species. During the recent years, translocation for the purpose of re-establishing endangered animals into their native habitats has become increasingly popular. As per IUCN (1998) guidelines, reintroduction is an attempt to establish a species in an area which was once a part of its historical range, but from which it has been extirpated or become extinct and through successful reintroduction, re-establishment of a particular animal can be achieved. However, some species conservation groups do not support releasing captive bred animals as a means of proper conservation measure to save the animal from extinction and the results made so far are not encouraging. According to European Association for Aquatic Mammals (EAAM 2004), "the success of reintroduction to the wild will depend upon resources, methodologies and techniques which still need to be tested". However, others suggest that using captive animals for release programme can be beneficial when certain criteria are fulfilled such as (i) the length of the captive breeding program does not exceed a reasonable time frame (e.g. 20 generations), (ii) introduction of captive born individuals should be kept at low levels (e.g. 1 or 2 individuals per generation), so that captive-born animals are only used as supplemental genetic stock and (iii) the size of the captive population is reasonably large (relatively low inbreeding depression). Available information demonstrates that translocation of native game species have been more successful (81–86 percent) than translocation and reintroduction of endangered species for conservation purposes (44–53 percent). This suggests that the use of translocation and reintroduction as tools for the conservation of endangered animals needs to be further improved in order to increase success rates.

8.2.1 Release Protocol

There are several aspects regarding the release of animals in a reintroduction programme. Release of a particular captive bred animal have been broadly categorized as either "hard release" (immediate release, with little or no provisioning) or "soft release" (acclimatization period, sometimes with prolonged provisioning). Soft releases are often better for captive-born animals, and can enhance reintroduction success. Soft releases usually include additional aspects of pre- and post- release monitoring, which include behavioural training, preventive health care, socialization, acclimatization and provisioning. Other criteria for successful release operations include accurate timing of release, as seasons have profound implications for successful breeding and/or survival. The survival and success of reintroduction also depends on environmental and social factors such as food availability, weather conditions and temperatures, as well as, the breeding season of the existing wild population. Nevertheless, genetic considerations need to be properly taken care of in order to reduce the risk of inbreeding depression, population decline and irreversible genetic loss.

8.2.2 Selection of Animal for Successful Release

Criteria for the selection of individual animal include:

- The degree in which the animal is inbred, as well as, its generational length of time in captivity.
- The gender and age at the time of release of the animal should be taken into consideration. In most cases, females can integrate better into an existing population, however, males tend to travel greater distances and can establish larger areas. Again, adults are more likely to survive than juveniles, but that juveniles are more likely to breed and are therefore important in boosting the genetic viability of future generations.
- Since captive-born animals are more prone to infectious diseases and pathogens, the health status of the animals is also important for both of the reintroduced animals, as well as, the existing wild population. Diseased individuals, if released, have the potential to wipe out existing populations.
- Temperament of the released individual is also important. So, appropriate selection of animals based on certain behavioural traits is one of the prime requisites for successful *ex-situ* conservation efforts.

8.2.3 Problems Associated with Reintroduction

- **Excess number of captive bred individuals:** One of the biggest problems associated with captive breeding and the reintroduction of the offspring into the wild is the production of surplus animals due to over enthusiasm.
- **Lack of infrastructure:** In reality, there is always an excess stock of bred offspring ready to be reintroduced. However, there is limited provision in terms of infrastructure to accommodate and release them properly. Either they could be rehabilitated in other zoos to improve their genetic pool or to reintroduce them forcibly into substandard habitats.
- **Post release monitoring:** Another big problem is the post release monitoring which is expensive and requires trained personnel.
- **Uncertainty of acceptance of captive breed animals by their wild counterparts:** It has been noticed that despite of a successful captive breeding programme and proper reintroduction protocols, the captive bred individual are not always accepted by their wild counterparts. Huge amount of time, effort and money involved in the process of captive breeding becomes completely futile, if the captive-bred individual is unable to select a mate from the wild and successfully reproduce.

8.3 ADVANTAGES OF CAPTIVE BREEDING

1. Zoos are able to recreate the natural habitat of the captured animals and the enclosures are able to protect animals from any predator ensuring proper care, better food, good health and prevent malnutrition.
2. Another benefit of keeping endangered animals in captivity is to offer scientists the opportunity to study and learn everything possible about the

particular species regarding their management, protection and restoration and to initiate best possible conservation measures.

3. Public education and awareness through entertainment is of utmost importance for sustainability and well-being of both wildlife and humans.

8.4 CHALLENGES OF CAPTIVE BREEDING

Although the basic objective is to increase the species population size and to reduce the risk of extinction within the wild, there are several disadvantages with captive breeding programme as well.

1. It can remove last few remaining individuals from the wild, resulting in extinction of the species in the wild.
2. Since, the animals are bred in captivity, there is often a high risk of inbreeding (i.e. mating between two closely related individuals as a result of a small gene pool), which might result in inbreeding depression. Inbred population may undergo genetic drift where genes may disappear completely ultimately leading to decrease in immunity to diseases and phenotypic abnormalities. If the phenomenon of inbreeding is not adequately taken care of, then the captive bred individuals might also adversely affect the natural selection of the species by putting pressures on the remaining population and the species that prey on them (Holt et al., 2004). However, if they survive over a sufficient number of generations, then inbred populations can regain "normal" genetic diversity as suggested by McGreevy et al., (2011).
3. Since captive breed animals miss critical learning periods during captivity, on release they face a lot of behavioural problems. Most of them are not able to hunt or forage for food leading to starvation, incapability in avoiding predators and are not able to find ample shelter thus, ultimately die. Therefore, these animals should be trained to learn the natural behaviour through proper training within the captive setup, so that the probability of survival in the wild would increase and match with that of their wild counterpart.
4. Captive breeding techniques are usually difficult to implement for highly mobile species like some migratory birds (like cranes) and fishes (like hilsa). For species like large cetaceans (whales, dolphins etc.), it is more difficult to meet their biological requirements in captivity, especially the vast amount of space required to keep large populations.

8.5 CONSERVATION BREEDING—A BRIEF IDEA

Conservation breeding of certain selected species is carried out throughout the globe in various zoos. This complements *in-situ* conservation and is often considered to be the only hope for the survival of certain species which are facing serious threats to survive in nature (Saha and Mazumdar, 2009). 'Conservation breeding' may be defined as breeding of certain threatened species in captivity or semi-captive condition maintaining optimum heterozygosity in the species and the offspring are released in the wild as and when appropriate and desirable. In fact, maintaining heterozygosity (or in other words protecting genetic diversity of a stock) in conservation breeding is most important in order to avoid inbreeding depression. So far 61 species of endangered animals have been considered for conservation breeding in different Indian zoos (Anonymous, 2008). However, all past efforts of conservation breeding were not successful, either due to lack of proper breeding stock or due to lack of proper infrastructure in several zoological parks.

8.5.1 Aims and Objectives of Conservation Breeding

- Breeding for the purpose of maintaining optimum level of heterozygosity in the species, avoiding breeding between kins and protecting genetic diversity within a breed._
- Endangered species which have no chance of survival in the wild, a last chance is through conservation breeding under ex-situ condition.
- Raising stocks for rehabilitating them in the wild as and when appropriate and desirable.

8.5.2 Planning of Conservation Breeding

Under any planned and coordinated 'Conservation Breeding Programme', of critically endangered wild animal in India, following steps are essential:

- Selection of species for 'Conservation Breeding Programme'
- Generate data on approximate number of the animals of the species in the wild, as well as, in the zoos
- Identification of coordinating and participating zoos
- Availability of animal enclosures in coordinating and participating zoos
- Existence/creation of off-display enclosures in coordinating zoos
- Identification of 'founders' (animals that will be bred in captive condition)

- ❒ Marking of 'founders' (through ring, ear tag, transponders etc.)
- ❒ Preparation of animal history sheets and animal observer sheets of the 'founders' by respective zoos
- ❒ Compilation and updating of studbook by the national studbook keeper
- ❒ Liaison with the international studbook keeper of the species, if any
- ❒ Assess the possibility of acquiring the 'founders' from the foreign zoos (if required) and get the details of zoos from where the 'founders' can be acquired
- ❒ Physical health check-up of the 'founders' at the veterinary hospitals within the zoo or in national referral centre
- ❒ Genetic health check-up of 'founders' using blood samples or body parts with the help of LaCONES, Hyderabad
- ❒ Preparation of the 'Conservation Breeding Management Plan' for the species

8.5.3 Prerequisites for Success

- ❒ Vast majority of captive animals overall are known hybrid or of unknown origin, hence are not suitable for this purpose. Only whose ancestry could be traced through documentary evidences of a single subspecies and originally captured from the wild can be considered for conservation breeding.
- ❒ The population has to be large
- ❒ Selection of breed should be carefully determined
- ❒ Degree of endangerment, endemism should be considered
- ❒ Taxonomically distinct or flagship taxa should be given priority
- ❒ High educational or research importance
- ❒ The budget is another important criteria
- ❒ Philosophy and directions of zoos, as well as, visitors profile are important
- ❒ Bio-geographic locations and climate should be taken in to consideration
- ❒ Should be done in cooperation with several zoos holding same species

8.5.4 Merits and Limitations of Conservation Breeding

Some of the merits and limitations of conservation breeding are briefly outlined in Table 8.1 below:

Table 8.1 Merits and Limitations of Conservation Breeding

Merits	*Limitations*
❒ Conservation breeding and subsequent release of the newborns to wild habitat is complementary to *in-situ* conservation ❒ Only hope for the survival of some species — extremely threatened in the wild ❒ Threat of inbreeding in small population could be avoided in conservation breeding as in this method breeding of the animal is totally controlled and can be manipulated at will ❒ Number of offspring should be limited ❒ Increased reproductive rate. ❒ Provide materials for basic and applied research	❒ Conservation breeding only concerns endangered or threatened species ❒ Very expensive and needs spacious enclosures and massive infrastructure ❒ High level of coordination is required for success ❒ Careful selection of most genetically suitable pairings for breeding in order to preserve the maximum amount of genetic diversity ❒ Lack of proper knowledge on the biology and behaviour of the target animals leads to total failure ❒ Indiscriminate release of over-breed or surplus animals interferes with population dynamics and behaviour leading to stress, panic and change in social behaviour of wild populations.

8.5.5 Selected Case Studies of Conservation Breeding

CASE STUDY I: RED PANDA *Ailurus Fulgens* Cuvier, 1825
(*see* Plate IV)

Present Status: IUCN: Endangered; CITES: Appendix–I; WPA- Schedule–I.

Distribution: Red panda is distributed in different areas throughout the Himalayas, from Nepal, Bhutan and India eastwards to upper Myanmar, southern Tibet and certain provinces of South China like West Yunnan, Sichuan and Shaanxi. In India, they are found in the parts of Sikkim, West Bengal and Arunachal Pradesh.

Habitat: Red panda lives in the areas with temperate moist climates in the Himalayas above 3,000 m or so. They prefer to live in the forests with a mixture of deciduous and coniferous trees above and bamboo and rhododendrons below. They are arboreal in nature and spend most of their time sleeping on treetops in the evergreen forests. They make their nests in hollow trees or dens.

Marks of Identification

- Head round; rostrum shortened; the ears are large, erect and pointed.
- The body of red panda is covered with long, coarse guard hair and the undercoat is soft, dense and wooly. The fur on the upper sides of its body is reddish-brown, while ventrally it is glossy black.
- The furry tail is marked with about 12 alternating red and buff rings and is not prehensile.
- The face is predominantly white with reddish-brown 'tear' marks under its eyes.
- Legs are black and the soles of feet are covered with dense white hair.
- There is no sexual dimorphism in color and size between males and females.
- Head and body length: 51–63.5 cm; shoulder height: 27.3–28.3 cm and tail length: 28–48.5 cm. Weight in between 3.70–6.20 kg.

Behaviour and Social Organisation

Red pandas are nocturnal and remain most active during dusk, dawn and in the night. They spend the day mostly sleeping on the trees. While resting, they curl up in the topmost branches, with its bushy tail wrapped over its head or lies along a branch with its head tucked away under its chest between its forelegs. In the evening, it descends to the ground and hunts for food and climbing back in the morning. Male home range generally overlaps with the home ranges of more than one females and may even expand during the mating season. Individuals scent mark their territories and home ranges with urine and secretion from anal glands using the soles of their feet.

Food and Feeding Behaviour

Although basically a carnivore, they have shifted mostly into herbivorous habit. In the wild, the red panda searches for roots, succulent grasses, leaves and fallen fruits. Eggs, insects and grubs may also be the part of the diet depending upon their individual taste. Red pandas feed on fresh bamboo leaves at the base of the stalk and do not eat the stalk itself. Ninety percent of the diet consists of bamboo leaves and the rest consist of bamboo shoots, fruits and berries.

Reproductive Behaviour

Red panda is a solitary animal, usually seeking a partner only during mating season from the end of December to the middle of February. The female begins to carry nest materials such as sticks, grasses and leaves etc. to a suitable nest site. In the wild, they build their nest in the hollow of a tree trunk generally located high up from the ground or inside a rock crevice. After a gestation period of 112–158 days the female gives birth of one to four blind cubs weighing 110–130 g during May–June. After birth, the mother cleans the cubs and in this way can immediately recognize each by knowing its smell. After one week, the mother leaves the nest to clean herself. The cubs start to open their eyes about 18 days later, but not fully until 30 to 40 days. The new litter remains at the nest for twelve weeks. After leaving the nest, they still remain with their mother, weaning around 6–8 months of age. The cubs will stay with their mother until the next cubs are born in the following summer. The young attains adult size at around 12 months and become sexually mature at around 18 months.

Behaviour in Captivity

They can survive up to 14 years in captivity, but probably a lot less in the wild. They survive and breed well in captivity. In captivity, they should be provided with a nutritionally balanced diet and the dietary ingredients should be fresh and of good quality. Every effort should be taken to avoid spoilage of food. It is suggested that the animals be fed with dry biscuits at least twice per day. If possible 200 g of fresh bamboo leaves should be offered daily to each animal. Fruits and vegetables are not important nutritionally to the diet of the red panda. Fresh water must be available to all animals at all times of day. They commonly suffer from parasitic infections, hemorrhagic enteritis, pneumonia, pasteurellosis, canine distemper and central nervous system disorders etc. However, many have died due to old age.

In captivity, a red panda is placid, inoffensive and within a short time becomes tame and docile. Its movement is awkward and slow on the ground but it is an excellent climber. It rests in a curled fashion on the tree tops. Often found to be walking over the branches of the trees, playing with its mates. In captivity, it is generally a very silent animal, but when angry or otherwise irritated it utters a "sharp spitting hiss".

Threats

Due to their shy and secretive nature and their largely nocturnal habits, observation of red panda is difficult. Therefore, population figures in the wild are determined by population density estimates and not direct counts. In 2001, the wild population in India was estimated at between 5,000 and 6,000 individuals. However, the recent population estimation reveals a very grim scenario for this species. It has been estimated that 225–370 individuals strive in 650 sq km of suitable forest in Sikkim (Ziegler et al., 2010) and 55–60 individuals in West Bengal (Bahuguna et al., 1998; Pradhan et al., 2001; Mallick 2010; Roka and Jha 2014). Besides, Arunachal Pradesh supposedly holds the largest Red Panda population in India, but there have been fewer site-specific studies (Choudhury 2001; Ghose and Dutta 2011; Glatston et al., 2015). Estimates for Nepal indicate only a few hundred individuals. There are no records from Bhutan or Myanmar.

Massive habitat loss has been noticed in its native range across Nepal, China, India, Myanmar and Bhutan due to reckless human interference such as poaching, hunting etc. n the recent past, poaching and illegal trade of skins and meat have increased due to greater demand in China and the trade of live Red Panda for pets, also seems to be increasing (Glatston et al., 2015). An exponential and rapid growth of human population has increased the pressure on their habitat for use in farming and housing. There is also a great demand for firewood. This has fragmented the temperate forests, leading to segregation of red panda populations and increased the risk of inbreeding within these smaller groups.

Conservation Initiatives

Conservation efforts around the world include designating protected areas and captive breeding programs. The species is listed on Appendix–I of CITES. This sweet and gentle creature was classified as 'vulnerable' by the IUCN 'Red List' since 2008, with a decrease in population of over 40 percent in the last 50 years. But, in 2015 red panda is listed as Endangered as 50 percent population decline has been recorded in last two decades over the last three generations, which is feared to continue, and probably intensify, in the next three generations (Glatston et al., 2015).

The red panda is protected in all range countries, and hunting is illegal. However, conservation efforts are highly variable between countries. In India, Red Pandas are reported from 19 protected areas of Sikkim, West Bengal and Arunachal Pradesh (viz. Lachung Reserve Forest, Kanchendzonga National Park, Barsey Rhododendron Sanctuary, Maenam Wildlife Sanctuary, Pangolakha Wildlife Sanctuary, Kyongnosla Alpine Sanctuary, Shingba Rhododendron Sanctuary, Singalila National Park, Neora Valley National Park, Kamlang Wildlife Sanctuary, Eaglesnest Wildlife Sanctuary, Zemithang Valley Community Forest, Nuranang Valley Community Forest, Mehao Wildlife Sanctuary, Mandla-Phudung Community Forest, Anjaw Reserve forest, Mechuka-West Siang Community Forest, Mouling National Park and Dibang Wildlife Sanctuary). China has 46 protected areas covering about 65 percent of red panda habitat, but most of these PAs are inflicted with poor law enforcement and large scale grazing and collection of non-timber forest products (Wei et al., 2011; Glatston et al., 2015), In Nepal, known populations occur in Langtang National Park, Sagarmatha National Park, Makalu Barun National Park, Rara National Park, Annapurna Conservation Area, Kanchenjunga Conservation Area, Gaurishankar Conservation Area, Manaslu Conservation Area and in Dhorpatan Hunting Reserve; Bhutan has five protected areas that support red panda populations and Myanmar has 26 protected areas, of which at least one hosts the population.

In addition, Global Species Management Plan (GSMP) has been implemented for red pandas held in zoos around the world (Glatston et al., 2015).

Conservation Underway

The IUCN/SSC Mustelid, Viverrid and Procyonid Specialist Group have initiated a Conservation Action Plan for this species. It recommends further research into the ecology and distribution of the red panda, so that key areas of habitat can be protected. The extent and intensity of current threats need to be quantified so that effective conservation measures can be implemented. Wildlife corridors should be established to link fragmented areas of habitat. Captive breeding should continue, but it is important to ensure that red pandas are no longer taken from the wild to supplement zoo populations. Further research is required to determine the degree of genetic variation within red panda throughout their range to ascertain the number of distinct groupings or subspecies. Until only recently, zoos and other wildlife institutions have made conservation breeding programs more important and some of these breeding programmes have the intention to reintroduce the offspring back into the wild. The number of individuals released from conservation breeding is normally quite small. It is also very important to try and decrease the amount of inbreeding that may occur within the captive populations.

In situ initiatives

A community-managed forest in Ilam dstrict of eastern Nepal is home to fifteen red pandas which generate household income through tourism activities, including home stays. Villagers in the high-altitude areas of Arunachal Pradesh have formed the Pangchen Red Panda Conservation Alliance, comprising five villages with a community-conserved forest area of 200 sq km at an altitude of 2,500 m to over 4,000 m.

In captivity

The red panda is quite adaptable to live in captivity and is common in zoos worldwide. As of 2006, the international studbook listed more than 800 individuals in zoos and parks around the world. Of these, 511 individuals of subspecies *A. f. fulgens* were kept in 173 institutions and 306 individuals of subspecies *A. f. styani* were kept in 81 institutions. The Knoxville Zoo, Tennessee has the largest number of captive red panda births in the Western Hemisphere (101 as of August 2011). Recently, three red panda cubs were born in captivity at Hamilton Zoo in New Zealand in

December, 2012. The Padmaja Naidu Himalayan Zoological Park, Darjeeling, India successfully bred more than forty red pandas and successfully released four captive-bred individuals to the wild in August and November 2003. The International Studbook is currently maintained at Rotterdam Zoo in the Netherlands and with the International Red Panda Management Group, they coordinate the Species Survival Plan (SSP) in North America, the European Endangered Species Programme in Europe and other captive-breeding programs in India, Japan, Australia and China and provides guidance and technical expertise on research and long-term management of the species in captivity. Later, World Association of Zoos and Aquariums (WAZA) launched the Global Species Management Plans (GSMPs) in the year 2003, through which the long-term, captive survival of many species can be ensured. As the first step in the GSMP process, a special workshop on red panda was convened in Rotterdam Zoo in April 2012. This was attended by all the regional coordinators and a working plan for the GSMP, including a captive breeding master plan for the next six years (one red panda generation) was approved by the WAZA Committee for Population Management at its meeting in October 2012. This official recognition enhances the global program and brings a lot more advantages like greater regional support for inter-regional transfers; more sharing of ideas and experience; increased uniformity of management; stronger links with range state partners; reduced legislative impediments to cross-border shipping; additional commitment of resources and especially greater prominence of the species. The main objective should be for all captive breeding programmes, is the reintroduction of the offspring into the natural habitat and their subsequent acceptance by the wild community. It is hoped that the red panda GSMP will become a model for other global program in the future so that many more species can benefit from worldwide population management.

Conservation Breeding of Red Panda in Padmaja Naidu Himalayan Zoological Park, Darjeeling

The Padmaja Naidu Himalayan Zoological Park, Darjeeling took a serious initiative to conserve this rare species through planned conservation breeding programme. The park is ideally situated within the natural distribution zone of the red panda and has had earlier records of successful breeding of red panda in captivity along with proper infrastructural facilities. There are at least two protected areas (Singhalila National Park and Neora Valley National Park) still having wild red panda populations in the region. A planned conservation breeding project as a part of the Global Captive Breeding Master Plan was initiated in 1990's in Darjeeling Zoo in response to the international conservation efforts. It is a unique effort aimed at planned conservation breeding and multiplication, to ensure their survival and reintroduce them back into the wild. The program started with existing nine animals — four wild caught animals already living in the zoo and five zoo-bred animals imported from European countries. The park had one male (Basant) and three females (Amita, Chanda and Divya) all of wild origin in stock at the beginning of the project. Hence, one male 'Oscar' (d.o.b. June 29, 1992) was brought from Rotterdam Zoo on April 1, 1993 to augment the existing populations of four red panda in the zoo. The first successful (planned) breeding of red panda occurred on 20.06.1994. When two cubs "Ekta" and "Friend" were born to 'Basant' and 'Amita''. Subsequently, Hari' (male, d.o.b. June 30, 1993, Rotterdam), Gora (male, d.o.b. —June 25, 1993, Colone) and Indira (female, d.o.b.—June 26, 1993, Madrid) arrived in Darjeeling on November 10, 1994 to introduce new blood and to continue the program. Again 'Omin' (Original name Tsambo) (male, d.o.b.—July 17, 1994, Rotterdam) and 'Vicky' (female, d.o.b. June 26, 1994, Antwerp) were further added into the already existing stock on December, 25, 1996. Later 'Vicky' (renamed as Prity) along with 'Jugal' (male, Darjeeling Zoo born) were shifted to Gangtok (Sikkim) zoo to start a subsidiary conservation breeding center over there. In the last 10 years there were total 38 births of red panda in captivity in Darjeeling zoo. At the same time, the pair at Gangtok zoo has also started breeding. The project at Padmaja Naidu Himalayan Zoological Park, Darjeeling is one of the most successful and only breeding programme (along with one subsidiary center at Gangtok) of the species in its natural distribution zone. All the record keeping of the program and animals has been made in collaboration with the International Studbook Keeper of the species at Rotterdam (Netherland). Steady research and studies are also being undertaken so that this very special and sensitive project can become a model for other such conservation breeding projects in suitable localities.

Diet Management: In captivity, the red panda is fed in the morning around 9 a.m. with fruits (apple, banana), sweet bread and a mix of egg, milk and honey. In the afternoon, they are provided with their natural diet—bamboo and water.

Breeding Management: Mating takes place at the end of December to February. After a gestation period of 112–158 days, the female gives birth to 1–4 blind cubs. The nesting period of the red panda is one month before parturition, when the animal starts collecting leaves to create a nest. In captivity, different cubing boxes, wooden and hollow, are provided and during nesting, they prefer calm and quiet surroundings. Any noise could disturb and stress the mother, which could lead to a mistreatment of the new born cub. After the birth, the mother and the cubs are kept together for 1 year time.

Reintroduction in the wild: During 2003–2004, the zoo attained a stable and genetically healthy population of twenty one red pandas and the preparation for their release in the wild has been initiated. After proper habitat feasibility studies and animal training, a total of four female red pandas were released in the Singhalila National Park for the first time following 'soft release' mode. Before final release, they were released in a semi-captive environment protected by fencing inside the jungle, where they are slowly habituated to eat only bamboos instead of captive diet and become ready for final release in the Singhalila National Park—the original home for red panda. Later, in 2003, two zoo-bred female pandas were released into the wild, as a trial for subsequent releases. Both pandas interacted naturally with their wild counterparts. While one was lost to a predator, the other female mated with a wild male and gave birth to next generation. This provides encouragement for the future reintroduction of this species, if required.

CASE STUDY II: SNOW LEOPARD *Panthera Uncia* (Schreber, 1775) (*see* Plate IV)

The snow leopard is one of the rarest and most interesting large carnivore inhabiting high mountains of Central Asia. This beautiful and shy animal is a striking symbol of the world's highest places and a good indicator of mountainous ecosystems (Shrestha et al., 2009). Snow leopard are persistently sought after and hunted for their valuable fur. Its soft colouring and luxuriant coat is scarcely rivaled.

Present Status: IUCN : Endangered; CITES : Appendix I; WPA : Schedule–I.

Distribution: Snow leopard is found in Afghanistan, Bhutan, India, certain places in China, Kazakhstan, Kyrgyzstan, Mongolia, Nepal, Pakistan, Russia, Tajikistan (Pamir-Altai range), and Uzbekistan. In India, the snow leopard is known to occur across the Himalayan range, including the western states of Jammu and Kashmir, Himachal Pradesh, Uttar Pradesh, and the eastern states of Sikkim and Arunachal Pradesh.

Habitat: Being a resident of the mountains, snow leopards typically inhabit rugged terrains such as steep slopes with bluffs, ridges broken by outcrops and valleys interrupted by rocks and cliffs, with arid and semi-arid shrub land, grassland or alpine meadows above the tree-line at an altitude of 3000–4500 m (McCarthy et al., 2003). Snow leopard generally avoids dense forests. In summer months, they occasionally go above 5500 m in the Himalayan range. However, at the onset of winter, like other animals of hilly areas, snow leopards also migrate to low levels of 600–1500 m into the oak, fir and rhododendron forests. At present, approximately 4,000–6,500 snow leopards remain in the wild.

Marks of Identification

- The snow leopard is distinctive in the shortness of its muzzle, its high forehead and vertical chin.
- It has long, thick smoky grey fur with dark-grey rosettes and black spots on its limbs, allows it to camouflage superbly. The wooly under fur is pure white, the grey is sometimes tinged with buff.
- Newborns are darker than the adults.
- The spots are unbroken and distinct on the head, nape and lower parts of the limbs. On the body they break up into larger, paler rosettes. The rosettes are less pronounced in the luxuriant winter coat.
- It has a round head, broad paws and a long round tail with hair that is equally long all around the tail and the tail is characteristically very long and thick.
- It has large, well-cushioned paws in comparison to its body, a strong chest and short forelimbs that enable it to leap around the cliff side.
- The female weighs 35–40 kg and the males are slightly heavier, weighing about 45–75 kg. Head to body length: 100–130 cm, tail length: 90 cm.

Behaviour and Social Organisation: The snow leopard can be either crepuscular or nocturnal. They generally take rest during daytime and hunt at night. They are excellent rock climbers and prefer travelling along linear features such as major ridgelines, gullies and along the base or crest of broken cliffs. Snow leopards are solitary and hunt alone, but at times a pair of snow leopards may travel together, especially during the breeding season and pairs have been observed hunting together. Very little is known about the lifestyle of these secretive cats. They are very agile and prefer the rocky cliffs, where they can hide and, therefore, stalk their prey better. So, they often congregate in those rocky cliffs to hunt and play. They mark their territories with urine, faeces and scraping the ground. Unlike other large cats, they do not roar.

Food and Feeding Behaviour: Snow leopards predate upon wild pigs, gorals, Himalayan tahrs, markhors, takins, musk deer and argalis. But their favourite prey species are blue sheep and ibex. In addition, marmots, hares and pikas are important among small mammals. Sometimes they are also reported to kill large birds. Besides, different kinds of livestock represent a significant prey item in some parts of their habitat. Generally in the summer months, they get the opportunities to prey upon domestic goats, sheep or ponies from their grazing grounds. Their home range varies from 12–39 sq km, but may exceed up to 400 sq.km where the food source is scanty. They hunt by stalking and ambushing birds and mammals in those higher elevations.

Snow leopard is an opportunistic predator, capable of killing prey three times heavier than them. It stalks its prey, creeping up and then grabbing it in a sudden sprint. The snow leopard is a superb jumper, executing long jumps covering 6 –15 m through air. They often rest on cliffs, in trees or on other elevated spots, which are not climbed but simply reached by jumping up. Unlike common leopard, snow leopards begin eating their prey from the posterior portion of the body. First the belly is opened and the viscera are eaten; then the snow leopard begins feeding on the muscles from the rump area, moving towards the front of the prey. The relatively low food supply in the high altitude terrains does not permit them to form social hunting groups, except during mating season when male and female hunt together or when a female hunts with her young. Snow leopards stay within their territories and do not migrate extensively.

Reproductive Behaviour: The breeding season occurs towards the end of winter. Mating usually takes place between late January and mid-March. Gestation period is about 90–105 days. In the months of June or July the female give births to 1–5 cubs in a well concealed den. They open their eyes at around nine days and are weaned at 2 months. The cubs remain with their mother until they become independent after around 18–22 months. The young become sexually mature at 2–3 years of age. Lifespan varies between 15–18 years in the wild.

Conservation Initiatives

In 1980, the American Association of Zoological Park and Aquarium (AAZPA) had introduced the Species Survival Plan (SSP) with the objective of strengthening and coordinating captive breeding program to ensure the survival of endangered species. In 1981, the International Snow Leopard Trust was formed to fulfill the objective of SSP concept and acted as apex body for snow leopards research across the globe. Numerous agencies are working to conserve the snow leopards and its threatened mountain ecosystems. These include the Snow Leopard Trust, the Snow Leopard Conservancy, the Snow Leopard Network, the Cat Specialist Group and the Panthera Corporation. These groups and numerous national governments of the snow leopard's range, nonprofit organizations and donors from around the world discussed on various issues and challenges for better conservation management of this precise gift of nature. In 2008, International Conference on Range-wide Conservation Planning for Snow Leopards was held in Beijing, China where important areas for Snow Leopard conservation (termed as Snow Leopard Conservation Units) was prioritized and a framework for the development of national action plans was designed (Jackson et al., 2008). Snow Leopard Network (SLN) was also set up in 2008 to bring individuals and organisations working on Snow Leopard under a common platform to ensure better coordination, cooperation and information sharing.

In situ initiatives

The total wild population of the snow leopard was estimated to lie between 4,080–6,590 with highest population in China followed by Mongolia, India, Nepal, Kyrgyzstan, Pakistan, Tajikistan, Kazakhstan, Russia, Bhutan, Afghanistan and Uzbekistan. A "surprisingly healthy" population of snow leopards has been found living at 16 locations in the isolated Wakhan Corridor in northeastern Afghanistan, giving rise to hopes for survival of wild snow leopards in that region. India has about 200–600 snow leopards, mostly in the alpine zones and snow clad mountain stretches of Himalayas. So, special attention must be given to *in situ* mode of conservation for this unique animal. Presently, Mongolia, Pakistan, Nepal and Russia have National Action Plans for Snow Leopard Conservation. India had also developed Project Snow Leopard for the conservation of this species, but this project did not receive adequate funding and did not become widely popular as some other species conservation programmes (Anonymous, 2007).

Snow Leopard in Captivity

Historical Overview

Snow leopards have been kept under human care since 1851, when the first specimen was exhibited in Antwerp Zoo (Sunquist and Sunquist, 2002) and first cub was born as early as in 1910. Authentic report on captive population first came in to existence during 1950s and has gained proper attention since 1976 after initiation of maintenance of International Stud Book. The first regional breeding program was launched in North America in the year 1984. During 1990s breeding programme was started in Japan, the then Russia, Australia and India. At the beginning of 2008, there were 445 specimens exhibited over 205 institutions, and involved a total of 239 females in global conservation breeding programme. Snow leopards are held in captivity in different zoos of the country (Table 8.2). In captivity, they are unlikely to show off their full capabilities and personalities. In captivity they can survive up to 21 years.

Table 8.2 Captive Population under Breeding Programme in India in 2013

Zoo	*Male*	*Female*	*Unsexed*	*Total*
Gangtok	0	1	0	1
Nainital	0	0	0	0
Kufri	0	0	0	0
Darjeeling	5	5	0	10
Total	5	6	0	11

Conservation Underway

The Padmaja Naidu Himalayan Zoological Park, Darjeeling is dedicated to conservation of wildlife. It started work on captive breeding project of this rare species in the year 1983. Past record of captive management of snow leopard in Indian zoos was not encouraging and it took almost 100 years to achieve the desired result. An ideal site for this purpose was selected at north-western corner of the Jawahar Parbat (Birch Hill) at an altitude of 2,100 m (latitude of 27º N and longitude 88ºE) in the district of Darjeeling, West Bengal after thorough inspection and approval by the experts Dr. Ingo Rieger and D. Walzthoeny in July 1983. This was the first instance of an Asian zoo participating in the Snow Leopard Master Plan under the leadership of Mrs. Helen Freeman, President of the International Snow Leopard Trust and coordinator of the "Species Survival Plan" for snow leopards.

A pair of unrelated snow leopards ('Kashi', the female and 'Vishnu' the male) were flown to Darjeeling Zoo respectively from Zurich Zoo and Helsinki Zoo on 21st March 1986. The female was born on 26th August 1983 in the Zurich Zoo and the male was born on 23rd June 1978 in Helsinki Zoo. Another pair ('Hank' male and 'Persia' female) came to Darjeeling Zoo from U.S. Zoo in the year 1989. The pair gave birth to two female cubs on May 20th, 1989. This was the first successful breeding of snow leopards in Darjeeling Zoo. 'Quizil' (male), 'Quila' and 'Quetta' (both females) were later added to the collection in the year 1992 to introduce new blood and continue breeding program. Another male 'Tyson' arrived at Darjeeling on January 27th, 2000 for the same purpose. Besides, two wild/rescued females 'Neeta and Meeta' from Leh-Ladakh region of Jammu and Kashmir were also air lifted to Darjeeling on May 17th, 2000. Unfortunately, Meeta died within few days of her arrival. In the last twenty years there are in total forty six births of snow leopards in captivity in the Padmaja Naidu Himalayan Zoological Park, Darjeeling and the project is one of the most successful and only breeding program of the species in South East Asia. All the record keeping of the whole programme is maintained by the International Stud Book Keeper of the species at Helsinki. Steady research and studies are also being continued to present this very special and sensitive project as a model for other such Conservation Breeding Project. As on May, 2006, there were 12 snow leopards (6 males and 6 females.). Next step taken was to have at least 4–5 stable captive populations of snow leopards at different high altitude zoos in the country, before any release/stocking in the wild can be planned. As such, in 2004, a pair each comprising a male and female snow leopard was sent from Darjeeling Zoo to Gangtok, Nainital and Shimla Zoos to start subsidiary breeding centers in those Himalayan Zoos. A new off display breeding centre with proper release facilities has been initiated at Topkey Dhara, Darjeeling with an objective of investigating and studying behavior and breeding biology and ecological adaptations of the species under semi-captive and simulated natural condition (Rai, 2013).

Dietary Management

In captivity, they are fed with chicken, mutton and beef on alternate days and raw eggs and boiled water every day. Apart from this they may be fed with whole prey or carcasses, meat mixer, bones and some slab meat. Approximately 700 kg of prey is required to feed an adult according to health condition and age of animals. Since overeating may lead to metabolic disorders and obesity resulting in increased risk of liver and heart diseases and respiratory problem, they are kept unfed, once in every week in captivity. Obese cats are also at greater risk of developing diabetes and arthritis. Clean water should be made available all times; a few drops of Vitamin A concentrate may be supplemented. One time feeding preferably during late hours of the day is sufficient except nourishing mother, whose total ration may be divided in to 2–3 equal meals. Bones and full prey should be included in the diet in order to reduce dental plaque formation.

Behavioural Management

Since captive environment differs from the wild situations in a number of ways such as lack of life threatening challenges by predators, hunger, diseases etc., they show abnormal level of behaviour in captivity either showing reduced or hyper activity. In captivity, they are more active early in the morning and again in the evening (Freeman, 1975). In captivity, normal behaviour is often replaced by abnormal or "stereotypic" behaviour due to spatial constraints or shrinkage of home range such as pacing, head-loss, aggressiveness, tameness, over eating or food refusal, aberrant appetite, auto-mutilation etc. (Clubb and Mason, 2007). Stereotypic behaviour is thought to be an indication of stress.

Health Management

The common ailments in captivity include mycotic pneumonia, ovarian dysgerminoma, pancreatic carcinoma, demodicosis, canine distemper, viral infection, osteomyelitis and number of fungal infections. Besides, Multiple Ocular Coloboma (MOC), septicemia, loose stool with different types of parasitic load, brittle bone in cubs are common. Pneumonia is common among new born characterized by rusty sputum, running nose, sniffing, and chest pains accompanied by fever with nagging cough. Pleurisy is also very common due to inflammation of pleural epithelium of the lung.

Population Management

The impact of small population size among endangered species is a major concern in conservation breeding. Population in captivity may deteriorate due to loss of genetic diversity, inbreeding depression, reduced fitness, genetic adaptations to captivity and accumulation of deleterious alleles and all these factors may jeopardize the objective of *ex-situ* conservation. The main objective of *ex-situ* conservation is to produce and manage the captive population in such a way that in long run, there will be a viable population of the species with a minimum of 90 percent of the original genetic diversity retained. To overcome all these short-comings, World Association of Zoo's and Aquarium (2005) recommended the need for population management and called for increased attention towards the management of animals at the population level, so as to ensure availability of healthy and viable species for the foreseeable future and to retain the founder's genetic diversity as unchanged as possible over time, such that the population may serve as a genetic reservoir for the species concerned. Although management of captive population is time consuming, expensive and sometimes risky, it has got several advantages. Since it is a genetic reservoir and as good as their wild counterpart, it may be used for reintroduction and improved animal welfare. It can prevent production of inbred animals as they often suffer from vast assortment of ailments like reduced longevity, inanition, metabolic disorders, morphological deformities, organ malformations, impaired reproductive traits, modified temperament, immunological imbalance, reduced temperature tolerance and susceptibility to stress.

Environmental Enrichment

Environmental enrichment is probably the most common means of tackling abnormal repititive behaviours (Menon et al. 2007). The successful enrichment involves improvement of the physical condition of the captive; prevent boredom as well as improvement in their biological monitoring. It provides a balance between risk factors associated with enrichment and maintaining appropriate behaviour and promote physical and psychological well-being of the captive animal. Enrichment programme was undertaken to overcome stereotypic, self-destructive abnormal behaviour in the captivity as they are deprived of certain essential components of living like mate finding and selection, home range patrolling, homing etc. Loud noise, construction works, expectation for food once a day and being locked inside enclosures contribute towards stereotypy. So enrichment programme is essential for better quality of life, make them well adjusted, curious, active and healthy.

Transportation

Conservation breeding programme involves regular exchange of animals, for which one of the major constrain is proper and safe transportation. During transportation enough care must be taken regarding cage size and specification as per specimen's need, amount and right type of food, distance to be travelled, veterinary care etc. Males need to be transported in separate, individual cages. Cages should be properly cleaned at regular intervals, disinfected, provided with proper resting beds and temperature should be under control.

Quarantine

Proper quarantine of newly arrived animals is an essential part of a preventive medicine programme. Although, it is expected that they are devoid of any transmissible disease, still there are chances of exposure during transportation. Ideally, a new animal be housed in a separate enclosure from that of the resident ones for at least one month under the supervision of a keeper who does not have any contact with the resident animals. During this period full physical examinations, hematological and biochemical profile and parasitological investigations are to be carried out. After the completion of quarantine period, complete physical checkup must be carried out before releasing it into the display area.

Stud Book Maintenance

Stud book is primarily a compilation and source of genealogical data of individual animals in a particular zoo population. It can suggest, recommend, coordinate and facilitate regarding selection of breed and other operational issues towards successful breeding of animals concerned.

Preventive Measures

- Enclosures along with food containers should be cleaned thoroughly on daily basis using detergents and disinfectants
- Maintain proper hygiene and sanitation with well managed drainage system
- Fumigation at regular intervals
- Regular monitoring of parasitic load
- Vaccination against respiratory viruses is recommended

Precautions

Before Birth

- To achieve maximum breeding success in captivity, optimal environment is to be provided to the pregnant female
- Privacy and freedom from disturbances influence the breeding success, there must be some provision of off exhibit maternity den for pregnant female

- During the week before parturition and at least first week after birth foot and vehicle traffic should be monitored around the den
- During pregnancy, extra food must be made available to meet the demands of growing fetus
- Special attention must be given during or imminent parturition
- The breeding room should be kept warm, dry and moisture free
- Hand rearing should not be encouraged

During cub rearing

- General hygiene and cleanliness of the rearing room must be ensured, as well as, keeping record of inside temperature and humidity
- Use musk and gloves while handling the cubs
- Document daily activity pattern like feeding, sleeping, playing and grooming time, as well as, respiration rate
- Maintain rearing diary to keep accurate record of daily activities
- Provide proper bedding facilities for rest, which must be changed at regular intervals
- Place a dehumidifier inside rearing room, especially during monsoon
- In captivity, major cause of mortality is related to the behavioural stress. So, measures must be taken to minimize unnecessary stress.

Challenges

Within a short period time PNH Zoological Park showed promising results in managing and breeding of snow leopard in captivity. But, there were several instances of cub mortality, absence of genetic variability among the existing population and health related problems. Study showed that cubs between 1 to 6 years of age are most vulnerable as maximum mortality occurred during this age period. This may be linked to some diseases like pneumonia and rickets which may be due to high humidity inside and lack of sufficient direct sunlight respectively (Rai, 2013).

CASE STUDY III: PYGMY HOG *Porcula Salvania* (Hodgson, 1847) (*see* Plate IV)

The pygmy hog is the smallest and rarest wild hog species in the world and has been given the highest conservation priority as critically endangered species by the IUCN. It is one of the most sensitive indicators of critical changes in grassland quality and composition. This species was once widespread across India, Nepal and Bhutan, but now is restricted only in some protected areas of Assam. The current global population is about 150 individuals or fewer.

Present Status: IUCN–Critically Endangered; CITES–Appendix–I. WPA–Schedule–I.

Distribution: The distribution of pygmy hog is restricted to the Terai region of India, Nepal and Bhutan. In India, the pygmy hog is restricted to the plains of Brahmaputra River in south and south-east Assam. Some isolated populations are also found in Manas Biosphere Reserve and Barnadi Wildlife Sanctuary in northwest Assam and very few locations in northern West Bengal (Narayan et al., 2008).

Habitat: Pygmy hog prefers dense, tall riverine wet grasslands (dominated by *Saccharum spp., Themeda sp., Narenga sp.* etc.) commonly referred to as 'thatch land' and forest habitat (Oliver and Deb Roy 1993; Narayan et al., 2008).

Marks of Identification

- Pygmy hog is the world's smallest pig having a total body length of about 50–70 cm and shoulder height of 25 cm. Male pygmy hogs weigh about 8–9 kg, females are smaller than males.
- Adult pygmy hog are gray-brown to black in appearance and have no crest on back.
- The young are lighter in appearance and with reddish stripes.
- Ears are very small and they have characteristically very short tail, which is sometimes not visible.
- The male hog generally possesses small tusks.

Behavioural Biology: Pygmy hogs groom each other and make soft grunting sound at the time of foraging, which keep them together. Both the sexes build unique nests by scraping and digging the forest floor in a very characteristic manner and also use piles of grass and other vegetation to lay in the floor of the burrow. Pygmy hogs generally use these burrows for sleeping at night. They are nocturnal in habit. Their sense of smell is acute, while the sight and hearing are moderately developed.

Food and Feeding Behaviour: The pygmy hogs are omnivorous in nature and feed on roots, tubers, crops and other vegetable matters, as well as, insects, other invertebrates and also rodents and small reptiles. They feed during early in the morning and late in the evening.

Reproductive Behaviour: Reproduction is highly seasonal and births take place during the dry months or with the onset of monsoon (April and May). Gestation period is about 100 days. The females generally give birth to 2–6 young. In the wild, they make small nests by digging a small trench and lining it with vegetation. They can survive up to 10–12 years in the wild.

Social Organization: The pygmy hog is non-territorial and is found to live in small family groups consisting of 4–5 individuals, which sometimes may reach up to 20 individuals. Generally one or more adult females are accompanied by juveniles. Adult males remain solitary, but join the females or family groups during breeding season. The home range of pygmy hog extends up to 0.25 sq km.

Threats: Loss and degradation of habitat due to human settlements, agricultural encroachments, dry-season burning, livestock grazing, commercial forestry and flood control schemes are the main threats for pygmy hog (Narayan et al., 2008).

Conservation Initiatives

According to IUCN, pygmy hog is designated as Critically Endangered, whereas its local status is Rare and it is placed in the Schedule–I of Wildlife (Protection) Act, 1972 providing the animal a nationwide legal protection. Most of the areas of their concentration have been declared as protected areas. Being in the Appendix–I of CITES, prevents any part of it from being used in international trade.

Preservation of its habitat in the north and northeastern India, particularly in Assam need to be prioritized and field data should be collected to understand the present population status and distribution of pygmy hog. An enclosure at Manas Biosphere Reserve has been created recently, where a good number of pygmy hogs could be protected, studied and bred. Pygmy Hog Conservation Programme (PHCP) under the umbrella of a formal 'International Conservation Management and Research Agreement' (originally signed at New Delhi in 1995 and later renewed as a Memorandum of Understanding in 2001) between the Ministry of Environment and Forests, Government of India and IUCN SSC Pigs Peccaries and Hippo Specialist Group, Durrell Wildlife Conservation Trust (DWCT), the Forest Department, Government of Assam is one of the major research and conservation programme (Narayan and Deka 2002; Narayan 2006; Narayan et al., 2008). The primary aim of this collaborative program is conservation of the pygmy hogs and other endangered species of tall grasslands of the region through field research, captive breeding and reintroduction after adequate restoration of degraded former habitats.

Captive Breeding

After the introduction of PHCP in the year 1995, a dramatic increase in the success of captive breeding has been noticed. One of the main objectives of the programme was to establish a well-planned conservation breeding project for the species as an insurance against their possible early extinction in the wild and as a source of animals for reintroduction purpose.

In the year 1996, six (2 male, 4 female) pygmy hogs were captured from Manas National Park, Assam to start the captive breeding program in Basistha, near Guwahati, with the goal of reintroducing captive bred individuals back in the wild. Later, five more hogs were caught and released at the capture site fitted with radio collar. The population almost doubled within one year duration from 18 to 35 through planned breeding. By 2002, it became 75 through successful breeding and addition of wild caught individuals. Although two more enclosures and a quarantine facility were constructed at Basistha, the unanticipated and rapid increase in the captive population created accommodation problems, leading to the forced restriction on breeding in captivity. Subsequently, a much larger facility was established at Potasali near Nameri National Park in Assam, which includes four stocking enclosures and four pre-release enclosures with near natural habitat.

Reintroduction

At the same time, surveys were carried out to identify possible release sites for the possible transfer of some of them back in to the wild. Two potential reintroduction sites were identified in Sonai-Rupai Wildlife Sanctuary and Nameri National Park, both in Sonitpur district of Assam bordering Bhutan and Arunachal Pradesh. Habitat management through proper restoration and scientific management were made and in the year 2008, a total of 16 hogs (7 males, 9 females) had been released into the Sonai-Rupai Wildlife Sanctuary, after proper acclimatization under simulated natural condition at pre-release centre at Potasali in the Nameri Tiger Reserve for five months. They were kept in the pre-release enclosures under minimum human contact and hogs began to behave like wild animals within a few weeks and shifted to Sonai-Rupai for final release. At present 50–60 hogs are maintained in captivity and 12–14 are being released every year. By the end of 2013, a total 60 individuals have been released successfully in the wild. Since the animals at Basistha Centre are the only captive pygmy hogs in the world, there is an urgent need to develop an alternative research and breeding site along with pre-release enclosures to avoid any catastrophe at the present location.

Community level conservation initiatives and awareness campaign have been started in the fringe villages of Manas, Nameri and Sonai-Rupai as it is almost impossible to save the species without the cooperation of the local population. Capacity building and training program are also being carried out for the frontline protection staff in the above protected areas.

REVIEW QUESTIONS

1. What is meant by captive breeding? Mention advantages and challenges of captive breeding.
2. What is reintroduction? Why is it controversial? Mention the problems associated with reintroduction of captive breeds.
3. What do you mean by conservation breeding? How does it differ from *ex-situ* conservation? Mention the prerequisite for successful Conservation breeding. What are the advantages and limitations of conservation breeding?
4. State the present status of Red Panda. Give an idea regarding their distribution. Comment on their food and feeding behaviour.
5. Give an account on the conservation management of captive Red Panda in India.
6. Mention the preferred habitat of snow leopard and their distribution in Indian context. Elaborate the conservation initiative undertaken in India for the survival of this species.
7. What are the precautions to be taken during captive management of snow leopard?
8. State the present status of pygmy hog. Comment on its habitat preferences and distribution in India. Mention different unique behaviours of this animal. Elaborate different conservation initiatives undertaken in India for its sustainable conservation.

REFERENCES

Anonymous, Snow Leopard Project Stalled: Ambitious Plans to Conserve Himalayan Snow Leopards Face Fund Crunch. *Sikkim Express*, 2007.

Anonymous, Concept paper on in-situ and *ex-situ* linkage—conservation breeding of endangered wild animal species in India, In: Proceedings of International Conference on India's Conservation Breeding Initiative. MoEF, GoI. 2008.

Bahuguna, C.C., Dhaundyal, S., Vyas, P. and Singhal, N. Red panda in Darjeeling at Singalila National Park and adjoining forest: a status report, *Small Carnivore Conservation* **19**, 11–12, 1998.

Choudhury, A., An overview of the status and conservation of the red panda *Ailurus fulgens* in India, with reference to its global status. *Oryx* **35**, 250–259, 2001.

Clubb, R. and Mason, G.J., Natural behavioural biology as a risk factor in carnivore welfare: How analysing species differences could help zoos improve enclosures. *Applied Animal Behaviour Science*, **102**, 303–328, 2007.

EAAM, European Association for Aquatic Mammals: Statement on release of long-term captive cetaceans, 2004. Retrieved from http://www.eaam.org/position_statement_on_releases/

Freeman, H., A Preliminary Study on the Behaviour of Captive Snow Leopards, *International Stud Book*, **15**, 217–222, 1975.

Ghose, D. and Dutta, P.K. Status and distribution of the Red Panda, *Ailurus fulgens fulgens*, in India, pp. 357–374. In: *Red Panda, biology and conservation of the first panda* (Glaston, A.R., ed.), Academic Press, London, UK, 2011.

Glatston, A., Wei, F., Than Zaw and Sherpa, A. *Ailurus fulgens*, The IUCN Red List of Threatened Species 2015: e.T714A45195924, 2015. Retrieved from: http://dx.doi.org/10.2305/IUCN.UK.2015-4.RLTS.T714A45195924.en.

Holt, W.V., Picard, A.R. and Prather, R.S., Wildlife conservation and reproductive cloning, *Reproduction*, **127**, 317–324, 2004.

IUCN, *IUCN guidelines for re-introductions*, IUCN/SSC Re-introduction Specialist Group, Gland, Switzerland, 1998.

Jackson, R., Mallon, D., McCarthy, T., Chundaway, R.A. & Habib, B. *Panthera uncia*. The IUCN Red List of Threatened Species 2008: e.T22732A9381126, 2008. Retrieved from: http://dx.doi.org/10.2305/IUCN.UK.2008.RLTS.T22732A9381126.en.

Mason, G., Clubb, R., Latham, N., and Vickery, S., Why and how should we use environmental enrichment to tackle steriotypic behaviour? *Applied Animal Behaviour Science*, **102**, 163–188, 2007

McCarthy, T.M., Allen, P.M., Fox, J., Chapron, G., Jackson, R.M., Mishra, C. and Theile, S., *Snow leopard survival strategy*, ISLT, Seattle, 2003.

Mallick, J.K. Status of the Red Panda *Ailurus fulgens* in the Neora Valley National Park, Darjeeling District, West Bengal, India, *Small Carnivore Conservation*, **43**, 30–36, 2010.

McGreevy, TJ-Jr., Dabek, L., and Husband, T.P., Genetic evaluation of the Association of Zoos and Aquariums Matschie's tree Kangaroo (*Dendrolagus matschiei*) captive breeding program. *Zoo Biology*, **30**, 636–646, 2011.

Narayan, G. Pygmy Hog Conservation Programme—an update. *IUCN/SSC Pigs, Peccaries, and Hippos Specialist Group (PPHSG) Newsletter*, **6**, 14–15, 2006.

Narayan, G. and Deka, P.J. Pygmy Hog Conservation Programme in Assam, India. *IUCN/SSC Pigs, Peccaries, and Hippos Specialist Group (PPHSG) Newsletter*, **2**, 5–7, 2002.

Narayan, G., Deka, P. and Oliver, W. *Porcula salvania*. The IUCN Red List of Threatened Species 2008: e.T21172A9254675, 2008. Retrieved from: http://dx.doi.org/10.2305/IUCN.UK.2008.RLTS.T21172A9254675.en.

Oliver, W.L.R., and Deb Roy, S., The Pygmy Hog (*Sus salvanius*)—Chapter 5.3. In: *Pigs, Peccaries and Hippos Status Survey and Action Plan*, IUCN/SSC Pigs and Peccaries Specialist Group & IUCN/SSC Hippo Specialist Group. 1993.

Pradhan, S., Saha, G.K. and Khan, J.A. Ecology of the Red Panda *Ailurus fulgens*in the Singhalila National Park, Darjeeling, India. *Biological Conservation*, **98**, 11–18, 2001.

Rai, S., *Study of Snow leopard (Uncia uncia) at Padmaja Naidu Himalayan Zoological Park, Darjeeling (Project Report)*, Padmaja Naidu Himalayan Zoological Park, Darjeeling, 2013. Retrieved from: http://www.pnhzp.gov.in/publication/Study%20of%20Snow%20Leopard.pdf

Roka, B. and Jha, A.K. Census of Red Panda (*Ailurus fulgens*) at Singalila National Park and its surrounding area, Darjeeling, West Bengal, India. *Zoo's Print* **29**, 11–14, 2014.

Saha, G.K. and Mazumdar, S., Wildlife conservation: Indian initiative through ages, *Wesleyan Journal of Research*, **2**,1, 40–47, 2009.

Shrestha, R., Wikramanayake, E., Thapa K, et al., 2009**.** Estimating snow leopard populations in Nepal Himalaya. In: *Proceedings of 23rd International Congress for Conservation Biology*, Society for Conservation Biology, Beijing, China.

Sunquist, M. and Sunquist, F. *Wild Cats of the World* (1st. ed.), University of Chicago Press, Chicago, 2002, ISBN 978-0-22-677999-7

Wei, F., Zhang, Z. and Liu, Z. Conservation initiatives in China, pp. 409–418. In: *Red Panda, biology and conservation of the first panda* (Glaston, A.R., ed.), Academic Press, London, UK, 2011.

World Association of Zoo's and Aquarium (WAZA), *Building a Future for Wildlife – The World Zoo and Aquarium Conservation Strategy*, World Association of Zoo's and Aquarium, Bern, Switzerland, 2005.

Ziegler, S.A., Melisch, G., Sharma, R., Ghose, B.K., Chakraborty, P.S., Shrestha, R., Ghose, P., Legshey, D., Pradhan, K., Bhutia, H., Tambe, N.T., and Sinha, S., Sikkim – Im Zeichen des Roten Panda. *Zeitschrift des Kölner Zoos*, **53**, 79–92, 2010. Retrieved from http://www.traffic.org/non-traffic/non-traffic_pub12.pdf

9

SPECIAL MANAGEMENT PROGRAMME OF WILD ANIMALS IN INDIA

9.1 WILDLIFE MANAGEMENT PROJECTS IN INDIA

To protect the endangered flora and fauna of our country, the Government, non-government organizations, different institutes and universities have initiated several special conservation projects. Private sectors have also started to get involved in conserving the rich natural wealth of this country as part of their 'corporate-social responsibility' to increase peoples' awareness in order to bring about a change in their attitude towards wildlife. A few of these conservation projects are also funded by several foreign organizations and multinational corporates.

9.2 PROJECT TIGER

'Project Tiger' is one of the most successful wildlife conservation projects being run in this country over the years. Tigers are present at the apex of the food chain and, hence, are considered as the indicator of the stability of the ecosystem. Therefore, to support a viable tiger population, a habitat should possess a good prey base which, in turn, will depend on undisturbed forest vegetation. 'Project Tiger', thus in the name of conserving tigers, actually aims to conserve the entire ecosystem.

9.2.1 Origin of 'Project Tiger'

About 40,000 tigers lived in the wilderness of this country in the beginning of the 20th century. Various anthropogenic pressures, deforestation and disturbance of viable tiger habitats, particularly in the second half of the 20th century, led to rapid decline in tiger populations of this country. In addition, poaching for international trade for its skins, bones and other body parts, as well as, reduction of their natural prey populations were other threats to these large cats. In the year 1969, serious concern was voiced about the threat to several species of wildlife and the shrinkage of wilderness in India in the General Assembly meeting of International Union for Conservation of Nature and Natural Resources (IUCN) in Delhi. Alarm was raised and a national ban on tiger hunting was imposed in 1970. In 1972, the Wildlife (Protection) Act came into force and initially a task force was set up to formulate a project for tiger conservation with an ecological approach. First ever all India tiger census was conducted in 1972, which revealed the existence of only 1827 tigers. Subsequently, 'Project Tiger' was launched on April 1, 1973.

The project started as a 'Central Sector Scheme' and received full assistance of Central Government till 1979–80. Later, it became a 'Centrally Sponsored Scheme' from 1980–81, with equal sharing of expenditure between the centre and the states. The World Wide Fund for Nature (WWF) has given an assistance of US$ 1 million in the form of equipment, expertise and literature. The overall administration of the project is monitored by a 'Steering Committee'. For proper execution of the project, the respective state governments appointed a 'Field Director' for each reserve, who is assisted by the field and technical personnel. The Chief Wildlife Wardens in various states are responsible for the field execution. A full-fledged 'Director' of the project centrally coordinates the work for the country.

9.2.2 Aims and Objectives of 'Project Tiger'

'Project Tiger' aims to conserve tigers in specially constituted 'tiger reserves' in different bio-geographical regions present throughout India. Main objectives of Project Tiger include:

- Identifying the limiting factors and to mitigate them by suitable management
- Prohibition of any anthropogenic activities, as well as, elimination of all forms of biotic disturbances from the core area
- Rationalization of activities in the buffer zone, where only 'conservation oriented land use' are allowed
- Restricting the habitat management only to repair the damages done to the ecosystem by human and other interferences, so as to facilitate recovery of the ecosystem to its natural state
- Monitoring the faunal and floral changes over time.
- Carrying out research about wildlife
- Carefully avoiding the management practices, which tend to push the wildlife populations beyond the carrying capacity of the habitat

9.2.3 Implementation of 'Project Tiger'

Initially nine tiger reserves covering an area of about 13,017 sq km were established during 1973–74 in different states by the central and state governments. These nine reserves were Manas (Assam), Palamau (Bihar), Similipal (Orissa), Corbett (Uttar Pradesh), Kanha (Madhya Pradesh), Melghat (Maharashtra), Bandipur (Karnataka), Ranthambhore (Rajasthan) and Sundarbans (West Bengal). All these tiger reserves were created on a 'core-buffer' strategy and a minimum core of 300 sq km with a sizeable buffer was recommended for each project area and suitable 'Management Plans' were drawn up for each tiger reserve.

9.2.4 Achievements of 'Project Tiger'

The main achievements of this project are fire protection through suitable preventive and control measures, excellent habitat recovery and consequent increase in the tiger population in the reserve areas. Populations of tigers in India have been estimated to range within 1,706–1,909 in 2010 (Jhala et al., 2011), which have increased to an estimated 2,226 individuals in 2014 (George, 2015 and Jhala et al., 2015). Apart from tigers, populations of all other wild animals have also increased within the project areas. Over the years, the number of tiger reserves also increased significantly, from a mere 28 reserves in 2006 to 50 reserves in 2016 covering an area of 71,207.10 sq. km (Project Tiger, 2016).

In the subsequent 'Five Year Plans', the main thrust was to enlarge the core and buffer zones in certain reserves, intensification of protection and eco-development in the buffer zones of existing tiger reserves, creation of additional tiger reserves and strengthening of the research activities. Wireless communication system and outstation patrol camps have also been developed within the tiger reserves to deter the poachers away from these reserves. Voluntary village relocation has been done in many reserves, especially from the core area. In Kanha, Bandipur and Ranthambhore, all the villages have been shifted from the core and after relocation, the villagers have been provided with alternate agricultural lands and other community benefits. The area around the buffer is now contemplated as a 'zone of multiple uses' by the neighbouring communities, to bring compatibility between the reserves and the local community in order to involve the locals in tiger conservation. Complementary inputs for eco-development and voluntary village relocation provided earlier in separate projects have now been merged as an umbrella scheme with Project Tiger. Through such 'restorative management' and 'intense protection', the tiger populations in the tiger reserve areas have increased. Recently important tiger reserves of this country have been linked in GIS domain for better management and crime detection. Moreover, 'National Tiger Monitoring and Habitat Evaluation System' has been developed using information and communication technology for dissemination of information through web.

9.2.5 Limitations of 'Project Tiger'

Certain shortcomings of 'Project Tiger', as well as, the limitations and challenges of the prevalent situation of wildlife conservation parse, were brought into limelight after the complete disappearance of tigers from the Sariska Tiger Reserve in Rajasthan. Investigation of the cause of this recent 'tiger crisis' in Sariska revealed a broader problem of wildlife conservation in this country. Apart from a very small segment of the society, the conservation movement has often not integrated the rural people and not even inculcated among majority of the urban people. Since thousands of indigenous communities depend on tiger habitats, these protected areas cannot be viewed in isolation from the surrounding socio-economic realities and developmental priorities of the Government. This calls for a cross-sectoral and multidisciplinary approach. Regional planning and active community participation around tiger reserves with integrated land use planning is of utmost importance in our country for effective tiger conservation.

9.2.6 Recommendations

Some of the recommendations in the 'Tiger Task Force Report' endorsed by the National Finance Commission include:

- Creation of two separate departments of 'Environment' and of 'Forests and Wildlife' within the Ministry of Environment and Forests
- Creation of a sub-cadre of wildlife specialists and professionals within the forestry services
- Delegate greater power to Project Tiger Directorate
- Periodic independent audit of each Tiger Reserve
- Recruit local persons to protect the protected areas
- Integrate the traditional hunting tribes and communities living around the protected areas in the conservation efforts
- People living in the forest fringe areas and relying heavily on forest resources are to be provided with alternate livelihood
- Deploy additional security forces, particularly for the reserves which are threatened with insurgency
- Create special bureau to deal with the menace of wildlife crime and development of appropriate forensic facilities to assist them
- A closer bilateral relationship with Peoples' Republic of China, as this country has often been found to be the destination country in various illegal consignments of wildlife articles
- Introduction of more scientific method of estimating tiger population and habitat monitoring
- Greater emphasis on research to assist better conservation
- Developing linkages with local people to help both people and wildlife to co-exist
- Proper regulation and management of tourism

In spite of all odds, Project Tiger was a pioneering effort of a unique kind and is undoubtedly one of the most successful initiatives to conserve the dwindling tiger population of this country. This is basically an ecosystem-based conservation project, where optimum presence of tiger indicates that the complex ecosystem is in its prime health. Tiger is an apex predator. So, population of all wild herbivores will also have to be increased in the project areas to sustain a healthy population of tigers. A viable tiger population in a habitat, indicates the presence of a good prey base, which in turn will only sustain if there is healthy and undisturbed forest vegetation. Project Tiger thus had shown how a mega species could be used to create support for conservation of diverse and representative ecosystems, along with its faunal and floral diversity, water, soil and wilderness.

9.3 PROJECT ELEPHANT

9.3.1 Origin of 'Project Elephant'

Project Elephant is a centrally sponsored scheme for conservation of a mega herbivore that often comes in conflict with human population. Asian elephants require large amount of food and fodder to thrive. As most of the forests in the elephant ranges are fragmented, so they often raid the crops cultivated in and around their forested habitat and subsequently indulge in conflict with human beings. To mitigate this human-elephant conflict and to improve the elephant habitat, Project Elephant was launched in February 1992 to provide required financial, technical and scientific assistance to the elephant range states of India. This project is also a part of the international programme for 'Monitoring of Illegal Killing of Elephants (MIKE)' which has been initiated under the aegis of the Convention on International Trade in Endangered Species of Fauna and Flora (CITES).

9.3.2 Aims and Objectives of 'Project Elephant'

The vision of this project was to ensure long-term survival of the viable population of elephants in their natural habitats. Project Elephant Action Plan thus includes:

- Acquisition of land and creation of plantation to act as corridors
- Removal of encroachments and settlements in the elephant ranges to facilitate free movement for elephants
- Plantation of suitable fodder plants in elephant habitats
- Eradication of weeds
- Mitigation of conflict through prompt action and compensation schemes

9.3.3 Implementation of 'Project Elephant'

Central assistance is given to thirteen elephant range states *viz.* Assam, Arunachal Pradesh, Meghalaya, Nagaland, Tripura, West Bengal, Jharkhand, Uttar Pradesh, Orissa, Kerala, Tamil Nadu, Andhra Pradesh and Karnataka to enable them to provide financial assistance for habitat management, to mitigate man-elephant conflict, payment of *ex-gratia* relief for loss of life and properties, strengthening of anti-poaching measures, capture and translocation of problematic elephant populations etc. The main activities of Project Elephant include:

- Research on issues related to management and *in-situ* conservation of Asiatic elephant
- Ecological restoration of existing natural habitats and providing migratory routes (corridors) between different elephant ranges

- Eradication of various weeds (like *Eupatorium, Lantana, Mimosa* etc.) from elephant habitats and replacing them with bamboo and other grass species
- Mitigation of man-elephant conflict in general, especially in crucial habitats with high frequency of conflict
- Ensuring proper and prompt compensation to the people for the loss of life and properties due to human-elephant conflict
- Strengthening of anti-poaching activities and patrolling for protection of wild elephants from poaching and other unnatural causes of death
- Veterinary care for the diseased wild elephants and immunization of domestic livestock against communicable diseases
- Development of strategies to minimize pressures of human and their domestic livestock on crucial elephant habitats
- Improvement of the quality of life of the people inhabiting the fringe areas through various eco-development projects in order to reduce their dependence on forest resources
- Awareness generation among the villagers living both within and around the periphery of elephant habitats and corridors (particularly in the conflict areas). A series of campaigns, workshops, seminars, meetings etc. should be carried out through schools and community organizations. Such awareness programmes should address the need of elephant conservation, make them understand the complexity of the problem and restore a sense of compassion for elephants
- Organizing regular state level consultative meetings to involve the local people in the conservation action programme
- Development of scientific management plan to ensure survival of a viable population of wild Asiatic elephants along with conservation of elephant habitats in India

9.3.4 Achievements of 'Project Elephant'

So far 32 Elephant Reserves (ERs) have already been declared in this country and several others are under consideration. Some of the elephant reserves are Shivalik ER (Uttarakhand), Uttar Pradesh ER (Uttar Pradesh), Eastern Dooars ER (West Bengal), Mayurjharna ER (West Bengal), Kameng ER (Arunachal Pradesh), South Arunachal ER (Arunachal Pradesh), Sonitpur ER (Assam), Dihing-Patkai ER (Assam), Kaziranga-Karbi Anglong ER (Assam), Dhansiri-Lungding ER (Assam), Chirang-Ripu ER (Assam), Intanki ER (Nagaland), Garo Hills ER (Meghalaya), Singhbhum ER (Jharkhand), Mayurbhanj ER (Orissa), Mahanadi ER (Orissa), Sambalpur ER (Orissa), Mysore ER (Karnataka), Wayanad ER (Kerala), Nilambur ER (Kerala), Anamudi ER (Kerala), Periyar ER (Kerala), Nilgiri ER (Tamilnadu), Coimbatore ER (Tamilnadu), Anamalai ER (Tamilnadu), Srivilliputtur ER (Tamilnadu), Rayala ER (Andhra Pradesh), etc. As an outcome of this project the elephant population in India has increased from just over 27000 (Range: 27657–27682) in 2007 to about 30000 (Range: 29391–30711) in 2012.

9.3.5 Limitations of 'Project Elephant'

Several limitations and challenges are also associated with the implementation of 'Project Elephant' in this country. Poaching is a major challenge in the conservation of Asian Elephants. Also many elephants die every year being hit by trains in different parts of this country, particularly in areas where railway tracks run through the forested habitats. Despite several joint meetings between railway and forest departments in the problem areas and many awareness campaigns with the train drivers, little success has been achieved and elephant mortality in railway tracts is still a burning reality. Rural and agricultural landscapes of this country are highly populated and often expand encroaching the adjoining forested areas. Declaring large stretches of lands as 'Elephant Reserves' in such a scenario is often very difficult. Moreover, elephants often come out of the protected areas into the adjoining human-dominated landscapes and indulge in conflict. Scientific data needs to be generated through adequate research to properly address these issues. Timely allocation of appropriate funds is very important to tackle some of the challenging issues in the elephant range states.

9.3.6 Recommendations

For effective and better conservation of Asiatic elephants in the country, Elephant Task Force recommended that Elephant Reserves should be the basic management unit and suggested that the entire Elephant Reserve should also be notified as Ecologically Sensitive Areas (ESA) under the Environment Protection Act. The limits of an Elephant Reserve should preferably lie within state boundaries and the boundaries of the interstate reserves need to be unified and re-aligned.

Besides, the land use policies in elephant habitats, as well as, in the elephant corridors need to ensure prevention of further fragmentation of habitat. Encroachment in corridors and elephant reserves have to be made punishable and fine be imposed. In this regard, imposing a minimum fine of ₹10 lakhs and imprisonment of not less than two years for the offenders has been recommended by the Elephant Task Force, which has to be incorporated in the Wildlife (Protection) Act.

9.4 OPERATION RHINO

9.4.1 Origin of 'Operation Rhino'

The Greater one-horned rhinoceros (*Rhinoceros unicornis* Linnaeus) once ranged across the northern part of the Indian subcontinent throughout the Indo-Gangetic Plain and Brahmaputra river basins, from Pakistan to the Indo-Myanmar border, including parts of Nepal, Bangladesh and Bhutan and also may have existed in Myanmar, southern China and Indochina. One-horned rhinos were common in northwestern India and Pakistan until around 1600. But they disappeared from most of this region shortly thereafter and declined sharply throughout their range over the next three hundred years. Their population drastically reduced mainly due to excessive hunting, poaching and illegal wildlife trade. Extensive habitat loss and frequent floods in their distribution range are few other major threats to survival of these mega herbivores. In the year 2013, a total of 41 rhinos were killed in Assam by the poachers. Rhino horns are often used in traditional Chinese medicines and other Oriental medicines for treatment of a variety of ailments like epilepsy, fevers and strokes. Rhino horns are also considered to be aphrodisiacs and are believed to have healing powers. Despite global ban on international trade in rhino horns, even today the volume of illegal trade is quite large and persists throughout Asia. Recently, many extremist groups armed with sophisticated weapons in North-east India have also been involved in both poaching and smuggling of rhino horns. Ever increasing human population and subsequent demand for land for agriculture, habitations and other developmental activities, have resulted in large scale habitat conversion. Large stretches of alluvial plain grasslands have almost disappeared from the former distribution range of rhinos leading to human-rhino conflicts and easier accessibility for hunters. Grazing by domestic livestock is another cause of habitat degradation. Besides, annual floods in Brahmaputra inundate a large portion of the rhino habitat in Kaziranga. Few rhinos drown and some others which successfully take refuge in the highlands are often killed by the poachers. The destruction and fragmentation of habitats by human activities, often prevents migration and genetic exchange among populations. Consequently, some local populations have become isolated and resulted in "inbreeding".

Till the end of 17th century, rhinoceros were extremely common and widespread in the Indo-Gangetic plains of the north, central and south-eastern parts of the country. But, presently this species is confined, as small populations, in the riparian grasslands, shallow and dense woodlands in a few protected areas in India. Only 100 rhinos remained in wild in the early 1900s and by 1908, the population had fallen to around 12 individuals in Kaziranga, one of the main ranges of rhinos.

In the early 1900s, officials became concerned at the rhino's reducing numbers. In 1910, rhino hunting in India became prohibited. The species has been included on CITES Appendix–I since 1975. Anti-poaching measures have been intensified by regular patrolling, constitution of special protection force, strengthening communication networks, provision of better arms for staff, coordination of law enforcement agencies, incentives and rewards, publicity/ nature education/awareness generation and eco-development activities for fringe villages. Habitat improvement works have been undertaken through canopy manipulation in woodlands, planting of indigenous fodder grasses, weed eradication, fire control, grazing control of domestic livestock, flood protection through embankment and soil moisture conservation works.

Conservation in Kaziranga was affirmed as a proposed reserve forest in the year 1905 and was crowned as a Wildlife Sanctuary in the year 1950 and was accredited as a National park in the year 1974. UNESCO designated Kaziranga National Park as a World Heritage Site in December 1985. Kaziranga celebrated its Centenary in 2005 with at least 1,700 rhinos (70 percent of the world's population). The other protected areas in Assam where this species occurs include Orang National Park and Manas National Park. The species also occurs in Dudwha National Park in the state of Uttar Pradesh, and in the Jaldapara Wildlife Sanctuary and Gorumara National Park in the state of West Bengal.

Recently, the Indian and Nepal governments have taken major steps towards Indian rhinoceros conservation, The 'Indian Rhino Vision 2020' (IRV 2020), is a joint conservation initiative of the Department of Environment and Forests, Government of Assam along with the International Rhino Foundation (IRF), World Wide Fund for Nature (WWF-India), Wildlife Trust of India (WTI), Aaranyak and several local community based organizations with major funding support from Bodoland Territorial Council, U.S. Fish & Wildlife Service and WWF-US (WWF International AREAS Programme).

9.4.2 Aims and Objectives of 'Operation Rhino'

The vision of this ambitious project is to increase the Indian rhino population and attain a population of 3,000 wild rhinos by the year 2020 spread among seven protected areas of Assam. This project thus aims to secure the long-term viability of wild rhinoceros in Assam and to encourage their population growth by expanding their distribution and to reduce the risks like inbreeding depression, disease and mass mortality.

9.4.3 Implementation of 'Operation Rhino'

Government of Assam had set up a task force for translocation of rhinos within Assam, commonly known as Rhino Task Force, in June 2005 (vide Notification No. FRW24/2005/15 dated 30.06.2005) involving officials and conservationists from both Government and non-government sectors. The Task Force was entrusted to ensure conservation of rhinos in Assam through protection, habitat management and range expansion which is to be achieved through 'wild-to-wild' translocation from two source populations (present inside Kaziranga National Park and Pobitora Wildlife Sanctuary) to Manas National Park and Dibru-Saikhowa National Park, as well as in other protected areas like Laokhowa, Bura Chapori, Kochpora and possibly Orang. The task force received immediate support from two international organizations World Wide Fund for Nature (WWF) and International Rhino Foundation (IRF) to undertake activities for the conservation of rhinos in Assam and also to create new populations in Assam through translocation. To implement the aims of IRV 2020, the Task Force set up two expert groups:

- **The security assessment group** to assess the current state of security in the potential areas for rhino conservation and suggest ways to strengthen it.
- **The habitat assessment group** to determine the feasibility of the project in these identified areas.

Work for enhancing protection to rhino habitats across Assam started in 2007 as the main activity of IRV 2020, mainly in Manas, Kaziranga and Orang National Parks and Pobitora Wildlife Sanctuary. Besides, a Translocation Core Committee (TCC) was set up in November 2007, whose roles were to plan, execute, and monitor the capturing, transportation and releasing of the rhinos from the source protected area to the target destination.

More than 85 percent of the world's greater one-horned rhino population inhabits Kaziranga National Park in Assam, India. Having most of the animals in one population puts it at risk from catastrophes such as floods or disease outbreaks, which could lead to a serious population decline. Pobitora Wildlife Sanctuary holds about 90 rhinos in less than 18 sq. km. Such density is well above the carrying capacity of this PA, which leads to an increased risk of rhino-human conflict as animals move out of the park and into agricultural areas to forage for food. Similarly, Pobitora has been chosen as a high-priority source for translocation because it boasts of the highest density of rhinos in the world. Translocations will lessen pressure on Pobitora's rhinos for food and space and hopefully reduce the number of rhinos straying into nearby villages.

On the other hand, Manas National Park has been selected as the first site to receive translocated rhinos. Rhinos were once common in the park, but violent civil conflict beginning in 1989 caused massive damage to the park's infrastructure, including destruction of anti-poaching camps, roads and villages. Therefore, after months of meticulous planning, the IRV 2020 Translocation Core Committee decided to begin translocations from Pobitora to Manas.

The implementation stage involved locating, capturing, transporting, and releasing rhinos. The first round of IRV 2020 translocations occurred in April 2008, when two male rhinos were moved from Pobitora to Manas. IRV 2020 general protocols call for four animals to be translocated at once and released within 24 hours of darting.

The post-release stage involves continued protection of the rhinos from poaching and monitoring them to ensure they have adapted well to the new surroundings. The team uses both standard traditional methods and radio telemetry to monitor rhinos on a regular basis. Each rhino was fitted with a radio collar so that the released animals could be adequately monitored. This allowed the teams to determine where they were, how were they moving and with which other rhinos they may be associating. WWF-India will oversee long-term monitoring of the animals and translocations of rhinos in Manas National Park were carried out in two phases:

- **Phase I (2005–2008):** Field assessments were carried out, infrastructure facilities were improved and the levels of security were elevated in Manas. This Phase 1 of IRV 2020 mainly included intensive field work to improve levels of protection for existing populations.
- **Phase II (2008–2012):** Phase II began with the first rhino translocations from Pobitora Wildlife Sanctuary to Manas National Park in April 2008. On February 19th, 2012, the first rhino translocation from Kaziranga National Park was undertaken. So far, 18 rhinos have been translocated to Manas from Pobitora and Kaziranga under IRV 2020 and four from the Centre for Wildlife Rehabilitation and Conservation as part of rehabilitation programme of WTI and the Government of Assam.
- Presently following activities are going on as part of IRV 2020:
  - Post release rhino monitoring in Manas
  - Monitoring of source rhinos (for translocation) in Kaziranga and Pobitora
  - Community based awareness programmes and confidence-building measures in Manas

- Training and orientation for frontline staff of Forest Department on monitoring, patrolling and legal issues
- In Orang National Park, enhancement of protection through supplying necessary fuel, bicycles, lights etc.
- Supply of fuel for vehicles to rhino bearing areas
- Health camps for departmental elephants and livestock, mainly in Manas

The task force has now identified the Laokhowa-Burachapori complex for reintroducing rhinos. The habitat team and the security team has made certain recommendations in this connection, which are being implemented with the help of funds from WWF, IRF, USFWS and the Government. The Government of India has given permission for the relocation of 10 rhinos in the first batch from Kaziranga to Laokhowa-Burachapori.

9.4.4 Achievements of 'Operation Rhino'

The population of the species recovered spectacularly during the last century in both India and Nepal through strict protection and rigorous conservation efforts. The population has turned around from approximately 200 individuals at the beginning of the 20th century to presently over 3,000 in the Terai Arc Landscape of India and Nepal, and the grasslands of Assam and north Bengal in north-east India. Thus, the species was moved from Endangered to Vulnerable status in 2008. The recovery of this species is a conservation success story which demonstrates the effectiveness of increased enforcement measures, ambitious conservation programmes and strong partnerships between local communities and Government authorities.

9.4.5 Limitations of 'Operation Rhino'

Incidents of poaching is still continuing both at Manas and Kaziranga, possibly due to the shortage of security staff, lack of forest camps, dilapidated roads, lack of sufficient number of vehicles and wireless communication infrastructure. Recent incidents have made it clear that the poachers intelligently exploit the annual flood situations. With increasing population of rhinos, more suitable habitats within their distribution range need to be declared as protected areas and the areas of the existing protected areas also need to be increased and realigned in order to reduce the incidence of rhinos straying out in the adjoining human dominated landscapes. But, with the burgeoning human population around the existing rhino habitats of this country, declaring new PAs as well as increasing the boundary of the designated PAs is undoubtedly a very challenging task.

9.4.6 Recommendations

1. Prevent Poaching of Rhinos: Strict anti-poaching measures and internationally coordinated response to block the illegal trade channels through improved field intelligence is essential. It is also of paramount importance to ensure strict enforcement of wildlife laws, as well as, to strengthen anti-poaching equipments and operations in protected areas. Following are some of the recommendations pertinent to curb the menace of poaching and illegal trafficking of rhino horns:

- The vulnerable areas with high incidences of rhino poaching need to be identified and anti-poaching posts be set-up at such strategic points, along with increased frequency of foot-patrolling, ambush patrolling, night patrolling etc. so that no intruder can slip into the area and kill animals.
- Regular "Area Dominance" by armed Assam police might serve as a strong deterrent to the poachers and other anti-socials.
- River police outposts should be set up at convenient places to increase river patrolling from Brahmaputra.
- Ex-army and police personnel may also be engaged to patrol vulnerable points outside protected areas. Besides, local youth may be motivated in volunteering to take active part in this effort.
- It should be made mandatory on the part of police and forest personnel deployed in Kaziranga to remain in full uniform with name badge and photo identity cards to avoid any confusion and possible mistaken identity.
- Logistic support like efficient wireless communication system, with sufficient number of mobile phones, binoculars, night-vision devices, flash lights, search lights, sophisticated weapons like AK-47, AK-56 and number of vehicles should be increased for proper vigilance.
- To receive information in advance on the movement of poachers and wildlife smugglers, a reliable informer network should be developed involving local youth on payment basis to minimize the incidence of crime.

2. Habitat and Corridor Restoration: As rhino population is increasing, they need additional space to live and breed. Therefore, it is important to improve connectivity between existing protected areas by securing habitat corridors. Most frequented animal corridors of Kaziranga across the national highway need to be identified and long flyovers be constructed over these areas so that animals can pass beneath those flyovers to Karbi Hills during natural disasters without any risk of being run over by speeding vehicles or being killed by the poachers. Besides, areas with healthy population of rhinos need to be declared as protected areas. Also, landscapes in former rhinos habitats are to be restored for further wild to wild translocation of rhinos. There is a need to protect rhinos during the annual flooding of Kaziranga National Park and its contiguous areas. Restoration of wildlife corridors north and south of the Brahmaputra river and creating secure migration paths for the animals on the ground may also be beneficial. This will also provide an escape route for rhinos during annual floods.

3. Prevent Habitat Degradation: Many areas in the present rhino distribution range require targeted programmes to control invasive plants, to prevent the spread of woodland and to limit the extent of grazing by domestic livestock.

4. Human-Rhino Conflict Mitigation: It is also important to reduce human-wildlife conflicts around these areas and this might involve fencing. Alternatively farmers may be encouraged to plant unpalatable species like mint, chilly etc. In Pabitora, specific recommendations have been made to increase the quality of feeding habitat of rhino within the sanctuary through meticulous manipulation and checking livestock grazing. Measures should be taken to maintain water holding mechanisms within the sanctuary during winter, so that less number of rhinos stray out of the sanctuary.

5. Community Participation: The protected areas covering the rhino habitat of India and Nepal are surrounded by dense human population. So, it is vital to ensure that communities that live around rhino reserves are sympathetic to and benefit from the rhinos around them. Several projects to improve local livelihoods might, in turn, involve them into the conservation effort and support community-based anti-poaching operations.

6. Socio-Political Factors: The future of the rhino will depend not only on ecological and natural factors, but also on socio-political factors. The need is urgent to initiate social welfare projects in favour of the locals. The Forest Department and the NGOs need to work together to achieve this uphill task.

9.5 LION CONSERVATION PROJECT

9.5.1 Origin of 'Lion Conservation Project'

Asiatic lion (*Panthera leo persica*) was once distributed in a wide range across north India, from Punjab in the north, to Jharkhand in the east, to Narmada river in the south, and as far west as northern Morocco and Greece. Large scale hunting is one of the major factors that decimated these majestic animals from most of its former domain. Prior to and after independence, conditions in Gir deteriorated rapidly due to widespread destruction of private forests, construction of hydro-electric projects involving mass clearance of forests, unabated shooting, reduction of natural habitat due to rapid increase of agriculture, water pollution, etc. Besides, drastic reduction of their natural prey base of wild ungulates, resulting increased cattle killing by the lions leading to greater amount of human-lion conflict. Alarmed by this bleak scenario, the 'Lion Conservation Project' was initiated in 1972 and a five year plan was proposed by the Government of Gujarat to protect the Asiatic lions inside the Gir forests, which serve as their last refuge in this country.

9.5.2 Aims and Objectives of 'Lion Conservation Project'

The main objectives of Lion Conservation Project were:

- to restore habitat and increase the number of prey species of Asiatic lions
- to increase the number of Asiatic lions in their natural habitat

Moreover, the hydrological value of lion habitats, essential for farming in the peripheral areas, are also taken into account in the recent conservation efforts to gain people's support. This approach has not only enhanced the prospects of lion conservation, but has also led to marked recovery of dry deciduous forests and scrub-savanna ecosystems of the entire area.

9.5.3 Implementation of 'Lion Conservation Project'

About 1450 sq km forests of Kathiawar district in Gujarat that served as the last refuge of Asiatic lions were immediately designated as 'Gir Sanctuary'. In the early 1970s prey population of Asiatic lions (like nilgai, spotted deer, sambar etc.) declined sharply, even inside the Gir forests. Besides, large numbers of cattle were illegally brought inside the park by the local *Maldhari* community as good quality grazing fields outside became scarce. With reduced natural prey, this increase in the number of cattle served as a bonanza for the lion prides. As a consequence, the incidences and frequency of cattle killing by lions increased, subsequently elevating the human-lion conflict. Therefore, almost 600 resident *Maldhari* families and their livestock and hundreds of thousands of cattle that seasonally grazed in Gir were relocated in 1973. Other conservation measures undertaken include addressing human-lion conflict through timely compensation and eco-development support to local communities.

9.5.4 Achievements of 'Lion Conservation Project'

With such successful and strict implementation of Lion Conservation Project, grazing pressure of the domestic animals gradually reduced which allowed the vegetation to recover and as a consequence, wild herbivores bounced back ten-fold. As the number of cattle reduced and more wild prey became available, the feeding habits of Asiatic lions in Gir have changed back to their 'normal pattern' with wild ungulates. With all these conservation initiatives, the lion population has increased more than two-fold from 177 in 1968 to 523 individuals in 2015 within the protected area of Gir. The Gir Sanctuary spreads over 1153.42 sq km area in Junagadh and Amreli districts of Saurashtra. At present a core area of 258.71 sq km is declared as 'National Park'. This is one of the best protected areas of the country with proper vigilance and the ecological balance is properly maintained.

9.5.5 Limitations of 'Lion Conservation Project'

- The number of Asiatic lions has almost crossed the carrying capacity of Gir and, except for Girnar, other adjoining forest areas are too small to accommodate them. Besides, the wilderness areas of Asiatic lions are presently surrounded by non-forested habitats, agricultural fields and human habitations. So the lions are compelled to invade the surrounding areas leading to unwanted incidences of human-lion conflict. Atleast 100 animals are outside the Gir Forest protected area (Breitenmoser, 2008). A recent census revealed that about 40 lions have left the overcrowded Gir Sanctuary and are striving outside the park in human habitations. As more rural people aspire for urban lifestyles, they may become less tolerant of lions in their surroundings.
- Moreover, protecting lions outside protected areas from the poachers is also very much difficult. Therefore, the main challenge of conservation of Asiatic lions lies outside the protected Gir forests.
- In spite of best effort, more than 2,000 *Maldharis* are still living within the sanctuary and are reluctant to relocate.
- People are often not impressed with the compensation scheme of the Forest Department, as the amount is too low and covers only a part of their cost. In addition to that, the procedure is also very lengthy and at times is not very transparent.
- As most of the present day Asiatic lions have originated from very few individuals, hence, their variability is very little due to small gene pool and most of the adult males (70-80%) are with deformed sperm. Such a precarious proportion of deformed sperm can even lead to infertility in a pride.
- As most of the Asiatic lions are presently striving only in Gir forests. Hence, outbreaks of disease or natural disasters might lead to the total destruction of this lion subspecies.

9.5.6 Recommendations

- The afforestation programmes in grasslands and savannah areas of the Gir forest should be avoided as far as possible.
- The habitat of the lions should be improved. One of the ways of ensuring this is by thinning of the teak stands, which will lead to the opening up of the forest canopy.
- The relationship between the Asiatic lions and people has been largely amicable. After living close to humans for at least 200–300 years, Asiatic lions in Gir are remarkably at home with people. They generally seem to avoid attacking people and stay out of trouble. Villagers are also remarkably tolerant of these large predators. It is essential to conserve and promote such conservation ethics of coexistence.

Text Box 9.1 Asiatic Lion Reintroduction Project

Population of Asiatic lion in a single area (Gir Forest) are always under potential risk of epidemics, natural disasters and other anthropogenic factors. Therefore, under the 'Asiatic Lion Reintroduction Project', Kuno Wildlife Sanctuary at Madhya Pradesh is being developed to create a near natural habitat to relocate the excess population of the Gir's lions. The aim is to establish a second independent population of Asiatic lions. However, the sanctuary is still not fully complete and many steps are required to be undertaken to create that perfect habitat for the royal animal.

9.6 CROCODILE CONSERVATION PROJECT

9.6.1 Origin of the Project

According to IUCN, 96–98 percent of the gharial population has declined since 1946 and in 2007 their population was estimated to be around 200–300 breeding adults. Due to such drastic population decline in the past 70 years, gharial is listed as 'Critically Endangered' in the IUCN Red List of Threatened species and enlisted under Schedule–I of the Wildlife (Protection) Act, 1972 to accord highest level of protection nationwide. To bring back this population from the verge of extinction, 'Project Crocodile' was initiated by the Government of India with financial support from the United Nations Development Fund and Food and Agriculture Organization in the year 1975. This project included an intensive 'captive breeding and rearing programme' with an aim to restock depleted gharial habitats.

9.6.2 Aims and Objectives

- To protect the remaining population of crocodilians in their natural habitat by creating sanctuaries
- To promote captive breeding
- To rebuild natural population quickly through 'grow and release' or 'rear and release' technique
- To take-up researches to improve management
- To build up a level of trained personnel for better continuity of the project through training imparted at project-sites and through the Central Crocodile Breeding and Management Training Institute, Hyderabad
- To intimately involve the local people in crocodile and gharial conservation

9.6.3 Implementation

Crocodile conservation programs have been undertaken in India and Nepal, based on the establishment of protected areas and restocking them with captive breed individuals. Eggs were purchased from Nepal and one male gharial was flown in from the Frankfurt Zoo (Germany) as one of the founding animals of the breeding programme. During the first phase of the project (1975–1982), sixteen crocodile rehabilitation centers and five crocodile sanctuaries (including the National Chambal Sanctuary and Katerniaghat Wildlife Sanctuary) were established in India.

However, initially the progress was not satisfactory due to mismanagement, growing and uncontrolled anthropogenic pressures (including depletion of fish resources), as well as, lack of knowledge on adaptation, migration and other key biological aspects of this species. Virtually nothing was known from the rest of the gharial's range in India, except from National Chambal Sanctuary, and to a certain extent in Katerniaghat Wildlife Sanctuary and Corbett Tiger Reserve, where regular population monitoring has been carried out. In 1991, funds were withdrawn for the captive-breeding and egg-collection programs. Later, Gharial Species Recovery Plan (GSRP) suggested for an overall population assessment of the existing populations, which could be used as a baseline for measuring the effectiveness of past recovery efforts and also to address the shortcomings. In early 1995, a 'Population and Habitat Viability Analysis (PHVA)' was conducted to plan future strategies (Rao et al., 1995) and based on its recommendation, egg collection and captive rearing started again. Juvenile gharials were reared to about a meter or more in length and then released into the wild.

9.6.4 Reintroduction and Restocking

Gharials are initially bred in captivity in the National Chambal Sanctuary in Uttar Pradesh, and in the Gharial Breeding Centre in Nepal's Chitwan National Park, where they are generally grown for two to three years and average about one metre in length, when released. Over 3,000 juveniles have been released at 12 sites. The major release sites are the Chambal river (1,718 released 1979–1993), Ramganga river (257 released 1982–1994), Girwa river (172 released 1979–1994) and the Sharada river (105 released 1986–1992), all in the Ganges drainage, and in the Mahanadi river in Orissa (609 released 1977–1989).

In December 2010, the Ministry of Environment and Forests, Government of India launched a National Tri-State Chambal Sanctuary Management and Coordination Committee for gharial conservation on 1,600 sq km of the National Chambal Sanctuary along the Chambal River in Madhya Pradesh, Rajasthan and Uttar Pradesh. The committee comprised of representatives from various concerned government departments of the three states and various leading NGOs (like Madras Crocodile Bank Trust, The Gharial Conservation Alliance, Development Alternatives, ATREE, WWF, India) and was entrusted to plan strategies for protection of gharials and their habitat, involving further research on gharial ecology and socio-economic evaluation of dependent riparian communities. Funding for this new initiative was ensured as a sub-scheme of the 'Integrated Development of Wildlife Habitats' with an annual amount of 50–80 million Indian rupees for five years.

9.6.5 Achievements

Current wild population is estimated to be in excess of 1,500 individuals, of which more than 1,000 are found in the Chambal River with around 64 nests per year at 15 different sites (Rao and Singh, 1994). More than seven thousand crocodilians have been restocked including about 4000 gharial (*Gavialis gangeticus*), 1800 mugger (*Crocodylus palustris*) and 1500 salt-water crocodiles (*Crocodylus porosus*). There are nine protected areas covering nearly 3000 sq km area in this country, at present, which are designated for gharial management.

Nepal also adopted similar programme in 1978 and 432 individuals were released to the wild between 1978–1994. Pakistan is also trying to improve the status of this unique animal. Although the Gangetic gharial is virtually extirpated in Pakistan, there are plans to start a restocking effort with assistance from Indian institutions.

9.6.6 Limitations

High cost of captive breeding and the paucity of additional 'release sites' are two major limitations of gharial conservation in this country. The negative effects of agriculture and fishing also restrict successful gharial populations to a few stretches along isolated and protected rivers. Though not completely extirpated, gharial remain in very few number at sites of smaller releases such as the Satkoshia Gorge (Mahanadi river), Ken and Son rivers and several other areas and no significant population increase has been noticed. Another important factor is that some individuals migrate out of protected areas, indulge in conflict with the riverside human populations and sometimes even get killed. In recent past, such human-crocodile conflicts have drastically affected the population of crocodiles in the country.

9.6.7 Recommendations

Rivers under gharial conservation network, as well as, those considered to be potential habitat for crocodiles need to be revived and rejuvenated. River-linking, and large irrigation projects need to be critically assessed as improper implementation might threaten the very existence of these species and might put all these years' effort in jeopardy. In addition to these, following initiatives are to be taken on a priority basis for successful gharial conservation along with other crocodilian species in this country:

- population modeling and scientific studies on migration of these reptilians
- analysis of genetic diversity and the effects of a bottleneck in the founder stock
- preparation of a 'National Management Plan' in India and implementation of the recommendations of the Gharial PHVA
- continued and improved restocking activities
- coordinated surveys and continuous monitoring of protected and restocked populations, as well as, periodic reanalysis of the status of the species
- increased public education and awareness to make local communities co-beneficiaries of all conservation initiatives

Independent conservation programmes are in effect in each country. But, international coordination for gharial management and conservation between the neighbouring countries is of paramount importance.

1. Coordinated Gharial Conservation Initiative between India and Nepal: Many rivers with gharial populations run across India and Nepal. In such situations, coordinated management efforts of these shared populations would enhance conservation effectiveness. Therefore, joint surveys, trainings, comparison of population trends and coordinated regulations and protection should be developed. Other neighbouring countries reported to have former gharial distribution should also join hand in such conservation initiatives. More captive rearing centres similar to those in India and Nepal are needed to supply animals for restocking in protected areas.

2. Status survey: Although the gharial is considered to be extinct in Myanmar, small populations may still exist in isolated areas. Surveys need to be conducted to assess the current status of gharial in the Irrawaddy and Kaladan river systems in Myanmar.

3. Expansion of restocking programme: The vast majority of the releases of gharial in Nepal have been into the Narayani river system. Additional sites in eastern and western Nepal need to be identified and included in the restocking programme.

The Indian Crocodile Conservation Project is considered among the successful conservation initiatives in the world. Restocking is maintaining this species in some protected localities such as the Chambal river and sustaining but smaller populations in the Mahanadi and other localities require continued replenishment. It has pulled back this once threatened crocodilians from the brink of extinction and placed them on path of recovery. The project has not just produced a large number of crocodiles, but has contributed towards conservation of a number of related species as well.

REVIEW QUESTIONS

1. State the objectives of "Tiger Project". Highlight significant achievements of the project. What is 3rd Tiger Crisis? Mention the limitations of the project. Elaborate recommendations of tiger tusk force regarding Tiger conservation.
2. Give a comprehensive account on the origin, implementation and achievements of Elephant Project. Mention the limitation of Project Elephant.
3. Give an update on "Operation Rhino" with a note on its limitations.
4. Write short notes on:
   (a) Crocodile project
   (b) Gir Lion project

REFERENCES

Breitenmoser U., Mallon D.P., Ahmad Khan J. and Driscoll C. (2008). *Panthera leo* ssp. *persica*. The IUCN Red List of Threatened Species 2008: e.T15952A5327221. Retrieved from: http://dx.doi.org/10.2305/IUCN.UK.2008.RLTS.T15952A5327221.en.

George, N., India counts more wild tigers, credits conservation [Online], Associated Press, 2015. Retrieved from: http://bigstory.ap.org/articlefe18af60d7fd428ab35f993d5a57107f/india-counts-more-wild-tigers-2014-credits-conservation.

Jhala, Y.V., Qureshi, Q., and Gopal, R. (Eds.), The status of tigers in India 2014, National Tiger Conservation Authority, New Delhi & The Wildlife Institute of India, Dehradun, India, 2015, Retrieved from: http://projecttiger.nic.in/WriteReadData/LetestNews/Document/Tiger%20Status%20booklet_XPS170115212.pdf.

Jhala, Y.V., Qureshi, Q. and Sinha, P.R. (Eds.), Status of tigers, co-predators and prey in India, 2010 (TR 2011/003), National Tiger Conservation Authority, Govt. of India, New Delhi, and Wildlife Institute of India, Dehradun, India, 302 pp, 2011, Retrieved from: http://projecttiger.nic.in/WriteReadData/PublicationFile/Tiger_Status_oct_2010.pdf

Project Tiger, List of Core and Buffer Areas of Tiger Reserves of India, 2016. Retrieved from: http://projecttiger.nic.in/content/109_1_ListofTigerReservesCoreBufferAreas.aspx

Rao, R.J., Basu D., Hasan S.M., Sharma B.B., Molur S. and Walker S. (Eds). Report of the Population and habitat viability assessment (PHVA) workshop for Indian Gharial (16–18 January 1995). 99 pp, 1995, Retrieved from: http://zooreach.org/downloads/ZOO_CAMP_PHVA_reports/1993_Indian_Gharial_report.pdf

Rao, R.J. and Singh, L.A.K., Status and conservation of gharial in India. In: Crocodiles: Proceedings of the 12th Working Meeting of the Crocodile Specialist Group, IUCN, Gland, pp. 84-97, 1994.

10

MAN AND WILDLIFE

10.1 HUMAN-WILDLIFE CONFLICT

Human-wildlife conflicts occur in various parts of the globe and exist in many different dimensions. Protected areas are presently islands of forested habitats surrounded by agricultural lands or other human-influenced ecosystems and incidences of human-animal conflicts are often high in areas adjoining the porous margins of the protected areas. Many people living in the forest fringe areas often incur the cost of living with wildlife without receiving much direct tangible benefits out of such co-existence. Rapid rise in human population and subsequent fast expansion of rural, urban and agricultural landscapes are encroaching many wilderness areas of this country, which leads to the degradation and loss of habitat. Unplanned and non-ecofriendly developmental projects (like construction of roads, railway tracts and dams) are also reducing the migration paths, foraging areas and breeding grounds of many wild animals. With gradually shrinking forested lands, wild animals are forced to live in proximity to human habitations thereby leading to and also elevating the incidences of conflict (Manoj et al., 2013).

Definition: Human-wildlife conflict (HWC) may be defined as any interactions between human and wildlife that results in negative impact on the social, economic and cultural life of human beings, as well as on the conservation of wildlife populations or on the environment.

10.2 CAUSES AND CONSEQUENCES OF HUMAN-WILDLIFE CONFLICTS

A series of direct and indirect negative interactions between human and wildlife leads to conflict. Human-wildlife conflicts are influenced by many factors and are therefore, often difficult to understand and manage. Throughout the globe, incidences of human-wildlife conflicts are mainly caused for one or more of the following factors (Distefano, 2013):

- ❒ human population explosion
- ❒ loss of natural forests due to encroachment of agricultural land and/or settlements within the forests
- ❒ changes in land-use pattern (habitat loss, degradation and fragmentation) and subsequent loss of habitat for the species in conflict
- ❒ seasonal decline in availability of food (or prey) within the protected areas
- ❒ lure of better foraging opportunities in the forest fringe areas
- ❒ higher abundance of a particular species in a given habitat (local overabundance)
- ❒ uncontrolled tourism leading to influx of more tourists inside nature reserves with greater access to its different corners
- ❒ competitive exclusion of wild herbivores by large livestock population

- climate change and other stochastic events (like flood, fire etc.)

Human-wildlife conflict leads to further detrimental effects to both human and wildlife in many ways. Human populations suffer economic loss due to destruction of agricultural crops by herbivores, predation of livestock by carnivores, damage to house and other immovable properties, as well as, loss of lives in extreme forms of conflict. Such conflicts also lead to alarming changes about the perception of wildlife among the affected people. Such changes are loss of appreciation and negative attitude towards wildlife and in extreme cases might even lead to retaliatory killing of the wild beasts. Such negative changes in peoples' perception about wildlife harmfully affect the natural fabric of co-existence. In addition, wildlife also suffer from injuries and deaths due to accidents in roads and railway tracts cutting through the forests. In many countries, the scenario becomes even worse when body parts of the animal killed in retaliation enter illegal trade.

10.3 MITIGATION OF CONFLICT—AN OVERVIEW

Several studies were carried out in India in various multi-use landscapes with high frequency of human-wildlife conflicts, which indicated that every incidence of conflict is unique. Mitigation measures therefore, mostly depend upon the region of the conflict, religious belief, cultural demography, species involved and social make up. Hence, local conflicts need to be understood and addressed in response to local agendas.

As compared to anywhere else in the world, people in most parts of India are remarkably tolerant of wildlife damage. Many conflicts may be avoided (or mitigated) through prompt, innovative and appropriate participatory approaches. Putting up barriers between man and animal, shifting the problem animals or illegal encroachers out of the conflict zone etc. are some of the interim solutions adopted to mitigate human-animal conflict. In our country adopting some simple measures may reduce the conflict scenario considerably. For instance, keeping livestock, dogs and other domesticated pets inside predator-proof enclosures in night may effectively reduce livestock killing by predatory carnivores. Similarly, crop depredation by herbivores can also be reduced by setting up barriers in the form of trenches or fences. Intensive methods to protect the crops need to be adopted particularly during the peak cropping season when the chance of raiding is also high. Time and type of crop also need to be selected carefully as each ungulate and herbivores have their own favourite crop. Elephants, blackbucks and many others do not damage crops like chilly, *jeera*, *karela* and *aloe vera* etc. So, buffer area of such inedible or less preferred crop may help reduce crop damage to a certain extent. In most exposed sites it is often better to go for scientific and sustainable alternatives to the current cropping pattern and grow unpalatable cash crops, which are not damaged by wild herbivores. 'Crop insurance' against damage by wild animals, particularly in agricultural lands around the major protected areas, need to be initiated. All these measures require extra costs. Hence, funds need to be raised to assist local people to adopt necessary preventive measures in conflict prone zones. Because it is better to spend money to prevent conflict, than to compensate after the conflict when damage has occurred.

In spite of these simple measures adopted at local scale, the final solution lies in proper landscape-level planning and local/site-level implementation. For example, protection of natural forests, reduction in the rate of deforestation, reversing the trend of ongoing fragmentation of many wilderness areas, restoration of many migratory corridors, proper buffer zones around wildlife habitats may reduce human wildlife interface and subsequent conflicts to a large extent. Finally, dialogue and collaboration between diverse stakeholders involved and affected by conflict with wildlife and designing appropriate management strategies involving all of them is an obvious necessity. Still some degrees of low level conflicts will always persist. In such situations rapid mitigating strategies and a quick compensation system needs to be in place. Compensations should commensurate with the damage and must be paid promptly with complete transparency in the entire process.

10.4 HUMAN-WILDLIFE CONFLICTS IN INDIA—AN OVERVIEW

Presently, human-wildlife conflict is of paramount threat to wildlife and is going to be one of the most important issues of wildlife conservation in India. Severe conflict between crop grazing ungulates like Indian bison, nilgai, blackbucks, wild boars that live in proximity to human habitats are frequently reported from many parts of India. For instance, conflict with the Indian bison (or *gaur*) is a major concern in northern West Bengal. Their numbers in the forests of this region has almost doubled. Such rapid increase is largely due to the decline in large carnivore population (mainly tigers) in this region, which served as their main predators. As a consequence of sharp rise in population, gaurs often stray outside forests in the adjoining human habitations and crop fields in search of fodder leading to severe conflict and often cause serious damage for both. Likewise, robust populations of blackbuck of the Great Indian Bustard Wildlife Sanctuary often venture outside the sanctuary and damage crops in the adjoining agricultural lands. Ungulates usually do not venture outside Tadoba Tiger Reserve (Maharashtra) during monsoon when food is plenty inside the forests, but in the drier season they raid into the adjoining agricultural lands which serve as better sources of food and water during this period. Another conflict scenario in different parts of this country involves several species of macaques. Seven species of macaques are found in India. Most of them are threatened by anthropogenic pressures like hunting, trapping and habitat loss. On the other hand, disturbances caused by certain species of macaques include crop-raiding, kitchen-raiding, damage to household articles while entering houses, occasional bites and injuries. Rhesus macaque (*Macaca mulata*) is the most feared among all species. Uttarakhand and Himachal Pradesh are two badly affected hill states of northern India due to rhesus macaque-human conflict. In Himachal Pradesh these primates were reported to be responsible for 53% of all crop damage between 2007-2009 accounting for a gross financial loss of about 100 crore rupees in agriculture and 75 crore rupees in horticulture (Radhakrishnan and Sinha, 2010). In such scenario, insurance schemes or compensation for macaque-caused damage and injuries essentially need to be implemented. In many towns and cities of northern India rhesus macaques are reported to grievously injure many people and hence, have been labeled as 'simian terrorists'. Mitigation and preventive management measures proposed to control this major conflict include surgical sterilization or immune-contraception of macaques and proper garbage management. Driving away macaques from human populated sites is also very essential, for which some area in adjoining wilderness areas need to be demarcated and declared as 'monkey sanctuaries'. Problem troops (or individuals) need to be identified, captured and relocated within these sanctuaries.

Similar measures have been taken to confine the macaques in a particular portion of urban Delhi. They are often chased away from residential areas (sometimes using trained langurs) and monkey-proof fences are installed in Asola Bhati Wildlife Sanctuary where these problem monkeys are relocated.

Human-carnivore conflicts always evoke strong emotions, particularly in conflicts that end with fatal consequences. Any carnivore is usually wary of human beings and never attempts a human kill unless a meticulous risk assessment assures it of certain levels of safety threshold. In most instances where a human is killed usually have some of the following factors in common:

- the victim was alone and ventured inside or very close to a forest.
- the victim was unaware of the presence of the predator, thereby giving it enough undisturbed time to observe and stalk
- the victim was either sitting or was in a posture that in the darkness of the forest resembled the posture of wild natural prey

Most of the big cats in this country, as well as throughout their distribution ranges, are suffering from significant habitat loss and decline in their prey species within the remaining habitat. Hence, these carnivores are often forced to move into the marginal areas searching for food. In these areas they often predate upon domestic livestock or attack human and involve in a conflict scenario with humans. So, lack of understanding of their biology, absence of sufficient prey base in their habitat and increased familiarity with human beings due to close proximity and frequent encounters have been summarized as the main reasons for the conflict with large carnivores.

Conflict with elephants, common leopards and Indian tigers are often involved in major conflict scenarios in different parts of this country. Therefore, Human-Elephant, Human-Leopard and Human-Tiger conflicts are separately discussed hereunder.

10.5 HUMAN-ELEPHANT CONFLICT

10.5.1 Human-Elephant Conflict Scenario in India

Mega-herbivores require large areas to fulfill their resource requirements. Radio telemetry studies revealed that an elephant requires a home range measuring between 100 and 1000 sq km. Being migratory in nature, elephants also tend to migrate in herds from one habitat patch to another and the traditional narrow strips of habitat that are used by them to move between two such patches are called 'elephant corridors'. Ever expanding agricultural lands and settlements have compelled these mega herbivores to survive in highly fragmented, degraded and compressed habitats. Elephants are distributed in only over 3 percent of India's land surface, but conflicts with the elephants are reported from all elephant range states. Encroachment of elephant habitats or disruption of elephant corridors are the main reasons behind human-elephant conflicts. However, the incidences and intensity of such conflicts are particularly high in human habitations adjoining elephant habitats.

The human-elephant conflict is often characterized by:

(i) Depredation of crops (crop raiding)
(ii) Destruction of house and properties by elephants
(iii) Injury to human beings and, at times, mortality
(iv) Injury to the elephants and retaliatory killing

There have been incidences of crop damage ever since human beings have converted the natural forests of elephants into agricultural lands. Over the years, expansion of agricultural areas in the elephant ranges resulted in increased competition for habitat, food and access to water. As a result, elephants become more aggressive, elevating the conflict and increased number of human or elephant casualties. Around 400 people and nearly 100 elephants are killed in retaliation every year on average in this country (Sukumar and Murali, 2010). In 2001, 11 elephants were poisoned in the reserve forests around Nameri WLS (Assam) due to illegal encroachment of forests. Extensive crop damage occur while herds are compelled to migrate from one forest patch to another through surrounding agricultural fields enroute in a highly fragmented habitat. In India, herds of elephants damage crops of over 10,000 sq km agricultural lands annually affecting the livelihoods of at least 5,00,000 farmers by such persistent attacks (Sukumar and Murali, 2010). Foraging theory states that any animal tends to optimize its nutrient uptake in least possible time and effort. Hence, crop raiding by the elephants' herds is quite obvious as these cultivated crops serve as concentrated source of highly palatable and nutrient rich sources of food at one place in contrast to the coarse wild grasses of the forests. In brief, human-elephant conflicts are mainly consequences of our own actions. Elephants are just trying to survive by compensating their resource requirements from human habitats, which they earlier used to meet up from their natural habitats.

Despite of heavy loss of life and property, the farmers are still more tolerant and are generally reluctant to harm them as they relate elephants with lord *Ganesha*. But frequent conflicts may quickly erode this culture of tolerance. Alarmingly, Elephant Task Force (ETF) report revealed that the number of sites and intensity of human-elephant conflict have increased over last two decades. Rise in *ex-gratia* payments made towards crop destruction and human casualty is an index of such rising trend of conflict.

10.5.2 Human-Elephant Conflict Mitigation Strategies

Human-elephant conflict can be minimized by adopting following measures:

1. Introduction of Barriers

Introduction of trenches, fences and other barriers are one of the simplest and age-old strategies devised to prevent elephants from crop raiding in many parts of the globe. Trenching is one of the main traditional deterrent strategies followed in India to prevent elephants entering agricultural fields. Electric fencing is another successful deterrent strategy which was highly successful in stopping elephants to enter the crop fields and human habitations. The nonlethal pulses of high voltage power carried along steel wires give an unpleasant shock to a raiding elephant, thereby deterring it away from the agricultural field. In some other instances barriers were constructed by thorny plants and bee hives along the perimeter of farms to create a 'biofence'. Delivering chilli's pungency through a variety of means like smoke, spray, paste smeared on a rope surrounding the crops are other such strategies adopted to keep away elephants from crop lands. The type of barrier to be implemented depends upon:

- Location of the agricultural field
- Types of crops in the agricultural field
- Time and intensity of crop raiding by the elephants
- Number of elephants in the crop raiding herd
- Motivation among the farming community to maintain the barrier

However, it is important to ensure that the barriers enclose human settlements and not the elephant habitat and such barriers should by no means impede the migration of the elephants. Otherwise, the conflict might increase leading to higher loss of life and property.

2. Crop Guarding

The simplest, widespread and perhaps the oldest practice is to guard crops by 'watcher squads' with drums and crackers in the night from tree top *machans* or ground level *tunsis* (shacks surrounded by a trench used in northern West Bengal and Assam). Vigilant farmers in these *machans* or *tunsis* make cacophonic sounds by beating drums, plates or other noisy elements and light up fire crackers to scare the animals away from the agricultural fields. Forest Departments in northern West Bengal and Assam has formed 'elephant chasing squads' in every division to assist the farmers in driving away the herds of crop raiding elephants.

3. Farming Non-palatable Crops

Another strategy is to farm non-palatable crops along the elephant ranges. Such changes in cropping patterns with alternate inedible cash crops, particularly in the agricultural fields enclosing the forests, are one of the extremely effective long-term mitigation measures. Farming chilly was found successful in reducing conflict in certain areas within the elephant ranges.

4. Securing Elephant Corridors

Securing corridors of elephant movements are the fourth major strategy. Most of the elephant corridors in this country have settlements and are affected by resulting anthropogenic pressures (Menon et al., 2005). So, these mega-herbivores often need to pass through agricultural land, tea gardens and human settlements to reach from one forested patch to another, further resulting in high conflict in areas situated enroute. Besides, roads and railway tracts passing through these corridors are another major threat for the survival of elephants. It is undoubtedly crucial to maintain and safeguard the elephant corridors to ensure free passage of elephants between connected habitats to reduce conflict and ensure long-term viability of the population.

5. Extermination of Problem Elephants

Culling of rogues or capture of problem herds are also practiced in some countries. However, culling should only be adopted if the rogue animals are precisely identified. Another way is to capture the problem elephants from the wild and domesticate them for various forestry activities. In Indian context, capture of elephants is often not encouraged as:

- capturing an elephant often increases aggression in the herd and results in greater conflict
- appropriate site selection for release of a captured elephant is of major concern
- translocation of captured elephants is problematic as the wild elephants often do not accept an elephant raised in captivity
- cost of maintaining an elephant in captivity is very high and apart from a few forestry operations, the utility of captive elephants are gradually decreasing in the modern context

10.5.3 Challenges in Human-elephant Conflict Mitigation in India

All strategies to deter elephants away from the agricultural fields usually show initial promise as the elephants are wary of and usually stay away from anything new and unusual. But in due time they develop counter strategies to surpass these obstacles set up by human wisdom. Therefore, in several instances setting up such barriers between man and the raiding elephant herds often act as temporary alleviation strategy.

Success of trenching depends on proper maintenance of trenches. If not maintained properly the elephants may easily pass through such barriers. Desperate elephants have even devised various means to get through electric fences. As the wood is non-conductor of electricity, they topple down large tree trunks over the live wires and easily move over the tree trunk without getting electric shock. Many individuals have also discovered that their tusks are non-conductors of electricity. It is recorded that the bulls of a herd pull up or rip the live wires using their tusk and then entire herd move through the gap. They even use the soles of their feet to step on the wires and some even run into them to bring the posts and wires down.

Guarding crops from elephant is undoubtedly a dangerous occupation. In spite of large body, elephants are almost invisible at night due to their dark coloration. In the past men in a large extended family took turns to guard their crop in night. But, now in smaller families there are not much members to share such crop guarding duties. Therefore, a farmer is often compelled to spend several sleepless nights during the cropping season as hiring guards is often not affordable for many poor and marginal farmers. The price of inadvertently falling asleep after a long day's labour is catastrophic leading to the loss of the entire family's sustenance for the next few months. In this context, forming a team with farmers of adjoining farms and sharing crop guarding duties or creation of voluntary youth groups to watch for elephants from *machans* seems to be a an alternative. Setting up of trip wire alarms may also be useful to alert sleeping farmers about the presence of elephants in field.

Farmers in elephant ranges often complain that the methods traditionally successful in deterring elephants to enter the croplands have often failed recently in most of the places as the elephants have become habituated to the strategies such as drum beating, fire, shooting in air (Sukumar and Gadgil, 1988). Hence, farmers in northern West Bengal and Assam have adopted more invasive strategies. They chase elephants using *mashal* (a spear tip surrounded by a flaming ball of rags), *birio* (indigenous sling shots), poison arrows, flaming arrow heads, burning jute and cycle tyres. Some of these cause serious injuries to the raiding elephants and make them more aggressive. If repeatedly chased away, the elephants become more irritable and these frustrated elephants charge humans, which often result in fatal consequences. In areas where farming has become unsustainable due to high conflict and damage caused by elephants, the farmers migrate to cities for work leaving their family to guard the crops. In worse cases of conflict, people kill elephants with home-made guns, electric wires hooked up to high tension cables and poison or explosive-filled pumpkin baits.

Apart from these temporary mitigation strategies, protecting existing elephant habitats and corridors and enriching the habitat by planting fodder, trees, and bamboo plants in elephant country seems to be the only long-term, feasible, landscape-level solution to reduce human-elephant conflicts in many parts of this country. Elephant Task Force (ETF) in this regard, has suggested for establishment and management of 10 elephant landscapes and recommended to address and mitigate human-elephant conflict issues with utmost concern.

10.6 HUMAN-TIGER CONFLICT

10.6.1 Human-Tiger Conflict Scenario in India

Human beings are not a natural prey of tigers as these carnivores have evolved to predate upon large ungulates and the bipedality of human beings in complete contrast with the posture of their quadruped prey. But, tiger habitat has shrunk to less than 5 percent of its historical distribution and three tiger subspecies have gone extinct (Gurung et al., 2006). Presently tiger habitat extends through one of the most densely inhabited regions of the world. Human populations across majority of tiger distribution range are increasing further and much faster than the average global rate. In India, small populations of tigers mostly dwell inside isolated protected areas. Larger landscapes of tiger habitat comprise of protected reserves, multiple-use forests, agricultural lands, as well as, rural and urban areas. So in dearth of food and other vital resources inside those forests, tigers often venture out in the adjoining human landscapes often resulting in cattle lifting, cattle killing, as well as, death and injuries to human. Human killing and livestock depredation are the main issues of human-tiger conflict in this country, which might negatively affect the entire process of tiger conservation.

Some of the following factors are usually associated with tigers straying out of the forests into human habitations:

- The tiger is being displaced from its territory after losing a territorial fight.
- Inadequacy of number of natural prey in the tiger habitat.
- Injured and aged tigers find it difficult and are often unable to predate upon wild prey.
- In search of safe refuge with easy prey during breeding or littering time.
- In a landscape where human habitations and villages are closely intermingled within forests.
- Accidental killing or mauling of human by a tiger is often an outcome of an instinctive aggressive behaviour of a tiger for self-defense.

High conflict areas are largely restricted to the edges of protected reserves along with some multiple-use and plantation forests (Chauhan, 2011). Large numbers of the tiger attacks on human or cattle lifting have been noted to occur around protected area boundaries of tiger habitats. Agricultural lands in forest fringe areas often provide favourable resting, hiding and ambush cover for tigers. Immature tigers often reside in these sub-optimal habitats when prime habitats are occupied by the mature resident individuals. Majority of human casualties occur between 16:00–20:00 hours, male casualties were more than female casualties and most of the victims were between 25–30 years (Chauhan, 2011). Such high incidences of tiger attack on young males may possibly because they frequently enter forests in search of non-timber forest produce and extensively move inside the forests.

10.6.2 Possible Causes of Human-Tiger Conflict

1. Killing of Livestock

Tigers often kill domestic ungulates inside government owned forests or in the forest fringe areas, where the density of wild prey is low and large number of cattle and other livestock graze. These livestock and cattle are relatively easier to hunt as compared to their natural prey inside forests.

2. Accidental Injury or Killing of Humans

Tigers may maul or kill human but very rarely and only during unexpected encounters. Such incidences usually occur if people come too close to a tigress with cubs inside forests. Tigers often kill people sitting or bending over as a human might resemble natural prey to a tiger in dense environment in such posture (Gurung et al., 2006). Outside forests injury or killing of people by tiger mostly occurs when a tiger entering human settlements in search of livestock are surrounded by agitated mob.

3. Man-eating Behaviour

There have been reports of some tigers turning into 'man-eaters' and persistently stalking human beings as prey species. It has been documented in extremely rare occasions in parts of India. Such man-eating behaviour is manifested in an unusually persistent form among the tigers of *Sundarbans* mangroves. Loss of fear of humans and subsequently considering them as prey turns a tiger into man-eater. Though, the ecological factors that turn a tiger to 'man-eater' have not been scientifically proven.

10.6.3 Human-Tiger Conflict Mitigation Strategies

1. Translocation of Problem Tiger

Capture of a 'problem tiger' and moving it away from the site of conflict has wide social acceptability and is often adopted in case of human-tiger conflicts.

2. Guarding, Barriers and Aversive Conditioning

Guarding is an effective and traditional approach. Most tiger attacks on livestock occur under free-ranging conditions. Hence, this approach involves employment of human herders to guard livestock, particularly those grazing in tiger habitats. Barriers made of wooden poles, wire mesh and nylon netting are also being used to prevent tigers from entering human habitations. Uses of nylon nets have been extensively implemented in the *Sundarbans* to prevent tigers venturing out of the mangroves and entering villages. 'Electrified human dummies' have also been deployed for aversive conditioning of tigers in some of the conflict zones.

3. Compensatory and Ex-gratia Payments

Although financial aid can never fully compensate the loss suffered by the victim's family, yet such ex-gratia payments may mitigate the local hostility towards tigers to some extent. Government schemes for such compensation for human lives lost to tigers are found to be effective. But, compensations for predation of livestock by tigers are not so effective due to massive scale of cattle kill by tigers and high expenses involved in verifying the claims.

Nevertheless, government compensation procedures are very lengthy and the amount of money is also much lower than the actual market value of the livestock killed. As a solution to this problem, WWF-India had initiated a 'cattle compensation scheme' in 1997 around various tiger reserves and wildlife sanctuaries where the threats to the livestock were high. The compensation was equivalent to a nearby market rate and was usually paid within two days of kill through local NGOs. Besides, informers of cattle kills were paid a reward and cattle carcasses were disposed of by burial or burning after inspection to prevent the poisoning of carcasses. In several instances, WWF-India had also borne the costs of the funeral of victims killed in tiger attacks.

4. Relocation of Human Settlements from Tiger Habitats

Relocation of human settlements from tiger habitats is a proactive strategy and has been effectively implemented under the wildlife conservation schemes of the Government of India to mitigate tiger-human conflicts. Such relocation of human settlements from the tiger habitat has also helped in recovery of wild tiger populations from the brink of extirpation in several Indian protected areas through reducing further habitat fragmentation, habitat restoration and subsequent increase of the herbivore (prey) population.

In addition to these, following measures are also recommended to reduce human-tiger conflict:

- People should be alert and vigilant while in the forest fringe areas or inside forests, particularly in the region with high incidences of conflicts.
- Protection and improvement of tiger habitat need to be carried out through restoration of prey base, so that the tigers do not stray outside the forests in search of food.
- Mitigation strategies should be devised through discussion with local people.
- Relocation of villagers outside tiger reserves with attractive rehabilitation package.
- Imposing restriction on livestock grazing inside tiger reserves.
- People depending largely on the tiger habitat for livelihood should be trained and provided with alternative suitable livelihood options (tourist guides, self-help groups, etc.) to reduce their dependence on forests.
- Cattle should never be left unattended by the herders in high conflict zones of forest fringe areas.

In human dominated landscapes support of the local community is critical for successful conservation of tigers. So, local communities need to be educated about the need for tiger conservation. For this purpose regular and frequent campaigns need to be organized in conflict prone areas to make these people aware of tiger behaviour and biology and also to inculcate a sense of compassion among them for tigers. Most importantly affected local communities should essentially be included and involved in tiger conservation initiatives and their opinion should be considered with due importance.

10.6.4 Challenges in Human-Tiger Conflict Mitigation in India

It is a fact that capture and random translocations of 'problem tigers', though fairly popular strategy, but are not long term practical solutions to human-tiger conflicts. Studies revealed that the displaced carnivores often exacerbate problem and even lead to conflicts in new areas.

Translocation of tigers may not have the desired conservation outcome or conflict mitigation goal due to the following reasons:

- In a free-ranging tiger population precise identification of a 'problem tiger' is hardly possible.
- Safe capture of a tiger straying inside human habitations is difficult due to overcrowding of people.
- Most problem tigers get injured during the process of capture and handling and often lose their canines in steel cages that are commonly used in transportation.
- Many tigers straying in human habitations are either weak or old individuals which have been

evicted from their ranges by more vigorous rivals. Such tigers are unfit for relocation into the wild.

- Wild tigers do not adapt well in captivity and after certain extent of human contact successful reintroduction of the captive tigers back into the wild is often not possible.
- Most of the Indian zoos cannot afford to keep problem tigers anymore.
- Due to the scarcity of high quality tiger habitat without conflict potential, relocations might result in new situations of conflict.
- As the tigers are territorial in nature, hence the translocation of a tiger even into a large reserve with adequate prey base might still result in competition for territory with the existing tiger population thriving there. Such competition lead to the elimination of either the introduced tiger or the resident tiger.

Wildlife biologists suggested 3,000 sq km area as the ideal size of a tiger reserve. But in India, due to its ever-expanding population, the size of the tiger reserves is often less than half of this recommended area. Tiger Task Force had predicted that with habitat and prey base restoration as the number of tigers increase inside tiger reserves, eventually, some of these territorial carnivores will be compelled to come out of these protected areas and roam outside core and buffer zones. Over the years this prediction has come to reality in most areas resulting in human-tiger conflicts.

10.7 HUMAN-LEOPARD CONFLICT

10.7.1 Human-Leopard Conflict Scenario in India

Human-leopard conflicts due to leopards 'straying' into settlements, causing human causalities and the retaliatory killing of leopards have also been on the rise. Shrinking natural habitat and dwindling prey base of leopards, as well as, increase in livestock and other animals around human habitations have resulted in frequent venturing of these carnivores out of wilderness areas into the human habitation in various parts of this country. Incidences of leopard straying into human habitation are widespread in this country. Conflict situations are fairly high in the states of Uttarakhand, Himachal Pradesh, Jammu and Kashmir and Karnataka, tea gardens of northern West Bengal, Assam, Western Ghats and in the suburbs of Bengaluru, Mumbai and Guwahati.

Tea gardens of northern West Bengal act as one of the major areas of human-leopard conflict. According to Manoj et al., (2013), majority of leopard attacks in western Dooars usually happen in and around various tea gardens. It is to be noted that several tea gardens have greatly encroached the forests of northern West Bengal shrinking natural leopard habitat. Moreover, the presence of domestic hens and ducks, feral pigs and dogs, cattle, goats and other livestock often attract leopards as these are easy prey in comparison to wild herbivores.

10.7.2 Possible Causes of Leopard Straying

Leopards are territorial carnivores, highly adaptable and can dwell near human habitations. Feral animals and unattended livestock are probably important prey of leopards living outside protected areas in India (Athreya and Belsare, 2007). But, leopards are usually reclusive in nature and generally avoid people even in these human dominated landscapes. Occasionally, they attack humans mainly out of fear when they meet in wrong circumstances. So, it was believed that leopards usually stay in the wilderness areas inside tall undisturbed forests and make occasional visit to human habitation, croplands, tea gardens and coffee plantations possibly for the following reasons:

- old age, debilitating injuries and broken canines
- dearth of wild prey and/or little water inside the forests
- infrastructure development disturbing the natural habitat of leopards
- increase in the number of leopards in a particular area
- improper disposal of corpses
- loss of fear of people

But, a recent telemetry study carried out in Maharashtra revealed that the radio-collared leopard stayed in the refuge of sugarcane fields all day and emerged at night to hunt easy prey in abundant supply (Lenin, 2010). Some populations have even become resident in agricultural fields, tea and coffee estates. This study showed that leopards are being sustained in high densities in many rural areas for the easy availability of livestock, stray dogs and feral pigs. A large number of leopards have also been killed in retaliation by bullets, poisoning and using snares.

10.7.3 Human-Leopard Conflict Mitigation Strategies

To reduce conflict with leopards, existing cattle shed should be strengthened and other domestic animals should be kept inside "leopard-proof" enclosures in night. The farmers should avoid entering agricultural fields in night or before dawn. For watering the distant farm in night automatic timers are to be fitted with water pumps. If visit to the cropland in dark is unavoidable, then the farmers should be in groups, with bright torches, talking loudly among themselves. These simple measures might greatly reduce the chances of people and leopard meeting under wrong circumstances.

Cleaning up of garbage, on the other hand, might largely reduce the number of free-ranging pigs and feral dogs. It is advisable that local health and municipal authorities take necessary steps to control feral animal population, which in turn would reduce the number of leopards and their frequency of visits around human habitations (Athreya and Belsare, 2007).

Residents should quickly be paid appropriate amount of *ex-gratia* in case of attacks or deaths of humans and loss of livestock. Animal replacement might be prospective than compensatory funds.

State wildlife departments must launch awareness drives among local schools, local administrative bodies (like gram sabha, gram panchayat, eco-development committees, JFM groups, biodiversity management committees etc.) and residents about the importance of leopards, possible causes of leopard straying and preventive measures to be taken.

10.7.4 Challenges in Human-Leopard Conflict Mitigation in India

Indian cultural tradition and religious beliefs have made most of the villagers and farmers amazingly tolerant and sympathetic to leopards. But, with frequent conflicts these values evade very fast and people indulge in retaliatory killing of these carnivores. It is to be understood that mere sighting of a leopard in the vicinity of human habitations does not necessarily mean that the animal needs to be captured. In most cases the animal tries to get away. But, once sighted, the villagers often start chasing the animal and/or start pelting stones. The leopard gets scared, confused and attacks in self-defense. In such a scenario, trained people are needed to mitigate conflict. Proper crowd management is a prime requisite for successful rescue operation. Absence of competent and trained staff results in delay and unsuccessful rescue operations, often resulting in death of the leopard straying into human habitats. Under pressure of the local mass, sometimes wildlife officials are compelled to declare a straying leopards as 'man-eater' and order its elimination.

Translocation of 'problem leopards' is carried out routinely all over India. This is perhaps the most common way of dealing with animals caught in problem situations. However, as in many other species, trapping and random translocation does not necessarily provide long term solutions to the conflict situations. So, trapping should be reduced as much as practicable and should only be done following Section II of the Wildlife Protection Act, 1972. Moreover, translocation of problem leopards may be detrimental to the conservation of the leopard species for the following reasons:

- Leopards, especially older individuals, attempt to head back to their territories after translocation.
- Translocation of many leopards into a particular forest could lead to increased leopard populations there, which might again stray into the adjacent human dominated areas.
- Arbitrary removal of leopards could lead to increased conflicts. Because, the space vacated by a captured animal might soon be occupied by another leopard and the newly released animals might come into conflict at the fringes of protected areas.

So, translocation of leopard should only be done after obtaining adequate knowledge of the species' biology through strict and scientific monitoring using appropriate wildlife telemetry (radio-collar) techniques. Finally, each case of human-leopard conflicts needs to be thoroughly investigated. Because, a leopard killed in retaliation might enter the grey market of illegal wildlife trade due to huge demand for leopard skin, bones and other body parts.

REVIEW QUESTIONS

1. Enumerate the causes for "Man-Wildlife Conflict". Give an account on the Man-Elephant Conflict with special reference to North Bengal. Elaborate the mitigation strategies undertaken to minimize Man-Elephant conflict. Enumerate the challenges during the implementation of those mitigation strategies.
2. Mention possible causes of Man-Tiger Conflict. Give an account on the measures to be taken to minimize the Man-Tiger conflict.
3. Give an account on Man-Leopard conflict in India. Suggest measure to control Man-Leopard conflict.

REFERENCES

Athreya, V.R. and Belsare, A.V., *Human — leopard conflict management guidelines*, Kaati Trust, Pune, India, 2007.

Chauhan, N.P.S., Man-eating and cattle-lifting by tigers and conservation implications in India. In: *Proceedings of 8th European Vertebrate Pest Management Conference* 2011, doi: 10.5073/jka.2011.432.097

Distefano. E., *Human-Wildlife Conflict Worldwide: Collection of Case Studies, Analysis of Management Strategies and Good Practices,* 2013, Retrieved from: http://www.fao.org/sard/common/ecg/1357/en/hwc_final.pdf

Gurung, B., Smith, J.L.D., McDougal, C. and Karki, J., *Tiger Human Conflicts: Investigating ecological and sociological issues of tiger conservation in the buffer zone of Chitwan National Park, Nepal*, WWF-Nepal, 2006.

Lenin, J., Sugarcane leopards. *Current Conservation*, **4**, 4, 22–27, 2010.

Manoj, K., Bhattacharya, R. and Padhy, P.K. Forest and wildlife scenarios of northern West Bengal, India: a review. *International Research Journal of Biological Sciences*, **2**, 7, 70–79, 2013.

Menon, V., Tiwari, S.K., Easa, P.S. and Sukumar, R., *Right of Passage – Elephant Corridors of India (Cons. Ref. Ser. No. 3)*, Wildlife Trust of India, New Delhi, 2005.

Radhakrishna, S. and Sinha, A., Dr. Jekyll and Mr Hyde: The Strange Case of Human-Macaque Interactions in India, *Current Conservation*, **4**, 4, 39 – 40, 2010.

Sukumar, R. and Gadgil, M., Male-female differences in foraging on crops by Asian Elephants. *Animal Behaviour*, **36**, 1233–1235, 1988.

Sukumar, R. and Murali, L. Elephants, People & the Battle for Peaceful Coexistence. *Current Conservation*, **4**, 4, 6–11, 2010.

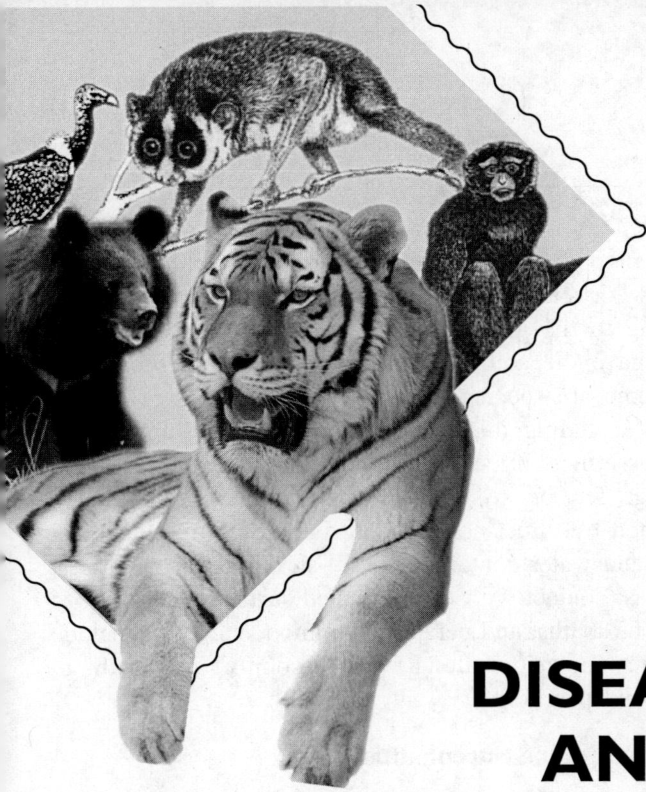

11

WILDLIFE HEALTH: DISEASES OF WILD ANIMALS AND THEIR MANAGEMENT

Several diseases threaten the survival of number of species in the wild, as well as in the captive conditions. The diseases are broadly categorized as:

- Diseases of animals in the wild and
- Diseases of animals in captivity

11.1 DISEASES OF ANIMALS IN THE WILD

11.1.1 Viral Diseases

Viruses are known to infect a wide range of hosts, including humans and wild animals. Wildlife populations, such as waterfowl, experience epizootics caused by viruses. Duck plague or duck viral enteritis may cause large die-offs in a localized area.

A. Canine Parvovirus

Canine parvovirus is a disease of canids (such as dogs, wolves etc). Individuals of all ages may get affected, but puppies and older dogs are more susceptible. The virus is related to feline panleukopenia and is transmitted between animals by oral contact through infected fecal material. This virus can survive in the environment for an exceptionally long time and usually causes intestinal infections resulting in severe diarrhoea and frequent vomiting. The stool typically contains blood and has a very characteristic odour. Affected animals usually do not eat and soon become extremely weak. Death often follows as a result of dehydration, shock and secondary infections.

B. Canine Distemper

Canine distemper is a disease of canids (such as dogs, foxes and wolves), mustelids (such as marten, otter, weasel, fisher and wolverine) and raccoons. All ages of these species may be affected, but young and older animals appear to be most susceptible. Although the virus cannot survive in the environment for very long time, still its mode of transmission is primarily through air by coughing of infected animals. Canine distemper initially causes lung infections. However, the virus can spread throughout body and affect other organs like intestinal tract, kidneys and central nervous system. Symptoms of the disease include signs of respiratory infection, such as mucous discharge from nose and eyes, as well as, difficulty in breathing. Dogs are usually depressed and may have diarrhoea. If the disease is persistent, animals may develop thickening of the pads of their feet or nose followed by neurological disorders such as muscle twitching, weakness, paralysis or seizures. Other symptoms include lack of coordination, circling or head pressing, depression etc. They may show little fear of humans, walk in circles, stagger or have convulsions.

Recently serological findings suggest that canine distemper virus (CDV) may be an emerging threat to Amur tigers (*Panthera tigris altaica*) in the Russian Far East (Goodrich et al., 2012; Seimon et al., 2013). More recently, several cases have been reported in wild tigers in India (ProMED, 2013). The morbilli virus causing canine distemper has been recorded in most families of terrestrial carnivores and is capable of causing very high mortality in some species like, African wild dogs, black-footed ferrets and has been implicated in population declines of the species concerned (Gilbert et al., 2014). Although, feline CDV infections have been recorded in captive large felids earlier, yet the importance of the virus as a threat to wild felines was not recognized until an outbreak affecting lions (*Panthera leo*) in the Serengeti in 1994, during which an estimated 1,000 animals (approximately 30 percent) disappeared (Roelke-Parker, 1996).

C. Rabies

Rabies is an infectious viral disease caused by a rhabdo virus, commonly seen in carnivorous species, both domestic and wild. In general, different strains of the virus are present in bats, dogs, foxes, skunks and racoons. Insectivorous bats are the only wildlife reservoir of rabies. Rabies causes an infection of local tissues and then spreads along nervous tissue to the brain and salivary glands, finally affecting the nervous system of humans and other mammals. At the beginning, there is a marked change in behaviour. The infected animal usually stops eating, becomes quiet and retreats from contact. In the next phase of the disease, animals become very excited or aggressive, followed by complete paralysis. This second aggressive phase is the most "furious" stage of rabies when the animal behaves in an irrational and vicious manner and may attack inanimate objects. This stage is also dangerous for other animals and humans. Paralysis initially begins in the throat and jaw muscles resulting in drooling of the animal with inability to swallow. Paralysis usually progresses quickly to other parts of the body, leading to delirium and convulsions and eventual death due to respiratory muscle paralysis.

D. Contagious Ecthyma

Contagious ecthyma is a viral disease that infects a number of wild ungulates and alternately known as 'contagious pustular dermatitis', 'scabby mouth' or 'sore mouth'. The causative virus is a parapoxvirus capable of infecting humans too, causing painful skin lesions in areas of contact and is characterized by mild to moderate lesions that disappear within weeks. The signs and symptoms of infection initiates with small swellings and pustules that enlarge and become covered with scabs and crusts. These proliferative lesions are usually present on the lips, oral tissues, muzzle, lower leg or coronary band above the hooves. In typical cases, lesions spontaneously heal within 2–4 weeks. The virus is very resistant to environmental conditions and has been recovered from crusts after 12 years. Although the numbers of animals affected in a group may be high, death appears to be rare and is usually associated with secondary bacterial infections. There is no treatment for the disease other than supportive care.

E. Avian Pox

The avian pox is a common name for a mild to severe and slow developing disease of birds caused by a virus belonging to the group of Avipox viruses. Most of these viruses have the ability to infect several species of birds while some are species specific. They infect large variety of birds including migratory waterfowl, wild raptors and many passerines. Infected birds may have warty lesions on head, legs, feet or any other unfeathered area. This virus is transmitted by direct contact with infected birds, ingestion of food and water contaminated by sick birds or carcasses, as well as, contact with contaminated surfaces such as bird feeders, birdbaths, and perches. Common symptoms include difficulties in vision, along with discomfort in breathing, feeding and perching.

F. Eastern Equine Encephalitis

Eastern equine encephalitis is caused by infection with a RNA virus belonging to the family Togaviridae. Replication of this virus may take place within mosquitoes, which can transmit the infection to vertebrate hosts (like birds and mammals, including humans). Clinical signs are usually noticed in non-indigenous birds, which include depression, tremors, paralysis of the legs, unnatural drowsiness, lethargy, profuse diarrhoea, voice changes, ataxia or loss of muscle coordination and involuntary circular movements, partial paralysis or paresis of the legs and neck prior to death.

G. Avian Influenza

Wild birds, especially waterfowl and shorebirds, have long been suspected to be a source for influenza infections in poultry, as well as, in human beings. Avian influenza viruses have been found in many bird species, but are most often found in migratory waterfowl, especially mallard duck.

H. Duck Plague

Duck plague is caused by a herpes virus. Infection often results in an acute, contagious and fatal disease. Only ducks, geese and swans are susceptible to duck plague.

I. Bluetongue Disease

Bluetongue is a viral disease of ruminants, more specifically of wild deer. It is a viral disease borne by midges. Wild and domestic sheep are also quite susceptible to this virus and can die of the disease.

11.1.2 Bacterial Diseases

Most of the bacteria that cause disease in wildlife might affect human beings as well. These infections are usually caused by mixed groups of bacteria, but they often involve Staphylococci and Streptococci.

A. Bumble Foot

Bumble foot is a chronic bacterial infection of the foot, usually with a type of Staphylococcus bacterium. It is very painful and debilitating, often involving the joints and toe-nail beds and in extreme cases, resulting in loss of the foot. Bumble foot is often noticed after an injury to the lower aspect of the foot, possibly from a sharp or abrasive object or from the unsuitable perching facilities.

B. Chlamydiosis

Chlamydiosis, also known as Ornithosis or Psittacosis, is quite prevalent among birds, particularly in psittacine birds, pigeons, raptors and finches. The infective agent is *Chlamydia psittaci*. The signs and symptoms include decreased or no appetite, resulting in emaciation, lethargy, respiratory signs, and a greenish blood-tinged diarrhoea. Conjunctivitis is another common symptom associated with this disease and varies in its severity. The disease may be acute and consequently the animal may die. In addition to birds, *Chlamydia* is also reported to infect koala bears (*Phascolarctos cinereus*) in Australia as a venereal infection, threatening viability of the species.

C. Leptospirosis

Leptospirosis is caused by *Leptospira* spp. and skunks, raccoons, opossums, Norway rats, mice and many other animals including domestic species are common victims of this disease.

D. Brucellosis (Undulant Fever)

The infectious agents are *Brucella* spp. and have been noticed in a wide variety of terrestrial and marine species. This is also an important zoonotic disease of human beings. Brucellosis is commonly transmitted to susceptible animals by direct contact with infected animals or with an environment that has been contaminated with discharges from infected animals.

E. Bubonic Plague

Occurs due to infection with *Yersinia pestis* and is prevalent among rats and ground squirrels. The signs include fever, pneumonia and swollen lymph nodes. However, infected wild rodents usually do not show clinical signs under normal conditions.

F. Salmonellosis

Salmonellosis has been recognized in all parts of the world but is most prevalent in regions with intensive animal husbandry. Infectious agent is *Salmonella* spp., commonly found in birds and reptiles. Many animals are persistent carriers. This facultative intracellular pathogen is commonly found in an environment with fecal contamination of the infected animals. Rodents and wild birds are also sources of infection for domestic animals. It often leads to disorders, including gastroenteritis, spontaneous abortions, and septicemia. Signs are often subclinical, but when present, include diarrhoea, vomiting, anorexia, lethargy, dehydration, weight loss, skin diseases, swollen lymph nodes and mild fever. This bacterial disease is also zoonotic, meaning it can be transmitted to humans.

G. Tularemia

Tularemia is an infectious zoonotic disease caused by a nonspore-forming, gram-negative coccobacillus bacterium, *Francisella tularensis*. This disease is also known as rabbit fever. Rodents (muskrats, beaver, voles and squirrels) and lagomorphs (rabbits and hares) are most commonly affected along with over 100 species of mammals and 25 species of birds. Two distinct forms of tularemia occur—one in rabbits and hares, spreading primarily through infected ticks. Humans are potentially at risk by the bite of infected ticks. The second form occurs in with fresh water associated rodents (like beaver, muskrat, and voles). Among domestic animals, sheep are the most common hosts, but clinical infection has also been reported in cats, dogs, pigs, and horses. Transmission is primarily through water contaminated from carcasses of animals dying of tularemia. Humans are exposed through handling live infected animals or carcasses, eating improperly cooked meat or from contaminated water. Animals usually die quickly, but if alive, they are very weak and ill. Disease varies depending upon the route of exposure to the bacteria. Initially flulike signs, such as fever, chills, nausea, headache and joint pains occur. Glands (or lymph nodes) may become swollen and painful and may break open and drain pus.

11.1.3 Protozoan Diseases

A. Giardiasis

Giardiasis refers to an intestinal infection that is caused by a protozoan parasite *Giardia intestinalis* (also known as *G. lamblia* and *G. duodenalis*). Giardiasis is a disease known from all over the world and is particularly common in resource-poor countries with low standards of sanitation facilities. This disease is quite prevalent among wild mammals and birds, specially, in beavers, muskrats and waterfowls. Transmission of this disease occurs through fecal contamination of water and hand-to-mouth transfer of cysts from feces of an infected animal. Waterfowl and aquatic species of mammals are most frequently affected. This protozoan infection is associated with a variety of intestinal symptoms like chronic diarrhoea, abdominal cramps, bloating, weight loss and frequent loose, pale stools.

B. Toxoplasmosis

Toxoplasmosis is caused by the protozoan parasite *Toxoplasma gondii.* Cats, including non-domestic species, are the definitive host, while many other mammals and birds can act as an intermediate host. Although wild animals are often cited as infectious agents for toxoplasmosis, the domestic cat is the only species that passes infective eggs in its faeces. Thus, infection is contracted through food or water that has been contaminated by cat faeces, or by eating the flesh of another animal that contains the parasite encysted in its muscles. Earthworms, flies and cockroaches are also reported to mechanically transmit the oocysts (Bettiol et al., 2000).

Clinical signs of this disease vary and include blindness, keratitis, chorioretinitis, neurological signs, depression, anorexia, fever, dyspnoea and even death.

11.1.4 Helminthic Infections

All species of wildlife carry their own complement of helminth intestinal parasites. There are two forms of disease caused by these parasites.

A. Cutaneous Larval Migrans (CLM)

CLM is a dermatitis infection caused by the penetration, invasion and migration of some parasitic larvae under the skin (Neafie and Meyers, 2000). These larvae usually have their origin from nematodes and rarely from insects (Nash, 1990). The infections are of great zoonotic importance, especially as occupational hazard and may happen to the victim either due to geohelminths (e.g., ascarids) or biohelminths (e.g., *Gnathostoma spinigerum*). The clinical features of CLM may vary from non-specific dermatitis to typical creeping eruptions, where the parasite undergoes a localized migration in or just under the skin, creating self-limiting inflammatory reactions. For this reason this disease is also known by other names like creeping eruption, sand worm, plumbers itch, duck hunters itch and epidermatitis linearis migrans (Neafie and Meyers, 2000).

B. Visceral Larval Migrans (VLM)

VLM is an uncommon parasitic infection most commonly caused by *Toxocara canis* and *Toxocara cati*. This disease occurs when the eggs of a parasite are ingested, then the immature larval forms penetrate the intestinal tract and migrate through various internal organs of the host in various parts of the body. The amoun t and severity of the disease depends on the organs affected. The most common one is *Baylisascaris* infection in racoons.

11.1.5 Mycotic Diseases

A. Aspergillosis

Infectious agent is *Aspergillus fumigatus.* This fungus is ubiquitous in nature. Animal hosts of *Aspergillus* are generally wild birds such as raptors or waterfowl. This fungus is responsible for respiratory infections.

B. Histoplasmosis

Causal agent is *Histoplasma capsulatum* and the usual hosts of this fungus are birds and bats. The parasite also occurs in skunks, rats, opossums, foxes and other animals. Majority of the animals develop mild respiratory infections.

C. White-nose Syndrome in Bats (WNS)

This disease is a rapidly-spreading lethal disease of wild bats, characterized by a white coating of fungal hyphae over the bat, often starting on the muzzle. The suspected causative agent is fungus *Geomyces destructans*, either as a primary pathogen or as an opportunist secondary infection.

11.1.6 Tick-borne Diseases

Infections to a variety of ticks are common phenomenon in case of wild animals. *Dermacentor albipictus* is usually seen on deer species, particularly moose, less commonly on livestock and is rarely found on humans. *D. andersoni* occur on many mammals. The immature larval and nymphal stages are on rabbits or small rodents, with adult ticks on larger wildlife, deer, livestock, dogs and humans. *Ixodid pacificus* has a similar host range as *D. andersoni*, with immature larval and nymphal stages on mice and lizards and adult ticks on dogs, deer, humans and horses. Heavy tick loads can be debilitating, as seen in one host winter tick on moose. A single moose may carry tens of thousands of ticks. Each tick can remove a significant amount of blood and causes irritation at the site of attachment. The moose rubs and scratches, often resulting in a significant loss of hair in a characteristic pattern over the neck and body. Heavy tick burdens can weaken animals by direct blood loss, loss of body heat due to hair removal and decrease in the rate of feeding. Death can result, particularly in young animals in early spring due to poor nutrition and severe weather conditions.

A. Lyme Disease

Lyme disease is a bacterial disease spread through the bite of an infected tick (vector). Lyme disease is generally caused by three species of *Borrelia viz. B. burgdorferi, B. afzelii*, and *B. garinii.* The last two species are more frequently reported from Asia (Vasudevan and Chatterjee, 2013). Wild mammals (especially small rodents, deer, weasels, bats etc.) carry the bacteria in nature and ticks get infected when they feed blood of these infected animals. Such infected ticks then bite and spread the bacteria to other uninfected animals or humans. However, little is known about the signs and symptoms in wild animals. But, in humans the symptoms might vary usually involving a multisystem inflammatory disorder with a wide spectrum of skin manifestations, skin rash and joint pain (arthritis).

B. Rocky Mountain Spotted Fever

Infectious agent is *Rickettsia rickettsi*. The disease is generally restricted to the summer months in areas where the dog tick (*Dermacentor variabilis*) and wild animal hosts are abundant.

11.1.7 Mite-borne Diseases

A. Mite-borne Mange

Mite-borne Mange is a type of skin infection caused by microscopic mite *Sarcoptes scabei*. It is quite commonly reported in coyotes and has also been reported in other wild and domestic species like red fox and wolves throughout the world, and also in humans. *Sarcoptes* mites spend their entire life cycle within the skin of the host and are transmitted by direct contact between animals. The mites burrow through the skin causing severe reactions and inflammation. The skin weeps fluid, thickens, darkens, with concominent hair loss and thick crusts are formed. Severely affected animals loose body weight, behave strangely and die of hypothermia.

11.1.8 Duck Leeches

Blood sucking leeches of the genus *Theromyzon* are known to feed directly in the nasal passages, trachea, and beneath the nictitating membrane of the eyes of migratory birds, particularly in aquatic bird species. Affected waterfowl include northern pintail, teal, American wigeon, northern shoveler, ring-necked duck, canvasback, redhead, lesser scaup, bufflehead, gadwall, ruddy duck, white-winged scoter, surf scoter, trumpeter swan, tundra swan, geese etc.

11.2 DISEASES OF ANIMALS IN CAPTIVITY

A. Avian *Aspergillus*

Avian *Aspergillus* infection generally occurs among penguins, pheasants and waterfowls. Usually recorded in chicks, young and adult pheasants and chicks of less than one week of age are most susceptible. Clinically characterized by increased respiration, gasping, drowsiness, dozing, and dullness with ruffled feathers in 1–10 days old pheasant chicks. In adults, sign and symptoms include weight loss, markedly elevated WBC counts, and in later stages, dyspnea. Death may occur due to the formation of localized aspergilloma inside the trachea or due to fungal septicemia. Treatment includes oral or intravenous or nebulized antifungal medications. Proper cleaning and disinfection of feed and water utensils and improvement of hygienic condition is recommended.

B. Infectious Pododermatitis (Bumble Foot)

Infectious pododermatitis (bumble foot) is a common disorder of captive birds and is characterized by lameness, inflammation, and swelling of the footpad due to localized bacterial infections, usually with a type of *Staphylococcus* bacterium, often involving the joints and toe-nail beds. In advanced stages, the infection may lead to chronic pododermatitis, septicemia, or amyloidosis. It may occur due to injury possibly from a sharp or abrasive object to the lower aspect of the foot. Infection leads to obesity or unilateral limb problems (trauma, arthritis). It is very painful and debilitating and ultimately results in loss of the foot.

C. Avian Mycobacteriosis

Avian mycobacteriosis is a chronic problem in many captive birds. But, wild animals like marsupials and young primates may also be contaminated when exposed to the infected birds. In case of marsupials the common manifestations include lung or bone lesions, which are unresponsive to most therapies.

D. Mammalian Tuberculosis

Mammalian tuberculosis is not uncommon among zoo animals, specially in primates, hoofed mammals and elephants. Interpretation of intradermal tuberculin tests can be problematic in nondomestic species due to the occurrence of nonspecific responses. When a test is suspicious or positive, a complete health evaluation should be performed.

E. Mandibular Osteomyelitis (Lumpy Jaw)

Mandibular osteomyelitis (lumpy jaw) is a common problem of small ruminants and macropods (wallabies and kangaroos). It can occur secondarily after oral trauma, or dental disease. The common signs generally include localized facial swelling and a foul oral odour or discharge. Treatment consists of lancing the abscess, debriding infected bone, removing affected teeth if indicated by radiographs and treating with systemic antibiotics.

F. Marek' Disease

Recorded in captive pheasants by Sah et al., (1982) and caused by a virus belonging to the Herpes virus group. Symptoms include lameness, paralysis and loss of weight and numerous grayish white nodules (2–3 mm) in the liver and larger greyish pink tumorous nodules on both the lungs. Also spleen and kidneys are moderately enlarged and grayish discolouration is seen. Breast muscles also appear grayish and lusterless. Lesions are discernable in the heart muscles, skin, testes, sciatic and vagus nerves.

11.2.1 Animal Healthcare and Management in Captivity

As proposed in Wildlife (Protection) Act, 1972, the following basic criteria must be taken in to consideration for proper maintenance of captive animals.

- The animals shall be handled only by the staff having experience and training in handling the individual animals. Every care shall be taken to avoid discomfort, behavioural stress or physical harm to any animal.
- Every zoo shall have facilities for restraining and handling wild animals.
- The condition and health of all animals in the zoo shall be checked every day by a competent person. If any abnormalities are detected such as if the animal is found sick, injured, or unduly stressed then the matter shall be reported to the veterinary officer for providing treatment expeditiously.
- Routine examination including parasite checks shall be carried out regularly and preventive medicines (including vaccination) be administrated as per schedule.
- Each zoo shall maintain animal history sheets and treatment cards, especially for endangered species.
- Every large and medium zoo shall have a full-fledged veterinary unit with basic diagnostic facilities, comprehensive range of drugs and a reference library on animal health care and upkeep.
- Each veterinary unit shall have isolation and quarantine wards to take care of newly arriving animals and sick animals as to minimize the chances of infections spreading to other animals of the zoo.
- Any animal that dies in a zoo shall be subjected to a detailed post-mortem examination.
- Each zoo shall have proper facility for disposal of carcasses without affecting the hygiene of the zoo.
- An active behavioural training programme enables improved health care. Through positive reinforcement, amphibians, reptiles, birds and mammals in zoo settings have been trained to perform behaviours on command that facilitate accomplishment of various management or medical procedures.

11.2.2 Routine Management

Hoof and nail trims are necessary when overgrowth occurs and are most often required in ruminants, equids, elephants, rhinoceros and larger carnivores. These procedures should be conducted on a regular basis to avoid excessive overgrowth. Elephant foot care is especially important to prevent chronic musculoskeletal problems and can usually be accomplished in an awake elephant through training. Many other species require chemical immobilization for foot care. Dentistry in zoo animals presents unique problems. Since the roots of canine teeth in primates and carnivores are more extensive than the exposed crown, simple traction and rotation cannot remove such teeth intact; so dislodging with a dental elevator is essential. A small electric drill or bone chisel is used to remove a section of alveolar bone around the root. Root canal treatments are done when a large canine tooth is fractured and viable pulp exposure occurs. The incisor teeth of rodents, beavers, porcupines, and capybaras, grow continually and interfere with their ability to feed. This can be manipulated by supplying coarse feed or logs as a routine practice. Periodontal disease in zoo animals is treated by routine cleaning and by providing adequate chewing substances to supplement the soft, prepared diets fed to many zoo animals. Bone fractures are repaired with splints, casts, surgical fixation, or a combination of these methods. Newer lightweight, strong, waterproof, fiberglass casting material is very much useful. Due to excellent management, husbandry, nutrition and veterinary care, many zoo animals live to advanced ages. Care of geriatric specimens is becoming increasingly common, including such disorders as diabetes, heart failure, chronic arthritis and neoplasia. The same diagnostic and therapeutic principles of management of these disorders in humans or domestic animals may be successfully applied to the care of affected zoo animals.

REVIEW QUESTIONS

1. Give an account on different viral diseases of the wild animals.
2. Write short notes on: (a) Protozoal diseases of wild animals (b) Marek's disease (c) Diseases of captive animals.
3. Give an idea on the diseases encountered in wild animals in captivity. Discuss in brief the routine management strategies in captivity to control diseases.

REFERENCES

Bettiol, S.S., Obendorf, D.L., Nowarkowski, M., Milstein, T. and Goldsmid, J.M., Earthworms as paratenic hosts of toxoplasmosis in eastern barred bandicoots in Tasmania, *Journal of Wildlife Diseases*, **36**, 145–148, 2000.

Gilbert, M., Miquelle, D.G., Goodrich, J.M., Reeve, R., Cleaveland, S., Matthews, L. and Joly, D.O., Estimating the potential impact of canine distemper virus on the Amur tiger population (*Panthera tigris altaica*) in Russia, *PLoS ONE*, **9,** 10, e110811, 2014. Retrieved from: http://www.plosone.org/article/info%3Adoi%2F10.1371%2Fjournal.pone.0110811

Goodrich, J.M., Quigley, K.S., Lewis, J.C.M., Astafiev, A.A., Slabi, E.V., Miquelle, D.G., Smirnov, E.N., Kerley, L.L., Armstrong, D.L., Quigley, H.B. and Hornocker, M.G., Serosurvey of Free-ranging Amur Tigers in the Russian Far East, *Journal of Wildlife Diseases*, **48**, 1, 186–189, 2012.

Nash, T., Visceral larva migrans and other unusual helminth infections. In: Mandell, G., Douglas, R., Bennett, J., (Eds.). *Principle and Practice of Infectious Diseases*, Churchill Livingstone, New York, 1990.

Neafie, R.C. and Meyers, W.M., Cutaneous larva migrans. In: Strickland, G.T. (Eds.) *Hunters Tropical Medicine and Emerging Infectious Diseases*. Sounders, Philadelphia, pp. 797–799, 2000.

ProMED, (2013) Archive Number 20140114.2172144. Retrieved from: http://promedmail.org.

Roelke-Parker, M.E., Munson, L., Packer, C., Kock, R., Cleaveland, S., Carpenter, M., O'brien, S.J., Pospischil, A., Hofmann-Lehmann, R., Lutz, H., Mwamengele, G.L.M, Mgasa, M.N., Machange, G.A., Summers, B.A. and Appel, M.J.G., A canine distemper virus epidemic in Serengeti lions (*Panthera leo*), *Nature*, **379**, 441–445, 1996.

Sah, R.L., Mall, M.P. and Mohanty, G.C., Cutaneus candidiasis in Japanese quail (*Coturnix coturnix japonica*), *Mycopathologia*, **80**, 33–37, 1982.

Seimon, A.T., Miquelle, G.D. and Chang, Y.T., Canine Distemper Virus: an Emerging disease in Wild Endangered Amur Tigers (*Panthera tigris altaica*), *mBio*, **4**, 4, 1–6, 2013. doi:10.1128/mBio.00410-13

Vasudevan, B. and Chatterjee, M., Lyme borreliosis and skin. *Indian J Dermatol*., **58**, 167–74, 2013.

12

WILDLIFE TRADE: ASSESSMENT, DOCUMENTATION, PREVENTIVE MEASURES

12.1 WHAT IS WILDLIFE TRADE?

Poaching and illegal trade is considered as second major threat to the survival of various species of wild flora and fauna after habitat loss. Among all illegal trades in the world, wildlife trade is considered to be the next in value to narcotics. Any illegal trade is very difficult to quantify precisely due to its clandestine nature. Nevertheless, the value of illegal import-export and conduit of several wildlife articles is estimated to be over US $20 billion annually (Wyler and Sheikh, 2008). In scale and volume, illegal wildlife trade ranges from locally bartered single item to tons of commercial consignments shipped all over the world. The wildlife contrabands include live pets, hunting trophies, tourist souvenirs, fashion accessories, cultural artifacts, animal parts for traditional medicines, wild meat for human consumption (bush meat), wild orchids etc. to name a few. Such unsustainable and illegal wildlife trade for high profit margins directly threatens the survival of many species in the world.

Lack of awareness and initiatives among the judiciary, low conviction rate, lack of appropriate anti-poaching operations, high profit margin to the poachers, poverty and unemployment of the villagers, particularly in the forest fringe villages, are some of the causes responsible for such voluminous illegal trade. Distinction between anti-poaching and anti-smuggling is not often understood clearly. Although every year different enforcement authorities seize various wildlife articles, but the conviction rate of these wildlife criminals are very low. Moreover, the smugglers often involve the unemployed youth of the forest fringe villages by paying meager amount (as compared to the profit the smugglers earn from illegal trade of wildlife articles) for killing and collection of certain wildlife trophies. These poor people, often unaware of the legal provisions, risk of their life, commit crime by poaching and trading the wildlife trophies and often end up being convicted.

Definition Wildlife crime is contravening any domestic or international law concerning wildlife which includes poaching (unlawful killing), unlawful possession or trade of wildlife articles be it for food, fun or to cater to the domestic or international trade market.

Illegal wildlife trade involves the illicit procurement, conduit of any transport and supply of wild flora and fauna, parts and derivatives thereof, in contravention of international or domestic laws and treaties.

12.1.1 Illegal Wildlife Trade—a Major Threat to Wildlife

Illegal wildlife trade adds to the plight of the wildlife which is already suffering from habitat loss throughout the globe. Rampant poaching of a species for illegal trade often leads to the extinction of the species with adverse 'ripple effects' as all species are interconnected and depend on each other. Thus, extinction of one might adversely affect or even threaten several other species. Mass killing and illegal wildlife trade has already led to the extinction of passenger pigeon, West Indian monk seal, great auk and Steller's sea cow. Many large vertebrates (like elephant, rhino, tiger, leopard, lesser wild cats, bear, musk deer etc.) along with several other species are now on the verge of extinction due to illegal poaching and trade in their body parts.

Some of the potential threats due to illegal wildlife trade are summarized in Table 12.1 below:

Table 12.1 Potential threats of Illegal Wildlife Trade

- Number of the species frequently poached and traded in large volume often decline rapidly and if the species disappear from an area then the species diversity of the area also reduces.
- The risk of extinction, at least locally, looms large particularly on species, which is already rare or known to have historically low population levels.
- Adverse impact on ecosystem occurs when species important for ecosystem functioning are reduced.
- Non-native species sometimes get introduced to a new ecosystem through illegal wildlife trade, particularly during trafficking of live animals as pets. Uncontrolled and rapid growth of these non-native species threatens the survival of many indigenous species.
- These invasive species often exert harmful effects on native animals and plants, thereby disrupt ecosystems and even lead to environmental damage and economic loss for mankind.
- Illegal trade in wildlife may also potentially spread several animal-borne diseases.

Apart from threatening the survival of the species in trade, poaching and illegal trade often threaten the existence of several other associated flora and fauna and ultimately dismantle a very intricate system that has come to existence over a million years of evolution.

Besides, reduction in the key wildlife population also leads to the loss of revenue due to reduced tourist attraction. Sariska Tiger Reserve in Rajasthan is one such example. This tiger reserve was one of the favoured tourist destinations particularly for tiger sighting. But, persistent non-sighting of tigers and more alarmingly not even any indirect evidence of the tigers' presence (like pugmarks, scratch marks on trees etc.) in 2004 raised a national debate and questioned the presence of tigers in Sariska. The Rajasthan Forest Department argued that "the tigers had temporarily migrated outside the reserve and would be back after monsoon season", which was then backed by the Project Tiger as presence of 16 tigers were reported in the previous year. In January 2005, journalist Jay Mazoomdaar published an article in Indian Express claiming that there were no tigers left in Sariska. Soon after this news Rajasthan Forest Department and the Project Tiger Director declared an "emergency tiger census" in Sariska and the Central Bureau of Investigation, India's premier intelligence agency, conducted a probe. Two months intensive survey finally unearthed that there were indeed no tigers left in Sariska and for such disappearance poaching was considered to be one of the major causes. Such local extinction of tigers from Sariska Tiger Reserve in 2005 is commonly known as 'Sariska Shock'. Subsequently, tourism at Sariska Tiger Reserve suffered enormously due to the disappearance of tigers from this protected area. In the year 2004–05 while Sariska was in news for decline of tiger numbers, the tiger reserve still recorded a footfall of 57,323 tourists. But, in the very next year after the absence of tigers was reported (i.e. in 2005–06), numbers of tourists showed a steep decline to 24,607. However, it picked up a little to reach 30,614 in 2006–07. This reduced visitor numbers due to 'Sariska Shock 2005' was also felt dramatically in the local economy (Wheeler, 2009). Apart from decline in revenue generation from tourism and loss of livelihood of local people depending on tourist visits, higher incidences of illegal crime also elevate the economic costs of surveillance, patrolling, enforcement and litigation.

12.1.2 Wildlife Trade—Global Perspective

Any trade persists and even flourishes, if there is demand. The primary motivation to engage in illegal wildlife trade appears to be huge economic gain for the criminals who make profits by catering to the continued demand for wildlife trophies in many parts of the globe through a network of supply chains. The demand for wildlife trophies and articles are ubiquitous and the United States, Peoples' Republic of China and the several countries of European Union are reported to be the regions with highest demand for legally obtained wildlife. As the demand for such legally obtained wildlife exists, the illegal trade comes into the scenario and flourishes by catering to the shortfall of supply from the legally procured wildlife trophies. The United States is thus also one of the major destinations of illegal wildlife products and it is evident that Mexico, Canada, Peoples' Republic of China, Philippines, Hong Kong, Russia, Thailand, Italy and South Africa are the major exporters of those illegal articles. The global trade of illegal wildlife varies according to regions and cultures. It has been noticed that the countries with rich biological heritage having weak governance and poor law enforcement are often vulnerable to illegal wildlife trade.

12.1.3 Wildlife Trade—Indian Scenario

In India, killing of any wildlife is prohibited under law. But, people residing in the remote forest fringe areas or inside forests, have few options of income generation. People are also presently moving from traditional subsistence lifestyle to cash economy in many such areas. Despite of the fact that, cash income from the sale of wildlife products often involves punishments or penalties or even death due to an attack by the wild beasts, still people living in the remote and forest fringe areas with limited access to capital, land or livestock, sometimes consider harvest of wildlife and other forest resources as best return for their labour input. This is a fairly regular incidence in the Sundarbans, where villagers without permit enter the mangroves risking their lives in search of honey and fishermen move in the creeks in search of fishes. Even the persons with permits sometimes move beyond the permissible zones for additional yields. If these persons are killed by tigers in the non-permissible zone then they do not even receive the ex-gratia from the government.

On the other hand, poaching of one-horned rhinoceros for its horn has been a serious problem at Kaziranga, Assam. But in these areas the problem of poaching is often linked with insurgency problems. Some terrorists often kill rhino to cater to the high demand for rhino horns in certain parts of China across the border. They cut the horns from frontal portion of skull of the butchered rhinoceros and sell them to some international smuggling groups in China who, in exchange, provide them with arms and ammunitions. Between 1980 and 2005 the park has lost around 567 rhinoceros to poachers, which implies that approximately 23 rhinos were slaughtered per year. Maximum poaching cases were recorded in between 1980 and 1997 (Mathur et al., 2006), then the poaching incidences fairly reduced in the subsequent years and again surged in the year 2012 when more than 40 one-horned rhinos were killed inside Kaziranga National Park.

Since 1950s, wildlife trade has accelerated owing to a growing demand from the rising population, particularly from the well off people of urban areas. According to some, the illegal wildlife trade is increasing, whereas others opine that the increased magnitude of such illegal trade might be the outcome of more investigations on wildlife crime (Brack, 2009).

Indian scenario of poaching of four mega species (viz. *Elephas maximus*, *Rhinoceros unicornis*, *Panthera tigris* and *Panthera pardus*) revealed that the reported cases of poaching of *Panthera pardus* is manifold higher than the other three species (Figure 12.1).

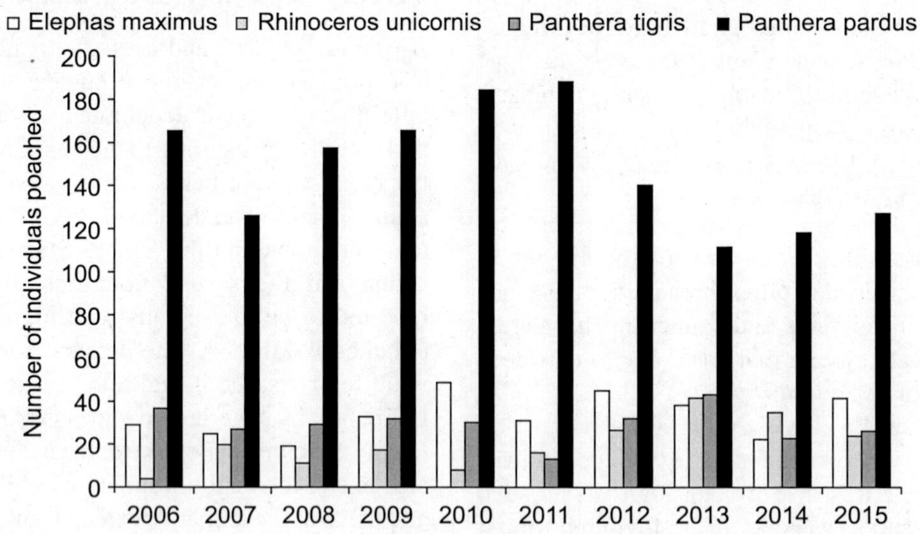

Figure 12.1 Reported cases of poaching of major wild animals in India during 2006–2013 (Source: WPSI).

It is to be noted that out of these four species, enough conservation initiatives have been accorded for *Elephas maximus*, *Rhinoceros unicornis*, *Panthera tigris* respectively under the aegis of Project Elephant, IRV 2020 and Project Tiger. But, initiatives and awareness for the Common Leopard conservation is still scanty. Subsequently, the poaching of leopard has been found to be maximum as leopard parts are now possibly serving as an alternative to tiger skin and other body parts.

Tiger, common leopard, one-horned rhinoceros, barking deer, sambar, spotted deer, hog deer, golden jackal, wild boar, serows, pythons, Ganges river dolphin, gharial, etc are often poached in this country, yet very few of the wildlife articles are seized. Because many of the illegal wildlife articles are traded in a clandestine way and often goes unnoticed. West Bengal sharing long international boundaries with several countries is often considered as safe haven for trafficking of these illegal wildlife commodities. Kolkata and Siliguri are two established trade centres in illegal wildlife trade. Similarly, there are many other states and cities in this country which have major trade routes and trade centres due to their strategic geographical location and proximity to international borders.

12.1.4 Major Articles in Wildlife Trade

A. Bear Parts

The adult bears are trapped and killed to collect their gall bladder and extract bear bile, while their cubs (few weeks old) are collected live. Bear bile is used in oriental medicines in the Far East, especially in China, Japan, Korea and Taiwan. It is also reported to be used in the Tibetan and Ayurvedic medicines in India (Menon and Kumar, 1998). Himalayan black bear (*Selenarctos thibetanus*) and sloth bear (*Melursus ursinus*) are commonly killed for their gallbladders (Menon and Kumar, 1998). These bears are killed in different areas of their distribution range, particularly in the Himalayas, often using leg-hold traps (Figure 12.2) or by shooting. Apart from gall bladders and bile of all species of bear, their paws, meat and fat are also traded illegally (Mills and Serveehn, 1991).

FIGURE 12.2 Illustration of capture and removal of bear gall bladder for bear bile trade.

Once a mother bear is captured or killed, the bear cubs are then captured live and are traded to the *kalandars*, who force the bear cubs to perform and dance using cruel techniques. Claws of the infant bears are ripped out and canines are broken off. Then a red hot poker is pushed up through the bear's snout and out through the delicate muzzle and nose. A rough rope is threaded through the open wound and this wound is never allowed to heal. So, whenever the handler jerks the rope upwards, the bear soon stands on its hind legs. This is not a dancing step, but the bear stands up actually to escape pain (Figure 12.3).

FIGURE 12.3 Schematic representation of 'Dancing Bear' trade.

B. Musk

Musk or *kasturi* is a very expensive natural perfume fixative and was extensively used earlier in the perfume industries to produce exquisite fragrance. Besides, musk is also widely used in the traditional medicine system in China (Unani and Tibetan schools of medicine), as well as, within this country (in Ayurveda). For all these purposes, musk is collected from the abdominal gland (commonly called as 'musk pod') present in the males of Himalayan musk deer. From India, musk pods are mainly traded in the countries like Hong Kong, Bhutan and Nepal. Few farms are known to exist in the western Himalaya, but they do not produce musk commercially due to various limitations. Musk is extracted from the musk pods, which are mostly collected by incessantly poaching musk deers (Menon et al., 1997) and is traded as whole pods, musk grain or in liquid form. The pods are traded as 'catties' and collection of one 'catty' (i.e. 630 g of musk pods) require killing of at least 24 adult male deers. Despite the fact that musk pods are available only from the male deer, yet it is to be noted that many more musk deers (including females and juveniles) are indiscriminately killed. To kill these secretive and nocturnal deers, the poachers strategically place large numbers foot snares and leg-hold traps in various parts of Himalayan forests where they inhabit. Apart from this species, musk is also collected from small Indian civet (*Viverricula indica*) and the large Indian civet (*Viverra zibetha*).

C. Ivory

Tusks of two living elephant species, Asiatic elephant (*Elephas maximus*) and African elephant (*Loxodonta africana*), are the major source of ivory. In addition to that, dentines collected from the tusk (teeth) of hippopotamus, walrus, wild boar etc. are also called ivory while bones of whales and camels are often reported to be used in the trade as substitutes. Ivory is used to build 'hanko' (signature stamps used by Japanese people), ornaments and artifacts (Fig. 12.4 A & B). 'Ivory Triangle' (People's Republic of China, Hong Kong and Macao) is reported to be the second largest destination for illegal ivory after Japan (Menon, 2002).

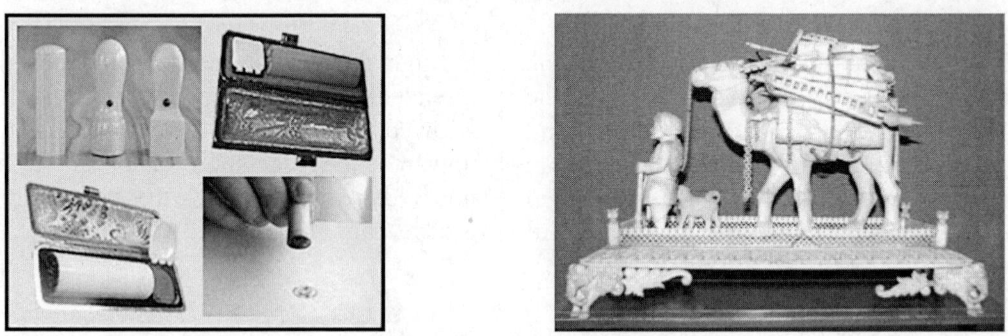

FIGURE 12.4 (A) Japanese name seal (Hanko) and (B) A piece of art made of ivory (Photo Dr. Subhendu Mazumdar).

Besides, as fine carvings are easier to be made on the tusks of Asiatic elephants, hence they are called 'soft ivory'. This type of ivory fetch higher price than the 'hard ivory' obtained from African elephants (Menon et al., 1997). Therefore, ivory from the Asiatic elephants are in relatively greater demand in trade thereby making the species *Elephas maximus* more vulnerable.

In addition to that, only the males have tusks in Asiatic elephants, while the females and the juveniles possess short *tushes* which are not valued in the illegal trade. Hence, the male tuskers are selectively poached. An estimated 100 male elephants were killed in the country every year by ivory poachers between 1980 and 1986 (Arivazhagan and Ramakrishnan, 2010). Selective hunting of male elephants for tusks led to increasingly female-biased sex-ratio. Ivory poaching has led to an adult male to female ratio of 1:25 as was observed in the Mudumalai Tiger Reserve, Nilgiris (Arivazhagan, 2005) in contrast to the normal sex-ratio of 1:3 to 1:4. Such skewed sex-ratio leads to reduction in genetic variation and demographic changes may occur through decreases in female mating success (Sukumar et al. 1998)

D. Tiger and Leopard Parts

Tiger and leopard are killed for their skins which have high demand in international market and are used as decorative items or fashion accessories. Tiger and leopard's bone and teeth are also believed to drive away evil influences. Undercover investigations, raids and seizures of tiger and leopard bones further revealed their demand in traditional Chinese medicine for curing bad ulcers, muscle cramps, rheumatism, abdominal pain, typhoid, malaria, hydrophobia etc. Most other body parts of a tiger like eye ball, nose, teeth, whiskers, claws, flesh, fat, bile, blood, stomach, penis and even the faeces are used in Tibetan and Chinese medicine.

Apart from retaliatory killing in some high-conflict zones of the country, these large carnivores are usually poached using fire arms, steel traps and by poisoning their 'kill' (poison baits). Poaching and illegal trade in tiger parts led to the 2nd and 3rd tiger crisis in India. Leopard is often poached as an alternative of tiger skin and bone and is hunted more often than tigers.

E. Rhino Horn

All five species of rhinoceros living in the world, including the greater one-horned rhino *Rhinoceros unicornis*, are endangered due to illegal trade in rhino horn. Although not scientifically proven, yet rhino horns are used to treat fever, high blood pressure, paralysis and is even considered as aphrodisiac in Oriental and Tibetan medicine. Far east countries, particularly China, are the main destination of such illegal trafficking of rhino horns. Futher, it has been reported that the horns of Asiatic rhinos are considered more valuable and fetch five times more price than African rhino horns. Moreover, trafficking rhino horn from the north-eastern states of India across the border to China is relatively easier as compared to the transit of rhino horns from Africa. In India, Dimapur of Nagaland is a major rhino-horn trade centre in the trade route to Myanmar. Similarly, Siliguri of West Bengal is also another such infamous trade centre for illegal trafficking of rhino horns to Nepal and Bhutan (Menon and Kumar, 1998). To meet the demand of the Far east countries, greater one-horned rhinoceros is brutally poached throughout its distribution range in India for their horns mostly by shooting, as well as, pit poaching, poisoning and electrocution using high tension live wires hanging in their paths.

F. Pelt Trade

Illegal pelt trade in India is reported to include about 20 species, of which 18 are either endangered or vulnerable (Fitzgerald, 1989). Large cats in such trade include tiger, common leopard, snow leopard, clouded leopard and desert cat, fishing cat, jungle cat, marbeled cat and leopard cat are amongst the lesser cats which are often traded in thousands. Such voluminous trade leads to a steady decline of these species. As many of these species, particularly the lesser cats, are crepuscular and nocturnal, therefore, such decline often goes unnoticed and sometimes even lead to 'local extinction' of the species. Red panda, golden jackal, Bengal fox, common otter, Indian smooth-coated otter and occassionally yak, goral, spotted deer, weasels and civets are some other species recorded in the pelt trade.

G. Reptile Skin

In 1977, when the trade was legal, India exported four million snake skins worth above US $ 60 million. In addition to that, about a million of lizard skins and two million crocodile skins were used to be traded anually in the past, which itself indicate the huge demand and massive volume of global trade in reptile skin. Such mammoth demand for reptile skins is basically to produce fashion accessories such as handbags, wallets, belts, boots etc. Tortoise shell, carapaces, leather etc. are often used to produce traditional musical instruments, belts, purses, decorative wall mounts and many other souvenirs. Presently any trade in skin or any other parts of reptiles is illegal in this country. But, the demand still exists. Hence, reptile skins are illegally procured and traded by some wildlife criminals operating in this country. Price of reptilian skin in such illegal trade largely depends upon the species and the width of the skin, but not much on the length of the skin. Russell's Viper, Checkered Keelback, Common Ratsnake, Spectacled Cobra, Monocled Cobra, Caspian Cobra, King Cobra, Indian Python, Banded Krait, Common Monitor Lizard, Yellow Monitor Lizard, Water Monitor Lizard, Marsh Crocodile and Saltwater Crocodile are some of the common Indian reptiles recorded to be traded illegally. In India more than half of the skins thus illegally traded are of non-poisonous rat snakes.

Chennai, Agra and Pune were reported to be the places where the reptile skins were tanned and the destination countries of various seized illegal consignments of reptile skins were found to be the economically rich countries in USA, Europe, Middle East and Far East.

Text Box 12.1 Illegal Trade in 'Shahtoosh' Shawls Threaten the Survival of 'Chiru'

Shahtoosh (king of wool) is one of the finest natural fibers of the world and are called 'ring shawls' as standard sized shawls passes through a finger ring. In spite of being exceptionally soft with a feather light quality, manufacture and trade in Shahtoosh shawls are illegal. The shawls are woven of the underwool of Tibetan antelope (*Pantholops hodgsoni*), commonly known as '*Chiru*'. These Tibetan antelopes are endemic to Chang Tang pastures of the Tibetan Plateau and a small population migrates to north-eastern Ladakh. An estimate revealed that in 1995 only around 75,000 animals were left in the wild. For collection of the underwool several individuals of this endemic antelope are ruthlessly killed threatening the very existence of the species. After poaching the underwool of *chiru* is used for weaving *Shahtoosh* shawls, horns are used in Tibetan medicine and their meat is consumed by the locals. Presently, the fashion crazy and wealthy people in the developed countries of Europe, North America, Far East, Middle East, Australia and South Africa are the main consumers of *Shahtoosh.*

H. Live Animals

Several live animals of various taxa (such as snakes, tortoises, birds, small mammals, etc.) are commonly traded as pets both in domestic and international markets. Meat, fat and eggs of turtles are secretly sold in various markets (particularly in Uttar Pradesh, Bihar and West Bengal) and are mostly used for local consumption. Some are also smuggled live for the demand of their parts in traditional medicine and for production of various commercial items. Besides, out of 31 species of turtles and tortoises found in India, 26 species are reported to be traded mostly to keep as live pets. One-fifth of world's bird species are also reported in international trade, of which 6 percent belongs to endangered species. Between 1970 and 1976, 13 million birds were exported from India of which 80 percent were either munias or parakeets (Fitzerland, 1989). Such export of live birds was banned in 1990 and in the very next year the ban was imposed on the domestic trade of any live Indian species. Many species of mammals are also traded live of which the most common ones are the bears, langurs and macaques.

I. Fur Trade

Illegal fur trade mainly operates in the north and north-east India. Jammu and Kashmir is the main processing centre of fur products and the big cities and hill stations of this country are the major domestic market. Both, raw fur and the processed products, are smuggled out of India to various destinations of Asia, as well as in east European countries (Menon and Kumar, 1998).

J. Other Trade Items

- Antlers — Chital, sambar, swamp deer, barking deer and hog deer
- Swiftlet nests — Edible nest swiftlets (*Collocalia fuciphaga* and *Collocalia unicolor*)
- Frog legs — Frogs belonging to Family Ranidae (*Rana* spp.)
- Ornamental Fishes — Guppies (Poecilidae), mollies (Cyprinodontidae), sword tails (*Xiphophorus* spp.), tetras (*Hyphessobrychon* spp.), Asian boney tongue (*Sclerophagusformosus*)
- Corals — Stony corals (mostly *Fungia*, *Acropora*, *Pocillopora*, *Porites*), blue corals (*Heliopora*), fire corals (*Millepora*), gorgonian corals (*Gorgonacea*) and black corals (*Antipathacea*).
- Lepidopterans — Mostly butterflies of the swallow-tail family.
- Spiders — Tarantulas and many other poisonous and brightly coloured spiders.
- Shells — Turban shell (*Turbo* spp.) and top shell (*Trochus* spp.)
- Medicinal and Ornamental Plants like ladies slipper orchids (*Paphiopedilium* spp.). Out of 2500 species of medicinal plants in India, at least 2000 species are used in traditional medicines.
- Timber — 41 species of tropical trees are endangered due to timber trade.

12.1.5 Underlying Causes of Illegal Wildlife Trade

Numerous factors explain the persistence and suspected rise in illegal wildlife trade throughout the globe. Some of the factors responsible for poaching and illegal trade in India are summarized in Figure 12.5.

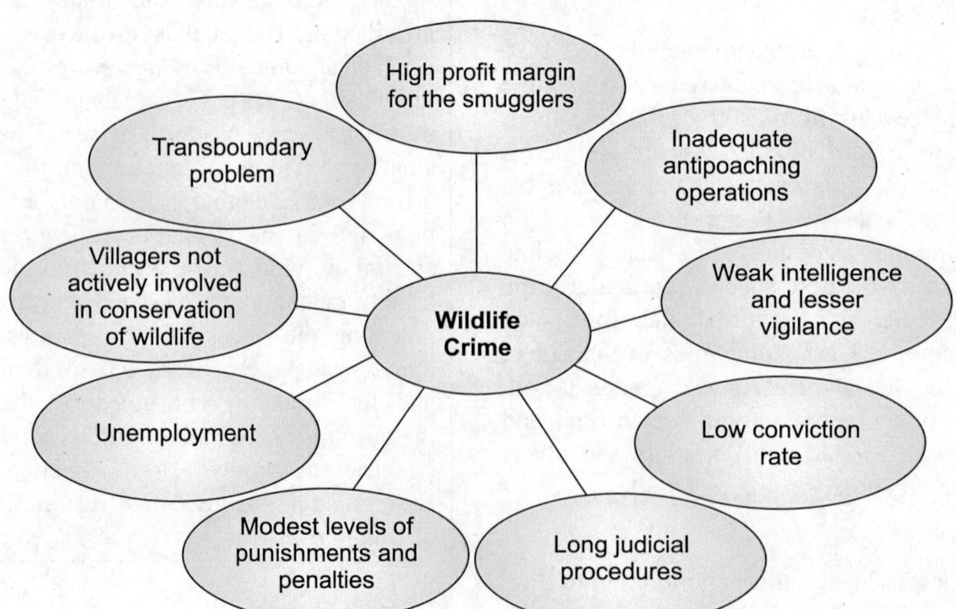

FIGURE 12.5 Summary on factors responsible for poaching and illegal trade.

A. Hunting as a Source of Livelihood and Traditional culture

Small-scale hunters and traders, particularly in the developing countries, often have little alternatives to generate subsistence-level incomes. On the other hand, hunting certain animals is a fundamental part of the culture, religion or traditions of some indigenous and tribal communities. Wildlife criminals often employ these poor traditional hunters in lieu of meager money to procure the wildlife trophy for them. As a result, often these people are caught red handed by the concern authorities while the 'kingpin' stays safe and continues with the notorious crime. Therefore, these poor and traditional hunters need to be considered differently and properly interogated to catch the international wildlife criminals who engage them in this trade purely for profit.

B. Unemployment and Poverty

In addition to the indigenous and tribal hunting communities, unemployed and poor people of the forest fringe villages are also engaged by the wildlife smugglers for poaching and illegal trafficking of wildlife articles.

C. High Demand and Profit Associated with Wildlife Trafficking

Demand for wildlife articles often exceeds what the market can legally supply. As a result, the prices of illegal wildlife products become very high. There are many potential buyers who are willing to pay even this higher amount. As certain wildlife species become more endangered and rare, its price increases in the gray markets even more. So there is always very high profit associated with illegal wildlife trade and trafficking which give more financial benefit to the smugglers. Hence, the mafias operating from the cities are the driving force behind poaching and most of the wildlife derivatives are smuggled outside India.

D. Inadequacy in Capacity Building and Anti-poaching Operations

Measures to curb the menace of poaching are practically non-existent in the non-protected areas, which are also vital from the species and habitat conservation perspective. Many foresters, particularly at the level of Range Officers and below, are not properly equipped and often not adequately trained of the legal provisions. This lack of knowledge of the provisions of pertinent laws (*viz.* WPA, CrPC, IPC etc.) among the frontline forest staffs is a major lacuna in booking the convict. Therefore, offenders often get released on bail from the court and roams free if the appropriate sections of pertinent laws are not properly mentioned in the charge sheet.

E. Weak Intelligence and Lesser Vigilance

Intelligence gathering and continuous vigil is critical to control any crime, as also for illegal wildlife trade. Development and maintenance of informer network to generate information on poaching and other wildlife crime has not always been given due importance. Therefore, proper and timely information on the trade is not available in many parts of the country. In addition, intensive patrolling in sensitive areas is often not possible due to shortage of staff.

F. Low Conviction Rate and Modest Levels of Punishments and Penalties

Risk of conviction or penalties related to wildlife crime is substantially less as compared to other trafficking crimes. As for example, punishment is much higher for similar crime involving human (homicide and human trafficking), as these kind of crime are considered to be more odious than wildlife crimes. Officials regulating the national and trans-boundary trade, often are either unaware of the list of wildlife articles prohibited in trade or fail to properly identify the contraband wildlife articles. Apart from the dearth of adequate resources, infrastructure, expertise, lack of awareness and strong political will are the major reasons behind this limited enforcement capabilities and low conviction rate in cases related to wildlife crime. Due to lesser vigilance, long judicial procedures, low conviction rate, modest levels of punishments and penalties often encourage the organized international criminals to indulge in heinous wildlife crimes for 'high profit at low risks'.

G. Long Judicial Procedures

Judicial process is very lengthy in many of the wildlife cases and most often the convicts roam free due to bail granted by the court.

H. Villagers not Actively Involved in Conservation of Wildlife

In the past, the forest fringe villagers and tribal people were not consulted prior to any policy implementation that might affect their livelihood. People of the villages present inside the protected areas were often forcefully thrown out of their homes in the name of 'relocation'. The importance of these people in wildlife conservation was never realized until recent past. As a consequence, they were alienated from the conservation movements. Although some initiatives have been taken recently to include these people in wildlife conservation, yet the efforts are not adequate, at least, to stop wildlife trade.

I. Trans-boundary Problems

India shares long international terrestrial boundary with various countries like Nepal, Bhutan, China, Bangladesh and Pakistan and some of which are destinations of various illegal wildlife articles. Therefore, species inhabiting in the wilderness areas adjoining these international borders are more vulnerable. Criminals often trespass the international border, commit poaching in the areas adjoining borders and go back to their native country making the combat efforts by the local authorities very much difficult.

12.1.6 Illegal Wildlife Trade—*Modus Operandi*

In common perception, a poacher is a man with gun who shoots animals. But, this may not always necessarily be true. Actually poaching takes place in various ways. A poacher may also be a humble looking local person who silently kill animals by setting up poisoned baits (poisoned carcasses), laying down snares and traps on the trails used by animals. Similar to any other crime, illegal wildlife trade also functions grossly involving a network of criminals operating at different levels (Figure 12.6).

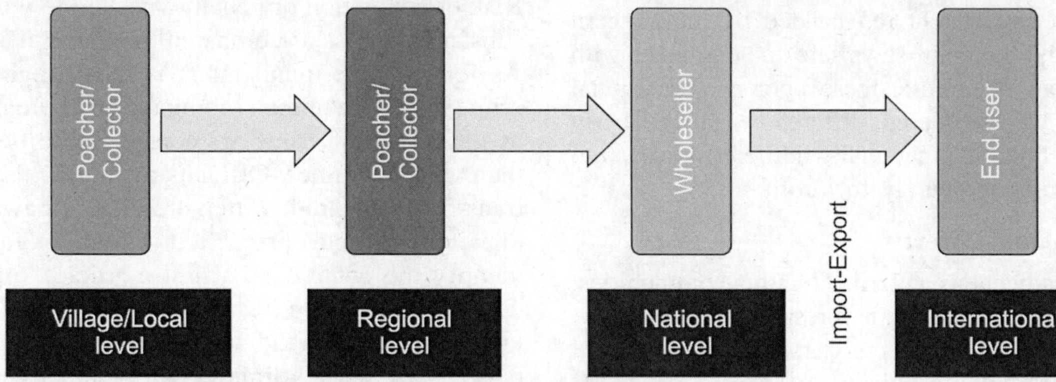

FIGURE 12.6 Different operational levels of wildlife crime.

Some village level hunters often kill and trade wildlife parts for subsistence cash income. Few others carry the illegal article from one place to another within the country or even across the borders and such transport of the contraband are at times facilitated by some corrupt officials. Criminal organizations involved in illegal wildlife trade are sometimes found to be involved in other organized crimes like drug, ammunitions and human trafficking, terrorism etc. and operate more often in states with political instability and weak enforcement. Finally the consumers willing to pay for such contrabands are the ultimate criminals. Therefore, the criminal may range from a poor villager to a wealthy international smuggler and the last one often gets away at the expense of the former.

12.1.7 Smuggling of Wildlife Products

Menon and Kumar (1998) elaborated the following ways by which the wildlife products are often smuggled within and out of the country.

(i) Concealment: The contraband article has traditionally been smuggled concealed within secret compartments within luggage or hidden between large numbers of legal items.

(ii) Misdeclaration of Species and Numbers Being Traded:

- **Misdeclaring species:** Species prohibited to be traded are falsely labeled as legal species. For example, peafowl chicks are often labeled as domestic hen chicks.
- **Misdeclaring numbers:** Larger than permitted number of individual of a particular species are often traded by declaring wrong numbers on papers.

(iii) Forged Permits and False Claims: Traders often claim that the wildlife article is captive-bred, cultivated or non-protected species and even produce 'Legal Procurement Certificate' (LPC) and trade permits. The LPC, trade permits or customs forms are often stolen or forged. Such forgery of permits is difficult to be detected as the officials may not always be familiar the LPCs of all exporting countries.

(iv) Manipulating Legal Stocks and Re-export: Some wildlife products, like fur, are legally traded in Jammu and Kashmir. The wildlife criminals used this opportunity to legalize their illegitimate stock. Illegally procured fur by killing animals from other states of India were also found to be smuggled to Jammu and Kashmir where it is mixed with the legal stock, thus, gets legalized. Similarly, in the past, when ivory, reptile skin etc were allowed to be imported to India for crafting, then items of Indian origin were also added to the stock while re-exporting. This was very difficult to regulate as the amount of wastage during crafting could not be measured and hence, the amount of laundering of indigenous articles could also not be quantified.

(v) Using Safe Countries: In some countries wildlife trade is legal and therefore, many wildlife articles from their countries of origin are smuggled to those countries from where these articles re-emerge as legal stocks. Dubai was one such 'safe countries' for illegal wildlife trade.

(vi) Other Methods: In the past, rhino horns, ivory, tiger parts, *shahtoosh* shawls and many other banned wildlife articles has been found to be smuggled involving the diplomats as they are rarely checked at borders and check posts due to their diplomatic immunity. Another very common technique adopted by the wildlife traders is transfer of wildlife items like reptile skins, furs, bristles and hairs, shahtoosh, feather and sometimes even ivory and musk pods using mail and courier services (Menon and Kumar, 1998). It has also been noticed that certain websites are presently being used for online sale of some illicit items.

12.1.8 Measures against Illegal Trade

India has a long history of conservation which is a part of our tradition and ethics. Most of the wild flora and fauna of this country are, at present, protected by law. Government of India has set up various agencies, policies and made its laws quite unambiguously. A large number of agencies are involved, directly or indirectly, to curb wildlife crime. Apart from Ministry of Environment and Forests at Central Government level and several forest and wildlife departments at the state level, local Police, Army, Indo-Tibetan Border Police, Border Security Force and Coastguards may act as '***Anti-Poaching Agencies***'. Similarly, '***Anti-Smuggling Agencies***' include Wildlife Preservation Department (Govt. of India), Customs, Railway Protection Force (RPF), Central Bureau of Investigations (CBI) along with their Interpol unit, as well as, Police, Border Security Force and Indo-Tibetan Border Police. The technical support and guidance to all these anti-poaching and anti-smuggling agencies are to be provided by the Wildlife Institute of India (WII), central and regional forensic laboratories, Zoological Survey of India (ZSI), Botanical Survey of India (BSI), Honorary Wildlife Wardens and several NGOs working for wildlife conservation.

India has also been one of the earliest members of the Convention on International Trade in Endangered Species of Wild Fauna and Flora (CITES) since 1973. Along with the Wildlife (Protection) Act 1972, the wildlife criminals may also be punished under provisions specified in other legislations *viz.* The Indian Penal Code 1860, The Arms Act 1959, The Prevention of Cruelty to Animals Act 1960, Customs Act 1962, The Code of Criminal Procedure 1974, Foreign Trade (Development and Regulation) Act 1992, The Biological Diversity Act 2002 etc.

Despite the presence of various such agencies, laws and policies, poaching and illegal trade in wildlife continue to flourish in recent times setting aside the inherent conservation ethos. Therefore, a number of recommendations to control poaching and unlawful trade of wildlife have been mentioned in the report of the Committee on Prevention of Illegal Trade in Wildlife and Wildlife Products (MoEF, 1994). Some of the important measures to curb wildlife crime are appended below.

- ❒ An anti-poaching strategy as a part of the existing working plan has to be in place.
- ❒ Policies on wildlife trade need to be in absolute harmony at international, national and regional levels.
- ❒ Controlling of wildlife crime must be given similar priority as has been accorded in curbing other heinous crimes.
- ❒ To identify properly the illegal wildlife articles, as well as, to effectively distinguish the fakes from the originals, capacity-building in molecular techniques like DNA Bar coding facilities, development of database and documentation might be very useful.
- ❒ Regular patrolling by sufficient number of forest guards with adequate arms and ammunitions, communication devices, vehicles and a very active informer network, particularly in the source and transit points of the established trade routes is essential to combat wildlife crime.
- ❒ The personnel engaged in combating wildlife crime should be trained and empowered to act in this field. Training should involve arms handling, ambush and counter-ambush, undercover operations, identification of species, interrogation and litigation.
- ❒ Local people should be involved through frequent village-level meeting and setting up of village-patrols, particularly in forest-fringe areas in order to promote mass awareness and activism.
- ❒ Proper sensitization of authorities like police, panchayat etc. about the importance and threat of wildlife, as well as, the means to curb wildlife crime is very essential.
- ❒ Packages and parcels should be scanned properly in the postal departments.
- ❒ Employing sniffer dogs to detect wildlife products at various transit points is another very efficient technique to detect illegal wildlife trafficking.
- ❒ Working in close association with the international, national and regional NGOs and having collaboration with regional and national media help in many ways.

Wildlife crime is no different from many other crimes like narcotics, arms and ammunitions, trafficking of humans etc. and any country must get rid of illegal wildlife trade as these criminals are a part of general crime syndicate.

REVIEW QUESTIONS

1. "Illegal Trade of wildlife—a major threat to wildlife management"—elaborate.
2. What are the major articles in wildlife trade? Identify the underlying causes behind illegal wildlife trade.
3. Suggest measures against illegal trade.

REFRENCES

Arivazhagan, C., Population dynamics of Asian Elephant (*Elephas maximus*) in Southern India. [PhD thesis] Bharathidasan University, Trichy, 2005.

Arivazhagan, C. and Ramakrishnan, B. Conservation perspective of Asian Elephants (*Elephas maximus*) in Tamil Nadu, Southern India. *IJBT* 1 (Special Issue): 15–22, 2010.

Brack, D., Combatting international environmental crime. In: White, R.D. (Ed.), *Environmental Crime: A Reader*, pp. 485–492, Willan Publishing, Cullompton, UK, 2009.

Fitzerland, S., *International Wildlife Trade: Whose Business is it?* World Wildlife Fund, Washington DC, 1989.

Mathur, V.B., Sinha, P.R. and Mishra, M., *UNESCO EoH Project_South Asia Technical Report-Kaziranga National Park*, UNESCO, 2006. Retrieved from: http://www.enhancingheritage.net/docs/UNESCOEoH_Project_South_Asia_Technical_Report_04_v1.pdf

Menon, V. and Kumar, A., *Wildlife Crime: An Enforcement Guide*, WPSI and Nataraj Publishers, Dehra Dun, 1998.

Menon, V., *Tusker: The Story of the Asian Elephant*, Penguin India, New Delhi, 2002.

Menon ,V., Sukumar, R. and Kumar, A., *A God in Distress: Threats of Poaching and the Ivory Trade to the Asian Elephant in India*, Wildlife Protection Society of India, New Delhi, India, 1997.

MoEF, *Report of the Committee on Prevention of Illegal Trade in Wildlife and Wildlife Products*, MoEF, New Delhi, 1994

Mills, J. and Servheen, C., *The Asian Trade in Bears and Bear Parts*, WWF, Washington, D.C., 1991.

Sukumar, R., *The Asian Elephant: Ecology and Management*, Cambridge University Press, Cambridge, 1989.

Sukumar, R., Ramakrishnan, U. and Santosh, J.A., Impact of poaching on an Asian elephant population in Periyar, southern India: a model of demography and tusk harvest, *Animal Conservation*, 1: 281–291, 1998.

Wheeler, M., *The Role the Tiger Plays in Local Economies: Sariska—a Case Study*. TRAFFIC, WWF-India, 2009.

Wyler, L.S. and Sheikh, P.A., *International Illegal Trade in Wildlife: Threats and U.S. Policy*, United States Congressional Research Service Report, Washington, DC, 2008.

13

WILDLIFE LEGISLATION: ADMINISTRATIVE MEASURES AND LAWS

13.1 HISTORICAL BACKGROUND OF WILDLIFE LEGISLATION

Conservation is an ardent article of faith in India. One of the earliest conservation acts was passed by Emperor Ashoka in the 3rd century B.C. Since independence, India has taken significant steps to conserve wildlife and its habitat through several administrative measures such as establishment of legislation, notifying protected areas and undertaking special conservation projects to protect the threatened wildlife of India. The ethos of conservation are also reflected in the Constitution of India. Besides, several laws have been implemented to conserve various flora and fauna of this country. The Indian Board for Wildlife was constituted in 1952 to advise the Government on measures to be adopted for the conservation of wilderness areas along with various life and resources found there. The contributions of the Indian Board for Wildlife in this regard have been widely admired and respected. Wildlife (Protection) Act was passed in 1972 followed by Forest Protection Act in 1980. The Wildlife (Protection) Act, 1972, is a comprehensive central legislation affording legal measures for the protection of the wild animals. It not only provided countrywide legal protection to the endangered animals but also specified the provisions for setting up protected areas, as well as, regulation of trade and commerce in wild animals, animal parts, products and trophies.

The country adopted National Wildlife Action Plan in 2002 to meet the new challenges in wildlife conservation. The National Board for Wildlife was constituted in September 2003 as a statutory authority, with full strength of law of the land behind it and is now entrusted with the responsibility for providing thrust to conservation activities. Over the years, 103 national parks, 536 wildlife sanctuaries, 67 conservation reserves and 26 community reserves have been created in India in order to protect critical ecosystems, as well as, to preserve the genetic resources of unquantifiable commercial and non-commercial values.

The concept of setting up of biosphere reserves evolved under the Man and Biosphere (MAB) programme of UNESCO. Biosphere reserves are notified for conserving the biological diversity of a representative ecosystem including flora, fauna and micro-organisms. These biosphere reserves provide facilities for education and awareness generation along with the scope of ecological research.

In addition to the notification of various Protected Areas, several 'conservation projects' have been taken up for several endangered species to restore their population and bring them back from the verge of extinction. Apex predators, as well as, several keystone and umbrella species were selected for such 'conservation projects'. Because, these species are often on the top of the food web or have a large home range, so it implies that to protect the selected target species their entire habitat needs to be conserved. Thus, in the name of conserving a single species actually an entire ecosystem is protected and many other species those which are an integral part of that ecosystem are also benefitted. Gir Lion Sanctuary Project (1972), Project Tiger (1973), Himalayan Musk Deer Ecology and Conservation Project (1974), Manipur Brow-antlered Deer Project (1977),

Project Hangul (1970), Crocodile Breeding Project (1975), Operation Rhino (1992), Project Elephant (1971) are few success stories of the conservation projects in India.

Apart from protecting the flora and fauna of our country through national legislation, India has played a significant role in the global scenario of wildlife conservation through international lobbying. India is a signatory to the Convention on International Trade in Endangered Species of Wild Fauna and Flora (CITES).

13.2 LEGAL PERSPECTIVES OF WILDLIFE CONSERVATION

The need of nature and wildlife conservation has been incorporated in the Indian constitution. In addition to that, several national legislative measures have been adopted for the protection of wildlife in the country.

13.2.1 Indian Constitution

Directive Principles and State Policy

Article 48–A of Directive Principles of State Policy pronounces that *"The state shall endeavour to protect and improve the environment and to safeguard the forests and wildlife of the country"*.

Fundamental Duty of the Citizens of India

Article 51–A interalia states that: *"It shall be the duty of every citizen of India to protect and improve the natural environment including forests, lakes, rivers and wildlife and to have passion for living creatures."*

The 42nd Amendment of constitution in 1976 has incorporated forest and wildlife in the concurrent list, which means above and beyond controlling the protection and preservation of wildlife, Central Government can acquire certain forests and wildlife sanctuaries of national importance under the powers of acquisition of property [Entry 42 of Union list]. The 73rd Amendment of constitution in 1992 has, to some extent, linked the panchayats to environment protection and conservation.

13.2.2 National Acts Related to Wildlife Conservation

The state and central authorities have made several acts from time to time to protect wildlife and check their decline. Some important acts are:

1. Madras Wild Elephant Preservation Act, 1873
2. All India Elephant Preservation Act, 1879
3. Wild Birds and Animals Preservation Act, 1912
4. Bengal Rhinoceros Preservation Act, 1932
5. Bombay Wild Animals and Wild Birds Protection Act, 1951
6. Assam Rhinoceros Protection Act, 1954
7. Indian Wildlife (Protection) Act, 1972
8. Forest Protection Act, 1980
9. The Biological Diversity Act, 2002

13.3 DECLARATION OF NATIONAL / STATE ANIMALS AND PLANTS

An alternative and effective way of conserving indigenous wildlife is to assign them a status quo. Accordingly, the Government of India has declared tiger (*Panthera tigris*) as national animal, Indian peafowl (*Pavo christatus*) as national bird, banyan (*Ficus benghalensis*) as national tree, Lotus (*Nelumbo nucifera*) as national flower and mango (*Mangifera indica*) as national fruit of India. Similarly, each state has declared one each of mammal, bird, tree and flower as their state mammal, state bird, state tree and state flower respectively (Table 13.1). This, in turn, ensures protection of those species within the state. It is the responsibility of the state to take up necessary legislative procedures to declare them, to ensure their conservation and to take necessary steps to increase their population size, especially in the relevant conservation areas within the state.

Table 13.1 List of State Mammals, Birds, Trees and Flowers of Different States of India (Source: Sinha, 2001; Venkataraman et al., 2012)

State/Union Territories	*Mammal*	*Bird*	*Tree*	*Flower*
Andhra Pradesh	Blackbuck *Antilope cervicapra*	Indian roller *Coracias benghalensis*	Neem	*
Arunachal Pradesh	Hoolock gibbon *Bunopithecus hoolock hoolock*	Great Indian hornbill *Buceros bicornis*	Hollong	Lady slipper orchid
Assam	Indian one-horned rhinoceros *Rhinoceros unicornis*	White winged wood duck *Asarc, ornis, scutulata*		

(*Contd...*)

Table 13.1 List of State Mammals, Birds, Trees and Flowers of Different States of India (Source: Sinha, 2001; Venkataraman et al., 2012) (*Contd...*)

State/Union Territories	*Mammal*	*Bird*	*Tree*	*Flower*
Bihar	Gaur *Bos frontalis*	Parakeets	Peepal	Kachnar
Chhattisgarh	Wild buffalo *Bubalus bubalis*	Hill myna *Gracula religiosa*	*	*
Goa	Gaur *Bos frontalis* Lambert 1804	Ruby throated yellow bulbul *Brachypus gularis*	Asna	*
Gujarat	Asiatic lion *Panthera leo persica*	Greater flamingo *Phoenicopterus rubber*	*	*
Haryana	Blackbuck *Antilope cervicapra*	Black francolin *Francolinus francolinus*	Peepal	Lotus
Himachal Pradesh	Snow leopard *Uncia uncia*	Western tragopan *Tragopan melanocephalus*	Deodar	Rhododendron
Jammu & Kashmir	Hangul *Cervus elaphus hanglu*	Black-necked crane *Grus nigricollis*	Chinar	Lotus
Jharkhand	Indian elephant *Elephas maximus*	Asian koel *Eudynamys scolopacea*	Sal	Palash
Karnataka	Spotted deer *Axix axix*	Asian koel *Eudynamys scolopacea*	Sandal	Lotus
Kerala	Indian elephant *Elephas maximus*	Great Indian hornbill *Buceros bicornis*	Coconut	Kanikonna
Madhya Pradesh	Swamp deer *Cervus duvaucelii*	Paradise fly catcher *Terpsiphone paradise*	*	*
Maharashtra	Indian giant squirrel *Rattufa indica*	Green imperial pigeon *Ducula aenea*	Mango	Jarul
Manipur	Manipur brow-antlered deer *Cervus eldi eldi*	Mrs. Hume's pheasant *Syrmaticus humiae*	Toon	Shirhoy lilly
Meghalaya	Clouded leopard *Neofelis nebulosa*	Hill myna *Gracula religiosa*	Gamari	Lady slipper orchid
Mizoram	Serow *Naemorhedus sumatraensis*	Mrs. Hume's pheasant *Syrmaticus humiae*	Iron wood	Red wanda
Nagaland	Binturong *Arctictis binturong*	Blyth's tragopan *Tragopan blythii*	Alder	Rhododendron
Orissa	Sambar *Cervus unicolor*	Indian roller *Coracias benghalensis*	Banyan	Lotus
Punjab	Blackbuck *Antilope cervicapra*	Eastern goshawk *Astrus gentilis gentilis*	Sheesham	*
Rajasthan	Chinkara *Gazella bennettii*	Great Indian bustard *Ardeotis nigriceps*	Khejri	Rohira
Sikkim	Red panda *Ailurus fulgens*	Blood pheasantis *Ithaginis cruentus affinis*	Rhododendron	Nobile orchid
Tamil Nadu	Nilgiri tahr *Nilgiritragus hylocrius*	Emerald dove *Chalcophaps indica*	Palmera palm	Kandhal
Tripura	Phayre's leaf monkey *Trachypithecus phayrei*	Green imperial pigeon *Ducula aenea*	Agar	Nageshwar

(*Contd...*)

Table 13.1 List of State Mammals, Birds, Trees and Flowers of Different States of India (Source: Sinha, 2001; Venkataraman et al., 2012) (*Contd...*)

State/Union territories	*Mammal*	*Bird*	*Tree*	*Flower*
Uttarakhand	Himalayan musk deer *Moschus chrysogaster*	Himalayan monal *Lophophorus impejanus*	Burans	Brahm kamal
Uttar Pradesh	Swamp deer *Rucervus duvaucelii*	Sarus crane *Grus antigone*	Ashok	Brahm kamal
West Bengal	Fishing cat *Prionailurus viverrinus*	White-throated kingfisher *Halcyon smyrnensis*	Chatian	Shephali
Andaman and Nicobar Islands	Dugong *Dugong dugong*	Andaman wood pigeon *Carpophaga palumboides*		
Chandigarh	*	*		
Dadra and Nagar Haveli	Striped hyna *Hyaena hyaena*	Lesser golden-backed woodpecker *Dinopium benghalensis*		
Daman and Diu	*	*		
Lakshadweep	Butterfly fish	Sooty tern *Sterna fuscata nubilosa*	Bread fruit	*
National Capital Territory of Delhi (NCT)	Blue bull *Boselaphus tragocamelus*	Shaheen falcon *Falco peregrinus peregrinator*		
Puducherry	Indian palm squirrel *Funambulus palmarum*	Asian koel *Eudynamys scolopacea*		
***** To be declared***				

13.4 BRIEF ACCOUNT ON IMPORTANT ACTS RELATED TO WILDLIFE CONSERVATION

A. Indian Wildlife (Protection) Act, 1972

It is an "*Act to provide for the protection of wild animals, birds and plants and for matters connected therewith or ancillary or incidental thereto with a view to ensuring the ecological and environmental security of country*".

This Act:

- is applicable all over India, except Jammu and Kashmir which has its own Act for conservation of wildlife
- prohibits hunting of any wild animals listed in its schedules except mice, rats, common crow and fruit bats
- sets down the rules for setting up any protected area and the regulations to be observed inside the protected areas
- clearly defines the punishments and penalties against committing crimes related to wildlife and violating several provisions of the Act

Genesis: There was a growing concern worldwide to conserve our wildlife wealth, specially on the plight of endangered species of plants and animals. During early seventies policy makers realized that the survival of wild life and its habitat would be jeopardized unless a uniform, well-structured law is enacted across the country.

Despite extinction being a natural phenomenon and inevitable outcome of evolution, it is also true that the rate of extinction becomes rapid due to human activities and different sorts of interferences such as habitat loss and degradation, over exploitation of natural resources, as well as, uncontrolled trade of wild animals and their body parts. To overcome all these problems and to provide legal protection to our wild heritage, a revolutionary attempt was initiated with the introduction of Wildlife (Protection) Act in the year 1972. Based on the recommendations of the Indian Board of Wildlife (IBWL), the Act was passed by the parliament in 1972 to provide legal protection to wildlife in general and threatened species in particular.

The Act consists of seven distinct chapters:

Chapter I: Preliminary (include short title, extent, commencement and definitions)

Chapter II: Authorities to be appointed or constituted under the Act

Chapter III: Hunting of wild animals

Chapter IIIA: Protection of specified plants

Chapter IV: Protected areas (including sanctuaries, national park, and closed areas)

Chapter IVA: Central Zoo Authority and recognition of Zoos

Chapter IVB: National Tiger Conservation Authority (new chapter incorporated in Wildlife (Protection) Amendment Act, 2006)

Chapter IVC: Tiger and Other Endangered Species Crime Control Bureau (new chapter incorporated in Wildlife (Protection) Amendment Act, 2006)

Chapter V: Trade or commerce in wild animals, animal articles and trophies

Chapter VA: Prohibition of trade or commerce in trophies, animal articles, etc. derived from certain animals

Chapter VI: Prevention and detection of offences

Chapter VIA: Forfeiture of property derived from illegal hunting and trade (new chapter incorporated in wildlife (protection) amendment act, 2002).

Chapter VII: Miscellaneous

As per demand of the time initially the Act allowed hunting permits to some extent and permitted regulated trade of certain wildlife article like ivory, far, skin and other derivatives. However, under legal coverage traders misused this provision and acquired fresh stocks by financing poachers. Subsequently, two amendments to the Act were made in 1986 and 1991 to overcome such loopholes and to make it strong enough to deter wildlife crime. These amendments incorporated new provisions including instructions related to zoo management, protection of plants and prohibition of trade in animal articles. The 1986 amendment was challenged by wild life traders in Delhi high court and initially they were successful in obtaining a stay order. Though the 1986 amendment imposed a ban on trade in Asian ivory, it was not challenged by ivory traders as they were not affected because they declared all their stock to be made from imported African ivory. Later, in the year 1989, international trade in African ivory was banned by CITES and being a signatory to CITES, India also imposed ban on export/ import of African ivory and carvings. Subsequently, the 1991 amendment imposed a ban on trade in imported ivory too. The traders immediately went to the Delhi high court and obtained stay order. In 1992, the stay order was vacated through untiring efforts of Government and other NGOs and the amendment finally came into force.

Later, a major breakthrough occurred by an amendment in the year 2002 to minimize anomalies and to make it more meaningful. The Wildlife Protection (Amendment) Act, 2002 came operational from 1st April 2003. This is a comprehensive revision of the initial Act through significant shift in attitudes and approaches to make it more acceptable to the common people. Such revisions were based on sets of recommendations suggested by 'expert committee' after analyzing the ground realities. New concepts of protected areas in the form of "Conservation Reserves" and "Community of Protected Areas Reserves" have been put forward to involve local people in conservation efforts. On one hand, this Act in its new form accommodates the concern of local people for enjoying benefits within ecologically sustainable limits from the natural resource on their door steps. On the other hand, it also incorporates stringent measures to conserve our rich wild heritage towards desirable goals. In fact, it is a revised regulatory mechanism that is not anti-people in nature, rather a need-based intervention to restore national and social interest. Wild animals are enlisted in five different 'Schedules' specified in the WPA (Text Box 13.1) and are provided with stringent protection under legislation, strict control measures are imposed to safeguard these scheduled species and the hunting is altogether banned.

Text Box 13.1 Schedules of Wildlife (Protection) Act, 1972

Schedule I: Includes rare and threatened animals
Schedule II: Includes animals that enjoy special game status
Schedule III: Includes big games (wild animals)
Schedule IV: Includes small games (wild animals)
Schedule V: Includes vermins (wild animals)

Unique features of Indian Wildlife (Protection) Act

- **Section 9** of the act prohibits hunting of any wild animals specified in Schedule I, II, III and IV. There are also stricter provisions and procedures to deal with the stocks of wildlife articles held by the dealers, transportation of wildlife and deterrent punishment to the poachers.
- Suggests the constitution of National Board for Wildlife (statutory authority) instead of Indian Board for Wildlife (advisory body). Similarly, State Wildlife Advisory Boards became converted into State Board of Wildlife.
- Empowers individuals and NGOs to file wildlife court cases.
- Suggest changes in the constitution of "Protected Areas" under **Section 18**, presently treated as "Deemed Protected Areas".
- As per **Section 26A** subsection 3, "no alteration of the boundaries of a sanctuary shall be made by the state Government except on the recommendation of the national board. Similar changes in case of national parks under **Section 35** have been recommended.
- According to **Section 33**, no construction of commercial tourist lodges, zoos and safari parks shall be undertaken inside the sanctuary except prior approval of the national board. This is very

crucial to check uncontrolled growth of structures inside the sanctuary.

- **Section 35** clause 6 states that no person shall destroy, exploit or remove any wild animal or deprive any wild animal of its habitat within such national parks except under and in accordance with permit granted by the Chief Wildlife Warden. No such permit shall be granted unless the state Government, being satisfied that such destruction, exploitation or removal of wildlife from the national park is necessary for the improvement and better management of wildlife therein.
- **Section 36A** introduces the concept of establishment of "Conservation Reserves" on Government owned land only in consultation with local communities which will enable creation of corridors and give protection to habitats adjoining sanctuary and national parks.
- **Section 36C** introduces the concept of formation of "Community Reserves" on private or community owned lands in collaboration with local communities, including village Panchayat, to provide protection to many species located outside National Park and Sanctuary.
- **Section 38** depicts the functions of Central Zoo Authority and provides recognition of zoos.
- According to **Section 39**, wild animals are Government property and no person shall acquire, keep, transfer, damage or destroy them without prior written permission from the Chief Wildlife Warden.
- As stated in **Section 40A**, the Act will enable Central Government to give another opportunity to such persons who has not yet declared wild animals and articles in their possession, to declare such items and to register them and procure ownership certificates against the declared items from concerned authorities.
- **Section 44** prohibits dealing in animal articles and trophy without proper license.
- **Section 48A** imposes a restriction on the transportation of wildlife.
- **Section 51** depicts the penalties which are detailed below:
  - Any person who contravenes any provisions of this Act (or any rule or order made thereunder) or who commits a breach of any of the conditions of any license or permit granted under this Act, shall be guilty of an offence against this Act.
  - On conviction, the offenders will be punishable with imprisonment for a term which may extend to three years or with fine which may extend to twenty five thousand rupees or with both.
  - If the offence committed is in relation to any animal specified in Schedule I or Part II of Schedule II, or meat of any such animal, animal article, trophy or uncurled trophy derived from such animal or where offence relates to hunting in or altering the boundaries of a sanctuary or a national park, such offence shall be punishable with imprisonment for a term which shall not be less than one year but may extend to six years and also with fine which shall not be less than five thousand rupees.
  - In the case of a second or subsequent offence of the nature mentioned in this sub-section, the term or imprisonment may extend to six years and shall not be less than two years and the amount of fine shall not be less than ten thousand rupees.
- **Section 60A** lays down a system of rewards to persons who render assistance in the detection of wildlife offences.
- According to **Section 61**, the Central Government may add or delete any entry to or from any Schedule or transfer any entry from one Part of a Schedule to another Part of the same Schedule or from one Schedule to another by notification, if it is of opinion that such changes are useful and necessary. On the issue of a notification, the relevant Schedule shall be deemed to be altered accordingly, provided that every such alteration shall be without prejudice to anything done or omitted to be done before such alteration.
- According to **Section 62**, the Central Government may declare any wild animal (other than those specified in Schedule – I and Part II of Schedule – II) to be vermin for any area and for such period as may be specified by notification therein. So long as such notification is in force, such wild animal shall be deemed to have been included in Schedule V.

Limitations Despite of such a stringent act, proper and successful enforcement of the provisions of WPA is still a major challenge. Being plagued with illiteracy and poverty, even today many citizens of this country view animals as resources and should be used at will. Besides, India has been one of the leading suppliers of the most coveted wildlife products (like tiger parts, rhino horns, ivory, live birds and mammals etc.) in the past and is strategically placed between the consumer countries. Although, at present, hunting and trade in wildlife is ban in this country, still the demand exists and in many parts of this country wildlife is illegally killed and traded. Many people in this country are unaware of the existence of this Wildlife (Protection) Act and do not even know that trespassing, trade and trafficking of wildlife are criminal offences. Strange but true, that even some of the protectors of wildlife and custodians of law are not completely familiar with various provisions of this Act. Lastly a law by itself cannot control crime, rather it needs active participation.

B. Biological Diversity Act, 2002

India is a signatory to the Convention on Biological Diversity (CBD) since February 1994 and is one of the first few countries to have enacted an appropriate comprehensive legislation to achieve the objectives of the convention. As signatory to the CBD, India has met three positive obligations, *viz.*

(i) *Submission of a status report* – A report entitled "Status of Biodiversity in India" was prepared in 1997 and submitted in 1998;

(ii) *Submission of National Biodiversity Strategy and Action Plan (NBSAP)* – The report was prepared over a period of three years and submitted in October, 2002 and

(iii) *Enacting laws to protect biodiversity of the country* – The Biological Diversity Act, 2002, passed on December 11, 2002 came into force on February 5, 2003, followed by the formation of the Biological Diversity Rules, 2004.

The Biological Diversity Act, 2002 provides necessary statutory and administrative mechanism at the national level to implement the objectives of CBD. This Act aims to conserve biological diversity and associated traditional knowledge and wisdom. It also ensures sustainable use of the biodiversity components and fair and equitable sharing of the benefits arising out of the use of biological resources, knowledge and for matters connected therewith or incidental thereto. Another major intent of this legislation is to prevent biopiracy and to prohibit unethical use of various bio-resources of this country and their associated knowledge.

As per the provisions of the Biological Diversity Act, 2002, a three tier system has been implemented to conserve the biodiversity and traditional knowledge. **National Biodiversity Authority (NBA)** is the apex body constituted by the Government of India under which every state are to create the **State Biodiversity Board (SBB)**. The lowest and perhaps the most important tier is the **Biodiversity Management Committee (BMC)** formed at the local level, which is constituted with the actual custodians of biodiversity of that area. BMCs take initiative to prepare and publish the **Peoples' Biodiversity Registers (PBRs)** where biodiversity of that particular area, along with the associated traditional knowledge and practices are documented.

Text Box 13.2 Regulation of Access to Biological Diversity – At A Glance

1. Certain persons not to undertake Biodiversity related activities without approval of National Biodiversity Authority. (Section 3)
2. Results of research not to be transferred to certain persons without approval of National Biodiversity Authority except certain collaborative research projects. (Section 4). Certain person in the above two sections refers to
   (a) a person who is not a citizen of India;
   (b) a citizen of India, who is a non-resident as defined in clause (30) of section 2 of the Income Tax Act, 1961;
   (c) a body corporate, association or organization –
      (i) not incorporated or registered in India; or
      (ii) incorporated or registered in India under any law for the time being in force which has any non-Indian participation in its share capital or management.
3. Application for intellectual property rights not to be made without approval of National Biodiversity Authority. (Section 6)
4. Prior intimation to State Biodiversity Board for obtaining biological resource for certain purposes. (Section 7)

No person, who is a citizen of India or a body corporate, association or organization, which is registered in India, shall obtain any biological resource for the purpose of commercial utilization, or bio-survey and bio-utilization for commercial utilization except after giving prior intimation to the State Biodiversity Board concerned. However, the provisions of this section shall not apply to the local people and communities of the area, including growers and cultivators of biodiversity, and vaidyas and hakims, who have been practicing indigenous medicines.

13.5 IMPORTANT CONVENTION FOR WILDLIFE CONSERVATION

A. Convention on International Trade in Endangered Species of Wild Fauna and Flora (CITES)

The Convention on International Trade in Endangered Species of Wild Fauna and Flora (CITES) came into effect in the year 1975. As the name suggests, this convention aims to prevent and/or regulate international trade in different parts of endangered species. CITES is a major step towards wildlife conservation because it provides cooperation at the international level to curb trans-boundary illegal trade, which is presently considered to be the second biggest illegal trade after narcotics. India is a signatory to this convention.

This convention controls the trade of all the species listed in its 'Appendix'. There are three Appendices under CITES (Text Box 13.3). Appendix–I, II and III contains the lists of species which are provided with different levels or types of protection from over-exploitation.

Text Box 13.3 Appendices of CITES

Appendix–I contains species that are most endangered among the CITES-listed animals and plants, and are threatened with extinction. CITES generally prohibits commercial international trade of these species (or their body parts). However, trade may be allowed under exceptional circumstances (e.g. for scientific research), where such trade need to be authorized by the granting of both export permit (or re-export certificate) and import permit. (Article III of the Convention)

Appendix–II contains species that are not necessarily threatened with extinction at present, but may become so unless trade is strictly controlled. It also includes so-called "look-alike species", i.e. species which look like those of species listed under Appendix–I for conservation purpose (Article II, paragraph 2 of the Convention). International trades in Appendix–II species may be authorized by granting of an export permit or re-export certificate. No import permit is necessary for these species under CITES (It is to be noted that import permit may be required in some countries that have taken stricter measures than CITES requires). Permits or certificates for these Appendix–II species should only be granted if the relevant authorities are satisfied that certain conditions are met, above all that trade will not be detrimental to the survival of the species in the wild. (Article IV of the Convention)

Appendix–III is a list of species included as per the request of a Party that already regulates trade in the species and that needs the cooperation of other countries to prevent unsustainable or illegal exploitation (Article II, paragraph 3, of the Convention). International trade in species listed in Appendix III is allowed only on presentation of the appropriate permits or certificates (Article V of the Convention).

Source: http://www.cites.org/eng/app/index.shtml

The countries which are signatory to this convention are referred to as the 'Parties' and these parties cannot import or export the species that is listed under the CITES without proper licenses. Species may be added to or removed from Appendices–I and II, or moved between them, only by the Conference of the Parties (CoP), either in regular meetings or through postal procedures. But species may be added to or removed from Appendix–III at any time and by any Party unilaterally (although the Conference of the Parties has recommended that changes be timed to coincide with amendments to Appendices–I and II).

Implementation of CITES: In each country, there is specific administrative setup to implement the provisions of the Convention. In India, Inspector General of Forests and the Director of Wildlife Preservation, Government of India, have been designated as the management authorities of the CITES. The Director, Zoological Survey of India; the Director, Botanical Survey of India and the Director, Central Marine Research Institute are the authorities for the scientific and technical inputs. To regulate the international trade, four ports (*viz.* Mumbai, Delhi, Kolkata and Chennai) are controlled by the Wildlife Preservation Wing and is supervised by the Deputy Directors posted at these places for regulating the trade (*viz.* Deputy Director—Northern Region, Deputy Director—Southern Region, Deputy Director—Eastern Region and Deputy Director—Western Region).

B. Ramsar Convention on Wetland

The *Convention on Wetlands of International Importance* especially as waterfowl habitat (commonly known as the *Ramsar Convention or Wetlands Convention*) is an intergovernmental treaty that provides the framework for national action and international cooperation for the conservation and 'wise use of wetlands' and their resources. 'Wise use of wetlands' is defined as the conservation and sustainable use of wetlands and their resources, for the benefit of mankind. This international treaty for the conservation and sustainable utilization of wetlands was adopted in Ramsar, Iran on 2nd February 1971 and came into force in December 1975. 'Ramsar sites' are wetlands considered to be of international importance.

Mission of the Ramsar Convention: The *Ramsar Convention's* mission is to ensure the conservation and wise use of all wetlands through local and national actions and international cooperation, in order to contribute towards achieving sustainable development throughout the world.

All Parties of the Ramsar Convention commit themselves to work towards the "three pillars" of the Convention:

(i) designation of wetlands of international importance as Ramsar sites
(ii) promotion of the wise-use of all wetlands in the territory of each country
(iii) international co-operation with other countries to further ensure the wise-use of wetlands and their resources

There are currently 168 Contracting Parties to the Ramsar Convention and the member countries are present throughout the globe in all geographic regions. Upon joining, each Contracting Party is obliged to designate at least one wetland site for inclusion in the List of Wetlands of International Importance. Till December 2014, globally 2,186 wetlands have been designated as 'Ramsar Sites' covering more than 20,00,000 sq km area. In India, 26 sites have been designated as "Wetlands of International Importance" or Ramsar sites expanding over a total surface area of 12,119.03 sq km. The *Ramsar Convention* is the only global environmental treaty that deals with one particular ecosystem, i.e. wetlands.

13.6 GOVERNMENT ORGANIZATIONS, INSTITUTES IN CONSERVATION INITIATIVES

To protect the endangered flora and fauna of our country, the government, non-government organizations, different institutes and universities have initiated several special conservation projects. Most of these projects are either funded by the Ministry of Environment and Forests, several government departments or has been taken up by several non-governmental organizations. Few of these projects are funded by several foreign organizations and multinational corporates as well.

13.6.1 Present Administrative Set-up in the Centre and State

Scientific forest management in this country was introduced even before independence. The Imperial Forest Department was established by the British Raj in 1864. Dr. Dietrich Brandis, a German forest officer, was appointed as Inspector General of Forests in 1866. In 1867, the Imperial Forestry Service was set up.

After independence, the modern Indian Forest Service (IFS) was established in 1966 as per the *All India Services Act 1951*. The prime objectives of Indian Forest Service were protection and conservation of forests and wildlife resources, as well as, regeneration of forests of this country. The Ministry of Environment and Forests (MoEF) became the nodal agency in the administrative structure of the Central Government for planning, promotion, co-ordination and overseeing the implementation of India's environmental and forestry policies and programmes. These programmes and policies are implemented through the IFS cadres. In addition to being entrusted with senior positions in the Central Secretariat, State Secretariats and various assignments under Central Staffing Scheme, the IFS officers also work in various national organizations related to management of forests, wildlife and environment such as Forest Survey of India (FSI), Wildlife Institute of India (WII), Indian Council of Forestry Research and Education (ICFRE), Indira Gandhi National Forest Academy (IGNFA), Directorate of Forest Education, Wildlife Crime Control Bureau (WCCB), etc.

Moreover, forest and wildlife is in the 'concurrent list'. Therefore, protection of wildlife is the joint responsibility of the central and state Governments. Hence, each state of this country has also set up a department to conserve forest and wildlife and to successfully implement the policies and programmes of the MoEF.

Important decisions are taken by state Government through the minister of Forest and Environment. The management of this department is done by the Secretary, Forests and Environment (an officer of IAS cadre) in consultation with Principal Chief Conservator of Forests (PCCF). PCCF is the Head of Forest Force and also the administrative head of the State Forest Directorate. He is usually assisted by the Additional Principal Chief Conservator of Forests.

The administrative hierarchy of posts in the Forest Departments of the Central and State Governments is as follows in the descending order:

- Director General of Forests – highest post at Centre, selected from amongst the senior-most PCCFs of states.
- Principal Chief Conservator of Forests (PCCF) – highest post in a State
- Additional Principal Chief Conservator of Forests
- Chief Conservator of Forests (CCFs)
- Conservator of Forests (CF)
- Divisional Forest Officer/Deputy Conservator of Forests
- Assistant Conservator of Forests (Probationary Officer)
- Range Officer
- Beat Officer

However, this administrative set up varies in different states. State government has the discretion to alter this structure depending on the availability of the officials and to successfully implement various policies. For instance, a new post of Principal Chief Conservator of Forests (Wildlife and Biodiversity) along with a separate Wildlife Wing has been created in the state of West Bengal for better management of wildlife and biodiversity of the state. He is assisted by one Additional Principal Chief Conservator of Forests.

13.6.2 Leading Institutes for Wildlife Conservation

In addition to the Ministry of Environment and Forests, Government of India and state forest departments, many organizations and NGOs play instrumental role for the conservation of wildlife of this country. The list of such organizations is exhaustive and some important organizations are Forest Research Institute (FRI), Central Zoo Authority (CZA), Sálim Ali Centre for Ornithology and Natural History (SACON), Wildlife Crime Control Bureau (WCCB), National Tiger Conservation Authority (NTCA), Centre for Ecological Sciences (CES), The National Museum of Natural History (NMNH), The Centre for Environment Education (CEE), Wildlife Institute of India (WII), Zoological Survey of India (ZSI), Botanical Survey of India (BSI), etc. Amongst these institutions, WII (Text Box 13.4) and ZSI (Text Box 13.5) play very important roles in conservation of faunal resources of this country.

Text Box 13.4 Wildlife Institute of India—A Leading Organization in Wildlife Research

Wildlife Institute of India (WII) is an internationally reputed autonomous institution under the Ministry of Environment and Forests, Government of India. The institute was established in 1982, accorded autonomy in April 1986 and is presently located at picturesque landscape in Chandrabani, Dehradun. The mandate of this acclaimed Institution is to train government and non-government personnel on biodiversity related issues through training programmes and academic courses. WII is actively engaged in research in different parts of this country on biodiversity, endangered species, wildlife forensics, spatial modelling, eco-development and climate change. It also extends scientific advice on matters of conservation and management of wildlife resources.

The prime concern of the Institute is to build capacity and develop skills for providing solutions to problems of wildlife conservation in general and protected area management in particular. Nevertheless, the ultimate goal is the dissemination of the skills to ground level for use by wildlife managers. Over the years WII developed as a centre of excellence in wildlife science to nurture the development of wildlife science and promote its application in conservation.

WII has not only popularized wildlife studies and careers in this country, but the trained personnel from this premier institute have significantly contributed in protecting Indian wilderness. The Institute also maintains a number of databases viz. (i) National Wildlife Database (NWD) on species, habitats and protected areas (ii) Zoo database; (iii) Officer trainee database; (iv) Research project database; (v) Bibliographic database etc. WII has very good infrastructure and research facilities for wildlife forensic studies, remote sensing and GIS, as well as, well equipped laboratories and herbarium. The institute has a wonderful collection of books and journals on wildlife in their electronic library.

Website: http://www.wii.gov.in/

Text Box 13.5 Zoological Survey of India – A Premier Organization in Faunal Survey and Documentation

The Zoological Survey of India (ZSI) is a premier Indian organization in zoological research. ZSI was established on 1st July, 1916 as a national centre to promote faunal survey, exploration and research leading to the advancement in our knowledge of the various aspects of the exceptionally rich animal life of this country. The Conservation and Survey Division in the Ministry of Environment and Forests, Government of India coordinates the activities of the ZSI. This is the only taxonomic organization in the country involved in the study of all kinds of animals from Protozoa to Mammalia, occurring in all possible habitats.

Presently, ZSI has its headquarters at Kolkata and 16 regional field stations located all over the country in different geographic locations. This central institute is actively engaged in the studies and surveys to explore the fauna of various states, important ecosystems and different conservation areas. Besides, ZSI is one of the nodal organizations entrusted to carry out status surveys of endangered species, range of ecological studies and conduct environmental impact assessments. Further, it also extends identification and advisory services, training and extension services in the field of animal taxonomy and library facilities.

Website: http://zsi.gov.in/

13.6.3 Leading NGO's of India for Wildlife Conservation

1. World Wide Fund for Nature–India (WWF–India)

WWF–India is a conservation organization working to build a healthy living planet for future generations mainly through Biodiversity Conservation and Footprint Reduction. WWF–India was established as a Charitable Trust on 27 November 1969 with a mission to stop the degradation of the planet's natural environment and build a future in which humans live in harmony with nature. Over the years, its perspective has broadened to reflect a more holistic understanding of conservation issues of Indian wildlife.

Website: www.wwfindia.org/

2. TRAFFIC

TRAFFIC, the wildlife trade monitoring network, is the leading non-governmental organization working globally to combat trade in wild animals and plants in the context of both biodiversity conservation and sustainable development. TRAFFIC was established in 1976. This organization aims to ensure that trade in wild flora and fauna do not pose threats to the conservation of nature.

Website: www.traffic.org/

3. Wildlife Trust of India (WTI)

WTI is a leading Indian nature conservation organization committed to conserve wildlife and its habitat and to work for the welfare of individual wild animals, in partnership with communities and Governments. A team of 150 dedicated professionals in WTI work towards achieving its vision of a secure natural heritage, particularly in six priority landscapes of India.
Website: www.wti.org.in/

4. Bombay Natural History Society (BNHS)

BNHS is a national wildlife research organization promoting the cause of nature conservation since 1883. The guiding principle of BNHS has been that conservation should be based on scientific research. This tradition was exemplified by its former president, world renowned ornithologist Dr. Sálim Ali. Presently, this NGO is working for the cause of conservation across India in diverse habitats. BNHS has been designated as a Scientific and Industrial Research Organization (SIRO) by Department of Science & Technology, Government of India and is the partner of Bird Life International in India. Extensive outreach activities of BNHS through communications, advocacy and education are other arenas of conservation initiatives by this premier NGO of this country.
Website: www.bnhs.org/

5. Ashoka Trust for Research in Ecology and the Environment (ATREE)

ATREE is a research institution in the areas of biodiversity conservation and sustainable development. The mission of ATREE is to generate rigorous interdisciplinary knowledge by actively engaging the academia, policy makers, practitioners, activists, students and wider public audiences in order to promote *'socially just'* environmental conservation and sustainable development. ATREE plays the role of a model knowledge-generating organization focusing on applied science through research, education and action that influence policy and practice of nature conservation, natural resource management and sustainable development.
Website: www.atree.org/

REVIEW QUESTIONS

1. State the unique features of Wildlife (Protection) Act of India, 1972. Mention its limitations.
2. Elaborate Biological diversity Act.
3. What are the missions of the Ramsar convention.
4. Elaborate the role of NGO's in conservation initiatives of Indian wildlife.

REFERENCES

CITES, *Appendices,* 2015. Retrieved from: https://www.cites.org/sites/default/files/eng/app/2015/E-Appendices-2015-02-05.pdf

Sinha, B.C., *Book of State Animal, Bird, Tree and Flower*, Wildlife Institute of India, Dehradun, 2001

Venkataraman, A., Chattopadhyay, A. and De, J.K., *National and State Animals of India*, Zoological Survey of India, Kolkata, 2012.

Important Links:

http://nbaindia.org/uploaded/Biodiversityindia/Legal/15.%20Wildlife%20(Protection)%20Act,%201972.pdf

http://wbbb.gov.in/Legislations/rules/TheBiologicalDiversityAct2002.pdf

http://www.wii.gov.in/

http://zsi.gov.in/

www.atree.org/

www.bnhs.org/

www.traffic.org/

www.wti.org.in/

www.wwfindia.org/

INDEX

COLOUR PLATES

A. Standard True Colour Composite of Kolkata
(Source: Google Earth)

B. Standard False Colour Composite of Kolkata
(Source: http://fas.org/irp/imint/docs/rst/Sect16/Sect16_10.html)

Figure 6.26 (A) True-colour Composite; (B) False Colour Composite.

Plate I

4.1 Himalayan salamander (Sketch: Dr. Subhendu Mazumdar)

4.2 Olive Ridley turtle (Sketch: Dr. Subhendu Mazumdar)

4.3 Great Indian bustard (Sketch: Dr. Subhendu Mazumdar)

4.4 Bengal florican (Sketch: Dr. Subhendu Mazumdar)

4.5 Jerdon's courser (Sketch: Dr. Subhendu Mazumdar)

4.6 White-rumped vulture (Sketch: Dr. Subhendu Mazumdar)

Plate II

4.7 Hoolock gibbon (Sketch: Abesh Sanyal)

4.8 Slender loris (Sketch: Abesh Sanyal)

4.9 Brow-antlered deer (Photo: Rudraprasad Das)

4.10 Himalayan musk deer (Photo: Dr. Dipankar Ghose)

4.11 Blackbuck (Photo: Rudraprasad Das)

4.12 Greater one-horned rhinoceros (Photo: Rudraprasad Das)

Plate III

4.13 Asian elephant (Photo: Rudraprasad Das)

4.14 Fishing cat (Photo: Dr. Subhendu Mazumdar)

4.15 Indian tiger (Photo: Dr. Subhendu Mazumdar)

4.16 Asiatic lion (Photo: Dr. Subhendu Mazumdar)

4.17 Himalayan black bear (Photo: Dr. Subhendu Mazumdar)

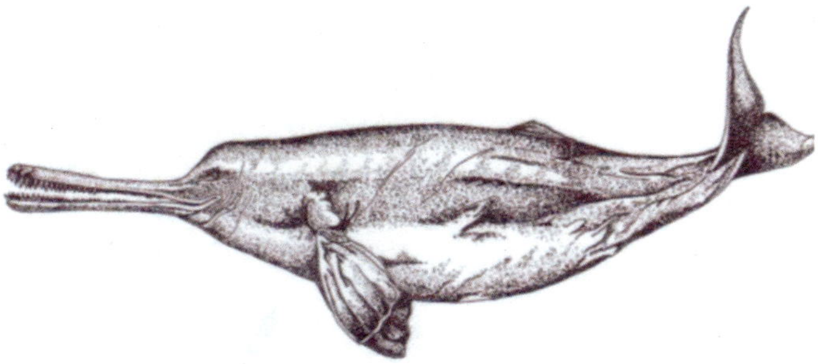

4.18 Ganges river dolphin (Sketch: Abesh Sanyal)

Plate IV

Red Panda in captivity at Padmaja Naidu Himalayan Zoological Park, Darjeeling (Photo: Dr. Subhendu Mazumdar)

Snow Leopard in captivity at Padmaja Naidu Himalayan Zoological Park, Darjeeling (Photo: Supriyo Dalui)

Female Pygmy Hog with juveniles and male Pygmy Hog in captivity (Photo: Rudraprasad Das)